A GUIDE TO INTERNATIONAL CONGRESS
REPORTS IN MUSICOLOGY
1900–1975

Garland Reference Library of the Humanities (Vol. 118)

A GUIDE TO INTERNATIONAL CONGRESS REPORTS IN MUSICOLOGY
1900–1975

John Tyrrell and Rosemary Wise

Garland Publishing, Inc., New York & London

1979

First published 1979 by
GARLAND PUBLISHING, INC. New York.
Also published in Great Britain by
The Macmillan Press Ltd., London and Basingstoke

Library of Congress Cataloging in Publication Data

Tyrrell, John.
  A guide to international congress reports in
musicology, 1900–1975.
  (Garland reference library of the humanities;
v. 118)
  Includes indexes.
  1. Music – Congresses – Bibliography. 2. Music –
Congresses – Indexes. I. Wise, Rosemary, joint author.
II. Title.
ML113.T95   780'.16   77–83364
ISBN 0–8240–9839–0

CONTENTS

Preface   vii

Acknowledgements   xi

How to Find a Congress Report   xiii

Chronological List of Congress Reports   1

Index of Places   245

Index of Titles, Series and Sponsors   247

Index of Authors and Editors   259

Subject Index   283

PREFACE

Music congress reports have long been a problem for scholars, bibliographers and librarians. How does one find them in a library? How should one catalogue them to make them more accessible? Many systems are used, so that without a full reference and some degree of imagination one can often fail to find a given congress report in a large library. The problem is made more acute for the musicologist by the fact that many useful papers on music appear not in musicological but in interdisciplinary congress reports, often unfamiliar territory to him. The result is that much valuable material is neglected, either because it seems that it cannot be found, or because it was not known about in the first place. The urgent need for a bibliographical guide to congress reports in music is filled only partially by Marie Briquet's *La musique dans les congrès internationaux (1835–1939)* (Paris: Heugel, 1961 = Publications de la Société française de musicologie ii/10) since her listings end before the postwar escalation of congresses in music.

Our first aim then was to enable someone with only the scantiest information – the place or date of a congress, a half-remembered title, or the name of a sponsoring organization – to identify the report of any congress held between 1900 and 1975 likely to turn up in a musicological bibliography. By consulting the indices (see 'How to find a congress report', p. xiii) the reader will be led to a full entry which will give him enough information to tackle the various approaches used by libraries for cataloguing congress reports.

Our second aim has been to list the musicological contents of each congress and provide a full subject index of the papers, thus bringing together and making more accessible a fascinating wealth of material. Our purposes have been practical rather than historiographical: we have not sought, for instance, to reconstruct congresses whose reports were never published.

As a starting point we have taken 1900, the year of the first congress entirely devoted to musicology for which a report was published. Our closing date, 1975, has been chosen in the knowledge that our listings of the last few years will be incomplete: publications as cumbersome and complicated as the larger international congress reports understandably take more than two or three years to come out. Despite the helpfulness of organizers, editors and publishers it has not been possible to include some of the major musicological congresses of 1974 and 1975. We are particularly sorry not to be able to list the reports of the 1974 congress of the Gesellschaft für Musikforschung in Berlin, the 1974 Schoenberg congress in Vienna, the 1975 Haydn congress in Washington, and the 1975 Bach congress in Leipzig, none of which had been published before we went to press. In spite of these omissions we felt it more helpful to bring our closing date as far forward as we dared rather than to take an earlier one and thus exclude the substantial number of recent reports that had been published.

We have considered all publications within these dates which, through their presentation and manner of publication, could reasonably be regarded as congress reports and which would normally be catalogued as such in a library. There are

exceptions: some isolated congress reports have been published in periodicals and we have listed these when they are clearly presented as congress reports. However, congress papers dispersed throughout different periodicals, or several issues of the same periodical, have been excluded, as have been whole periodical series made up of the published proceedings of societies (such as the Royal Musical Association or the American Musicological Society), even when organized into regular conferences like those held by the IFMC, the Yugoslav folklorists or the Flemish philologists. There is less need for such congresses to appear in our *Guide*: they will always be cited with their periodical title rather than a congress title and should thus be easier to find in libraries.

Similarly we have excluded reports whose congress origins have been disguised during the course of editing. Thus while including books made up of several congress reports (e.g. the three symposia in *Musicology and the Computer*, 1965, or the two 1954 Palermo congresses) where distinction is made between the individual congresses, we have not covered such congresses as those that gave rise to some of the *Studien zur Wertungsforschung*, where contributions from several congresses have been edited into a single undifferentiated sequence.

With the aim of keeping the book within reasonable bounds we have excluded congress reports in subject areas of less than central interest to the musicologist, such as music education, dance, music copyright, music therapy, sound recording techniques, though we have retained isolated papers on these topics in more general congress reports. In interdisciplinary congress reports we have attempted to select papers only of musicological interest, e.g. papers on Meistersinger research are included when dealing with music but not when dealing only with poetry. While the chief focus of our selection has been on international congress reports, we have also included the reports of purely national congresses where the distinction of the participants or the nature of their contributions have seemed to us to be of international interest.

Each congress report listed is given a code (see 'How to find a congress report', p. xiii) which precedes the main details of the congress: the published title of the report (in bold) and the place and full date of occurrence, if known. The indented lines supply details of sponsorship and publication:

Sponsor. The name of the organization sponsoring the congress is expressed in English where a standard form exists (e.g. in international congresses). Where several sponsors are given we have listed them all or, if differentiation is made in the report, only the chief ones (in general we have sought to include active sponsors, and to exclude patrons). For international congresses we have given the names of international sponsors and omitted those of the national or local organizers (less likely to be used in a library catalogue), though where a congress has been held jointly by an international organization and a quite different national body (e.g. 59 CAM, 74 KRP) we have given both. Sometimes a series of congresses has taken place without the apparent instigation of a formally constituted sponsoring organization. In such cases we have given, in place of a sponsor, the name of the series. We have not listed as sponsors the names of committees specially formed to organize individual congresses devoted to a person, place or event; such sponsors are less likely to be used in a cataloguing system than the name of the person, place or event being celebrated.

Publication information includes editor (where designated as such), publisher, place and date of publication, and publication series, if applicable. Where a book of résumés or preliminary papers is issued but superseded by a full report (e.g. 61

OKH) we have listed only the full report. If, however, the congress has generated more than one report we have listed the most comprehensive and referred to the others in the publication details (e.g. 57 PAR). When reports have been issued in more than one language we have chosen one (English, if available) for the main listing and referred to the others in the publication information.

A list of authors, papers and their page numbers follows. Main papers, or papers delivered at plenary sessions, are separated from the others by a space. Untitled papers have in general been excluded as has material dealing with the organization of the congress, as well as welcoming or farewell addresses, unless these were intended as musicological contributions. We have excluded the titles of papers which were delivered but which have not been printed in the report, but have listed résumés and full papers without differentiation. Printed discussions, whether at round tables or in response to individual papers, have been listed if particularly substantial. Versions of authors' names are generally given as they appear in the individual reports though obvious errors have been corrected.

We are aware that in a book of this scope there will undoubtedly be congress reports omitted which meet all the criteria set out earlier in this preface. All additions and corrections (sent to us at the Music Department, University of Nottingham) are welcomed and will be considered for any future supplement or edition.

JOHN TYRRELL
ROSEMARY WISE

ACKNOWLEDGEMENTS

The completion of this book would not have been possible without the generous help of many individuals and institutions. We would like to thank in particular Professor Israel Adler and Dr Bathja Bayer, Jewish Music Research Centre, Jerusalem; Professor Ryuei Akiyama, Tokyo College of Music Library; Dr Anthea Baird, University of London Library; Dr John Bergsagel, University of Copenhagen; Dr Ludwik Bielawski, Polish Academy of Sciences, Warsaw; Dr Irmgard Bontinck, International Institute for Music, Dance and Theatre in the Audio-visual Media, Vienna; Miss Kathryn Bosi, Biblioteca Berenson, Villa i Tatti, Florence; Mr Julian Budden, BBC; Professor Peter Crossley-Holland, University of California at Los Angeles; Professor Hans Heinrich Eggebrecht, University of Freiburg im Breisgau; Professor Ludwig Finscher, University of Frankfurt; Mrs Grete Fischer, Institut für Aufführungspraxis an der Hochschule für Musik und Darstellende Kunst, Graz; Dr Micheline Galley, International Association of Studies on Mediterranean Civilizations, Paris; Professor Graham George, International Folk Music Council; Dr Walter Gürtelschmied, International Music Centre, Vienna; Dr Hans Haase, Herzog August Bibliothek, Wolfenbüttel; Miss Elizabeth Hart, UK branch of International Association of Music Libraries; Dr Marcia Herndon, University of Texas at Austin; Professor Wiley Hitchcock, Brooklyn College, City University of New York; Dr Shlomo Hofman, Tel-Aviv; Istituto di storia delle tradizioni popolari, University of Rome; Dr Jean Jacquot, Centre national de la recherche scientifique, Paris; Dr Masakata Kanazawa, Christian University, Tokyo; Professor Israel Katz, Columbia University; Professor Winfried Kirsch, University of Frankfurt; Kraus Reprint, Kraus-Thomson Organization Ltd; Professor Don Krummel, University of Illinois; Professor Josef Kuckertz, Consociatio internationalis musicae sacrae, Rome; Mrs J. Lambrechts-Douillez, Museum Vleeshuis, Antwerp; Dr Andrew D. McCredie, University of Adelaide; Mrs Zofia Mossakowska, Polish Music Centre, Warsaw; Mrs Teresa Muraro, Fondazione Giorgio Cini, Venice; Musikhistoriska museet, Stockholm; Dr Alena Němcová, Czech Music Information Centre, Brno; Leo S. Olschki, Florence; Professor Wolfgang Osthoff, University of Würzburg; Dr Rudolf Pečman, University of Brno; Dr Susanne Popp, Max-Reger-Institut, Bonn; Dr Milan Poštolka, National Museum, Prague; Dr Miguel Querol, Instituto español de musicologia, Barcelona; Dr Wolfgang Rehm and Dr Dietrich Berke, Bärenreiter Verlag, Kassel; Mr Lothar Röhr, Harrassowitz, Wiesbaden; Mrs Salwa El-Shawan, Berlin; Verlag A. Schendl, Vienna; Dr Hans-Joachim Schulze, Bach-Archiv, Leipzig; Mr Peter Stadlen, London; Dr Dimitrije Stefanović, Serbian Academy of Arts and Sciences, Belgrade; Professor Rudolf Stephan, Free University of Berlin; Ms Chrystal Stillings Smith, University of Illinois Press; Dr Erich Stockmann, Humboldt University of Berlin; Professor Wolfgang Suppan, Institut für Musikethnologie an der Hochschule für Musik und darstellende Kunst, Graz; Segreteria Generale, Ufficio pubbliche relazioni, Comune di Mantova; Professor Giuseppe Vecchi, University of Bologna; M. André Veinstein, International Society for Performing Arts, Libraries and

Museums, Paris; Professor Charles Warren, Eisenhower College; Professor Edith Weber, Sorbonne, Paris; Associate Professor James Webster, Cornell University; Mr Paul Wilson, The Music Library, University of Birmingham; Dr Helmut Wirth, Hamburg; Professor Emila Zanetti, Biblioteca musicale governative del Conservatorio de musica 'S. Cecilia', Rome; Mrs Friederike Zimmerman, Universal Edition, Vienna; Dr Pierluigi Petrobelli, University of London King's College; Horniman Museum; Professor Otto Kolleritsch, Institut für Wertungsforschung an der Hochschule für Musik und Darstellende Kunst in Graz; Arno Volk Verlag Hans Gerig K. G., Cologne.

This book began as a bibliographical tool for use within the editorial offices of *The New Grove Dictionary of Music and Musicians* and we owe much to all our former colleagues there who contributed so willingly to its growth. Without the interest and encouragement of the chief editor, Dr Stanley Sadie, and the senior text editors, Dr Nigel Fortune and Professor Ian Bent, it would not have been published. The vigilance of the proof readers, Paulène Fallows, Judith Nagley and Ruth Thackeray, alerted us to some of our earliest congress reports; many of these were successfully located in London libraries by the resourcefulness of William Conner and Duncan Chisholm; Geoffrey Norris transliterated many of the Russian congresses. The manuscript was typed with great accuracy and fortitude by Kate Harney. We have been particularly fortunate in the help given by former colleagues now no longer in England: Bruce Carr in Detroit, and Elizabeth Bartlett in Paris, who both spent many hours on our behalf following up odd hunches and incomplete references. We òwe a special debt of gratitude to Brad Robinson. He encouraged this project from its earliest beginnings and provided many ideas for its organization and scope. And from Berlin he worked unceasingly, tracking down congress reports that had eluded us everywhere else while at the same time discovering many more that were completely new to us.

JOHN TYRRELL
ROSEMARY WISE

How to Find a Congress Report

Each separately published congress report has been given a code based on the last two digits of its date of occurrence and, in general, on the first three or four letters of its place of occurrence. Two or more congresses in the same town in the same year are differentiated by superscript figures.

1 If you know the place of occurrence
   look in the *Index of Places*.

2 If you know the date of occurrence
   look in the *Chronological List of Congress Reports*.
These are arranged alphabetically by town within one year. If you fail to find it look back to an earlier year: it is possible that your date of occurrence may turn out to be a publication date.

3 If you know the title
   look in the *Index of Titles, Series and Sponsors*.
Titles are listed under the first distinctive word, omitting numerals and words such as 'Proceedings', 'Bericht', 'Atti' etc. The words 'Congress' (Kongress, Tagung, Convegno etc.) or 'International Congress' (Congrès international etc.) are used to show series of congresses or are indexed if there is no other distinctive word in the title.

4 If you are looking for one congress from a series
   look in the *Index of Titles, Series and Sponsors*.
Most series are listed under the standard English name of the congress with cross-references from standard forms in other languages.

5 If you know the sponsoring organization
   look in the *Index of Titles, Series and Sponsors*.
International sponsors of the chief musicological series are generally given in a standard English form. However, where relevant, cross references are included which give the names of the sponsors in foreign languages.

6 If you know the editor of a musical congress report
   look in the *Index of Authors and Editors*.

7 If you know the author of a particular paper
   look in the *Index of Authors and Editors*.

8 If you know the main subject area dealt with in the congress
   look first in the *Index of Titles, Series and Sponsors*.
If this fails to locate the congress, look at the *Subject Index* which includes topics of individual papers, groups of papers and whole congresses.

9 If you know the topic of a particular paper
   look in the *Subject Index*.

THE CONGRESS REPORTS

00 MUN Akten des fünften internationalen Kongresses katholischer Gelehrten
Munich 24–8 September 1900
(Munich: Herder, 1901)

5 Kultur- und Kunstgeschichte
SCHMID, A. Kirchengesang nach den Liturgikern des Mittelalters 327
KIENLE, A. Über den Choral bei den Cisterciensern 328
Mac CREA, D. Gregorian music in our churches 330

HABERL, F. X. Was ist im XIX. Jahrhundert für die Kenntnis altklassischer Werke kirchlicher Tonkunst geschehen 331
EISENRING, C. Karl Greith, der grösste schweizerische Kirchenmusiker 338
MOSER, J. Klavierklang und Resonanzbodenkonstruktion 347

00 PAR¹ Congrès international de musique (Ier session): Exposition universelle de 1900: compte rendu – rapports – communications
Paris 14–18 June 1900
Exposition universelle de 1900
(Paris: Secrétariat général du Congrès, 1901)

d'INDY, V. Unification de l'orchestration des harmonies et fanfares 11
d'INDY, V. De l'utilité des écoles de chefs d'orchestre et de la généralisation de l'étude de l'instrumentation 14
MILLIET, P. Étant donné l'influence que la critique peut exercer sur le développement de l'art musical, n'y a-t-il pas lieu d'émettre un voeu relatif à la manière dont elle s'exerce? 15
COMBARIEU, J. De l'évolution du drame lyrique 19
COMBARIEU, J. L'état doit-il jouer dans les théâtres et concerts subventionnés un rôle de protecteur à l'égard des oeuvres des maîtres tombés dans le domaine public 21
LYON, G. Généralisation de l'emploi du diapason normal: étude des moyens de le rendre obligatoire 28
d'INDY, V. Transformation des instruments dits simples en instruments chromatiques: définition des instruments chromatiques 31
CANAT de CHIZY Régularisation des indications et appareils métronomiques 31
FRÉMOND Régularisation des indications métronomiques 34
BAUDOT Utilité d'un appareil enregistreur des mouvements des oeuvres musicales 38

HELLOUIN, F. Simplification de la notation musicale 38
MAHILLON, V. Utilité de désigner les sons de l'échelle chromatique par des numéros 39
BAUDOT Avantages et inconvénients du tempérament au point de vue de la pratique musicale 41
d'INDY, V. Emploi d'un signe distinctif accompagnant les clefs de fa et de sol dans les partitions vocales et instrumentales pour les parties s'entendant à l'octave 42
d'INDY, V. Y a-t-il utilité à employer la note réelle dans l'écriture musicale? 44
CHÉRION Y a-t-il utilité à reconstituer les maîtrises? Dans le cas de l'affirmative, quels sont les moyens pratiques pour parvenir à cette reconstitution? 46
de RILLÉ, L. and DUREAU, T. De l'utilité du développement des sociétés orphéoniques (chorales, symphonies, harmonies, fanfares), et des moyens d'améliorer leur répertoire 49
ERGO, E. Réforme de l'enseignement et de la science de l'harmonie suivant le système des fonctions tonales du Dr Hugo Riemann 56
RADIGUER Situation des chefs de musique militaire 62

00 PAR²   Congrès international d'histoire de la musique tenu à Paris à la Bibliothèque de l'Opéra du 23 au 29 Juillet 1900 (VIIIᵉ section du Congrès d'histoire comparée): documents, mémoires et voeux
Paris 23–9 July 1900
    Exposition universelle de 1900
     ed. J. Combarieu (Paris: Librairie Fischbacher, 1901)

1 Musique grecque
RUELLE, E.   Le chant gnostico-magique des sept voyelles grecques   15
POIRÉE, É.   Chant des sept voyelles: analyse musicale   28
LALOY, L.   Le genre enharmonique des Grecs 39
GRASSI LANDI, B.   Observations sur le genre enharmonique   57
REINACH, T.   L'harmonie des sphères   60
TIERSOT, J.   Le premier hymne delphique   63
REINACH, T.   Sur la transcription du premier hymne delphique   65
POIRÉE, E.   Une nouvelle interprétation rythmique du second hymne à Apollon   70

2 Musique byzantine
THIBAUT, R. P.   Assimilation des 'êchoi' byzantins & des modes latins avec les anciens tropes grecs   77
THIBAUT, R. P.   Les notations byzantines   86
GAÏSSER, H.   L'origine & la vraie nature du mode dit 'chromatique oriental' ·   93

3 Musique du moyen âge
A Musique religieuse
HOUDARD, G.   La notation neumatique (discussion GAÏSSER, H. 113)   103
HOUDARD, G.   La notation neumatique considérée dans son sens matériel extérieur   116
GRASSI LANDI, B.   Observations relatives à l'interprétation des notes neumatiques du chant grégorien   124
GAÏSSER, H.   L'origine du 'tonus peregrinus' 127
SACCHETTI, L.   Le chant religieux de l'Église orthodoxe russe   134

B Musique profane
AUBRY, P.   La légende dorée du jongleur   155
BRENET, M.   Un poète-musicien du XVᵉ siècle: Eloy d'Amerval   165

4 Musique moderne
TIERSOT, J.   Des transformations de la tonalité & du rôle du dièze & du bémol depuis le moyen âge jusqu'au XVII siècle   175
CHILESOTTI, O.   Musiciens français: Jean-Baptiste Besard & les luthistes du XVIᵉ siècle   179
ROLLAND, R.   Notes sur l' 'Orfeo' de Luigi Rossi & sur les musiciens italiens à Paris, sous Mazarin   191
SHEDLOCK   Purcell & Bach   210
LONGO, A.   Observations sur la valeur historique des compositions pour clavecin de Dominique Scarlatti   213
LINDGREN, A.   Contribution à l'histoire de la 'Polonaise'   215
HUMBERT, G.   Les principes naturels de l'évolution musicale   221
BONAVENTURA, A.   Progrès & nationalité dans la musique   226
KROHN, I.   De la mesure à 5 temps dans la musique finnoise   241
LANDORMY, P.   Des moyens d'organiser en France une ligue pour la protection & le développement de l'art musical   246
GÉROLD, T.   De la valeur des petites notes d'agrément & d'expression   251

5 Varia
SAINT-SAËNS, C.   [on the reform of musical notation]   261
HÉLOUIN   Histoire du métronome en France   264
MEERENS   Réforme du système musical   270
CARILLO, J.   La nomenclature des sons   276
GARIEL, E.   De la nécessité de méthodiser l'enseignement de la musique en lui appliquant une base scientifique   281
PARENT, H.   De l'enseignement élémentaire du piano en France au point de vue de la vulgarisation de la musique   289
DAURIAC, L.   La pensée musicale   296
COMBARIEU, J.   Le vandalisme musical   298

00 PAR³   Annales internationales d'histoire: Congrès de Paris: Congrès international d'histoire comparée
Paris 24–8 July 1900
    (Paris: A. Colin, 1901–2 / R Nendeln: Kraus, 1972)

Vol. v Histoire des sciences (1901)
TANNERY, P.   Lettres inédites adressées au Père   Mersenne [music discussed in Pierre Trichet's letters]   311

00 PAR⁴   IVᵉ congrès international de psychologie: Compte rendu des séances et texte des mémoires
Paris 20–26 August 1900
        ed. P. Janet (Paris: Félix Alcan, 1901/R Nendeln: Kraus, 1974)

RICHET, C.   Note sur un cas remarquable de   KRUEGER, F.   Ueber Consonanz und Disso-
précocité musicale   97   nanz   455

00 PAR⁵   [2ᵉ] Congrès international des traditions populaires
Paris 10–12 September 1900
        (Paris: E. Lechevallier, E. Leroux and J. Maisonneuve, 1902)

BLÉMONT, E.   La tradition poétique   44   Europe   71
PINEAU, L.   Les vieux chants populaires   VOULÉTICH-VOUKASSOVITCH, V.   La moreska et
scandinaves   62   le juge gras (le roi du village) dans l'île de
THOMAS, N. W.   La danse totémique en   Cuozola (Dalmatie)   77

00 PAR⁶   Mémoires de musicologie sacrée lus aux assises de musique religieuse à la Scola Cantorum
Paris 27–9 September 1900
        Scola Cantorum
        (Paris: Édition de la Scola Cantorum, [1900])

GASTOUÉ, A.   L'art grégorien: les origines   CLERVAL   La musique religieuse à Notre-Dame
premières   1   de Chartres   47
AUBRY, P.   Les raisons historiques du rythme   AUBRY, P.   Les jongleurs dans l'histoire: Saint
oratoire   19   Julien-des-Ménétriers   57
VILLETARD, H.   Recherche et étude de fragments   QUITTARD, H.   G. Carissimi et le XVIIᵉ siècle
. de manuscrits de plain-chant   29   italien   75
PARISOT, J.   Essai d'application de mélodies   PIRRO, A.   Les formes de l'expression dans la
orientales à des chants d'église   39   musique de Heinrich Schütz   95

02 HAM   **Verhandlungen des XIII. internationalen Orientalisten-Kongresses**
Hamburg 4–10 September 1902
International Congress of Orientalists
(Leiden: E. J. Brill, 1904/*R* Nendeln: Kraus, 1968)

03 DIN   Congrès de Dinant: compte rendu
            Dinant 9–13 August 1903
            Fédération archéologique et historique de Belgique (17th congress); Société archéo-
            logique de Namur
            ed. E. de Pierpont (Namur: Ad. Wesmael-Charlier, 1904)

MORIN, G.   Les AOI de la chanson de Roland   565

03 ROM   Atti del [III] congresso internazionale di scienze storiche
            Rome 1–9 April 1903
            (Rome: R. Accademie dei Lincei, 1904–7/R Nendeln: Kraus, 1972)

Vol. viii Storia dell'arte musicale e drammatica
(1905)
RAMORINO, F.   Dell'opportunità di pubblicare
in edizione critica gli 'scriptores musici latini' 3
BARINI, G.   Sulla opportunità di compilare una
raccolta di indici e cataloghi dei codici musicali
italiani esistenti negli archivi, nelle biblioteche e
nelle collezioni pubbliche e private, per servire
di base ad una serie di edizioni critiche delle
opere dei nostri classici   7
BARINI, G.   Sulla necessità di render più completo e proficuo l'insegnamento della storia
della musica negli istituti musicali, ponendo
constantemente in relazione la produzione
musicale con la storia civile e del costume e con
le altre manifestazioni della vita intellettuale nel
tempo in cui fiorirono i singoli compositori e si
svolsero le varie forme musicali   11
RASI, L.   Della costituzione di un museo dell'arte
drammatica italiana   17, 139
BONAVENTURA, A.   Sull'ordinamento della
musica e dei libri relativi nelle pubbliche
biblioteche   19
ZAMBIASI, G.   Sullo svolgimento storico-critico
dei principii e criteri seguiti nel dare base
scientifica alla musica   27

VESSELLA, A.   Sulla evoluzione storica della partitura di banda   43
PAGLICCI-BROZZI, A.   Opportunità di racco-
gliere le antiche et tradizionali fanfare dei comuni italiani   51
SALVAGNINI, F. A.   Francesco Caffi, musicologo
veneziano, 1778–1874   55
CAMETTI, A.   Un nuovo documento sulle origini
di Giovanni Pierluigi da Palestrina: il testa-
mento di Jacobella Pierluigi (1527)   87
FAVARA, A.   Le melodie tradizionali di Val di
Mazzara   93
GAÏSSER, U.   I canti ecclesiastici italo-greci 107
TRAVERSARI-SALAZAR, P. P.   L'arte in America:
storia dell'arte musicale indigena e popolare,
arie, canzoni, poesie, strumenti e danze   117
CHILESOTTI, O.   Gli 'Airs de court' del 'Thesaurus harmonicus' di J. B. Besard   131
CHILESOTTI, O.   Trascrizioni da un codice musicale di Vincenzo Galilei   135
RADICIOTTI, G.   Teatro e musica in Roma nel
secondo quarto del secolo XIX (1825–50) 157
VILLANIS, L. A.   Alcuni codici manoscritti di
musica del secolo XVI posseduti dalla Biblioteca nazionale di Torino   319

05 ALG   Actes du XIVe congrès international des orientalistes
          Algiers 19–26 April 1905
          International Congress of Orientalists
          (Paris: E. Leroux, 1906–8/*R* Nendeln: Kraus, 1968)

Vol. iii Langues musulmanes (1907)
DESPARMET, J.   La poésie arabe actuelle à Blida
et sa métrique   437

05 ROM   Atti del V congresso internazionale di psicologia
          Rome 26–30 April 1905
              ed. S. Sanctis (Rome: Forzani e C. Tipografi del Senato, 1905/*R* Nendeln: Kraus,
          1974)

iii/1 Psicologia sperimentale
KRUEGER, F.   Die Messung der Sprechmelodie
als Ausdrucksmethode   245

iii/3 Psicologia patologica
INGEGNIEROS, J.   Disturbi del linguaggio musicale negli isterici   476

05 STRS   **Acta generalis cantus gregoriani studiosorum conventus/Bericht des internationalen
          Kongresses für gregorianischen Choralgesang/Compte rendu du congrès international de
          plain-chant grégorien**
          Strasbourg 16–19 August 1905
          (Strasbourg: F. X. Le Roux, 1905)

POTHIER, J.   La catholicité du chant de l'église
romaine   13
MATHIAS, F. X.   Der Choral im Elsass   19
FOUCAULD   Simple observation sur le caractère
du rythme grégorien dans la psalmodie   29
WAGNER, P.   Ueber den traditionellen
Choral   32
WAGNER, P.   Der traditionelle Choralvortrag
und seine geschichtliche Begründung   40
OTT, K.   Die Entwicklung des mailändischen
Chorals   55
ROJO, C.   Le chant grégorien en Espagne   63
WAGNER, P.   Wie müssen die Melodien der Vati-
kanischen   Choralausgabe   ausgeführt
werden?   71
GASTOUÉ, A.   Sur l'intérêt de l'étude des traités
du moyen-âge et de deux traités perdus   80

ANDOYER   Le rythme oratoire, principe de la
méthode grégorienne   88
HORN, P.   Die Choralfrage in Schule, im Lehrer-
und Priesterseminar   100
WAGNER, P.   Ueber die Zweckmässigkeit der
Choralrestauration   und   ihre   praktische
Durchführung   106
MATHIAS, F. X.   Die Choralbegleitung   117
MARXER   Untergang St. Gallischer Choral-
pflege im ausgehenden Mittelalter und in neuer
Zeit   123
GASTOUÉ, A.   Comment on peut s'inspirer des
anciens pour l'accompagnement du chant
romain   133
AMELLI   De Guidonis Aretini, eiusque assecla-
rum gestis, in conventibus internationalibus
oratio Aretii, Romae et Argentinae   141

06 BAS **Bericht über den zweiten Kongress der Internationalen Musikgesellschaft zu Basel**
Basle 25–7 September 1906
International Musical Society
(Leipzig: Breitkopf & Härtel, 1907)

1 Bibliographie, Bibliothekswesen (chairman SPRINGER, H.)
SPRINGER, H. Über den Stand der musikalischen Bibliographie 1

SONNECK, O. G. Der Ausbau von Musik-Bibliotheken 6
Discussion: Eitner's Quellenlexikon; Zeitschriftenschau 7

2 Notationskunde (chairman WOLF, J.)
WOLF, J. Über den Stand der Notationskunde 8

DECHEVRENS, P. A. 'La rhythme du chant grégorien' 17
RUNGE, P. Über die Notation des Meistergesangs 17
MÜNZER, G. Zur Notation der Meistersinger 27
STAIGER, R. Über die Notation des Meistergesangs 34
BERNOUILLI, E. Zur Notation des Meistergesangs 35
SPRINGER, H. Die musikalischen Blockdrucke des 15. und 16. Jahrhunderts 37
KROHN, I. Zweckmässige Notation von Psalmen und andern rezitativischen Gesängen 47
GEISLER, C. Neue Notation für Gesangsmusik 48
KROHN, I. Zur Einheitlichkeit der Notenschlüssel 55

3 Vergleichende Musikforschung, Akustik, Tonpsychologie (chairman von HORNBOSTEL, E.)
von HORNBOSTEL, E. Über den gegenwärtigen Stand der vergleichenden Musikwissenschaft 56

SCHMIDT, W. Über die Musik westafrikanischer und ozeanischer Neger 60
LALOY, L. Notes sur la musique cambodgienne 61
KROHN, I. Über das lexikalische Ordnen von Volksmelodien 66
SCHMIDT, H. Über die Registerausbildung der menschlichen Stimme (Methode Nehrlich-Schmidt) 74
KROHN, I. Das akustische Harmonium der Universität zu Helsingfors 75
POLAK, A. J. Briefwechsel mit dem Direktor der

School of Music in Tokio, betr. die Harmonisierung japanischer Melodien 83

4 Ästhetik (chairmen ECORCHEVILLE, J., SEIDL, A.)
MARSCHNER, F. Wertbegriff als Grundlage der Musikästhetik 86
MOOS, P. Theodor Lipps als Musikästhetiker 87
WITASEK, S. Zur allgemeinen Analyse des musikalischen Genusses 111
ABERT, H. Die spätantike Musikästhetik und ihre Bedeutung für das Mittelalter 128
SEIDL, A. Lässt sich Ästhetik mit Aussicht auf Erfolg an Konservatorien lehren? 129

5 Musikgeschichte des Altertums und Mittelalters bis zum 16. Jahrhundert (chairmen WOLF, J., WAGNER, P., THÜRLINGS, A.)
GRAF, E. Über den Stand der altgriechischen Musikforschung 154
WAGNER, P. Über den gegenwärtigen Stand der mittelalterlichen Musikforschung 161

GASTOUÉ, A. Sur les origines de la forme 'sequentia' du VIIe–IXe siècles 165
MASSON, P.-M. L'humanisme musical en France au XVIe siècle: la musique 'mesurée à l'antique' 170
THÜRLINGS, A. Die soggetti cavati dalle vocali in Huldigungskompositionen und die Herculesmesse des Lupus 183
KOLLER, O. Wie könnte ein thematischer Katalog der Messen-, Motetten- und Madrigalliteratur des XV. u. XVI. Jahrhunderts eingerichtet werden? 194

6 Instrumentalmusik (chairmen NEF, K., OBRIST, A., HAMMERICH, A.)
NEF, K. Zur Forschung über die ältere Instrumentalmusik 195
SEIFFERT, M. Zur Forschung über die ältere Klavier- und Orgelmusik 200

SCHERING, A. Die freie Kadenz im Instrumentalkonzert des 18. Jahrhunderts 204
OBRIST, A. Dürfen oder sollen der Entwicklung der modernen Instrumentation Grenzen gezogen werden? 211
OBRIST, A. Sollen Musiker und Musikhistoriker die Entwicklung der Klavierspielapparate för-

dern, bekämpfen oder zu beeinflussen suchen?   212

7 Oper, Oratorium, Lied (chairmen ECORCHE-VILLE, J., SCHIEDERMAIR, L.)
SCHIEDERMAIR, L. Über den Stand der Operngeschichte   212

SCHERING, A. Die Anfänge des Oratoriums 216
SCHIEDERMAIR, L. Die neapolitanische Oper des 18. Jahrhunderts   217

8 Musikinstrumente (chairman HAMMERICH, A.)

BUHLE, E. Über den Stand der Instrumentenkunde   217

HAMMERICH, A. Zur Frage nach dem Ursprung der Streichinstrumente   225
LEICHTENTRITT, H. Ältere Bildwerke als Quellen der musikgeschichtlichen Forschung   230
OBRIST, A. Die historische und künstlerische Bedeutung der Wiederbelebung altertümlicher Musikinstrumente   234
CLAUDIUS, C. Die schwedische Nyckelharpa   242

06 QUE   **Congrès international des Américanistes: XVe session**
                Quebec 10–15 September 1906
                   International Congress of Americanists
                   (Quebec: Dussault & Proulx, 1907/*R* Nendeln: Kraus, 1968)

Vol. i (1907)
GAGNON, E. Les sauvages de l'Amérique et l'art musical   179

08 FRA   **Bericht über den III. Kongress für experimentelle Psychologie**
                ~rankfurt am Main 22–5 April 1908
                    Gesellschaft für experimentelle Psychologie
                    ed. F. Schumann (Leipzig: Johann Ambrosius Barth, 1909)

RÉVÉSZ, G.   Über Orthosymphonie (eine merkwürdige parakustische Erscheinung   243

08 VIE   **Verhandlungen des XVI. internationalen Amerikanisten-Kongresses**
                Vienna 9–14 September 1908
                    International Congress of Americanists
                    ed. F. Heger (Vienna: A. Hartleben, 1908/R Nendeln: Kraus, 1968)

PRESS, K.T.   Das Fest des Erwachens (Weinfest)
bei den Cora-Indianern   489
BRETON, A. C.   Survivals of ceremonial dances
among Mexican Indians   513

WALLASCHEK, R.   Über den Wert phono-
graphischer Aufnahmen von Gesängen der
Naturvölker   557
HARTMANN, C. V.   The photographone   563

09 GEN   VIme congrès international de psychologie: rapports et comptes rendus
          Geneva 2–7 August 1909
              ed. E. Claparède (Geneva: Librairie Kündig, 1910/R Nendeln: Kraus, 1974)

DAURIAC, L.   Quelques exemples de ce que peut
devoir la psychologie générale à la psychologie
musicale   630

09 LIÈ   Annales du XXIe congrès
          Liège 31 July – 5 August 1909
              Fédération archéologique et historique de Belgique
                  ed. J. Brassinne and L. Renard-Grenson (Liège: Henri Poncelet, 1909)

Vol. ii Rapports et mémoires (1909)
BERGMANS, P.   Le Collegium musicum fondé à
Hasselt au XVIe siècle   517
DWELSHAUVERS   Programme des recherches à
faire dans les fonds musicaux de la province de
Liège   643
BERGMANS, P.   De l'intérêt qu'il y aurait à
dresser un inventaire général des instruments de
musique anciens disséminés dans les musées et
les collections privées de Belgique   666
DWELSHAUVERS   La forme musicale, embryon

de sonate, adoptée par Jean-Noël Hamal dans
son opus I doit-elle être considerée comme une
antériorité aux 'Sonate a tre' de Stamitz? 722
LAVOYE, L.   Note sur la musique au pays de
Liégè aux Xe, XIe et XIIe siècles   746
van den BORREN, C.   Guillaume Dufay   865
VITRY, P.   Le tombeau de Henry du Mont,
musicien liégeois, établi en France au XVIIe
siècle   917
LAVOYE, L.   L'art musical belge pendant la
Renaissance   953

09 VIE   Haydn-Zentenarfeier: III. Kongress der Internationalen Musikgesellschaft: Bericht
          Vienna 25–9 May 1909
              International Musical Society
                  (Vienna: Artaria & Co/Leipzig: Breitkopf & Härtel, 1909)

ADLER, G.   [Franz Joseph Haydn: Festrede] 45
MALHERBE, C.   L'internationalisme dans la
musique   56
MACKENZIE, A.   Gedächtnisrede auf Mendels-
sohn   60
HEUSS, A.   Gedächtnisrede auf Händel   67

1a–c Alte und neue Musikgeschichte
GAISSER, U. A.   Die acht Kirchentöne in der
griechisch-albanesischen Überlieferung   83
RUNGE, P.   Über die Notation des Meisterge-
sanges (Berichtigung und Ergänzung des Referats auf dem Baseler Kongress 1906)   84
HENNERBERG, C. F.   Diè schwedischen Orgeln
des Mittelalters   91
HAMMERICH, A.   Bericht über eine alte grie-

chische Lyra von Elfenbein aus der Mykenä-
Zeit   99
LUDWIG, F.   Die mehrstimmige Musik des 11.
und 12. Jahrhunderts   101
AUBRY, P.   L'ars mensurabilis et les proses litur-
giques au XIIIe siècle   108
d'INDY, V.   Quand c'est formée la fugue telle
qu'on enseigne actuellement dans les grands
conservatoires de l'Europe?   108
SCHWARTZ, R.   Zur Akzidentienfrage im 16.
Jahrhundert   109
KROYER, T.   Zum Akzidentienproblem im Aus-
gang des 16. Jahrhunderts   112
WOLF, J.   Die Akzidentien im 15. und 16.
Jahrhundert   124
BERNOULLI, E.   Hinweis auf gewisse Alterations-

zeichen in Drucken des 16. Jahrhunderts 126
CHILESOTTI, O. Le alterazioni cromatiche nel secolo XVI° 128
ARNHEIM, A. Über das Musikleben in Bremen im 17. Jahrhundert 135
WUSTMANN, R. Über Bearbeitung älterer und ausländischer Gesangstexte 136
d'INDY, V. De la sophistication de l'oeuvre d'art par l'édition 137
BIENENFELD, E. Neue Versuche zur Veränderung der klassischen Sinfonieform 141
HEUSS, A. Einige grundlegende Begriffe für eine historische Darstellung der musikalischen Dynamik 144
LEICHTENTRITT, H. Zur Vortragspraxis des 17. Jahrhunderts 147
CESARI, G. Die Entwicklung der Monteverdischen Kammermusik 153
JACHIMECKI, Z. Südliche Einflüsse in der polnischen Musik 156
HAAS, R. Zur Frage der Orchesterbesetzungen in der zweiten Hälfte des 18. Jahrhunderts 159
GANDOLFI, R. La Cappella musicale della Corte di Toscana (1539–1859) 167

1d Geschichte der Oper

NAGEL, W. Kleine Beiträge zur Geschichte der Oper in Darmstadt 184
ABERT, H. Zur Geschichte der Oper in Württemberg 186
CALMUS, G. Das Théâtre de la Foire des Lesage (Paris 1712–1738) und seine Bedeutung für die Entwicklung der Komischen Oper in Frankreich, England und Deutschland 193
SANDBERGER, A. Richard Wagners 'Liebesverbot' 194
GOLDSCHMIDT, H. Die Reform der italienischen Oper des 18. Jahrhunderts und ihre Beziehungen zur musikalischen Ästhetik 196
SCHERING, A. Geschichtliches über das Verhältnis von Oper und Oratorium 207
SANDBERGER, A. Neue Forschungen zu Caccini und Monteverdi 208
GREGOR, J. Die historische Dramaturgie in der Geschichte der Oper 208

1e Lautenmusik

ECORCHEVILLE, J. Über die Lautenkommission 211
SIMON, A. Die Lautenmusikbestände der Königl. Bibliothek in Berlin 212
KOCZIRZ, A. Über die Notwendigkeit eines einheitlichen, wissenschaftlichen und instrumentaltechnischen Forderungen entsprechenden Systems in der Übertragung von Lautentabulaturen 220

2 Exotische Musik und Folklore

POLLAK, H. W. Ausrustung der von Akademien und Gesellschaften zu entsendenden Reisenden, mit besonderer Rücksicht auf musikwissenschaftliche Zwecke 224

GÖTZ, J. Stand der Volksliedforschung in Mähren und Schlesien 226
GÖTZ, J. Die Fiedelmusik in der Iglauer Sprachinsel 227
ZODER, R. Über den Takt des Ländlers in Oberösterreich 228
KROHN, I. Über die typischen Merkmale der finnischen Volksliedmelodien in den Abteilungen A I und A II 230
LINEFF, E. Über neue Methoden des Folklores in Russland 233
LAUNIS, A. Die Pentatonik in den Melodien der Lappen 244
POMMER, J. Juchzer, Rufe und Almschreie aus den österreichischen Alpenländern 248
ANDERSSON, O. Altnordische Streichinstrumente 252
ANDERSSON, O. Altertümliche Tonarten in der Volksmusik mit besonderer Berücksichtigung der finnländischen 259
POMMER, J. Das Volkslied in Österreich: Unternehmen des k. k. Ministeriums für Kultus und Unterricht 266
HOSTINSKÝ, O. Mitteilungen über das tschechische Volkslied in Böhmen und Mähren 268
KUBA, L. Einiges über das istro-dalmatinische Lied 271
KOLESSA, F. Über den melodischen und rhythmischen Aufbau der ukrainischen (kleinrussischen) rezitierenden Gesänge, der sogenannten Kosakenlieder 276
SCHMIDT, W. Über Musik und Gesänge der Karesau-Papuas, Deutsch-Neu-Guinea 297
von HORNBOSTEL, E. M. Über Mehrstimmigkeit in der aussereuropäischen Musik 298
THUREN, H. Über die folkloristische Sammlung in Kopenhagen 303

3 Theorie, Ästhetik, Didaktik

SCHIEDERMAIR, L. Bemerkungen zum musikhistorischen Unterricht an hohen und mittleren Schulen 306
AIKIN, W. A. Die Phonologie in der Gesangslehre 309
ROSENTHAL, F. Die Musik als Eindruck. II 315
GOW, G. C. Harmonic problems of to-day 322
KRUEGER, F. Die psychologischen Grundlagen der Konsonanz und Dissonanz 330
HABÖCK, F. Der Gesangsunterricht in den Schulen 333
MOOS, P. Die Ästhetik des Rhythmus bei Theodor Lipps 345
BRANDSMA, E. Die Tonverhältnisse in der alten und neuen Musik 353
STÖHR, A. Das psychophysiologische Problem der Klangfarbe 360
ANTCLIFFE, H. Inductive and comparative criticism as applied to the art of music 364
GEISLER, C. Der Schulgesang und die Notationsfrage 368
MALHERBE, C. La graphologie dans les écritures musicales 371

ZAMPIERI, G. L'insegnamento della teoria della musica e del solfeggio nel r. Conservatorio di Milano 374
ZAMPIERI, G. I programmi d'insegnamento della storia della musica nel r. Conservatorio di Milano 381
ZAMPIERI, G. La notazione della partitura d'orchestra secondo il sistema Giordano 382
D'ANGELI, A. Novità, varietà, necessità del ritmo 384
KROHN, I. Reform der Taktbezeichnung 386
DAURIAC, L. Note sur l'inspiration musicale 402
GANDILLOT, M. Base rationiste du système musical 407
SCHMITZ, E. Das Verhältnis der Musikwissenschaft zur Populärliteratur und Musikkritik 422

4 Bibliographie, Organisationsfragen und Musikalische Länderkunde
SPRINGER, H. Die internationale Verzeichnung der älteren Musikliteratur 428
HENNERBERG, C. F. Schwedische Haydn-Handschriften 429
ECORCHEVILLE, J. Le catalogue du fonds de musique ancienne de la Bibliothèque nationale à Paris 432
MALHERBE, C. Observations relatives à l'établissement d'un catalogue des autographes musicaux dans les principales bibliothèques de l'Europe 433
MANTUANI, J. Katalogisierung des deutschen Liedes 434
MANTUANI, J. Katalogisierung der katholisch-liturgischen Texte 437
MANTUANI, J. Über die Umarbeitung von Riemanns Opernhandbuch 439
de OLIVEIRA-LIMA, M. La musique au Brésil (au point de vue historique) 443
SONNECK, O. G. Das Musikleben Amerikas vom Standpunkte der musikalischen Länderkunde 446
STANLEY, A. A. Music in American universities 459
SACCHETTI, L. Les principaux moments de l'histoire de la musique profane en Russie 466
BERNOULLI, E. Über die Schweizerische Musikgesellschaft 473
BEHREND, W. Musikalische Länderkunde Dänemarks 484
SQUIRE, W. B. Music in England 489
DAUBRESSE, M. Rapport sur l'enseignement musical en France 507

FLEURY, L. De la situation économique des musiciens d'orchestre en France 515
de LA LAURENCIE, L. Essai d'application des methodes graphiques à l'étude de la bibliographie musicale 526
LEVYSOHN, S. Die Pflege der Haydnschen Musik in Dänemark 529

5a Katholische Kirchenmusik
SCHNABL, K. Charakteristik der Kirchenmusik 531
MÜLLER, H. Zur Urgeschichte des deutschen Kirchenliedes 532
WEINMANN, K. Alte und moderne Kirchenmusik: historisch-kritische Bemerkungen zur Theorie und Praxis 537
SCHNERICH, A. Die textlichen Versehen in den Messen Josef Haydns und deren Korrektur 542
SCHNERICH, A. Die Wiener Kirchenmusikvereine 544
SCHNERICH, A. Kirchenmusikalische Denkmalpflege 546
WAGNER, P. Über gregorianischen Choral 550
WIDMANN, W. Einrichtung historischer Musikwerke für Aufführungen 557
MOISSL, F. Über die Notwendigkeit unterbehördlicher Durchführungsvorschriften zum Motu proprio vom 22. November 1903 567

5b Evangelische Kirchenmusik
SANNEMANN, F. Grundsätze evangelischer Kirchenmusik 576

5c Orgelbaufragen
SCHWEITZER, A. Die Reform unseres Orgelbaues auf Grund einer allgemeinen Umfrage bei Orgelspielern und Orgelbauern in deutschen und romanischen Ländern 581
EHRENHOFER, W. E. Einheitliche Gestaltung des Spieltisches unter spezieller Berücksichtigung der Pedalfrage 607
HAERPFER, F. Erfahrungen über Aufstellung und Intonation von modernen Orgeln 611
LYON, G. Utilité d'une numération logique des sons de l'échelle chromatique qui permette à première vue de se rendre compte de la note dont il s'agit et de l'octave où elle se trouve 616
RUNG-KELLER, P. S. Reform des Orgelbaues 621
SCHWEITZER, A. and MATHIAS, X. Internationales Regulativ für Orgelbau 636

11 BOL   Atti del IV congresso internazionale di filosofia
            Bologna 5–11 April 1911
            International Congress of Philosophy
            (Genoa: A. F. Formaggini, n.d./R Nendeln: Kraus, 1968)

Vol. iii (n.d.)
TORREFRANCA, F.   L'intuizione musicale quale
sintesi a priori estetica   513

11 LON   Report of the Fourth Congress of the International Musical Society
            London 29 May – 3 June 1911
            International Musical Society
            ed. C. Maclean (London: Novello, 1912)

[English résumés of all papers on pp. 52–77]
ADLER, G.   Zur Periodisierung der Musikgeschichte [résumé]   76
ECORCHEVILLE, J.   L'internationalisme dans la
musique [résumé]   76
FRIEDLAENDER, M.   German folk-songs, with
reference to English and American folk-songs
[résumé 59]
PARRY, C. H. H.   The meaning of ugliness in
. art   77
WOLF, J.   English influence on the evolution of
music   83

1 History (chairmen BARINI, G., de RODA,
C., SANDBERGER, A., WOLF, J.)
ANDERSSON, O.   The introduction of orchestral
music into Finland   90
ARNHEIM, A.   Englische Suitenkomponisten des
XVII. Jahrhunderts und ihre in Deutschland
erschienenen Sammlungen   93
BERNOULLI, E.   Eine Handschrift mit rhyth-
misierten Meistersängermelodien   99
CUMMINGS, W. H.   Matthew Locke, composer
for the church and theatre   100
DENT, E. J.   Giuseppe Maria Buini   106
FRERE, W. H.   Key-relationship in early medi-
eval music   114
HAMMERICH, A.   Musical relations between
England and Denmark in the XVII cen-
tury   129
HENNERBERG, C. F.   Einige Dokumente, den
Abt Georg Joseph Vogler betreffend   134
de LA LAURENCIE, L.   Les pastorales en musique
au XVIIme siècle en France avant Lully et leur
influence sur l'opéra   139
OPIENSKI, H.   Les premiers opéras polonais et
leur influence sur l'époque de la jeunesse de
Chopin   146

PROD'HOMME, J.-G.   La musique et les musiciens
en 1848 [résumé]   149
PRUNIÈRES, H.   Notes sur les origines de
l'ouverture française, 1640–1660   149
SONNECK, O. G.   Ciampi's 'Bertoldo, Bertoldino
e Cacasenno': a contribution to the history of
pasticcio [résumé 71]
SQUIRE, W. B.   Who was 'Benedictus'?   152
STEIN, F.   Mitteilungen über eine in Jena aufgefundene   mutmassliche   Jugendsymphonie
Beethovens [résumé]   158
TORREFRANCA, F.   La sonata italiana per cembalo nella prima metà del settecento e i concerti
di Giovanni Platti, 1740 [résumé]   158

2 Ethnology (chairmen ECORCHEVILLE, J.,
FRIEDLAENDER, M., NORLIND., T.)
ANDERSSON, O.   Violinists and dance-tunes
among the Swedish population of Finland to-
wards the middle of the XIX century   159
FELBER, E.   Die Musik in den Märchen und
Mythen der verschiedenen Völker   167
FELBER, E.   Das Gesetz der Zahlenverschiebung
in Märchen und Mythos und sein Einfluss auf
die Skalenbildung [résumé]   178
KEEL, F.   Some characteristics of British folk-
song   179
KOLESSA, P.   Ueber den rhythmischen Aufbau
der ukrainischen Volkslieder [résumé]   184
LAUNIS, A.   Ueber die Notwendigkeit einer ein-
heitlichen Untersuchungsmethode der Volks-
melodien   185
LINEFF, E.   Psalms and religious songs of Russ-
ian sectarians in the Caucasus   187
NORLIND, T.   Die polnischen Tänze ausserhalb
Polens   201
SANNEMANN, F.   Ueber eine ungedruckte
Sammlung deutscher Volkslieder mit ihren

Singweisen in der Altmark und im Magdeburgischen aus Volksmunde gesammelt von Ludolf Parisius [résumé] 205
SIHLEANU, S. De la musique populaire dans les pays roumains [résumé] 205

3 Theory, Acoustics, and Aesthetics (chairmen CALVOCORESSI, M. D., RIETSCH, H., TORREFRANCA, F.)
ANTCLIFFE, H. Musical form and the symphonic poem 206
de BERTHA, A. Les 'Rhapsodies hongroises' de Franz Liszt 210
CALVOCORESSI, M. D. Psychophysiology the true road to necessary reforms in musical aesthetics 224
ERGO, E. Des causes et des conséquences du manque d'unité dans plusieurs branches de la science musicale [résumé] 227
GANDILLOT, M. Sur le langage musical 228
GRIVEAU, M. Le sens et l'expression de la musique pure 238
KROHN, I. Ueber die Methode der musikalischen Analyse 250
FULLER MAITLAND, J. A. The interpretation of musical ornaments 259
MENCHACA, A. Nouveau systeme de notation musicale 267
SACHS, M. E. Das temperierte 19-Tonsystem und eine dafür passende Schrift 279
THELWALL, W. H. Mathematical analysis of the tempered chromatic scale [résumé 74]
WELLESZ, E. Die Aussetzung des Basso Continuo in der italienischen Oper 282

4 Church Music (chairmen MATHIAS, F. X., MÜLLER, H., SANNEMAN, F., STANLEY, A. A.)
BEWERUNGE, H. The metrical cursus in the antiphon melodies of the mass [résumé 54]
BIEHLE, J. Theorie des Kirchenbaues vom Standpunkte des Kirchenmusikers 286
HADOW, J. H. The influence of secular idiom upon English music [résumé 61]
MATHIAS, F. X. Subjektivität und Objektivität in der katholischen Kirchenmusik [résumé] 303
MÜLLER, H. Prinzipielles zur katholischen Kirchenmusik 303
ROOTHAM, C. B. Choir-boy training 307
WEINMANN, K. Zur Geschichte der Kirchenmusik im 17. und 18. Jahrhundert [résumé]312

5 Musical Instruments (chairmen FEDELI, V., HAMMERICH, A., SCHEURLEER, D. F.)
CARILLO, J. Sur la nécessité d'élever le niveau artistique de la musique militaire 313
DURANT, F. Instruments en cuivre omnitoniques à 6 pistons dépendants 314
GALPIN, F. W. The origin of the clársech or Irish harp 317
KRAUS, A. Italian inventions for instruments with a keyboard 324

MATTHAY, T. Principles of pianoforte teaching 326
NORLIND, T. Die englische Lautenmusik zur Zeit Shakespeare's [résumé] 331
ORLANDINI, I. Il Dattilapero 332
PIAZZANO, G. Le fonotomo – diviseur des sons [résumé] 332
de RODA, C. Les instruments de musique en Espagne au XIIIme siècle 332
PEREIRA de SAMPAIO, J. Harmonium tessaradécatonique [résumé] 333
SCHEURLEER, D. F. Iconography, of musical instruments 334
SPIRO-ROMBRO, A. Proposals for improving elementary 'violin methods', and hints for teaching the violin to children 337
STANLEY, A. A. The value of a collection of musical instruments in universities 341
WILLFORT, E. S. An 'encyclopaedic method' of pianoforte teaching 346
WOLF, J. Ueber Guitarren-Tabulaturen [résumé] 354

6 Bibliography, Organization, Contemporary Questions, etc. (chairmen HENNERBERG, C. F., SEIFFERT, M., SOMIGLI, C., SONNECK, O. G., SPRINGER, H.)
FEDELI, V. L'insegnamento della composizione negli istituti musicali 355
FLOOD, W. H. G. Irish musical bibliography 359
GÜTTLER, H. Die Pantomine W. A. Mozarts und ihre Aufführung 363
KARLYLE, C. E. International voice-training [résumé 62]
McNAUGHT, W. G. Introductory to 'tonic-sol-fa' 364
MAYER-REINACH, A. Vorschläge zur Herausgabe von Vokalmusik des XV.–XVII. Jahrhunderts 365
van REYSSCHOOT, D. De quelques réformes dans la notation des partitions d'orchestre d'édition dite 'populaire' 366
SEIFFERT, M. Neuausgabe der englischen Virginalmusik [résumé] 369
SEIFFERT, M. Generalkatalog der in englischen öffentlichen und privaten Bibliotheken befindlichen älteren Musikalien bis 1800 [résumé] 369
SIMON, A. Lute music in Berlin libraries [résumé 71]
SOMIGLI, C. Les mécanismes laryngiens et les timbres vocaux 370
SPIRO, F. Ueber eine Revision der Beethoven-Gesamtausgabe 372
SPRINGER, H. Die jüngsten Fortschritte der Musikbibliographie 377
STANLEY, A. A. Provincial music festivals in the United States 377
SUMMERS, J. Musical education in Australia, 1863–1911 [résumé 73]
WOITINEK, J. Ein neuer Schultafel-Apparat für den Gesangs-Klassen Unterricht [résumé] 385

11 MAL   **Annales du XXIIe congrès**
Malines 5–10 August 1911
Fédération archéologique et historique de Belgique
ed. H.-J.-B. Coninckx (Malines: L. & A Godenne, 1911)

Vol. ii Rapports & mémoires (1911)

van Doorslaer, G. Le carillon, son origine et son développement 353

Peeters, T. Oude kempische liederen en dansen 467

van Aerde, R. Les ménestrels communaux malinois et joueurs d'instruments divers, établis ou de passage à Malines de 1311 à 1790 507

van Doorslaer, G. Notes sur les facteurs d'orgues malinois 605

van Doorslaer, G. Connaît-on des documents relatifs au séjour de Jérôme Frescobaldi à Malines? 733

van Doorslaer, G. Connaît-on des documents relatifs au séjour de Jean-Ladislav Dussek à Malines? 735

Bergmans, P. Simon, maître de vièle (1313) 761

Jorissenne, G. Facteurs d'orgues dans le pays de Liège 885

Dwelshauvers Programme des recherches faites ou à faire dans les fonds musicaux de la province de Liège 891

van den Borren, C. L'esthétique expressive de Guillaume Dufay dans ses rapports avec la technique musicale du XVe siècle 899

11 ROM   **Rapport sur la musique contemporaine française** [Congrès de musique de l'Exposition internationale de Rome]
Rome 4–11 April 1911
Section d'histoire musicale de l'Institut français de Florence
ed. P.-M. Masson (Rome: Armani et Stein, 1913)

Masson, P.-M. Préface [on the evolution of French music since 1861] 5

Brenet, M. La musicologie 15

Malherbe, C. La musique dramatique 21

Huré, J. La musique religieuse et la musique chorale 63

Carraud, G. La musique symphonique 77

Landormy, P. La musique de chambre 103

Lalo, C. La philosophie de la musique 117

Anglas, J. La science des sons dans ses rapports avec la musique 127

Koechlin, C. La pédagogie musicale 139

de Bricqueville, E. La facture instrumentale 151

Baudin, G. La législation 157

12 BERL   **Bericht über den V. Kongress für experimentelle Psychologie**
                Berlin 16–20 April 1912
                    Gesellschaft für experimentelle Psychologie
                    ed. F. Schumann (Leipzig: Johann Ambrosius Barth, 1912)

13 BERL   [I.] **Kongress für Ästhetik und allgemeine Kunstwissenschaft: Bericht**
Berlin 7–9 October 1913
[International Congress on Aesthetics; Kongress für Ästhetik und allgemeine
Kunstwissenschaft]
(Stuttgart: Ferdinand Enke, 1914)

Moos, P.   Über den gegenwärtigen Stand der
Musikästhetik   416
Myers, C. S.   Beitrag zum Studium der Anfänge
der Musik   430
Heusz, A.   Der geistige Zusammenhang zwischen Text und Musik im Strophenlied   444
Sievers, E.   Demonstrationen zur Lehre von den
klanglichen Konstanten in Rede und
Musik   456
Ohmann, F.   Melodie und Akzent: experimentelle Untersuchungen über ihre Beziehungen 476

Penkert, A.   Die musikalische Formung von
Witz und Humor   482
Schering, A.   Zur Grundlegung der musikalischen Hermeneutik   490
Wetzel, H.   Dur und Moll im diatonischen
Tonkreise   501
Guttmann, A.   Kunst und Wissenschaft des
Gesanges   511
Riemann, H.   'Gignomenon' und 'Gegonos'
beim Musikhören   533

13 GHE   **Annales du XXIIIᵉ congrès**
Ghent 8–13 August 1913
Fédération archéologique et historique de Belgique
ed. G. vanden Gheyn (Ghent: W. Siffer, 1914)

Vol. iii Mémoires de la section d'archéologie et des
sous-sections de l'histoire de l'art et de la
musicologie (1914)
2 Musicologie
van Aerde, R.   Deux contrats de facteurs
d'orgues belges inconnus: XVIIᵉ et XVIIIᵉ
siècles   243
Klemantaski, L.   La musique flamande en
Angleterre   254
Arnheim, A.   Belgische Komponisten des 17.
und 18. Jahrhunderts und ihre Beziehungen zu
Deutschland   262
Bayart   Drogon de St Winnoc et quelques

autres compositeurs d'offices liturgiques aux
XIᵉ et XIIᵉ siècles   280
van Aerde, R.   Quelques documents inédits
concernant la musique dans un village   285
van Aerde, R.   Les Tuerlinckx, facteurs
d'instruments de musique à Malines, XVIIIᵉ et
XIXᵉ siècles   311
Prod'homme, J. G.   Lettres inédites de Lesueur,
Boieldieu et Cherubini au compositeur anversois Janssens   339
Prod'homme, J. G.   Fétis, Bibliothécaire du
Conservatoire de Paris   347

14 GÖT   **Bericht über den VI. Kongress für experimentelle Psychologie**
Göttingen 15–18 April 1914
Gesellschaft für experimentelle Psychologie
ed. F. Schumann (Leipzig: Johann Ambrosius Barth, 1914)

KATZ, D. Über einige Versuche im Anschluss an die Tonwortmethode von Karl Eitz   86, 141

RÉVÉSZ, G. Über musikalische Begabung   88, 134

RÉVÉSZ, G. Neue Versuche über binaurale Tonmischung   90

STUMPF, C. Über neuere Untersuchungen zur Tonlehre   305

15 WAS   **Proceedings of the Nineteenth International Congress of Americanists**
                  Washington 27–31 December 1915
                      International Congress of Americanists
                      ed. F. W. Hodge (Washington: Secretary, 1917/*R* Nendeln: Kraus, 1968)

Folklore and tradition

21 PAR   Actes du congrès d'histoire de l'art
Paris 26 September – 5 October 1921
Société de l'histoire de l'art français
(Paris: Presses universitaires de France, 1923–4)

Vol. ii/2 (1924)
4 Histoire de la musique
SQUIRE, W. B. L'iconographie musicale [in English]   731
FULLER MAITLAND, J. A. Les influences réciproques internationales en musique   735
PINCHERLE, M. Autour d'une histoire de la harpe   742
GENTILI, A. L'histoire de la théorie dans l'enseignement de la musique [in Italian]   754
JOSZ, R. and ROCHELLE, E. Essai d'une théorie de l'évolution de l'art musical, conforme aux conceptions scientifiques modernes de l'évolution   759
RAUGEL, F. Le Chant de la Sibylle d'après un manuscrit du XIIᵉ siècle, conservé aux Archives de l'Hérault   774
GASTOUÉ, A. L''Alarme' de Grimache (vers 1380–1390) et les chansons polyphoniques du moyen âge   784
BORGHEZIO, G. Poésies latines et françaises mises en musique conservées dans un manuscrit inconnu de la Bibliothèque capitulaire d'Ivrée [in Italian]   790
BONELLI, L. Les joueurs de flûte avignonnais au service de la République de Sienne au XVᵉ siècle [in Italian]   802
RAUGEL, F. Josquin des Prés à la Collégiale de Saint-Quentin   807
BERNOULLI, E. Sur la notation de rythmes complexes dans deux imprimés du XVIᵉ siècle   810
PEDRELL, F. Les échanges musicaux entre la France et la Catalogne au Moyen Age: Le Français Jean Brudieu, musicien catalan   823
TORRI, L. La seule composition musicale connue de Jean d'Arras [in Italian]   829
van den BORREN, C. Deux recueils peu connus d'Orlande de Lassus   833
de FREITAS-BRANCO, L. Les contrepointistes de l'École d'Evora   846
NEF, K. L'influence de la musique française sur le développement de la suite   853
BOGHEN, F. Bernardo Pasquini   856
PRUNIÈRES, H. Un opéra de Paolo Lorenzani   867
TESSIER, A. Un document sur les répétitions du 'Triomphe de l'Amour' à Saint-Germain-en-Laye (1681)   874
CHIGI SARACINI, G. Un musicien siennois du XVIIIᵉ siècle: Azzolino Bernardino Della Ciaia, prêtre et chevalier de Saint-Étienne [in Italian]   895
BRUNOLD, P. Un livre de pièces de clavecin de J.-F. d'Andrieu   918
KLEMETTI, H. Aperçu de l'histoire musicale finlandaise   922
LOGOTHETI La contribution française à l'étude de la chanson populaire grecque   929
BURLINGHAM HILL, E. La musique aux Etats-Unis [in English]   935

21 TUR   La vita musicale dell'Italia d'oggi: Atti del Iᵒ congresso italiano di musica
Turin 11–16 October 1921
Rivista musicale italiana, Santa Cecilia, Il pianoforte
(Turin: Fratelli Bocca, 1921)

FEDELI, V. La cultura musicale in Italia   33
FARA, G. Il folklore   43
VATIELLI, F. L'edizione (musica e letteratura musicale)   49
ALALEONA, D. Educazione musicale del popolo e sua organizzazione nella scuola e nella vita cittadina   58
PIZZETTI, I. Gli istituti musicali italiani   78
BAS, G. Iniziazione musicale degli esecutori: precedenza di un'adeguata preparazione artistica a qualsiasi studio tecnico   91
FERRARIA, L. E. L'educazione del senso ritmico col metodo Jaques-Dalcroze (ginnastica ritmica)   96
CORIO, E. Organizzazioni economiche fra musicisti e loro rapporti   114
CORIO, E. Assicurazioni sociali   126
CESARI, G. Critica musicale   139

22 RIO   **Annaes do XX congresso internacional de Americanistas**
Rio de Janeiro 20–30 August 1922
International Congress of Americanists
(Rio de Janeiro: Imprensa nacional, 1924–32/*R* Nendeln: Kraus, 1968)

Vol. i (1924)
1 Ethnologia
DENSMORE, F. Rhythm in the music of the
American Indian   85

23 BRUS   Compte rendu du Ve congrès international des sciences historiques
Brussels 9–15 April 1923
(Brussels: M. Weissenbruch, 1923/R Nendeln: Kraus, 1972)

X Histoire de l'art et archéologie
1 Histoire de l'art
de LA LAURENCIE, L.   Les femmes et le luth en
France aux XVIe et XVIIe siècles   366
KREPS, J.   Le développement des neumes   366
CORNETTE, A.   Liszt le romantique   368

van den BORREN, C.   Quelques manuscrits autographes de Gossec   369
TIRABASSI,   A.   Notation   mensurelle: la
transcription inexacte du temps parfait   370
CLOSSON, E.   Les instruments de musique
disparus   371

23 LEIP   Bericht über den VIII. Kongress für experimentelle Psychologie
Leipzig 18–21 April 1923
Gesellschaft für experimentelle Psychologie
ed. K. Bühler (Jena: Gustav Fischer, 1924)

JUHÁSZ,   A.   Wiedererkennungsversuche   auf
musikalischem Gebiete   182

24 BAS   Bericht über den musikwissenschaftlichen Kongress in Basel: veranstaltet anlässlich der Feier des 25jährigen Bestehens der Ortsgruppe Basel der Neue Schweizerischen Musikgesellschaft Basle 26–9 September 1924
Neue Schweizerische Musikgesellschaft: Ortsgruppe Basel
ed. W. Merian (Leipzig: Breitkopf & Härtel, 1925/R Wiesbaden: Dr Martin Sändig, 1969)

NEF, K.   Seb. Virdungs Musica getutscht   7
ABERT, H.   Grundprobleme der Opern-geschichte   22
ADLER, G.   Internationalismus in der Ton-kunst   36
ALTMANN, W.   Die Schaffung einer internationalen Bibliographie der Musikliteratur   51
ANGLÈS, H.   Cantors und Ministrers in den Diensten der Könige von Katalonien-Aragonien im 14. Jahrhundert   56
BECKING, G.   Zur Typologie des musikalischen Schaffens   67
BERNOULLI, E.   Dokumente zur Geschichte des Liedes und Tanzes aus dem 16. Jahrhundert   72
BOEPPLE, P.   Theoretisches und Praktisches zur Rhythmik der neuesten Musik   80
van den BORREN, C.   La musique pittoresque dans le manuscrit 222 C 22 de la Bibliothèque de Strasbourg (XVᵉ siècle)   88
BUNDI, G.   Ein musikhistorisches Kuriosum aus dem Oberengadin   106
CHERBULIEZ, A. E.   Über die Anwendung der Sieversschen Theorien auf die musikalische Interpretation   110
DENÉRÉAZ, A.   L'harmonie moderne et les phénomènes d'ordre 'complémentaire'   118
ERPF, H.   Einige Begriffe zur Harmonik der neueren Musik   125
FISCHER, W.   Zur Chronologie der Klaviersuiten J. S. Bachs   127
FRIEDLAENDER, M.   Eigenleben von Volksliedmelodien   131
GAGNEBIN, H.   Divers courants qui se sont manifestés dans la musique suisse romande pendant les cinquante dernières années   147
GRAESER, W.   Joh. Seb. Bachs 'Kunst der Fuge'   151
GURLITT, W.   Burgundische Chanson- und deutsche Liedkunst des 15. Jahrhunderts   153
GYST, F.   Über Zusammenhänge zwischen Ton und Farbe   177
HAAPANEN, T.   Denkmäler des gregorianischen Gesanges in Finnland   184
HANDSCHIN, J.   Über den Ursprung der Motette   189

HEUSS, A.   Das Orchestercrescendo bei Beethoven   201
von HORNBOSTEL, E. M.   Die Entstehung des Jodelns   203
JEPPESEN, K.   Das 'Sprunggesetz' des Palestrinastils bei betonten Viertelnoten (halben Taktzeiten)   211
KROHN, I.   Die Kirchentonarten   220
KROYER, T.   Die threnodische Bedeutung der Quart in der Mensuralmusik   231
MERIAN, W.   Die Tänze in den deutschen Orgeltabulaturen   243
MERSMANN, H.   Beethovens Skizzen vom Standpunkt phänomenologischer Musikbetrachtung   244
MOSER, H. J.   Musikalische Probleme des deutschen Minnesangs   259
MÜLLER-BLATTAU, J. M.   Zum Verhältnis von Wort und Ton im 17. Jahrhundert   270
NOACK, F.   Die Tabulaturen der hessischen Landesbibliothek zu Darmstadt   276
RIHOUËT, Y.   Un motet de Moulu et ses diverses transcriptions pour orgue   286
RIPOLLÈS, V.   Breves anotaciones a la Epistola Farçida de San Esteban (German résumé 308)   293
SACHS, C.   Die Musik im Rahmen der Schwesterkünste   310
SCHERING, A.   Das Problem einer Philosophie der Musikgeschichte   311
SEIFFERT, M.   Grundaufgaben der Musikwissenschaft und das Bückeburger Forschungsinstitut   317
SONDHEIMER, R.   Sinfonien aus dem 18. Jahrhundert in den Basler Sammlungen Lucas Sarasin und Collegium musicum   321
SPRINGER, H.   Beziehungen zwischen Oper und Volksmusik im Settecento   326
TIRABASSI, A.   Histoire de l'harmonisation à partir de 1600 à 1750   328
TOCH, E.   Melodielehre   334
TORREFRANCA, F.   Influenza di alcuni musicisti italiani vissuti a Londra su W. A. Mozart (1764–65)   336
UNGER, M.   Beethovens Handschrift   363
URSPRUNG, O.   Der vokale Grundcharakter des diskantbetonten figurierten Stils   364

WERNER, T. W.   Anmerkungen zur Motetten-   WOLF, J.   Altflämische Lieder des 14./15. Jahr-
kunst Josquins   375   hunderts und ihre rhythmische Lesung   376

24 BERL   Zweiter Kongress für Ästhetik und allgemeine Kunstwissenschaft: Bericht
                Berlin 16–18 October 1924
                Gesellschaft für Ästhetik und allgemeine Kunstwissenschaft
                Zeitschrift für Ästhetik und allgemeine Kunstwissenschaft xix (Stuttgart: Ferdinand
                Enke, 1925)

JACOBY, H.   Voraussetzungen und Grundlagen   SCHÜNEMANN, G.   Beziehungen neuer Musik zu
einer lebendigen Musikkultur   281   exotischer und frühmittelalterlicher Tonkunst
MERSMANN, H.   Zur Phänomenologie der   (supplementary papers JARNACH, P.   421, von
Musik (supplementary papers BECKING,   HORNBOSTEL, E.   424)   411
G. 388, PLESSNER, H. 392)   372   MOSER, H. J.   Die Stilverwandtschaft zwischen
ABERT, H.   Geistlich und Weltlich in der Musik   der Musik und den anderen Künsten (sup-
(supplementary papers von KEUSSLER,   plementary papers ANSCHÜTZ, G.   439,
G. 405, SCHERING, A. 408)   397   SACHS, C. 443)   425

24 NAP   Atti del V congresso internazionale di filosofia
                Naples 5–9 May 1924
                International Congress of Philosophy
                ed. G. Della Valle (Naples, Genoa and Città di Castello: Società anonima editrice
                Francesco Perrella, 1925/*R* Nendeln: Kraus, 1968)

Vol. ii Estetica
BIEHLE, H.   L'influenza dell'Italia sulla musica
tedesca   110

25 BRUG   Congrès jubilaire
Bruges 3–5 August 1925
Fédération archéologique et historique de Belgique (26th congress)
(Bruges: Les presses Gruuthuuse, 1925)

9 Musicologie (chairman BERGMANS, P.)
DENÉRÉAZ, A. De la musique à l' 'Harmonie des
spheres'   221
BERGMANS, P. L'imprimeur Gérard de Lisa,
chantre maître de chapelle à Trevise (1463–
1496)   222
van den BORREN, C. Sur Benedictus de Opitiis et
deux de ses oeuvres recemment publiées en
facsimile   223
van den BORREN, C. L'histoire de la musique
dans l'enseignement universitaire   223
PUGH, R. Les Silbermann: leur oeuvre dans la
région alsacienne   224
van DOREN, R. Le rôle joué par l'Abbay de

Saint-Gall   dans   la   diffusion   du   chant
romain   225
KREPS, J. Aux sources de notre écriture musicale
européenne: Xᵉ siècle   226
HOOD [FLOOD], W. H. G. Belgium's musical
debt to Ireland   228
van DOORSLAER, G. Severin Cornet, compo-
siteur-maître de chapelle 1530–1582   229
PLAMENAC, D. La chanson de L'Homme armé
et MS.VI:E.40 de la Bibl. nationale de
Naples   229
BORGHEZIO   Un codice vaticano trecentesiodi
rime musicale   231

25 LEIP   **Bericht über den I. musikwissenschaftlichen Kongress der Deutschen Musikgesellschaft in Leipzig**
Leipzig 4–8 June 1925
Deutsche Musikgesellschaft
(Leipzig: Breitkopf & Härtel, 1926/R Wiesbaden: Dr Sändig, 1969)

SCHERING, A. Musikwissenschaft und Kunst
der Gegenwart   9
WAGNER, P. Germanisches und Romanisches
im frühmittelalterlichen Kirchengesang   21
ADLER, G. Das obligate Akkompagnement der
Wiener klassischen Schule   35

1 Bibliographie der Musik (chairman
SCHWARTZ, R.)
ALTMANN, W. Die geschichtliche Entwicklung
der Katalogisierung musikalischer Hand-
schriften   49
OREL, A. Zur Quellenkunde für neuere Musik-
geschichte   51
SPRINGER, H. Wissenschaftliche und produktive
Musikbibliographie   54
HAAS, R. Zur Bibliographie der Operntexte   59

**2 Vergleichende Musikwissenschaft und In-
strumentenkunde** (chairman SACHS, C., repre-
sented by HEINITZ, W.)
HEINITZ, W. Asymmetrien in Gebrauchston-
leitern   67
JAHNN, H. H. Entstehung und Bedeutung der
Kurvenmensur für die Labialstimmen der
Orgel   71

KINSKY, G. Stand und Aufgaben der neueren
Instrumentenkunde   78
LACHMANN, R. Musik und Tonschrift des
Nô   80
SCHÄFER, O. (im Auftrage von K. Laker) Das
musikalische Sehen   94
RABSCH, E. Instrumentenkunde und ver-
gleichende Musikwissenschaft in der Schule 98

3 Methodik der Musikwissenschaft (chairman
ADLER, G.)
BÜCKEN, E. Zur Frage der Begrenzung und
Benennung der Stilwandlung im 18. Jahr-
hundert   103
DANCKERT, W. Personale Typen des Melodie-
stils   108
MEYER, K. Zur musikalischen Wiss-
enschaftslehre   113
MIES, P. Werdegang und Eigenschaften der De-
finition in der musikalischen Stilkunde   120

4 Musikalische Jugenderziehung und Organisation
(chairman KESTENBERG, L.)
JÖDE, F. Wege zur Polyphonie in der Erziehung   127
KÜHN, W. Grundlinien zu einer Theorie der

musikalischen Erziehung 134
BENNEDIK, F. Tonwort und Musikerzie-
hung 142
EBEL, A. Einrichtung und Aufgaben der musik-
pädagogischen Organisation 150
MÜNNICH, R. Die Behandlung musikästheti-
scher Probleme in der höheren Schule 159
RABSCH, E. Musikwissenschaft in der
Schule 165

5 Theorie der Musik (chairman THIEL, C.)
KLATTE, W. Stimmführung im homophonen
Satz und Stufentheorie 171
LANDÉ, F. Die Dissonanz als harmonisch-
melodisches Mischgebilde 181
JEPPESEN, K. J. J. Fux und die moderne Kont-
rapunkttheorie 187
MÜLLER-BLATTAU, J. Das pädagogische Pro-
blem des Kontrapunkts und der Fuge 189
KROHN, J. Methode für Ausbildung zur Mel-
odik 190

**6a-b Geschichte der Musik im Altertum und
Mittelalter** (chairman WOLF, J.)
WOLF, J. Über den Wert der Aufführungspraxis
für die historische Erkenntnis 199
EICKHOFF, P. Die Bedeutung des Viertakters als
herrschenden Prinzips in der griechisch-
römischen Metrik und Rhythmik 203
URSPRUNG, O. Wirklich so viel griechische Ein-
flüsse in der mittelalterlichen Musik? 206
HANDSCHIN, J. Notizen über die Notre Dame-
Conductus 209
LUDWIG, F. Die mehrstimmige Messe des 14.
Jahrhunderts 218
OREL, A. Zur Kompositionstechnik im Zeitalter
der Trienter Codices 219
WERNER, T. W. Über innere Kriterien für die
vokale oder instrumentale Bestimmung älterer
Musik 225
ANGLÈS, H. Orgelmusik der Schola Hispanica
vom 15. bis 17. Jahrhundert 227
GURLITT, W. Über Prinzipien und zur Ge-
schichte der Registrierkunst in der alten Orgel-
musik 232
BRUGER, H. D. Probleme der deutschen
Lautenmusik des 18. Jahrhunderts 237

**6c-d Geschichte der Musik von 1600 bis zum Tode
Beethovens** (chairman FISCHER, W.)
HASSE, K. Palestrina, Schütz, Bach und
Beethoven im Lichte der Stilwandlungen 245
FISCHER, W. Zur Geschichte des Fugenthe-
mas 246
NETTL, P. Spuren des Wiener Liedes in der
zweiten Hälfte des 17. Jahrhunderts 247
OPPEL, R. Melodische und architektonische Ge-
setze bei Bach 250
KELLER, H. Der Artikulationsstil der Bach-
schen Instrumentalwerke 251
NOACK, F. Die Opern von Christoph Graupner
in Darmstadt 252

SONDHEIMER, R. Anfänge des Wiener Stils in
der Sinfonie des 18. Jahrhunderts 260
GYSI, F. Mozart als Kritiker 266
DEINHARDT, H. Übersetzungsfragen im beson-
deren Hinblick auf die Opern Mozarts 270
SCHMITZ, A. Beethovens Religiosität 274
MÜLLER-BLATTAU, J. Die deutsche Kontra-
punktlehre des 17. Jahrhunderts 280
FROTSCHER, G. Ein Danziger Orgelbuch des 18.
Jahrhunderts 284
WERNER, T. W. Aus der Frühzeit des un-
begleiteten Männergesangs 286

**6e Geschichte der romantischen und modernen
Musik** (chairman SCHÜNEMANN, G.)
MERSMANN, H. Die Lage der abendländischen
Musik um 1900 289
BECKING, G. Klassik und Romantik 292
KALLENBACH-GRELLER, L. Die Klangwerte der
modernen Musik 297
HÁBA, A. Welche Aufgaben bietet die Viertel-
tonmusik der Musikwissenschaft? 304
ABER, A. Das Problem der Stilbühne bei den
Werken Richard Wagners (supplementary
paper APPIA, A. 314) 312

6f1 Katholische Kirchenmusik (chairman
MÜLLER-PADERBORN, H.)
KROMOLICKI, J. Zum Stil des neuen kirchen-
musikalischen Schaffens 321
MÜLLER, H. Zur Editionstechnik bei
Kirchenmusikwerken der klassischen Vokal-
periode 322
WEINMANN, K. Palestrina und das Oratorium
des hl. Filippo Neri 323
WEISSENBÄCK, A. Was bedeutet die neue litur-
gische Bewegung für die Kirchenmusik? 329
LECHTHALER, J. Die melodische Nachzeich-
nungstechnik in den kirchlichen Werken Alex-
ander Uttendals 335
KROYER, T. Das Orgelbuch Cod. Ms. 153 der
Münchner Universitätsbibliothek 339
KURTHEN, W. Liszt und Bruckner als Messen-
komponisten 340
SAMBETH, H. M. Die Gregorianischen Melodien
in den Werken Franz Liszts mit besonderer
Berücksichtigung seiner Kirchenmusik-
Reformpläne 341
BALLMANN, W. Vom Wesen der liturgischen
Musik 343
MÜLLER, H. Neue Bestrebungen auf dem Ge-
biete des katholischen deutschen Kirchen-
liedes 350

6f2 Protestantische Kirchenmusik (chairman
SMEND, J.)
BALTHASAR, K. Kirchenmusik und neuere evan-
gelische Liturgik 353
MÜLLER, J. Bach-Psychologie 359
EICKHOFF, P. Nach welchem Rhythmus müssen
die Melodien der deutschen evangelischen Kir-
chenlieder gesungen werden? 360

SCHERING, A. Zur Choralrhythmik 365
EPSTEIN, P. J. A. Herbsts geistliche Kompositionen 368
GÜTTLER, H. Die Monumentaloratorien des Königsberger Kantors George Riedel (1676–1738) 373

6g Musikalische Landeskunde (chairman SCHIEDERMAIR, L.)
MOSER, H. J. Ziele und Wege der musikalischen Lokalforschung 381
WERNER, A. Die praktische Durchführung der lokalen Musikforschung in Sachsen-Thüringen 385
OBERBORBECK, F. Schwäbische Reichsstädte als Träger deutscher Musikkultur im 18. Jahrhundert 391
RATTAY, K. Die Musikkultur des deutschen Ostens im Zeitalter der Reformation 393
KRUTTGE, E. Zur Musikgeschichte Westfalens 397
KURTHEN, W. Zur Renaissancebewegung des 19. Jahrhunderts im Rheinlande 398
SCHIEDERMAIR, L. Die Musik des Rheinlandes 401

7 Ästhetik der Musik (chairman SCHERING, A.)
MOOS, P. Beziehungen der jüngsten Musikwissenschaft zur Ästhetik (supplementary papers MERSMANN, H. 410, ERPF, H. 412) 405, 414
von KEUSSLER, G. Sinnestäuschungen und Musikästhetik 416
STEPHANI, H. Das Verhältnis von reiner und pythagoreischer Stimmung als psychologisches Problem (supplementary papers WICKE, R. 421, HEINITZ, W. 425) 417
MERSMANN, H. Die Bedeutung der Substanzgemeinschaft für die Analyse von Instrumentalmusik (supplementary paper REUTER, F. 429) 428
STEGLICH, R. Über das Formhören des Barock 430
FROTSCHER, G. Bachs Themenbildung unter dem Einfluss der Affektenlehre (supplementary paper BAUER, M. 439) 436
HEUSS, A. Die genetische Methode, gezeigt an Lied und Arie (supplementary paper MIES, P. 444) 442
WIEHMAYER, T. Über die Grundfragen der musikalischen Rhythmik und Metrik 445
SCHERING, A. Betonungs- und Gewichtsprinzip 460

25 MUN Bericht über den IX. Kongress für experimentelle Psychologie
Munich 21–5 April 1925
Gesellschaft für experimentelle Psychologie
ed. K. Bühler (Jena: Gustav Fischer, 1926)

BREHMER, F. Untersuchungen über Melodienauffassung und melodische Begabung des Kindes 140

WICKE, R. Untersuchungen zur Gegensätzlichkeit von Dur und Moll 240

26 FRE/B Bericht über die [I] Freiburger Tagung für deutsche Orgelkunst
Freiburg im Breisgau 27–30 July 1926
Musikwissenschaftliches Institut der Universität Freiburg im Breisgau
ed. W. Gurlitt (Augsburg: Bärenreiter, 1926)

GURLITT, W. Die Wandlungen des Klangideals der Orgel im Lichte der Musikgeschichte 11
WALCKER, O. Zur Geschichte der Orgelmensuren und ihrer Bedeutung für die Kunst des Orgelbaues 43
JAHNN, H. H. Gesichtspunkte für die Wahl zweckmässiger Pfeifenmensuren 50
FLADE, E. Gottfried Silbermann als Orgelbauer 59
FISCHER, W. Die konzertierende Orgel im Orchester des 18. Jahrhunderts 68
FROTSCHER, G. Zur Registrierkunst des 18. Jahrhunderts 70
JUNG, H. Wege zu einem einheitlichen Aufbau von Disposition und Spieltisch 76
SCHERING, A. Zur Frage der Orgelmitwirkung in der Kirchenmusik des 15. Jahrhunderts 87

BÖSER, F. Orgel und Liturgie 92
MÜLLER-BLATTAU, J. M. Über Erziehung, Bildung und Fortbildung der Organisten 99
LEHMANN, F. Die neue Orgel als Instrument der Volksbildung 110
MUND, H. Geschichte und Bedeutung des Orgelhäuses 114
HASSE, K. Max Reger und die deutsche Orgelkunst 122
KELLER, H. Die deutsche Orgelmusik nach Reger 130
ERPF, H. Orgel und zeitgenössische Musik 134
LUEDTKE, H. Das Oskalyd als neuzeitliche Versuchsorgel 139
BESSELER, H. Erläuterungen zu einer Vorführung ausgewählter Denkmäler der Musik des späten Mittelalters 141

26 GEN Compte rendu du Ier congrès du rythme
Geneva 16–18 August 1926
Institut de rythmique de Genève
ed. A. Pfrimmer (Geneva: Secrétariat de l'Institut Jaques-Dalcroze, 1926)

RISLER, J. Le rythme de la musique grecque 5
BOVET La liberté relative du rythme dans le chant grégorien 10
DAVID, L. L'accent d'intensité et le geste de l'expression rythmique de la mélodie grégorienne 15
KREPS, J. Le 'nombre musical' chez saint Augustin et au moyen âge 21
OPIENSKI, H. Le rythme dans l'exécution de la musique vocale 26
CHERBULIEZ, A.-E. L'unité du temps et sa division: problème psychologique fondamental du rythme musical 33
DENÉRÉAZ, A. Rythmes humains et rythmes cosmiques 39

REFARDT, E. Rhythmische Analysen 70
CHERBULIEZ, A.-E. Polyrythmique exotique 71
LEVY, E. Métrique et rythmique: definitions et basses 76
MARTIN, F. La notation du rythme 82
JAQUES-DALCROZE, E. Rythmes d'hier, d'aujourd'hui et de demain et leur enseignement dans les écoles de musique 92
PFRIMMER, A. L'utilité de la méthode Jaques-Dalcroze par le chef d'orchestre et les musiciens d'orchestre 179
GIESE, F. Körperrhythmus in Leben und Kunst der Völker 350

26 GRON   **VIIIth International Congress of Psychology: Proceedings and Papers**
Groningen 6–11 September 1926
(Groningen: P. Noordhoff, 1927/*R* Nendeln: Kraus, 1974)

WYNN JONES, L.   Experimental studies in consonance and rhythm   448

26 ROM   **Atti del XXII congresso internazionale degli Americanisti**
Rome 23–30 September 1926
International Congress of Americanists
(Rome: Riccardo Garroni, 1928/*R* Nendeln: Kraus, 1968)

Vol. ii (1928)
3 Etnologia
BÉCLARD-d'HARCOURT, M.   Le système pen-
taphone dans les chants des Copper-
Eskimos   15

27 BEL   Deuxième congrès international des études byzantines
Belgrade 11–16 April 1927
International Association of Byzantine Studies
ed. D. Anastasijević and P. Granić (Belgrade: Impr. de l'État, 1929)

Květ, J.   L'antiphonaire de Sedlec conservé à la   Gastoué, A.   Documents latins du moyen-âge
Bibliothèque de l'Université de Prague   155   sur le chant byzantin   157

27 BERL   Bericht über den deutschen Kongress für Kirchenmusik
Berlin 19–22 April 1927
Staatliche Akademie für Kirchen- und Schulmusik in Charlottenburg, Berlin
(Kassel: Bärenreiter, 1928)

Gennrich, D.   Die gegenwärtigen Bedingungen   Lechthaler, J.   Der katholische Organist als
für die Vorbildung unserer Kirchenmusiker 11   Baumeister des liturgischen Gesamtkunst-
Smend, J.   Die notwendige Beziehung zwischen   werkes   62
dem Kirchenmusiker und dem Vertreter des   Wagner, P.   Ästhetik des Gregorianischen Ge-
Predigtamts   22   sanges   71
Plath, J.   Die liturgischen Aufgaben des Organ-   Johner, D.   Wie gelangen wir zu einem wür-
isten und Chordirigenten   32   digen Vortrag des Gregorianischen Cho-
Wolf, J.   Die Aufgaben des Evangelischen Kir-   rals?   81
chenmusikers in geschichtlicher Beleuch-   Müller, H.   Einiges über klassische kirchliche
tung   41   Polyphonie   102
Moser, H. J.   Die Musikwissenschaft in der   Müller, H.   Das katholische deutsche Kirchen-
Ausbildung des Kirchenmusikers   48   lied   110
Gölz, R.   Die heutige Lage der evangelischen   Reimann, W.   Die Orgel als Kult- und Konzert-
Kirche auf dem Gebiete des Gottesdienstes 55   instrument   112

27 BON   Bericht über den X. Kongress für experimentelle Psychologie
Bonn 20–23 April 1927
Gesellschaft für experimentelle Psychologie
ed. E. Becher (Jena: Gustav Fischer, 1928)

Guttmann, A.   Experimentelle Untersuchungen über die Vierteltonmusik   118

27 FRE/S   Bericht über die Dritte Tagung für deutsche Orgelkunst
Freiberg in Sachsen 2–7 October 1927
ed. C. Mahrenholz (Kassel: Bärenreiter, 1928)

Mahrenholz, C.   Der gegenwärtige Stand der   Hasse, K.   Die geistigen und religiösen Grund-
Orgelfrage im Lichte der Orgelgeschichte 13   lagen der Orgelmusik seit Bach   46
Mahrenholz, C.   Orgel und Liturgie   58
Liturgischer Tag   Mendelssohn, A.   Die Orgel im Gottes-
Frotscher, G.   Kult-, Kirchen- und Konzertor-   dienst   72
gel   43

QUOIKA, R. Gregorianischer Choral und Orgel 78

SMEND, J. Die Synthese von Text und Ton im deutschen Choral und deren Bedeutung für das Orgelspiel 83

WÖRSCHING, J. Beruf und Bedeutung des Organistenamtes für den Lehrerstand und das deutsche Volk 87

Historischer Tag

BLUME, F. Die Orgelbegleitung in der Musik des 17. Jahrhunderts 95

SCHNORR von CAROLSFELD, E. Statistische Mitteilungen über die Orgeln im Bereich der evangelisch-lutherischen Landeskirche des Freistaates Sachsen 102

FLADE, E. Der Zukunftswerk des Silbermannorgel 103

GURLITT, W. Die musikwissenschaftliche Bildung des Organisten 110

HANDSCHIN, J. Die Orgelbewegung in der Schweiz 116

LÖFFLER, H. J. S. Bach und die Orgeln seiner Zeit 122

MOSER, H. J. Über deutsche Orgelkunst 1450–1500 133

MUND, H. Joachim Wagner, ein Alt-Berliner Orgelbauer 139

RUBARDT, P. Arp Schnitger 149

ZILLINGER, E. Über die ästhetische Durchbildung der Organisten 176

Orgelbautechnischer Tag

GEYER, J. Schwierigkeiten eines einheitlichen Aufbaues der Orgeldispositionen und des Orgelspieltisches 182

JAHNN, H. H. Monographie der Rohrflöte 189

KELLER, H. Der Spieltisch 197

LENK, A. Etwas vom Rollschweller 204

POPPEN, H. Die Einstimmung der heutigen Orgel 206

27 HAL Dritter Kongress für Ästhetik und allgemeine Kunstwissenschaft: Bericht
Halle 7–9 June 1927
Gesellschaft für Ästhetik und allgemeine Kunstwissenschaft
ed. W. Liepe, *Zeitschrift für Ästhetik und allgemeine Kunstwissenschaft* xxi (Stuttgart: Ferdinand Enke, 1927)

2 Vorträge und Verhandlungen zum Problemkreise Rhythmus

BAENSCH, O. Rhythmus in allgemein philosophischer Betrachung (supplementary paper to T. Ziehn's) 202

von WALTERSHAUSEN, H. W. Rhythmus in der Musik (supplementary papers von KEUSSLER, G. 270, OREL, A. 273) 260

3 Vorträge und Verhandlungen zum Problemkreise Symbol

SCHERING, A. Symbol in der Musik (supplementary papers BAUER, M. 388, MOOS, P. 393) 379

27 VIE Beethoven-Zentenarfeier: Internationaler musikhistorischer Kongress
Vienna 26–31 March 1927
(Vienna: Universal Edition, 1927)

Beethoven (chairmen MARX, J., FISCHER, W., GRAF, M.)

SCHIEDERMAIR, L. Beethoven und das Rheinland 7

KAUFMANN, P. Aus der Bonner Gesellschaft in Beethovens Jugendzeit 11

CLOSSON, E. Les particularités flamandes de Beethoven 16

WEINMANN, K. Beethovens Verhältnis zur Religion 19

TIERSOT, J. Les autographes de Beethoven à la Bibliothèque du Conservatoire de Paris 25

SIMON, A. Über einige amerikanische Beethoven-Ausgaben 26

OREL, A. Zum Begriff der Wiener Klassik 29

SPRINGER, H. Beethoven und die Musikkritik 32

HASSE, K. Art und Wesen der Tonsprache Beethovens 35

NAGEL, W. Beethoven Romantiker? 40

WILLNER, A. Die innere Einheit der klassischen Symphonie 43

DENÉRÉAZ, A. Beethoven et les rythmes cosmiques 45

WELLESZ, E. Die dramaturgische Bedeutung des Fidelio 48

MERSMANN, H. Beethovens zyklisches Formprinzip 52

MÜLLER-BLATTAU, J. Beethoven und die Variation 55

KROHN, I. Die Form des ersten Satzes der Mondscheinsonate 58

KAMIŃSKI, L. Neue Beiträge zur Entwicklung der Polonaise bis Beethoven 66

HEINITZ, W. Eine Studie zur dynamischen Schichtung in Beethovenschen Sonatenthemen 75

EINSTEIN, A. Beethoven und die Polyphonie 79

STEPHANI, H. Enharmonik ('Polare Harmonik') bei Beethoven 83

IWANOW-BORETZKY, M. Ein Moskauer Skizzenbuch von Beethoven 88

GURLITT, W. Robert Schumann in seinen Skizzen gegenüber Beethoven 91

MIKULICZ, K. L. Skizzen zur III. und V. Symphonie und über die Notwendigkeit einer Gesamtausgabe der Skizzen Beethovens 95

ROSENTHAL, F. Auftakt und Abtakt in der Thematik Beethovens 97

MARSCHNER, F. Zählzeit, Tempo und Ausdruck bei Beethoven 100

STEGLICH, R. Über Dualismus der Taktqualität im Sonatensatz 104

SCHNERICH, A. Das konfessionnelle Element bei Beethoven 107

ŠIROLA, B. Haydn und Beethoven und ihre Stellung zur kroatischen Volksmusik 111

PROD'HOMME, J. G. Les débuts de Beethoven en France 116

WOLF, J. Beethoven Kirchenmusiker? 123

KROLL, E. E. T. A. Hoffmann and Beethoven 128

VIANNA da MOTTA, J. Beethoven in Portugal 132

HAAS, R. Zum Kanon im Fidelio 136

OPIENSKI, H. Chopins Sonaten und ihr Verhältnis zum Beethovenschen Stil 138

Musikgeschichte (chairmen FICKER, R., OREL, A., WELLESZ, E.)

MEYER, K. Über die Melodiebildung in den geistlichen Spielen des früheren Mittelalters 145

HANDSCHIN, J. Über frühes und spätes Mittelalter 149

GOMBOSI, O. J. Quellenmässige Belege über den Einfluss der Chansonkunst auf die deutsche Liedmusik in der zweiten Hälfte des fünfzehnten Jahrhunderts 152

JEPPENSEN, K. Die Textlegung in der Chansonmusik des späteren 15. Jahrhunderts 155

ANGLÈS, H. Die mehrstimmige Musik in Spanien vor dem 15. Jahrhundert 158

GRAFCZYŃSKA, M. Die Polyphonie am Hofe der Jagellonen 164

URSPRUNG, O. Der kunst- und handelspolitische Gang der Musikdrucke von 1462–1600 168

CAUCHIE, M. Les chansons à trois voix de Pierre Cléreau 175

MOSER, H. J. Paul Hofhaimer als Orgelkomponist 181

PRUSIK, K. Das englische Madrigal um 1600 186

MERIAN, W. Das Verhältnis von Tabulaturtänzen des 16. Jahrhunderts zu vorhandenen Fassungen für mehrere Instrumente 189

SCHWARTZ, R. Zur Musikkultur der Renaissance 193

SCHERING, A. Die Kunstpraxis der Diminution 195

SCHNEIDER, C. Zur Frühgeschichte der Oper in Salzburg (bis 1650) 196

ROSENTHAL, K. A. Zur Stilistik der Salzburger Kirchenmusik des 17. Jahrhunderts 202

NOACK, F. Landgraf Ernst Ludwig von Hessen-Darmstadt als Komponist 205

KAUL, O. Ausstrahlungen der Wiener Vorklassik nach Würzburg 208

KAHL, W. Geschichte, Kritik und Aufgaben der K. Ph. E. Bach-Forschung 211

GÜTTLER, H. Kant und sein musikalischer Umkreis 217

KÖLTZSCH, H. Das Gestaltungsproblem in der Instrumentalmusik Franz Schuberts 222

Kirchenmusik (chairmen MÜLLER, H., WEISSENBÄCK, A.)

MÜLLER, H. Beethovens Missa solemnis und das Motu proprio des Papstes Pius X. über Kirchenmusik 229

URSPRUNG, O. Das Wesen des Kirchenstils: Zusammenfassung 232

WAGNER, P. Über den altspanischen, mozarabischen Kirchengesang 234

HAAPANEN, T. Zur Verbreitung der romanischen und germanischen Tradition im gregorianischen Gesang 237

KOSCH, F. Der Rhythmus im Choral der Solesmenser 240

FELLERER, K. G. Der Stile antico in der katholischen Kirchenmusik des 18. Jahrhunderts 244

JÁROSY, D. Die historische Entwicklung der ungarischen Kirchenmusik 247

LECHTHALER, J. Die stilistischen Strömungen in der Kirchenmusik der Nachkriegszeit 257

Bibliographie (chairmen HAAS, R., OREL, A.)

SPRINGER, H. Aufgaben der Gesellschaft für wissenschaftliche Musikbibliographie 263

SCHNEIDER, C. Musikbibliographie in Österreich 265

DEUTSCH, O. E. Über die bibliographische Aufnahme von Originalausgaben unserer Klassiker 268

NOACK, F. Organisation und wissenschaftliche Nutzbarmachung der Arbeit in den Seminaren 273

ZOBELEY, F. Praktische Probleme der Musikbibliographie 276

SCHMIDT-PHISELDECK, J. Datierung der Musikalien 279

ALTMANN, W. Über thematische Kataloge 283

HAAS, R.   Die Erhaltung der musikalischen Meisterhandschriften   290

HITZIG, W.   Bedeutung der Verlagsarchive für die Musikforschung   292

NETTL, P.   Die Notwendigkeit einer Textbücherbibliographie   296

Methodologie, Ästhetik, Psychologie, Instrumentenkunde, Vergleichende Musikwissenschaft (chairmen LACH, R., FELBER, E.)

GRAESER, W.   Neue Bahnen in der Musikforschung   301

MIES, P.   Stilkundliche Probleme bei Beethoven   304

NADEL, S.   Die Hauptprobleme der neueren Musikpsychologie   307

MOOS, P.   Hermann Siebeck als Musikästhetiker   312

FELBER, E.   Die orientalischen Notationen und unsere Notenschriftreform   317

LACHMANN, R.   Zur aussereuropäischen Mehrstimmigkeit   321

GUNTEBRÜCH, R.   Über die Mehrstimmigkeit im österreichischen Volksgesang   326

KOTEK, G.   Der Jodler in den österreichischen Alpen   331

RIEGLER, E.   Das rumänische Volkslied und die Instrumentalmusik der Bauern   340

MILLET, L.   La chanson populaire et l'art choral en Catalogne   351

PUJOL, F.   L'oeuvre du 'Chansonnier populaire de la Catalogne'   355

KALLENBACH-GRELLER, L.   Die historischen Grundlagen der Vierteltöne   359

KLIER, K. M.   Volkstümliche Querflöten und die Maultrommel in den österreichischen Alpen   373

GEIRINGER, K.   Gaudenzio Ferraris Engelkonzert im Dome von Saronno: ein Beitrag zur Instrumentenkunde des 16. Jahrhunderts   378

BERGMANS, P.   Les carillons belges et la musique de carillon   382

TETZEL, E.   Rhythmus und Vortrag   385

BIEHLE, H.   Schuberts Lieder als Gesangsproblem   388

28 NEWY Proceedings of the Twenty-third International Congress of Americanists
New York 17–22 September 1928
International Congress of Americanists
(New York, 1930/*R* Nendeln: Kraus, 1968)

Ethnology
HERZOG, G. Musical styles in North America   455
MICHELSON, T. Note on Fox Gens festivals 545

STRELNIKOV, I. D. La música y la danza de las tribus indias Kaa-Ihwua (Guarani) y Botocudo   796

28 OSL VIᵉ congrès international des sciences historiques: Résumés des communications présentées au congrès
Oslo 14–18 August 1928
(Oslo: Comité d'organisation du congrès, 1928/*R* Nendeln: Kraus, 1972)

15 Histoire des nations nordiques
BONNEROT, J. Saint-Saëns en Scandinavie en 1897   397

28 PRA Art populaire: Travaux artistiques et scientifiques du Iᵉʳ congrès international des arts populaires
Prague 1928
Institut international de cooperation intellectuelle
(Paris: Duchartre, 1931)

Vol. ii (1931)
3 Études sur les techniques
La musique
MERSMANN, H. Buts et méthode d'une étude musicale des chants populaires   97
KUTHY-TEREY La musique populaire dans la vie pratique et dans l'enseignement   101
BENEDITO, R. Le folklore musical à l'école 102
NADEL, S. Sur la structure des systèmes de gammes et le problème du 'cycle' dans la musique primitive   102
PERNOT, H. Chants et mélodies populaires: résolution adoptée par le congrès des arts populaires   104
van HOOGENHOUCK-TULLEKEN Le chant populaire au Canada   105
KUNST, J. Quelques notes sur la musique javanaise moderne   107
DURAN, S. M. La musique aborigene et populaire de l'Equateur   117
ALLENDE, U. La musique populaire chilienne   118

KENNEDY, D. Chants populaires anglais 124
PSACHOS, C.-A. Le chant populaire hellénique de l'antiquite a nos jours   126
BARTÓK, B. Les recherches sur le folklore musical en Hongrie   127
FUJII, K., ORIGUCHI, N. and KODERA, Y. Considérations sur la musique populaire au Japon   129
TANABE, H. Les études récentes concernant les instruments de musique du Japon   130
SANDVIK, O. M. La musique populaire norvégienne   130
BREDICEANU, T. Historique et état actuel des recherches sur la musique populaire roumaine   133
RIEGLER-DINU, E. La hora, le maquam et la chanson populaire de l'Orient européen 140
VÁCLAVEK, B. Les chansons profanes tchèques devenues populaires   141
HORAK, J. L'état actuel de l'étude des chansons populaires en Tchécoslovaquie   146
STRÁNSKÁ, D. L'état actuel de la chanson popu-

laire dans les Monts des Géants (Krko-
noše) 148
REPP, F. La chanson populaire de l'îlot linguis-
tique allemand de Spiz en Slovaquie 150
KOLESSA, P. Les formations anciennes et nouvelles dans les mélodies populaires ukra-
niennes 150
CASTRILLO HERNANDEZ, G. Le chant populaire
de la Vieille Castille 151
GUZMAN, A. Deux chansons de la province de
Palencia 154
SERRA y BOLDU, V. Les 'goigs' ou 'gozos',
poèmes religieux chantés en Catalogne 155
de SAN SEBASTIAN, J. A. La musique populaire
basque 155
MARTIN GONZALEZ, C. Les chansons et les
danses dans un village de Tolède 158
de las CUEVAS, E. Les chansons de noce dans la
province de Léon 158
ORTIZ DIAZ, D. L. Refrains et chansons de la
vallée de Iguna (Santander) 159
MARTINEZ TORNER, E. Bibliographie du folklore musical espagnol 159

La danse et le théâtre
HOUSTON, E. La musique, la danse et les cérémonies populaires du Brésil 162
KENNEDY, D. La renaissance de la musique et de
la danse populaire en Angleterre 164
KUBA, L. La danse slave: ses principales formes
et leur signification 166
BURCHENAL, E. Les danses populaires caractéristiques des États-Unis 166
LOUDON, E. Les cérémonies et les poèmes
dansés des Indiens Pueblos 168

RÉGNIER, H. Les danses populaires fran-
çaises 169
LAJTHA, L. Les jeux et les danses populaires en
Hongrie 172
BORRELLI, N. La tarentelle en Campanie 175
ALFORD, V. Quelques danses du Pays basque
français 177
NOTO SOEROTO Le caractère de la danse jav-
anaise 181
ZICH, O. Les particularités rythmiques des
danses populaires tchécoslovaques 184
KODERA, Y., KTANO, H. and ORIGUCHI, N. Les
danses populaires japonaises 185
DOMINGUEZ BERRUETA, J. Les couplets et la
musique de la jota aragonaise 187
del ARCO y GARAY, R. La jota aragonaise 187
MASOLIVER MARTINEZ, J. R. La 'dance' de
Hijar (Province de Teruel) 188
del ARCO y GARAY, R. Les couplets et les
'dances' dans le Haut-Aragon (Espagne) 189
ZALDIVAR, J. Les danses populaires cata-
lanes 190
ARAMON y SERRA, R. La 'danza' et la danse du
cierge de Castelltersol 191
PIERA GELABERT, M. La danse des gitanes du
Vallès 192
GRASES GONZALEZ, P. Les danses du Panadés
(Los bailes del Panadès) 192
de SAN SEBASTIAN, J. A. Les danses bas-
ques 193
KODERA, S. Les kagura, les représentations
populaires bouddhiques et les nouvelles représentations populaires au Japon 194
CIERNAK, J. Le théâtre populaire ancien et mo-
derne en Pologne 200

28 VIE Bericht über den internationalen Kongress für Schubertforschung
Vienna 25–9 November 1928
(Augsburg: Dr Benno Filser, 1929)

FRIEDLAENDER, M. Ansprache zur Ein-
führung 1
HAAS, R. Schubertforschung und Meister-
archiv 27
OREL, A. Schubert und Wien 37
BÜCKEN, E. Schubert und die Klassik 47
LACH, R. Schubert und das Volkslied 57
KŘENEK, E. Franz Schubert und wir 69
KÖHLER, F. Zur Abstammung Schuberts 77
MÜLLER, R. F. Die Körpergrösse Franz
Schuberts 81
PROD'HOMME, J. G. Les oeuvres de Schubert en
France 87
MARX, J. Schuberts Lied 111
MIES, P. Mehrfache Bearbeitung gleicher Texte
bei Schubert 117
GÜNTHER, F. Zur Darstellung Schubertscher
Lieder 125
van der STRAETEN, E. Schuberts Behandlung
der Streichinstrumente mit besonderer Berück-

sichtigung der Kammermusik 131
STEFAN, P. Schuberts geistige Haltung und
Bedeutung 141
WOLF, J. Die Schuberthandschriften der
preussischen Staatsbibliothek in Berlin 147
KINSKY, G. Schuberthandschriften in deut-
schém Privatbesitz 155
FRIEDLAENDER, M. Zur Handschriftenkunde
Schuberts 167
DEUTSCH, O. E. Zum thematischen Katalog der
Werke Schuberts 173
NOWAK, L. Franz Schuberts Kirchenmusik 181
KAHL, W. Schuberts lyrisches Klavierstück 189
KÖLTZSCH, H. Schuberts Sonaten 199
HAUSLEITHNER, A. Franz Schuberts Gesänge
für Männerstimmen 209
VRIESLANDER, O. Das Organische in Schuberts
'himmlischer Länge' 219
DECSEY, E. Franz Schubert als Tanz-
musiker 233

29 FLOR   Atti del I congresso nazionale delle tradizioni popolari
Florence 8–12 May 1929
Comitato nazionale per le tradizioni popolari
(Florence: Rinascimento del libro, 1930)

SANTOLI, V. Di una nuova raccolta di canti   FARA, G. La musica del popolo   211
popolari toscani   66   BONAVENTURA, A. L'archivio delle voci   215

29 NEWH   Ninth International Congress of Pyschology: Proceedings and Papers
New Haven, Connecticut 1–7 September 1929
(Princeton, New Jersey: Psychological Review Company, 1930/R Nendeln: Kraus,
1974)

Theory and history of psychology (chairman   SEASHORE, R. H. Individual differences in rhyth-
WARREN, H. C.)   mic motor coördinations   385
GUTTMANN, A. Ist die Vierteltonsmusik   STANTON, H. M. Psychological tests: a factor in
möglich?   203   admission to the Eastman School of
                                                   Music   406
Psychology of music (chairman SEASHORE, C. E.) VERNON, P. E. The psychology of music: its
HEINLEIN, C. P. The effect of the musical modes   scope and methodology   461
on the amplitude of tapping and on the nature of
pianoforte performance   217   **Aesthetics** (chairman LANGFELD, H. S.)
HOLLINSHEAD, M. T. The vibrato in violin   PRATT, C. C. Schopenhauer's theory of
playing   224   music   350
LARSEN, W. S. The rôle of tests of musical   RUCKMICK, C. A. Musical appreciation: a study
aptitude in an instrumental music-program in a   of the higher emotions   372
public school   284   SANBORN, H. C. The problem of music   379
PETERSON, J. and SMITH, W. F. Habituation
effects of the equally tempered musical   **Experimental psychology** (chairman KÖHLER, W.)
scale   338   SEASHORE, C. E. The rôle of experimental
SCHOEN, M. The nature of the musical   psychology in the science of art and
mind   383   music   384

29 ROM   Primo congresso mondiale delle biblioteche e di bibliografia
Rome and Venice 15–30 June 1929
Ministerio della educazione nazionale: Direzione generale delle accademie e bib-
lioteche
(Rome: Libreria dello Stato, 1931–3)

Vol. ii (1931)
Regole internazionali per la compilazione dei cat-   graphie der Erstdrucke   332
aloghi
BONAVENTURA, A. L'ordinamento della musica   Vol. iii (1931)
nelle biblioteche italiane e le relazioni   **Il Libro italiano, bibliografia e biblioteche ital-**
bibliografico-musicali con le altre nazioni 188   **iane**
                                                   2 Studi bibliografici in Italia
Bibliografia internazionale redazione di un codice TORREFRANCA, F. La bibliografia della musica
internazionale per bibliografi   theorica e la necessità di una bibliografia
DEUTSCH, O. E. Internationale Musikbiblio-   italiana a tutto l'ottocento   105

30 ANT   Congrès d'Anvers 1930: annales
Antwerp 16–21 August 1930
Fédération archéologique et historique de Belgique (27th congress)
ed. P. Rolland (Antwerp: V. Resseler, 1930–31)

Vol. ii (1931)
JUTEN, G. C. A.   Jacob Obrecht   441
LENAERTS, R. B.   Nederlandsche polifoniese

liederen uit de XVᵉ en XVIᵉ eeuwen   453
van DOORSLAER, G.   Aperçu sur la pratique de la
musique vocale à Malines au XVᵉ siècle   465

30 ATH   IIIᵉᵐᵉ Congrès international des études byzantines
Athens 12–18 October 1930
International Association of Byzantine Studies
ed. A. C. Orlandos (Athens: Imprimerie Hestia, 1932)

HOËG, C.   L'état actuel de l'étude de la musique
byzantine   263
ANTONIADIS, S.   La musique byzantine rendue
par les 'ondes Martenot'   265
PSACHOS, C.   Histoire, art, parasémantique et
tradition de la musique byzantine   266

MERLIER, MME M.   Les particularités melo-
diques de la chanson populaire grecque   267
PAPADIMITRIOU, A.   Peri tēs Heptanēsō idio-
rrhythmou byzantinēs mousikēs tēs kaloumenēs
Krētikēs [Rhythmic peculiarities of so-called
Byzantine music]   268

30 BON   Bericht über die I. Tagung der Internationalen Gesellschaft für experimentelle Phonetik
Bonn 10–14 June 1930
Internationale Gesellschaft für experimentelle Phonetik
ed. P. Menzerath (Bonn: Gebr. Scheur, 1930)

BEATTY, R. T.   The sensation of pitch in listening
to vibrato singing   15
SELMER, E. W.   Vorschläge zu Zeitnormungen
bei Melodieaufnahmen   31

HENDRIK, K.   Notenvorlage und Kymogra-
phionaufnahme   42
JONES, S.   Two methods of measuring intonation   49

30 HAM[1]   Verhandlungen des XXIV. internationalen Amerikanisten-Kongresses
Hamburg 7–13 September 1930
International Congress of Americanists
ed. R. Grossmann and G. Antze (Hamburg: Friederichsen, De Gruyter & Co.,
1934/R Nendeln: Kraus, 1968)

Ethnographie
van PANHUYS, L. V.   Quelques chansons et quelques danses dans la Guyane néerlandaise 207

POSPÍŠIL, F.   The present condition of choreographic research in Northern, Central and
Southern America   212

30 HAM^2 Vierter Kongress für Ästhetik und allgemeine Kunstwissenschaft: Bericht
Hamburg 7–9 October 1930
Gesellschaft für Ästhetik und allgemeine Kunstwissenschaft
ed. H. Noack, *Zeitschrift für Ästhetik und allgemeine Kunstwissenschaft* xxv,
supplement (Stuttgart: Ferdinand Enke, 1931)

STECHOW, W. Raum und Zeit in der graphischen und musikalischen Illustration (discussion 127) 118

RIEZLER, W. Das neue Raumgefühl in bildender Kunst und Musik (discussion 205) 179

SCHNEIDER, M. Raumtiefenhören in der Musik 207

MERSMANN, H. Zeit und Musik 216

30 LIÈ Société internationale de musicologie premier congrès Liége: compte rendu/Internationale Gesellschaft für Musikwissenschaft erster Kongress Lüttich: Kongressbericht/International Society for Musical Research First Congress Liége: Report
Liège 1–6 September 1930
International Society for Musical Research (International Musicological Society)
(Burnham, Bucks: International Society for Musical Research/Plainsong & Mediaeval Music Society, 1931)

van den BORREN, C. Du rôle international de la Belgique dans l'histoire musicale 17

FELLOWES, E. H. The English madrigal of the sixteenth century 33

GURLITT, W. Franz-Joseph Fétis und seine Rolle in der Geschichte der Musikwissenschaft 35

PIRRO, A. Remarques sur l'exécution musicale de la fin du 14e au milieu de 15e siècle 55

ANGLÈS, H. La polyphonie religieuse péninsulaire antérieure à la venue des musiciens flamands en Espagne 67

AUDA, A. Léonard Terry, professeur, compositeur, chef d'orchestre et musicologue liégeois 73

BERNET-KEMPERS, K. P. Die wallonische und die französische Chanson in der ersten Hälfte des 16. Jahrhunderts 76

BIEHLE, H. Die textlichen Grundlagen als Gesangsproblem 81

CAUCHIE, M. Les Psaumes de Janequin (description seule) 86

CHARLIER, C. 'L'Écho', périodique liégeois au XVIIIème siècle 87

DELPORTE, J. La Messe 'Christus resurgens' de Louis van Pulaer (†1528) 91

van DOORSLAER, G. Paul van Winde, organiste à la Cour impériale de Vienne (†1598) 93

DREIMÜLLER, K. Neue Neumenfunde (aus dem ehemaligen Benediktiner-Abtei München-Gladbach, Rheinland) 100

EINSTEIN, A. Filippo di Monte als Madrigalkomponist 102

FELLERER, K. G. Das Partimentospiel, eine Aufgabe des Organisten im 18. Jahrhundert 109

FELLOWES, E. H. The Ouseley Library at Tenbury 112

FRYKLUND, D. Eine schwedische Sammlung von Briefen von und an Fétis 113

GÜTTLER, H. Johann Reichardt, ein preussischer Lautenist 118

GURLITT, W. Ein Lütticher Beitrag zur Adam von Fuldafrage 125

HAAPANEN, T. Eine Introitensammlung in finnischer Sprache von Jahre 1605 132

HANDSCHIN, J. Die Rolle der Nationen in der Mittelalterlichen Musikgeschichte 138

HANDSCHIN, J. Zur Musikästhetik des 19. Jahrhunderts 139

HARASZTI, E. Le question tzigane-hongroise au point de vue de l'histoire de la musique 140

HARDING, R. The pianoforte from 1709 to 1851 146

HEINITZ, W. Die Erfassung des subjektivmotorischen Elements in der musikalischen Produktion Primitiver 148

HERTZMANN, E. Adrian Willaert im Rahmen der Chansonentwicklung 154

JEPPESEN, K. Die mehrstimmige italienische Lauda am Anfang des 16. Jahrhunderts 155

KROHN, I. Fr. Aug. Gevaerts Stellung zum gregorianischen Gesang 158

LAVOYE, L. Sur une pièce vocale à 4 voix extraite d'un manuscrit de l'ancienne abbaye de Saint-Trond 165

LENAERTS, R. La chanson polyphonique néerlandaise aux 15e et 16e siècles 168

MASSON, P.-M. Rameau et Beethoven 174

MATHIAS, F. X. Die Pragmatik der Orgelbaugeschichte des 18. Jahrhunderts im Lichte des Pariser Silbermann-Archivs 182

XVᵉ Congrès international d'anthropologie et d'archéologie préhistorique: IVᵉ Session de l'Institut international d'anthropologie
Portugal 21–30 September 1930

see 31 PAR

31 HAM   **Bericht über den XII. Kongress der Deutschen Gesellschaft für Psychologie**
Hamburg 12–16 April 1931
Deutsche Gesellschaft für Psychologie
ed. G. Kafka (Jena: Gustav Fischer, 1932)

GUTTMANN, A.   Das Tempo und seine Vari-
ationsbreite   341

31 LEID   **Actes du XVIIIᵉ congrès international des orientalistes**
Leiden 7–12 September 1931
International Congress of Orientalists
(Leiden: J. Brill, 1932/R Nendeln: Kraus, 1968)

EDWARDS, E. D.   The establishment of schools of
secular music by Ming Huang of the T'ang
dynasty   121

31 PAR   **XVᵉ Congrès international d'anthropologie et d'archéologie préhistorique (suite): Vᵉ Session
de l'Institut international d'anthropologie**
Paris 20–27 September 1931 [second half; first half of congress, and IVᵉ Session de l'Institut
international d'anthropologie, held in Portugal 21–30 September 1930]
Institut international d'anthropologie
(Paris: Librairie E. Nourry, 1933/R Nendeln: Kraus, 1970)

VÉKOVITCH, D.   Chants populaires de femmes
serbes   710
de VAUX-PHALIPAU   Moeurs des Serbes de
Lusace d'après les chansons populaires   715

IRZA-NOUR   Keuroghlou,   poète   populaire
turc   725
BUGIEL, V.   Quelles sont les premières phases de
la poésie des peuples primitifs?   793

31 SAL   **Bericht über die musikwissenschaftliche Tagung der Internationalen Stiftung Mozarteum in
Salzburg**
Salzburg 2–5 August 1931
Internationale Stiftung Mozarteum
ed. E. Schenk (Leipzig: Breitkopf & Härtel, 1932)

SCHIEDERMAIR, L.   Das deutsche Mozartbild 1
LACH, R.   Mozart und die Gegenwart   12
SCHRADE, L.   Mozart und die Romantiker   22
OREL, A   Mozart in der Kunstanschauung
Franz Grillparzers   39
SCHENK, E.   Mozarts mütterliche Familie   45
FISCHER, W.   Die Stetigkeit in Mozarts
Schaffen   69

PAUMGARTNER, B.   Zur Synthese der symphonischen Musik Mozarts   72
TORREFRANCA, F.   Mozart e il quartetto italiano   79
CHERBULIEZ, A.-E.   Zur harmonischen Analyse
der Einleitung von Mozarts C-Dur Streichquartett (K.V. 465)   103
CHERBULIEZ, A.-E.   Stilkritischer Vergleich von

Mozarts beiden g-moll Sinfonien von 1773 und 1788   112
ENGEL, H.   Mozarts Konzertwerke   120
DANCKERT, W.   Mozarts Menuettypen   129
NETTL, P.   Mozarts Prager Kontertänze   133
FELLERER, K. G.   Mozarts Litaneien   136
NETTL, P.   'Sethos' und die freimauerische Grundlage der 'Zauberflöte'   142
CHERBULIEZ, A.-E.   Zwei Passauer handschriftliche Klavierauszüge von Mozarts 'Figaro' und 'Don Juan der Schwelger' (1789)   150
LEWICKI, E.   Die Stimmcharaktere im 'Idomeneo'   158

WALLERSTEIN, L.   Mozarts 'Idomeneo' in der Wiener Bearbeitung   161
KAUL, O.   Zur Instrumentation Mozarts   167
STEGLICH, R.   Das Tempo als Problem der Mozartinterpretation   172
BÖHME, E. W.   Mozart in der schönen Literatur   179
HAAS, R.   Mozartforschung und Meisterarchiv   298
SCHENK, E.   Organisation der Mozartforschung   302
ENGEL, H.   Musiksoziologie und musikalische Volkskunde   304

31 UDIN   **Il congresso nazionale delle tradizioni popolari**
Udine 5–8 September 1931
Comitato nazionale italiano per le tradizioni popolari
Lares ii/3 (Florence: Società editrice 'Rinascimento del Libro', 1931)

GOIDÀNICH, P. G.   Proposta di una fonofilmoteca internazionale linguistico-folkloristica   10

32 AMS   **Proceedings of the [First] International Congress of Phonetic Sciences**
Amsterdam 3–8 July 1932
International Society of Phonetic Sciences
Archives néerlandaises de phonétique expérimentale, viii–ix
(The Hague: Martinus Nijhoff, 1933) [also published separately Harlem: J. Enschedé
et fils, n.d.]

BERNET KEMPERS, K. P. Das Entstehen von Tonsystemen   130
BECKING, G. Der musikalische Bau des Montenegrinischen Volksepos   144
FEUCHTWANGER, E. Das Musische in der
Sprache und seine Pathologie   205
TRAUTWEIN, F. Über elektrische Synthese von Sprachlauten und musikalischen Tönen mit Demonstrationen   291

32 CAIR   **Recueil des travaux du congrès de musique arabe**
Cairo 28 March – 3 April 1932
Royaume d'Égypte: Ministère de l'instruction publique
(Cairo: Boulac, 1934)

II Partie technique
1 Commission de l'enregistrement (includes list of recorded examples p. 109 and report by LACHMANN, R. 127)   89
2 Commissions des modes, des rythmes et de la composition   131
INSTITUT de MUSIQUE ORIENTALE Genres de composition musicale arabe employés en Egypte   166
EL GAREM, A. Rapport sur la composition 171
d'ERLANGER, R. Report [in arabic]   176
INSTITUT de MUSIQUE ORIENTALE Communication sur les rythmes employés en Egypte et leur décomposition en rythmes simples (bassit) et composés (aaraye) avec des exemples tirés de mélodies composées sur ces rythmes   399

DARWICHE, A. Communication sur les rythmes employés en Syrie et spécialement à Alep, et leur décomposition en mesures simples et composés, avec des exemples de mélodies composées sur ses rythmes   433
Rythmes employés en Iraq et spécialement à Bagdad   .   516
Rythmes employés en Tunisie, au Maroc et en Algérie   521
INSTITUT de MUSIQUE ORIENTALE Maqamates employés en Egypte et leur décomposition en genres   529
Maqamates employés chez les Marocains et spécialement en Tunisie   583
3 Commission de l'échelle musicale   593
4 Commission de l'enseignement   605
Supplement of photographs of instruments etc.

32 COP   **Papers read to the X. International Congress of Psychology at Copenhagen, 1932**
Copenhagen 1932
Acta psychologica i/1 (The Hague: Martinus Nijhoff, 1935/*R* Nendeln: Kraus, 1975)

BAHLE, J. Zur Psychologie des Einfalls und der Inspiration im musikalischen Schaffen   7
SEASHORE, C. E. Psychology of the vibrato in music and speech   212

32 LAP   Actas y trabajos científicos del XXV° congreso internacional de Americanistas
La Plata 24 November – 4 December 1932
International Congress of Americanists
(Buenos Aires: Coni, 1934/R Nendeln: Kraus, 1968)

Vol. i (1934)
Etnografía
DENSMORE, F.   The music of the North American Indians   119

VEGA, C.   La flauta de Pau andina   333
VEGA, C.   Escalas con semitonos en la música de los antiguos peruanos   319

32 LIÈ   Congrès de Liège 1932: annales
Liège 1932
Fédération archéologique et historique de Belgique (29th congress)
ed. J. Dumont and P. Harsin (?Liège, n.d.)

Musicologie
van den BORREN, C.   Hugo et Arnold de Lantins   263

CHARLIER, C.   Un manuscrit musical mosan de 1728   273
BRAGARD, R.   André de Pape   289

32 STRS   Compte rendu du congrès d'orgue tenu à l'Université de Strasbourg
Strasbourg 5–8 May 1932 [1934 given in error on title page]
ed. F. X. Mathias (Strasbourg: Société strasbourgeoise de Librairie 'Sostralib', 1934)

Part IV

1a Technique de la facture d'orgue
GEYER, J.   Fautes à éviter dans la disposition des jeux   114
RUPP, E.   Les sommiers et la traction de l'orgue   115
BÉRENGER de MIRAMON, MARCHAL, A., DUFOURCQ, N. and GONZALEZ, V.   La doctrine parisienne de l'orgue   125
DILLENSEGER, R. P.   La puissance organale mise en proportion avec le cubage des sanctuaires et des salles de concert   129
MATHIAS, F. X.   L'emplacement des orgues dans les sanctuaires   134
COUPLEUX, L.   L'orgue des ondes   139

1b Technique de la musique d'orgue
CELLIER, A.   L'improvisation   141
MATHIAS, F. X.   La continuité dans l'évolution de l'expression organale et ses conséquences pour la pédagogie musicale de l'heure présente   146
CELLIER, A.   Le rôle de l'orgue dans le culte protestant   148

PIZOT-MONNIER, Mme P.   De l'orgue dans le culte protestant   151
MATHIAS, F. X.   L'orgue dans le culte catholique   157

2 Esthétique de la facture d'orgue et du jeu d'orgue
MATHIAS, F. X.   L'orgue dans la culture musicale de tous les siècles   159
MATHIAS, F. X.   L'orgue au service du culte catholique   162

3 Histoire de l'orgue
GEYER, J.   Un orgue à 52 tuyaux, 4 jeux, sommier à coulisses, de l'an 228   164
MATHIAS, F. X.   L'orgue dans l'antiquité chrétienne   166
GÉROLD, T.   Strasbourg dans l'histoire de l'orgue   172
PIRRO, A.   Orgues et organistes en Alsace et en Lorraine du XIVᵉ au XVIIIᵉ siècle   177
PIRRO, A.   Orgues et organistes de Haguenau de 1491 à 1525   182
DUFOURCQ, N.   Le grand orgue de la Chapelle de l'Ecole Royale Militaire   187
RAUGEL, F.   Les orgues de Bruckner   195

33 FLOR   Atti del primo congresso internazionale di musica
Florence 30 April – 4 May 1933
I Maggio musicale fiorentino
(Florence: Felice Le Monnier, 1935)

[includes résumés in Italian for non-Italian articles]

CESARI, G. Le funzioni, i metodi, gli scopi della critica musicale   11

PANNAIN, G. La critica musicale come critica d'arte   18

RONGA, L. Nuove tendenze nella critica musicale europea   31

LUALDI, A. Due nuove vie per la musica: radio e film sonoro   43

COEUROY, A. Problèmes intérieurs et extérieurs de radio   52

MOOSER, R.-A. Le contrôle de la critique musicale sur les auditions radiophoniques   61

FLEISCHER, H. Neue Musik und mechanische Musik   68

COLACICCHI, L. Il disco e la musica   76

MAINE, B. Some effects of mechanized music   84

VUILLERMOZ, É. La musique mécanique et la culture musicale   93

EBERT, C. Moderne Opernregie   105

KOCH, L. Schallplattenmusik   109

ROSBAUD, H. Problem der Programmgestaltung und der künstlerisch-technischen Wiedergabe im deutschen Rundfunk   118

ROSSI-DORIA, G. Tendenze dell'odierno teatro musicale italiano   125

MACHABEY, A. Rapport sur le théâtre musical en France   139

EINSTEIN, A. Le tendenze attuali dell'opera tedesca   169

BONAVIA, F. L'opera in Inghilterra   183

SESSIONS, R. L'opera negli Stati Uniti   188

BEKKER, P. Organisation des Operntheaters   194

DELLA CORTE, A. Ricerca intorno alle 'vicende degli stili del canto in rapporto alla cultura musicale e alla pedagogia stilistica'   203

MILA, M. Musica e ritmo nel cinematografo   209

FÜRST, L. Prinzipien musikalischer Gestaltung im Tonfilm   216

CASELLA, A. Scambi musicali   223

DENT, E. J. International exchange in music   226

STEFAN, P. Ein Völkerbund der Musik   233

PRUNIÈRES, H. Des rapports artistiques internationaux considérés du point de vue de la musique, de la musicologie et des musiciens   239

de SCHLOEZER, B. Comprendre la musique   250

PARENTE, A. Il problema dell'interpretazione musicale   259

GATTI, G. M. Dell'interpretazione musicale   268

33 LEIP   Bericht über den XIII. Kongress der Deutschen Gesellschaft für Psychologie
Leipzig 16–19 October 1933
Deutsche Gesellschaft für Psychologie
ed. O. Klemm (Jena: Gustav Fischer, 1934)

BAHLE, J. Die Gestaltübertragung im vokalen Schaffen zeitgenössischer Komponisten   112

34 PRA   Actes du huitième congrès international de philosophie
Prague 2–7 September 1934
International Congress of Philosophy
(Prague: Comité d'organisation du congrès, 1936/R Nendeln: Kraus, 1968)

CUCLIN, D.   Musique, art, science et philosophie   1073

34 SOF   Actes du IVᵉ congrès des études byzantines
Sofia 10–15 September 1934
International Association of Byzantine Studies
ed. B. D. Filov, *Bulletin de l'Institut archéologique bulgare* ix–x (Sofia: Imprimerie de la
Cour, 1935–6)

Vol. i (1935)
PETRESCU, I. D.   Les principes du chant d'église
byzantin   242

34 TRT   Atti del III congresso nazionale di arti e tradizioni popolari
Trento 8–11 September 1934
Comitato nazionale italiano per le arti popolari
(Rome: Opera nazionale dopolavoro, 1936)

CARAVAGLIOS, C.   Metodi ed orientamenti nelle
ricerche delle tradizioni popolari musicale   76
LIUZZI, F.   Della raccolta dei canti popolari a
cura della commissione tecnica del Comitato
nazionale per le arti popolari   111
TORREFRANCA, F.   Le prime villote a quattro e
loro importanza storica ed estetica   182

3 Musica e danze
COLACICCHI, L.   Canti popolari di Cio-
ciaria   289
FARA, G.   Canzone popolare, canto del popolo,
etnofonia   335
GABRIEL, G.   Laofonografia   347
GIRALDI, R.   La liuteria italiana come arte
popolare   350
LUNELLI, R.   La fisarmonica e il Trentino   352

LUNGHI, F. L.   Sulla scheda Caravaglios per la
raccolta dei canti popolari   360
MAFFIOLETTI, M.   L'aderenza spirituale ed es-
pressiva della poesia alla musica nei canti del
popolo italiano nel Risorgimento   368
NATALETTI, G.   I poeti a braccio della campagna
romana   383
NATALETTI, G.   Il disco e il film sonoro nella
ricerca e nelle trascrizioni della musica
popolare   392
PARTINI, R.   Elementi e sviluppi nel canto
popolare   393
TIBALDI CHIESA, M.   Canzoni popolari
valdostane   397

5 Letteratura popolare
BARBI, M.   Poesia e musica popolare   511

34 TÜB   **Psychologie des Gemeinschaftslebens: Bericht über den XIV. Kongress der Deutschen
          Gesellschaft für Psychologie**
          Tübingen 22–6 May 1934
              Deutsche Gesellschaft für Psychologie
              ed. O. Klemm (Jena: Gustav Fischer, 1935)

35 BRUS¹   **Actes et travaux du congrès international pour l'étude du XVIIIᵉᵐᵉ siècle en Belgique**
                Brussels 27–30 July 1935
                    Société des amis du Prince de Ligne
                    ed. F. Leuridant (Brussels: Éditions des *Annales Prince de Ligne*, 1936)

Vol. i (1936)
LUNSSENS, M. Sur la musique nouvelle de 'Colette et Lucas', comédie du Prince de Ligne   306

Vol. ii (1936)
van der LINDEN, A. La musique et la danse dans les Pays-Bas au XVIIIᵉ siècle   197
LAVOYE, L. Le théâtre musical Liégeois au XVIIIᵉ siècle   212

35 BRUS²   **XVIᵉ Congrès international d'anthropologie et d'archéologie préhistorique: VIᵉ Assemblée générale de l'Institut international d'anthropologie**
                Brussels 1–8 September 1935
                    Institut international d'anthropologie
                    (Brussels: Impr. médicale et scientifique, 1936/R Nendeln: Kraus, 1969)

TORII, R. Les gongs-cloches au Japon   990

36 JEN   **Gefühl und Wille: Bericht über den XV. Kongress der Deutschen Gesellschaft für Psychologie**
Jena 5–8 July 1936
Deutsche Gesellschaft für Psychologie
ed. O. Klemm (Jena: Gustav Fischer, 1937)

3 Gefühl und Wille im Zusammenhang
BAHLE, J.   Gefühl und Wille im musikalischen
Schaffen   194

36 ROM   **Atti del V congresso internazionale di studi bizantini**
Rome 20–26 September 1936
International Association of Byzantine Studies
(Rome: Istituto per l'Europa Orientale, 1939–40 = Studi bizantini e neoellenici 6)

Vol. ii (1940)
5 Liturgia e musica
D'ANGELI, A.   La musica bizantina o neogreca
è il tramite fra la ellenica o classica e la gregoriana?   479
PETRESCO, I. D.   La lecture des manuscrits musi-
caux byzantins des Xe, XIe, XIIe siècles   507
SUÑOL, G.   Rapporti tra la musica bizantina e la
musica latina liturgica, specialmente il canto
ambrosiano   540
TILLYARD, H. J. W.   Neumes byzantins primitifs:
système Cioslin: un nouveau principe de dé-
chiffrement   542
WELLESZ, E.   Lo stadio attuale delle ricerche nel
campo della musica sacra bizantina   546

37 FLOR   Atti del secondo congresso internazionale di musica
Florence and Cremona 11–20 May 1937
Il Maggio musicale fiorentino
(Florence: Felice Le Monnier, 1940)

[includes résumés in Italian for non-Italian articles]

de SCHLOEZER, B.   La fonction sociale du compositeur 9

LORIA, A.   Il pubblico e la musica 15

DI SAN MARTINO, E.   La musica contemporanea e la società dei concerti 25

MARKEVICH, I.   Les musiciens et le public 31

PANNAIN, G.   Il problema del pubblico 36

LUCIANI, S. A.   La musica, arte postuma 42

CUVELIER, M.   Les relations entre la musique contemporaine et le public, considérées avec l'organisation de manifestations musicales 47

CASELLA, A.   Musica contemporanea e pubblico 57

BECK, C.   La musique et le public 68

HÖFFER, P.   Komponist und Konzertkrise 75

LAJTHA, L.   La musique d'aujourd'hui et le public 83

GAVAZZENI, G.   Il compositore e l'attitudine del pubblico verso la musica moderna 90

WELLESZ, E.   Der Musiker und sein Publikum 98

MALIPIERO, G. F.   I rapporti fra compositore e pubblico 103

KRENEK, E.   Le point de vue du compositeur contemporain au sujet de l'attitude du public vis à vis des oeuvres modernes 108

REICH, W.   Il gusto musicale nella luce della statistica 113

RAZZI, G.   La musica lirica e sinfonica nella sua diffusione attraverso la radio 118

BONDEVILLE, E.   La radiophonie et la musique contemporaine 125

MOOSER, R.-A.   La radio et son influence sur le goût musical 129

ROSBAUD, H.   Der Rundfunk als Erziehungsmittel für das Publikum 135

COLLAER, P.   La culture musicale par la radiophonie 145

SCHAEFFNER, A.   Le disque: sa porté, ses défaillances, ses conséquences 156

COPPOLA, P.   La funzione educatrice del disco 166

RONGA, L.   La funzione educatrice della scuola 172

VUILLERMOZ, É.   Les responsabilités de la critique 180

LESSONA, M.   Il gusto del pubblico e la musica contemporanea: funzione educatrice della critica giornalistica 185

TORREFRANCA, F.   Ciò ch'è vivo nella musica del passato 195

GERIGK, H.   Wiedergabepraxis älterer Opern in Deutschland (vom letzten Drittel des 18. Jahrhunderts bis etwa 1830) 205

DELLA CORTE, A.   I problemi concernenti la rappresentazione della opere antiche 210

BRILLOUIN, J.   Éléments psycho-physiologiques du problème de la musique à l'écran 219

VERETTI, A.   Varie forme di musica nel film 228

DE FEO, S.   La musica nel cinematografo 232

PASINETTI, F.   Cenno storico sulla collaborazione della musica col film della nascita del cinema a oggi nei diversi paesi europei: Italia 239

DEBENEDETTI, G.   In sala o sullo schermo? 245

ROLAND-MANUEL   La musique prise dans le sujet, élément matériel du film et la musique composée pour le film, éléments formel de l'oeuvre d'art 253

MILHAUD, D.   Wagner, Verdi ed il film 257

INNAMORATI, L.   I problemi della registrazione musicale 261

CAVALCANTI, A.   Music can provide only interior rhythm 265

EMMANUEL, M.   La création du violon et ses conséquences 283

VATIELLI, F.   Rapporti della musica violonistica con l'ultima litteratura per liuto 292

WELLESZ, E.   Italienische Musiker am österreichischen Hof 299

HINDEMITH, P.   La 'viola d'amore' 309

TORREFRANCA, F.   Profunda umanità di una rivoluzione musicale 314

RONGA, L.   Creazione dello strumento e creazione della musica 324

37 PAR¹   Congrès international de musique sacrée, chant et orgue
Paris 19–25 July 1937
Exposition internationale des arts et techniques de 1937, Paris
(Paris: Desclée/De Brouwer, 1938)

JACOB, G. La vie de l'Union des maîtres de chapelle et organistes au cours de ses premières vingt-cinq années   31

MEUGÉ, J. Communication sur la bibliothèque et le bulletin de l'Union des maîtres de chapelle et organistes   37

TOURNEMIRE, C. L'orgue à travers les siècles 41

GAJARD Le chant grégorien   55

EMMANUEL, M. Le chant liturgique de l'église romaine ne doit pas être harmonisé   66

LE GUENNANT, A. La crise des offices solennels et le chant grégorien   72

BONNET, J. Le chant grégorien dans la littérature d'orgue   76

POTIRON, H. Les équivalences modales dans le chant grégorien   79

GASTOUÉ, A. Les Gildes de Sainte-Cécile   94

PRIM Pour l'application intégrale, sincère et filiale des directives pontificales en matière de musique sacrée   100

GASTOUÉ, A. Du style dans l'interprétation du chant grégorien   109

OSSORGUINE, M. Exposé de l'histoire de la musique religieuse en Russie   122

DELPORTE L'école musicale française des XVᵉ–XVIᵉ siècles   130

BRUN Le clergé et la musique d'église   135

AUDA, A. Ce que sont les modes grégoriens 140

VIVET, A. La musique sacrée en France depuis la Révolution   147

ROBLOT Les cantiques à l'église   158

BERTHIER P. Le cantique et son usage actuel   163

DUFOURCQ, N. Les tendances de la facture d'orgues française contemporaine   171

RAUGEL, F. La commission des orgues au service des monuments historiques   182

de LIONCOURT, G. Le cantique grégorien   184

AURIOL [BUSSER, H.] La musique sacrée   191

37 PAR²   Onzième congrès international de psychologie: rapports et comptes rendus
Paris 25–31 July 1937
ed. H. Piéron and I. Meyerson (Agen: Imprimerie Moderne, 1938/R Nendeln: Kraus, 1974)

1 Symposia: Du mouvement à la conduite
1 Morphologie du mouvement
FRAISSE, P. La structure temporelle des mouvements volontaires rythmés   51

III Commissions
7 La pensée constructive et l'invention
BAHLE, J. Konstruktiver Arbeitstypus und In-spirationstypus im Schaffen der Komponisten   285

LALO, C. L'invention artistique   293

IV Communications
MARCUSE, I. Il talento musicale nei movimenti della scrittura   397

37 PAR³   Deuxième congrès international d'esthétique et de science de l'art
Paris 7–11 August 1937
International Congress on Aesthetics
(Paris: Félix Alcan, 1937)

Vol. i (1937)
III Sociologie et culture
2 Folklore et nationalités
SCHAEFFNER, A. Musique, danse et danse des masques dans une société nègre   308

HUMBERT-SAUVAGEOT Diversité des ambiances créées par les musiques exotiques   315

VIGE-LANGEVIN Causes de la régression de la chanson populaire   318

MARCEL-DUBOIS, C. L'esthétique et la technique des danses populaires   322

3 Individu, société, culture
LALO, C. Sur les valeurs culturelles et sociales des beaux-arts   358

Vol. ii (1937)
IV Histoire et critique
1 Histoire de l'esthétique
JANSSENS, A. J.   Les fonctions psychologiques de la musique selon Aristote   18
BUKOFZER, M.   Hegel's Musikaesthetik   32

V Science de l'art et techniques
3 L'art littéraire
SILBERSTEIN, L.   Les catégories musicales dans les sciences littéraires   213

4 Musique
WIORA, W.   Das musikalische Kunstwerk und die systematische Musikwissenschaft   223
MASSON, P.-M.   La notion de musicalité   227
PRUNIÈRES, H.   Le symbolisme dans la création musicale   232
KOECHLIN, C.   Comment compose-t-on?   236
BIEHLE, J.   Aesthetik des Orgelklanges und des Orgelspiels   239
FERRAZ de MESQUITA, R.   'L'intuition scientifique' dans les élaborations d'"art pur' manifestée dans les 'fugues' de Bach   243
LOYONNET, P.   Étude sur la formation de la langue musicale de Beethoven   247
STANI-DUCOUT, M.   Le chant et la danse: recherche de synthèse de la danse et de la musique   251
RIABOUCHINSKY, Mme V.   Sur la création dans l'interprétation musicale   254

CROIZA, C.   L'art lyrique et l'interprétation   256

6 Architecture et urbanisme
BEAUDOUIN, E.   La lumière et le son sur la Seine à l'Exposition internationale de 1937   337

7 Théâtre et cinema
ROLAND-MANUEL   Rythme cinématographique et rythme musical   364

VI L'art contemporain
1 Humanisme ou formalisme
VALENSI, H.   La tendance musicaliste de la peinture   402
3 Destins de la musique et de la danse
LE FLEM, P.   Les courants de la musique contemporaine   453
LOURIÉ, A.   De l'harmonie dans la musique contemporaine   458
EMMANUEL, M.   La polymodie   462
MALIPIERO, J. F.   La musique comme force anti-esthétique   464
de MARÉ, R.   Évolution du ballet de 1900 à nos jours   466
von LABAN, R.   Wege zur Aesthetik der Tanzkunst   474
LIFAR, S.   Les grands courants de la chorégraphie à travers le XXᵉ siècle   478
BRENN, F.   Das Sein der musikalischen Welt   506
GAGNEBIN, H.   Les psaumes huguenots   510

37 PAR[4]   Travaux du 1ᵉʳ congrès international de folklore
Paris 23–8 August 1937
(Tours: Arrault et Cie, 1938 = Publications du Département et du Musée national des arts et traditions populaires)

Traditions et littératures orales
HEISKE, W.   Träger, Art der Verbreitung und Wanderung des Volksliedes   140
PINCK, L.   La circulation des chants, vue de la Lorraine   145
GAUTHIER-VILLARS, M.   Les cantiques populaires de Marie-Madeleine   151
CHOTTIN, A.   Le chant et la danse berbères dans le folklore européen   154

Méthodologie
BRAILOIU, C.   Technique des enregistrements sonores   286
DÉVIGNE, R.   Enregistrements sonores   287
STERN, P.   Étude de la musique populaire de tradition orale   290
de DONOSTIA, J. A.   Quelques observations sur la façon de recueillir les chansons en pays basque   290

Musique – Théâtre – Danse – Fêtes
MARCEL-DUBOIS, C.   L'instrument musical pop-

ulaire en France   377
KARPÉLÈS, M.   The folk dance revival in England, with special reference to folk dancing in school   382
CHEVAIS, M.   Participation de la jeunesse scolaire à des fêtes et cortèges folkloriques   387
DELARUE, P.   Les chants populaires régionaux à l'école et dans les fêtes scolaires et post-scolaires   389
SZABOLCSI, B.   Die Volksmusik in der Schule und in der Nachschulbildung   394
HAENNI, G.   La chanson populaire dans la famille et à l'école   397
DAVE, E.   Fêtes folkloriques de la jeunesse à Namur   399
de la FARGE, G.   Le folklore à l'école, l'instrument musical populaire   401
TEXIER, M.   Danses et chants folkloriques dans l'enseignement   403

38 BAY   Charakter und Erziehung: Bericht über den XVI. Kongress der Deutschen Gesellschaft für
          Psychologie
          Bayreuth 2–4 July 1938
          Deutsche Gesellschaft für Psychologie
          ed. O. Klemm (Leipzig: Johann Ambrosius Barth, 1939)

IV Charakter
1 Vererbung
WELLEK, A. Zur Vererbung der Musikbe-
gabung und ihrer Typen   133

38 COP   Congrès international des sciences anthropologiques et ethnologiques: compte rendu de la
          deuxième session
          Copenhagen 1–6 August 1938
          Congrès international des sciences anthropologiques et ethnologiques
          (Copenhagen: Einar Munksgaard, 1939)

E (b) Ethnographie africaine
SCHAEFFNER, A. Contribution à l'étude des
instruments de musique d'Afrique et
d'Océanie   268

38 FLOR   Atti del terzo congresso internazionale di musica
          Florence 30 April – 4 May 1938
          III Maggio musicale fiorentino
          (Florence: Felice le Monnier, 1940)

[includes résumés in Italian for non-Italian articles]
de SCHLOEZER, B. La musique ancienne et le goût moderne   7
PANNAIN, G. La critica e la musica del passato   16
VUILLERMOZ, É. Le goût moderne et la musique du passé   21
DELLA CORTE, A. Il pubblico-popolo di oggi e di domani   27
GAVAZZENI, G. Umanesimo del musicista italiano   33
HANDSCHIN, J. Réflexions dangereuses sur le renouveau de la musique ancienne 40
LORIA, A. Il gusto moderno e la musica del passato   58
BÜCKEN, F. Die Musik als Stil- und Kultur-problem   67
COPEAU, J. L'interprétation des ouvrages dramatiques du passé   77
PRUNIÈRES, H. Que doit-il sortir de la crise que traverse actuellement la musique? 78
PARENTE, A. Musicisti, critici, interpreti e pubblico di fronte alla musica del passato 81
MILHAUD, D. La tradition   89
WALLECK, O. Die Regie der Oper   94
DEBENEDETTI, G. 'L'Oratorio di Via Belsiana'   102
VENTURINI, G. Del modo di rappresentare le opere del passato e dell'"Amfiparnasso' di Orazio Vecchi 108
SALVINI, G. La regìa moderna del melodramma   114
BESSELER, H. Sulla disposizione delle masse orchestrali e corali negli ambienti destinati alle esecuzioni profane e religiose nell'età barocca 121
CASELLA, A. Errori (e pretesi errori) di alcune partiture illustri   120
GUI, V. Letture e interpretazioni delle partiture   136
COPPOLA, P. Rievocazioni di un maestro gir-

ovago (dal vecchio repertorio a Maurizio
Ravel)   143
COLLAER, P. Renaissance de la musique
ancienne   147
GRAF, H. L'opera quale 'Festspiel'   161
JEPPESEN, K. Palestrina e l'interpretazione 166

BONTEMPELLI, M. Il nuovo classicismo della
musica moderna   172
SCHAEFFNER, A. Musique primitive ou exotique
et musique moderne d'occident   176
RONGA, L. La musica 'senza storia'   186

38 FRA   **Bericht über den internationalen Kongress Singen und Sprechen in Frankfurt am Main 1938**
Frankfurt am Main 10–15 October 1938
(Munich and Berlin: R. Oldenbourg, 1939)

Musikgeschichte

OSTHOFF Der Gesangstil der frühdeutschen
Oper   11
MÜLLER-BLATTAU Arie und Lied   17
GOSLICH Deklamation und instrumentale
Symbolik im begleiteten Kunstgesang   27
ZWIRNER, E. Schallplatte und Tonfilm als
Quellen sprech- und gesangskundlicher
Forschung   30
DEBUS Das Lautdenkmal deutscher Mund-
arten   34

Gesangspädagogik

PIETZSCH Fragen des Opernnachwuchses 116
GÉRAR, M. Zur Einführung in den folgenden
Vortrag   120
WICART La phonation optime pour la parole et
le chant; les contrôles auditifs et visuels pour son
enseignement   122
MOLL Wie können wir die Phonetik dem Sing-
und Sprechunterricht dienstbar machen? 128
EMGE Die klassischen Schulwerke der Singe-
kunst als Grundlagen für den Sängernach-
wuchs   132
TROMMER Reform der Gesangspädagogik 137
STRECK Die Stimmdiagnose als Grundlage der
modernen Stimmbildung und Hilfsmittel gegen
pädagogische Pfuscharbeit   140
MARTIENSSEN-LOHMANN, F. Übereinstimmung
und Abweichung in der Stimmausbildung der
männlichen und der weiblichen Stimme 143
RÜHLMANN Ideale Schuleinrichtungen für
Opernnachwuchs   147
MANUCCI de GRANDIS, I. La tecnica del respiro
in rapporto all'arte del canto e della parola 151
SCOLARI Le due maniere di cantare sorte
all'inizio dell'800   155
CAIRATI Gibt es einen geschmacklichen,
technischen oder methodischen Unterschied
zwischen dem italienischen und dem deutschen
Gesang, oder beruht der Unterschied nur auf
dem verschiedenen Aufbau der beiden
Sprachen?   161
BORUTTAU Die Beschaffenheit des harten
Gaumens und deren Bedeutung für die
Stimmabgabe   165
FORCHHAMMER, J. Stützen und Stauen   168

KOHMANN Gesangstechnik und Gesangs-
methode   172
FORCHHAMMER, V. Die Rutz-Sieversschen
Beobachtungen   175

Chorleiter

RÜHL Ausbildung und Schulung des Opern-
chorsängers im Hinblick auf die Praxis des
Repertoiretheaters   178
SOMMER Das Singen im Dienste der
Volkserziehung   181
RICHTER Was muss der Kapellmeister von der
Behandlung der Stimme des Sängers bei der
Einstudierung einer Oper wissen?   184
THIEL Heimatkunde im Schulgesang   188
SCHREMS Der Chordirigent als Führer-
persönlichkeit   191
MIEDERER Der Knabenchor als Kultur-
faktor   196

Film, Stimme und Bewegung

SEIDEL Wirkungsmöglichkeiten und Anforder-
ungen des Tonfilmes für Sprecher und Sän-
ger   196
WEISSBACH Konzertgesang im Rundfunk 199
FITZ Stimme und Leibesübung   199
GANSS Opernregie im Rundfunk   202

Schauspiel, Oper, Konzert

HARTMANN Die Erziehung zur Durchgeist-
igung des Sängerdarstellers   211
NIEDECKEN-GEBHARD Die Aufgaben und
Probleme monumentaler Festspielgestal-
tung   213
ROENNEKE Die Ausdrucksfähigkeit des
Gesanges und der Sprache als Grundlage
schöpferischer, dramatischer Gestaltung 218
KÖHLER-HELFFRICH Dialog in der Oper 225

Biologie

TRENDELENBURG, W. Zur Frage der Register-
bruchstellen   234
GUTZMANN Der Stimmbruch unter gesunden
und krankhaften Verhältnissen   241
WETHLO Intonation beim Singen   253

Sprecherziehung

RUTH Das Phonogrammarchiv der Akademie

der Wissenschaften in Wien und sein Wirken im Dienste der Sprach- und Musikwissenschaft und der Sprech- und Gesangsausbildung 279
HÄNDCHEN Singen und Stimmbildung in der NS.-Gemeinschaft 'Kraft durch Freude' 293
THOMAS Über die Aussprache beim chorischen Singen 295
TRAUTWEIN Die technische Akustik in Schule und Praxis des Singens und Sprechens 298

Psychologie
SCHOLE Die Vokalität der einfachen Töne und das Singen von Vokalen in hoher Stimmlage 301
STAUDER Grundfragen des Hörens 305
WARDE Die Beziehungen zwischen Sprache und Gesang 308
LOEBELL Die Rufstimme im Lichte der Experimentalphonetik 311
WÜNSCH Grenzgebiete der Musik- und Sprachforschung 315

KREICHGAUER Akustische Probleme der Opern- und Sprechbühne 319
STICHTENOTH Der Gesang in der Kritik der Tagespresse 322
SCHULZ-DORNBURG Das musikalische Wort im Wandel der Zeiten 326
SCHROTH Die Bedeutung des Singens in der Kameradschaftserziehung des NSD.-Studentenbundes 331
BRÄUTIGAM Deutsche Volkslieder aus Jugoslawien 336

Rundfunk
SCHLENGER Gibt es mikrophongeeignete Stimmen, und welches sind ihre Kennzeichen? 339
SCHWAIGER Das Problem der Übertragungstreue bei Sprache und Gesang 348
GÖRNER Kammerchor im Rundfunk 352
SCHNAPP Dynamikbeschränkung bei Schallübertragungen und Schallaufzeichnungen 365

38 FRE/B   Bericht über die zweite Freiburger Tagung für deutsche Orgelkunst
Freiburg im Breisgau 27–30 June 1938
Musikwissenschaftliches Institut der Universität Freiburg im Breisgau
ed. J. Müller-Blattau (Kassel: Bärenreiter, 1939)

MAHRENHOLZ, C. Die Kleinorgel: Grundfragen ihres Baues und ihres Klanges 8
MEHL, J. G. Die Denkmalpflege auf dem Gebiet der Orgelbaukunst 20
SCHUKE, K. Positiv und Kleinorgel vom Standpunkt des Orgelbauers 37
FELLERER, K. G. Die alte für Kleinorgel bestimmte Orgelmusik 43
AULER, W. Weltliche Musik auf dem Positiv 55
WALCHA, H. Die Kleinorgel im Gottesdienst und in den geistlichen Hausmusik 63
KLOTZ, H. Das alte Positiv und die neue Kammerorgel 64
HAAG, H. Die Orgel im weltlichen Bereich: Geschichtliches und Grundsätzliches 78
EHMANN, W. Orgel und Volkslied 88

FROTSCHER, G. Die Wechselbeziehungen zwischen Orgelmusik und Orgelbau in Geschichte und Gegenwart 98
THIENHAUS, E. Orgelbaufragen im Lichte der akustischen Forschung 104
SUPPER, W. Die dreimanualige Übungsorgel: ein Beitrag zur Kleinorgel 110
MERTIN, J. Erfahrungen mit der Kleinorgel 118
KLUYVER, P. and BOUMAN, A. Hausorgeln in Holland 125
MÜLLER-WALT, T. Die Toggenburger Bauernorgeln 132
RIEBER, K. Kleinorgeln in Oberbaden 136
MÜLLER-BLATTAU, J. Orgel und Gegenwart 144

38 GHE   Proceedings of the Third International Congress of Phonetic Sciences
Ghent 18–22 July 1938
International Society of Phonetic Sciences
ed. E. Blanquaert and W. Pée (Ghent: Laboratory of Phonetics of the University, 1939)

General linguistics and phonology

WÜNSCH, W. Grenzgebiete der Musik- und Sprachforschung 72
ZWIRNER, E. Schwankungen der Mundlage beim Singen einzelner Laute 77

Technics
GRÜTZMACHER, M. Ein neuer Tonhöhenschreiber, seine Anwendung auf mathematische, phonetische and musikalische Probleme,
nach gemeinsamen Versuchen mit W. Lottermoser 105

Physiology and pathology
LABARRAQUE, L. La science phonetique, base essentielle de l'éducation de la voix chantée 207

Phonetics of particular languages
BURSSENS, A. Le Luba, langue à intonation, et le tambour-signal 503

38 NAM **Congrès de Namur 1938: annales**
Namur 23–9 July 1938
Fédération archéologique et historique de Belgique (31st congress)
ed. J. Balon (Namur, n.d.)

van der LINDEN, A.   Note sur une ordonnance du
Conseil des Finances relatifs aux pianos et aux
clavecins (9 Janvier 1786)   430

38 ZUR **Communications présentées au congrès de Zurich** [VIIIe Congrès international des sciences
historiques]
Zurich 24 August – 4 September 1938
Bulletin of the international committee of historical sciences x (Paris: Presses universitaires de France, 1938/R Nendeln: Kraus, 1977)

12 Histoire des idées (philosophie, beaux-arts, littérature)
HANDSCHIN, J.   Die Entstehung der Sequenz   604
HANKISS, J.   Le drame populaire et la société   650
CHERBULIEZ, A.-E.   Le problème de la périodicité dans l'histoire de l'art musical par rapport aux beaux-arts en général et à la poesie   655

39 ALG   Sixième congrès international d'études byzantines: résumés des rapports et communications
[Algiers 2–7 October 1939; planned but did not take place]
International Association of Byzantine Studies
(Paris: Comité d'organisation du congrès, 1940)

WELLESZ, E. La musique byzantine et ses relations avec le chant grégorien dans la musique du moyen âge   113

39 FEZ   Ecos del Magrib: El primer congreso de música marroquí celebrado en Fez
Fez 6–10 May 1939
(Tangiers: Tánger, 1940)

[all papers printed in Spanish, French and Arabic]
1 Cronica del congreso
Ensayo de nuevas posibilidades de música europea, inspirada en la hispano-musulmana   26
El repertorio tradicional   32
Las orquestas marroquíes   40
Modernización de las orquestas marroquíes   44
Las orquestas árabes de Argelia y Túnez   48
Música popular marroquí   50

Cuestiones técnicas generales   58
Conclusiones del congreso   60

2 Memoria presentada al congreso
Trabajos de recopilación de música indigena realizados en la Zona de Protectorado Español en Marruecos   68
Esquema de nueve nubas menores   74
Esquema de la once nubas más conocidas transcritas en Tetuán   90

39 FLOR   Atti del secondo convegno nazionale di studi sul Rinascimento
Florence 7–8 May 1939
Centro nazionale di studi sul rinascimento, Florence
(Florence: Clarior, 1940)

GHISI, F. La musica   52

39 MEX   [XXVIIth International Congress of Americanists]
Mexico City 5–15 August 1939, Lima 7–16 September 1939
International Congress of Americanists
Vigesimoseptimo congreso internacional de Americanistas: Actas de la primera sesion, celebrada en la Cuidad de Mexico en 1939 (Mexico: Secretaria de educación publica, 1942/R Nendeln: Kraus, 1976)

Vol. ii (1942)
8 Problemas actuales de las poblaciones indigena y negra de America

CAMPOS, R. M. La música popular mexicana de hoy   441

Actas y trabajos científicos del XXVII° congreso internacional de Americanistas (Lima: Libreria e Imprenta Gil, 1940–42/*R* Nendeln: Kraus, 1976)

Vol. ii (1942)
Arte – linguistica – folklore
GARCES BEDREGAL, M.   Evolución técnica de la música peruana, gama eptafónica   25

39 NEWY   **Papers read at the International Congress of Musicology**
New York 11–16 September 1939
American Musicological Society
ed. A. Mendel, G. Reese and G. Chase (New York: Music Educators' National Conference for the American Musicological Society, 1944)

General (chairman SMITH, C. S.)
SEEGER, C.   Music and government – field for an applied musicology   11
PLAMENAC, D.   Music of the 16th and 17th centuries in Dalmatia   21
DENT, E. J.   La rappresentazione di anima e di corpo   52
JEPPESEN, K.   Venetian folk-songs of the Renaissance   62

Primitive and folk music in North America (chairman HERZOG, G.)
JACKSON, G. P.   Some enemies of folk-music in America   77
BUCHANAN, A. M.   Modal and melodic structure in Anglo-American folk music – a neutral mode   84
LAMSON, R.   English broadside ballad tunes of the 16th and 17th centuries   112
BAYARD, S. P.   Aspects of melodic kinship and variation in British-American folk-tunes   122
HERZOG, G.   African influences in North American Indian music   130

EINSTEIN, A.   Mozart's handwriting and the creative process   145

Ancient, medieval and Renaissance music (chairman REESE, G.)
STRUNK, O.   Some motet-types of the 16th century   155

SACHS, C.   The mystery of the Babylonian notation   161
GOMBOSI, O.   New light on ancient Greek music   168
SMIJERS, A.   Music of the Illustrious Confraternity of Our Lady at 's-Hertogenbosch from 1330 to 1600   184
LIUZZI, F.   Notes sur les *Barzelette* et les *Canzoni a ballo* du quattrocento italien, d'après des documents inédits   193
ELLINWOOD, L.   The French Renaissance of the 12th century in music   200

Music and science (chairman MILLER, D. C.)
ORTMANN, O.   The psychology of tone-quality   227
HAYDON, G.   Alfred Day and the theory of harmony   233
BUKOFZER, M. F.   The evolution of Javanese tone-systems   241
TAYLOR, D.   Music written for radio   251
MILLER, D. C.   Musical tone-color   267

Hispanic session (chairman CHASE, G.)
LANGE, F. C.   'Americanismo musical'   273
SÁNCHEZ de FUENTES, E.   The musical folklore of Cuba   284
ROIG, G.   Some problems confronting musicians in the Americas   289

40 VEN   **Atti del IV congresso nazionale di arti e tradizioni popolari**
Venice September 1940
Comitato nazionale italiano per le arti popolari
(Rome, Opera nazionale dopolavoro, 1942)

FARA, G.   Etnofonia e civiltà mediterranea 106

4 La nostra letteratura popolare
ABIUSO, V.   I canti e le ninne-nanne popolari sarde   357
BAINCHI, G.   Valore spirituale ed impronta etnica dei nostri canti di guerra   365
BOLLINI, G.   Il mare nei canti popolari lombardi   369
FARA, S.   Il ballo tradizionale del popolo di

Sardegna   382
PAOLONE, E.   La musica del popolo nelle sur origini – caratteri fondamentali e riflessi   403
SANTOLLINO, R.   Il mare nei canti popolari napoletani   409
SCHIRÒ, G.   Poesia e musica tradizionali degli italo-albanesi   410
SINICROPI, E.   Canti popolari ennesi   423
TANCREDI, G.   Canti e balli garganici   428

45 DAK   **Première conférence internationale des Africanistes de l'ouest: comptes rendus**
            Dakar 19–25 January 1945
                International West African Conference
                (Paris: Institut français d'afrique noire, 1950–51)

Vol. ii (1951)
3 Le milieu humain
DUCHEMIN, G.-J.   Autour d'un arc musical du
    Saloum oriental   248

47 BIS   Conferência internacional dos Africanistas ocidentais: 2.ª conferência
Bissau 8–17 December 1947
International West African Conference
(Lisbon: Ministério das colónias, junta de investigaçcões coloniais, 1950–52)

Vol. v (1952)
iii/2a Meio humano
DUCHEMIN, G. J.   Deux arcs renforcés de Guinée
Française   127
BALANDIER, G. and MERCIER, P.   Notes sur les

théories musicales maures à propos de chants
enregistrés   135
ROUGÉ, G.   Note sur les travaux d'ethnographie
musicale de la mission Ogooué-Congo   193

47 PAR   Actes du XXVIIIᵉ congrés international des Américanistes
Paris 25–30 August 1947
International Congress of Americanists
(Paris: Société des Américanistes, 1948/R Nendeln: Kräus, 1976)

4 Ethnologie
STESSER-PÉAN, G.   Danse des aigles et danse des

jaguars chez les Indiens Huastèques de la région
de Tantoyuca   335

47 PRA   Hudba národů: sborník přednášek, proslovených na 1. mezinárodnim sjezdu skladatelů a
hudebních kritiků v Praze / Musique des nations: 1ᵉʳ Congrès international des com-
positeurs et critiques musicaux à Prague
Prague 16–26 May 1947
Syndikát českých skladatelů/Syndicat des compositeurs tchèques
(Prague: Syndikát českých skladatelů, 1948) [printed in Czech and French throughout]

BENGTSSON, I.   Skandinávská hudba [Scandi-
navian music]   13
BOKESOVÁ, Z.   Slovenská hudba [Slovak
music]   16
BUSH, A.   Britští skladatelé dneška [British com-
posers today]   22
CAVALLINI, E.   O nové harmonické řeči [The
new harmonic language]   25
CUVELIER, M.   Jeunesses musicales   28
HÁBA, A.   Souměrnost evropského tónového
systému [Symmetry in the European tonal
system]   31
KAMBUROV, I.   Rytmické zvláštnosti bulharské
lidové a umělecké hudby [Rhythmic traits of
Bulgarian folk and art music]   37
ŁOBACZEWSKA, S.   Kritika a její vztah k moderní
hudbě [Criticism and its relation to modern
music]   41
MENON, N.   Kam spěje indická hudba? [Which
way is Indian music going?]   44
POLLAK, F.   Soudobá hudba mezi orientem a

okcidentem [Contemporary music between the
west and east]   48
RACEK, J.   Vznik a počátky barokního hudeb-
niho slohu v Čechách (příspěvek k dějinám
italské jednohlasé písně v českých zemích) [The
origin and beginnings of Baroque musical style
in Bohemia (contribution to the history of
Italian monody in Czech lands)]   51
SMITH, C. S.   Hudba v severní a jižní Americe
(náčrt) [Music in North and South America
(outline)]   62
STANISLAV, J.   O masové písni a jejim dnešním
významu [Mass songs and their meaning to-
day]   64
SYCHRA, A.   Hudební estetika a kritika [Musical
aesthetics and criticism]   69
ŠOSTAKOVIČ [Shostakovich], D.   Svaz sovět-
skych skladatelů [The Union of Soviet Com-
posers]   75
YÖNETKEN, H. B.   Turecká hudba [Turkish
music]   82

48 AMS   Proceedings of the Tenth International Congress of Philosophy
Amsterdam 11–18 August 1948
International Congress of Philosophy
ed. E. W. Beth and H. J. Pos (Amsterdam: North-Holland Publishing Company,
1949/R Nendeln: Kraus, 1970)

Vol. i (1949)
10 Aesthetics
BLAUKOPF, K.   The aesthetics of musical humanism from Diderot to Hanslick   534

48 BRUS   Congrès international des sciences anthropologiques et ethnologiques: compte-rendu de la
troisième session
Brussels 1948
Congrès international des sciences anthropologiques et ethnologiques
ed. F. M. Olbrechts and H. van Geluwe (Tervuren: Musée royal de l'Afrique centrale,
1960)

HAUSE, H. E.   Terms for musical instruments in   van PANHUYS, L. C.   Some remarks on Dutch
the Sudanic languages: a linguistic approach to   songs   265
culture   103   van PANHUYS, L. C.   Music in Latin America,
HERSKOVITS, M. J.   Afrobahian cult music 105   Surinam and Curaçao   266

48 EDIN   Twelfth International Congress of Psychology: Proceedings and Papers
Edinburgh 23–9 July 1948
(Edinburgh and London: Oliver and Boyd, 1950/R Nendeln: Kraus, 1974)

WING, H. D.   Standardized tests of musical
aptitude   129

48 FLOR   Atti del quinto congresso di musica presieduto da Ildebrando Pizzetti
Florence 14–17 May 1948
XI Maggio musicale fiorentino
(Florence: Barbèra, 1948)

D'AMICO, F.   Il compositore moderne e il lin-   pressioni del linguaggio musicale   45
guaggio musicale   11   LUPI, R.   Armonia di gravitazione   51

MILA, M.   La musica e il linguaggio musi-   BIANCHI, G.   La musica nella realtà della nostra
cale   25   vita   55
PARENTE, A.   Il problema del linguaggio come   DAMERINI, A.   La musica nella vita della scuola
problema morale   33   contemporanea   62
MORTARI, V.   La crisi del sistema temparato e i   RONGA, L.   Aspetti del costume musicale
problemi del linguaggio musicale   39   contemporaneo   66
GUERRINI, G.   Il tramonto di due gloriose es-   LUCIANI, S. A.   Inflazione musicale   73

TORREFRANCA, F. Perchè non v'è osmosi tra arte e pubblico?   75
FRAZZI, V. Il superamento della tonalità ed il nuovo concetto armonico   89

MANTELLI, A. Problemi di linguaggio nell'opera di Strawinsky   97
VERETTI, A. Il problema del linguaggio della musica moderna   105
RINALDI, M. Funzione della tecnica nel linguaggio musicale   109
PANNAIN, G. Chiarimenti sul concetto di linguaggio   115
PIOVESAN, A. Offerte e divieti del linguaggio

musicale contemporaneo   119
LUCIANI, S. A. La crisi del sistema temperato   129
GIAZOTTO, R. Teatro di provincia e sovvenzioni   133
LUALDI, A. 'La ballata della morte' e una parolina di Aristotele   140
BORRELLI, E. Dal neoclassicismo alla dodecafonia   146
GHISI, F. Le influenze 'ultramontane' e la musica europea   153
FLEISCHER, H. Discutendo il problema linguistico   156
HERMET, A. Musicologia e musica   157

48 PAR[1]   Actes du XXIe congrès international des orientalistes
             Paris 23–31 July 1948
             International Congress of Orientalists
             (Paris: Société asiatique de Paris, 1949)

1 Égyptologie
HICKMANN, H. Sur l'enquête musicologique de la saison 1947–1948   71

48 PAR[2]   Actes du VIe congrès international d'études byzantines
             Paris 27 July – 2 August 1948
             International Association of Byzantine Studies
             (Paris: Comité français des études byzantines, 1950–51)

Vol. ii (1951)
5 Archéologie, histoire de l'art
PALIKAROVA-VERDEIL, R. La musique byzan-
tine chez les slaves (Bulgares et Russes) aux IXe et Xe siècles   321

48 TUR   V Congresso nazionale di tradizioni popolari
          Turin 9–12 September 1948
          Società di etnografia italiana, Rome
          Lares xx/1–2 (Florence: Leo S. Olschki, 1954)

2 Popolo e risorgimento
TRON, E. Canzoni popolari valdesi del risorgimento   44

4a Letteratura popolare
BRONZINI, G. B. La canzone della 'finta monacella': nuove versioni e loro classificazione   83
TRON, E. Cenno sui canti popolari delle Valli Valdesi   106

4b Musica e danza popolare
FARA, G. Sardegna persistenza dell'ethos artistico mediterraneo   120
GHISI, F. Antiche melodie popolari nelle Valli Valdesi   123

49 BAS   Société internationale de musicologie quatrième congrès Bâle: compte rendu / Internationale Gesellschaft für Musikwissenschaft vierter Kongress Basel: Kongressbericht / International Musicological Society Fourth Congress Basle: Report
Basle 29 June – 3 July 1949
International Musicological Society
ed. Schweizerische musikforschende Gesellschaft Ortsgruppe Basel (Kassel and Basle: Bärenreiter, [1951])

HANDSCHIN, J.   Musicologie et musique   9
LANG, P.-H.   Stylistic elements in the Classic era   22
JEPPESEN, K.   Zur Kritik der klassischen Harmonielehre   23
ALBRECHT, H.   Zur Frage eines neuen musikalischen Quellenlexikons   37
AMELN, K.   Die Anfänge der deutschen Passionshistorie   39
ANGLÈS, H.   Der Rhythmus der monodischen Lyrik des Mittelalters und seine Probleme   45
ANGLÈS, H. , L'oeuvre de l'Institut espagnol de musicologie   50
BAKE, A.   Der Begriff Nâda in der Indischen Musik   55
BESSELER, H.   Katalanische Cobla und Alta-Tanzkapelle   59
BRĂILOIU, C.   A propos du jodel   69
BRENN, F.   Die gregorianischen Modi nach dem Speculum musicae   72
BRENN, F.   Das Wesensgefüge der Musik   75
BROCKHOFF, M. E.   Zur Methodik der musikwissenschaftlichen Analyse   80
BUKOFZER, M. F.   The Caput Masses and their plainsong   82
ENGEL, H.   Ein Beitrag zur Prosodie im 16. Jahrhundert   83
ENGEL, H.   Vom Sinn und Wesen der Musik in Werken und Deutung der Gegenwart   96
FERAND, E. T.   'Zufallsmusik' und 'Komposition' in der Musiklehre der Renaissance   103
von FICKER, R.   Probleme der Editionstechnik mittelalterlicher Musik   109
von FISCHER, K.   Bemerkungen zu Beethovens Variationenwerken   111
FOKKER, A. D.   Expériences musicales avec les genres musicaux de Leonhard Euler contenant la septième harmonique   113
GAILLARD, A.   Petite étude comparée du 'note contre note' de Loys Bourgeoys (1547) et du Psautier de Jaqui (Goudimel 1565)   115
GEERING, A.   Die Nibelungenmelodie in der Trierer Marienklage   118
GERSTENBERG, W.   Motetten- und Liedstil bei Ludwig Senfl   121
GHISI, F.   La musique religieuse de Marco da Gagliano à Santa Maria del Fiore Florence   125

GIEGLING, F.   Sinn und Wesen des 'concertare'   129
GOMBOSI, O.   Key, mode, species   133
GURLITT, W.   Zur Bedeutungsgeschichte von 'musicus' und 'cantor' bei Isidor von Sevilla   134
HAMMERSCHLAG, J.   Sigel-Ornamente in ihren harmonischen Relationen   135
HANDSCHIN, J.   Eine umstrittene Stelle bei Guilelmus Monachus   145
HICKMANN, H.   Über den Stand der musikwissenschaftlichen Forschung in Ägypten   150
HOLST, I.   Ein Doppelchorwerk mit beziffertem Bass von Claudio Merulo   154
KELLER, H.   Über Bachs Bearbeitungen aus dem 'Hortus musicus' von Reinken   160
BERNET KEMPERS, K. P.   Die Jamisation   162
KICKTON, E.   Die Beziehungen der Tonkunst zur Philosophie (Logik, Ethik und Metaphysik)   166
KLOTZ, H.   Die Registrierkunst der französischen Organisten des 17. und 18. Jahrhunderts und das Bachspiel   172
LABHARDT, F.   Zur st. gallischen Sequenztradition im Spätmittelalter   176
LARSEN, J. P.   Gibt es eine definitive Version von Händels 'Messias'?   178
LENAERTS, R.   La missa parodia néerlandaise au 16e siècle   179
MIES, P.   Der Charakter der Tonarten   181
NEF, W.   Das mehrsaitige 'Monochord'   182
SCHNEIDER, M.   Vom ursprünglichen Sinn der Musik   183
SMITS van WAESBERGHE, J.   Das Maastrichter Osterspiel (Beitrag zur Literatur der liturgischen Spiele)   184
STÄBLEIN, B.   Ambrosianisch-Gregorianisch   185
STEGLICH, R.   Beethovens 'überaus merkwürdige Akzentuation'   190
TORREFRANCA, F.   Problemi Vivaldiani   195
TORREFRANCA, F.   Prime ricognizioni della stile violoncellistico Plattiano   203
WIORA, W.   Die vergleichende Frühgeschichte der europäischen Musik als methodische Forschung   212
WOLFF, H. C.   Die ethischen Aufgaben der neuen Musik   221
ZENCK, H.   Zu Adriaen Willaerts 'Salmi spezzati'   226

49 CLU   À Cluny: Congrés scientifique: Fêtes et cérémonies liturgiques en l'honneur des saints Abbés
             Odon et Odilon: travaux de congrès
             Cluny 9–11 July 1949
             (Dijon: Société des amis de Cluny, 1950)

HESBERT, R.   Les témoins manuscrits du culte de   THOMAS, P.   Saint Odon de Cluny et son oeuvre
    saint Odilon   51   musicale   171

49 FLOR   Atti del sesto congresso internazionale di musica presieduto da Ildebrando Pizzetti
             Florence 18–21 May 1949
             XII Maggio musicale fiorentino
             (Florence: G. Barbèra, 1950)

FLEISCHER, H.   Soggetto e oggetto nell'es-   de SCHLOEZER, B.   Expression et création   94
    pressione musicale   9   MILA, M.   Sul carattere inconsapevole
D'AMICO, F.   Che cos'è l'oggettivismo   17   dell'espressione artistica   98
RONGA, L.   Soggettivismo e oggettivismo   GRAY, C.   Soggettivismo ed oggettivismo
    nell'espressione musicale   27   nell'arte musicale   104
GENTILI, A.   L'insegnamento della com-   RINALDI, M.   Dal sentimento individuale alla
    posizione in rapporto alle tendenze mo-   realtà di tutti   108
    derne   33   PETRASSI, G.   L'insegnamento della compo-
DELLA CORTE, A.   Storia, cultura e 'tendenze'   sizione   116
    nell'insegnamento della composizione 39   NEUMANN, V.   La musique en Tchécoslova-
GHISI, F.   Per un richiamo alla tradizione   quie   121
    umanistica   49   DALLAPICCOLA, L.   Considerazioni sull'inseg-
DAMERINI, A.   Di una metodologia storicistica   namento della composizione   125
    nell'insegnamento della composizione 53   PINCHERLE, M.   De l'enseignement de la
TURCHI, G.   Cause, effetti ed alcuni rimedi 59   composition   130
STROBEL, H.   Lebendiger Kompositionsunter-   ANSERMET, E.   Subjectivisme et objectivisme
    richt!   67   dans l'expression musicale   138
PANNAIN, G.   Orientamento storico nell'in-   PIOVESAN, A.   Attualità dell'oggettivismo
    segnamento della composizione   70   musicale   146
GUERRINI, G.   La riforma nelle classi di   BORRELLI, E.   Soggetto ed espressione nella
    composizione   74   musica   153
PARENTE, A.   La favola dell'oggettivismo 78   BUCCHI, V.   Solitudine del musicista   161
ZAFRED, M.   Contributo ad una critica di alcune   LUALDI, A.   Il mantello della miseria   166
    posizioni formalistiche   87   HERMET, A.   Suono come 'mistero'   173

49 NEWY[1]   [XXIXth International Congress of Americanists]
             New York 5–12 September 1949
             International Congress of Americanists
             *Acculturation in the Americas: Proceedings and Selected Papers of the XXIXth
             International Congress of Americanists*, ed. S. Tax (Chicago: University of Chicago
             Press, 1952)

Acculturation and culture change   **Afroamerica**
GAMBLE, J. I.   Changing patterns in Kiowa   WATERMAN, R. A.   African influence on the
    Indian dances   94   music of the Americas   207
RHODES, W.   Acculturation in North American
    Indian music   121

The Civilisations of Ancient America: Selected Papers of the XXIXth International Congress of Americanists, ed. S. Tax (Chicago: University of Chicago Press, 1951)

[no articles on music in the collection]

Indian tribes of Aboriginal America: Selected Papers of the XXIXth International Congress of Americanists, ed. S. Tax (Chicago: University of Chicago Press, 1952)

KURATH, G. P. Matriarchal dances of the Iroquois   123

49 NEWY[2]   **Symposium on Local Diversity in Iroquois Culture**
New York 17 November 1949
American Anthropological Association
ed. W. N. Fenton (Washington DC: United States Government Printing Office, 1951 = Smithsonian Institution Bureau of American Ethnology Bulletin 149)

KURATH, G. P. Local diversity in Iroquois music and dance   109
FENTON, W. N. and KURATH, G. P. The Feast of the Dead, or Ghost Dance at Six Nations Reserve, Canada   139

50 FLOR   **La musica nel film** [preliminary papers for Settimo congresso internazionale]
Florence 1950
XIII Maggio musicale fiorentino
ed. L. Chiarini (Rome: Bianco e Nero, 1950 = Quaderni della Mostra internazionale
d'arte cinematografica di Venezia)

MASETTI, E. Introduzione ai problemi della musica nel film 7
Aspetti della musica nel film (COSTARELLI, N. 30 MARINUZZI, G. 35, ROSATI, G. 39, TOMMASINI, V. 43, VERETTI, A. 44)
ZECCHI, A. Particolare rilievo della musica in alcuni film 49
LUNGHI, F. L. La musica e il neo-realismo 56
CICOGNINI, A. Il film musicale 61
LARAGNINO, F. La musica nel disegno animato 63
GERVASIO, R. La musica nel documentario 69
VLAD, R. La musica nel documentario 72
FERRARA, F. La direzione dell'orchestra e la musica cinematografica 78
Tre opinioni (MALIPIERO, G. F. 80, PIZZETTI, I. 80, PETRASSI, G. 83)

LONGO, A. La critica cinematografica e la musica nel film 86
Il parere del regista, del mentatore e della critica (BLASETTI, A. 91, SERANDREI, M. 92, LUCIANI, S. A. 94)
CAVAZZUTI, E. Problemi della registrazione sonora e del missaggio 97
GAILLARD, M. F. La musica per film in Francia 107
IRVING, E. La musica per film in Inghilterra 114
AMFITHEATROF, D. La musica per film negli Stati Uniti 118
CHRENNIKOV, T. La musica per film nell'U.R.S.S. 129
VERDONE, M. Un breve scenario cinematografico di Alban Berg 135
VERDONE, M. Nota bibliografica 139

50 LEIP   **Bericht über die wissenschaftliche Bachtagung der Gesellschaft für Musikforschung**
Leipzig 23–6 July 1950
Gesellschaft für Musikforschung
ed. W. Vetter and E. H. Meyer (Leipzig: Peters, 1951)

GURLITT, W. Bach in seiner Zeit und heute 51
CHUBOW, W. N. Bach und die zeitgenössische musikalische Kultur 81
BESSELER, H. Bach und das Mittelalter 108
VETTER, W. Bachs Universalität 131
LAUX, K. Bach und die deutsche Nation 158
Discussion 180

1 Bachs Persönlichkeit (chairman BORRIS, S.)
DEHNERT, M. Neue Aufgaben der biographischen Bachforschung 193
GRAUPNER, F. Bach als Musikerzieher 201
BORRIS, S. Bachs Unterweisung im Tonsatz 210

2 Bachs Werk (chairman ANSCHÜTZ, G.)
SCHMIEDER, W. Bemerkungen zur Bachquellenforschung 219
SIEVERS, H. F. K. Griepenkerl und die neu aufgefundene Handschrift von Bachs h-moll-Messe 231
GURLITT, W. Zu Bachs Ostinato-Technik 240

BLANKENBURG, W. Die Bedeutung des Kanons in Bachs Werk 250
DÜRR, A. Stilkritik und Echtheitsprobleme der fruhen Kantaten Bachs 259
ANSCHÜTZ, G. Über Aufbauprinzipien in den Werken Bachs 270
HAHN, H. Der Symmetriebegriff in der Musik Bachs 277
OBERBORBECK, F. 'Vor deinen Thron tret ich hiemit': Bemerkungen zu Geschichte, Form und Aufführungspraxis von Bachs Lebensepilog 285

3 Bach in der Musikgeschichte (chairman SERAUKY, W.)
SERAUKY, W. Zum gegenwärtigen Stande der Bach- und Händelforschung 295
KNEPLER, G. Bemerkungen zum Wandel des Bachbildes 308
SCHMITZ, E. Bachs h-moll-Messe und die Dresdner katholische Kirchenmusik 320

LIEBE, A. Bachs Matthäuspassion in ihrer geschichtlichen Beurteilung 331

HAUSSWALD, G. Zur Sonatenkunst der Bachzeit 340

FREYSE, C. Unbekannte Jugendbildnisse Friedemann und Emanuel Bachs 349

ELLER, R. Bruckner und Bach 355

STEMPEL, M. Bach in Schweden 367

WOLFF, H. C. Bach und die Musik der Gegenwart 375

4 Zeit und Umwelt Bachs (chairman GURLITT, W.)

DRÄGER, H.-H. Zur mitteltönigen und gleichschwebenden Temperatur 389

FLADE, E. Bachs Stellung zum Orgel- und Klavierbau seiner Zeit 405

SZABOLCSI, B. Bach, die Volksmusik und das osteuropäische Melos 411

BARTHA, D. Bemerkungen zur Stilisierung der Volksmusik, besonders der Polonäsen, bei Bach 416

REBLING, E. Der Rationalismus, eine Grundlage des Bachschen Realismus 420

EGGEBRECHT, H. H. Bach und Leibniz 431

50 LÜN[1]   **Kongress-Bericht: Gesellschaft für Musikforschung Lüneburg 1950**
Lüneburg 16–20 July 1950
Gesellschaft für Musikforschung
ed. H. Albrecht, H. Osthoff, W. Wiora (Kassel and Basle: Bärenreiter, n. d.)

BESSELER, H. Charakterthema und Erlebnisform bei Bach 7

SCHMITZ, A. Die oratorische Kunst J. S. Bachs – Grundfragen und Grundlagen 33

1 Ältere Musikgeschichte (chairman OSTHOFF, H.)

STÄBLEIN, B. Alt- und neurömischer Choral 53

LIPPHARDT, W. Die Kyrietropen in ihrer rhythmischen und melodischen Struktur 56

TORREFRANCA, F. Guido d'Arezzo 60

AARBURG, U. Wechselbeziehungen zwischen Motiv und Tonart im mittelalterlichen Liede, insbesondere im Liede um 1200 62

GUDEWILL, K. Die Barform und ihre Modifikationen 65

STEPHAN, R. Einige Hinweise auf die Pflege der Mehrstimmigkeit im frühen Mittelalter in Deutschland 68

WIORA, W. Der mittelalterliche Liedkanon 71

GERBER, R. Die Textwahl in der mehrstimmigen Hymnenkomposition des späten Mittelalters 75

SCHAAL, R. Zur Methodik quellenmässiger Datierung der Werke Pierre de la Rues 80

BOETTICHER, W. Zur Chronologie des Schaffens Orlando di Lassos 82

TIBY, O. La scuola polifonica siciliana dei secc. XVI e XVII 89

STEGLICH, R. Zur Ausdruckskunst des Nürnberger Paumann-Kreises 91

REICHERT, G. Der Passamezzo 94

SIEVERS, H. Die Braunschweiger Tabulaturen 97

2 Neuere Musikgeschichte (chairman GERBER, R.)

GHISI, F. The oratorios of Giacomo Carissimi in Hamburg Staats-Bibliothek 103

WALLAU, R. Die kirchliche Bedeutung der Bachschen Musik 107

ENGEL, H. Über Form und Mosaiktechnik bei Bach, besonders in seinen Arien 111

DÜRR, A. Zur Chronologie der Weimarer Kantaten J. S. Bachs 120

EHMANN, W. Aufführungspraxis der Bachschen Motetten 121

von FISCHER, K. Zur Satztechnik von Bachs Klaviersuiten 124

GERSTENBERG, W. Zur Verbindung Präludium und Fuge bei J. S. Bach 126

HAAS, R. Bach und Wien 130

REDLICH, H. F. Anfänge der Bachpflege in England 1750–1850 131

FELLERER, K. G. Die Lehre vom Cantus gregorianus im 18. Jahrhundert 136

ABERT, A. A. Zum metastasianischen Reformdrama 138

GERBER, R. Unbekannte Instrumentalwerke von Chr. W. Gluck 140

STEGLICH, R. Zum Kontrastproblem Johannes Brahms – Hugo Wolf 140

KLUSEN, E. César Franck und die Überwindung der Nationalstile im späten 19. Jahrhundert 143

TANZBERGER, E. Jean Sibelius als Symphoniker 146

3 Musikalische Volks- und Völkerkunde: Vergleichende Musikforschung (chairman WIORA, W.)

SEEMANN, E. Mythen vom Ursprung der Musik 151

EMSHEIMER, E. Lappischer Kultgesang 153

BAKÉ, A. Die beiden Tongeschlechter bei Bharata 158

KUNST, J. Die 2000jährige Geschichte Süd-Sumatras im Spiegel ihrer Musik 160

HARICH-SCHNEIDER, E. Die Gagaku in der Musikabteilung des japanischen Kaiserhofes 168

ECKARDT, H. Die Ei und Saezuri, verschollene melismatische Gesangformen im japanischen Tanz 170

EMSHEIMER, E. Schallaufnahmen georgischer Mehrstimmigkeit 172

SALMEN, W. Vermeintliches und wirkliches Volkslied im späten Mittelalter 174

von der AU, H. Frühformen des deutschen Volkstanzes 178

HOERBURGER, F. Zum Problem des Umsingens von Volksliedmelodien 181

4 Ästhetik und Psychologie (chairman ENGEL, H.)

BRENCHER, K.-E. Zur Farbe-Ton-Forschung 187

CONRADIN, H. Das Problem der Bewegung in der Musik 189

SCHAEFER, H. J. Zur Ästhetik und Dramaturgie bei Wagner 192

MOOS, P. Gehören Gluck, Händel und Bach zur barocken Kunst ihrer Zeit? 195

MOSER, H. J. Musikalischer Erbgang und seelische Mutation 197

KRÜGER, W. Grundbegriffe und Periodizität in der abendländischen Musikgeschichte 200

WOLFF, H. C. Der Wert der Geschichte 202

BARUCH, G. W. Musikhistorische Aufgaben und Möglichkeiten des Rundfunks 204

5 Theorie, Pädagogik und Soziologie (chairman GERSTENBERG, W.)

SMITS VAN WAESBERGHE, J. Zur Entstehung der drei Hauptfunktionen in der Harmonik 209

BORRIS, S. Die Widersprüche zwischen älterer Harmonielehre und neueren Tonsatzlehren 211

ROHWER, J. Zur Überwindung des Formalismus in der musikalischen Tonarten- und Geschlechterlehre 213

NEUMANN, F. Probleme der Mehrklangsbildung 217

VALENTIN, E. Zur Soziologie des Musiklebens 220

ENGEL, H. Soziologisches Porträt Johann Sebastian Bachs 223

6 Akustik und Instrumentenkunde (chairman THIENHAUS, E.)

KREIDLER, W. Die Tonleiter als Tonspektrum 229

CREMER, L. Über unser zweifaches Tonhöhenempfinden 230

KOSCHEL, H. Hörmängel und ihre audiometrische Feststellung 231

STREICH, R. Das elektrische Musikinstrument im Spiegel der akustischen Forschung 233

THIENHAUS, E. Zur Frage der Glockenprüfung und Glockenbegutachtung 236

BERNER, A. Zum Klavierbau im 17. und 18. Jahrhundert 239

THIENHAUS, E. Vorführung stereophonischer Bandaufnahmen 243

50 LÜN²   **Zweiter Weltkongress der Musikbibliotheken Lüneburg 1950: Kongress-Bericht**
Lüneburg 20–22 July 1950
International Society of Music Libraries
ed. H. Albrecht (Kassel and Basle: Bärenreiter, 1951)

DENIS, V. Les buts et les moyens des bibliothèques des conservatoires 4

SIEBER, P. Die Bibliothek der Allgemeinen Musikgesellschaft Zürich 7

DAVIES, J. H. Music librarianship for broadcasting 15

BECKER-GLAUCH, I. Die englischen Musikbibliotheken in Deutschland 20

OTT, A. Wesen und Aufgabe einer musikalischen Volksbibliothek 24

NOWAK, L. Dienst am Leser: Aufgaben, Probleme, Lösungen 27

KRAGEMO, K. Konzertprogramme 31

RAUGEL, F. La bibliothèque de la maîtrise de la cathédrale d'Aix en Provence 33

MUELLER von ASOW, E. H. Der Gesamtkatalog der Musiker-Briefe 35

GAUKSTAD, Ö. Registrierung von Volksmusik 38

ZEHNTNER, H. Handschriftliche Musikernachlässe in Schweitzer Bibliotheken 41

HALM, H. Schallplattenarchiv und öffentliche wissenschaftliche Bibliotheken 46

FÉDOROV, V. Entente et organisation internationales pour le dépouillement des périodiques musicaux 49

STÄBLEIN, B. Der thematische Katalog der mittelalterlichen einstimmigen Melodien 52

CREMER, M. Das Schicksal der Musikabteilung der ehemaligen Preussischen Staatsbibliothek 55

STAM, H. Die Stiftung Donemus 56

FÉDOROV, V. Échange et prêt entre bibliothèques musicales 57

50 LUX Mélanges colombaniens: Actes du congrès international de Luxeuil
Luxeuil 20–23 July 1950
Association des amis de St Colomban, Luxeuil
(Paris: Editions Alsatia, 1951; Bibliothèque de la Société d'histoire ecclésiastique de la France)

2 Saint Colomban, sa vie et son oeuvre
COUSIN, P. La psalmodie chorale dans la Règle de Saint Colomban 179

4 Le culte de Saint Colomban
DUFT, J. Saint Colomban dans les manuscrits liturgiques de Saint-Gall 317
HESBERT, R. J. Les compositions rythmiques en l'honneur de Saint Colomban 327

50 ROM Atti del [I] congresso internazionale di musica sacra
Rome 25–30 May 1950
Pontificio istituto di musica sacra; Commissione di musica sacra per l'Anno santo
ed. I. Anglès (Tournai: Desclée & Cie, 1952)

1 Questioni pratiche
ALBERTI, G. Campane 'a festa' suonate mediante movimento a rotazione 28
DE BONIS, A. Formazione tecnica dei musicisti di chiesa 30
BUSSON, M. De la nécessité d'un Graduel à l'usage des petites églises 34
DALLA LIBERA, E. Nei paesi latini è necessario fomentare il canto del popolo nel tempio; per conseguire ciò dobbiamo cominciare dalla scuola elementare 37
DEAN, A. The laity and the liturgy 41
DELACROIX, S. Musique sacrée et pastorale 44
ECCHER, C. Necessità di formare nei paesi latini cappelle musicali con cantori volontari per l'esecuzione della sacra polifonia 49
HABERL, F. Die liturgisch-seelsorgliche und musikalische Notwendigkeit der Schaffung eines kirchlichen und weltlichen Einheitsliederkanons für jede Nation 53
IPPEL, A. and SCHMIDT-GÖRG, J. Eine tönende Musikgeschichte 55
LENNARDS, J. L'éducation musicale des enfants 57
LILLIE, H. W. R. The vocal training for the clergy 59
MAILLET, F. L'Apostolat social, artistique et spirituel des Manécanteries 60
MALCOLM, G. La musica nell'Ufficiatura liturgica della Cattedrale di Westminster 62
da MOTTA e ALBUQUERQUE, J. B. La musica sacra nel Brasile 66
NEUMANN, P. Die Organisation der Kirchenmusikpflege 69
PRIM, J. De l'indispensable base juridique et financière de la musique sacrée 73
ROMITA, F. De studio ac praxi musicae sacrae in Seminariis juxta praescripta S. Sedis 77
ROSSINI, C. Necessità delle scuole diocesane di musica sacra 80

ROUSSEL, G. Les Maîtrises d'enfants et les Offices liturgiques 82
SMIJERS, A. Il faut unir l'oeuvre des diverses Associations de Ste Cécile et de S. Grégoire, en conservant leur autonomie et leur caractère national 87
SCHREMS, T. Rom–Regensburg: Kirchenmusikalische Beziehungen 90
TACK, F. Das zeitgenösische kirchenmusikalische Schrifttum in Deutschland 93
TELEU, W. Die Organisation und soziale Stellung der Kirchenmusiker in Deutschland 96

2 Canto orientale e bizantino
HICKMANN, H. Quelques observations sur la musique liturgique des Coptes d'Egypte 100
HØEG, C. L'Octoechus Byzantin 107
LAILY, P.-A. Difficulté de la notation Byzantine et projet de la remplacer par une notation occidentale adaptée 108
STRUNK, O. The classification and development of the early Byzantine notations 111
PALIKAROVA-VERDEIL, R. Les notations musicales employées dans les églises slaves au IXᵉ siècle 114
RUBIO, S. Manuscritos musicales de la liturgia bizantina que se conservan en la biblioteca del Monasterio de El Escorial 119
DI SALVO, B. La notazione paleobizantina e la sua trascrizione 123
DI SALVO, B. La tradizione orale dei canti liturgici delle colonie Italo-Albanesi di Sicilia comparata con quella dei codici antichi bizantini 129
WELLESZ, E. Kontakion and Kanon 131
WERNER, E. The common ground in the chant of church and synagogue 134

Relazioni e canti di musiche orientali dei collegi orientali romani

KAFTANGIAN, G. Il canto liturgico armeno 149
DAYAN, L. I canti armeni attraverso la tradizione dei secoli 152
MARANGOS, N. Rito bizantino-greco 155
PICHLER, L. Antichi canti bulgari e russi 158
MOUSSES, K. La musique liturgique chaldéenne 164
JARGY, S. La musique liturgique syrienne 166

3 Canto gregoriano
AGUSTONI, L. La scomposizione del neuma 172
ALTISENT, M. Las melodías gregorianas para los 'Propios' nuevos 177
BOMM, U. Historismus und gregorianischer Vortragstil 179
BROU, L. L'Antiphonaire wisigothique et l'Antiphonaire grégorien au début du VIIIᵉ siècle 183
CARDINE, E. De l'édition critique du Graduel: nécessité, avantages, méthode 187
CARRAZ, P. L'accent et l'ictus dans la métrique latine 192
CATTANEO, E. Sul canto ambrosiano 196
CISTERCIAN MONK, Conspectus historicus de cantu in Ordine cisterciensi 199
DELALANDE, D. L'insuffisance du système d'écriture guidonien, ou l'existence de plusieurs notes mobiles dans le système grégorien 202
FROGER, J. Les divers états du Calendrier dans le Graduel romain 207
GAJARD, J. Du rôle des principales familles de manuscrits dans la restauration de la leçon grégorienne authentique 212
GHISLANZONI, A. Importanza dello studio del canto gregoriano per la formazione dei musicisti di oggi e di domani 220
HESBERT, R.-J. Les pièces de chant des messes 'Pro defunctis' dans la tradition manuscrite 223
HESBERT, R.-J. Groupes neumatiques à signification mélodique 229
HOURLIER, J. Le domaine de la notation messine 236
HUGLO, M. Origine de la mélodie du Credo 'authentique' de la Vaticane 240
LE GUENNANT, A. Le mouvement grégorien en France 245
LIPPHARDT, W. Gregor der Grosse und sein Anteil am römischen Antiphonar 248
POTIRON, H. La question modale 255
SANDEN, H. Neumen ohne Linien: neue Forschungen 259
SCHWAKE, G. De cantu gregoriano in ore populi 265
SMITS van WAESBERGHE, J. L'évolution des tons psalmodiques au moyen âge 267
STÄBLEIN, B. Zur Frühgeschichte des römischen Chorals 270
THOMAS, P. Principes de la théorie modale hexacordale dans les théoriciens médiévaux et principalement dans Guy d'Arezzo 276

4 Musicologia
BESSELER, H. Johannes Ciconia, Begründer der Chorpolyphonie 280
CORBIN, S. L'Office en vers 'Gaude, Mater Ecclesia' pour la Conception de la Vierge 284
DENIS, V. La musique et la musicologie dans les universités catholiques 287
de DONOSTIA, J. A. El canto popular religioso en España 291
FEININGER, L. Necessità di catalogare la musica esistente nelle cattedrali e negli archivi parrocchiali 295
FEININGER, L. Orazio Benevoli (1605–1672) 298
FELLERER, K. G. Die kirchliche Monodie um 1600 299
von FICKER, R. Der Choral als symbolische Idee in der mittelalterlichen Mehrstimmigkeit 303
GAZÉ, A. L'oeuvre de l'Université catholique d'Ottawa (Canada) au point de vue de la musique sacrée 304
GHISI, F. L'Ordinarium Missae nel XV secolo ed i primordi della parodia 308
LENAERTS, R. B. La musique sacrée en Belgique au XVIIIᵉ siècle 311
PIRROTTA, N. Considerazioni sui primi esempi di Missa parodia 315
PUJOL, D. Manuscritos de música neerlandesa conservados en la Biblioteca del Monasterio de Montserrat 319
QUEROL, M. La música religiosa Española en el s. XVII 323
RONGA, L. Nota sulla vocalità Palestriniana 327
TORREFRANCA, F. Grecia e Occidente: valore cristiano della polifonia 330
ZEHRER, F. L'interpretazione moderna della polifonia sacra classica: difetti de evitare 336

5 Organo e musica organistica
BÉVENOT, L. L'orgue McClure à tempérament non-égal 342
BONNET, A. Musique d'orgue et chant grégorien 344
GERMANI, F. L'organo barocco nell' idea moderna 348
JEPPESEN, K. Die älteste italienische Orgelmusik 351
KELLER, H. Die Orgel-Messe im 'Dritten Teil der Klavier-Übung' von Johann Sebastian Bach 354
LUNELLI, R. Apologia dell'organo tradizionale 356
GUILLAUME, M. Etude sur le choral 'Notre Père au Royaume des Cieux' de J. S. Bach 359
PIECHLER, A. Die Phrasierung der Orgelwerke Bachs 363
SANGIORGIO, C. Le caratteristiche dell'organo liturgico 367
QUOILIN, R. Zur Entstehung der italienisch-österreichischen Barockorgel 371
WALTER, R. Bemerkungen zu Orgelbau und Orgelspiel in Deutschland 380

51 IES Atti del primo congresso internazionale di studi spontiniani
Iesi, Maiolati, Fabriano, Ancona 6–9 September 1951
(Fabriano: Gentile, 1954)

CAFFARELLI, F. Spontini grande italiano e grande europeo 7

GHISLANZONI, A. Sintesi della produzione giovanile Spontiniana 13

TRAGLIA, G. Umiliazioni giovanili e reazioni nell'età matura in Gaspare Spontini 23

BELARDINELLI, A. Documenti Spontiniani inediti 27

FELLERER, K. G. L'importanza de La Vestale nella produzione operistica di Spontini 33

ROLANDI, U. Tre parodie de La Vestale 41

CAFFARELLI, F. Documentazioni Spontiniane inedite: l'Epistolario 48

SERVOLINI, L. Inediti Spontiniani a Forlì 50

OSTHOFF, H. L'idea drammatica e lo stile musicale nelle opere di Gaspare Spontini 53

CAFFARELLI, F. Il rapporto di G. Spontini intorno alla riforma della musica sacra 59

GHISLANZONI, A. Gaspare Spontini e la musica bandistica 70

BELARDINELLI, A. Le Ateniesi di De Jouy 81

GLINSKI, M. Spontini direttore d'orchestra 86

GHISLANZONI, A. I rapporti fra Spontini e Mendelssohn 95

ENGEL, H. L'opera 'Agnese di Hohenstaufen' di Spontini 105

TORREFRANCA, F. Gaspare Spontini e l'opera tedesca 129

51 OCH Der Barock, seine Orgeln und seine Musik in Oberschwaben: zugleich der Bericht über die Tagung in Ochsenhausen 1951
Ochsenhausen 29 July – 5 August 1951
Gesellschaft der Orgelfreunde
ed. W. Supper (Berlin and Darmstadt: Carl Merseburger, 1952)

2 Die kulturgeschichtlichen Referate

SIEGELE, W. Musik des oberschwäbischen Barock 40

QUOIKA, R. Über die österreichische und oberschwäbische Barockorgel 59

SCHAHL, A. Die Wallfahrtskirche von Steinhausen 67

REICHERT, G. Beziehungen württembergischer Musiker zum Hamburger Organistenkreis 70

3 Die auf den süddeutschen Orgelbarock bezugnehmenden Referate

QUOIKA, R. Zur Technologie der süddeutschen Barockorgel 76

BÖSKEN, F. Der mittelrheinische Orgelbau zur Zeit des Aufenthalts Joseph Gablers in Mainz 78

GOTTRON, A. Joseph Gabler in Mainz 82

GINDELE, C. Der Anteil Beurons an der Rettung der Ottobeurer Orgeln 84

RAUGEL, F. Die Barockorgel in Frankreich 87

4 Die oberschwäbische Barockorgel

LOTTERMOSER, W. Die Akustik der oberschwäbischen Barockorgeln 119

6 Beiträge zum Orgelbau der Gegenwart

KOPP, R. Das Portativ für zeitnahes Schulsingen 141

SPÖRRI, O. Die neuzeitliche kleine Orgel in der Schweiz 144

BÖHRINGER, H. Das Spezifische des 'katholischen' Orgelbaus 148

7 Die Aussprache mit den Entschliessungen

NEUMANN, H. J. Die Elektro-Orgel in der Kirche 155

51 PAL   Atti dello VIII congresso internazionale di studi bizantini
Palermo 3–10 April 1951
International Association for Byzantine Studies
, (Rome: Associazione nazionale per gli studi bizantini, 1953 = Studi bizantini e
neoellenici, ed. S. G. Mercati, 7–8)

Vol. ii (1953)
Liturgia e musica
DI SALVO, B.   Lo sviluppo dei modi della musica

bizantina dal sec. XIII alla riforma di Chry-
santhos   405

51 PAR   Troisième congrès international des bibliothèques musicales Paris: actes du congrès
Paris 22–5 July 1951
International Association of Music Libraries
ed. V. Fédorov (Kassel and Basle: Bärenreiter, 1953)

FÉDOROV, V.   La commission provisoire: Le con-
grès: Le status   18
BLUME, F.   Die Frage eines internationalen
Quellenlexikons der Musik   20
ZEHNTNER, H.   A propos de la refonte d'un
*Répertoire international des sources musi-
cales*   24
HILL, R. S.   The U.S. position on the *International Inventory of Musical Sources*   28
GIRARDON, R.   Rapport sur la nécessité d'un
nouveau Recueil international des sources
musicales   32
HILL, R. S.   Some pros and cons regarding an
international code for cataloging practical
music   37
PIRROTTA, N.   Fondi musicali non inventariati
nè catalogati   46

LUTHER, W. M.   Die Mikrokopie von Auto-
graphen, Unica und sonstigen musikalischen
Wertstücken; ihr Austausch innerhalb der Welt
und ihre Sicherung gegen Zerfall und
Vernichtung   48
DENIS, V.   Échanges et prêts internationaux de
musique   56
KING, A. H.   An international scheme for publishing summaries of articles in musical
periodicals   62
DAVIES, J. H.   Broadcasting music libraries 65
DUCKLES, V. H.   The place of gramophone re-
cording in a university music library   65
MYERS, K.   Phonograph records in American
public libraries   71

51 STIS   Conferencia internacional de Africanistas occidentales: 4.ª conferencia
Santa Isabel, Fernando Póo 1951
International West African Conference
(Madrid: Dirección general de Marruecos y Colonias, 1954)

Vol. ii Trabajos presentados a la III.a sección
(medio humano) (1954)
PEPPER, H.   Considérations sur le langage tam-

bourine et autres langages musicaux d'Africa
central, sur la pensée musicale africaine   165

51 STOC   Thirteenth International Congress of Psychology: Proceedings and Papers
Stockholm 16–21 July 1951
(? Stockholm, n.d./*R* Nendeln: Kraus, 1974)

ROIHA, E.   On the psychology of musical time
(measure)   210

52 BERN   Bericht über den [I.] internationalen Kongress für Kirchenmusik in Bern / Compte rendu du [Iᵉ] congrès international de musique sacrée à Berne
Berne 30 August – 4 September 1952
(Berne: Paul Haupt, 1953 = Publikationen der Schweizerischen Musikforschenden Gesellschaft ii/3)

HANDSCHIN, J. Die Kirchenmusik und die Frage der Wiedervereinigung der Kirchen   9
GURLITT, W. Die Kirchenorgel in Geschichte und Gegenwart   23
ILJINE, V. Der gemeinsame Ursprung des gregorianischen und des altrussischen Neumengesangs   38
van der HORST, A. Fragen der Chorerziehung   40
KROHN, I. Errungenschaften und Aussichten der finnischen Kirchenmusik   41
BLANKENBURG, W. Die evangelische Kirchenmusik in Deutschland im Lichte der Liturgie   42

FELLERER, K. G. Palestrina   43
NIEVERGELT, E. Zeitgenössische evangelische Kirchenmusik   50
RIMBAULT, L. Le Psautier huguenot, lien universel d'amitié entre les peuples   52
RAUGEL, F. La musique sacrée à la Chapelle des rois de France   55
JEANS, S. Anglikanische Kirchenmusik   57
ZACHARIASSEN, S. Aktuelle Orgelbaufragen und Möglichkeiten zu ihrer praktischen Lösung   62
SCHIESS, E. Grundzüge des neuen Orgelbaues, Erfahrungen und Erkenntnisse der letzten Jahrzehnte   65

52 CAM   Proceedings of the Thirtieth International Congress of Americanists
Cambridge 18–23 August 1952
International Congress of Americanists
(London: Royal Anthropological Institute, 1955)

YEOMANS, W. The musical instruments of pre-Columbian Central America   54

52 UTR   Société internationale de musicologie cinquième congrès Utrecht: compte rendu / Internationale Gesellschaft für Musikwissenschaft fünfter Kongress Utrecht: Kongressbericht / International Society for Musical Research Fifth Congress Utrecht: Report
Utrecht 3–7 July 1952
International Society for Musical Research (International Musicological Society)
(Amsterdam: Vereniging voor nederlandse muziekgeschiedenis/G. Alsbach & Co., 1953)

MASSON, P.-M. Les tâches internationales de la musicologie   11
SCHRADE, L. Renaissance: the historical conception of an epoch   19
von FICKER, R. Grundsätzliches zur mittelalterlichen Aufführungspraxis   33
ANGLÈS, H. Les musiciens flamands en Espagne et leur influence sur la polyphonie espagnole   47

ANTONOWYTSCH, M. Die Mehrstimmigkeit in den ukrainischen Volksliedern   55
BESSELER, H. Die Besetzung der Chansons im 15. Jahrhundert   65
BODKY, E. New contributions to the problem of the interpretation of Bach's keyboard works   73
van den BORREN, C. A propos de quelques messes de Josquin   79
BROCKHOFF, M. E. Die Kadenz bei Josquin 86

BUKOFZER, M. F. Interrelations between conductus and clausula 96

CHAILLEY, J. Pour une philologie du langage musical 100

CLERCX-LEJEUNE, S. Johannes Ciconia de Leodio 107

CUDWORTH, C. L. Pergolesi, Ricciotti and the Count of Bentinck 127

DANISKAS, J. Analytische Studien über die Kompositionstechnik der burgundischen Schule 132

DART, T. English music and musicians in 17th century Holland 139

DITTMER, L. A. The ligatures of the Montpellier manuscript 146

EGGEBRECHT, H. H. Aus der Werkstatt des terminologischen Handwörterbuchs 155

ENGEL, H. Die Entstehung des italienischen Madrigales und die Niederländer 166

FELLERER, K. G. Musikalische Beziehungen zwischen den Niederlanden und Deutschland im 17. Jahrhunderts 181

VON FISCHER, K. C. P. E. Bachs Variationenwerke 189

FOKKER, A. D. The qualities of the equal temperament by 31 fifths of a tone in the octave 191

GAILLARD, A. Essai sur le rapport des sources mélodiques des Pseaulmes cinquantes de Iean Louis (Anvers 1555) et des 'Souterliedekens' (Anvers 1540) 193

GLAHN, H. Entwicklungszüge innerhalb des evangelischen Kirchengesanges des 16. Jahrhunderts im Lichte vergleichender Quellenforschung 199

GURLITT, W. Ein begriffsgeschichtliches Wörterbuch der Musik 211

HAMEL, F. J. S. Bach als geistesgeschichtliche Erscheinung 218

HARRISON, F. Ll. The Eton College Choirbook (Eton College MS 178) 224

HICKMANN, H. Quelques nouveaux documents concernant le jeu de la harpe et l'emploi de la chironomie dans l'Egypte pharaonique 233

HUSMANN, H. Die mittelniederländischen Lieder der Berliner Handschrift Germ. 8° 190 241

KAHL, W. Niederländische Werke aus den Bestanden der alten Kölner Jesuitenbibliothek 252

KOLNEDER, W. Das Frühschaffen Antonio Vivaldis 254

KOOLE, A. Report on the inquiry into the music and instruments of the Basutos in Basutoland 263

KUNST, J. Gamelan music 271

LENAERTS, R. Les manuscrits polyphoniques de la Bibliothèque capitulaire de Tolède 276

LIESS, A. 'Umdeutung' als musikgeschichtlicher Grundbegriff 282

van der LINDEN, A. La place de la Hollande dans l'Allgemeine musikalische Zeitung (1798 1848) 293

MOSER, H. J. Die Niederlande in der Musikgeographie Europas 296

OSTHOFF, H. Zur Echtheitsfrage und Chronologie bei Josquins Werken 303

PLAMENAC, D. New light on Codex Faenza 117 310

QUITIN, J. L'intervention du Gouvernement hollandais dans la création du Conservatoire royal de musique de Liège in 1826 327

RAUGEL, F. Anciennes orgues françaises 335

SALMEN, W. Das Liederbuch der Anna von Köln und seine Beziehungen zu den Niederlanden 340

SCHRÖDER, A. E. Les origines des Lamentations polyphoniques au XVe siècle dans les Pays-Bas 352

SEEGER, C. Preface to the description of a music 360

SMITS van WAESBERGHE, J. Das niederländische Osterspiel 371

STÄBLEIN, B. Die Tegernseer mensurale Choralschrift aus dem 15. Jahrhundert: etwas Greifbares zur Rhythmik der mittelalterlichen Monodie 377

TEUBER, U. Bemerkungen zur Homophonie im 16. Jh. 384

TIBY, O. Emanuele d'Astorga: aggiunte e correzioni da apportare alle ricerche del Prof. Hans Volkmann 398

TORREFRANCA, F. Origine e significato di repicco, partita, ricercare, sprezzatura 404

WARD, J. The 'folia' 415

WERNER, E. New studies in the history of the early octoechos 428

WIORA, W. Die Melodien der 'Souterliedekens' und ihre deutschen Parallelen 438

WOLFF, H. C. Der Stilbegriff der 'Renaissance' in der Musik der alten Niederländer 450

ZAGIBA, F. Die Entstehung des Slavischen liturgischen Gesanges im 9. Jahrhundert nach westlichem und östlichem Ritus 456

52 VIE   Actes du IVe congrès international des sciences anthropologiques et ethnologiques
Vienna 1–8 September 1952
International Union of Anthropological and Ethnological Sciences
ed. R. Heine-Geldern and others (Vienna: Adolf Holzhausens Nfg., 1954–6)

53 BAM   **Bericht über den internationalen musikwissenschaftlichen Kongress Bamberg 1953**
Bamberg 15–19 July 1953
Gesellschaft für Musikforschung
ed. W. Brennecke, W. Kahl, R. Steglich (Kassel and Basle: Bärenreiter, 1954)

BLUME, F. Musikforschung und Musikleben 7

Musikerziehung und Musikwissenschaft (chairman OBERBORBECK, F.)
MOSER, H. J. Lage und Ziele der Musikpädagogik aus wissenschaftlicher Schau   27
GURLITT, W. Musikwissenschaftliche Forschung und Lehre in pädagogischer Sicht 33
Discussion: Musikerziehung und Musikwissenschaft (panel OBERBORBECK, F., LAAFF, E., MÜLLER-BLATTAU, J., KLAUSMEIER, F., EGGEBRECHT, H. H.)   38
SMITS van WAESBERGHE, J. Guido von Arezzo als Musikerzieher und Musiktheoretiker 44
HÖWELER, C. Zur internationalen Uniformität der Begriffe Metrum und Rhythmus   47
REUSCH, F. Versuch einer Tonraumlehre   50

Heutige Aufgaben der Instrumentenkunde (chairman STEGLICH, R.)
BERNER, A. Die Instrumentenkunde in Wissenschaft und Praxis   57
DRÄGER, H.-H. Das Instrument als Träger und Ausdruck des musikalischen Bewusstseins 67
LOTTERMOSER, W. Unterschiede in Klang und Ansprache bei alten und neuen Orgeln   75
MEHL, J. C. Die Barockorgel in Lahm (Itzgrund) im Zusammenhang des nord- und süddeutschen Orgelbaus ihrer Zeit und die Probleme ihrer Restaurierung   78
SERAUKY, W. Ausgewählte instrumentenkundliche Probleme in einem Musikinstrumenten-Museum   82
NEUPERT, H. Kopie und Rekonstruktion: Geschichte und Probleme des Neubaus von besaiteten Tasteninstrumenten   85
SENN, W. Forschungsaufgaben zur Geschichte des Geigenbaues   89
KARSTÄDT, G. Aufführungspraktische Fragen bei Verwendung von Naturtrompeten, Naturhörnern und Zinken   93
AMELN, K. Historische Instrumente in der gegenwärtigen Musikpraxis   96

Die Kompositionslehre des 16. und 17. Jahrhunderts (chairman OSTHOFF, H.)
GURLITT, W. Die Kompositionslehre des deutschen 16. und 17. Jahrhunderts   103
SCHMITZ, A. Die Kadenz als Ornamentum musicae   114

WALLIN, N. L. Zur Deutung der Begriffe Faburden–Fauxbourdon   120
BOETTICHER, W. Orlando di Lasso als Demonstrationsobjekt in der Kompositionslehre des 16. und 17. Jahrhunderts   124
QUOIKA, R. Die Musica des Jan Blahoslav 1569   128
FEDERHOFER, H. Die Figurenlehre nach Christoph Bernhard und die Dissonanzbehandlung in Werken von Heinrich Schütz   132
DAHLHAUS, C. Die Figurae superficiales in den Traktaken Christoph Bernhards   135
MAXTON, W. Johann Theile als Theoretiker 138
OREL, A. Die Kontrapunktlehren von Poglietti und Bertali   140
TORREFRANCA, R. Documenti definitivi sulla Partita   143
PFROGNER, H. Der Clavis in Andreas Werckmeisters 'Nothwendigsten Anmerkungen und Regeln, wie der Bassus continuus oder Generalbass wol könne tractiret werden'   149
GERSTENBERG, W. Generalbasslehre und Kompositionstechnik in Niedts 'Musikalischer Handleitung'   152

Der volks- und völkerkundliche Beitrag zur Musikgeschichte (chairman FELLERER, K. G.)
WIORA, W. Schrift und Tradition als Quellen der Musikgeschichte   159
SCHNEIDER, M. Arabischer Einfluss in Spanien?   175
ANGLÈS, H. Die Bedeutung des Volksliedes für die Musikgeschichte Europas   181
BAKE, A. A. Bemerkungen zur Entstehungsgeschichte eines Modus   184
SALMEN, W. Die altniederländischen Handschriften Berlin 8° 190 und Wien 7970 im Lichte vergleichender Melodienforschung   187
TIBY, O. L'origine popolare della Siciliana a la sua evoluzione dal trecento a Bach e ad Haendel   194
ZAGIBA, F. Die Funktion des Volksliedgutes in der Entwicklung der südeuropäischen Musikgeschichte   197
WÜNSCH, W. Die südosteuropäische Volksepik, die Ballade und das Tanzlied im Vergleich zu den Frühformen in der abendländischen Musikkultur   200
KOMMA, K. M. Volksmusikalische Grundlagen des Kompositionsstils der letzten Jahrzehnte in Böhmen und Mähren   203

VÄISÄNEN A. O. Jean Sibelius und die Volksmusik 207

KREIDLER, W. Der Wert des Atlas der deutschen Volkskunde für die Musikgeschichte 209

BOSE, F. Instrumentalstile in primitiver Musik 212

Singstil und Instrumentalstil in der europäischen Musik (chairman von FICKER, R.)

HUSMANN, H. Singstil und Instrumentalstil in ihren Voraussetzungen 219

BESSELER, H. Singstil und Instrumentalstil in der europäischen Musik 223

KRÜGER, W. Singstil und Instrumentalstil in der Mehrstimmigkeit der St. Martialepoche 240

REANEY, G. Voices and instruments in the music of Guilleaume de Machaut 245

GUDEWILL, K. Vokale und instrumentale Stilmomente in textlosen Kompositionen des Glogauer Liederbuches 248

WOLFF, H. C. Die Gesangsimprovisationen der Barockzeit 252

HAUSSWALD, G. Instrumentale Züge im Belcanto des 18. Jahrhunderts 256

ELLER, R. Nationale Bedingtheiten des europäischen Instrumentalstiles 259

HOFFMANN-ERBRECHT, L. Grundlagen der Melodiebildung bei Mussorgski 262

NESTLER, G. Ästhetische Grundlagen des Sing- und Instrumentalstils in der Musik der Gegenwart 266

Sondertagung der Internationalen Vereinigung der Musikbibliotheken, Bamberg 20 July 1953 (chairman HALM, H.)

LESURE, F. La datation des premières editions d'Estienne Roger (1697–1702) 273

RAUGEL, F. Bernard Jumentier (1749–1829) maître de chapelle de la Collégiale de Saint-Quentin et ses oeuvres inédites 279

SCHMIEDER, W. Musikbibliographische Probleme: ein Beitrag zur Theorie der Verzeichnung von Büchern über Musik 282

FERCHAULT, G. Essai de justification d'une bibliographie particulière à la philosophie de l'art musical 286

KAHL, W. Öffentliche und private Musiksammlungen in ihrer Bedeutung für die musikalische Renaissancebewegung des 19. Jahrhunderts in Deutschland 289

PAULI, F. W. Phonetische Dokumentation und Musikforschung 295

HALM, H. Über Verzeichnisse der Werke Beethovens 299

53 BRUS   Actes du XIème congrès international de philosophie
Brussels 20–26 August 1953
International Congress of Philosophy
(Amsterdam: North-Holland Publishing Company/Louvain: Editions E. Nauwelaerts, 1953/*R* Nendeln: Kraus, 1970)

x **Philosophie des valeurs: ethique – esthétique** (1953)
Esthétique
HARTMANN, H. Hauptprobleme der Musikphilosophie 271

53 NET   Proceedings of the First ICA-Congress: Electro-Acoustics
Netherlands 16–24 June 1953
International Commission on Acoustics, International Union of Pure and Applied Physics
ed. C. W. Kosten and M. L. Kasteleyn, reprinted in *Acustica* iv/1 (Zurich: S. Hirzel, 1954) [original distributed only among congress members]

6 Electro-acoustics applied to musical instruments

RICHARDSON, E. G. General review 212

BIERL, R. Neuere Ergebnisse der elektrischen Klangerzeugung und deren Beziehungen zu der mechanischen Klangerzeugung 218

GELUK, J. J. Electronic tuners for musical pitch 220

GEORGE, W. H. A sound reversal technique applied to the study of tone quality 224

GRÜTZMACHER, M. Über die Klänge von Glocken und Orgeln 226

KOK, W. Experimental study of tuning problems 229

LENIHAN, J. M. A. and McNEILL, S. An acoustical study of the Highland bagpipe 231

MEINEL, H. Zur Stimmung der Musikinstrumente 233

MERCER, D. M. A. The effect of voicing adjust-

ments on the tone quality of organ flue
pipes   237
MEYER-EPPLER, W. Welche Möglichkeiten be-
stehen für eine sinnvolle Anwendung elektroni-
scher Musikinstrumente?   239
MOLES, A. The characterization of sound objects by the use of the level recorder in musical
acoustics   241
PASQUALINI, G. Récents résultats obtenus dans
l'étude électroacoustique de la caisse

harmonique des instruments à archet   244
SKUDRZYK, E. Betrachtungen zum musikalischen Zusammenklang   249
THIENHAUS, E. Stereophonische Übertragung
klangschwacher Instrumente im Konzert-
saal   253
TRAUTWEIN, F. Elektroakustische Mittel in der
aktiven Tonkunst   256
YOUNG, R. W. Inharmonicity of piano
strings   259

53 PAR   **Musique et poésie au XVIᵉ siècle**
Paris 30 June – 4 July 1953
Centre national de la recherche scientifique: sciences humaines
ed. J. Jacquot (Paris: Centre national de la recherche scientifique, 1954, 2/1974 = Le
choeur des muses, ed. J. Jacquot)

WALKER, D. P. Le chant orphique de Marsile
Ficin   17
POPE, I. La musique espagnole à la cour de
Naples dans la seconde moitié du XVᵉ siècle35
BRIDGMAN, N. La frottola et la transition de la
frottola au madrigal   63
THIBAULT, G. Musique et poésie en France au
XVIᵉ siècle avant les Amours de Ronsard 79
SAULNIER, V. L. Maurice Scève et la musi-
que   89
LEBÈGUE, R. Ronsard et la musique   105
STEVENS, D. La chanson anglaise avant l'école
madrigaliste   121
WESTRUP, J. A. L'influence de la musique
italienne sur le madrigal anglais   129
JACQUOT, J. Lyrisme et sentiment tragique dans
les madrigaux d'Orlando Gibbons   139
'ELLERS, W. La mélancolie au début du XVIIᵉ
siècle et le madrigal anglais   153
LESURE, F. Éléments populaires dans la chanson
française au début du XVIᵉ siècle   169
LEVY, K. J. Vaudeville, vers mesurés et airs de
cour   185

DART, T. Rôle de la danse dans l''ayre'
anglais   203
VERCHALY, A. Poésie et air de cour en France
jusqu'à 1620   211
CHAILLEY, J. Esprit et technique du chro-
matisme de la Renaissance   225
YATES, F. A. Poésie et musique dans les
'Magnificences' au mariage du duc de Joyeuse,
Paris, 1581   241
GHISI, F. L''aria di maggio' et le travestissement
spirituel de la poésie profane en Italie   265
SCHRADE, L. L''Edipo Tiranno' d'Andrea
Gabrieli et la Renaissance de la tragédie grec-
que   275
PIRROTTA, N. Tragédie et comédie dans la
Camerata fiorentina   287
QUEROL-GAVALDA, M. Importance historique
et nationale de romance   299
CLERCX, S. L'Espagne XVIᵉ siècle, source
d'inspiration du génie héroïque de Monte-
verdi   329
Discussion   345

53 THE   **Pepragmena tou th' diethnous byzantinologikou synedriou** [Acts of the ninth international
Byzantine congress]
Thessaloniki 12–19 April 1953
International Association of Byzantine Studies
ed. S. Kyriakides, A. Xyngopoulos, P. Zepos (Athens: Typographeion Myrtidē 1955–
8 = Hellenika, supplement 7)

Vol. ii (1956)
Theologia
HOEG, C. Quelques remarques sur les rapports
entre la musique ecclésiastique de la Russie et la
musique byzantine   120
KARA, Z. I. Hē orthē hermēneia kai metagraphē

ton byzantinōn mousikōn cheirographōn [The
true interpretation and transcription of
Byzantine manuscript music]   140
STRUNK, O. S. Salvatore di Messina and the
musical tradition of Magna Graecia   274

54 ARR   La Renaissance dans les provinces du Nord (Picardie – Artois – Flandres – Brabant – Hainaut)
Arras 17–20 June 1954
Centre national de la recherche scientifique
ed. F. Lesure (Paris: Centre national de la recherche scientifique, 1956 = Le choeur des muses, ed. J. Jacquot)

van der LINDEN, A. Comment désigner la nationalité des artistes des provinces du Nord à l'époque de la Renaissance   11
van den BORREN, C. Musicologie et géographie   19
BAUTIER-RÉGNIER, A.-M. L'édition musicale italienne et les musiciens d'Outremonts au XVIᵉ siècle (1501–1563)   27
BRIDGMAN, N. Les échanges musicaux entre l'Espagne et les Pays-Bas au temps de Philippe le Beau et de Charles-Quint   51
CHAILLON, P. Les musiciens du Nord à la cour de Louis XII   63
KREPS, J. Le mécènat de la cour de Bruxelles (1430–1559)   169
THIBAULT, G. Le concert instrumental dans l'art flamand au XVᵉ siècle et au début du XVIᵉ   197

54 CAM   Proceedings of the Twenty-third International Congress of Orientalists
Cambridge 21–8 August 1954
International Union of Orientalists
ed. D. Sinor (London: Royal Asiatic Society, 1957/R Nendeln: Kraus, 1968)

4 Iranian, Armenian and Central Asian Studies
PATMAGRIAN, A. L'utilisation des éléments folkloriques dans le chant liturgique arménien au XIIᵉ siècle   173

54 FER   Torquato Tasso
Ferrara 16–19 September 1954
(Milan: Marzorati, 1957)

RONGA, L. Tasso e la musica   187

54 PAL   Atti del congresso internazionale di musiche popolari mediterranee e del convegno dei bibliotecari musicali
Palermo 26–30 June 1954
(Palermo: Ministero della pubblica istruzione, Assessorato per la pubblica istruzione della regione siciliana, 1959)

[Congresso internazionale di musiche popolari mediterranee]
TIBY, O. La tradizione del anto popolare in Sicilia e nelle regioni mediterranee   37
AMADES, J. La canzone ritmica catalana   47
BAUD-BOVY, S. Sur quelques aspects de là chanson populaire dans l'île de Crète   53
BORREL, E. A propos du folklore israélite de Salonique   57
BRĂILOIU, C. Un type mélodique méditerranéen   59

CERVELLI, L. Polifonia e monodia nel canto religioso popolare del cinquecento 63

COLLAER, P. À propos de deux chansons bulgares et espagnoles 71

KALOMIRIS, M. L'évolution de la musique en Grèce 75

TOSCHI, P. Etnofonia e musica popolare siciliana e sarda 89

WIORA, W. Volks- und Kunstmusik in der griechisch-römischen Antike 91

TIBALDI CHIESA, M. I canti popolari siciliani e la musica greca negli studi de Ettore Romagnoli 95

BRĂILOIU, C. Melodie, ritme, strumenti e simboli nelle danze mediterranee 101

AMADES, J. Strumenti di musica popolare in Catalogna 115

AMADES, J. Simbolismo delle danze catalane 123

GALANTI, B. Analogie di forme e ritmi nelle espressioni coreutiche mediterranee 127

GARCÍA MATOS, M. Strumenti musicali folkloristici di Ibiza: gli aerofoni melodici 133

GERSON-KIWI, E. Sintesi e simboli degli stili popolari in Israele 153

MARCEL-DUBOIS, C. Les éléments musicaux et la danse d'une cérémonie rituelle de français méditerranées 161

NASELLI, C. Riti prenunziali; il ballo sul letto, i canti del letto 163

NATALETTI, G. Il grido nelle danze mediterranee 181

TANI, G. Origini autoctone e paleolitiche della danza italiana 183

TORREFRANCA, F. La musica siciliana e dei popoli mediterranei nella storia della musica europea 189

ANGLÉS, I. La musica medioevale sacra in Sicilia 205

BRIDGMAN, N. Quelques editions rares de musique italienne du seizième et dixseptième siècle dans les bibliothèques de France 215

CLERCX-LEJEUNE, S. Le premier séjour en Italie de Joannes Ciconia (1358–1367) 223

DI SALVO, B. Alcune tradizioni musicali liturgiche orientali e la tradizione scritta dei codici bizantini medioevali 229

FELLERER, K. G. Probleme der mittelmeerischen Musik in Frühchristlichen Gesang 237

GEORGIADES, T. Un esempio di polifonia primordiale della Grecia 243

HANDSCHIN, J. La question du chant 'vieux-romain' 245

HUCKE, H. Improvvisazione nella Schola cantorum romana 259

LI GOTTI, E. La questione dello strambotto alla luce delle recenti scoperte 263

MOMPELLIO, F. Le musiche ad una ed a due voci del palermitano Sigismondo d'India 267

MOSER, H. J. De Mari Interno quasi vinculo musico gentium accolentium 271

OSTHOFF, W. Le forme più antiche della passacaglia nella musica italiana 275

STÄBLEIN, B. Una sconosciuta sequenza dello stile arcaico in Italia 289

VALABREGA, C. La millenaria musica·ebraica e Ernest Bloch 295

WOLFF, H. C. Der Siciliano bei J. S. Bach und G. Fr. Haendel 301

SCHNEIDER, M. Studi e proposte per un corpus delle musiche popolari mediterranee 311

PORRINO, E. Per un corpus delle musiche popolari mediterranee 325

NATALETTI, G. I canti greco-albanesi di Sicilia, Calabria e Molise 329

Relazione e communicazioni sul tema del convegno dei bibliotecari musicali

PIRROTTA, A. Compiti regionali, nazionali, ed internazionali delle biblioteche musicali 331

de AZEVEDO, L. H. C. L'UNESCO et la coopération internationale entre les Bibliothèques musicales 341

DAMERINI, A. Per l'incremento delle biblioteche nei conservatori di musica 349

FÉDOROV, V. L'Association internationale des bibliothèques musicales: son organisation, ses tâches: ses rapports avec les groupes nationaux et locaux 353

GHISLANZONI, A. Per un catalogo unico nazionale delle biblioteche musicali 359

LESURE, F. Les bibliothèques musicales comme centres de documentation 363

SARTORI, C. Uno schedario regionale nella biblioteca musicale del capoluogo della regione 369

54 PAR[1]   **La musique instrumentale de la Renaissance**
Paris 28 March – 2 April 1954.
Centre national de la recherche scientifique: Journées internationales d'études
ed. J. Jacquot (Paris: Centre national de la recherche scientifique, 1955 = Le choeur
des muses, ed. J. Jacquot)

THIBAULT, G.   Le concert instrumental au XVe siècle   23
HARASZTI, E.   Les musiciens de Mathias Corvin et de Béatrice d'Aragon   35
HEARTZ, D.   Les styles instrumentaux dans la musique de la Renaissance   61
DART, T.   Origines et sources de la musique de chambre en Angleterre (1500–1530)   77
STEVENS, D.   Les sources de l'"in nomine"   85
NOBLE, J.   Le répertoire instrumental anglais (1550–1585)   91
COLE, E.   L'anthologie de madrigaux et de musique instrumentale pour ensembles de Francis Tregian   115
BRENNECKE, W.   Musique instrumentale d'après un manuscrit allemand (Ratisbonne, ms. A.R. 940/41)   127
MEYER, E. H.   L'élément populaire dans les danses instrumentales allemandes jusqu'à la guerre de Trente Ans   139
LISSA, Z.   La formation du style national dans la musique instrumentale polonaise de la Renaissance   149
CAPE, S.   À propos d'enregistremen's de danses du moyen âge et de la Renaissance   163
GOMBOSI, O.   À la recherche de la forme dans la musique de la Renaissance: Francesco da Milano   165
de MORCOURT, R.   Le livre de tablature de luth de Domenico Bianchini (1546)   177
LUMSDEN, D.   De quelques éléments étrangers dans la musique anglaise pour le luth   197
PUJOL, E.   Les ressources instrumentales et leur rôle dans la musique pour vihuela et pour guitare au XVIᵉ siècle et au XVIIᵉ   205
KASTNER, S.   Rapports entre Schlick et Cabezón   217
WARD, J.   Les sources de la musique pour le clavier en Angleterre   225
DART, T.   Le manuscrit pour le virginal de Trinity College, Dublin   237
JACQUOT, J.   Sur quelques formes de la musique de clavier élisabéthaine (d'après des oeuvres inédites de John Bull)   241
HARDOUIN, P.   La composition des orgues que pouvaient toucher les musiciens parisiens aux alentours de 1600   259
DUFOURCQ, N.   Remarques sur le clavier (clavecin et orgue) dans la première moitié du XVIIᵉ siècle   269
FROIDEBISE, P.   Sur quelques éditions de musique d'orgue ancienne   277
BENEDETTI-MICHELANGELI, F.   Principe d'édition des oeuvres de clavier anciennes   287
KASTNER, S.   Le 'clavecin parfait' de Bartolomeo Jobernardi   293
SARTORI, C.   Une pratique des musiciens lombards (1582–1639), l'hommage des chansons instrumentales aux familles d'une ville   305
CLERCX, S.   La toccata, principe du style symphonique   313
LAUNAY, D.   La fantaisie en France jusqu'au milieu du XVIIᵉ siècle   327
HECKMANN, H.   Influence de la musique instrumentale du XVIᵉ siècle sur la rythmique moderne du XVIIᵉ   339
SOURIS, A.   Problèmes d'analyse   347
Discussion   359

54 PAR[2]   **Radio, musique et société: Actes du congrès international sur les aspects sociologiques de la musique à la radio**
Paris 27–30 October 1954
Centre d'études radiophoniques
Cahiers d'études de radio-télévision 3–4 (Paris: Presses universitaires de France, 1955)

1 Transformation des structures sociales par la musique à la radio

CAPLOW, T.   The influence of radio on music as a social institution   279
MALETZKE, G.   Der Mensch im publizistischen Feld   292
RÖSSEL-MAJDAN, K.   Das fundamentale Problem der Phonokopie   302
GOUZOU, L.   Modification de la classe paysanne française par la musique à la radio   310
ECKANOVE, C. A.   Remarques sur la qualité artistique de la musique à la radio   318
MOREUX, S.   Reproduction mécanique du son et création musicale   331
ROSSEAU, N.   Des responsabilités de la radio dans les rapports musicaux et sociaux   335
GIROD, R.   Recherches sociologiques et développement de la culture musicale   338

PORTE, J. Problèmes posés par une étude par sondage de l'auditoire radiophonique 344.

KÖNIG, R. Sur quelques problèmes sociologiques de l'émission radiophonique musicale notamment sur les difficultés d'adaptation socio-culturelle à de nouvelles données techniques 348

2 Continuité et valeur culturelle de la musique à la radio

BRELET, G. La radio purifie et confirme la musique 367

MOLÈS, A. Facteurs physiques influençant l'écoute musicale et la cristallisation du groupe auditif 379

SOUDERES, V. Les possibilités d'évolution rapide des jeunes compositeurs grâce à la radio 391

LOCKSPEISER, E. The greed of music 394

LABROCA, M. Valeur éducative des cycles musicaux illustrés 396

3 Evolutions des règles sociales et culturelles en fonction de la musique à la radio

CHAILLEY, J. La radio et le développement de l'instinct harmonique chez les auditeurs 401

DEMUTH, N. The music was specially composed 413

TAL, J. Die musiksoziologische Einflussphäre des israelitischen Radios 419

van DIJK, H. La musique à la radio (aspects sociologiques à la suite de quelques recherches hollandaises) 425

BLUM, K. Plus und Minus 430

BELVIANES, M. Musique et radio 432

ROCHE, C. Essai sur l'attitude de l'auditeur de musique à la radio 437

TEMPREMENT, J. La musique à la radio 441

ALISKY, M. Mexico's musical microphones: instruments of cultural integration for the republic 446

4 Nature, développement et champ d'influence des programmes musicaux

DOVAZ, R. Nature, développement et champs d'influence des programmes musicaux 449

LANDOWSKI, W. L. Le rôle actuel du disque radiodiffusé dans l'enseignement de la musique 458

BRISTIGER, M. The problem of folkmusic in the Polish radio on the background of social and cultural changes in Poland 462

KNIGHT, F. E. Radio music used therapeutically and the need for research 468

STUCKENSCHMIDT, H. H. Limitation au sens auditif de l'événement musical 473

DOSSE Place de la musique à la radio dans la vie des candidats bacheliers 479

MORIN, E. 'Matérialité' et 'magie' de la musique à la radio 483

PONTZEN, T. Les émissions musicales en tant qu'objets d'une attention indirecte 487

HOEBAER, R. Extension de la radio en Belgique: le comportement des auditeurs vis-à-vis de certains programmes musicaux et les possibilités offertes par la radio en matière de culture musicale 494

5 Processus d'établissement et d'organisation des programmes musicaux

ISAACS, L. The musician in the radio 507

ANNEN, F. Pour une 'radio absolue' 515

LIEBERMANN, R. Radio und neue Musik 518

COSTÈRE, E. Audience de la musique d'aujourd'hui 521

WINCKEL, F. Ueber die Schwankungserscheinungen in der Musik 526

MARIE, J.-E. La radiodiffusion devant le problème de l'initiation à la musique contemporaine 534

WANGERMÉE, R. La vulgarisation de la musique par la radio 538

ADLER, F. Presuppositions of and design for a quantitative study in the sociology of radio music 550

DUMONT, C. La signification sociologique de la musique légère dans le cadre des émissions radiophoniques 559

54 ROU   Jumièges: Congrès scientifique du XIIIᵉ centenaire
Rouen 10–12 June 1954
(Rouen: Lecerf, 1955)

Histoire: rayonnement de Jumièges

MARILIER, J. L'office rythmé de saint Philibert à Tournus et Dijon 335

HESBERT, R.-J. L'hymnologie de saint Philibert: les hymnes de Tournus et Mâcon 343

La vie à Jumièges: vie liturgique

HESBERT, R.-J. Les manuscrits liturgiques de Jumièges 855

HESBERT, R.-J. Les manuscrits musicaux de Jumièges 901

CORBIN, S. Valeur et sens de la notation alphabétique, à Jumièges et en Normandie 913

DUFT, J. Le 'presbyter de Gimedia' apporte son Antiphonaire à Saint-Gall 925

CHAILLEY, J. Jumièges et les séquences aquitaines 937

HESBERT, R.-J. Les séquences de Jumièges 943

HESBERT, R.-J. Les tropes de Jumièges 959

HESBERT, R.-J. La composition musicale à Jumièges: les Offices de saint Philibert et de saint Aycadre 977

54 STAD   Orgelbewegung und Historismus: Tagungsberichte
Stade 12–15 July 1954; Malmö and Copenhagen 12–14 April 1955; Hanover 5–12 May
1955
Gesellschaft der Orgelfreunde
ed. W. Supper (Berlin: Merseburger, 1959)

Bericht über das 2. Orgeltreffen der GDO in Stade
SUPPER, W.   Die nord- und süddeutsche
Barockorgel, ein stilistischer Vergleich – und
eine Synthese?   15
KLOTZ, H.   Orgelbewegung und Historismus 25
BÖHRINGER, H.   Die Orgel als geistliche
Aufgabe   34
FOCK, G.   Die Hauptepochen des norddeutschen
Orgelbaues bis Schnitger   36
HOPPE, A.   Die Klassizität des norddeutschen
Orgelbaus   48

Bericht über das 3. Orgeltreffen der GDO in Malmö-Kopenhagen
SUPPER, W.   Über die Pflege von Orgeln mit
Denkmalwert   56

ANDERSEN, G. P.   Die Gestaltung des Orgel-
gehäuses   58
QUOIKA, R.   Warum bauen wir Orgeln mit
mechanischer Traktur   59

Bericht über die internationalen Orgeltage in Hannover
UTERMÖHLEN, R.   Orgel und Kirchenraum   75
RÖSSLER, E. K.   Klangfunktion, Orgelsatz und
Orgelbau heute   82
SUPPER, W.   Wo historisieren wir – und wo eilen
wir voraus?   89
VIDERÖ, F.   Dietrich Buxtehude   97
JEANS, S.   Orgeln und Orgelmusik in England
vom 16. bis zum 18. Jahrhundert   97

54 VIE   Zweiter internationaler Kongress für katholische Kirchenmusik: zu Ehren des Heiligen Papstes
Pius X: Bericht
Vienna 4–10 October 1954
(Vienna: Exekutivkomitee des II. Internationalen Kongresses für katholische Kirchen-
musik, 1955)

Musik der Ostkirchen
WELLESZ, E.   Ein Überblick über die Musik der
Ostkirchen: Stand, Aufgaben und Probleme 76
WERNER, E.   Die Ursprünge der Psalmodie 82
SWAN, A. J.   Something about the 'Znam-
enny'   87
ZAGIBA, F.   Wie wird die westliche Liturgie in
kirchenslawischer Sprache noch heute gepflegt?
(discussion 91)   89
PICHLER, L.   Zur Reform der russischen
Kirchenmusik   93

Gregorianik
LE GUENNANT, A.   Le chant grégorien dans
l'oeuvre pastorale de Pie X   98
CARDINE, E.   L'interprétation traditionnelle du
chant grégorien   105
SMITS van WAESBERGHE, J.   Neues über die
Schola Cantorum zu Rom   111
HUCKE, H.   Die Tradition des Gregorianischen
Gesanges in der römischen Schola Cantorum   120
HESBERT, R.   La restitution critique des mélodies
grégoriennes et les manuscrits de Klosterneuburg   124
d'ALMENDRA, J.   L'actuel mouvement grégorien
au Portugal   127
FIUMARA, U.   Antiphonale Lectionarium Mo-
nasterii Fontis Avellanae   129

GAUGUSCH, F.   Die Choralpflege auf dem
Lande   138
HUGLO, M.   Vestiges d'un ancien répertoire
musical de Haute-Italie   142
MATHÉ, A.   Beschouwingen over het ritme der
gregoriaanse muziek   146
ZAGIBA, F.   Probleme, Aufgaben und
Organisation der österreichischen Choral-
forschung   149

Vokalpolyphonie
ANGLÈS, H.   Die Bedeutung der Vokalpolyphonie für die römische Liturgie   154
CHAILLEY, J.   La musique religieuse contemporaine en France (discussion 170)   162

Instrumentale Kirchenmusik
SCHENK, E.   Instrumentale Kirchenmusik   174
DAMILANO, P.   Le laudi Filippine: storia ed
interpretazione (discussion 187)   184
MERTIN, J.   Über Aufführungspraxis histori-
scher Sakralmusik   188

Liturgie und Volksgesang
JUNGMANN, J. A.   Liturgie und Volksgesang 194
SCHMIT, J. P.   Liturgie und Volksgesang (discussion 206)   203
FEDERHOFER, H.   Die älteste schriftliche Überlieferung deutscher geistlicher Lieder in Steiermark   208

Orgel
ZACHARIASSEN, S.   Aktuelle Orgelbaufragen 214
KLOTZ, H.   Tradition und Historismus im
Orgelbau heute   225
EIBNER, F.   Die Verwendung elektro-akustischer
Instrumente beim Gottesdienst (discussion
239)   230
LITAIZE, G.   L'improvisation liturgique   241
MORETTI, C.   Definizione di organo   243
QUOIKA, R.   Die Passauer Orgelbauschule und
ihr Wirken in Österreich   246
QUOIKA, R.   Über den Orgelbaustil Abbate F. X.
Chrismanns   249
SUPPER, W.   Werktreue und heutiger
Orgelbau   251
WALTER, R.   Gregorianischer Choral und
gottesdienstliches Orgelspiel   254

Neue Kirchenmusik
LEMACHER, H.   Neue Kirchenmusik   260
KORNFELD, F.   Chinas katholische Kirchen-
musik im Aufbruch einer Zeit   265
LIESS, A.   Das Sakrale in der profanen Gegen-
wartsmusik (discussion 271)   269

CARDUCCI-AGUSTINI, E.   Necessità di una val-
utazione cristiana dell'arte musicale e della sua
storia   274
RADOLE, G.   Richiamo all'interiorità   279

Kirchenmusik als Beruf
HILBER, J. B.   Kirchenmusik als Beruf (discussion 287)   282
LÓPEZ GODOY, R. J.   La musica sagrada y el
canon 1264   288

Erziehung zur Kirchenmusik
LENNARDS, J.   Erziehung zur Kirchenmusik an
den Grundschulen   296
OVERATH, J.   Die Erziehung zur Kirchenmusik
an den höheren Schulen und Seminaren (discussion 309)   303
HECHT, T.   Der Primat der Stimme in der katholischen Kirchenmusik   312
ZAGIBA, F.   Das Studium der Kirchenmusik-
wissenschaft an den Universitäten und theolog-
ischen Hochschulen   316

Organisation der Kirchenmusik
GOTTRON, A.   Die Organisation der Kirchenmusik (discussion 328)   320

54 WÉG   **Les colloques de Wégimont [I]: Cercle international d'études ethno-musicologiques** [Ethno-
musicologie I]
Wégimont 19–26 September 1954
Cercle international d'études ethno-musicologiques
ed. P. Collaer (Brussels: Elsevier, 1956)

SCHAEFFNER, A.   Ethnologie musicale ou musicologie comparée?   18
BUKOFZER, M. F.   Observations on the study of
non-western music   33
COLLAER, P.   État actuel des connaissances relatives à la perception auditive, l'émission
vocale et la mémoire musicale: conclusions au
sujet de la mesure des fréquences vibratoires et
des rythmes   37
SCHNEIDER, M.   Les fondements intellectuels et
psychologiques du chant magique   56
BRAILOIU, C.   Le rythme enfantin   64
MARCEL-DUBOIS, C.   Extensions du domaine

d'observations directes en ethnographie mus-
icale française   97
WIORA, W.   Gesungene Erzählung als Strophen-
lied   120
ROUGET, G.   À propos de la forme dans les
musiques de tradition orale   132
LAJTHA, L.   À propos de l'"intonation fausse'
dans la musique populaire   145
GRENI, L.   Über Vokaltradition in norwegischer
Volksmusik   154
MAQUET, J.-N.   La musique chez les Pende
et les Tshokwe   169

55 ARR Visages et perspectives de l'art moderne: peinture – poésie – musique
Arras 20–22 June 1955
ed. J. Jacquot (Paris: Centre national de la recherche scientifique, 1956)

FRANCÈS, R. La musique moderne et l'auditeur 163

SOURIS, A. Les sources sensibles de la musique sérielle 175

PHILIPPOT, M. Electronique et technique compositionnelles 183

55 AVIG Actes et mémoires du 1ᵉʳ congrès international de langue et littérature du midi de la France
Avignon 7–10 September 1955
Congrès international de langue et littérature du midi de la France
(Avignon: Palais du Roure, 1957 = Publications de l'Institut méditerranéen du Palais du Roure, Avignon 3)

C Études sur l'ancienne langue d'oc: langues anciennes

HUSMANN, H. Les époques de la musique provençale au moyen-âge 197

55 BRUS Quatrième congrès international des bibliothèques musicales Bruxelles: actes du congrès
Brussels 11–18 September 1955
International Association of Music Libraries
ed. V. Fédorov, *Fontes artis musicae* iii (Kassel and Basle: Bärenreiter, 1956)

Preliminary reports

LE COSQUINO de BUSSY, J. R. Le rôle et la place de la lecture publique dans l'éducation musicale contemporaine 35

DUCKLES, V. H. The rôle of the public library in modern musical education 37

SCHAEFFNER, A. Les tâches scientifiques et pédagogiques des phonothèques musicales 39

MILLER, P. L. Educational and scientific aspects of the record library 41

BLUME, F. Problèmes musicologiques d'un Répertoire des sources musicales [in German with French résumé] 44

LESURE, F. Quelques conséquences bibliographiques et téchniques d'un Répertoire international des sources musicales 49

CLERCX-LEJEUNE, S. Le bibliothécaire musical: sa formation professionelle 51

de MOURA REIS PEQUENO, M. La formation professionelle du bibliothécaire musicale [in Spanish with French résumé] 57

DAVIES, J. H. The contribution of radio music libraries to national and international musical life 62

GRASBERGER, F. À propos des échanges de musique [in German with French résumé] 68

ROUGET, G. Le disque et la bande comme matière d'échanges 70

Written communications

ACERENZA, E. Formación profesional de un bibliotecario de música 74

BECHERINI, B. Catalogues généraux et catalogues spécialisés dans les bibliothèques musicales 76

MOLL ROQUETA, J. Les bibliothèques musicales publiques: les aspects nationaux du problème [in Spanish with French résumé] 81

MOLL ROQUETA, J. La formation professionelle d'un bibliothécaire musical [in Spanish with French résumé] 84

CHAMRATH, G. C. Die Rechte der Schallplatte und des Tonbandes (International record libraries commission) 86

BRITTEN, V., CLOUGH, F. F. and CUMING, G. Problems of an international gramophone record catalogue 95

LINDBERG, F. A survey of the musical resources of Scandinavia, with particular reference to their use in broadcast performances 109

STRARAM, E. Problèmes relatifs à l'éstablissement d'un inventaire international des oeuvres dont les matériels d'exécution n'existent qu'à de très rares exemplaires 112

MEYLAN, P. Étude comparative sur les bibliothèques musicales publiques dans différent pays (International public music libraries) 116

OTT, A. Wirkungsmöglichkeiten in öffentlichen Musikbibliotheken 122

SCHIØRRING, N. Public music libraries: international co-operation 132

Papers read at the conference

LE COSQUINO de BUSSY, J. R. Le rôle et la place

de la lecture publique dans l'éducation musicale contemporaine – quelques nouveaux aspects de la question 138

DUCKLES, V. H. The rôle of the public library in modern musical education: an American appraisal 140

LESURE, F. Le RISM: deux ans d'expérience 144

MILLER, C. K. Phonograph records in U. S. public libraries 146

REINHOLD, H. Aufbau und Verwendungsmöglichkeiten einer Discothek wertvoller Gesangsaufnahmen im Sendebetrieb 148

PAULI, F. W. Die deutschen Rundfunk-Musikbibliotheken: ihre Organisation, ihre internationalen Arbeitsmöglichkeiten 153

CLERCX-LEJEUNE, S. Le bibliothécaire musical 155

Bericht über die internationalen Orgeltage
Hanover 5–12 May 1955

see 54 STAD

55 IST **X. Milletlerarasi Bizans Tetkikleri Kongresi Tebliğleri / Actes du X. congrès international d'études byzantines**
Istanbul 15–21 September 1955
International Association for Byzantine Studies
(Istanbul: Istanbul Matbaasi', 1957)

3 Littérature – philologie – musique

MANGANARO, G. Cyprien le Mage et la chanson de Lioghenniti 284

SCHIRÒ, G. Les canons inédits de Joseph l'Hymnographe dans les plus anciens manuscrits de Grottaferrata 286

SCHLÖTTERER, R. Aufgaben und Probleme bei

der Erforschung der byzantinischen Musiktheorie 287

STRUNK, O. Two stichera on the death of the Emperor Nicephorus Phocas 294

WELLESZ, E. Akathistos Hymnos (poetry and music) 297

Bericht über das 3. Orgeltreffen der GDO
Malmö and Copenhagen 12–14 April 1955

see 54 STAD

55 ROY   Les fêtes de la Renaissance [I]: **Journées internationales d'études**
Royaumont 8–13 July 1955
Association internationale des historiens de la Renaissance et l'humanisme (I^e congrès)
ed. J. Jacquot (Paris: Centre national de la recherche scientifique, 1956, 2/1973 = Le choeur des muses, ed. J. Jacquot)

JACQUOT, J.   Joyeuse et triomphante entrée   9
LEBÈGUE, R.   Les représentations dramatiques à la Cour des Valois   85
SCHRADE, L.   Les fêtes du mariage de Francesco dei Medici et de Bianca Cappello   107
WALKER, D. P.   La musique des intermèdes Florentins de 1589 et l'humanisme   133
GHISI, F.   Un aspect inédit des intermèdes de 1589 à la cour médicéenne et le développement de courses masquées et des ballets équestres devant les premières décades du XVIIe siècle   145
LESURE, F.   Le recueil de ballets de Michel Henry (vers 1620)   205
TANI, G.   Le Comte d'Aglié et le ballet de cour en Italie   221
ROUSSET, J.   L'eau et les tritons dans les fêtes et ballets de cour (1580–1640)   235

STEVENS, D.   Pièces de théâtre et 'pageants' à l'époque des Tudor   259
CUTTS, J. P.   Le rôle de la musique dans les masques de Ben Jonson   285
STERNFELD, F. W.   Le symbolisme musical dans quelques pièces de Shakespeare présentées à la cour d'Angleterre   319
SHIRE, H. M. and ELLIOTT, K.   La fricassée en Écosse et ses rapports avec les fêtes de la Renaissance   335
BEERLI, C. A.   Quelques aspects des jeux, fêtes et danses à Berne pendant la première moitié du XVIe siècle   347
QUEROL-GAVALDA, M.   Le Carnaval à Barcelone au début du XVIIe siècle   371
WINTERNITZ, E.   Instruments de musique étranges chez Filippino Lippi, Piero di Cosimo et Lorenzo Costa   379

55 WÉG   Les colloques de Wégimont II – 1955: **L'ars nova: Recueil d'études sur la musique du XIVe siècle**
Wégimont 19–24 September 1955
(Paris: Société d'édition 'Les belles lettres', 1959 = Bibliothèque de la Faculté de philosophie et lettres de l'Université de Liège 149)

van den BORREN, C.   L'ars nova   17
von FISCHER, K.   L'influence française sur la notation des manuscrits du trecento [discussion only]   27
SCHRADE, L.   The chronology of the ars nova in France (discussion 59)   37
HOPPIN, R. H. and CLERCX, S.   Notes biographiques sur quelques musiciens français du XVIe siècle (discussion 88)   63
PIRROTTA, N.   Cronologia e denominazione dell'ars nova italiana (discussion 104)   93
CLERCX, S.   Johannes Ciconia et la chronologie des mss. italiens Mod. 568 et Lucca (Mn) (discussion 122)   110
von FISCHER, K.   Chronologie des manuscrits du trecento [discussion only]   131
APEL, W.   Remarks about the isorhythmic motet (discussion 144)   139

GHISLANZONI, A.   Les formes littéraires et musicales italiennes au commencement du XIVe siècle (discussion 162)   149
CLERCX, S.   Les accidents sous-entendus et la transcription en notation moderne: introduction (discussion 181)   167
REANEY, G.   Musica ficta in the works of Guillaume de Machaut (discussion 203)   196
GHISI, F.   La persistance du sentiment monodique et l'évolution de la polyphonie italienne due XIVe au XVe siècle (discussion 223)   217
von FISCHER, K.   À propos de la répartition du texte et le nombre de voix dans les oeuvres italiennes du trecento [discussion only]   232
BECHERINI, B.   Poesia e musica in Italia ai primi del XV secolo (discussion 250)   239
PERROY, E.   Le point de vue de l'historien   261

56 CAG   **Atti del VI congresso nazionale delle tradizioni popolari**
Cagliari, Nuoro and Sassari 25 April – 1 May 1956
Centro per la documentazione e la difesa del folklore italiano, Gubbio; Centro
etnografico Sardo, Cagliari; Società di etnografia italiana, Rome
Lares xxii (Florence: Leo S. Olschki, 1956)

GABRIEL, G. La fonografia del folklore
musicale   120
DOMPÉ, G. 'Is musicas' a Tonara   123

CARPITELLA, D. Prospettive e problemi nuovi
degli studi di musica popolare in Italia   175

56 CAM/M   **Proceedings of the Second ICA Congress: Sound and Man**
Cambridge, Massachusetts 17–23 June 1956
International Commission on Acoustics, International Union of Pure and
Applied Physics
ed. R. B. Lindsay (New York: American Institute of Physics, 1957)

b Architectural and musical acoustics
BIGGS, E. P. A musician and his acoustical
environment   50
KUHL, W. Optimal acoustical design of rooms
for performing, listening, and recording   53
MEYER, E. Physical measurements in rooms and
their meaning in terms of hearing conditions   59
SMALL, A. M. and MARTIN, D. W. Musical
acoustics: aims, problems, progress, and fore-
cast   68

56 FLOR   **Actes du VIIIᵉ congrès international d'histoire des sciences**
Florence and Milan 3–9 September 1956
Union internationale d'histoire et de philosophie des sciences
(Florence: Gruppo italiano di storia delle scienze/Paris: Herman, 1958 = Collection
de travaux de l'Académie internationale d'histoire des sciences 9)

Vol. i (1958)
1a Storia della matematica
BIREMBAUT, A. Les frères Engramelle   149

56 HAM   **Bericht über den internationalen musikwissenschaftlichen Kongress Hamburg 1956**
Hamburg 17–22 September 1956
Gesellschaft für Musikforschung
ed. W. Gerstenberg, H. Husmann and H. Heckmann (Kassel and Basle: Bärenreiter,
1957)

LARSEN, J. P. Ein Händel-Requiem   15
HUSMANN, H. Antike und Orient in ihrer
Bedeutung für die europäische Musik   24
MOBERG, C.-A. Das Musikleben in Schwe-
den   33

ABERT, A. A. Wort und Ton   43
BACHMANN, W. Bilddarstellungen der Musik im
Rahmen der artes liberales   46
BERNHARDT, K.-F. Zur musikschöpferischen
Emanzipation der Frau   55

BIMBERG, S. Die variable Reaganz des musikalischen Hörens 58

BLANKENBURG, W. Die Nachwirkung der artes liberales in den reformatorischen Gebieten und deren Auflösungsprozess 60

BOETTICHER, W. Die Magnificat-Komposition Orlando di Lassos 62

DAHLHAUS, C. Zwei Definitionen der Musik als quadrivialer Disziplin 64

DITTMER, K. Ethnologie und Musikethnologie 66

DRÄGER, H.-H. Die 'Bedeutung' der Sprachmelodie 73

DÜRR, A. Gedanken zu J. S. Bachs Umarbeitungen eigener Werke 75

EGGEBRECHT, H. H. Zum Wort-Ton-Verhältnis in der 'Musica poetica' von J. A. Herbst 77

ELLER, R. Zur Frage Bach–Vivaldi 80

ENGEL, H. Zur italienischen Prosodie 85

ENGELBRECHT, C. Eine Sonata con voce von Giovanni Gabrieli 88

ERDMANN, H. Wesen und Form des Fichtelbarger 90

FACK, H. Zur Anwendung der Informationstheorie auf Probleme des Hörens 91

FEDER, G. Das barocke Wort-Ton-Verhältnis und seine Umgestaltung in den klassizistischen Bach-Bearbeitungen 95

FEDERHOFER, H. Zur Einheit von Wort und Ton im Lied von Johannes Brahms 97

FELDMANN, F. Mattheson und die Rhetorik 99

HAHN, K. Johannes Kuhnaus 'Fundamenta Compositionis' 103

HAMEL, F. Die Industrieschallplatte als Mittlerin des musikgeschichtlichen Erbes 105

HARICH-SCHNEIDER, E. Über die Gilden blinder Musiker in Japan 107

HEINITZ, W. Hamburg und die Vergleichende Musikwissenschaft 109

HERZOG, E. Sinnbildung und deren Träger in Sprache und Musik 111

HOFFMANN-ERBRECHT, L. Die Rostocker Praetorius-Handschrift (1566) 112

HUCKE, H. Die beiden Fassungen der Oper 'Didone abbandonata' von Domenico Sarri 113

HÜSCHEN, H. Die Musik im Kreise der artes liberales 117

JEANS, S. Geschichte und Entwicklung des Voluntary for Double Organ in der englischen Orgelmusik des 17. Jahrhunderts 123

KAHMANN, B. Über Inhalt und Herkunft der Handschrift Cambridge Pepys 1760 126

KLINKENBERG, H. M. Der Zerfall des Quadriviums in der Zeit von Boethius bis zu Gerbert von Aurillac 129

KOCH, F. Moderne Aufnahmetechnik 133

KRÜGER, W. Wort und Ton in den Notre-Dame-Organa 135

LIEBE, A. Wortforschung als Methode zur Wesensbestimmung des Tones 140

LINHARDT, W. Über die Funktionen der verschiedenen Traktursysteme der Orgel 142

LISSA, Z. Semantische Elemente der Musik 145

LOTTERMOSER, W. Akustik und Musik 148

MOHR, W. Wort und Ton 157

MOSER, H. J. Der melodische Mehrterzenverband 162

MÜLLER, L. Das optische Bild akustisch guter Raüme 168

NIEMÖLLER, K. W. Ars musica – ars poetica – musica poetica 170

POLOCZEK, F. Das Räuber-Volkslied in dem Gebiet des Tatra-Gebirges 172

RAWP-RAUPP, J. 'Unsere Krieger ziehen aus dem Kampfe heim' – ein altsorbisches episches Lied 175

REANEY, G. 'Quid est musica' in the Quatuor principalia musicae 177

REINECKE, H. Akustik und Musik 179

REINHARD, K. Tanzlieder der Turkmenen in der Südtürkei 189

REINOLD, H. Grundverschiedenheiten musikwissenschaftlichen und soziologischen Denkens und Möglichkeiten zu ihrer Überwindung 193

RICHTER, L. Platons Stellung zur praktischen und spekulativen Musiktheorie seiner Zeit 196

SCHMIEDEL, P. Ein unsymmetrisches Tonsystem 202

SCHNEIDER, M. Entstehung der Tonsysteme 203

SCHRAMMEK, W. Das Buxheimer Orgelbuch als deutsches Liederbuch 211

SENN, W. Der Wandel des Geigenklanges seit dem 18. Jahrhundert 213

SIEGMUND-SCHULTZE, W. Wort und Ton bei Robert Schumann 216

SMITS VAN WAESBERGHE, J. Matthaei Herbeni Trajectensis 'De Natura Cantus ac Miraculis vocis' (1496) 219

SØRENSEN, S. Eine neu gefundene Buxtehude-Kantate 221

SOWA, G. Eine neu aufgefundene Liederhandschrift mit Noten und Text aus dem Jahre 1544 223

STEPHAN, R. Über sangbare Dichtung in althochdeutscher Zeit 225

STOCKMANN, E. Kaukasische und albanische Mehrstimmigkeit 229

VÄISÄNEN, A. O. A. Yrjö Kilpinens Kanteletar-Lieder 231

VOGEL, M. Über die drei Tongeschlechter des Archytas 233

WOLFF, H. C. Rekonstruktion der alten Hamburger Opernbühne 235

WORBS, H. C. Eine unbekannte Liederhandschrift aus dem Anfang des 18. Jahrhunderts 239

WÜNSCH, W. Die musikalisch-sprachliche Gestalt des Zehnsilblers im serbokroatischen Volkspos 241

56 PAR   Les influences étrangères dans l'oeuvre de W. A. Mozart
Paris 10–13 October 1956
Centre national de la recherche scientifique: sciences humaines
ed. A. Verchaly (Paris: Centre national de la recherche scientifique, 1958)

WALIN, S. Sur les conditions générales de l'internationalisme de Mozart   9
SCHENK, E. Mozart incarnation de l'âme autrichienne   17
LANDON, H. C. R. La crise romantique dans la musique autrichienne vers 1770: quelques précurseurs inconnus de la Symphonie en sol mineur (KV 183) de Mozart   27
WIRTH, H. Mozart et Haydn   49
SCHMID, E.-F. L'héritage souabe de Mozart 59
FELLERER, K. G. Mozart et l'école de Mannheim   85
de NYS, C. Mozart et les fils de Jean-Sébastien Bach   91

VALABREGA, C. Mozart et le goût italien 117
TAGLIAVINI, L.-F. L'opéra italien du jeune Mozart   125
BARTHA, D. Mozart et le folklore musical de l'Europe centrale   157
DOBIÁŠ, V. Wolfgang-Amédée Mozart et la musique tchèque   183
SYCHRA, A. W.-A. Mozart et la musique populaire tchèque   189
FORTASSIER, P. Le récitatif dans l'écriture instrumentale de Mozart   199
HESS, E. Remarques sur l'authenticité de l'Ouverture KV 311a = Anh. 8   227
Discussion   239

56 PHIL   Men and Cultures: Selected Papers of the Fifth International Congress of Anthropological and Ethnological Sciences
Philadelphia 1–9 September 1956
International Union of Anthropological and Ethnological Sciences
ed. A. F. C. Wallace (Philadelphia: University of Pennsylvania Press, 1960)

2 Theory and method
KURATH, G. P. and CHILKOVSKY, N. Jazz choreology   152

3 Culture change and culture history
RHODES, W. The Christian hymnology of the

North American Indians   324

4 Ethnography
McALLESTER, D. P. The role of music in western Apache culture   468

56 PRA   Internationale Konferenz über das Leben und Werk W. A. Mozarts: Bericht
Prague 27–31 May 1956
Svaz československých skladatelů [Union of Czechoslovak Composers]
ed. P. Eckstein (Prague: Svaz československých skladatelů, n.d.)

SCHMID, E. F. Mozarts Lebenswerk, seine Bergung und Erschliessung   15
du JOURDIN, G. M. Mozart in Paris   26
RACEK, J. Beitrag zur Frage des 'mozartschen' Stils in der tschechischen vorklassischen Musik   34
VALABREGA, C. Mozart und der Geist der italienischen Musik   44
ŠTĚDROŇ, B. Mozart und Mähren   51
HÁBA, A. Wolfgang Amadeus Mozart und die weitere Entwicklung der Musik   56
VETTER, W. Mozart und Bach   61
LOULOVÁ, O. Das tschechische Volkslied im Werke von Jan Křtitel Vaňhal   70
STÁDNÍK, M. W. A. Mozart und neue Betrachtungen über A. Rejcha   79

PILKOVÁ, Z. Das Melodram Jiří Bendas im Zusammenhang mit der Mozartproblematik   85
LOBACZEWSKA, S. Mozarts Sonate F-Dur (K. V. 533) als Problem des klassischen Stils   95
KNEPLER, G. Mozart – eine Gestalt der bürgerlichen Aufklärung   98
MARTYNOV, I. Mozart und die russische Kunst   106
VANCEA, Z. Stand und Ergebnisse der rumänischen musikwissenschaftlichen Forschung über die Beziehungen der Werke Mozarts zu Rumänien   112
YÖNETKEN, H. B. Mozart und die türkische Musik   118
KÖHLER, S. Instrumentation als Ausdrucks-

kunst im Opernschaffen Wolfgang Amadeus
Mozarts 121
MARKL, J. Mozart und das tschechische Volks-
lied 127
POŠTOLKA, M. Leopold Koželuh, ein Zeitge-
nosse Mozarts 135
SIEGMUND-SCHULTZE, W. Zur Frage der
Beziehungen zwischen Mozarts Vokal- und
Instrumentalmusik 146
GOLÉA, A. Mozart und die französische Re-
volution 156
SÝKORA, V. J. František Xaver Dušek 159
HUMMEL, W. Die Mozart-Gedenkstätten Salz-
burgs 167
OČADLÍK, M. Voraussetzungen wissenschaft-
licher Mozartforschung in Böhmen 175
SZABOLCSI, B. Die 'Exotismen' Mozarts 181
STEMPEL, M. Mozart in Schweden 189
VOKOS, G. Die Ästhetik der Mozartschen Kom-
positionen 193
VALENTIN, E. Das Kind Mozart 196
EL HEFNY, M. Ägyptens Verehrung für
Mozart 200
SMETANA, R. Mozart und das tschechische
Volk 202

MEYER, E. H. Mozarts polyphone Tradition 210
RUBIN, M. Mozart und die Probleme der mo-
dernen Musik 225
WITOLD, J. Mozarts Humanismus 230
HOŘEJŠ, A. Die tschechoslowakische Musik-
wissenschaft und Mozart 236
HUSMANN, H. Zur Entwicklung der mozart-
schen Sonatenform 241
HOLEČKOVÁ-DOLANSKÁ, J. Wie man Mozart
singen soll 246
HRABUSSAY, Z. Mozartdokumente im Archiv
der Stadt Bratislava 253
HRUŠOVSKÝ, I. Das klassische Musikschaffen
der Mozartzeit in der Slowakei 256
KRATOCHVÍL, J. Betrachtungen über die Ur-
fassung des Konzerts für Klarinette und des
Quintetts für Klarinette und Streicher von
W. A. Mozart 262
NĚMEČEK, J. Das Problem des 'Mozartismus'
und die tschechischen Dorflehřer 272
TARANTOVÁ, M. Das Echo von Mozarts Werk
in der Epoche der Wiedergeburt des tschechischen Volkes 282

56 STOM Conferéncia internacional dos Africanistas ocidentais: 6.ª sessào
São Tomé 21–8 August 1956
Scientific Council for Africa South of the Sahara
(Comissão de cooperação técnica na África ao sul do Sara, [1957])

Vol. v Ciências hûmanas: comunicações [1957]
BARROS, M. Folclore musical da Ilha de São

Tomé (yelhas danças, suas músicas y cantares)
(with Spanish, English and French résumés) 101

56 VEN Atti del III congresso internazionale di estetica
Venice 3–5 September 1956
International Congress on Aesthetics
ed. L. Pareyson (Turin: Edizioni della *Rivista di estetica*, Istituto di estetica
dell'Università di Torino, 1957)

Problemi delle varie arti
VALENSI, H. De l'art de la musique et de l'art
abstrait 638
OBERTI, E. Tecnica e linguaggio musicale 642
SIOHAN, R. Un micro-organisme sonore 647
ROGNONI, L. Tecnica e linguaggio nella musica
postweberniana 651
PARAIN VIAL, J. L'expérience musicale et
l'harmonisation de textes poétiques 657

DELLA CORTE, A. Preliminari di critica musicale 660
LIFAR, S. L'évolution technique et esthétique de
la danse académique 664

Storia dell'estetica
FABRO, C. Estetica mozartiana nell'opera di
Kierkegaard 706

56 VIE   **Bericht über den internationalen musikwissenschaftlichen Kongress Wien Mozartjahr 1956**
Vienna 3–9 June 1956
Gesellschaft zur Herausgabe von Denkmälern der Tonkunst in Österreich; Österreichische Akademie der Wissenschaften
ed. E. Schenk (Graz and Cologne: Hermann Böhlaus Nachf., 1958)

ALLORTO, R.   Mozart e Clementi   1

ALTAR, C. M.   Wolfgang Amadeus Mozart im Lichte osmanisch-österreichischer Beziehungen   5

ANGLÈS, H.   Die alte spanische Mensuralnotation: praktische Winke, um den Rhythmus der monodischen Lyrik des Mittelalters besser kennenzulernen   7

BARBLAN, G.   Le orchestre in Lombardia all'epoca di Mozart   18

BARTHA, D.   Die ungarische Musikforschung des letzten Jahrzehnts: ein Literaturbericht   22

BECHERINI, B.   Le sonate per pianoforte di W. A. Mozart: problemi di esecuzione contemporanea   28

BECK, H.   Probleme der venezianischen Messkomposition im 16. Jahrhundert   35

BERNET KEMPERS, K. P.   Mahler und Willem Mengelberg   41

BESSELER, H.   Mozart und die deutsche Klassik   47

BIMBERG, S.   Die Polarität bei der Rezeption der Tonalitäten   55

BOETTICHER, W.   Die französische Chansonkomposition Orlando di Lassos   60

BOLLERT, W.   Bemerkungen zu Mozarts Klavierkonzert F-Dur (K.V.459)   66

BREAZUL, G.   Zu Mozarts Zweihundertjahrfeier   69

BRIQUET, M.   Contribution à la vie parisienne de Mozart (1764)   75

CHAILLEY, J.   A propos de quatre mesures de l'"Entführung': la renaissance de la modalité dans la musique française avant 1890   78

CHOMIŃSKI, J.   Der Entwicklungscharakter der Harmonik im Mittelalter und in der Renaissance   92

COGNI, G.   Grundzüge einer neuen Musikpsychologie   99

CVETKO, D.   J. B. Novak – ein slowenischer Anhänger Mozarts   103

von DADELSEN, G.   Zu den Vorreden des Michael Praetorius   107

DAYAN, L.   Il pluricromatismo nella musica armena   112

DEININGER, H. F.   Zur Genealogie Wolfgang Amadeus Mozarts   116

DELLA CORTE, A.   Il culto di Mozart e la cultura nell'ottocento italiano   128

DI CLEMENTE, R.   Può la spiritualità di Mozart esercitare una funzione nel caos degli indirizzi musicali di oggi?   132

DJURIĆ-KLAJN, S.   Un contemporain de Mozart, Ivan-Mane Jarnović   134

DONATH, G.   Gefühlscharaktere in den Themenkontrasten der klassischen Sonatenform   139

DREIMÜLLER, K.   Gedanken und Anregungen zur musikalischen Bibliographie und Quellenkunde   143

EBENSTEIN, Y. J.   Musik und Musiker in Israel, dem Grenzland zwischen Asien und Afrika   148

ELLER, R.   Geschichtliche Stellung und Wandlung der Vivaldischen Konzertform   150

ERDMANN, H.   Mozart in norddeutscher Resonanz   156

ESPIAU de la MAESTRE, A.   Mozarts weltanschauliche Bedeutung in der modernen französischen Literatur   170

FALVY, Z.   Die neuesten ungarischen Ergebnisse auf dem Gebiete der mittelalterlichen musikalischen Paläographie   176

FEDERHOFER, H.   Die Funktionstheorie Hugo Riemanns und die Schichtenlehre Heinrich Schenkers   183

FEICHT, H.   Die Kenntnis Mozarts in Polen   191

FELIX, W.   Die Entwicklung des dramatischen Konfliktes in den Opern Mozarts als Ausdruck der gesellschaftlichen Auseinandersetzungen seiner Zeit   195

FELLERER, K. G.   Kirche und Musik im frühen Mittelalter   199

FERAND, E. T.   Über verzierte 'Parodiekantaten' im frühen 18. Jahrhundert   203

GEORGIADES, T.   Zur Lasso-Gesamtausgabe   216

GHISI, F.   Alcune canzoni storiche nelle valli Valdesi del Piemonte   220

GHISLANZONI, A.   Influenze favorevoli e sfavorevoli dei moderni studi storici e musicologici sugli indirizzi estetici e tecnici della creazione musicale di oggi   227

GOTTRON, A.   Mozart und die musikgeschichtliche Situation in Mainz zu seiner Zeit   230

GRADENWITZ, P.   Reihenkomposition im Orient   238

GRAF, W.   Zum Inhalt in der Musik der Naturvölker   242

GRASBERGER, F.   Zur Symbolik der 'Zauberflöte'   249

GREGOR, J.   Typen der Regie der Oper im 20. Jahrhundert   253

HEINITZ, W.   Pulsationsprobleme in Mozartscher Musik   261

HERMELINK, S.   Zur Chiavettenfrage   264

HETSCHKO, A.   Die Bedeutung des kulturellen Erbes in Musikerziehung und Musikgestaltung der Deutschen Demokratischen Republik   272

HUSMANN, H. Die Alleluia und Sequenzen der Mater-Gruppe 276

JONAS, O. Mozart-Handschriften in Amerika 285

KAHL, W. Zur Frage nach Schuberts früher Vollendung 289

KALOMIRIS, M. Die Musik Mozarts in Griechenland 294

KAST, P. Zu Biographie und Werk Jean Moutons 300

KELLER, H. Die Bedeutung der Artikulationszeichen in den Handschriften und frühen Drucken Mozarts 304

KING, A. H. The Mozart Bi-Centenary Exhibition in the British Museum 305

KOSCH, F. Die Enzyklika 'Musicae sacrae disciplina' Pius' XII. und die Vota des Wiener Kirchenmusikkongresses 309

KROHN, I. Formale und ideelle Einheitlichkeit der Symphonien Anton Bruckners 313

LARUE, J. Die Datierung von Wasserzeichen im 18. Jahrhundert 318

LEBEAU, E. Une succursale officieuse de Johann Anton André à Paris, de 1802 à 1806 324

LEHMANN, D. Der russische Komponist und Musikforscher Alexander Nikolajewitsch Serow und sein Mozart-Bild 328

LESURE, F. L'oeuvre de Mozart en France de 1793 à 1810 344

LEVI, V. Das Schicksal der Mozart-Opern in Italien 348

LIM, W. S. Present status of music in Korea 350

LINHARDT, W. Über die Funktionen verschiedener Orgeltraktur-Systeme 352

LISSA, Z. Über den nationalen Stil von F. Chopin 355

LIVANOVA, T. N. Motsart i russkaya muzikal'naya kultura [Mozart and Russian musical culture] 365

LOBACZEWSKA, S. Die Analyse des musikalischen Kunstwerkes als Problem der Musikwissenschaft 373

LOTTERMOSER, W. Der akustische Entwurf und Abgleich moderner Orgeln 378

LOTTERMOSER, W. Die akustische Prüfung von Violinen 384

LUIN, E. J. Mozarts Opern in Skandinavien 387

MEIER, B. Glareans 'Isagoge in musicen' (1516) 397

MEYER, E. H. Das Konfliktelement in Mozarts Instrumentalmusik, 402

MIES, P. Der zyklische Charakter der Klaviertänze bei Franz Schubert 408

MOLDENHAUER, H. From my autograph collection: C. Ph. E. Bach – Dittersdorf – Mozart 412

MORIN, G. Wolfgang Amadeus Mozart und Schweden 416

MOSER, H. J. Österreich auf der Musiklandkarte Europas 421

MUELLER von Asow, E. H. Musikerepistolographie 430

MÜLLER-BLATTAU, J. Beethovens Mozart-Variationen 434

MUROI, M. Der gegenwärtige Stand der Musik in Japan 440

NESTLER, G. Über den Begriff der 'Mannigfaltigkeit im Einfachen' (J. J. Winckelmann) in der Musik der Wiener Klassik 443

NEWMAN, S. Mozart's G minor Quintet (K. 516) and its relationship to the G minor Symphony (K. 550): new evidence derived from a study of the autograph sources 447

NOWAK, L. 'Urfassung' und 'Endfassung' bei Anton Bruckner 448

OSTHOFF, H. Die Psalm-Motetten von Josquin Desprez 452

PFAFF, M. Die Laudes-Akklamationen des Mittelalters 457

PFANNHAUSER, K. Die Mozart-Gesamtausgabe in Österreich 462

PFROGNER, H. Zur Theorieauffassung der Enharmonik im Zeitalter Mozarts 471

QUARANTA, F. Mozart fra gli operai 477

QUELLMALZ, A. Musikalisches Altgut in der Volksüberlieferung Südtirols 481

QUOIKA, R. Die Generalbassimprovisation nach Josef Seger 490

RACEK, J. Zur Frage des 'Mozart-Stils' in der tschechischen vorklassischen Musik 493

RADOLE, G. Giacomo Gorzanis, 'leutonista et cittadino della magnifica città di Trieste' 525

RATNER, L. G. Eighteenth century theories of musical period structure 531

RAUGEL, F. Paris, fidèle au souvenir de Mozart 535

SAKVA, K. Chaykovskiy o Motsarte [Tchaikovsky on Mozart] 537

SALMEN, W. Die internationale Wirkungsweite fahrender Musiker im Dienste der Herzöge von Österreich 544

SCHMIDT-GÖRG, J. Die besonderen Voraussetzungen zu einer kritischen Gesamtausgabe der Werke Ludwig van Beethovens 548

SCHMIEDER, W. Grenzen und Ziele der Musikdokumentation 551

SCHOENBAUM, C. Die Kammermusikwerke des Jan Dismas Zelenka 552

SCHREIBER, O. Max Regers musikalischer Nachlass 563

SCHUH, W. Über einige frühe Textbucher zur 'Zauberflöte' 571

SERAUKY, W. W. A. Mozart und die Musikästhetik des ausklingenden 18. und frühen 19. Jahrhunderts, 579

SIEGMUND-SCHULTZE, W. Zur Frage des Mozartschen Stils 586

SIMBRIGER, H. Die heutige Situation der Zwölftonmusik 593

SMITS van WAESBERGHE, J. Die rheno-mosamosellanische Neumenschrift 599

ŠTĔDROŇ, B. Mozart und Mähren 603

STEPHENSON, K.   Zur Soziologie des Studenten-
liedes   608
STOCKMANN, E.   Albanische Volksmusikinstru-
mente   612
SYCHRA, A.   Die Bedeutung des Skizzen-
studiums für die wissenschaftliche Analyse mus-
ikalischer Werke   616
SZABOLCSI, B.   Mozart und die Volksbühne 623
TACK, F.   Die musikgeschichtlichen Vorausset-
zungen der christlichen Kultmusik und ihre
Bedeutung für den gregorianischen Vortrags-
stil   633
TAPPOLET, W.   Le séjour de Wolfgang-Amadeé
Mozart à Genève en 1766   637
TENSCHERT, R.   Der Tonartenkreis in Mozarts
Werken   640
TERENZIO, V.   Il problema del preromanticismo
e l'arte mozartiana   643
VANCEA, Z.   Die sozialen Grundlagen der rumänischen Kunstmusik   647
van der MUEREN, F.   L'histoire de la musique et
la comparaison avec les autres arts   653
VETTER, W.   Mozart im Weltbild Richard Wagners   657
VOLBACH, W. R.   Die Synchronisierung von Ak-
tion und Musik in Mozarts Opern   661
WALLON, S.   Romances et vaudevilles français
dans les variations pour piano et pour piano et
violon de Mozart   666

WEISE, D.   Zur Gesamtausgabe der Briefe
Beethovens durch das Beethoven-Archiv
Bonn   673
WELLEK, A.   Die ganzheitspsychologischen As-
pekte der Musikästhetik   678
WESSELY-KROPIK, H.   Romanus Weichlein: ein
vergessener österreichischer Instrumental-
komponist des 17. Jahrhunderts   689
WESSELY, O.   Beiträge zur Lebensgeschichte von
Johann Zanger   708
WINCKEL, F.   Die Wirkung der Musik unter
dem Gesichtspunkt psychophysiologischer
Erscheinungen   727
WINTERNITZ, E.   Mozarts Raumgefühl   736
WÖRNER, K. H.   Mozarts Fugenfragmente 743
WOLFF, H. C.   Palestrina und Schönberg – zwei
Extreme der europäischen Musik   749
WORBS, H. C.   Komponist, Publikum und Auf-
traggeber: eine Untersuchung an Mozarts
Klavierkonzerten   754
WÜNSCH, W.   Volksmusikpflege und Wissen-
schaft   758
ŽIVKOVIĆ, M.   Tonale Grundlage in Volksme-
lodien einiger Gebiete Jugoslawiens   760
von ZSCHINSKY-TROXLER, E. M.   Mozarts
Violinkonzerte in spieltechnischem Vergleich
mit denen zeitgenössischer italienischer Violin-
komponisten   765

56 WÉG   **Les colloques de Wégimont III – 1956: Ethnomusicologie II**
Wégimont 15–21 September 1956
Cercle international d'études ethno-musicologiques
ed. P. Collaer (Paris: Société d'édition 'Les belles lettres', 1960 = Bibliothèque de la
Faculté de philosophie et lettres de l'Université de Liège 157)

SCHNEIDER, M.   Sociologie et mythologie
musicales   13
SALMEN, W.   Zur sozialen Schichtung des
Berufsmusikertums im mittelalterlichen Eura-
sien und in Afrika   23
SCHAEFFNER, A.   Situation des musiciens dans
trois sociétés Africaines   33
SCHIØRRING, N.   Musical folklore and ethnomusicology in Denmark   51
MARCEL-DUBOIS, C.   Le toulouhou des Pyrénées
centrales: son usage rituel, ses variétés   55
COLLAER, P.   Le tambour à friction (II), et
idiophones frottés   91

GRIMAUD, Y.   Note sur la musique vocale des
Bochiman !Kung et des pygmées Babinga 105
COLLAER, P.   Chants et airs des peuples de
l'extrême-Nord   127
JANKOVIĆ, L. S. and JANKOVIĆ, D. S.   Sur les
traces du plus ancien héritage culturel de la
danse et de la musique traditionnelles
Yougoslaves   149
GÜNTHER, R.   Eine Studie zur Musik in Ruanda
(I)   163
KAUFMANN, H. E. and SCHNEIDER, M.   Lieder
aus den Naga-Bergen (Assam)   187

57 BRUS   Fêtes et cérémonies au temps de Charles Quint: Fêtes de la Renaissance II
Brussels, Antwerp, Ghent, Liège 2–7 September 1957
Association internationale des historiens de la Renaissance (IIe congrès)
ed. J. Jacquot (Paris: Centre national de la recherche scientifique, 1960, 2/1976 = Le choeur des muses, ed. J. Jacquot)

KAST, P.   Remarques sur la musique et les musiciens de la chapelle de François Ier au Camp du Drap d'Or   135
BAILLIE, H.   Les musiciens de la chapelle royale d'Henri VIII au Camp du Drap d'Or   147

BRIDGMAN, N.   La participation musicale à l'entrée de Charles Quint à Cambrai, le 20 janvier 1540   235
HEARTZ, D.   Un divertissement de palais pour Charles Quint à Binche   329

57 CAM/M   Instrumental Music: a Conference at Isham Memorial Library
Cambridge, Massachusetts 4 May 1957
Department of Music, Harvard University
ed. D. G. Hughes (Cambridge, Mass.: Harvard University Press, 1959 = Isham Library Papers 1)

KINKELDEY, O.   Dance tunes of the fifteenth century (panel FERAND, E., HERTZMANN, E., REESE, G.)   3
LANDON, H. C. R.   Problems of authenticity in eighteenth-century music (panel DOWNES, E. O., GEIRINGER, K., LARUE, J., STRUNK, O.)   31

WERNER, E.   Instrumental music outside the pale of Classicism and Romanticism (panel BRODER, N., GROUT, D. J., SMITH, C. S.)   57
PISTON, W.   Problems of intonation in the performance of contemporary music (panel KENTON, E., LUENING, O., MENDEL, A.)   70

57 CHIE   VII Congresso nazionale delle tradizioni popolari
Chieti 4–8 September 1957
Società di etnografia italiana, Rome
ed. B. M. Galanti, *Lares*, xxv (Florence: Leo S. Olschki, 1959)

CARPITELLA, D.   Le registrazioni di cantori popolari in Abruzzo   160
GUILIANTE, G.   Saltarella: ritmo vecchio e nuovo   164
GHISI, F.   Le fonti musicali in Piemonte di alcuni canti narrativi popolari   230
MARICA, P. and SILESU, F.   La settimana santa a Sanluri   237
TRINCHIERI, R.   Il canto a braccio tra pastori-poeti nel Monterealese   267

ALBERTINI, A. M.   Studio su nuove versioni della canzone della 'finta monacella'   442
MAYER, M. V.   Il canto lirico monostrofico in Abruzzo   449
PICCOLOTTI, D.   Il canto popolare in rapporto agli usi e costumi del popolo Abruzzese   473
CIRESE, A. M.   Natura e valori del canto popolare secondo Pietro Ercole Visconti (1830)   523

57 MUN   **Akten des vierundzwanzigsten internationalen Orientalisten-Kongresses München**
Munich 28 August – 4 September 1957
International Union of Orientalists
ed. H. Franke (Wiesbaden: Deutsche morgenländlische Gesellschaft, 1959/R Nendeln: Kraus, 1968)

10 Indologie
GAUR, G. D.   Folksongs of Kuru Pradesh   573

57 NEU/S   **Le luth et sa musique**
Neuilly-sur-Seine 10–14 September 1957
Centre national de la recherche scientifique: sciences humaines
ed. J. Jacquot (Paris: Centre national de la recherche scientifique, 1958, rev. 2/1976 = Le choeur des muses ed. J. Jacquot)

JACQUOT, J.   Objectifs et plan de travail   13

DISERTORI, B.   Remarques sur l'évolution du luth en Italie au XVe siècle et au XVIe   19

BINKLEY, T. E.   Le luth et sa technique   25

DISERTORI, B.   Contradiction tonale dans la transcription d'un 'Strambotto' célèbre   37

THIBAULT, G.   Un manuscrit italien pour luth des premières années du XVIe siècle   43

HEARTZ, D.   Les premières 'Instructions' pour le luth (jusque vers 1550)   77

SCHEIT, K.   Ce que nous enseignent les traités de luth des environs de 1600   93

POULTON, D.   La technique du jeu du luth en France et en Angleterre   107

DART, T.   La méthode de luth de Miss Mary Burwell   121

MURPHY, R. M.   Fantaisie et Recercace dans les premières tablatures de luth du XVIe siècle   127

BOETTICHER, W.   Les oeuvres de Roland de Lassus mises en tablature de luth   143

VERCHALY, A.   La tablature dans les recueils français pour chant et luth (1603–1643)   155

WARD, J.   Le problème des hauteurs dans la musique pour luth et vihuela au XVIe siècle   171

NOSKE, F.   Remarques sur les luthistes des Pays-Bas (1580–1620)   179

WILKOWSKA-CHOMIŃSKA, K.   A la recherche de la musique pour luth (expériences polonaises   193

LESURE, F.   Recherches sur les luthistes parisiens à l'époque de Louis XIII   209

DART, T.   La pandore   225

DISERTORI, B.   Le liuto soprano   231

PRYNNE, M. W.   Comment noter et conserver les mesures des luths anciens   239

DORFMÜLLER, K.   La tablature de luth allemande et les problèmes d'édition   245

MOE, L. H.   Le problème des barres de mesure (étude sur la transcription de la musique de danse des tablatures de luth du XVIe siècle)   259

PODOLSKI, M.   Recherche d'une méthode de transcription formelle   277

SOURIS, A.   Tablature et syntaxe (remarques sur le problème de la transcription des tablatures de luth)   285

LUMSDEN, D.   Un catalogue international des sources de la musique pour luth (les leçons d'une étude des sources anglaises)   297

Discussion   Problèmes d'édition   303

JACQUOT, J.   Premiers résultats acquis – perspectives d'avenir [revised version in 2nd edition as 'Résultats et perspectives' 313]   311

Un souvenir et une inspiration [obituary for G. Thibault, in 2nd edition only 311]

57 PAR   **Actes au troisième congrès international de musique sacrée Paris – 1er – 8 juillet 1957: Perspectives de la musique sacrée à la lumière de l'encyclique Musicae sacrae disciplina**
Paris 1–8 July 1957
(Paris: Édition du congrès, 1959); abridged version in French only published as La musique sacrée au IIIème congrès international de musique sacrée – Paris – juillet 1957 in La revue musicale nos. 239–40 (Paris: Éditions Richard-Masse, 1957)

1 Les principes
MIRANDA y GOMEZ   La enciclica 'Musicae sacrae disciplina' (French 126)   121

ROGUET   Valeur pastorale de la musique sacrée   131

ROMITA, F.   I principi della legislazione musicale

sacra secondo l'enciclica 'Musicae sacrae disciplina' (French 147) 137

CHAILLEY, J. La révision du critère historique dans les problèmes de la musique d'église 156

2 La musique religieuse de l'école française.

DUFOURCQ, N. France et Italie: la place occupée par Michel-Richard Delalande dans la musique occidentale aux XVIIᵉ et XVIIIᵉ siècles 171

SAMSON, J. Propositions sur la qualité 178

3 Le chant grégorien

MORILLEAU Valeur pastorale du chant grégorien à la lumière des enseignements pontificaux 187

GAJARD, J. La valeur artistique et religieuse toujours actuelle du chant grégorien 198

SMITS van WAESBERGHE L'état actuel des recherches scientifiques dans le domaine du chant grégorien 206

MONETA-CAGLIO, E. Stato attuale della ricerche concernenti il canto ambrosiano (French 222) 218

BIHAN, J. Le mouvement grégorien dans le monde 226

MADSEN, C. Gregorian chant in the United States of America (French 251) 241

OBAMA, J. Les réussites du chant grégorien au Cameroun 260

CARDINE, J. Neumes et rythme 264

DELALANDE De quelques renseignements mélodiques à tirer de manuscrits purement neumatiques 277

4 Le chant des églises d'orient

DUMONT Diversité des rites orientaux et enrichissement de la spiritualité catholique 287

WELLESZ, E. The work done by the editors of 'Monumenta musicae byzantinae' (French 300) 294

WERNER, E. Dead Sea Scrolls contain musically revealing elements (French 312) 305

ANTONOWYCZ, M. Participation des fidèles d'Ukraine aux chants liturgiques 319

DAYAN La publication des 'Hymnes de l'Église arménienne' 324

DYKER Vestiges d'un style calliphonique dans le chant oriental au XIIIᵉ siècle 326

LEVI, L. Les neumes, les notations bibliques et le chant protochrétien 329

FORET, R. Les églises d'orient et la musique moderne 339

von GARDNER, J. Le Psautier chanté en slavon au XVIIIᵉ siècle 346

5 L'orgue et les instruments à l'église

AHRENS, J. Die Liturgie und die Orgelmusik (French 361) 355

TAGLIAVINI, L. Le rôle liturgique de l'organiste des origines à l'époque classique 367

REBOULOT, A. L'organiste liturgique au XXᵉ siècle et sa formation 373

DENIS, P. Le véritable problème des orgues électroniques 380

FRAILE, G. El órgano litúrgico (French 390) 385

Communication of La S. Congrégation des Rites (1949) on electronic instruments (discussion 394) 389

de AMEZUA, G. Les orgues électroniques 407

MARTIN, C. Orgues électroniques d'hier et de demain 412

MEYERS, H. Problèmes actuels de facture d'orgues 423

6 La polyphonie sacrée

LESURE, F. Les éditions scientifiques de musique polyphonique 431

WOLFF, C.-H. Einige moderne Kompositionen des 'Ordinarium Missae' (French 442) 437

PRIETO, J. I. Orientaciones de la música moderna religiosa en España (French 451) 447

Discographie religieuse établie par les soins de l''Académie du Disque français' [extracts] 454

7 Le chant populaire religieux

AGUSTONI, L. Culte chrétien et chant populaire 469

GELINEAU, J. La valeur catéchétique du chant populaire 476

KAELIN Qualité musicale et chant populaire 484

HESBERT Structure grégorienne et chant en français 494

BÉCLARD D'HARCOURT, M. Cantiques folkloriques français retrouvés en Louisiane 509

HAJTAS The vernacular religious songs in Hungary since 1932 (French 518) 515

8 La musique sacrée en pays de mission

COSTANTINI La musique sacrée dans les missions 523

SASTRE Le sacré et la musique négro-africaine 526

ACHILLE, T. E. Les négro-spirituals, musique populaire sacrée 530

PRIM, J. L'enquête mondiale sur la musique sacrée dans les pays de mission 538

OBAMA, J. Enquête sur l'emploi de la musique indigène dans les chrétientés africaines 547

ROZING, P. Vortrag über indonesische Musik (French 555) 552

PAROISSIN, R. Musique d'Asie 559

PAROISSIN, R. Enquête sur la musique missionnaire en Extrême-Orient 564

BASILE Le dilemme de la musique religieuse indigène en Afrique du Sud 567

9 Problèmes de structure et d'enseignement

PIZZARDO L'importance de l'enseignement de la musique dans les Séminaires 577

ALCINI, J. L'insegnamento della musica sacra nei Seminari (French 589) 580

OVERATH, J. Die 'Associatio sub titulo S Caeci-

lia pro universis Germanicae linguae terris' als Typ einer Landesorganisation für Kirchenmusik (French 606) 599

SCHMIT, J. P. Une création de l'encyclique: le responsable diocésain de la musique sacrée 613

ROUSSEL, G. Le rôle exemplaire des maîtrises de cathédrales 618

HERTZ, O. Pour que tous nos enfants apprennent à l'école comment chanter à l'église 623

VYVERMAN, J. Le programme des instituts supérieurs de musique sacrée 626

BROCKBERND, B. La radio au service d'une meilleure musique religieuse 630

10 Organisation internationale de la musique sacrée

KOSCH, F. Die Auswirkungen des II. Internationales Kirchenmusikkongresses (Wien, 1954) (French 639) 635

MAILLET, F. La Fédération internationale des 'Pueri cantores' 643

ANGLÈS, H. Organisation internationale de la musique sacrée 646

HUCKE, H. Zum Plan eines Lexikons der katholischen Kirchenmusik (French 653) 650

de NYS, C. Une nouvelle collection de disques 'Les archives sonores de la musique sacrée' 656

---

57 TOD **Iacopone e il suo tempo: Convegni del Centro di studi sulla spiritualità medievale I**
Todi 13–15 October 1957
Centro di studi sulla spiritualità medievale
(Todi: Accademia Tudertina, 1959)

BECHERINI, B. La musica italiana dalla laude iacoponica alla laude fiorentina del XV secolo 105

PERICOLI, M. Lauda drammatica e dramma sacro a Todi 133

---

57 VEN¹ **Studi goldoniani: Atti del convegno internazionale di studi goldoniani**
Venice 28 September – 1 October 1957
Comune di Venezia; Istituto veneto di scienze lettere ed arti; Istituto di lettere musica e teatro, Fondazione Giorgio Cini, Venice
ed. V. Branca and N. Mangini (Venice and Rome: Istituto per la collaborazione culturale, 1960)

DELLA CORTE, A. Il libretto e l'influenza di Goldoni 567

DE' PAOLI, D. Il librettista Carlo Goldoni e l'opera comica veneziana 571

DE SANCTIS, G. B. Toni di opera buffa in alcune scene goldoniane 593

---

57 VEN² **Arte neoclassica: atti del convegno**
Venice 12–14 October 1957
Istituto di storia dell'arte, Fondazione Giorgio Cini, Venice
(Venice and Rome: Istituto per la collaborazione culturale, 1964)

CUMAR, R. Antonio Miari, musicista bellunese del primo ottocento 105

57 WÉG   Les colloques de Wégimont IV – 1957: Le 'Baroque' musical: Recueil d'études sur la musique du XVIIe siècle

Wégimont 9–14 September 1957

(Paris: Société d'édition 'Les belles lettres', 1963 = Bibliothèque de la Faculté de philosophie et lettres de l'Université de Liège 171)

CLERCX, S.   Le terme Baroque, sa signification, son application à la musique (discussion 30) 17

WOLF, R. E.   Renaissance, Mannerism, Baroque: three styles, three periods (discussion 69)   35

van der MUEREN, F.   Limites géographiques du Baroque (discussion 87)   83

QUEROL, M.   La polyphonie religieuse espagnole au XVIIe siècle (discussion 98)   91

COLLAER, P.   Lyrisme baroque et tradition populaire (discussion 125)   109

KASTNER, M.   Le rôle des tablatures d'orgue au XVIe siècle dans l'avènement du Baroque musical (discussion 142)   131

MASSENKEIL, G.   Zur Frage der Dissonanzbehandlung in der Musik des 17. Jahrhunderts (discussion 171)   151

LAUNAY, D.   Á propos d'une messe de Charles d'Helfer: le problème de l'exécution des messes réputées a capella en France, aux XVIIe et XVIIIe siècles (discussion 194)   177

LEBEAU, E.   La musique des cérémonies célébrées à la mort de Marie-Thérèse, reine de France (discussion 214)   200

WANGERMÉE, R.   Principes d'interprétation, introduction [discussion only]   223

STEVENS, D.   L'interprétation de la musique de Claudio Monteverdi (discussion 248)   241

FROIDEBISE, P.   Interprétation de la musique d'orgue et réalisation des gloses [discussion only]   255

FLAGEL, C.   Exposé sur la vielle à roue ·fait à l'occasion du Colloque de Wégimont 1957 260

Discussion   267

58 AIX   Actes et mémoires du IIᵉ congrès international de langue et littérature du midi de la France
Aix 2–8 September 1958
Congrès international de langue et littérature du midi de la France
(Aix: Centre d'études provençales de la Faculté des lettres d'Aix, 1961)

PETIOT, A.   La musique des troubadours   105

58 BRN   Leoš Janáček a soudobá hudba: Mezinárodní hudebně vědecký kongres, Brno 1958 [Leoš
Janáček and contemporary music: international musicological congress, Brno 1958]
Brno 19–26 October 1958
(Prague: Knižnice Hudebních rozhledů, 1963)
[all Czech papers printed with German résumés; all German and French papers with
Czech résumés]

RACEK, J.   Leoš Janáček a jeho postavení v české a světové hudební kultuře [Janáček and his place in Czech and international musical culture]   37

ANDREJEV, A.   Leoš Janáček a Bulharsko [Janáček and Bulgaria]   75

ČERNOHORSKÁ, M.   Význam nápěvků pro Janáčkovu operní tvorbu [The significance of speech melodies for Janáček's operatic works] (discussion LÉBL, V. 202)   77

ECKSTEIN, P.   O režijní koncepci a inscenačním slohu v Janáčkových operách [The direction and style of staging in Janáček's operas] (discussion FELSENSTEIN, W. 86)   81

FLOTHUIS, M.   Der Widerhall von Janáčeks Musik in Holland und die Möglichkeiten das Interesse für sein Werk zu fördern   94

GARDAVSKÝ, Č.   Janáček a psychologie hudební tvorby [Janáček and the psychology of composition]   98

HÁBA, A.   Hudební sloh Janáčkův a jeho současníků [The musical style of Janáček and his contemporaries]   117

HÁBA, A.   Janáčkovo pojetí harmonie [Janáček's conception of harmony]   121

HELM, E.   Janáčkovo postavení ve vývoji novodobé hudby [Janáček's place in the evolution of contemporary music]   123

HOLEČKOVÁ-DOLANSKÁ, J.   K pěveckým problémům Janáčkových oper [Problems in the singing of Janáček's operas] (discussion SOBIESKY, B. 279)   124

HOLLÄNDER, H.   Das monothematische Prinzip der Glagolitischen Messe   129

HRABAL, F.   K otázce hudební tektoniky Výletu pana Broučka do XV. století [The musical structure of 'Mr Brouček's Excursion to the 15th Century']   132

CHLUBNA, O.   Janáčkovy názory na operu a jeho úsilí o nový operní sloh [Janáček's views on opera and his striving for a new operatic style]   140

JANEČEK, K.   Stavba Janáčkových skladeb [The structure of Janáček's compositions]   150

JIRÁNEK, J.   K některým otázkám vztahu Leoše Janáčka k české a světové hudbě [Questions on Janáček's relations with Czech and world music]   155

KARÁSEK, B.   Svět Janáčka dramatika (Rysy kritického realismu v jeho operním díle) [The world of Janáček the dramatist (traits of critical realism in his operatic works)]   162

KÖHLER, S.   Leoš Janáčeks Progressivität und der musikalische Modernismus in der westlichen Welt (discussion FESCHOTTE, J. 90)   169

KRAUSE, E.   Über Versäumnisse der internationalen Musikkritik   176

KRESÁNEK, J.   Tonalita v primitivnej a l'udovej hudbe [Tonality in primitive music and folk music]   182

KUNDERA, L.   K otázce interpretace Janáčkových děl [The interpretation of Janáček's works]   189

LÉBL, V.   Postavení osobnosti Leoše Janáčka v české hudební kultuře [The place of Janáček's personality in Czech musical culture]   198

LOEWENBACH, J.   Dramatický princip Leoše Janáčka a M. P. Musorgského [The dramatic principles of Janáček and Musorgsky]   205

MARKL, J.   Janáčkova nápěvková teorie a český písňový typ instrumentální [Janáček's speech-melody theory and the instrumental type of Czech song]   217

MIES, P. Skizzen, Fassungen und Ausgaben-typen 220

MŁODZIEJOWSKI, J. Janáčkova hudba v Polsku [Janáček's music in Poland] 226

NOVÁČEK, Z. Niektoré podmienky osobitosti u Janáčka, Orffa a Schönberga [Some conditions in the personality of Janáček, Orff and Schoenberg] 236

OČADLÍK, M. Janáček a Stravinskij (discussion FESCHOTTE, J. 90 and GOLDSCHMIDT, H. 111) 240

PALA, F. Mladý Janáček a divadlo [The young Janáček and the theatre] 244

PEČMAN, R. Symfonické dílo Leoše Janáčka v pojetí Břetislava Bakaly [Janáček's symphonic works interpreted by Bakala] 250

PLAVEC, J. Janáčkova tvorba sborová [Janáček's choral works] 254

RISINGER, K. Problém konsonance a disonance v soudobé hudbě [The problem of consonance and dissonance in contemporary music] 261

RIHTMAN, C. O otázce nesoučasnosti přízvuku slova a přízvuku nápěvu v lidové hudbě [Divergence in verbal stress and melodic stress in folk music] 265

SERAUKY, W. Vorläufer in der europäischen Musikgeschichte und Musikästhetik zu Janáčeks Sprachmelodie 267

SMOLKA, J. Příspěvek k poznání vnitřního řádu Janáčkovy melodiky a tematické práce [Recognition of the inner laws of Janáček's melodic and thematic development] 275

SPIES, L. Janáčeks Theorie der Sprachmelodie – ein Instrument des Naturstudiums – nicht eine Kompositionsmethode (discussion LÉBL, V. 202) 281

STRAKOVÁ, T. K problematice Janáčkovy opery Osud [Problems in Janáček's opera 'Fate'] 289

STŘELCOVÁ, V. Několik poznámek k pěvecké interpretaci Janáčkova dramatického slohu [Remarks on the singer's interpretation of Janáček's dramatic style] 294

SYCHRA, A. Vztah hudby a slova jako jeden z nejzávažnějších problémů Janáčkova slohu [The relationship of word and music as one of the most serious problems of Janáček's style] 298

ŠTĚDROŇ, B. K inspiraci Janáčkových Listů důvěrných [The inspiration of Janáček's 'Intimate Letters'] 315

ŠTĚDROŇ, B. Lidové kořeny Její pastorkyně [The folk roots of 'Jenůfa'] 317

VÁLEK, J. Konkrétnost zobrazení – základ Janáčkova symfonismu posledního období [Concrete depiction: the basis of Janáček's symphonic works of his final period] 323

VANCEA, Z. Janáček und die führenden Komponisten der südosteuropäischen Schulen: Bartók, Enescu, Kodály 330

VETTERL, K. Otázky tvůrčího a reprodukčního stylu v lidové písni [Questions of creative and reproductive styles in folk music] 345

VOLEK, J. Živelná dialektika a její klady i nedostatky v teoretických názorech Leoše Janáčka [Essential dialectics, its virtues and its inadequacies in Janáček's theoretical views] 352

VYSLOUŽIL, J. Janáčkova tvorba ve světle jeho hudebně folkloristické teorie [Janáček's works in the light of his folk-music theory] 361

VYSLOUŽIL, J. Janáček jako kritik [Janáček as critic] 377

WASSERBAUER, M. K režijnímu pojetí Janáčkových oper [The director's conception of Janáček's operas] (discussion FELSENSTEIN, W. 86) 381

WELLEK, A. Fortschritte in der Theorie der Konsonanz und Dissonanz 387

WÖRNER, K. H. Katjas Tod, die Schlussszene der Oper Katja Kabanowa von Leoš Janáček 392

58 COL   **Bericht über den Siebenten internationalen musikwissenschaftlichen Kongress Köln 1958**
Cologne 23–8 June 1958
International Musicological Society
ed. G. Abraham, S. Clercx-Lejeune, H. Federhofer, W. Pfannkuch (Kassel and Basle: Bärenreiter, 1959)

BRAILOIU, C. N. Musicologie et ethnomusicologie aujourd'hui 17

BOYDEN, D. D. The violin and its technique: new horizons in research 29

ENGEL, H. Werden und Wesen des Madrigals 39

ALDRICH, P. Obligatory improvisation or ornaments ff

ANGLÈS, H. Die zwei Arten der Mensuralnotation der Monodie des Mittelalters 56

ARNOLD, D. The influence of ornamentation on the structure of early 17th century church music 57

BADURA-SKODA, E. Zur Appoggiaturenfrage 58

BAKE, A. A. Rhythmischer Kontrapunkt auf einer Rahmentrommel aus Ceylon 60

BARKECHLI, M. Les rythmes caractéristiques de la musique iranienne 61

BARTHA, D. Zum Harmoniebegriff in der Musik Béla Bartóks 63

BECHERINI, B. Communications sur Antonio Squarcialupi et notes au Cod. Med. Palatino 87 , 65

BERNER, A. Untersuchungsprobleme und Wertungsprinzipien an Musikinstrumenten der Vergangenheit 66

BLANKENBURG, W. Kanonimprovisationen im 16. und Anfang des 17. Jahrhunderts 68

BOETTICHER, W. Zum Spätstilproblem im Schaffen Orlando di Lassos 69

BOSE, F. Rhythmusprobleme in instrumental begleiteter primitiver Musik 72

BRENN, F. Ockeghems spiritueller Rhythmus 73

BRINER, A. Wandlungen des Zeitempfindens im Harmoniebewusstsein 74

BRIQUET, M. Deux motets inédits de Montéclair (1667–1737) 75

CERVELLI, L. Italienische Musikinstrumente in der Praxis des Generalbassspiels: das Arpichord 76

CHAILLEY, J. Philologie musicale: principes et premiers résultats 78

CHRISTENSEN, D. Heterogene Musikstile in dem Dorfe Gabela (Herzegovina) 79

CROLL, G. Zur Vorgeschichte der 'Mannheimer' 82

CVETKO, D. Ein unbekanntes Inventarium Librorum Musicalium aus dem Jahre 1620 84

DABO-PERANIĆ, M. Le sens de l'harmonie chez les Grecs 85

DAHLHAUS, C. Über den Dissonanzbegriff des Mittelalters 87

DJURIĆ-KLAJN, S. Correspondance inédite de Johannes Brahms 88

DUCKLES, V. The lyrics of John Donne as set by his contemporaries 91

EGGEBRECHT, H.-H. 'Diaphonia vulgariter organum' 93

ENGELBRECHT, C. Die Psalmsätze des Jenaer Chorbuches 34 97

FÉDOROV, V. B. V. Asaf'ev et la musicologie russe avant et après 1917 99

FEININGER, L. Raum und Architektur in der vielchörigen römischen Kirchenmusik des 17. Jahrhunderts 100

FELLER, M. The new style of Giulio Caccini, member of the Florentine Camerata 102

FERAND, E. T. Zum Begriff der 'compositio' im 15. und 16. Jahrhundert 104

von FISCHER, K. Neues zur Passionskomposition des 16. Jahrhunderts 107

GARROS, M. Les motets à voix seule de Guillaume Gabriel Nivers 108

GEIRINGER, K. Unbekannte Werke von Nachkommen J. S. Bachs in amerikanischen Sammlungen 110

GERSTENBERG, W. Grundfragen der Rhythmus-Forschung 113

GOLDSCHMIDT, H. Zu einer Neubewertung von Schuberts letzter Schaffenszeit (1828) 118

GUDEWILL, K. Melchior Franck und das geistliche Konzert 120

HARICH-SCHNEIDER, E. Ein Beitrag zur Quellenkunde Japanischer Musik 123

HAYDON, G. The Lateran Codex 61 126

HELGASON, H. Das Bauernorganum auf Island 132

HERMELINK, S. Zur Geschichte der Kadenz im 16. Jahrhundert 133

HERZOG, E. Harmonie und Tonart bei Janáček 136

HOFFMANN-ERBRECHT, L. Neue Dokumente zum Leben Thomas Stoltzers 139

HUCKE, H. Zum Problem des Rhythmus im Gregorianischen Gesang 141

HÜSCHEN, H. Der Harmoniebegriff im Musikschrifttum des Altertums und des Mittelalters 143

JIRÁNEK, J. Der Beitrag Zdeněk Nejedlýs zur Erforschung des Hussitischen Gesanges 150

KARSTÄDT, G. Neue Ergebnisse zur Buxtehude-Forschung 152

KIRBY, P. R. Physical phenomena which appear to have determined the bases and development of an harmonic sense among Bushmen, Hottentot and Bantu, as I have observed them in Southern Africa 154

KLUSEN, E. Gregorianischer Choral und frühprotestantisches Kirchenlied: neue Gesichtspunkte zur Beurteilung ihrer gegenseitigen Beziehungen 157

KNEPLER, G. Über einige geistige Schwierigkeiten der Musikforschung von heute 160

KÖHLER, K.-H. Zwei Grundtypen historischer Musiksammlungen 162

KRAFT, G. Thüringisch-sächsische Quellen zur musikphysiologischen Forschung des 17. und 18. Jahrhunderts 164

KRAUTWURST, F. Grundsätzliches zu einer Filiation geistlicher Musikhandschriften der Reformationszeit 166

KROLL, E. Die Musikkritiken E. T. A. Hoffmanns 169

KRÜGER, H. Die Verstimmung (scordatura, discordatura) auf Saiten-Instrumenten in Beziehung zur klanglichen Einrichtung der Instrumente und zum Tonsystem und ihre Folgen auf die Aufführungspraxis 172

KUTTNER, F. A. A 'Pythagorean' tone-system in China – antedating the early Greek achievements by several centuries 174

LARUE, J. Harmonic rhythm as an indicator of rhythmic function 176

LENAERTS, R. B. Improvisation auf der Orgel und der Laute in den Niederlanden (16. und 17. Jahrhundert) 177

LIPPHARDT, W. Ein unbekannter karolingischer Tonar und seine Bedeutung für die fränkische Choralüberlieferung 179

LISSA, Z. Die Kategorie des Komischen in der Musik 181

LUNDGREN, B. Johan Lorentz in Kopenhagen – organista nulli in Europa secundus 183

MACHATIUS, F.-J. Die Tempo-Charaktere 185

MACKERNESS, E. D. Mendelssohn and 'Charles Auchester' 188

MASSENKEIL, G. Bemerkungen zum 'Compendium musicae' (1618) des René Descartes 188

MÉNARD, R. Le problème de la mémorisation en musique copte garant de fidélité à la tradition 191

MIES, P. Die Quellen des op. 61 von Ludwig van Beethoven 193

MÜLLER-BLATTAU, J. Zur vokalen Improvisation im 16. Jahrhundert 195

MULLER, F. La technique de la réalisation variée dans la Tablature de Goerlitz (1650) de Samuel Scheidt 196

MUNRO, K. Haydn's keyboard arrangement of Symphony No. 96 in D 197

NATALETTI, G. Dix ans d'ethno-musicologie en Italie 198

NESTLER, G. Der Rhythmus in der Reihentechnik der Gegenwart 199

NETTL, B. Some historical aspects of ethnomusicology 200

NOMURA, F. Y. Gegenwärtige Probleme der Musikwissenschaft in Japan 201

NOSKE, F. Joannes Tollius, ein niederländischer Meister des Frühbarock 203

OTTO, I. Die instrumentenkundliche Auswertung der deutschen Lexika des 18. Jahrhunderts 207

PETZOLDT, R. Zur sozialen Stellung des Musikers im 17. Jahrhundert 210

PFROGNER, H. Zur Definition des Begriffes Atonalität 212

PLAMENAC, D. German polyphonic lieder of the 15th century in a little-known manuscript 214

RACEK, J. Drei unbekannte Autographentorsen W. A. Mozarts 216

RAUGEL, F. Saint-Césaire, précepteur du Chant gallican 217

REANEY, G. A note on conductus rhythm 219

REHM, W. Über ein Repertorium der Musik 221

REINECKE, H. Zum Problem des Hörens von Zusammenklängen und Klangfarben im Hinblick auf die akustische Funktion des Ohres 227

REINHARD, K. Eine von der rhythmischen Belebung abhängige Tempobezeichnung 229

ROHWER, J. Der Sonanzfaktor im Aufbau von Tonsystemen 230

RUBSAMEN, W. H. The Jovial Crew: history of a ballad opera 240

SERAUKY, W. Zur Neuinterpretation von Richard Wagners Werk 244

SIEGMUND-SCHULTZE, W. Probleme der Verdi-Oper 247

SMITS van WAESBERGHE, J. Zur ursprünglichen Vortragsweise der Prosulen, Sequenzen und Organa 251

SØRENSEN, S. Ein Kantaten-Jahrgang von Christian Ludwig Boxbert (1670–1729) 254

SYCHRA, A. Das Problem des Rhythmus im

Lichte der Beziehungen von Musik und Wort 255

SZABOLCSI, B. Über Form und Improvisation in der Kunst- und Volksmusik 257

SCHANZLIN, H. P. Zur Geschichte der Litanei im 17. Jahrhundert 259

SCHMID, H. Die Kölner Handschrift der Musica Enchiriadis 262

SCHNEIDER, M. Prolegomena zu einer Theorie des Rhythmus 264

STEGLICH, R. Über die Synkope 277

STEIN, F. Zum Problem der 'Jenaer Symphonie' 279

STEPHAN, R. Zur Cantio-Rhythmik 281

STESZEWSKI, J. Einige charakteristische Merkmale der Kurpischen Volksmusik 283

STEVENS, D. Ornamentation in Monteverdi's shorter dramatic works 284

TAPPOLET, W. Einige prinzipielle Bemerkungen zur Frage der Improvisation 287

van der VEEN, J. Problèmes structuraux chez Maurice Ravel 289

VETTER, W. Antike Polyphonie? 290

WAELTNER, E. L. Die 'Musica disciplina' des Aurelianus Reomensis 293

WINCKEL, F. Rekonstruktion historischer Klangstile unter dem Gesichtspunkt von Architektur und Raumakustik 295

WINTERNITZ, E. Quattrocento-Intarsien als Quellen der Instrumentengeschichte 300

WIRSTA, A. Theodore Akimenko – représentant de l'impressionisme de l'Europe de l'Est 302

WÖRNER, K. H. Harmoniebewusstsein und Symbolwandel in Schönbergs Oper 'Moses und Aron' 305

WOLFF, H. C. Orientalische Einflüsse in den Improvisationen des 16. und 17. Jahrhunderts 308

WÜNSCH, W. Zur Frage der Mehrstimmigkeit des alpenländischen Volksliedes 316

YOUNG, P. M. Some aspects of Handelian research 318

ZICH, J. Agogische Prinzipe der Wiedergabe 319

ZIMMERMAN, F. B. Advanced tonal design in the part-songs of William Byrd 322

Study groups

Lauten- und Gitarrentabulaturen (chairman BOETTICHER, W.) 329

La révision de la notion traditionelle de tonalité (chairman CHAILLEY, J.) 332

Musikalische Stratigraphie Afrikas (chairman COLLAER, P.) 334

Klassifikation der Operngeschichte (chairman GROUT, D. J.) 338

Composer and Publisher 1500–1850 (chairman KING, A. H.) 340

Dynamik und Agogik in der Musik des Barock (chairman KOLNEDER, W.) 343

Editionsprobleme des späten 18. Jahrhunderts

(chairman LARSEN, J. P.)   349
Der Musiker in der mittelalterlichen Gesellschaft
(chairman SALMEN, W.)   354
Die Tradition des 'Altrömischen' und des Grego-

rianischen Chorals (chairman SMITS van
WAESBERGHE, J.)   358
Der Terminus Variation (chairman SCHNEI-
DER, M.)   363

58 MARS   Acoustique musicale
Marseilles 27–9 May 1958
Centre national de la recherche scientifique
(Paris: Centre national de la recherche scientifique, 1959)

CHAILLEY, J. Le dynamisme des gammes et des accords dans les principaux systèmes acoustiques et son influence sur le développement de la musique   13

A Théorie de la gamme et la valeur des accords
BARKECHLI, M. Quelques idées nouvelles sur la consonance   21
FOKKER, A. Les cinquièmes de ton   29
BARKECHLI, M. L'évolution de la gamme dans la musique orientale   39
CHAILLEY, J. Le problème de l'harmonique 7 devant l'histoire musicale   47
TANNER, R. Le rôle de la fusion dans l'appréciation de justesse des accords   49
WINCKEL, F. Influence des facteurs psychophysiologiques sur la sensation de consonance-dissonance   61
BRILLOUIN, J. Réflexions sur les problèmes dits d'acoustique musicale   75
TANNER, R. Le problème des rapports simples: notion de psycharithme   83
DUSSAUT, R. Proposition de quelques réformes en théorie acoustico-musicale   103
RIETY, P. Le vocabulaire d'acoustique musicale d'après la formation du langage musical   111

B La physique des instruments à cordes et à vent
PIMONOW, L. La détermination de la qualité des instruments de musique au moyen du spectre sonore transitoire   119

TARNOCZY, T. Recherches sur le spectre de l'orgue en faisant sonner plusieurs touches à la fois   135
KREPS, J. Les synthèses sonores de l'orgue à tuyaux   145
YOUNG, R. W. Sur l'intonation de divers instruments de musique, du U.S. Navy electronics laboratory, San Diego 52, California   169
LOTTERMOSER, W. L'examen acoustique des violons dans la Physikalisch-Technische Bundenanstalt   185
BLADIER, B. Contribution à l'étude du violoncelle   193
RIMSKI-KORSAKOV, A. V. Les recherches sur le timbre des violons et guitares et sur l'excitation des vibrations d'une anche d'harmonium 203
CARRIÈRE Entretien d'un tuyau à anche libre   215
GUITTARD Calculs et mesures d'indépendances acoustiques   221
MERCIER, J. Étude de la stabilité des oscillations entretenues dans un tuyau sonore couplé à un tuyau mort   231
GRUTZMACHER Le spectre d'un son de cloche   239
RICHARDSON, E. G. L'acoustique des cors et des trompes   245
HUSSON, R. La physique du pavillon pharyngo-buccal dans la phonation   253

58 SJOS   Actas del XXXIII congreso internacional de Americanistas
San José, Costa Rica, 20–27 July 1958
International Congress of Americanists
(San José: Lehmann, 1959)

Vol. ii (1959)
I Etnomusicología
RAMÓN y RIVERA, L. F. Problemas de la grabación y transcripción musical de los tambores   603
MERRIAM, A. P. and SPIER, R. F. G. Chukchansi Yokuts songs   611

SMITH, M. B. Progress report on the study of African influences in the music of Panama 639
RAMÓN y RIVERA, L. F. Supervivencia de la polifonía popular en Venezuela   647
ARETZ, I. Un planteamiento de orígenes – El Maremare como expresión musical y coreográfica   649

58 TOD   Spiritualità cluniacense: Convegni del Centro di studi sulla spiritualità medievale II
Todi 12–15 October 1958
   Centro di studi sulla spiritualità medievale
   (Todi: Accademia Tudertina, 1960)

SCHMITZ, P.   La liturgie de Cluny   83

58 WAS   Symposium on Cherokee and Iroquois Culture
Washington 20 November 1958
   American Anthropological Association
   ed. W. N. Fenton and J. Gulick (Washington DC: United States Government Printing
   Office, 1961 = Smithsonian Institution Bureau of American Ethnology Bulletin 180)

KURATH, G. P. Effects of environment on   dance (discussion STURTEVANT, W. C.
Cherokee-Iroquois ceremonialism, music, and   197)   173

58 WÉG   Les colloques de Wégimont IV [= V] 1958–1960: Ethnomusicologie III [+IV]
Wégimont 7–12 September 1958; Wégimont 4–10 September 1960
   Cercle international d'études ethnomusicologiques
   ed. P. Collaer (Paris: Société d'édition 'Les belles lettres', 1964 = Bibliothèque de la
   Faculté de philosophie et lettres de l'Université de Liège 172)

COLLAER, P. Stratigraphie musicale et structures mélodiques   13
WACHSMANN, K. Problems of musical stratigraphy in Africa   19
COLLAER, P. Contributions à la méthode scientifique en ethnomusicologie   24
COMIŞEL, E. La musique de la ballade populaire
roumaine   39
NATALETTI, G. Alcuni strumenti di musica
popolari italiani: distribuzione geografica 75
STOCKMANN, D. and E. Die vokale Mehrstimmigkeit in Süd-Albanien   85

ROVSING-OLSEN, P. Enregistrements faits à
Kuwait et Bahrain   137
GRIMAUD, Y. Étude analytique de la danse
'Choma' des Bochimans !Kung   171
ESTREICHER, Z. Le rythme des Peuls Bor-
oro   185
SCHAEFFNER, A. Le tambour-sur-cadre quad-
rangulaire chez les Noirs d'Afrique et
d'Amérique   229
CHAILLEY, J. Ethnomusicologie et harmonie
classique   249

59 BUD   **Bericht über die internationale Konferenz zum Andenken Joseph Haydns** [I. internationale musikwissenschaftliche Konferenz]
Budapest 17–22 September 1959
Magyar tudományos akadémia [Hungarian Academy of Sciences]
ed. B. Szabolcsi and D. Bartha (Budapest: Akadémiai kiadó, 1961)

BARTHA, D.   Haydn als Opernkapellmeister 17
BESSELER, H.   Einflüsse der Contratanzmusik auf Joseph Haydn   25
FELLERER, K. G.   Joseph Haydns Messen   41
GEIRINGER, K.   Sidelights on Haydn's activities in the field of sacred music   49
HOŘEJŠ, A.   Haydn mit heutigen Augen gesehen   57
KREMLJEW, J.   J. Haydn und die russische Musikkultur   61
LANDON, H. C. R.   Survey of the Haydn sources in Czechoslovakia   69
LESURE, F.   Haydn en France   79
LIWANOWA, T.   Ranniye otkliky na iskusstvo Gaydna v Rossiy [Early comments on Haydn's works in Russia] (German 91)   85
MIES, P.   Joseph Haydns Singkanons und ihre Grundidee   93
MOLNÁR, A.   Der gestaltpsychologische Unterschied zwischen Haydn und Mozart   95

de NYS, C.   A propos du concerto pour deux cors et orchestre en mi bémol majeur   103
POŠTOLKA, M.   Joseph Haydn und Leopold Koželuh   109
SCHMID, E. F.   Joseph Haydn und die vokale Zierpraxis seiner Zeit, dargestellt an einer Arie seines Tobias-Oratoriums   117
SEEGER, H.   Zur musikhistorischen Bedeutung Albert Christoph Dies' und seiner Haydn-Biographie von 1810   131
SIEGMUND-SCHULTZE, W.   Mozarts 'Haydn-Quartette'   137
SYCHRA, A.   Über die Bedeutung von Beethovens Skizzen zur IX. Symphonie   147
SZABOLCSI, B.   Haydn und die ungarische Musik   159
VANCEA, Z.   Der Einfluss Haydns auf die rumänischen Komponisten des XIX. Jahrhunderts   177

59 CAM   **Music Libraries and Instruments: Papers read at the Joint Congress, Cambridge, 1959 of the International Association of Music Libraries and the Galpin Society**
Cambridge 30 June – 3 July 1959
International Association of Music Libraries (5th Congress); Galpin Society
ed. U. Sherrington and G. Oldham, *Hinrichsen's Eleventh Music Book* (London and New York: Hinrichsen, 1961)

II Music, librarianship, and instrument collections
1 Music and musicology
WESTRUP, J. A.   Practical musicology   25
GERHARD, R.   Concrete and electronic sound-composition   30
CVETKO, D.   National sources, their functions and interpretation in musicological research   37
2 Music librarianship
KING, A. H.   The music librarian and his tasks, national and international   40
America
DUCKLES, V.   The growth and organisation of music research libraries in the western United States   47

England
DUCK, L. W.   The public provision of music for choirs and orchestras   53
ANDERSON, K.   Public service for music: the use of standard methods in Liverpool's new music library   60
OLDMAN, C. B.   Panizzi and the music collections of the British Museum   62
Germany
VÖTTERLE, K.   Musikbibliothek und Musikverlag   67
SCHETELICH, H.   Der Gesichtskreis der Musikbüchereiarbeit in einer Gross-stadt der Deutschen Demokratischen Republik   75
OTT, A.   The rôle of music in public libraries of medium size   79

Scandinavia

LINDBERG, F. Scandinavian music libraries: their value for research and broadcasting 83

HEILMANN, I. Organisation of the music collection of the state library in Aarhus, Denmark 86

Scotland

LINTON, M. Music in Scottish libraries 88

ROLLAND, G. H. The music collection in the Mitchell Library 95

3 Record libraries

SPIVACKE, H. The preservation and reference services of sound recordings in a research library 99

SAUL, P. Preserving recorded sound 110

KÖHLER, K.-H. Zur Problematik der Schallplatten-Katalogisierung 116

REINHARD, K. Probleme und Erfahrungen in einem Musik-ethnologischen Schallarchiv 119

TERENZIO, V. Criteri per la classificazione e la catalogazione di una discoteca nelle biblioteche musicali 126

4 Collections of music and musical instruments

DOUILLEZ, J. Collections of musical instruments in Antwerp 128

THIBAULT, G. Les collections privées de livres et d'instruments de musique d'autrefois et d'aujourd'hui 131

5 Musical bibliography

Towards a definition of certain terms in musical bibliography (chairman HOPKINSON C; panelists DEUTSCH O. E., ELVERS, R., FÉDOROV, Y., HALM, H., van der LINDEN, A., NEIGHBOUR, O. W., ROSENTHAL, A., WEINHOLD, L.) 147

6 Classification of music; microfilms

COATES, E. J. The British catalogue of music classification 156

PLESSKE, H.-M. Zur Musikalien-Katalogisierung der Deutschen Bücherei 165

JURRES, A. From microfilm to microphone 169

HECKMANN, H. Musikalische Quellen auf Mikrofilmen 173

III Musical instruments

7 Keyboard instruments

BENTON, R. The early piano in the United States 179

JEANS, S. Water organs 189

DUFOURCQ, N. Pierre Baillon, facteur de clavecins, d'orgues, graveur de musique et organiste français 196

8 Barrel organ, string and wind instruments

BOSTON, N. The barrel organ 200

BAINES, A. Some points in the nomenclature of folk instruments 204

WINTERNITZ, E. The survival of the kithara and the evolution of the cittern 209

JACQUOT, J. The international catalogue of music for the lute and kindred instruments 214

MacGILLIVRAY, J. The cylindrical reed pipe from antiquity to the 20th century: its classification and scope 218

HOOD, M. The Javanese rebab 220

BERGMANN, W. Henry Purcell's use of the recorder 227

OLDHAM, G. Two pieces for 5-part shawm band by Louis Couperin 233

HEDLUND, H. J. James Hook and the patent voice flute 239

LUITHLEN, V. Musical treasures of the Vienna Art Museum 244

SKEAPING, K. The Karl Schreinzer collection of violin fittings 251

9 Representations of instruments and musicians

NICEWONGER, C. and NICEWONGER, H. Mediaeval musical instruments sculptured in the decorations of English churches 253

OTTO, I. Buchschmuck als instrumentenkundliche Quelle 256

LaRue, J. and HOLLAND, J. B. Stimmer's women musicians: a unique series of woodcuts 261

59 CER   **L'ars nova italiana del trecento: primo convegno internazionale**
Certaldo 23–6 July 1959
Centro di studi sull'ars nova italiana del trecento, Certaldo; International Musicological Society
ed. B. Becherini (Certaldo: Centro di studi sull'ars nova italiana del trecento, 1962)

FELLERER, G. La 'Constitutio docta Sanctorum Patrum' di Giovanni XXII e la musica nuova del suo tempo 9

von FISCHER, K. Les compositions à trois voix chez les compositeurs du trecento 18

GHISI, F. Rapporti armonici nella polifonia Italiana del trecento 32

BECHERINI, B. L'ars nova italiana del trecento: strumenti ed espressione musicale 40

PIRROTTA, N. Piero e l'impressionismo musicale del secolo XIV 57

HOPPIN, R. H. The Manuscript J. II. 9. in the Biblioteca nazionale of Torino 75

BRIDGMAN, N. La musique dans la société française de l'Ars nova 83

CLERCX-LEJEUNE, S. Les débuts de la Messe unitaire et de la 'Missa parodia' au XIV siècle et principalement dans l'oeuvre de J. Ciconia 97

FANO, F.   Punti di vista su l'ars nova   105
Conclusions   113
SEAY, A.   Paolo da Firenze: a trecento

theorist   118
BECHERINI, B.   Antonio Squarcialupi e il Codice
Mediceo-Palatino 87   141

59 HAL   Handel-Ehrung der Deutschen Demokratischen Republik: Konferenzbericht
Halle 11–19 April 1959
 ed. W. Siegmund-Schultze (Leipzig: Deutscher Verlag für Musik, 1961)

MEYER, E. H.   Händels polyphoner Ton   22
SIEGMUND-SCHULTZE, W.   Künftige Aufgaben
der Förderung und Pflege des Händelschen
Werkes   30

Händels Leben, Persönlichkeit und Umwelt
KRAFT, G.   Zur geistigen Umwelt des jungen
Händel   45
FELIX, W.   Händel und Weissenfels   53
BRAUN, W.   Echtheits- und Datierungsfragen im
vokalen Frühwerk Georg Friedrich Hän-
dels   61
SMITH, W. C.   Händels Leben in England 73
SASSE, K.   Händels Stellung zu den gesellschaft-
lichen Problemen.in England   81
FLEISCHHAUER, G.   Händel und die Antike 87
WOLFF, H. C.   Vom Wesen des alten Bel-
canto   95
STEGLICH, R.   Händels Sprachengebrauch 101

**Die Gestaltungsprinzipien bei Händel (insbesondere
im Übergang von der Oper zum Oratorium)**
SERAUKY, W.   Georg Friedrich Händels ital-
ienische Kantatenwelt   109
RAUGEL, F.   Händels französische Lieder 115
MÜLLER-BLATTAU, J.   Über Händels Früh-
Oratorien 'Esther', 'Deborah' und
'Athalia'   127
YOUNG, P. M.   Zur Interpretation des 'Saul' 131
HEINITZ, W.   Rezitativ-Gestaltung in Hän-
delschen Werken   135
LARSEN, J. P.   Tempoprobleme bei Händel, dar-
gestellt am 'Messias'   141
KNEPLER, G.   Die motivisch-thematische Arbeit
in Händels Oratorien   155
SIEGMUND-SCHULTZE, W.   Händels Melodik in
Oper und Oratorium   165
WEISMANN, W.   Choralzitate in Händels

Oratorien   173
RUDOLPH, J.   Über die biblische Gewandung
von Händels Oratorien   181

**Fragen der Pflege und Nachwirkung des Hän-
delschen Schaffens**
MIES, P.   Faksimile-Ausgaben von Werken
Händels und ihre Bedeutung   187
HUDSON, F.   Wasserzeichen in Händelschen Ma-
nuskripten und Drucken   193
HICKMANN, H.   Instrumentenkundliche und aufführungspraktische Probleme bei der Aufführung und stereofonischen Einspielung Händelscher Werke   207
USZKOREIT, H.-G.   Händel und Mendel-
ssohn   215
SYCHRA, A.   Romain Rollands Händel-Bild
heute gesehen   219
BROCK, H.   Händel und die Schulmusik   223
LAMMEL, I.   Die Pflege Händelscher Oratorien
durch die deutsche Arbeiter-Sängerbewe-
gung   229
STOMPOR, S.   Zu einigen Fragen der Interpret-
ation Händelscher Opern   235
ZSCHOCH, F.   Agrippina – eine satirische
Oper?   241
SEEGER, H.   Zu Fragen der Aufführungspraxis
von Händels Oratorien   245
ENGLÄNDER, R.   Händel auf der schwedischen
Bühne   251
BUSH, A.   Zum Problem der Verbreitung von
Händels Schaffen unter dem grossen Publikum,
besonders bei den Arbeitern und Bauern, durch
szenische Aufführungen seiner Oratorien 257
GRUBER, R. I.   Zur Händel-Pflege in der
Sowjetunion   261
KÖHLER, S.   Gestaltungsprinzipien Händels in
der sozialistischen Vokalsinfonik   265

59 KIE   [I.] **Internationaler Kongress der Volkserzählungsforscher in Kiel und Kopenhagen: Vorträge
und Referate**
Kiel and Copenhagen 19–22 August 1959
[International Society for Folk-Narrative Research]
 ed. K. Ranke (Berlin: Walter de Gruyter & Co, 1961 = supplement series to
Fabula: Zeitschrift für Erzählforschung, ed. K. Ranke, B2)

SOFER, Z.   Die Verwendung der Volksmusik in
der chassidischen Volkserzählung   406

59 ROY   **Les théâtres d'Asie**
Royaumont 28 May – 1 June 1959
Groupe de recherches sur le théâtre (CNRS): Conférences du théâtre des nations
(1958–9); Journées d'études de Royaumont
ed. J. Jacquot (Paris: Centre national de la recherche scientifique, 1961)

Chine
HIAO-TSIUN, M. Le théâtre de Pékin   89
TRAVERT, A. Caractères originaux et évolution
du théâtre pékinois   99

Japan
SIEFFERT, R. Le théâtre japonais   133

RENONDEAU, G. L'influence bouddhique sur les
Nô   163

Viet Nam
TRÂN VÂN KHÉ, Le théâtre vietnamien   203

JACQUOT, J. Craig, Yeats et le Théâtre
d'Orient   271

59 STU   **Proceedings of the Third International Congress on Acoustics**
Stuttgart 1 September 1959
International Commission on Acoustics, International Union of Pure and Applied
Physics
ed. L. Cremer (Amsterdam: Elsevier, 1961)

Vol. i Principles (1961)
3 Speech
MATHEWS, M. V. and GUTTMAN, N. Generation of music by digital computer   253

8 Roomacoustics
BERANEK, L. L. Audience and seat absorption
in halls for music   913
JORDAN, V. L. The building-up process of sound
pulses in a room and its relation to concert hall
quality   922

BURRIS-MEYER, H. and MALLORY, V. Die Verwertung moderner akustischer Methoden zur
Lösung von Problemen des Theaters und der
Oper sowohl klassischen wie auch moderner
Art   967
LUKACS, M. Subjektive Untersuchungen über
den Zusammenhang zwischen der Nachhallzeit
und dem musikalischen Tempo   979
BLAUKOPF, K. Nutzbarmachung neuerer
raumakustischer und electroakustischer
Erkenntnisse für die Musikwissenschaft   983

60 ATH   **Pepragmena tou d' diethnous synedrion aisthētikēs Athēnai 1960/Actes du IV congrès international d'esthétique Athènes 1960** [title also in English, Italian and German]
Athens 1–6 September 1960
International Congress on Aesthetics
ed. P. A. Michelis (Athens: Ellēnikē Organōtikē Epitropē, 1962)

D L'art et la technique moderne
REVAULT d'ALLONES, O.   Techniques modernes et renouvellement esthétique: le cas de la 'Musique concrète'   232

E L'art et la psychologie des profondeurs
OTTO, D.   Musical taste and personality   257

G Méthodes de recherche et vues nouvelles: écrits d'artistes, théorie de l'information, 'semantics', etc.
FRANCÈS, R.   L'information harmonique et les problèmes d'esthétique   353
H L'art, la science, le langage et la musique
JIRÁNEK, J.   About some principal aesthetic pro-

blems of further development of musicological research   422
PUCELLE, J.   La musique et le temps   425
SCHUELLER, H. M.   Musical expression: research in the last two decades   428
SIOHAN, R.   Musique et poésie en quête du hasard   432
SYCHRA, A.   About the problematic of experimental research of musical contents   435

J Méthode et interprétation
FUBINI, E.   L'interpretazione musicale   555

60 PAR[1]   **La résonance dans les échelles musicales**
Paris 9–14 May 1960
Centre national de la recherche scientifique: sciences humaines
ed. E. Weber (Paris: Centre national de la recherche scientifique, 1963)

1 Exposés inauguraux: La résonance dans les échelles musicales
DIDIER, A.   Le point de vue des physiciens   21
TOMATIS, A.   Le point de vue des physiologistes   33
WIORA, W.   Le point de vue des musicologues   37

2 Hypothèses de travail
CHAILLEY, J.   Hypothèses de travail   45

3 Objections et critiques
SIOHAN, R.   Les objections à la résonance   51
TANNER, R.   Critique de la théorie de 'la résonance'   63

4 Présence ou absence de la constante de quarte, de quinte et d'octave: son rôle structurel
HICKMANN, H.   Dans l'antiquité pré-hellénique   103
MACHABEY, A.   Dans la musique grecque antique et la polyphonie occidentale primitive 109
EL MAHDI, S.   Dans la musique orientale non pentatonique   123

WIORA, W.   Dans l'ethnomusicologie primitive   129
MARCEL-DUBOIS, C.   Dans l'ethnomusicologie européenne   143
SCHNEIDER, M.   Dans la consonance polyphonique primitive (la quinte, la quarte et la tierce)   149

5 Les échelles régulières du cycle des quintes et leurs déformations occasionnelles
TRAN VAN KHÊ   Dans le cadre du pentatonique   161
BARKÉCHLI, M.   Dans les cadres non pentatoniques   173

6 Les éléments de formation des échelles extérieurs à la résonance
COSTÈRE, E.   L'attraction   185
CHAILLEY, J.   L'égalisation   191
CANAC, F.   Les facteurs de consonance 199
DANIÉLOU, A.   Les déformations expressives 209
SCHAEFFNER, A.   Le timbre   215
ROUGET, G.   Facture instrumentale et résonance   223

7 Les polysystèmes des musiques de tradition orale
GRIMAUD, Y. Les polysystèmes des musiques de tradition orale peuvent-ils être intégrés à la résonance? 237

8 Le développement de la résonance dans les musiques évoluées
REGAMEY, C. Les théories de l'harmonie moderne 251

CHAILLEY, J. Occident du moyen-âge au XIXᵉ siècle 267
BARTHA, D. Occident au XXᵉ siècle: la musique de Bartok 279

CHAILLEY, J. Synthese et conclusions 291

60 PAR² VIᵉ Congrès international des sciences anthropologiques et ethnologiques
Paris 30 July – 6 August 1960
International Union of Anthropological and Ethnological Sciences
(Paris: Musée de l'Homme, 1962–4)

Vol. ii/2, ed. A. Leroi-Gourhan, P. Champion, M. de Fontanès (1964)
B6 Ethnomusicologie, arts et danses
CARPITELLA, D. Documenti coreutico-musicali sul 'tarantismo' ancora oggi esistente in Puglia 95
CZEKANOWSKA, A. Les anciennes mélodies de noce en Pologne 97
DREYFUS, S. Formes de musiques rituelles chez les Indiens d'Amérique du Sud 101
HYE-KERKDAL, K. Tanz im Alten China 105

de LARREA PALACIN, A. Recherches sur la musique hispano-arabe 107
RAVINA, M. Neue Israelische Folklore 109
REVAULT, J. Note sur les instruments traditionnels de musique populaire dans le Sud tunisien 113
ROUGET, G. Musique 'vodu' (Dahomey) 121
SCHAEFFNER, A. Musiques rituelles Baga 123
WIDSTRAND, C. Skolt Lapp songs of N. E. Finland 127

60 ROM Manierismo, Barocco, Rococò: concetti e termini: Convegno internazionale: relazioni e discussioni
Rome 21–4 April 1960
Classe di scienze morali, storiche e filologiche dell'Accademia nazionale dei Lincei
(Rome: Accademia nazionale dei Lincei, 1962 = Problemi attuali di scienza e di cultura, quaderno 52)

Sezione 'Musica'
DELLA CORTE, A. Il Barocco e la musica 361
BLUME, F. Begriff und Grenzen des Barock in

der Musik (discussion 385) 377
RONGA, L. Il Rococò musicale 387

60 STRT The Modern Composer and his World: a Report from the International Conference of Composers, held at the Stratford Festival, Stratford, Ontario, Canada, August 1960
Stratford August 1960
Canadian League of Composers
ed. J. Beckwith and U. Kasemets (Toronto: University of Toronto Press, 1961)

1 The composer in today's world
Composer and public (papers by LEGLEY, V. 3, KUKHARSKI, V. 5, FRANKENSTEIN, A. The critic's role 8; discussion 12)
Training of composers (papers by SUTERMEISTER, H. Letter to a young aspiring composer 17,

PAPINEAU-COUTURE, J. 20, de la VEGA, A. 24; discussion 32)
Composer and performer (papers by DOBIÁŠ, V. 35, SCHULLER, G. 37, FELDBRILL, V. 40; discussion 43)

2 The composer's métier

Serialism (papers by HAMILTON, I. 49, ROCHBERG, G. Duration in music 56, KRENEK, E. 65; discussion 71)

Some other paths (papers by DUTILLEUX, H. Diversities in contemporary French music 77, MYCIELSKI, Z. 86, REGAMEY, C. 91, SCHULLER, G. 97)

Opera and ballet (papers by BLOMDAHL, K.-B. Aniara 102, BADINGS, H. Experiences with electronic ballet music 106)

Synthetic means (papers by LeCAINE, H. 109, TAL, J. 116, USSACHEVSKY, V. 121; discussion 126)

Form (papers by HOLMBOE, V. On form and metamorphosis 134, BERIO, L. 140; discussion 145)

3 Summary

DUCHOW, M. Conference summary (discussion 157)   151

---

60 WAR[1]   The Book of the First International Musicological Congress devoted to the Works of Frederick Chopin
Warsaw 16–22 February 1960
ed. Z. Lissa (Warsaw: Państwowe Wydawnictwo Naukowe, 1963)

BELZA, I. Natsional'nïye istoki tvorchestva Shopena [National sources of Chopin's works]   23

CHAILLEY, J. L'importance de Chopin dans l'évolution du langage harmonique   30

CHOMIŃSKI, J. M. Die Evolution des Chopinschen Stils   44

HUSMANN, H. Die Stellung der Romantik in der Weltgeschichte der Musik   53

ŁOBACZEWSKA, S. La culture musicale en Pologne au début du XIXe siècle et ses relations avec la musique de Chopin   63

WIORA, W. Chopins Préludes und Etudes und Bachs Wohltemperiertes Klavier   73

1 Criticism of Chopin's style

ABRAHAM, G. Chopin and the orchestra   85

BECHERINI, B. Il dissolvimento della tonalità nelle opere di Federico Chopin   88

BIEGAŃSKI, K. Evolution de l'attitude de Chopin à l'égard du folklore (suivant ses mazurkas)   95

BIELAWSKI, L. Problem krakowiaka w twórczości Chopina [The problem of the Krakowiak in Chopin's works]   100

BOETTICHER, W. Über einige Spätstilprobleme bei Chopin   104

BORRIS, S. Chopins Bedeutung für den Chromatismus des XIX. Jahrhunderts   107

CHAILLEY, J. Une page d'album de Chopin à Emile Gaillard   111

CUKKERMAN, V. De l'emploi des genres et des formes dans l'oeuvre de Chopin   114

CZEKANOWSKA, A. Beiträge zum Problem der Modalität und der sogenannten 'halbchromatischen Leiter' bei Chopin   122

DOBROWOLSKI, J. Organizacja pola dźwiękowego u Chopina [The organization of regions of sound in Chopin]   127

DREYER, E.-J. Melodisches Formelgut bei Chopin   132

EIBNER, F. Die Stimmführung Chopins in der Darstellung Heinrich Schenkers   145

HERNÁDI, L. Einige charakteristische Züge in dem Chopinschen Klaviersatz   168

HŁAWICZKA, K. Ein Beitrag zur Verwandschaft zwischen der Melodik Chopins und der polnischen Volksmusik   176

HŁAWICZKA, K. Eigentümliche Merkmale Chopins Rhythmik   185

KOSZEWSKI, A. Pierwiastek walcowy w twórzości Chopina [The waltz element in Chopin's work]   196

KREMLEV, J. La place historique de l'harmonie de Chopin   202

LISSA, Z. Die Formenkreuzung bei Chopin 207

POCIEJ, B. Rola harmoniki w technice przetworzeniowej Chopina [The role of harmony in Chopin's transformation process]   213

PROSNAK, A. Niektóre zagadnienia wariacyjności etiud Chopina [Questions of variation technique in Chopin's études]   219

PROTOPOPOV, V. Variatsionnost' kak printsip razvitiya v muzïke Shopena [Variation as a principle of development in Chopin's music]   224

SANDELEWSKI, W. Les éléments du 'bel canto' italien dans l'oeuvre de Chopin   230

SKREBKOV, S. Novatorskiye chertï tematicheskovo razvitiya v muzïke Shopena [Innovatory features of thematic development in Chopin's music]   236

SŁAWIŃSKI, A. Rytm a harmonia w polonezach Chopina [Rhythm and harmony in Chopin's polonaises]   241

SOBIESKA, J. and SOBIESKI, M. Das Tempo rubato bei Chopin und in der polnischen Volksmusik   247

TURŁO, T. D. Funkcja harmoniczna figuracji u Chopina [The harmonic function of figuration in Chopin]   255

VOLEK, J. Die Bedutung Chopins für die Ent-

wicklung der alterierten Akkorde in der Musik des XIX. Jahrhunderts 259

2 Stylistic influences

BASSO, A. Chopin et l'esprit de la musique instrumentale baroque 271

CHMARA, B. Das Problem der Agogik der Nocturnos von Field und Chopin 275

CVETKO, D. Chopin chez les Slovènes au XIXᵉ siècle 281

FALCKE, W. Zu Chopins Aufenthalt auf Mallorca und zur Chopin-Überlieferung in Palma und Valldemosa 288

FRĄCZKIEWICZ, A. Koncerty fortepianowe Chopina jako typ koncertu romantycznego [Chopin's piano concertos as a type of Romantic concerto] 293

GAILLARD, P. A. Le lyrisme pianistique de Chopin et ses antécédents directs 297

HELMAN, Z. Wpływ Chopina na wczesną twórczość Karola Szymanowskiego [Chopin's influence on the early works of Szymanowski] 300

JIRÁNEK, J. Beitrag zum Vergleich des Klavierstils von Fryderyk Chopin und Bedřich Smetana 304

KACZYŃSKI, T. Texte poétique en tant que source d'inspiration musicale dans certains chants de Chopin et de Moniuszko 313

KROÓ, G. Einige Probleme des Romantischen bei Chopin und Liszt 319

LADMANOVÁ, M. Chopin und Smetana 324

LEHMANN, D. Satztechnische Besonderheiten in den Klavierwerken von Frédéric Chopin und Robert Schumann 329

LINDLAR, H. Chopin in der deutschen Musikkritik seiner Zeit 334

LISSA, Z. Über die Verbindungen zwischen der Harmonik von A. N. Skrjabin und der Harmonik von F. Chopin 335

MILSTEIN, J. Fortep'yannaya faktura Shopena i Lista [Piano texture in Chopin and Liszt] 341

OČADLÍK, M. Echa twórczości chopinowskiej u Bedřicha Smetany [Echoes of Chopin's works in Smetana] 347

OTTICH, M. Chopin und die Komponisten der nachfolgenden Generationen 350

PAWLISZYN, S. Elementy melodyki ukraińskiej w twórczości Chopina [Ukrainian melodic elements in Chopin's works] 355

PISCHNER, H. Die Bedeutung Chopins für Robert Schumann 363

PROCHÁZKA, J. The origin of 'The Prague Mazurka' in G major and Chopin's relations with Václav Hanka 365

PROSNAK, J. Elementy berżeretki francuskiej, 'sztajerka' i folkloru ukraińskiego w twórczości Chopina [Elements of the French bergerette, the Styrian waltz and Ukrainian folklore in Chopin's works] 374

RACEK, J. Les études faites par Leoš Janáček

dans les compositions pour piano de Frédéric Chopin 383

SIEGMUND-SCHULTZE, W. Chopin und Brahms 388

SÝKORA, V. J. Jan Ladislav Dusík, der älteste Vorgänger Chopins 396

TING SHAN-TEH What makes the Chinese people accept and appreciate Chopin's music 399

TOMASZEWSKI, M. Verbindungen zwischen den Chopinschen Liederwerken und dem polnischen populären Volks- und Kunstlied 404

VANCEA, Z. Der Chopin Schüler Carl Mikuli, ein Bindeglied zwischen rumänischer und polnischer Musikkultur 410

VASINA-GROSSMAN, V. Shopen i 'Moguchaya kuchka' [Chopin and the 'Mighty Handful'] 413

ZIELIŃSKI, T. Forma okresowa w mazurkach Chopina i w mazurkach Szymanowskiego [Periodic form in the mazurkas of Chopin and of Szymanowski] 415

3 Problems of performance

ALEKSEEV, A. Traditsii ispolneniya Shopena v Rossiyi i Sovetskom Soyuze [Performance traditions of Chopin in Russia and the Soviet Union] 421

CHECHLIŃSKA, Z. Das Problem der Form und die reelle Klanggestalt in Chopins Präludien 425

DRZEWIECKI, Z. Le style d'interprétation de Chopin dans la pédagogie polonaise contemporaine 430

HEINITZ, W. Physiologische Beobachtungen zur Werk-Ästhetik F. Chopins 433

HOFFMAN, A. Un grand interprète roumain de la musique de Chopin: Dinu Lipatti 436

KAŃSKI, J. Über die Aufführungsstile der Werke Chopins 444

REINHARD, K. Zur Frage des Tempos bei Chopin 449

URBAŃSKI, J. Das Chopin-Klavier auf der Basis der zeitgenössischen Phonographie 455

4 Editorial and bibliographical

EKIER, J. Le problème d'authenticité de six oeuvres de Chopin 463

HEDLEY, A. Some observations on the autograph sources of Chopin's work 474

KELDISH, J. Sovetskaya shopeniana [Soviet Chopiniana] 478

KOBYLAŃSKA, K. Sur l'histoire des manuscrits de F. Chopin 482

SKORUPSKA, Z. Chopiniana w zbiorach Biblioteki Kórnickiej [Chopiniana in the collections of the Kórnicki library] 488

5 Historical

APEL, W. Der Anfang des Präludiums in Deutschland und Polen 495

BARFUSS, F. Die polnische historische Oper in den Jugendjahren Chopins   503

BELZA, I. Rosyjsko–polskie stosunki muzyczne w wieku XVII i XVIII [Russian–Polish musical relations in the 17th and 18th centuries]   507

BIRKNER, G. Das Sequenzrepertoire in Pclen und die Stellung des Sequenz 'Jesu Christe rex superne'   510

BRENNECKE, W. Johannes Polonus, ein Musiker um 1600   514

ENGELBRECHT, C. Zur Vorgeschichte der Chopinschen Klavierballade   519

FEDERHOFER, H. Musikalische Beziehungen zwischen den Höfen Erzherzog Ferdinands von Innerösterreich und König Sigismunds III von Polen   522

FEICHT, H. Zur Entstehung zweier polnischer 'carmina patria'   527

HALSKI, R. C. The Polish origin of the polka   530

IDASZAK, D. Mazurek w polskiej muzyce XVIII wieku [The mazurka in Polish music of the 18th century]   538

JACQUOT, J. L'organisation internationale des recherches sur la musique pour luth et les sources polonaises   547

KAMIŃSKI, W. Frühmittelalterliche Musikinstrumente auf polnischem Gebiet   551

KMICIC-MIELESZYŃSKI, W. Sprawa pobytu Chopina w Gdańsku [News of Chopin's stay in Gdansk]   559

KRAFT, G. Polnische Folklore im Lied der Vormärz-Bewegung in Deutschland   560

MIAZGA, T. Prosa pro . defunctis 'Audi tellus'   565

MOKRÝ, L. Zu den Anfängen der Mehrstimmigkeit bei den Westslawen   567

MORTENSEN, A. O. The Polish dance in Denmark   572

de NYS, C. Note sur les polonaises de Wilhelm Friedemann Bach   578

PERZ, M. Handschrift Nr. 1361 der Öffentlichen Städtischen Raczyński-Bibliothek in Poznań – als neue Quelle zur Geschichte der polnischen Musik in der II. Hälfte des XV. Jahrhunderts   588

PROKOPOWICZ, M. Musique imprimée à Varsovie en 1800–1830   593

RUDZIŃSKI, W. Źródła stylu muzycznego Stanisława Moniuszki [Sources of Moniuszko's musical style]   598

SALMEN, W. J. F. Reichardt und die osteuropäische Volksmusik   601

SILBERMANN, A. Sozialpsychologische Aspekte im Wandel des Chopin-Idols   604

SNIŽKOVÁ, J. Contribution aux relations tchéco-polonaises au XVIᵉ – XVIIᵉ siècle   608

STADNICKI, K. Polski walc fortepianowy przed Chopinem [The Polish waltz for piano before Chopin]   613

ŠTĚDROŇ, B. Janáček und Polen   618

STESZEWSKA, Z. and STESZEWSKI, J. Zur Genese und Chronologie des Mazurkarhythmus in Polen   624

SUTKOWSKI, A. The Pelplin organ tablature (1620–1630) – a valuable musical document of Polish music culture in late Renaissance   628

SZCZEPAŃSKA, M. Niektóre zagadnienia polskiej muzyki lutniowej XVI wieku [Questions of Polish lute music of the 16th century]   630

SZWEYKOWSKI, Z. Proces przemian stylistycznych w muzyce wokalno-instrumentalnej epoki saskiej [The process of stylistic changes in the vocal and instrumental music of the Saxon era]   633

VOISÉ, W. 'Dodecachordon' d'Henri Glaréan d'après sa correspondance avec Jean Laski (Johannes à Lasco)   638

WILKOWSKA-CHOMIŃSKA, K. Nicolas de Cracovie et la musique de la Renaissance en Pologne   640

6 Problems of aesthetics

CHAINAYE, S. Frédéric Chopin et les Apocryphes   649

FAND, F. Vertu classique de Chopin   654

GAILLARD, P. A. Jugements portés sur Chopin par Mickiewicz d'après le Journal de Caroline Olivier   659

GERMAN, F. Chopin im Lichte unbekannter Memoirenquellen gesehen   662

GLIŃSKI, M. Les lettres de Chopin à Delphine Potocki   669

HORDYŃSKI, W. Nieznany list Chopina do Teresy Wodzińskiej [An unknown letter of Chopin to Teresa Wodzińska]   675

IWASZKIEWICZ, J. Styl literacki listów Chopina [The literary style of Chopin's letters]   679

JAKUBOWSKI, J. Z. Norwid i Chopin   684

KNEPLER, G. Die Bestimmung des Begriffes 'Romantik'   691

KREMLEV, J. L'importance mondiale de l'esthétique de Chopin   696

MOLNÁR, A. Die Persönlichkeit Chopins   701

MOSER, H. J. Chopin stilkundlich betrachtet   707

NOWAK-ROMANOWICZ, A. Ideologia Józefa Elsnera a Chopin [Elsner's ideology and Chopin]   713

SIENKIEWICZ, J. Zapomniany list Chopina (Chopin i Piotr Michałowski) [A forgotten letter of Chopin (Chopin and Piotr Michałowski)   718

SIMONIDES, J. Quelques problèmes des traductions de la correspondance de Frédéric Chopin   721

STARZYŃSKI, J. Chopin – Delacroix (comparaison d'esthétique)   725

SYCHRA, A. Ein Beitrag zur inhaltlichen Deutung von Chopins Schaffen   732

TATARKIEWICZ, W. Prądy filozoficzne epoki Chopina [Philosophical currents in the time of Chopin]   735

60 WAR^2 **Poetics/Poetyka/Poetika** [First International Conference of Work-in-Progress devoted to Problems of Poetics]
Warsaw 18–27 August 1960
Polska akademia nauk: Instytut badań literackich [Polish Academy of Sciences: Institute of Literary Research]
(Warsaw: Państwowe wydawnictwo naukowe/The Hague: Mouton, 1961)

Versification and sound-texture
TROST, P.   Das Metrum der litauischen Volkslieder   119

Problems of intonation
DAVIE, D.   The relation between syntax and music in some modern poems in English   203

The poetics of folklore
DINEKOV, P.   Nekotorïye osobennosti poetiki sovremennoy narodnoy pesni [Some characteristics of the poetics of contemporary folksong   487
ANDREYCHIN, L.   O poetike bolgarskikh narodnïkh pesen [The poetics of Bulgarian folksongs]   501
AUSTERLITZ, R.   The identification of folkloristic genres (based on Gilyak materials)   505
PEUKERT, H.   Die Funktion der Formel im Volkslied   525
DJOUDJEFF, S.   Vestiges de la métrique ancienne dans le folklore bulgare   537

Les colloques de Wégimont IV [= V] 1958–60: Ethnomusicologie III [+ IV]
Wégimont 4–10 September 1960

see 58 WÉG

61 BUD   Liszt – Bartók: Bericht über die zweite internationale musikwissenschaftliche Konferenz / Report of the Second International Musicological Conference
Budapest 25–30 September 1961
Magyar tudományos akadémia [Hungarian Academy of Sciences]
ed. Z. Gárdonyi and B. Szabolcsi, *Studia musicologica Academiae scientiarum hungaricae*, v (Budapest: Akadémiai kiadó, 1963; also published separately Budapest: Akadémiai kiadó, 1963)

Sőtér, I. Le populisme dans la littérature et la musique   11

Ferenc Liszt
Buchner, A. Liszt in Prag   27
Chomiński, J. M. Einige Probleme der Klangtechnik von Liszt   37
Federhofer, H. Die Diminution in den Klavierwerken von Chopin und Liszt   49
Felix, W. Liszts Schaffen um 1848 – Versuch zur Deutung seiner Programmatik   59
Gardavský, Č. Liszt und seine tschechischen Lehrer   69
Gárdonyi, Z. Nationale Thematik in der Musik Franz Liszts bis zum Jahre 1848   77
Goldhammer, O. Liszt, Brahms und Reményi   89
Helm, E. A newly discovered Liszt-manuscript   101
Hoffman, A. and Missir, N. Sur la tournée de concerts de Ferenc Liszt en 1846–47 dans le Banat, la Transylvanie et les pays roumains   107
Hrabussay, Z. Correspondance de Liszt avec des musiciens de Slovaquie   125
Hudec, V. Zum Problem des 'Lisztartigen' in Smetanas symphonischen Dichtungen 131
Jiránek, J. Liszt und Smetana   139
Kraft, G. Das Schaffen von Franz Liszt in Weimar   193
Lehmann, D. Bemerkungen zur Liszt-Rezeption in Russland in den vierziger und fünfziger Jahren des 19. Jahrhunderts 211
Michel, P. Franz Liszt als Lehrer und Erzieher   217
Molnár, A. Über Transkriptionen und Paraphrasen von Liszt   227
Nováček, Z. Liszts Bedeutung in den fortschrittlichen musikalischen Bewegungen Bratislavas   233
Očadlik, M. Die radikalen Demokraten – Liszt und Smetana   241
Petrov, S. Proizvedeniya Ferentsa Lista v Bolgarii [Liszt's works in Bulgaria]   249
Poštolka, M. Liszt und Böhmen im Spiegel der unveröffentlichten Korrespondenz 255
Rackwitz, W. Liszts Verhältnis zur Musik Georg Friedrich Händels   267

Searle, H. Liszt and 20th century music 277
Somfai, L. Die Metamorphose der 'Faust-Symphonie' von Liszt   283
Štědroň, B. Leoš Janáček und Ferenc Liszt   295
Suppan, W. Liszt und die Steiermark   301
Szelényi, I. Der unbekannte Liszt   311
Gárdonyi, Z. Schlusswort der Liszt-Sektion   333

Béla Bartók
Abraham, G. Bartók and England   339
Bodnár, G. Bartók et le mouvement 'Nyugat'   347
Bónis, F. Quotations in Bartók's music 355
Burlas, L. Neuerertum und Tradition in Bartóks Formenwelt   383
Chao Feng Bartók and Chinese music culture   393
Demény, J. Béla Bartóks Stellung in der Musikgeschichte des 20. Jahrhunderts 403
Dille, D. Les problèmes des recherches sur Bartók   415
Gorczycka, M. Neue Merkmale der Klangtechnik in Bartóks Streichquartetten 425
Járdányi, P. Bartók und die Ordnung der Volkslieder   435
Kerényi, G. and Rajeczky, B. Über Bartóks Volksliedaufzeichnungen   441
Kroó, G. Monothematik und Dramaturgie in Bartóks Bühnenwerken   449
Lesznai, L. Realistische Ausdrucksmittel in der Musik Béla Bartóks   469
Nest'yev, I. V. Bela Bartok v Rossii [Bartók in Russia]   481
Petrov, S. Bela Bartok i bolgarskaya musïkal'naya kul'tura [Bartók and Bulgarian musical culture]   491
Racek, J. Leoš Janáčeks und Béla Bartóks Bedeutung in der Weltmusik   501
Saygun, A. A. Quelques réflexions sur certaines affinités des musiques folkloriques turque et hongroise   515
Szabolcsi, B. Mensch und Natur in Bartóks Geisteswelt   525
Ujfalussy, J. Einige inhaltliche Fragen der Brückensymmetrie in Bartóks Werken 541
Vancea, Z. Einige Beiträge über das erste Ma-

nuskript der Colinda-Sammlung von Béla Bartók und über seine einschlägigen Briefe an
Constantin Brăiloiu 549
VOLEK, J. Über einige interessante Beziehungen
zwischen thematischer Arbeit und In-

strumentation in Bartóks Concerto für Orchester 557
WEISSMANN, J. On some problems of Bartók
research in connection with Bartók's biography 587

61 CAM/M   **Chanson & Madrigal 1480–1530: Studies in Comparison and Contrast: a
Conference at Isham Memorial Library**
Cambridge, Massachusetts 13–14 September 1961
Department of Music, Harvard University
ed. J. Haar (Cambridge, Mass.: Harvard University Press, 1964 = Isham Library
Papers 2)

BROWN, H. M. The genesis of a style: the
Parisian chanson, 1500–1530 (panel THIBAULT,
G., POPE-CONANT, I., LESURE, F.) 1
RUBSAMEN, W. H. From frottola to madrigal:
the changing pattern of secular Italian vocal

music (panel BRIDGMAN, N., D'ACCONE, F. A.,
PIRROTTA, N.) 51
HEARTZ, D. Les goûts réunis, or the worlds of
the madrigal and the chanson confronted (panel
HERTZMANN, E., JOHNSON, A., PALISCA, C.)
88

61 COL   **IV. Internationaler Kongress für Kirchenmusik in Köln**
Cologne 22–30 June 1961
Allgemeiner Cäcilien-Verband für die Länder der deutschen Sprache
ed. J. Overath (Cologne: Sekretariat des Allgemeinen Cäcilien-Verbandes,
1962 = Schriftenreihe des Allgemeinen Cäcilien-Verbandes für die Länder der
deutschen Sprache 4)

BALLIN, E. D. H. Urheberrecht am Scheideweg
(English 92, French 97) 87
SCHULZE, E. Kirchenmusik und Urheberrecht
(English 108, French 114) 102
KRINGS, A. Zur Aufführung von Kirchenmusik
des Mittelalters und der Renaissance 127
ROMITA, F. De institutis musicae sacrae eri-
gendis ad eiusdem musicae sacrae re-
staurationem juxta S. Pium X (German
142) 132

Musik der ostkirchlichen Liturgien
DI SALVO, B. Dall'essenza della musica nelle
liturgie orientali 155
TOZTKE, I. Unsere Verpflichtung gegenüber der
ostkirchlichen Musik 161

Musik der römischen Messliturgie
EBEL, B. Grundlagen des Verhältnisses von Kult
und Gesang (English 173, French 183, Italian
193) 163
LENAERTS, R. B. M. Probleme der Messe in
ihrer historischen Sicht (English 212, French

220, Italian 228) 202

Kirchenmusik in den Missionsländern
COUTURIER, C. Dimensions de l'adaptation
(German 242) 236
NOMURA, F. Y. Akkommodation und Kirchen-
musikpflege in Japan 247
OUEDRAOGHO, R. Rapport sur la musique re-
ligieuse au Mossi (German 268) 251
ALBUQUERQUE, W. Südindische klassische und
Volksmusik: die Ursprünge der indischen
Musik in der Legende 287
ALVARES, V. The apostleship of music with
regard to a fruitful missionary future in
India 304

Musikerziehung
WECHNER, B. Die kirchenmusikalische Er-
ziehung des Welt- und Ordensklerus 312
SMITS van WAESBERGHE, J. Die Ausbildung des
Kirchenmusikers 319
RONAN, J. E. Musical education and cathedral
choir schools 328

61 FLOR   **Arte pensiero e cultura a Mantova nel primo Rinascimento in rapporto con la Toscana e con il Veneto: Atti del VI convegno internazionale di studi sul Rinascimento**
Florence, Venice, Mantua 27 September – 1 October 1961
Istituto nazionale di studi sul Rinascimento, Florence
(Florence: G. C. Sansoni, 1965)

GALLICO, C. Civiltà musicale mantovana intorno al 1500   243

61 JER   **Third World Congress of Jewish Studies: Report**
Jerusalem 25 July – 1 August 1961
World Union of Jewish Studies; Hebrew University of Jerusalem
(Jerusalem: World Union of Jewish Studies, 1965)

[English résumés only; full Hebrew versions printed elsewhere in the volume]
Folklore and folk-art
ADLER, J. Le ms Vm¹ de la Bibliothèque nationale (Cantate pour une circoncision dans le Comtat venaissin au dix-septième siècle) 360
BAR-DAYAN, H. Music in the life of Vilna Jewry   360
EVENARI, H. 'Who is on Mount Horeb?' – a Piyyut and its melody from the Geniza   362

BAYER, B. Musical relics in Palestinian archaeology   364
SPECTOR, J. Problems of compatibility: non-western versus western traditions in Jewish music   365
GESHURI, M. S. Chants used in the study of the Talmud by Ashkenazi and oriental Jews 366
HERZOG, A. The Tora readings according to the Israeli Sephardic mode   369
GERSON-KIWI, E. Halleluia and Jubilus in oriental Jewish and Christian chant   371

61 NEWY   **Report of the Eighth Congress New York 1961**
New York 5–10 September 1961
International Musicological Society
ed. J. LaRue (Kassel and Basle: Bärenreiter, 1961–2)

Vol. i: Papers (1961)
Round tables
ANGLÈS, H. Der Rhythmus in der Melodik mittelalterlicher Lyrik   3
(chairman CHAILLEY, J.; discussion ii, 43)
STÄBLEIN, B. Die Unterlegung von Texten unter Melismen: Tropus, Sequenz und andere Formen   12
(chairman REICHERT, G.; discussion ii, 48)
GUDEWILL, K. Ursprünge und nationale Aspekte des Quodlibets   30
(chairman PLAMENAC, D.; discussion ii, 53)
LOWINSKY, E. E. Awareness of tonality in the 16th century   44
(chairman REESE, G.; discussion ii, 58)
ANTONOWYTCH, M. The present state of Josquin research   53
(chairman OSTHOFF, H.; discussion ii, 64)
VERCHALY, A. La métrique et le rythme musical au temps de l'humanisme   66
(chairman POPE-CONANT, I.; discussion ii, 67)
JACQUOT, J. La musique pour luth   75
(chairman NOSKE, F.; discussion ii, 72)

BRITTON, A. P. The singing school movement in the United States   89
(chairman LOWENS, I.; discussion ii, 77)
AUSTIN, W. Traditional forms in new musical idioms   100
(chairman MERSMANN, H.; discussion ii, 80)
WINTERNITZ, E. The visual arts as a source for the historian of music   109
(chairman THIBAULT, G.; discussion ii, 84)
WELLEK, A. Der gegenwärtige Stand der Musikpsychologie und ihre Bedeutung für die historische Musikforschung   121
(chairman DRÄGER, H.-H.; discussion ii, 88)
WEVER, E. G. The physiological bases of musical hearing: present state and problems of research   133
(chairman HUSMANN, H.; discussion ii, 93)
WACHSMANN, K. Criteria for acculturation 139
(chairman de AZEVEDO, L. H. C.; discussion ii, 97)
STEVENS, D. Problems of editing and publishing old music   150
(chairman BRODER, N.; discussion ii, 101)

Symposia

SCHNEIDER, M. Wurzeln und Anfänge der abendländischen Mehrstimmigkeit   161
WAITE, W. G. The era of melismatic polyphony   178
(chairman WIORA, W.; discussion ii, 107)

von FISCHER, K. Der Begriff des 'Neuen' in der Musik von der Ars nova bis zur Gegenwart   184
EGGEBRECHT, H. H. Der Begriff des 'Neuen' in der Musik von der Ars nova bis zur Gegenwart   195
(chairman LANG, P. H.; discussion ii, 112)

FELLERER, K. G. Beziehungen zwischen geistlicher und weltlicher Musik im 16. Jahrhundert   203
BOETTICHER, W. Zum Parodieproblem bei Orlando di Lasso   214
(chairman LENAERTS, R. B.; discussion ii, 118)

PINCHERLE, M. Des manières d'exécuter la musique aux XVIIᵉ et XVIIIᵉ siècles   220
DART, T. Performance practice in the 17th and 18th centuries: six problems in instrumental music   231
(chairman WESTRUP, J. A.; discussion ii, 122)

von DADELSEN, G. Bach-Probleme   236
EMERY, W. On evidence of derivation   249
(chairman MENDEL, A.; discussion ii, 127)

HUCKE, H. Die neapolitanische Tradition in der Oper   253
DOWNES, E. O. D. The Neapolitan tradition in opera   277
(chairman GHISI, F.; discussion ii, 132)

ENGEL, H. Die Quellen des klassischen Stiles   285
FEDER, G. Bemerkungen über die Ausbildung der klassischen Tonsprache in der Instrumentalmusik Haydns   305
(chairman LARSEN, J. P.; discussion ii, 135)

ABERT, A. A. Liszt, Wagner und die Beziehungen zwischen Musik und Literatur im 19. Jahrhundert   314
GUICHARD, L. Liszt, Wagner et les relations entre la musique et la littérature au XIXᵉ siècle   323
(chairman BERNET KEMPERS, K. P.; discussion ii, 140)

LESURE, E. Pour une sociologie historique des faits musicaux   333
HARRISON, F. Ll. The social position of church musicians in England   346
(chairman WINTERNITZ, E.; discussion ii, 146)

de AZEVEDO, L. H. C. Survivance et développement des diverses traditions européennes dans le continent américain   356
SEEGER, C. The cultivation of various European traditions in the Americas   364
(chairman SMITH, C. S.; discussion ii, 150)

SCHAEFFNER, A. Contribution de l'ethnomusicologie à l'histoire de la musique   376
SCHIØRRING, N. The contribution of ethnomusicology to historical musicology   380
(chairman COLLAER, P.; discussion ii, 153)

HÜSCHEN, H. Frühere und heutige Begriffe von Wesen und Grenzen der Musik   386
BABBITT, M. Past and present concepts of the nature and limits of music   398
(chairman FELLERER, K. G.; discussion ii, 158)

REINECKE, H. Musikwissenschaft und Schallplatte   404
MILLER, P. L. Musicology and the phonograph record   418
(chairman ABRAHAM, G.; discussion ii, 163)

THIBAULT, G. Du rôle de l'ornementation, improvisée ou écrite, dans l'évolution de la musique   425
ROUGET, G. Note sur l'ornementation en Afrique noire   427
CORBIN, S. Note sur l'ornementation dans le plain-chant gregorien   428
MARCEL-DUBOIS, C. Remarques sur l'ornementation dans l'ethnomusicologie européenne   439
TRAN VAN KHÊ Note sur l'ornementation au Vietnam   445
THIBAULT, G. L'ornementation dans la musique profane au moyen-âge   450
FERAND, E. T. A history of music seen in the light of ornamentation   463
(chairman DONINGTON, R.; discussion ii, 166)

Vol. ii: Reports (1962)
Public addresses
MENDEL, A. Evidence and explanation   3
BRIDGMAN, N. Mécénat et musique   19
OSTHOFF, H. Der Durchbruch zum musikalischen Humanismus   31

61 OKḤ   Actes du XII congrès d'études byzantines
Okhrida 10–16 September 1961
International Association for Byzantine Studies
(Belgrade: Naučno Delo, 1963–4)

Vol. i (1963)
WELLESZ, E. Melody construction in Byzantine chant (supplementary papers STRUNK, O. 365, STEFANOVIĆ, D. 375)   135

Vol. ii (1964)
Musicologie
FLOROS, C. Fragen zum musikalischen und metrischen Aufbau der Kontakien   563
LEVY, K. The Byzantine Communion-cycle and its Slavic counterpart   571

MARZI, G. Martyria e incipit nelle tradizione nomica   575
MILOJKOVIĆ-DJURIĆ, J. On the Serbian chant in the eighteenth century after the neumatic manuscripts from Chilandar   583
PEJOVIĆ, R. Instruments de musique dans l'art serbo-macedonien et byzantin   589
RAASTED, J. The production of Byzantine musical manuscripts   601
THODBERG, C. Chromatic alterations in the Sticherarium   607

61 TEH   The Preservation of Traditional Forms of the Learned and Popular Music of the Orient and the Occident: International Congress/La préservation des formes traditionalles [sic] de la musique savante et populaire dans les pays d'orient et d'occident: congrès international
Teheran 6–12 April 1961
International Music Council
ed. W. K. Archer (Urbana, Illinois: Center for Comparative Psycholinguistics, Institute of Communications Research, University of Illinois, 1964)

BORNOFF, J. The Teheran Congress   21
ARCHER, W. K. Introduction: The Musical Bride: some applications of evolution, culture and tradition   27
BARKÉCHLI, M. Introduction to the International Congress   49
BAUD-BOVY, S. The problems of the preservation of traditional forms   58
BRAGARD, R. Les musées instrumentaux, moyens de préservation des formes traditionnelles de la musique savante et populaire dans le pays d'orient et d'occident   63
CANAC, F. Faithfulness in the transmission of music as a means of preservation   73
CHAILLEY, J. Musique orientale et harmonie européenne   83
CHARPENTIER, J. Les musiques orientales peuvent-elles susciter des formes nouvelles chez les compositeurs occidentaux?   89
COWELL, H. The composer's world   99
CROSSLEY-HOLLAND, P. Music of the occidental type written by orientals   114
CVETKO, D. Les transformations sociales avant une influence sur la vie du musicien et sur sa position dans la société   125
DANIÉLOU, A. Establishment of the distinction between the main 'families' of music, according to the different fundamental systems   132
EL MAHDI, S. Les problèmes de la preservation des formes traditionnelles   141
GERSON-KIWI, E. The integration of dastgah and maqam in oriental–Jewish liturgies   146
HACOBIAN, Z. La tendance à l'hybridation: l'influence des conceptions occidentales   148

KÁRPÁTI, J. Quelques notes sur la musique traditionnelle et folklorique dans différentes régions du Maroc   163
TRẦN VAN KHÊ Basic principles of musical expression as they are found in modal music in the Far East   171
KOIZUMI, F. Contemporary music in occidental style and its problems in Japan   184
MENON, N. Basic principles of musical expression as they are found in the music of India   190
NKETIA, J. H. Continuity of traditional instruction   203
REINHARD, K. Cooperation with the musician – prospection, conservation, transcription and publication, classification   214
SAYGUN, A. A. Basic principles of musical expression as they are to be found in the modal music of the Middle East   222
SCHNEIDER, M. Basic principles: the variation, orient – occident   231
SPIRA, Y. Developments in Israel   240
STANISLAV, J. Some remarks on the development of musical creation among African peoples   244
VAZIRI, A.-N. Notation: means for the preservation or destruction of music traditionally not notated   251
VINOGRADOV, V. The experience of applying folk music traditions to professional music in the eastern republics of the U.S.S.R.   258
YUIZE, S. Means of preservation: preservation of traditional instruction   279
Discussion (chairman CHAILLEY, J.)   289

61 TOD   Pellegrinaggi e' culto dei santi in Europa fino alla 1ª Crociata: Convegni del Centro di studi
sulla spiritualità medievale IV
Todi 8–11 October 1961
Centro di studi sulla spiritualità medievale
(Todi: Accademia Tudertina, 1963)

MONTEROSSO, R.   Il culto dei Santi nella tradizione musicale medievale liturgica ed extralitur-
gica   181

61 TOK   Music – East and West: Report on 1961 Tokyo East–West Music Encounter Conference
Tokyo 17–22 April 1961
(Tokyo: Executive Committee for 1961 Tokyo East–West Encounter, 1961)

Music – East and West
SINGH, T. J.   The music of India   1
DANIÉLOU, A.   The music of India   5
SHIBA, S.   The music of Japan (gagaku)   9
YUIZE, S.   The music of Japan   15
GARFIAS, R.   Some effects of changing social
values on Japanese music   18
HOOD,.M.   The music of Indonesia   23
NOMURA, Y.   Religious music   26
CROSSLEY-HOLLAND, P.   Operatic and ballet
music   30
TOYAMA, K.   Concerts in Japan   36
SCHRADE, L.   Music's place in western life   40
DRAEGER, H. H.   Liturgical and religious
music   47
CROSSLEY-HOLLAND, P.   Asian music under the
impact of western culture   50
TRAN VAN KHE   Problems of Sino-Japanese
musical tradition today   54
McPHEE, C.   The music crisis in Bali today   60
DANIÉLOU, A.   Problems of Indian music tradi-
tion today   64
VISWANATHAN, T.   Problems of Indian music
tradition today   67
COWELL, H.   Oriental influence on western
music   71
SAKKA, K.   Western music in Japan   77
BHATIA, V.   Western music in India   82
MACEDA, J.   Western music in the Phillip-
pines   86
BEKKU, S.   The composer in Japan today   91
HIRASHIMA,M.   The   composer   in   Japan
today   99

Music education
STUCKENSCHMIDT, H. H.   Instruction in music as
part of general education   107
FRANKENSTEIN, A.   Instruction in music as part
of general education   110
ROY, R. L.   Instruction in music as part of
general education   115

ARIMA, D.   Musical education as part of general
education   119
CVETKO, D.   Instruction in music as part of
general education   123

Renewing the musical language
CARTER, E.   Extending the classical syntax 126
MOROI, M.   Electronic music   130
XENAKIS, I.   Stochastic music   134
HARRISON, L.   Refreshing the auditory per-
ception   141
THOMSON, V.   The philosophy of style   144
MIYAGI, M.   Renewing the musical language –
an eastern view   147
GRIMAUD, Y.   Notes on some aesthetic problems
of our time   152

Patronage of music
NOMURA, K.   Problems of music patronage in
the East   155
SINGH, T. J.   Patronage of music in India   159
SEEFEHLNER, E.   Patronage of music in the West:
the role of the maecenas in Europe   161
HAREWOOD   Patronage   of   music   in   the
West   165

Music and society
SINGH, T. J.   Presenting the eastern tradition
under conditions of mass distribution   170
TRAN VAN KHE   Presenting the eastern tradition under conditions of mass distribution 173
KITAZAWA, M.   Situation of creative art in the
industrial society   178
KELEMEN, M.   Situation of creative art in the
industrial society   181

Discussions
Music   and   listener   (chairman   STUCKEN-
SCHMIDT, H. H.)   183
Critics' forum (chairman THOMSON, V.)   202

62 BERN   Kirchenmusik in ökumenischer Schau: 2. internationaler Kongress für Kirchenmusik in Bern: Kongressbericht
Berne 22–9 September 1962
(Berne: Paul Haupt, 1964 = Publikationen der Schweizerischen Musikforschenden Gesellschaft ii/11)

ANGLÈS, H. Das Alte und das Neue in der heutigen Kirchenmusik und die Vereinigung der Christen 9

SÖHNGEN, O. Musik und Theologie 15

STIRNIMANN, H. Ökumenische Gedanken zur Kirchenmusik 21

GEORGIADES, T Sprachschichten in der Kirchenmusik 24

KOVALEVSKY, M. La musique liturgique orthodoxe russe 32

BOMM, U. Gregorianischer Choral als Kultgesang 38

SCHWEIZER, J. Vom legitimen Ort kirchlicher Musik im Gottesdienst der reformierten Kirchen der deutschen Schweiz 43

AMELN, K. Die Wurzeln des deutschen Kirchenliedes der Reformation 47

PIDOUX, P. Ergebnisse der Forschungen um den Hugenotten-Psalter 51

STÄBLEIN, B. Das Wesen des Tropus 55

WAGNER, J. Neue Aufgaben der katholischen Kirchenmusik im Zeitalter der pastoralliturgischen Erneuerung 60

BLANKENBURG, W. Offizielle und inoffizielle liturgische Bestrebungen in der Evangelischen Kirche Deutschlands 64

BRUNNER, A. Liturgisch-musikalische Möglichkeiten im reformierten Gottesdienst 68

GELINEAU, J. Psalmodie populaire 74

ZIMMERMANN, H. W. Neue Musik und Anbetung 79

LAURENT Neue Formen der Anbetung 84

DUFOURCQ, N. Interdépendance de la facture et de la musique d'orgue en France sous le règne de Louis XIV 88

KLOTZ, H. A propos de l'orgue de 1500 environ, de l'orgue brabançon de 1550 et de la manière de les jouer 91

JAKOB, F. Tendenzen des heutigen Orgelbaus 96

62 COP   Fourth International Congress on Acoustics
Copenhagen 21–8 August 1962
International Commission on Acoustics, International Union of Pure and Applied Physics
(Copenhagen: Organization Committee of the Fourth International Congress on Acoustics, 1962)
Congress Report I of the Fourth International Congress on Acoustics: Copenhagen, 1962: Contributed Papers, ed. A Kjerbye Nielsen (1962)

P5 Musical acoustics

LEIPP, E. La cavité buccale, paramètre sensible des spectres rayonnés par les instruments à vent 51

MARTIN, D. W. Musical implications of standardized tuning frequency 52

MEYER, J. Unharmonische Komponenten im 'Klang der Orgelpfeifen' 53

PIKLER, A. G. Musical transfer functions 54

PLOMP, R. and LEVELT, W. J. M. Musical consonance and critical bandwidth 55

M Room acoustics

KNUDSEN, V. O. Acoustics of music rooms 27

WINCKEL, F. Über den Einfluss der Deckenhöhe auf die Klangqualität in Konzertsälen 37

The Fourth International Congress on Acoustics: Congress Report II (1962) [Invited papers]

BERANEK, L. L. Rating of acoustical quality of concert halls and opera houses 15

YOUNG, R. W. A decade of musical acoustics 231

62 KAS   Bericht über den internationalen musikwissenschaftlichen Kongress Kassel 1962
Kassel 30 September – 4 October 1962
Gesellschaft für Musikforschung
ed. G. Reichert and M. Just (Kassel and Basle: Bärenreiter, 1963)

Generalthemen

Generalthema I: Die musikalischen Gattungen und ihr sozialer Hintergrund (chairman GERST-ENBERG, W.)
ENGEL, H. Die musikalischen Gattungen und ihr sozialer Hintergrund   3
WIORA, W. Die musikalischen Gattungen und ihr sozialer Hintergrund   15

von DADELSEN, G. Die Vermischung musikalischer Gattungen als soziologisches Problem   23
REANEY, G. The isorhythmic motet and its social background   25
ZIMMERMAN, F. B. Social backgrounds of the Restoration anthem   27
BUŽGA, J. Die soziale Lage des Musikers im Zeitalter des Barocks in den böhmischen Ländern und ihr Einfluss auf seine künstlerischen Möglichkeiten   28
YOUNG, P. M. Johann Christian Bach and his English environment   32
RIEDEL, F. W. Der 'Reichsstil' in der deutschen Musikgeschichte des 18. Jahrhunderts   34
FINSCHER, L. Zur Sozialgeschichte des klassischen Streichquartetts   37

Generaltheme II: Die Musik von 1830 bis 1914 (chairman OSTHOFF, H.)
BLUME, F. Die Musik von 1830 bis 1914: Strukturprobleme einer Epoche   40

WESTRUP, J. A. Die Musik von 1830 bis 1914 in England   51
OREL, A. Die Musik von 1830 bis 1914 in Österreich   54
WALLNER, B. Die Nationalromantik: Die Musik von 1830 bis 1914 in den Skandanavischen Ländern   60
HONEGGER, M. La musique française de 1830 à 1914   66
LOWENS, I. Amerikanische Demokratie und die Amerikanische Musik von 1830 bis 1914   74
CVETKO, D. Die Situation und die Probleme der slowenischen, kroatischen und serbischen Musik des 19. Jahrhunderts   80
STANTSCHEWA-BRASCHOWANOWA, L. Die Musik von 1830 bis 1914 in Bulgarien   85
GÁRDONYI, Z. Die Musik von 1830 bis 1914 in Ungarn   91

Freie Forschungsberichte
Antike / Mittelalter / 1450–1600 (chairman MÜL-LER-BLATTAU, J.)
VOGEL, M. Die Entstehung der Kirchentonarten   101

WENDLER, J. Zur Formeltechnik des einstimmigen mittelalterlichen Liedes   106
GÜNTHER, U. Das Ende der 'ars nova'   108
REICHLING, A. Die Präambeln der Hs. Erlangen 554 und ihre Beziehung zur Sammlung Ileborghs   109
JUST, M. 'Ysaac de manu sua'   112
PÄTZIG, G. Heinrich Isaacs 'Choralis Constantinus' – eine posthume Werksammlung   . 114
KIRSCH, W. Grundzüge der Te Deum-Vertonungen im 15. und. 16. Jahrhundert 117

1450–1600 (chairman BERNET KEMPERS, K. P.)
HOFFMANN-ERBRECHT, L. Heinrich Finck in Polen   119
RUBSAMEN, W. H. Sebastian Festa and the early madrigal   122
MEIER, B. 'Hieroglyphisches' in der Musik des 16. Jahrhunderts   127
STALMANN, J. Die reformatorische Musikschauung des Johann Walter   129
NIEMÖLLER, K. W. Grundzüge einer Neubewertung der Musik an den Lateinschulen des 16. Jahrhunderts   133
DÜRR, W. Zur mehrstimmigen Behandlung des chromatischen Schrittes in der Polyphonie des 16. Jahrhunderts   136
DEBES, L. H. Über den Stand der Forschungen zu Claudio Merulo   138
BOETTICHER, W. Zum Problem der Übergangsperiode der Musik 1580–1620   141
HIEKEL, H. O. 'Tactus' und Tempo   145

1600–1830 (chairman ABERT, A. A.)
FEININGER, L. Die katholische Kirchenmusik in Rom zwischen 1600 und 1800: eine unfassbare Lacune in der Musikgeschichte   147
KOLNEDER, W. Zur Frühgeschichte des Solokonzerts   149
MASSENKEIL, G. Über die Messen Giacomo Carissimis   152
BRAUN, W. Zur Parodie im 17. Jahrhundert   154
GERSTENBERG, W. 'Andante'   156
HAMANN, H. W. Neue Quellen zur Johann Joseph Fux-Forschung   158
RUHNKE, M. Zum Stand der Telemann-Forschung   161
SIEGELE, U. Zur Verbindung von Präludium und Fuge bei J. S. Bach   164
HECKLINGER, D. Tanzrhythmik als konstitutives Element in Bachs Vokalmusik   167
SIEDENTOPF, H. Zu J. S. Bachs Klaviersatz mit obligaten Stimmen: Instrument und Spieltechnik   170

MANN, A. Händels Fugenlehre – ein unveröffentliches Manuskript 172

1600–1830 (chairman REICHERT, G.)

HOLSCHNEIDER, A. Die musikalische Bibliothek Gottfried van Swietens 174

JURISCH, H. Zur Dynamik im Klavierwerk Ph. E. Bachs 178

FEDER, G. Zwei Haydn zugeschriebene Klaviersonaten 181

PLATH, W. Über Skizzen zu Mozarts 'Requiem' 184

PALM, A. Mozart und Haydn in der Interpretation Momignys 187

PFANNKUCH, W. Sonatenform und Sonatenzyklus in den Streichquartetten von Joseph Martin Kraus 190

MACHATIUS, F.-J. 'Eroica' (das transzendentale Ich) 193

KAISER, F. Die authentischen Fassungen des D-dur-Konzertes op. 61 von Ludwig van Beethoven 196

FEIL, A. Zur Rhythmik Schuberts 198

ELVERS, R. Rudolf Werckmeister, ein Berliner Musikverleger 1802-1809 200

1830–1914 (chairman FELLERER, K. G.)

SALMEN, W. Die Auswirkung von Ideen und Kompositionen Reichardts im 19. Jahrhundert 202

MOHR, W. Über Mischformen und Sonderbildungen der Variationsform 205

WERNER, E. Mendelssohns Kirchenmusik und ihre Stellung im 19. Jahrhundert 207

OTT, A. Die 'Ungarischen Rhapsodien' von Franz Liszt 210

JONAS, O. Eine private Brahms-Sammlung und ihre Bedeutung für die Brahms-Werkstatt-Erkenntnis 212

MIES, P. Über ein besonderes Akzentzeichen bei Joh. Brahms 215

KROSS, S. Rhythmik und Sprachbehandlung bei Brahms 217

FELLINGER, I. Zum Problem der Zeitmasse in Brahms' Musik 219

OSTHOFF, W. Die zwei Fassungen von Verdis 'Simon Boccanegra' 222

LIEBNER, J. Der Einfluss Schillers auf Verdi 222

1830–1914 (chairman ENGEL, H.)

KAST, P. Die Autographensammlung Campori und ihre musikalischen Schätze 226

WEYLER, W. Die Frage der flämischen Musik: ein Beitrag zur Klärung einer Begriffsverwirrung 229

SUPPAN, W. Die Romantische Ballade als Abbild des Wagnerschen Musikdramas 233

STOLLBERG, O. Die musikalisch-liturgische Bewegung in der zweiten Hälfte des 19. Jahrhunderts im Spiegel unbekannter Briefe und Aufzeichnungen dieser Zeit 236

MUELLER von ASOW, H. Komponierende Frauen 239

LIESS, A. Der junge Debussy und die russische Musik 241

BENARY, P. Das impressionistische Raumgefühl als Stilfaktor bei Debussy 244

KLUSEN, E. Gustav Mahler und das böhmisch-mährische Volkslied 246

Musik nach 1914 (chairman HÜSCHEN, H.)

LINDLAR, H. Debussysmen beim frühen Strawinsky 252

BORRIS, S. Strukturanalyse von Weberns 'Symphonie' op. 21 253

FLOROS, C. Kompositionstechnische Probleme der atonalen Musik 257

BERGMANN, R. Das Problem der Jazzmusik im heutigen Musikleben 260

SCHÄFFER, B. Präexistente und inexistente Strukturen 263

Systematisches/Pädagogisches (chairman WIORA, W.)

NEUMANN, F. Die Zeitgestalt als Grundbegriff der musikalischen Rhythmik 268

BERNET KEMPERS, K. P. Versuch eines vertieften Einblicks in den musikalischen Organismus 271

DAHLHAUS, C. Intervalldissonanz und Akkorddissonanz 272

BRENN, F. Tonsysteme in Equiton und Fawcettzahlen 275

BENGTSSON, I. Über Korrelation zwischen Durationsvariable und Rhythmuserlebnis 276

REINECKE, H.-P. Zur Frage der Anwendbarkeit der Informationstheorie auf tonpsychologische Probleme 279

NOLL, G. Jean-Jacques Rousseau als Musikerzieher 282

HERDIECKERHOFF, U. Die wissenschaftliche Selbstbegründung der Musikpädagogik 284

METZLER, F. Takt und Rhythmus in der freien Melodieerfindung des Grundschulkindes 286

HAMANN, F. Die Arbeit der Seminar-Musiklehrer und die Bedeutung dieses Standes für die Musikkultur 290

Methodisches/Instrumentenkundliches (chairman von DADELSEN, G.)

BECK, H. Zur musikalischen Analyse 291

HEINITZ, W. Zeitgemässe Aufführungsprobleme 293

MAXTON, W. Können die 'Denkmäler Deutscher Tonkunst' uns heute noch als Quellen zweiter Ordnung dienen? 295

BOSE, F. Die Fabrikation der nordischen Bronzeluren 298

BECKER, H. Zur Spielpraxis der griechischen Aulos 300

DROYSEN, D. Die Darstellungen von Saiteninstrumenten in der mittelalterlichen Buchmalerei und ihre Bedeutung für die Instrumentenkunde 302

van der MEER, J. H. Zur Geschichte des Klaviziteriums 305

OTTO, I.　Das Fotografieren von Musikinstrumenten zu wissenschaftlichen Zwecken　309
KARSTÄDT, G.　Das Instrument Gottfried Reiches: Horn oder Trompete?　311
BABITZ, S.　Das Violinspiel im 18. Jahrhundert und heute　313

Musikalische Volks- und Völkerkunde (chairman SALMEN, W.)
LIEBNER, J.　Ein verschollenes Werk von Béla Bartók　315
WÜNSCH, W.　Über Schallaufnahmen südosteuropäischer Volksepik in der Zeit von 1900 bis 1930　317
WERNER, E.　Statistische Gesetze der mündlichen Musiktradition und ihrer Erforschung　318

Arbeitsgruppen
1 Berufsfragen des jungen Musikwissenschaftlers (chairman LAAFF, E.)
LAAFF, E.　Berufsfragen des jungen Musikwissenschaftlers [survey]　321
SCHMIEDER, W.　Das Berufsbild des wissenschaftlichen Musikbibliothekars　323
NEUPERT, H.　Musikwissenschaftler und Instrumentenbau　323
REHM, W.　Der Musikwissenschaftler im Musikverlag　325
MÜLLMANN, B.　Der Musikwissenschaftler als Redakteur oder Musikkritiker　327
WIRTH, H.　Der Musikwissenschaftler beim Rundfunk　328
REINECKE, H.-P.　Der Musikwissenschaftler in der Schallplatten-Industrie　330
OBERBORBECK, F.　Pädagogische Berufsmöglichkeiten des Musikwissenschaftlers　331
LAAFF, E.　Berufsfragen des jungen Musikwissenschaftlers [conclusion]　333

2 Musikdokumentation (chairman SCHMIEDER, W.)
SCHMIEDER, W.　Gedanken über den Begriff, das Wesen und die Aufgaben der Musikdokumentation　334
REINECKE, H.-P.　Erläuterungen zur modernen Dokumentations-Technik　336
DEUTSCH, O. E.　Dokumentarische Biographien　337
STÄBLEIN, B.　Erfassung und Erschliessung mittelalterlicher Musikhandschriften　339
WEINHOLD, L.　RISM im Rahmen der Musikdokumentation　341
HECKMANN, H.　Zur Dokumentation musikalischer Quellen des 16. und 17. Jahrhunderts　342
BIRKNER, G.　Quellenlage und Katalogisierung des deutschen Volkslieds　345

3 Historische Musiktheorie (chairman FEDERHOFER, H.)
FEDERHOFER, H.　Historische Musiktheorie [survey]　348
SCHMID, H.　Plan und Durchführung des 'Lexicon Musicum Latinum' I: Erfassung und Erforschung der musikalischen Fachsprache des Mittelalters　349
WAELTNER, E.　Plan und Durchführung des 'Lexicon Musicum Latinum' II: Archivaufbau mit Hilfe maschineller Datenverarbeitung　351
REANEY, G.　Zur Frage der Autorenzuweisung in mittelalterlichen Musiktraktaten　353
APFEL, E.　Über das Verhältnis von Musiktheorie und Kompositionspraxis im späteren Mittelalter (etwa 1200-1500)　354
MEIER, B.　Musiktheorie und Musik im 16. Jahrhundert　356
FEDERHOFER-KÖNIGS, R.　Heinrich Saess und seine 'Musica plana atque mensurabilis'　359
SCHLÖTTERER, R.　Lehrmethoden des Palestrina-Kontrapunkts　361
BENARY, P.　Die Stellung der Melodielehre in der Musiktheorie des 18. Jahrhunderts in Deutschland　362
JONAS, O.　Zur realen Antwort in der Fuge bei Bach　364
FEDERHOFER, H.　Historische Musiktheorie [conclusion]　366

4 Strukturprobleme der Musik von heute (chairman STUCKENSCHMIDT, H. H.)
FROMMEL, G.　Tonalitätsprobleme der neuen Musik vom Standpunkt des Komponisten　367
DAHLHAUS, C.　Der Tonalitätsbegriff in der neuen Musik　370
ENGELMANN, H. U.　Fragen seriellen Kompositionsverfahren　374
KARKOSCHKA, E.　Zur rhythmischen Struktur in der Musik von heute　379
STUCKENSCHMIDT, H. H.　'Musique concrète'　388

62 MAG　　**Beiträge zu einem neuen Telemannbild: Konferenzbericht der I. Magdeburger Telemann-Festtage**
Magdeburg 3–5 November 1962
Arbeitskreis 'Georg Philipp Telemann' im Deutschen Kulturbund Magdeburg
(Magdeburg: Arbeitskreis 'Georg Philipp Telemann' im Deutschen Kulturbund Magdeburg, 1963)

SCHNEIDER, M.　Telemannpflege – eine unserer nationalen Aufgaben　7
SIEGMUND-SCHULTZE, W.　Georg Philipp Telemann　9
MEYER, E. H.　Zur Telemann-Deutung　17
WILKOWSKA-CHOMINSKA, K.　Telemanns Bezie-

hungen zur polnischen Musik   23
WOLFF, H. C.   Telemann und die Hamburger
Oper   38
FLEISCHHAUER, G.   Einige Gedanken zur Har-

monik Telemanns   50
MAERTENS, W.   Telemanns Orchestersuite mit
Hornquartett   64

62 MEX   **XXXV Congreso internacional de Americanistas: actas y memorias**
              Mexico City 20–25 August 1962
              International Congress of Americanists
              (Mexico City: Instituto nacional de antropologiá e historia, 1964)

Vol. iii (1964)
Folklore (chairman MENDOZA, V. T.)
FRANCO, J. L.   Sobre un grupo de instrumentos

musicales prehispánicos con sistema acústico no
conocido   369

62 PAR   **Debussy et l'évolution de la musique au XXᵉ siècle**
              Paris 24–31 October 1962
              Centre national de la recherche scientifique: sciences humaines
              ed. E. Weber (Paris: Centre national de la recherche scientifique, 1965)

SAUGUET, H.   Debussy, révolution perma-
nente   23
ROLAND-MANUEL   Debussy, tradition perma-
nente   27

1 Le langage de Debussy
ANSERMET, E.   Le langage de Debussy   33
CHAILLEY, J.   Apparences et réalités dans le
langage de Debussy   47
BARRAQUÉ, J.   Debussy ou l'approche d'une
organisation autogène de la composition   83
GERVAIS, F.   Debussy et la tonalité   97
d'ALMENDRA, J.   Debussy et le mouvement
modal dans la musique du XXᵉ siècle   109

2 L'esthétique de Debussy
SOURIS, A.   Poétique musicale de Debussy   133
LOCKSPEISER, E.   Quelques problèmes de la
psychologie de Debussy   141
SCHAEFFNER, A.   Debussy et ses rapports avec la
peinture   151
JAROCIŃSKI, S.   Quelques aspects de l'univers
sonore de Debussy   167
KREMLEV, J.   Tendances réalistes de l'esthétique
de Debussy   189
FÉDOROV, V.   Debussy, vu par quelques
Russes   199

3 L'influence de Debussy
RAAD, V.   Amérique (Etats-Unis)   215
de AZEVEDO, L. H. C.   Amérique latine   233
LOCKSPEISER, E.   Angleterre   239
STUCKENSCHMIDT, H.-H.   Autriche et Alle-
magne   241
d'ALMENDRA, J.   Espagne et Portugal   263
GERVAIS, F.   France   269
BARTHA, D.   Hongrie   273
MANTELLI, A.   Italie   289
ONNEN, F.   Pays-Bas (Belgique, Hollande)   291
ROVSING OLSEN, P.   Pays nordiques   301
JAROCIŃSKI, S.   Pologne   313
KREMLEV, J.   Russie   315

AUSTIN, W.   Quelques connaissances et opinions
de Schoenberg et Webern sur Debussy   319
LESURE, F.   Debussy et Edgard Varèse   333
ANSERMET, E.   Debussy et Robert Godet   339
Discussion: À propos de la publication des lettres
de Debussy   341
Discussion générale   345
WEBER, E.   Synthèse et conclusions   349

62 ROY   **Les tragédies de Sénèque et le théâtre de Renaissance**
              Royaumont 3–6 May 1962
              Groupe de recherches sur le théâtre (CNRS)
              ed. J. Jacquot (Paris: Centre national de la recherche scientifique, 1964)

STERNFELD, F. W.   La musique dans les tragédies élisabéthaines inspirées de Sénèque   139

62 SIN   Actes du colloque international de civilisations balkaniques
Sinaia, Romania 8-14 July 1962
Romanian National Commission of UNESCO; Romanian Academy
(Bucharest: Commission nationale roumaine pour l'UNESCO, 1963)

YÖNETKEN, H. B. Dimitrie Cantemir dans
l'histoire de la musique turque   145

62 STOC   Sixième congrès international des bibliothèques musicales Stockholm-Uppsala: actes du
congrès
Stockholm and Uppsala 13-18 August 1962
International Association of Music Libraries
ed. C. Johansson and F. Lindberg, *Fontes artis musicae* xi (Kassel and Basle:
Bärenreiter, 1964)

BENTON, R. Early musical scholarship in the
United States   12
DAVIDSSON, Å. Cultural background to col-
lections of old music in Swedish libraries   21
SARTORI, C. Le RISM et l'Italie   28

The profession of the music librarian
1 Library building (chairman LESURE, F.)
DORFMÜLLER, K. Die bauliche Einrichtung der
Musiksammlung der Bayerischen Staatsbib-
liothek, München   34
FREITAG, W. M. On planning a music
library   35
KÖHLER, K.-H. Bauliche und strukturelle
Verhältnisse der Musikabteilung der Deutschen
Staatsbibliothek, Berlin   49
2 The training of the music librarian (chairman

DAVIES, J. H.; papers FÉDOROV, V. 51,
STELLAN MÖRNER, C.-G. 53, PEMBERTON,
J. 54, PETERSEN, H. 55, SPIVACKE, H. 57)
3 International aspects (chairman ZEHNTER, H.;
papers JURRES, A. 60, PROKOPOWICZ,
M. 62)
4 The music librarian and his public (chairman
OTT, A.)
OTT, A. Possibilities of musical education in
public libraries   63
DORFMÜLLER, K. Der wissenschaftliche Musik-
bibliothekar und sein Publikum   66
ANNEGARN, A. The scientific music librarian
and his public   67
Further papers by DUCK, L. 68, SHEPARD,
B. 70

62 TOD   Il dolore e la morte nella spiritualità dei secoli XII e XIII: Convegni del Centro di studi sulla
spiritualità medievale V
Todi 7-10 October 1962
Centro di studi sulla spiritualità medievale
(Todi: Accademia Tudertina, 1967)

MONTEROSSO, R. Il dolore e la morte nell'espressione musicale dei secoli XII e XIII   261

62 WAR   Karol Szymanowski: Księga sesji naukowej poświęconej twórczości Karola Szymanowskiego [Book of the conference devoted to the works of Karol Szymanowski] Warsaw 23–8 March 1962 Uniwersytet warszawski ed. Z. Helman (Warsaw: Wydawnictwa Universytetu warszawskiego, 1964 = Prace Instytutu muzykologii Uniwersytetu warszawskiego ed. Z. Lissa) [all papers printed with English résumés]

BIELAWSKI, L.   Karol Szymanowski a muzyka Podhala [Szymanowski and the Highlanders' music]   8

CHOJAK, A.   Tradycje Szymanowskiego w polskiej muzyce współczesnej [Szymanowski's traditions in Polish contemporary music]   22

CHOMIŃSKI, J. M.   Szymanowski i muzyka europejska XX wieku [Szymanowski and 20th-century European music]   37

CZYŻOWSKI, S.   Problem stylizacji w Królu Rogerze [Stylization in Szymanowski's 'King Roger']   47

DRZEWIECKI, Z.   Kilka uwag o interpretacji utworów fortepianowych Szymanowskiego [A few remarks on the interpretation of Szymanowski's piano works]   67

GŁOWACKI, J.   Kolorystyka a technika skrzypcowa w twórczości Szymanowskiego [Colour devices and violin technique in Szymanowski's works]   75

GORCZYCKA, M.   Wpływy ideologii twórczej Szymanowskiego na kompozytorów polskich dwudziestolecia międzywojennego [Szymanowski's influence on Polish composers of the pre-war period]   86

HELMAN, Z.   Z zagadnień warsztatu twórczego Karola Szymanowskiego na materiale jego szkiców [Szymanowski's writing technique in the light of his sketches]   109

IWASZKIEWICZ, J.   Karol Szymanowski a literatura [Karol Szymanowski and literature]   126

KACZYŃSKI, T.   Zagadnienie autonomiczności i nieautonomiczności muzyki na przykładzie twórczości Karola Szymanowskiego [Absolute and programme music in Szymanowski's output]   136

KLEMM, E.   Zagadnienie techniki wariacyjnej u Regera i Szymanowskiego [Reger's and Szymanowski's variation technique]   142

LISSA, Z.   Szymanowski a romantyzm [Szymanowski and Romanticism]   161

ŁOBACZEWSKA, S.   Sonaty fortepianowe Szymanowskiego a sonaty Skriabina [Szymanowski's and Skryabin's piano sonatas]   177

NIESTIEW, I.   Nowe materiały do biografii Karola Szymanowskiego [New material towards Szymanowski's biography]   191

NOWACKI, K.   Rola folkloru góralskiego w 'Harnasiach' [Highlanders' folk art in 'Harnasie']   209

POCIEJ, B.   Faktura chóralna utworów Szymanowskiego [Choral writing in Szymanowski's works]   226

RUDZIŃSKI, W.   Zagadnienia struktury 'I Koncertu skrzypcowego' K. Szymanowskiego [Structural problems in Szymanowski's First Violin Concerto]   247

STARZYŃSKI, J.   Szymanowski a problematyka plastyki polskiej w XX-leciu międzywojennym [Szymanowski and Polish plastic arts of his day]   261

STĘSZEWSKI, J.   Pieśni kurpiowskie w twórczości Karola Szymanowskiego [The folksongs of the Kurpie regions in Szymanowski's works]   274

ŚWIERZEWSKI, S.   Karol Szymanowski w oczach krytyki polskiej [Karol Szymanowski in the light of Polish criticism]   294

TOMASZEWSKI, M.   Związki słowno-muzyczne w liryce wokalnej Szymanowskiego na materiale 'Słopiewni' [The relationship between word and music in Szymanowski's lyrical vocal works on the basis of his 'Słopiewni']   305

ZABŁOCKA, J.   Rymy dziecięce Karola Szymanowskiego [Szymanowski's 'Children's Rhymes']   334

ZIELIŃSKI, T. A.   Sonorystyka harmoniczna w trzecim okresie twórczości Szymanowskiego [Harmonic sonorities in Szymanowski's output of the third period]   345

63 BUD   **Europa et Hungaria: Congressus ethnographicus in Hungaria**
              Budapest 16–20 October 1963
              ed. G. Ortutay and T. Bodrogi (Budapest: Akadémiai kiadó, 1965)

VARGYAS, L.   The importance of the Hungarian ballads on the confines of occident and orient   325
ROMANSKA, Z.   Bulgarische und mazedonische Heldenlieder und historische Volkslieder über Persönlichkeiten aus der ungarischen Geschichte   333
UKHIKVADZE, G.   Doistoricheskaya gruzinskaya kostyanaya salamurifleyta [The prehistoric Georgian 'salamuri' bone flute]   451
AKHOBADZE, V. V.   Forma kollektivnovo truda 'nadi' i gruzinskaya chetïrekhgolosnaya pesnya 'naduri' [The form of the collective work 'nadi' and the Georgian four-part song 'naduri']   459
MARTIN, G.   East-European relations of Hungarian dance types   469

63 CART   **Primera conferencia interamericana de etnomusicologia: trabajos presentados**
              Cartagena de Indias, Colombia 24–8 February 1963
              Inter-American Music Council (CIDEM); Pan-American Union: Music Division
              ed. G. Espinosa, supplement to *Inter-American Music Bulletin*
              (Washington, DC: Union Panamericana, 1965)

AYESTARÁN, L.   Fétis, un precursor del criterio etnomusicológico en 1869   13
SEEGER, C.   Preface to a critique of music   39
HOOD, M.   The quest for norms in ethnomusicology   65
ARETZ, I.   Cantos navideños en el folklore venezolano   73
VEGA, C.   Música de tres notas   87
PARDO TOVAR, A.   Proyecciones sociológicas del folklore musical   107
ESPINOSA, L. C. and PINZÓN URREA, J.   La heterofonía en la música de los Indios Cunas del Darién   119
LIST, G.   Music in the culture of the Jibaro Indians of the Ecuadorian montaña   131
RAMÓN y RIVERA, L. F.   Cantos negros de la Fiesta de San Juan   153
LEACH, MacE.   Collecting techniques with special reference to ballads   177
RHODES, W.   A preliminary study of the Mazatec mushroom ceremony   187
MANZANARES, R.   Etnomusicologia hondureña   197
TAVARES de LIMA, R.   Música folclórica e instrumentos musicais do Brasil   203

63 KIE   **Norddeutsche und nordeuropäische Musik: Referate der Kieler Tagung 1963**
              Kiel October 1963
              Landeskundliche Abteilung des Musikwissenschaftlichen Instituts der Universität Kiel
              ed. C. Dahlhaus and W. Wiora (Kassel and Basle: Bärenreiter, 1965 = Kieler Schriften zur Musikwissenschaft 16)

1 Geschichtliche Zusammenhänge deutscher Musik mit Dänemark, Schweden und Norwegen
SØRENSON, S   Allgemeines über den dänischen protestantischen Kirchengesang   11
SCHIØRRING, N.   Nachwirkungen der Lobwasserpsalter in Dänemark   22
GRUSNICK, B.   Die Datierungen der Dübensammlung   27
KILIAN, D.   Buxtehudes Membra   32
GURVIN, O.   Über Beziehungen zwischen deutscher und norwegischer Musik   37
BENGTSSON, I.   Romantisch-nationale Strömungen in deutscher und skandinavischer Musik   42

HAHNE, G. Musikalische Zusammenhänge
zwischen Dänemark und Schleswig-Holstein im
19. Jahrhundert   48
EPPSTEIN, H. Aktuelle Tendenzen in der
schwedischen Musikpädagogik   56

2 Zur Geschichte der Musik in Norddeutschland
RIEDEL, F. W. Strenger und freier Stil in der
nord- und süddeutschen Musik für Tasteninstrumente des 17. Jahrhunderts   63
BREIG, W. Über das Verhältnis von Komposition und Ausführung in der norddeutschen
Orgel-Choralbearbeitung des 17. Jahrhunderts   71
REIMANN, M. Zur Editionstechnik von Musik
des 17. Jahrhunderts   83

KÜMMERLING, H. Gottorfer Bestände in der
Sammlung Bokemeyer   92
GUDEWILL, K. Musik an der Kieler Uni-
versität   95
WITTROCK, W. Volkslieder in Schleswig-
Holstein   100
DAHLHAUS, C. Cribrum musicum: der Streit
zwischen Scacchi und Siefert   108
BRAUN, W. Johann Sebastiani (1622–1683) und
die Musik in Königsberg   113
SCHWARZ, W. Von Musik und Musikern im
deutschen Osten: nach unveröffentlichten
Briefen an Robert Schumann aus den Jahren
1834 bis 1854   120

63 MER   **La storiografia nel mondo italiano ed in quello tedesco: Stato e problemi attuali nel quadro dell'unità culturale europea: Atti del IV convegno internazionale di studi italo-tedeschi / Das Geschichtsbild im deutschen und italienischen Sprachraum: Gegenwärtiger Stand und Probleme im Rahmen der europäischen Kultureinheit: Akten der IV. internationalen Tagung deutsch-italienischer Studien**
Merano 17–23 April 1963
Istituto culturale italo-tedesco in Alto Adige, Merano/Deutsch-italienisches Kultur-institut in Südtirol, Merano
(Merano: Istituto culturale italo-tedesco in Alto Adige, 1967)

Letteratura e arte
KARLINGER, F. Die nationale und die internationale Sprache der deutschen und italienischen Musik der Gegenwart (Italian résumé
417)   409
CAMBISSA, G. Influssi viennesi nella musica ital-

iana contemporanea (discussion 455; German
résumé 457)   447
GALLICO, C. Esperimenti e realizzazioni della
più recente avantguardia musicale: compositori
italiani a Darmstadt (German résumé
686)   679

63 MTA   **Montauban 1963: Actes des journées internationales d'étude du Baroque [I]**
Montauban 26–8 September 1963
Festival de Montauban
[*Baroque* i] (Toulouse: Association des publications de la Faculté des lettres et sciences humaines, 1965)

Thèmes généraux
LACAS, P.-P. Essai sur le Baroque en
organologie   25

Études d'ensemble
KASTNER, M. S. Quelques aspects du Baroque
musical espagnol et portugais   85

63 PRA   **I. Internationales Seminar marxistischer Musikwissenschaftler**
Prague 27 May – 1 June 1963
Beiträge zur Musikwissenschaft v/4 (Berlin: Neue Musik, 1963)

SYCHRA, A. Zur Problemstellung unseres
Seminars   245
JIRÁNEK, J. Zu einigen Grundbegriffen der

marxistischen Ästhetik (discussion 325)   261
UJFALUSSY, J. Zur Dialektik des Wirklichkeits-
bildes in der Musik (discussion 326)   275

GOLDSCHMIDT, H. Musikalische Gestalt und
Intonation   283
KNEPLER, G. Musikgeschichte und Geschichte
(discussion 345)   291
MARÓTHY, J. Von der Hagiographie zur
Historiographie   299

KRESÁNEK, J. Die gesellschaftliche Funktion
der Musik (discussion 348)   304
MOKRÝ, L. Soziologie und Marxismus   307
MAYER, G. Zur musiksoziologischen Frage-
stellung   311

63 ROY Le lieu théâtral à la Renaissance
Royaumont 22–7 March 1963
Centre national de la recherche scientifique: sciences humaines
ed. J. Jacquot (Paris: Centre national de la recherche scientifique, 1964, 2/1968)

**Le lieu théâtral hors d'Italie: diffusion de la scène 'à
l'italienne' au XVIIᵉ siècle**
AUBRUN, C. V. Les débuts du drame lyrique en
Espagne   423

JACQUOT, J. Les types du lieu théâtral et leurs
transformations de la fin du moyen âge au
milieu du XVIIᵉ siècle   473

63 STT Actas do congresso internacional de etnografia
Santo Tirso 10–18 July 1963
(Porto: Imprensa portuguesa, 1965)

Vol. ii (1965)
GIL, B. Panorama de la canción popular an-
daluza: consideración preliminar   85
KLUSEN, E. Beziehungen zwischen Volkslied-
forschung und Volksliedpflege   133
ALFAIATE MARVÃO, A. O folclore musical do
Baixo-Alentejo nos ciclos litúrgicos da
Igreja   147

MOURINHO, A. Aspecto e função da música
popular Mirandesa, profana e religiosa   177
MUÑOZ, M. A. Problemas de sistematización de
las danzas folklóricas   179
do PAÇO, A. Sogras e cunhadas no cancioneiro
popular e no adagiário   185
SAN VALERO APARISI, J. Las bandas de música
en la vida valenciana   337

63 TOD Chiesa e riforma nella spiritualità del secolo XI: Convegni del Centro di studi sulla spiritualità
medievale VI
Todi 13–16 October 1963
Centro di studi sulla spiritualità medievale
(Todi: Accademia Tudertina, 1968)

MONTEROSSO, R. Canto gregoriano e riforma
tra Cluniacensi e Cistercensi   191

63 VEN   **Venezia e la Polonia nei secoli dal XVII al XIX: convegno**
Venice 28 May – 2 June 1963
Fondazione Giorgio Cini, Venice; Polish Academy of Sciences
ed. L. Cini (Venice and Rome: Istituto per la collaborazione culturale, 1965 = Civiltà
veneziana studi 19)

CHOMIŃSKI, J. M.   La technique polychorale
vénitienne en Pologne   179

64 AMS Actes du cinquième congrès international d'esthétique
Amsterdam 24–8 August 1964
International Congress of Aesthetics
ed. J. Aler (The Hague and Paris: Mouton, 1968)

JURRES, A. Dutch musical composition in the middle of our century 15

2 Innovation et tradition
CORVER, G. M. A. Tradition et innovation musicales dans la pensée du compositeur Willem Pijper 171

McGLINCHEE, C. Shakespeare, Delacroix and Chopin 187

PORCELIJN, C. The position of Alphons Diepenbrock in the Dutch history of music 201

3 Colloque sur le non-finito
CHARLES, D. L'esthétique du 'non finito' chez John Cage 219

PUCELLE, J. L'achèvement des 'symphonies inachevées' 256

7 L'art et la vie
FISCHER, P. Sa tendre majesté la harpe 518

SMITS van WAESBERGHE, J. Der Niederländer in seinen tänzerischen, sprachlichen, und musikalischen Äusserungen 534

8 Les techniques nouvelles
KRAFFT, C. L'esthétique du nouveau Bayreuth 570

10 Colloque sur les problèmes du réalisme
FUBINI, E. Espressione e imitazione della natura nell'estetica musicale del settecento 626

12 L'oeuvre d'art et l'expérience esthétique
ASSELBERGS, A. 'Musical poetry' and organic composition 745

JACOBS, C. Some psychological remarks concerning the aesthetics of music 760

13 Le rôle du sentiment religieux dans les arts
NOMURA, F. Y. On Zen and musical aesthetics 843

14 Esthétique expérimentale
FULIN, A. Le langage musical des enfants 885

LEVELT, W. J. M. and PLOMP, R. The appreciation of musical intervals 901

16 La créativité artistique
BERNET KEMPERS, K. P. Die Affektenlehre und die Musikauffassung des neunzehnten Jahrhunderts 969

64 ATH IV International Congress for Folk-Narrative Research in Athens: Lectures and Reports
Athens 1–6 September 1964
International Society for Folk-Narrative Research
ed. G. A. Megas (Athens, 1965 = Laographia 22)

BREDNICH, R. W. Volkslied und Volkssage zum Verhältnis von 'Singen und Sagen' im Deutschland 42

64 BERL Bericht der Tagung zu Fragen der Arbeiterliedforschung
Berlin 28–30 April 1964
Deutsche Akademie der Künste, Berlin: Abteilung Arbeiterlied
Beiträge zur Musikwissenschaft vi/4 (Berlin: Neue Musik, 1964)

LAMMEL, I.   10 Jahre Arbeiterliedarchiv   255
KRAFT, G.   Stand und Koordinierung der wissenschaftlichen Forschung auf dem Gebiet des Arbeiterliedes in der Deutschen Demokratischen Republic (discussion 278)   267
STEINITZ, W.   Arbeiterlied und Arbeiterkultur   279
MEYER, E. H.   Aus der Tätigkeit der 'Kampfgemeinschaft der Arbeitersänger' (discussion 295)   289
ELSNER, J.   Der Einfluss der Arbeitermusikbewegung auf die Kampfmusik Hanns Eislers (discussion 307)   301

KLAUDER, K.   Lehren der deutschen Arbeitersängerbewegung für die heutige Chorpraxis   308
KARBUSICKÝ, V.   Das Arbeiterlied in der Geschichte und Gesellschaft (discussion 322)   317
HROVATIN, R.   Kategorisierung des Partisanenliedes in Jugoslawien   326
PLETKA, V.   Über einige methodische Probleme der Arbeiterlied-Forschung   332
LIBEROVICI, S.   Zur Schaffung neuer politischer Lieder in Italien   337
SEMMER, G.   Über die Ostermarsch-Lieder   339

64 BON Stil und Überlieferung in der Kunst des Abendlandes: Akten des 21. internationalen Kongresses für Kunstgeschichte in Bonn 1964
Bonn 14–19 September 1964
Comité international d'histoire de l'art
(Berlin: Gebr. Mann, 1967)

Vol. iii Theorien und Probleme (1967)
Rhetorik und Kunsttheorie
TEYSSÈDRE, B.   Peinture et musique: la notion d'harmonie des couleurs au XVIIᵉ siècle français   206

64 BRA Anfänge der slavischen Musik
Bratislava August 1964
Slovenská akadémie vied: Ústav hudobnej vedy [Slovak Academy of Sciences: Institute of Musicology] (Symposia I)
ed. L. Mokrý (Bratislava: Vydavateľstvo Slovenskej akadémie vied, 1966)

KOSCHMIEDER, E.   Wie haben Kyrill und Method zelebriert?   7
VAŠICA, J.   Slavische Petrusliturgie   23
MOKRÝ, L.   Der Kanon zur Ehre des hl. Demetrius als Quelle für die Frühgeschichte des kirchenslavischen Gesanges   35
FUKAČ, J.   Zu den Ergebnissen der Forschung über den musikalischen Charakter der Epoche Gross-Mährens   43
LAZAROV, S.   Die altbulgarische Musik und die Kyrillo-Methodianische Tradition   49
STEFANOVIĆ, D.   The beginnings of Serbian chant   55
STRUNK, O.   Zwei Chilandari Chorbücher   65
LEVY, K.   Die slavische Kondakarien-Notation   77
BELYAYEV, V. M.   Proizchozhdeniye znamennovo pospeva [The beginnings of Znamenny

chant]   93
ARRO, E.   Probleme der Provenienz des altrussischen kirchlich-kultischen Gesanges   101
SVAN, A. Yi. [Swan, A. J.]   O sposovakh garmonizatsi znamennovo pospeva [Ways of harmonizing Znamenny chant]   117
BACHMANN, W.   Das byzantinische Musikinstrumentarium   125
KAMIŃSKI, W.   Beiträge zur Erforschung der frühmittelalterlichen Musikinstrumente der Nordwest- und Ostslaven   139
ELSCHEKOVÁ, A.   Strukturelle Frühformen slavischer Volksmusik   147
KARBUSICKÝ, V.   Zu den historischen Wurzeln der Metrik der russischen Bylinen   165
VELIMIROVIĆ, M.   Preparation of an inventory of sources of old Slavic music   173

64 GRA¹   Die Kirchenmusik und das II. Vatikanische Konzil: Referate der Kirchenmusikwoche in Graz
Graz 3–7 March 1964
Akademie für Musik und darstellende Kunst in Graz: Abteilung für Kirchenmusik
(Graz: Verlag Styria, 1965)

ZAUNER, F. Die liturgische Konstitution und ihre Grundtendenzen   13
AMON, K. Die Funktionsteilung in der Liturgiefeier   33
HARNONCOURT, P. Neue Aufgaben der katholischen Kirchenmusik   51
KRONSTEINER, H. Das deutsche Kirchenlied in der Liturgiefeier   77
BOMM, U. Choralforschung und Choralpflege in der Gegenwart   91

LIPPHARDT, W. Möglichkeiten und Grenzen deutscher Gregorianik   121
MARCKHL, E. Kirchenmusik, Musikerziehung, Bildung   149
GUTFLEISCH, P. Der Kirchenmusiker als Beruf   167
NIKLAUS, H. and ROHR, H. Gesangliche Erziehung der Gemeinde   173
MAYER, J. E. Das Volk Gottes als singende Gemeinde   215

64 GRA²   Volksmusik südosteuropas: Beiträge zur Volkskunde und Musikwissenschaft anlässlich der I. Balkanologentagung in Graz 1964
Graz 6–9 May 1964
Akademie für Musik und darstellende Kunst in Graz
ed. W. Wünsch (Munich: Dr Dr Rudolf Trofenik, 1967 = Südosteuropa-Schriften, ed. W. Althammer, 7)

WÜNSCH, W. Über die Aufgaben der Musikwissenschaft in der Epenforschung   7
SCHMAUS, A. Probleme und Aufgaben der balkanischen Epenforschung   14
ŽGANEC, V. Über das Redigieren der Volksliedersammlungen   29
GAVAZZI, M. Die Namen der altslavischen Musikinstrumente   34
KRETZENBACHER, L. Südosteuropäische Primitivinstrumente vom 'Rummelpott'-Typ in

vergleichend-musikvoikskundlicher Forschung   50
WALDMANN, G. Mehrstimmiges Singen im slawischen Bauernlied   98
WOLFRAM, R. Altformen im Tanz der Völker des pannonischen und Karpatenraumes   109
KOMMA, K. M. Das böhmische Musikantentum   140
MICHAELIDES, S. The neohellenic folkmusic   153

64 HAM   Zeitgenössisches Musiktheater / Contemporary Music Theatre / Théâtre musical contemporain: Hamburg 1964: Internationaler Kongress / International Congress / Congrès international
Hamburg 16–23 June 1964
International Music Council (4th congress)
ed. E. Thomas (Hamburg: Deutscher Musikrat, 1966)

LABROCA, M. Le théâtre musical – hier et aujourd'hui   27
LIEBERMANN, R. Musiktheater oder Stagione   29

1 Die musikalische Sprache
STUCKENSCHMIDT, H. H. Stoff und Libretto 34
YARUSTOWSKI, B. Probleme des gegenwartigen Musiktheaters   37
de la MOTTE, D. Das Verhältnis zwischen Text und Musik   43

2 Stoff und Libretto
BOLL, A. Le livret – élément essential d'un renouveau du théâtre musical   48
DALLAPICCOLA, L. Livrets et paroles dans l'opéra   52
SAUGUET, H. Le sujet dans le théâtre musical contemporain   57
BLOMDAHL, K. B. and LINDEGREN, E. Fragment of an arctic conversation   59
ORFF, C. Das Libretto im zeitgenössischen Musiktheater   61

FORTNER, W.   Libretto und musikalische
Sprache   62
RENNERT, W.   Das zeitgenössische Musik-
theater bedarf zeitgenössischer Stoffe   63

3 Formen und Formelemente
BORRIS, S.   Das neue 'drama per musica'   66
MONK, E.   Der Einfluss Brechts   70
HELM, E.   Forms and components: mixed
forms   75
MILA, M.   Stravinsky et les nouvelles formes du
théâtre musical   78
CHEVREUILLE, P.   'La reine verte' de Maurice
Béjart   82

4 Inszenierung und musikalische Realisierung
KAŠLÍK, V.   Die Wiederbelebung der Oper   86
RENNERT, G.   Zur Regie des zeitgenössischen
Musiktheaters   90
HABUNEK, V.   Le metteur-en-scène dans le théâ-
tre musical contemporain   94
DUPONT, J.   Le rôle du décorateur dans la mise-
en-scène lyrique   96
MAXIMOWNA, I.   Die Bühnenbildner im heutigen
Theater   98
HENZE, H. W.   Zur Inszenierung zeitgenössi-
schen Musiktheaters   101
VEDOVA, E.   Réalisation scénique de 'In-
tolleranza 60' de Luigi Nono   103

5 Einflüsse der technischen Mittler
KRENEK, E.   Remarks on the influence of the
new technical media (electronics, cinema) on the
conception of works for the music stage
(opera)   108
TOMEK, O.   Zur Übernahme neuer musikali-

scher Bühnenwerke im Hörfunk   109
EGK, W.   Szenische Darstellung eines für den
Funk bestimmten Werkes   112
de LEEUW, T.   Introduction par l'auteur à l'opéra
'Alceste'   114

6 Erfahrungen orientalischer Theater
DANIÉLOU, A.   Les influences orientales dans le
théâtre musical contemporain   116
TRAN VAN KHE   Le théâtre musical de tradition
chinoise   121
KISHIBE, S.   The music of the Japanese Noh
plays   124
MENON, N.   The dance-drama of India   126
LI MAN KUEI   Chinese drama   130

Arbeitsgruppe A: Organisation
HAREWOOD   The place of contemporary music
in festivals   132
WALTER, F.   Enquête sur le théâtre musical
contemporain dans les festivals   134

Arbeitsgruppe B: Ausbildung
GRAF, H.   Training for opera   140
HÉRICARD, J.   La formation vocale dans l'opéra
contemporain   143
NEUMANN, A.   Young artists and contemporary
music theatre   145
PILARCZYK, H.   Kann man die moderne Oper
singen?   148
SITTNER, H.   Ausbildungsprobleme des sängeri-
schen Nachwuchses für das Musiktheater 151

BORNOFF, J.   Zeitgenössiches Musiktheater/
Contemporary music theatre/Théâtre musical
contemporain   153

64 MOS   VII mezhdunarodnïy kongress antropologicheskikh i etnograficheskikh nauk / VIIme Con-
grès international des sciences anthropologiques et ethnologiques
Moscow 3-10 August 1964
International Union of Anthropological and Ethnological Sciences
(Moscow: Nauka, 1968-71)

Vol. vii (1970)
15 Narodnaya muzïka/Musique populaire
COMIŞEL, E.   Les particularités stylistiques musicales des genres folkloriques au cours de différentes périodes historiques   221
VITOLIN', Ya. Ya.   Stilevïye osobennosti
latïshskoy narodnoy pesni godovovo
zemledel'cheskovo tsikla [Stylistic features of
Latvian folksong of the annual agricultural
cycle]   226
CHKHIKVADZE, G. Z.   Osnovnïye tipï gruzin-
skovo narodnovo mnogogolos'ya [Principal
types of Georgian polyphony]   ·   232
STOCKMANN, D.   Wandlungen des deutschen
Volksgesanges vom 19. Jahrhundert bis zur
Gegenwart   238

KAROMATOV, F. M.   O lokal'nïkh stilyakh uzbekskoy narodnoy muzïki [Local styles of Uzbek folksong]   243
STOIN, E.   K voprosu o svyazi teksta s muzïkoy v
bolgarskoy narodnoy pesne [Questions of the
connections between text and music in Bulgarian folksong]   248
TSITOVICH, G. I.   Novïye stilevïye chertï traditsionnoy belorusskoy narodnoy pesni [New
stylistic features of traditional Belorussian folk-
song]   253
GORDEYCHUK, N. M.   Sovremennaya ukrain-
skaya narodnaya pesnya [Contemporary U-
krainian folksong]   259
RIHTMAN, C.   Les formes polyphoniques dans la
musique traditionnelle Jougoslave   265

MUKHARINSKAYA, L. S. Partizanskiye pesni Belorussii i ikh slagateli (chertï stilya) [Belorussian partisan songs and their composers (stylistic features)]   268

PETROV, S. Muzikal'naya kul'tura banatskikh bolgar [The musical culture of the Banat Bulgarians]   272

SLAVYUNAS, Z. I. Litovskiye narodnïye trudovïye pesni 'sutartines' [Lithuanian 'sutartines' folk work songs]   278

LEON PEREZ, A. El area de la fiesta de bembe en Cuba   283

AKHOBADZE, V. V. Gruzinskiye narodnïye trudovïye pesni 'naduri' [Georgian 'naduri' folk work songs]   287

GORALI, M. Stranstvuyushchiye melodii [Wandering melodies]   291

DIAS, M. Gruppenbildende und individuelle Musikinstrumente in Moçambique   293

LEBEDINSKIY, L. N. Bashkirskaya protyazhnaya pesnya 'Zyul'khizya' [The Bashkir 'Zyul'-khizya' drawling song]   309

ALEKSEYEV, E. Ye. Novoye v traditsionnïkh stilyakh yakutskovo muzïkal'novo fol'klora 'd'ieretii ïrïa' i 'degeren ïrïa' [New information on traditional styles of Yakut folk music: 'd'ieretii ïrïa' and 'degeren ïrïa']   319

CHYURLIONITE, Ya. Stilisticheskiye osobennosti traditsionnoy litovskoy narodnoy melodii [Stylistic features of traditional Latvian folk melody]   325

ATAYAN, R. A. Komitas – sobiratel' armyanskoy narodnoy pesni [Gomidas as collecter of Armenian folksong]   329

TAMPERE, Kh. T. Stilevïye tipï melodiki estonskikh run [Melodic styles in Estonian runes]   334

BELYAYEV, V. M. Persdikskiye tesnifi (K voprosu o kvantitativnom stikhoslozhenii) [Persian tesnifs: on the question of quantitative versification]   340

NIGMEDZYANOV, M. N. Stilevïye osobennosti muzïkal'novo fol'klora tatar-kryashen [Stylistic features of the folk music of the Kriashen Tartars]   343

Simpozium: Narodnïye muzïkal'nïye instrumenti/Symposium: Instruments de musique populaire

STOCKMANN, E. Introduction (discussion KUNC, L. 396, ZHUBANOV, A. 404, KHADZHIMANOV, V. 409, BENTTSON, A. F. V. 411, VERTKOV, K. A. 413, PALYULIS, Z. 418, SMIRNOV, B. F. 422, SADOKOV, R. L. 427, RUDNEVA, A. V. 435, EL'DAROVA, E. M. 441, BELYAYEV, V. M. 447, VINOGRADOV, V. S. 449)   383

---

64 NEWD[1]   **Proceedings of the Twenty-sixth International Congress of Orientalists**
New Delhi 4–10 January 1964
        International Union of Orientalists
        (Poona: Bhandarkar Oriental Research Institute, 1966–70)

Vol. iii/2 ed. R. N. Dandekar (1970)
6d History and culture
VATSYAYAN, K. A history of Indian dance and music in mediaeval period   792

64 NEWD[2]   **Music East and West**
New Delhi 8–12 February 1964
        Indian Council for Cultural Relations
        ed. R. Ashton (New Delhi: Indian Council for Cultural Relations, 1966)

1 Evolution in music
DANIÉLOU, A. Conscious and haphazard evolution in music   11
DEODHAR, B. R. Evolution in Indian music 16
KHAN, A. The Tarana style of singing   22
MEYER, E. Evolution in music   24
SAMBAMOORTHY, P. Evolution of music with special reference to musical instruments   28
SHUKLA, N. N. Evolution in Hindusthani music   32

Discussion   38

2 The differences and similarities in musical structures of Indian and western music
KOELREUTTER, H. J. Indian and western music as an expression of different attitudes of consciousness   43
ASHTON, R. Basic details of variance between music in India and the West   48

STUCKENSCHMIDT, H.   Trends of improvisation in western music   57
JUNIUS, M.   On the differences and similarities of structure in Indian and western music   66
LUTZE, L.   Aspects of Indian music   73
RENSHAW, R.   Rhythmic structures in Indian and western music   77
KÁRPÁTI, J.   Bela Bartok and the East   90
Discussion   97

3 The psychology of the musician and the listener
CROSSLEY-HOLLAND, P.   Problems and opportunities in listening to the music of another civilisation   103
CVETKO, D.   The problem of the process of listening to and of making western and Indian music   112
SADAGOPAN, V. V.   Psychology of listening   118
SYCHRA, A.   Psychology of the listener from the experimental point of view   125
Discussion   129

4 Traditional music facing industrial civilization
GARFIAS, R.   Traditional music and the value of education   137
IYER, M. S.   Classical music under the impact of industrial change   143
TRAN VAN KHE   Far eastern musical tradition and the new rhythm   146
MAYOR, G.   The raag in the twentieth century   151
SHANKAR, R.   Hindusthani classical music and the demands of today   158
RAMACHANDRAN, N. S.   Classical music and the mass media (with special reference to South India)   166
ROY, R. L.   Traditional music between a culture and a civilization   171
SINGH, T. J.   Tradition and the inventive principle   179
VISWANATHAN, T.   Traditional music in South India: a dynamic force   186
Discussion   192

Concluding session   197

64 SAL   Bericht über den neunten internationalen Kongress Salzburg 1964
Salzburg 30 August – 4 September 1964
International Musicological Society
ed. F. Giegling (Kassel and Basle: Bärenreiter, 1964–6)

Vol. i Aufsätze zu den Symposia (1964)
Symposia
WIORA, W.   Idee und Methode 'vergleichender' Musikforschung (chairman BARTHA, D.; panel FELLERER, K. G., HEINS, E., KUTTNER, F. A., MARCEL-DUBOIS, C., POWERS, H. S., SCHNEIDER, M., WERNER, E.; discussion ii, 23)   3
LISSA, Z.   Musikalisches Hören in psychologischer Sicht (chairman SYCHRA, A.; panel ALBERSHEIM, G. L., BENGTSSON, I., GOLDSCHMIDT, H., REINECKE, H.-P., UJFALUSSY, J., BLINOWA, M; discussion ii, 38)   11
TAGLIAVINI, L. F.   Prassi esecutiva e metodo musicologico (chairman REESER, E.; panel GEIRINGER, K., RINGER, A. L., SCHLÖTTERER, R., SOMFAI, L.; discussion ii, 51)   19
HUSMANN, H.   Das Organum vor und ausserhalb der Notre-Dame-schule (chairman GEORGIADES, T. G.; panel CORBIN de MANGOUX, S., GEERING, A., GÖLLNER, T., HARRISON, F. Ll., SMITS van WAESBERGHE, J., STÄBLEIN, B., TREITLER, L.; discussion ii, 68)   25
FINSCHER, L.   Die nationalen Komponenten in der Musik der ersten Hälfte des 16. Jahrhunderts (chairman WESTRUP, J.; panel CHAMBURE Mme de, HEARTZ, D., LISSA, Z., MEYER, E. H., QUEROL-GAVALDÀ, M., RUBSAMEN, W. H.; discussion ii, 81)   37

PLATH, W.   Der gegenwärtige Stand der Mozart-Forschung (chairman GERSTENBERG, W.; panel DEUTSCH, O. E., ENGEL, H., GIEGLING, F., HAMANN, H. W., HESS, E., KNEPLER, G., KÖHLER, K.-H., LaRUE, J., NEUMANN, F., REHM, W., SENN, W.; discussion ii, 88)   47
SZABOLCSI, B.   Die Anfänge der nationalen Oper im 19. Jahrhundert (chairman ABRAHAM, G.; panel CVETKO, D., KROÓ, G., LONGYEAR, R. M., MARTYNOV, I., SYCHRA, A., TAWASTSTJERNA, E.; discussion ii, 98)   57
COLLAER, P.   Structures et domaines expressifs des systèmes musicaux contemporains (chairman BABBITT M.; panel BORETZ, B., FOKKER, A. D., FÜSSL, K., GOEHR, A., SALZMAN, E.; discussion ii, 110)   63

Vol. ii Protokolle von den Symposia und Round Tables: Vorträge und Kongressprogramm (1966)
PAUMGARTNER, B.   Vom Musiktheater Mozarts   3
OREL, A.   Österreichs Sendung in der abendländischen Musik   7
Round tables
Mündliche und schriftliche Tradition im Mittelmeerraum (chairman WERNER, E.; panel AVENARY, H., CORBIN, S., GÉGOU, F., GERSON-KIWI, E., REINHARD, K., SMOIRA-ROLL, M., WÜNSCH, W.)   121

La musique funéraire en Afrique noire: fonctions et formes (chairman ROUGET, G.; panel ARMSTRONG, R. G., CONNICK-MCCOLLESTER, R., de AZEVEDO, L.-H. C., DUVELLE, C., KOOLE, A. J. C., MARCEL-DUBOIS, C., SCHNEIDER, M., WACHSMANN, K. P.)   143

Der gegenwärtige Stand der Gregorianik-Forschung (chairman HUGLO, M.; panel FALVY, Z., FEICHT, H., HOLMAN, H.-J., SMITS van WAESBERGHE, J., STÄBLEIN, B., STRUNK, O.)   156

Byzantinische Elemente in der frühen slawischen Kirchenmusik (chairman KOSCHMIEDER, E.; panel ANTONOWYCZ, M., FLOROS, C., von GARDNER, J., GOŁOS, J., HUSMANN, H., KELDYSCH, J., MALI, J., MOKRÝ, L., STEFANOVIĆ, D., STRUNK, O., VELIMIROVIĆ, M., WERNER, E., WÜNSCH, W.)   167

Die Musikinstrumente in Europa vom 9. bis 11. Jahrhundert (chairman van der MEER, J. H.; panel BERNER, A., BOWLES, E. A., CHAMBURE Mme de, CRANE, F., DEVOTO, D., DRÄGER, H.-H., DROYSEN, D., HAMMERSTEIN, R., SMITS van WAESBERGHE, J., STAUDER, W., WINTERNITZ, E.)   176

Die Rolle Englands, Spaniens, Deutschlands und Polens in der Musik des 14. Jahrhunderts (chairman REANEY, G.; panel DITTMER, L. A., FEICHT, H., von FISCHER, K., GEERING, A., GÖLLNER, T., GÜNTHER, U., HARRISON, F. Ll., PEACOCK, P. E., STEVENS, D.)   188

Der Generalbass um 1600 (chairman SØRENSON, S.; panel ABRAHAM, L. U., BRAUN, W., LÓPEZ-CALO, J., HAACK, H., LAUNAY, D., MATHIASSEN, F., RUBSAMEN, W. H., VERCHALY, A., WESTRUP, J. A.)   201

Die Beziehungen zwischen Oper, Oratorium und Instrumentalmusik der Barockzeit (chairman WOLFF, H. C.; panel BARBOUR, J. M., BROOK, B. S., ELLÉR, R., ENGEL, H., GEIRINGER, K., GHISI, F., KOOLE, A. J. C., NOSKE, F., REDLICH, H. F., SUESS, J. G., VECCHI, G., ZIMMERMANN, F. B.)   212

Probleme der Schulbildungen in der Musik des 17. und 18. Jahrhunderts im österreichisch-italienischen Raum (chairman SCHENK, E.; panel BROOK, B. S., CVETKO, D., ENGLÄNDER, R., ESTRADA, G., HUCKE, H., KOOLE, A. J. C., RIEDEL, F. W., SUESS, J. G.)   226

Die Rolle der slawischen Völker in der Geschichte der europäischen Musik des 18. und 19. Jahrhunderts (chairman KELDYSCH, J.; panel CVETKO, D., FEICHT, H., JIRÁNEK, J., KNEPLER, G., LISSA, Z., RACEK, J., SCHWARZ, B., SPECTOR, I., ŠTĚDROŇ, B., VOLEK, T., WIRSTA, A.)   237

Die stilistische Einheit in Giuseppe Verdis Werk (chairman MILA, M.; panel GROUT, D. J., HOLMES, W. C., SIEGMUND-SCHULTZE, W., UGOLINI, G., UNDERWOOD, L.)   249

Die moderne Oper: Autoren, Theater, Publikum (chairman SCHUH, W.; panel BURLAS, L., GEIRINGER, K., LOWENS, I., PFANNKUCH, W., VOJTĚCH, I., WEIL, L.)   255

Analysis and synthesis of musical structures on the basis of information theory (chairman WINCKEL, F.; panel ALBERSHEIM, G., DONA, M., DRÄGER, H. H., FOKKER, A. D., RAHLFS, V., VOLEK, J., WATSON, J. M.)   261

Round Table der Union académique internationale über die geplante Ausgabe Corpus des Troubadours (chairman HUSMANN, H.; panel APEL, W., MONTEROSSO, R., STÄBLEIN, B., STRUNK, O., VECCHI, G.)   269

van der MEER, J. H. Mozarts Hammerflügel   273

65 AMS   **Acts of the VIIth International Congress of Libraries and Museums of the Performing Arts/Actes du VIIᵉ congrès international des bibliothèques-musées des arts du spectacle**
Amsterdam 6–9 September 1965
International Section for Performing Arts Libraries and Museums, International Federation of Libraries Associations
(The Hague: Netherlands Centre of the International Theatre Institute, 1967)

von GLEICH, C. C. J. Le 'Répertoire International des Sources Musicales' (R.I.S.M.) et les collections théâtrales   27

WOLFF, H. C. L'élaboration d'une bibliographie des documents illustrant l'histoire de l'opéra   29

65 BERL[1]   **II. Internationales Seminar marxistischer Musikwissenschaftler**
Berlin 22–6 June 1965
Beiträge zur Musikwissenschaft vii/4 (Berlin: Neue Musik, 1965)

MARÓTHY, J., UJFALUSSY, J. and ZOLTAY, D. Das Verhältnis zwischen ästhetischen und ideologischen Kategorien unter besonderer Berücksichtigung des zeitgenössischen Musikschaffens   257

MASEL, L. Über die Entwicklung der Sprache (Ausdrucksmittel) der zeitgenössischen Musik   278

ČERNÝ, M. Über die Kriterien der historischen Wertung der zeitgenössischen Musik   325

BROCKHAUS, H.-A. Über einige Probleme und Kriterien des Neuen in der zeitgenössischen Musik   328

RAȚIU, A. Aspekte der Ausdrucksmittel im Lichte der Entwicklung der zeitgenössischen Musik   337

JIRÁNEK, J. Der spezifische Charakter des musikalischen Inhalts in seiner historisch-gesellschaftlichen Bedingtheit   343

TOMESCU, V. Beiträge zur dialektischen Behandlung der musikästhetischen Probleme   347

BIMBERG, S. Einige Bemerkungen zum Tonalitätsbegriff   351

CHRISTOV, D. Perspektiven der nationalen musikalischen Tradition   359

MAYER, G. Zur Dialektik des musikalischen Materials   363

KUČERA, V. Zur Frage der Intonationssemantisierung der Struktur   377

GOLDSCHMIDT, H. Gedanken zu einer nicht-aristotelischen Musikästhetik   387

SYCHRA, A. Möglichkeiten der Anwendung der Kybernetik und der Informationstheorie in der marxistischen Musikwissenschaft   402

65 BERL[2]   **Artistic Values in Traditional Music: Proceedings of a Conference held in Berlin**
Berlin 14–16 July 1965
International Institute for Comparative Music Studies and Documentation, Berlin
ed. P. Crossley-Holland (Berlin: International Institute for Comparative Music Studies and Documentation, 1966)

1 Values

MENUHIN, Y. Artistic values   8

DANIÉLOU, A. Values in music   10

Discussion   19

2 Methods

TRAN VAN KHE Responsabilité des organisations pour la culture et l'éducation dans la préservation des traditions musicales des pays extrême-orientaux   23

NKETIA, J. H. K. The dimensions of musical studies   34

ARCHER, W. K. A quodlibet for Saraswathi: some observations on the possibilities and limit-

ations of scientific methods applied to the study of artistic values in traditional music 49
Discussion 94

3 Recent work
RHODES, W. The 'new' folk music 100
HOOD, M. Program of the Institute of Ethnomusicology, University of California, Los Angeles 108

CROSSLEY-HOLLAND, P. Work of the International Institute for Comparative Music Studies during the year 1964–1965 115
WINCKEL, F. Aspects of information theory in relation to comparative music studies 124
Discussion 127

65 BLM   **Music in the Americas**
Bloomington, Indiana 24–8 April 1965
Inter-American Music Council (CIDEM); Pan-American Union: Music Division
ed. G. List and J. Orrego-Salas (Bloomington: Indiana University Research Center in Anthropology, Folklore, and Linguistics, 1967 = Inter-American Music Monograph Series 1)

Papers read at the Second Inter-American Conference on Ethnomusicology
ARETZ, I. Raíces europeas de la música folklorica de Venezuela: el aporte indígena 7
AYESTARÁN, L. El tamboril afro-uruguayo 23
de AZEVEDO, L. H. C. Vissungos – Negro work songs of the diamond district in Minas Gerais, Brazil 64
DANNEMANN, M. La glosa en el folklore musical chileno 68
GILLIS, F. Hot rhythm in piano ragtime 91
HAYWOOD, C. Latin American music in the college curriculum: problems and prospects 105
LIST, G. The folk music of the Atlantic littoral of Colombia, an introduction 115
MANZANARES, R. Instrumentos musicales tradicionales de Honduras 123
MERRIAM, A. P. Music and the origin of the Flathead Indians: a problem in culture history 129
NETTL, B. Aspects of folk music in North American cities 139
RAMÓN y RIVERA, L. F. El Mestizaje de la música afro-venezolana 176
RODRÍGUEZ, F. de M. Metodología para la reconstrucción de las danzas folklóricas extintas 183
VEGA, C. Tradiciones musicales y aculturación en Sudamérica 220

Papers read at the First Inter-American Composers Seminar

ATEHORTÚA, B. La ejecución de nueva música 18
BECERRA, G. La ejecución de la nueva música 41
COGAN, R. The training of the composer 51
CORDERO, R. El público y la música viva 57
de la VEGA, A. Breves consideraciones en relación a la formación del compositor contemporáneo 78
GARCÍA MORILLO, R. Consideraciones sobre la formación del compositor 84
NOBRE, M. Insuficiência da notação convencional en face das novas exigências da música contemporânea a apontamentos sôbre uma possivel mundança de atitude de intérprete frente a essa problemática 148
PINILLA, E. Problemas que enfrenta el compositor contemporáneo de las Américas 158
POWELL, M. A note on the training of composition students 164
POZZI ESCOT La música contemporánea y el auditor 168
SOMERS, H. An evaluation of the facts preventing contemporary music from reaching the concert repertoire 213
VINCENT, J. State and private aid to music 251

Papers read at the Joint Session of Composers and Ethnomusicologists
SANDI, L. El nacionalismo, la música tradicional y el compositor latino americano 192
SEEGER, C. Tradition and the (North) American composer 195

65 BRA Methoden der Klassifikation von Volksliedweisen [Bericht über die I. Arbeitstagung der Study Group of Folk Music Systematization beim International Folk Musik Council] Bratislava 31 August – 4 September 1965
Slovenská akadémie vied: Ústav hudobnej vedy [Slovak Academy of Sciences: Institute of Musicology] (Symposia II); Study Group of Folk Music Systematization of the International Folk Musik Council
ed. O. Elschek (Bratislava: Vydavatel'stvo Slovenskej akadémie vied, 1969)

Allgemeines zur Klassifikation
MARKL, J. Zu einigen Fragen des folkloristischen Musik-Katalogs 11
SUPPAN, W. Das Deutsche Volksliedarchiv und die Katalogisierung von Volksweisen 17
WIORA, W. Zur Methode der vergleichenden Melodienforschung 31

Rhythmisch-metrische Klassifikationssysteme
BIELAWSKI, L. and STĘSZEWSKI, J. Zur Klassifikation der polnischen Volkslieder 47
GALKO, L. and POLOCZEK, F. Systematik der formbildenden Elemente der slowakischen Volkslieder 57
HOSCHOWSKY, J. W. Die Aufbauprinzipien des Elementarkatalogs der rhythmischen Versstrukturen 73
VETTERL, K. and GELNAR, J. Die Melodien-

ordnung auf der Basis der metrorhythmischen Formgestaltung 81

Melodische Klassifikationssysteme
ELSCHEKOVÁ, A. Technologie der Datenverarbeitung bei der Klassifizierung von Volksliedern 93
JÁRDÁNYI, P. Die neue Ordnung der ungarischen Volkslieder 123
RAJECZKY, B. Die Melodieordnung der Monumenta Monodica Medii Aevi I 135

Melodische Inzipitenklassifikation
DEUTSCH, W. Die Gesetze der Tonalität und das Melodien-Register 141
KVĚTOVÁ, R. Die neue Ordnung der tschechischen Volkslieder vom Standpunkt der Melodie-Inzipiten 145

65 BRN Operní dílo Leoše Janáčka: Sborník příspěvků z mezinárodního symposia [Janáček's operatic works: collection of papers from the international symposium] Brno October 1965
Moravské Museum, Brno; Universita J. E. Purkyně, Brno; Svaz československých skladatelů [Union of Czechoslovak composers]
ed. T. Straková (Brno: Moravské museum, 1968 = Acta janáčkiana 1)

RACEK, J. Das Musikdrama Leoš Janáčeks und seine Stellung im Opernschaffen des 20. Jahrhunderts 16

Janáčkův hudebně dramatický styl [Janáček's style of music drama]
ŠTĚDROŇ, B. Die Urfassung von Janáčeks Jenufa 23
SYCHRA, A. Zum semantischen Charakter von Janáčeks thematischer Arbeit 28
VYSLOUŽIL, J. Über die Bedeutung der sogenannten modalen Strukturen bei der Entstehung von Janáčeks musikdramatischem Stil 32
KÖHLER, S. Funktionswert musikalischer Strukturen im Opernschaffen Leoš Janáčeks 37

Nápěvky mluvy a současná opera [Speech melodies and contemporary opera]
RACEK, J. Zur Problematik von Janáčeks Theorie der Sprachmelodie und seiner Kompositionspraxis 43
ŠTĚDROŇ, B. Zu Janáčeks Sprachmelodien 46
FUKAČ, J. Zur Frage der Stil-Bedeutung der Sprachmotive L. Janáčeks 49
ŠTĚDROŇ, M. Leoš Janáček und die zweite Wiener Schule 55

BÁRTOVÁ, J. Die Volkstümlichkeit im Opernwerk Leoš Janáčeks und Bohuslav Martinů 60
PEČMAN, R. Janáček und Martinů als dramatische Typen 65
VAJDA, I. Janáček und die slowakische Oper 68
POLJAKOVA, L. Yanachek i russkaya kultura [Janáček and Russian culture] (German résumé 78) 72
CVETKO, D. Janáčkove opere v ljubljanskom gledališču [Janáček's operas on the Ljubljana stage] (German résumé 84) 80
DELLA CORTE, A. L'interessamento culturale italiano all'arte di Leoš Janáček 86
ORLANDO, S. Squardo di insieme allo stile operistico di Janáček di un compositore italiano 88

Edice a interpretace Janáčkových pramenů [The editing and interpretation of Janáček sources]
DÜRR, J. M. Editionsprobleme von Janáčeks Opern 94
JÍLEK, F. Zur Instrumentation von Janáčeks Opern 97
MACKERRAS, C. On the problems of interpretation of Janáček's orchestration 102

JIČÍNSKÝ, B.   Das Brodsche Paradox   105
PROCHÁZKA, J.   Brods Übersetzung des Lib-
rettos der Jenufa und die Korrekturen Franz
Kafkas   109
STUCKENSCHMIDT, H. H.   Betrachtungen zu
Leoš Janáčeks Brouček   114
HOROVÁ, E.   Zu der deutschen Bearbeitung der
Ausflüge des Herrn Brouček   117
PŘIBÁŇOVÁ, S.   Zum 'Libretto der Ausflüge des
Herrn Brouček   123
STRAKOVÁ, T.   Die Zwischenspiele in Káťa
Kabanová   125
LINK, J. D.   Janáčeks Ouvertüre Žárlivost und

ihre Beziehungen zur Oper Jenufa   131

Interpretace a inscenace Janáčkových oper [The
interpretation and staging of Janáček's operas]
KUNDERA, L.   Zu den Fragen der Interpretation
von Janáčeks Werk   141
VOGEL, J.   Zur Interpretation der Opern
Janáčeks   145
TELCOVÁ, J.   Zur Szenographie von Janáčeks
Opern   148
WASSERBAUER, M.   Regie/Probleme der Oper
Janáčeks 'Das schlaue Füchslein'   152

65 CARB   Vision 65: International Congress on New Challenges for Human Communications
Carbondale, Illinois 21-3 October 1965
International Center for Typographic Arts; University of Southern Illinois at
Carbondale
(New York: International Center for Typographic Arts, 1966)

KOENIG, G. M.   The second phase of electronic
music   169

65 COP   Nord–Sud: Colloque tenu les 16 et 17 septembre 1965 à Copenhague à l'occasion de la VIIIᵉ
Assemblée Générale du C.I.P.S.H.
Copenhagen 16-17 September 1965 .
Kongelige danske videnskabernes selskab; International Council for Philosophy and
Humanistic Studies (CIPSH)
(Copenhagen: Munksgaard, 1967)

von FISCHER, K.   Nord et sud dans la musique du
XIVe au XVIe siècle   31

65 DIJ   Septième congrès international des bibliothèques musicales Dijon: actes du congrès
Dijon 1-6 July 1965
International Association of Music Libraries
ed. V. Fédorov, Fontes artis musicae xii 1965 (Kassel and Basle: Bärenreiter, 1966)

4 Round tables
1 **Les centres de documentation musicale et leurs
techniques particulières** (chairman STRARAM,
E.: panel JURRÈS, A., HUYS, B., DAVIES, J. H.,
NICOL, K. L., SHEPARD, B.)
JURRÈS, A.   Les centres de documentation musicale et leurs techniques particulières   100
DAVIES, J. H.   The radio librarian and music
documentation techniques   106

II **Utilization of data processing techniques in
musical documentation** (chairman HECKMANN,
H.: panel BROOK, B. S., SCHIØDT, N.,

RECKZIEGEL, W., MEYLAN, R.)
BROOK, B. S.   Utilization of data processing
techniques in music documentation   112
SCHIØDT, N.   Data processing applied to Byzan-
tine chant   122
RECKZIEGEL, W.   Musikbibliographie und
Datenspeicher   123
MEYLAN, R.   Utilisation des calculatrices élec-
troniques pour la comparaison interne du réper-
toire des basses danses du quinzième siècle 128

III **The music librarian, the bibliographer, the
documentalist** (chairman NOSKE, F.; panel

KING, A. H., DONÀ, M., DUCKLES, V., SCHETELICH, H., WALLON, S., ZEHNTNER, H., CUDWORTH, C.)
KING, A. H. The music librarian, the bibliographer, the documentalist 135
CUDWORTH, C. Un 'répertoire de documents musicaux' 145

IV Audio-visual means of musical documentation (chairman SPIVACKE, H.; panel LINDBERG, F., LEBEAU, E., SAUL, P.)
LINDBERG, F. Quelques aspects de la documentation musicale audio-visuelle 147
LEBEAU, E. Le problème des publications originales de musique non imprimées à propos dc la recherche de la musique de film 150
SAUL, P. A documentation policy for a national sound archive 152

BROOK, B. S. The simplified 'Plaine and Easie Code System' for notating music: a proposal for international adoption 156

5 Séance de la Société française de musicologie: 'Le tempo dans l'exécution musicale du XVIIe et du XVIIIe siècles'; 'Le tempo dans la musique de tradition orale', 4 July 1965 (chairman de CHAMBURE, H.)
THIBAULT, G. Le 'Te Deum' de Lalande: minutage de l'époque 162
LAUNAY, D. Les rapports de tempo entre mesures binaires et mesures ternaires dans la musique française (1600–1650) 166
CUDWORTH, C. The meaning of 'vivace' in eighteenth century England 194
BROOK, B. S. Le tempo dans l'exécution de la musique instrumentale à la fin du XVIIIe siècle: les contributions de C. Mason et William Crotch 196
VERCHALY, A. Le tempo dans la 'musique mesurée à l'antique' 202
MARCEL-DUBOIS, C. Le tempo dans les musiques de tradition orale 204

6 Séance du Group français du Comité international des musées et collections d'instruments de musique, Beaune 6 July 1965
MARCEL-DUBOIS, C. Instruments de musique ethniques et musées spécialisés d'ethnologie 207
THIBAULT, G. Recherches effectuées au musée instrumental du Conservatoire de Paris (1962–1965) 209

65 GEN Deuxième congrès international du rythme et de la rythmique
Geneva 9–14 August 1965
Institut Jaques-Dalcroze, Geneva
(Geneva: Institut Jaques-Dalcroze, 1966)

MARTIN, F. Les sources du rythme musical 15
JAENICKE, G. Rhythmik als Mittel zur Ausbildung des Opernsängers 22
FALLER, R. Un esprit nouveau dans l'enseignement du solfège 136
WINCKEL, F. Rhythmus und Resonanz 141
REICHEL, B. L'improvisation 148
TAUBERT, K.-H. Die Beziehungen zwischen den klassischen Tänzen und der Rhythmik 154
ANSERMET, E. Les structures du rythme 156

65 JER Fourth World Congress of Jewish Studies: Papers
Jerusalem 25 July – 1 August 1965
World Union of Jewish Studies
(Jerusalem: World Union of Jewish Studies, 1967–8)

Vol. ii (1968) [Full Hebrew versions of all articles printed in vol. i]
GRADENWITZ, P. The religious works and thought of Arnold Schoenberg 147
SPECTOR, J. Written tradition and contemporary practice in the biblical cantillation of the Samaritans 153
WERNER, E. Scope and aims of Jewish music research (isolation or integration) 157
SHILOAH, A. The sources of Falaquera's chapter on music in his Sefer ha-mevaqqesh [English résumé] 207
SMOIRA, M. Musical ethos in the theory and practice of the Jews [English résumé] 207
AVENARY, H. Gentile song as a source of inspiration for Israel Naǧarah [English résumé] 208
ADLER, I. The new music fragment of Obadiah the Norman Proselyte and its importance for Jewish music research [English résumé] 209
SHMUELI, H. Music in mediaeval biblical exegesis [English résumé] 209

65 LIÈ Problèmes d'acoustique: 5e Congrès international d'acoustique: Rapports/Reports/Berichte
Liège 7–14 September 1965
International Commission on Acoustics, International Union of Pure and Applied
Physics
(Liège: Université de Liège, 1965 = Les congrès et colloques de l'Université de Liège 35)

Vol. i/b Conférences particulières/Specialized conferences/Sondervorträge (1965)

G Acoustique architecturale

CANAC, F. Equation canonique des théâtres antiques; rôle de l'angle d'écoute et de l'orchestre 13

KOSTEN, C. W. and de LANGE, P. A. The new Rotterdam concert hall – some aspects of the acoustic design 43

M Acoustique musicale

LEIPP, E. Méthode d'appréciation des qualités musicales d'un ensemble orgue-salle 51

MERCER, D. M. A. Organ pipe adjustments as a guide to theories of the mechanism of the pipe 52

CHIARUCCI, H., REIBAL, G., RIST, S., FERREYRA, B. Rapport entre la hauteur et le fondamental d'un son musical 53

MEYER, J. Die Richtcharakteristiken von Violoncelli 54

ISING, H. Über die Tonbildung in Orgelpfeifen 55

YOSHIDA, T. An investigation on how industrial music in Japan goes on 56

CASTELLENGO, M. and LEIPP, E. L'acoustique des cloches 61

MANLEY, D. M. J. P. The subjective judgement of liveness and quality of recorded music 62

LIENARD, J. S. L'usure des disques 63

LORENTE, M. Physical basis of musical tonality and consonance 64

BIERL, R. Musik-Elektronik – praktische Erfahrungen, Gegenwartsprobleme und Zukunftsfragen 65

SLAWSON, A. W. A psychoacoustic comparison between vowel quality and musical timbre 66

KOSHIKAWA, T., NAKAYAMA, T. and MIYAGAWA, R. On the designing method of reproduced sound quality using the multidimensional sensory and emotional scales 67

Vol. ii Conférences générales/General conferences/Allgemeine Vorträge (1965)

FOURDOUIEV, V. Evaluation objective de l'acoustique des salles 41

65 MARB Arbeit und Volksleben: Deutscher Volkskundekongress 1965 in Marburg
Marburg 1965
Deutsche Gesellschaft für Volkskunde, Leipzig
(Göttingen: Otto Schwartz & Co., 1967 = Veröffentlichungen des Instituts für mitteleuropäische Volksforschung an der Philipps-Universität Marburg-Lahn, ed. G. Heilfurth and I. Weber-Kellermann, A4)

6 Lied-, Musik- und Tanzforschung

KLUSEN, E. Musik zur Arbeit heute 306

SUPPAN, W. Volks-(völker-)kundliche und soziologische Gedanken zum Thema 'Musik und Arbeit' 318

ANDERLUH, A. Das Lied der Arbeit im deutschen Alpenland 325

STOCKMANN, E. Volksmusikinstrumente und Arbeit 331

65 MTS II congrés litúrgic de Montserrat
Montserrat 5–10 July 1965
Monestir de Montserrat
(Montserrat: Monestir de Montserrat, 1966–7 = Publicacions de l'Abadia de Montserrat 4)

Vol. iv Secció de música, ed. G. Estrada (1967)

UBEDA, J. Valor pastoral de la música en la litúrgia 15

BENET, S. Glossa a la ponència 'Valor pastoral de la música en la litúrgia' 27

Discussion 30

ALTISENT, M. Valor pastoral del cant
gregorià   35
PUIG I MATAS, Ll.   El cant gregorià com a
cant de la litúrgia romana   38
RIUS, J.   Les melodies en llengua popular elim-
inen el cant gregorià? Fins a quin punt s'ha de
conservar aquest cant?   41
CARCELLER, P.   Possibilitat d'adaptar la melodia
gregoriana a una traducció en llengua
popular   43
BARDOLET, S.   Interès musicològic del cant
gregorià   45
MORAGAS, B.   Reflexions sobre el cant gregorià
com a model per al nou cant litúrgic   48
PRAT, J.   Ús mixt musical entre melodies noves
en llengua popular i melodies en llatí 54
Discussion   56

PADRÓS, J.   Estructures del cant popular en la
litúrgia   67

CIVIL, F.   Glossa a la ponència 'Estructures del
cant popular en la litúrgia'   72
HOMS, J.   Notes sobre la funció de la música en la
litúrgia   74
SÀBAT, A.   La paraula en el cant litúrgic   75
COLS, D.   Cants de la missa amb estructura
sàlmica   78
CAMPS, G.   Necessitat de trobar un estil musical
que afavoreixi una bona traducció dels
salms   79
ESTRADA, G.   Avantatges i inconvenients de
l'estil salmòdic musical del P. J. Gelineau:
necessitat de buscar les estructures musicals més
adaptades a cada salm i a cada moment en el
qual es canta   80
Discussion   82

Valor pastoral de la polifonia
PÉREZ SIMÓ, A.   La polifonia en el gust del
poble   89
CIVIL, F.   Valor pastoral de la polifonia en
llengua vernacle fonamentada sobre el cant
popular   90
ESTRADA, G.   La polifonia en la nostra litúrgia
d'ara i de demà   93
Discussion   106

MOLL, X.   El cant en llengua viva a l'acció
litúrgica   113

VILANOVA, J.   Conservem el cant gregorià tant
com puguem   125
CERVERA, J. M.   Dos treballs a realitzar: els
recitatius i els himnes   127
MOLL, X.   Resposta a les dues intervencions
anteriors   128
PLANAS, J.   Experiències de cant litúrgic en llengua viva   129

VIVANCOS, J. M.   Notes amb vista a la reforma
del cant en l'acció litúrgica   131

Valor pastoral de la polifonia
TEMPRANO, I.   El canto popular litúrgico   136
ARNELLA, J.   El ritme en el futur del cant popular
religiós   137
MARTORELL, O.   Cant popular i música litúrgica
a Catalunya   138
RÖVENSTRUNCK, B.   Situació actual de la música
litúrgica a Alemanya   141
COLS, D.   Situació del cant popular litúrgic a
França, avui   144
GARCÍA, J. A.   La música del proprio de la
missa   147
ARRIZABALAGA, J. M.   Canto litúrgico en
euskera   151
MIRET, H.   Cant litúrgic en català   156
Discussion   162

VIRGILI, Ll.   Promoció de directors amb vista a
la participació popular   169

CERVERA, M.   Sobre els directors   173
BALLARÀ, J.   Les agrupacions corals, primer
auxiliar del director amb vista a la participació
popular en el cant religiós   174
RIBÓ, E.   Pedagogia de la direcció coral   176

SOLÀ, J. M.   Contribució de les institucions
d'ensenyament al cant litúrgic popular   179

CASTELLÀ, M. C.   El mètode Ward   190
TULLOT, M. T.   El mètode 'Orff-Schulwerk' 192
BONAL, M. D.   L'educació musical a l'escola 194
MARTORELL, A.   Una experiència d'educació
musical   197
CASULLERAS, J.   Estat actual de l'ensenyament
de la música al batxillerat   200

MARTORELL, O.   Mitjans de difusió   203

FÀBREGUES, A.   Les fitxes i edicions de cants
litúrgics   212

Valoració actual de l'orgue i dels instruments
GAMISSANS, J.   El servei litúrgic de l'orgue   219
MATHEU, A.   L'orgue i l'harmònium   222
VICTORI, Ll.   Els instruments electrònics   223
CASALS, J.   Comparació dels instruments elec-
trònics amb l'orgue   226
BLANCAFORT, G.   Tècnica de l'orgueneria, con-
strucció i collocació de l'orgue   228
TORRENT, M.   Consells per a l'adquisició d'un
orgue   231
GARCÍA, J. M.   La restauración de los órganos
históricos   233

65 NEWH   **Computers for the Humanities? A Record of the Conference sponsored by Yale University**
New Haven 22–3 January 1965
Yale University
(New Haven: Yale University, 1965)

5 Computers and the arts
BOWLES, E. A.   Computers in musicology   103

FERRETTI, E.   The computer as a tool for the
creative musician   107

65 NEWY   **Musicology and the Computer: Three Symposia**
New York 10 April 1965; 10 May 1965; 21 May 1966
American Musicological Society: Greater New York Chapter
ed. B. S. Brook (New York: City University of New York Press, 1970 = American
Musicological Society Greater New York Chapter Publications 2)

MITCHELL, W. S.   'A hitherto unknown – or – A
recently discovered . . .'   1

Musicology and the computer I
FORTE, A.   The structure of atonal music: practical aspects of a computer-oriented research
project   10
LOCKWOOD, L.   A stylistic investigation of the
masses of Josquin Desprez with the aid of the
computer: a progress report   19
BROOK, B. S.   Music documentation of the
future   28
Discussion BOWLES, E. A., MENDEL, A.   37

**Musicology and the computer II: input languages
to represent music**
BAUER-MENGELBERG, S.   The Ford-Columbia
input language   48
BROOK, B. S.   The Plaine and Easie Code   53
GOULD, M. J. and LOGEMANN, G. W.   Alpha-
meric language for music analysis   57
WENKER, J.   A computer oriented music not-
ation including ethnomusicological symbols 91
JACKSON, R. and BERNZOTT, P.   A musical input

language and a sample program for musical
analysis   130
KASSLER, M.   An essay toward specification of a
music-reading machine   151
Discussion and commentary ROTHENBERG, D.,
KASSLER, M., REGENER, E., LINCOLN, H. B.,
KUTTNER, F. A., LOGEMANN, G. W.   176

Musicology 1966–2000: A practical program
DITTMER, L.   Western-European music of the
Christian era before 1400: research and
publication   190
LARUE, J.   New directions for style analysis 194
LIPPMAN, E.   History of theory   198
LOCKWOOD, L.   Utopian proposals   204
PALISCA, C. V.   Stylistic change and the history
of ideas   211
ZIMMERMAN, F.   Musical biography and the-
matic cataloguing: two opposing aspects of
musicology in the 21st century   216
Discussion MENDEL, A.   222

Bibliography: Computer applications to music
and musicology   229

65 RAV   **Dante: Atti della giornata internazionale di studio per il VII centenario**
Ravenna 6–7 March 1965
Società di studi romagnoli
(Faenza: Fratelli Lega, 1965)

MONTEROSSO, R.   Musica e poesia nel 'De vulgari eloquentia'   83

65 STAV   **Apollinaire et la musique: actes du [4ème] colloque**
               Stavelot 27–9 August 1965
                    Amis de Guillaume Apollinaire: Journées Apollinaire
                    ed. M. Décaudin (Stavelot: Amis de Guillaume Apollinaire, 1967)

DAVIES, M.   La petite musique d'Apollinaire 43   Résumé of discussions   69
BELLAS, J.   Apollinaire et Poulenc: peut-on
mettre 'Alcools' en musique?   49   **Appendix**
POUILLIART, R.   Apollinaire et quelques   Les musiciens d'Apollinaire   99
musiciens   59   Poèmes d'Apollinaire mis en musique   103

65 WAR   **Actes du XIᵉ congrès international d'histoire des sciences**
               Warsaw, Toruń, Kielce, Kraków 24–31 August 1965
                    Union internationale d'histoire et de philosophie des sciences
                    ed. P. Czartorski (Wrocław: Ossolineum, 1967–8)

Vol. ii (1967)   BRISTIGER, M.   L'analyse musicale dans la musi-
2 Histoire des sciences de l'homme   cologie contemporaine   285
LISSA, Z.   Musicology and the universal history
of music   279

66 BRN   The Stage Works of Bohuslav Martinů: Collected Papers from the Colloquim of the Musical-
Dramatic Works of Bohuslav Martinů, held during the First International Musical Festival in
Brno on October 9th and 10th 1966/ Bohuslav Martinůs Bühnenschaffen: Sammelschrift des
Kolloquiums über das musikdramatische Werk von Bohuslav Martinů, das vom 9. bis 10.
Oktober in Brno stattfand
Brno 9–10 October 1966
    Mezinárodní hudební festival [International Musical Festival], Brno
    ed. R. Pečman (Prague: Czechoslovak Music Information Centre, 1967)

RACEK, J. Evolution créatrice de Bohuslav
    Martinů   19
ŠAFRÁNEK, M. Aus den Erinnerungen an Bo-
    huslav Martinů   25

General problems
ŠAFRÁNEK, M. Free form in the stage com-
    positions of Bohuslav Martinů   39
HALBREICH, H. Bohuslav Martinů und die Welt
    des Traumes   57
MIHULE, J. Der Mensch und die Welt im musik-
    dramatischen Schaffen Bohuslav Martinůs 75
TROJAN, J. Zur Problematik der Volkstüm-
    lichkeit im musikdramatischen Werk von Bo-
    ·huslav Martinů   97
PEČMAN, R. On the artistic types to which
    Bohuslav Martinů and Leoš Janáček belong (an
    attempt at a comparison on the basis of their
    dramatic works)   115

On the individual operas
POPELKA, I. The minute opera of Bohuslav
    Martinů   127

BÁRTOVÁ, J. Die Rundfunkoper Die Stimme des
    Waldes –ein Versuch Bohuslav Martinůs um
    eine neue Lösung der musikdramatischen Form
    (Beitrag zur Schaffensproblematik des Kom-
    ponisten in der 1. Hälfte der dreissiger
    Jahre)   159
FUKAČ, J. Zum Kompositionstyp der Oper
    Juliette   173
ŠTĚDROŇ, M. Zur Frage der 'Adaptation' der
    Oper Griechische Passion von Bohuslav
    Martinů   183
VYSLOUŽIL, J. The Ariadne of Bohuslav Mar-
    tinů (notes on the genesis, style and ideas of the
    work)   195

Miscellanea
COSMA, V. La musique de Leoš Janáček et de
    Bohuslav Martinů en Roumanie   207
NOSEK, V. The works of Bohuslav Martinů on
    the Brno operatic stage (remarks of
    dramaturgist)   221

66 BYD   Musica antiqua Europae orientalis: acta scientifica congressus I
Bydgoszcz and Toruń 10–16 September 1966
    Bydgoskie towarzystwo naukowe [Bydgoszcz Scientific Society]; Filharmonia po-
    morska imienia Ignacego Paderewskiego [Paderewski Pomeranian Philharmonia]
    ed. Z. Lissa (Warsaw: Państwowe wydawnictwo naukowe, 1966)

LISSA, Z. Ost-West-Probleme in der modernen
    Musikgeschichtsschreibung   19
KRĂSTEV, V. Puti razvitiya bolgarskoy
    muzïkal'noy kul'turï v period XII–XVIII sto-
    letii [Developmental paths of Bulgarian musical
    culture from the 12th to the 18th century] 45
VANICKÝ, J. Czech mediaeval and Renaissance
    music   69
VOLEK, T. Czech music of the seventeenth and
    eighteenth centuries   80
RIBARIČ, R. Die Hauptquellen und Probleme
    der slowakischen Musikgeschichte bis zum
    Ende des XVIII. Jahrhunderts   97
DJURIĆ-KLAJN, S. Certains aspects de la musi-

que profane serbe de l'époque féodale   117
STEFANOVIĆ, D. The Serbian chant from the
    15th to 18th centuries   140
CVETKO, D. La musique slovène du XVIᵉ au
    XVIIIᵉ siècle   164
KOVAČEVIĆ, K. Die kroatische Musik des
    XVII. und XVIII. Jahrhunderts   200
RAJECZKY, B. Mittelalterliche Mehrstimmigkeit
    in Ungarn   223
FALVY, Z. Musik in Ungarn bis zum Ende des
    XVI. Jahrhunderts   237
BÓNIS, F. Ungarische Musik im XVII.–XVIII.
    Jahrhundert   258

FEICHT, H. Die polnische Monodie des
Mittelalters   277
FEICHT, H. Quellen zur mehrstimmigen Musik
in Polen vom späten Mittelalter bis 1600   281
SZWEYKOWSKI, Z. M. Some problems of Bar-
oque music in Poland   294
NOWAK-ROMANOWICZ, A. Musik in den
Theaterformen des ehemaligen Polens   310
WĘCOWSKI, J. La musique symphonique po-
lonaise du XVIIIe siècle   334
LISSA, Z. Folk elements in Polish music from the
middle ages up to the 18th century   354
CHOMIŃSKI, J. M. Die Beziehungen der polni-
schen Musik zu Westeuropa vom XV. bis zum
XVII. Jahrhundert   383
COSMA, V. Aspects de la culture musicale sur le
territoire de la Roumanie entre le XIVe et le
XVIIIe siècle   403
CIOBANU, G. La culture musicale byzantine sur

le territoire de la Roumanie jusq'au XVIIIe
siècle   419
GHIRCOIAŞIU, R. Les mélodies roumaines du
XVIe–XVIIIe siècles   431
BRAZHNIKOV, M. Russkoye tserkovnoye peniye
XII–XVIII vekov [Russian ecclesiastical chant
from the 12th to the 18th century]   455
SKREBKOV, S. Evolyutsiya stilya v russkoy
khorovoy muzïke XVII veka [The evolution of
style in Russian choral music of the 17th
century]   470
KELDÏSH, YU. Voznikoveniye i razvitiye russkoy
operï v XVIII veke [The rise and development of
Russian opera in the 18th century]   489
SHREYER-TKACHENKO, A. Razvitiye ukrainskoy muzïki v XVI–XVII vekakh [The development of Ukrainian music from the 16th to
the 18th century]   507

66 CHIC   **Sacred Music and Liturgy Reform after Vatican II: Proceedings of the Fifth International Church Music Congress**
Chicago and Milwaukee 21–8 August 1966
Consociatio internationalis musicae sacrae
ed. J. Overath (Rome: Consociatio internationalis musicae sacrae, 1969); German version as *Musica Sacra und Liturgiereform nach dem II. Vatikanischen Konzil: V. Internationaler Kongress für Kirchenmusik*, ed. J. Overath (Regensburg: Pustet, 1969)

HENNIG, J. Liturgy and art   52
FELLERER, K. G. Liturgy and music   71
O'NEILL, C. E. Theological meaning of 'Ac-
tuosa participatio' in the liturgy   89
MIRANDA y GÓMEZ, M. D. Function of sacred
music and 'Actuosa participatio'   111, 235
GÖLLER, G. Structure of the Missa cantata in
the Roman liturgy   117
WERNER, E. Problem of congregational singing
and art singing in the liturgy   135

LENNARDS, J. Possibilities and limits of congregational singing   148
BOMM, U. Gregorian chant and liturgical singing in the vernacular   163
Discussions of practices in post-conciliar church
music [including proposals on setting vernacular texts to Latin compositions]   169
LANG, P. H. The 'Patrimonium musicae sacrae'
and the task of sacred music today   238

66 GRA   **Grazer und Münchener balkanologische Studien. i Zweite Grazer Balkanologen-Tagung 1966 'Das orientalische Element am Balkan'; ii Münchener Studien zu Geschichte und Volkskunde der Balkan-Länder**
Graz 11–14 May 1966
Akademie für Musik und darstellende Kunst in Graz
(Munich: Dr Dr Rudolf Trofenik, 1967; Beiträge zur Kenntnis Südosteuropas und des Nahen Orients, ed. H.-G. Beck and others, 2)

1 Zweite Grazer Balkanologen-Tagung 1966 'Das orientalische Element am Balkan'

GRAF, W. Zur sonagraphischen Untersuchung
von Sprache und Musik   40
REINHARD, K. Die gegenwärtige Praxis des
Epengesanges in der Türkei   83

RIHTMAN, C. Orientalische Elemente in der
traditionellen Musik Bosniens und der Herze-
gowina   97
WÜNSCH, W. Das orientalische Element am
Balkan als Thema der Musikgeschichte, Musikethnologie und Instrumentenkunde   106

66 LEIP   **Bericht über den internationalen musikwissenschaftlichen Kongress Leipzig 1966**
Leipzig 19–23 September 1966
Gesellschaft für Musikforschung
ed. C. Dahlhaus, R. Kluge, E. H. Meyer, W. Wiora (Kassel and Basle:
Bärenreiter/Leipzig: Deutscher Verlag für Musik, 1970)

GERSTENBERG, W. Goethes Dichtung und die Musik   3
SIEGMUND-SCHULTZE, W. Probleme des historischen Musikverständnisses   11

Symposium I: Fortschritt und Avantgardismus (chairman MEYER, E. H.)
BROCKHAUS, H. A. Fortschritt und Avantgardismus   25
DAHLHAUS, C. Fortschritt und Avantgarde   33
(panel BORRIS, S., von DADELSEN, G., ELSNER, J., FINSCHER, L., KIRCHMEYER, H., KÖHLER, S., MAYER, G., NOTOWICZ, N.   41)

Symposium II: Zum Begriff der Tonalität (chairman WIORA, W.)
VEIT, E. Zum Begriff der Tonalität   65
REINECKE, H.-P. Zum Begriff der Tonalität 72
(panel BESSELER, H., GOLDHAMMER, O., HÜSCHEN, H., KNEPLER, G., ROHWER, J., VOGEL, M.   79)

Symposium III: Zum Begriff der Klassik (chairman SALMEN, W.)
FINSCHER, L. Zum Begriff der Klassik in der Musik   103
GOLDSCHMIDT, H. Über die Einheit der vokalen und instrumentalen Sphäre in der klassischen Musik   139
(panel FEDER, G., KÖHLER K.-H., MAINKA, J., SCHOLZ, G., SEIFERT, W., WIORA, W. 127, 152)

HEYDE, H. Zur Bedeutung der synästhetischen Wahrnehmung kosmischer Lichterscheinungen für den altindischen Klangzauber   165
SCHULER, M. Zur Geschichte des Kantors im Mittelalter   169
GÖLLER, G. Zur Bezeichnung der Neumen in der germanischen Choralnotation   173
GÜNTHER, U. Zur Datierung des Manuskripts Modena, Biblioteca estense, αM. 5, 24 (Olim lat. 568)   175
DUNNING, A. Die 'aktuelle' Musik im Zeitalter der Niederländer   181
BENTE, M. Senfls Musik im Heidelberger Kapellkatalog: ein Beitrag zur Repertoireüberlieferung im 16. Jahrhundert   186
KÄMPER, D. La Gamba: Folia-Bearbeitungen für Instrumentalensemble um die Mitte des 16. Jahrhunderts in Italien   190
KIRSCH, W. Zum Verhältnis von Motettenstil und liturgisch-musikalischer Praxis im 16. Jahrhundert   196
MÜLLER-BLATTAU, W. Zur Dissonanzbehandlung bei Giovanni Gabrieli   201

DÜRR, W. and SIEGELE, U. Cantar d'affetto: zum Vortrag monodischer Musik   208
KROSS, S. Concerto – concertare und conserere   216
BRAUN, W. Zum Verhältnis zwischen Vokal- und Instrumentalmusik im 17. Jahrhundert   221
KÜMMERLING, H. Entdeckung und Verwendung der Subbasslage   227
BASELT, B. Actus musicus und Historie um 1700 in Mitteldeutschland   230
MASSENKEIL, G. Marc-Antoine Charpentier als Messenkomponist   237
JUST, M. Lecerf de la Viéville: comparaison de la musique italienne et de la musique française (1704–1706)   238
GRÜSS, B. Über die objektive Verlangsamung musikalischer Verläufe als Erscheinungsweise der historischen Entwicklung musikalischer Formen   242
STOCKMANN, B. Über die Relatio non harmonica als rhetorische Figur   245
HELLER, K. Die Bedeutung Johann Georg Pisendels für die deutsche Vivaldi-Rezeption   247
FLEISCHHAUER, G. Entwicklung und Stand der Magdeburger Telemann-Pflege   251
HOBOHM, W. Georg Philipp Telemann und seine Schüler   260
NEUMANN, W. Zur Frage instrumentaler Gestaltungsprinzipien in Bachs Vokalwerk   265
SCHULZE, H.-J. Beiträge zur Bach-Quellenforschung   269
FEDER, G. Eine Methode der Stiluntersuchung, demonstriert an Haydns Werken   275
OLIAS, G. Das Bach- und Beethoven-Bild im literarischen und musik-kritischen Werk Wladimir Fjodorowitsch Odojewskis   287
RICHTER, L. Tanzstücke des Berliner Biedermeier – Folklore an der Wende zur Kommerzialisierung   293
NIEMEYER, A. Franz Schuberts 'Lazarus'-Fragment und seine Beziehung zur Textdichtung   300
LEHMANN, D. Gibt es Gesetzmässigkeiten der Entstehung und Entwicklung nationaler Musikkulturen?   305
MARGGRAF, W. Die formale Entwicklung des Duetts in den Frühopern Giuseppe Verdis   310
FELLINGER, I. Unbekannte Entwürfe zu Robert Schumanns Klavierstücken op. 99 und op. 124   313
ROTHE, H.-J. Neue Dokumente zur Schumann-Forschung aus dem Leipziger Stadtarchiv 318

MOHR, W. Johannes Brahms' formenschöpferische Originalität, dargestellt am ersten Satz seiner Violinsonate, op. 108, und seiner Rhapsodie, op. 79 Nr. 2   322

BEYTHIEN, J. Die Violinsonate in G-Dur, op. 78, von Johannes Brahms – ein Beitrag zum Verhältnis zwischen formaler und inhaltlicher Gestaltung   325

MAINKA, J. Klangaufnahme und musikalisches Schriftzeichen – Gedanken zu Notation und Tradition in der Moderne   332

ŠTĚDROŇ, B. Zu Janáčeks Sprachmelodien   339

SCHUHMACHER, G. Zur Entwicklung der evangelischen Kirchenmusik in Deutschland seit 1945   347

MAYER, G. Über die musikalische Integration des Dokumentarischen   351

SCHAEFER, H. Charakter oder Typ? – Gedanken zu Problemen des zeitgenössischen Musiktheaters und der modernen Operninterpretation   357

STRELLER, F. Musikalische Sprachmittel in Werken der zeitgenössischen Musik (Bartók, Chatschaturjan)   362

HOKE, H. G. Überlegungen zu einer Theorie der Musikwissenschaft   372

CLEMENS, W. Zur wissenschaftlichen Grundlegung der Musikerziehung   375

WEHNERT, M. Zum Terminus 'Thema' in der Musik- und Sprachforschung der Gegenwart   380

HEINZ, R. Motivationen der musikhistorischen Forschung im 19. Jahrhundert   385

RUMMENHÖLLER, P. Der dialektische Theoriebegriff – zur Verwirklichung Hegelschen Denkens in Moritz Hauptmanns Musiktheorie   387

ELSSNER, M. Hegel und Vischer über Gegenstand, Inhalt und Form in der Musik   391

VOGEL, M. Lässt sich die Reine Stimmung verwirklichen?   397

JOST, E. Subjektive Dimensionen musikalischer Klangwahrnehmungen, dargestellt am Beispiel der Klarinette   407

DROYSEN, D. Akustische Untersuchungen an Tasteninstrumenten des 18. bis 20. Jahrhunderts   416

GRESS, F.-H. Gedanken zur Perspektive der Pfeifenorgel und ihrer universellen und ökonomischen Gestaltung   424

SCHRAMMEK, W. Welche Musikinstrumente gehören in ein Musikinstrumentenmuseum?   434

SEIDEL, E. Ein chromatisches Harmonisierungsmodell in Schuberts 'Winterreise'   437

SWING, R. Zur Beschreibung komplizierter harmonischer Abläufe in tonaler Musik (insbesondere in Werken der Wiener Klassik)   451

RECKZIEGEL, W. Ein subjektives Tempomass   459

KLUGE, R. Volksliedanalyse und -systematisierung mit Hilfe eines Rechenautomaten   460

LARUE, J. Some computer aids to musicology   466

SCHMIEDEL, P. Die Begriffe Melodie, Harmonie und Rhythmus und ihre Beziehung zum menschlichen Erleben sowie zur akustischen Schwingung   469

de la MOTTE-HABER, H. Die Abhängigkeit des Sonanzeindrucks von der Intervallstruktur   477

KÖTTER, E. Dimensionen der Musikbeurteilung bei elektrischer Übertragung   482

GÜLKE, P. Interpretation und die Wandlungen des musikalischen Hörens   487

NIEMANN, K. Mehrdimensionale Musikurteile in der soziologischen Forschung   490

REINECKE, H.-P. Über den Zusammenhang zwischen Stereotypen und Klangbeispielen verschiedener musikalischer Epochen   499

MICHEL, P. Musikpsychologische Untersuchungen über die optimale Entwicklung musikalischer Fähigkeiten in den ersten Lebensjahren   510

METZLER, F. Über Eigenart und Herkunft wechselrhythmischer Gestalten in der Melodieerfindung des zehn- bis vierzehnjährigen Volksschulkindes   516

MEHNER, K. Kommauntersuchungen beim einstimmigen begleiteten Singen   524

HÖCHEL, L. Zur Entwicklung des Intonationsgehörs im Bereich der Mehrstimmigkeit   529

ELSNER, J. Zum Problem des Maqām   535

KOJIMA, S. Tonale Strukturen und ihr tonsystematischer Zusammenhang im japanischen Volkslied   547

SCHÖNFELDER, G. Die melodische Gerüstgestalt Örlhuang und ihre Realisation   561

66 MANL   The Musics of Asia: Papers read at an International Music Symposium
Manila 12–16 April 1966
National Music Council of the Philippines; UNESCO National Commission of the
Philippines; International Music Council
ed. J. Maceda (Manila: National Music Council of the Philippines/UNESCO
National Commission of the Philippines, 1971)

HOOD, M.   Aspects of group improvisation in the
Javanese gamelan   16
MACEDA, J.   Classification and distribution of
musical instruments in the Philippines   24
POWERS, H.   A comparative approach to the
classification of ragas   38
TRÂN VAN KHÊ Elements of musical structure in
the Vietnamese tradition   77
MORTON, D.   The traditional instrumental music
of Thailand   90
GARFIAS, R.   On melody and mode in Japanese
court music   107
PIAN RULAN CHAO   The function of rhythm in

the Peking opera   114
SMITH, B.   The 'classical' music of Korea   132
CHOU WEN CHUNG   East and West, old and
new   143
de LEEUW, T.   What can we do for our musical
future?   147
XENAKIS, I.   Structures hors-temps   152
AMARADEVA, W. D.   Sinhalese music through
the ages and its modern trends   174
CHUANG PEN-LI   A study of some ancient Chin-
ese musical instruments   185
LIANG TSAI PING   Chinese music in Asia   191

66 MOR   Papers from the West Virginia University Conference on Computer Applications in Music
Morgantown, West Virginia 29–30 April 1966
West Virginia University
ed. G. Lefkoff (Morgantown: West Virginia University Library, 1967)

BROOK, B. S.   Music bibliography and the computer   9
FORTE, A.   Computer-implemented analysis of
musical structure   29
LEFKOFF, G.   Computers and the study of musical style   43

HILLER, L. A.   Programming a computer for
musical composition   63
COOK, C. C.   An introduction to the information
processing capabilities of the computer   89

66 MTA   Montauban 1966: Actes des journées internationales d'étude du Baroque [II]
Montauban 22–4 September 1966
[Baroque ii] (Montauban: Centre national de recherches du Baroque, 1967)

Le Baroque au théâtre
MATHIEU-ARTH, F.   Du masque à l'opera anglais   53

Théâtralité du Baroque
WOLF, R. E.   Musique du mal, musique du bien
dans le théâtre Baroque   119

Musicology 1966–2000: A Practical Program
New York 21 May 1966

see 65 NEWY

66 OXF¹ Proceedings of the XIIIth International Congress of Byzantine Studies
Oxford 5–10 September 1966
International Association for Byzantine Studies
ed. J. M. Hussey, D. Obolensky, S. Runciman (London: Oxford University Press, 1967)

VELIMIROVIĆ, M. The influence of the Byzantine chant on the music of the Slavic countries 119
STEFANOVIĆ, D. The influence of the Byzantine chant on the music of the Slavic countries (supplementary paper) 141
STRUNK, O. Byzantine music in the light of recent research and publication 245
SCHIRÒ, G. Problemi heirmologici (supplementary paper) 255
HUGLO, M. Relations musicales entre Byzance et l'Occident (supplementary paper) 267

66 OXF² Probleme mittelalterlicher Überlieferung und Textkritik: Oxforder Colloquium 1966
Oxford 18–24 September 1966
Institute of Germanic Studies, University of London; Institut für Ältere Deutsche Philologie der Philipps-Universität, Marburg
ed. P. F. Ganz and W. Schröder (Berlin: Erich Schmidt, 1968 = Publications of the Institute of Germanic Studies, University of London)

RÄKEL, H.-H. S. Liedkontrafaktur im frühen Minnesang 96
LOMNITZER, H. Zur wechselseitigen Erhellung von Text- und Melodiekritik mittelalterlicher deutscher Lyrik 118

66 SOF Actes du premier congrès international des études balkaniques et sud-est européennes
Sofia 26 August – 1 September 1966
International Association of South-East European Studies
(Sofia: Académie bulgare des sciences, 1967–71)

Vol. ii Archéologie, histoire de l'antiquité, arts (1969)

Arts

PETROV, S. Sur quelques nouveaux procédés méthodologiques de recherche sur le folklore musical en Bulgarie et les autres pays balkaniques 1041
TONČEVA, E. Die Neumentexte in der Palausow – Abschrift des Synodiks des Zaren Boril und ihre Stellung in der Geschichte der bulgarischen Mittelalterlichen Musik 1055
KAUFMANN, N. Die Mehrstimmigkeit in der Liederfolklore der Balkanvölker 1067
CIOBANU, G. Les liens folkloriques musicaux des peuples du Sud-Est de l'Europe 1085
KRADER, B. Serbian and Bulgarian wedding ritual song: a comparison of musical and other traits 1088
YÖNETKEN, H. B. Les rythmes boiteux (Aksak usuller) employés dans la tradition musicale turque et leurs commentaires actuels 1123

Vol. vii Littérature, ethnographie, folklore (1971)

Folklore

POKROVSKAYA, L. A. Narodnïye pesni gagauzov Moldavii i Ukrainï [Folksongs of Moldavia and the Ukraine] 731
ROMANSKA, T. Les chansons populaires des haïdouks bulgares comparées aux chansons à thèmes semblables des autres peuples slaves et balkaniques 755
PLANA, SH. Obshchiye motivï v revolyutsionnikh pesnyakh balkanskikh narodov [Common motifs in the revolutionary songs of the Balkan nations] 777
KONSTANTINOVIĆ, Z. Otto Dublislav von Pirch und das serbische Volkslied 883
DOBRAHINOVIĆ, G. Vuk Karadžić et le folklore bulgare 885
MLADENOVIĆ, Ž. Importance du recueil de chants populaires de Vuk Karadžić pour les études balkaniques et sud-est européennes 887
DOMOKOS, S. Les traits communs dans les ballades de type haïdouk des Balkans et de l'Europe centrale 903

66 VEN Atti del I° congresso internazionale di studi verdiani: Situazione e prospettive degli studi verdiani nel mondo
Venice 31 July – 2 August 1966
Istituto di studi verdiani, Parma
ed. M. Medici (Parma: Istituto di studi verdiani, 1969)

Indagini storiche, critiche, formali e stilistiche
BARBLAN, G. Spunti rivelatori nella genesi del 'Falstaff' 16
BERGER, R. Osservazioni sul 'Pater Noster' di Verdi 22
BERLIN, I. The 'naïveté' of Verdi 27
BRUNI, M. Funzionalità drammatica dell'accordo di quarta e sesta nello stile di Verdi 36
CAULA, G. A. Nuove tendenze della critica verdiana: la poetica verdiana e le esigenze della moderna filologia 40
CAVICCHI, A. Verdi e Solera: considerazioni sulla collaborazione per 'Nabucco' 44
CHUSID, M. The organization of scenes with arias: Verdi's cavatinas and romanzas 59
CONATI, M. L''Oberto, conte di San Bonifacio' in due recensioni straniere poco note e in una lettera inedita di Verdi 67
DUNNING, A. Verdi e lo storicismo musicale 93
EOSZE, L. Aspetti comuni dell'arte poetica di Verdi, Bartók e Kodály 97
GALLICO, C. La critica stilistica dell'opera di Verdi 106
GERHARTZ, L. K. Il 'Re Lear' di Antonio Somma ed il modello melodrammatico dell'opera verdiana: principi per una definizione del libretto verdiano 110
GHISI, F. Saper ancora considerare attuale l'esperienza melodrammatica verdiana 116
GRÄWE, K. D. Shakespeares Dramatische Charaktere und Verdis Operngestalten: über das Verhältnis von Dramentext und Opernlibretto 120
GUGLIELMI, E. Il 'Quartetto' di Verdi e la rinascita della musica strumentale in Italia 126
KOVÁCS, J. Zum Spätstil Verdis 132
LEIBOWITZ, R. Vérisme, véracité et vérité de l'interprétation de Verdi 145
LENDVAI, E. Verdi's Formgeheimnisse 157
LEVI, V. 'Stiffelio' e il suo rifacimento ('Aroldo') 172
LIEBNER, J. Les deux 'Macbeth' 176
LIPPMANN, F. Verdi e Bellini 184
MARCHESI, G. Verdi epico, Verdi crudele 197
MARTINOTTI, S. Appunti sulla religiosità verdiana 208
MATZ, M. J. The Verdi family of S. Agata and Roncole: legend and truth 216
MILA, M. La dialogizzazione dell'aria nelle opere giovanili di Verdi 222
PETROBELLI, P. Verdi e il 'Don Giovanni': osservazioni sulla scena iniziale del 'Rigoletto' 232
STROHM, R. Zum Verhältnis von Textstruktur und musikalischer Struktur in Verdis Arien 247

TEDESCHI, R. Il Risorgimento verdiano non sta nei libretti 252
TERENZIO, V. Due problemi di critica verdiana 257
UGOLINI, G. 'La traviata' e i rapporti di Verdi con l'opera verista 261
VÁRNAI, P. P. Contributo per uno studio della tipizzazione negativa nelle opere verdiane: personaggi e situazioni 268
VIOZZI, G. Note sul 'Corsaro' 276
ZIINO, A. L'edizione Del Monaco (Napoli, s.d.) de 'La traviata' 281

Il palcoscenico
ADAMS, J. C. The Verdi tenor and the modern culture 298
CELLETTI, R. L'interpretazione di Verdi nel secolo XIX 308
GARA, E. Come ha da essere un cantante verdiano? 314
GRAF, H. Verdi e la regia lirica 319
MARTINELLI, G. La mia conoscenza dell'opera verdiana 323
MURARO, M. T. Le scenografie delle cinque 'prime assolute' di Verdi alla Fenice di Venezia 328

Verdi in Italia e nel mondo
ADAMS, J. C. Verdi in Chicago 336
ALLORTO, R. Fortuna delle opere minori di Verdi in Italia nell'ultimo ventennio: schede per uno studio 342
CVETKO, D. Le opere di Verdi al Teatro Nobile di Lubiana 346
GUALERZI, G. Aspetti del repertorio e dell'interpretazione verdiana nel dopoguerra 351
KAUKO, O. Verdi en Finlande 361
KÜHNER, H. Verdi e la Germania 364
LABROCA, M. Verdi e Venezia 367
LEDESMA, J. L'interesse popolare e gli studi verdiani in Messico 375
MARTIN, G. La prima rappresentazione di 'Un ballo in maschera' a Boston, 15 marzo 1861 378
MASSARANI, R. Giuseppe Verdi a Rio de Janeiro 383
MERCÙ, P. Aspetti della critica verdiana presso gli Sloveni fino al 1918 413
NORDIO, M. Verdi: voce della Patria, incitamento e conforto per gli Italiani irredenti 417

Fonti, bibliografia, discografia
CADIEU, M. Les récents écrits français sur Verdi 422

DE LUIGI, M.   Incisioni delle opere verdiane dall'inizio della fonografia ad oggi   428

HOPKINSON, C.   Bibliographical problems concerned with Verdi and his publishers   431

LAWTON, D.   Per una bibliografia ragionata verdiana   437

NICASTRO, A.   Compiti e funzioni della rivista musicale in relazione allo studio dei problemi critici verdiani   443

PAVARANI, M.   Per una bibliografia e documentazione verdiana   446

STRUNK, O.   Verdiana alla Biblioteca del Congresso   452

TINTORI, G.   Bibliografia verdiana in Russia 458

67 BERL   Creating a Wider Interest in Traditional Music: Proceedings of a Conference held in Berlin
in Cooperation with the International Music Council
Berlin 12–17 June 1967
International Institute for Comparative Music Studies and Documentation, Berlin;
International Music Council
ed. A. Daniélou and others (Berlin: International Institute for Comparative Music
Studies and Documentation, n.d.)

DANIÉLOU, A.   Plurality of culture or synthesis
(discussion 24)   18
TRAN VAN KHE   The importance of traditional
music in non-European countries (discussion
41)   31
BOSE, F.   The importance of traditional music for
the western countries (discussion 54)   44
GARFIAS, R.   Various levels of traditional music
(discussion 60)   55

MARCEL-DUBOIS, C.   Le Musée des arts et traditions populaires – Paris   72
KISHIBE, S.   Means of preservation and diffusion
of traditional music in Japan   74
TRAN VAN KHE   Means of preservation and
diffusion of traditional music in Vietnam   81
MACEDA, J.   Means of preservation and diffusion
of traditional music – the Philippine situ-
ation   90
BRATA, S.   Means of preservation and diffusion
of traditional music in Indonesia (discussion
101)   94
ISMAIL, M.   Traditional music in the Sudan
(discussion 112)   104
NKETIA, J. H. K.   Traditional music in
Ghana   120
WACHSMANN, K.   Traditional music in
Uganda   128
NIKIPROWETZKY, T.   Means of preservation and

diffusion of traditional music in French-
speaking Africa   132
AROM, S.   The traditional music in the Central
African Republic   135
VATSYAYAN, K.   Means of preservation and dif-
fusion of traditional music in India   141
BARKÉCHLI, M.   Means of preservation and dif-
fusion of traditional music in Iran   150
EL MAHDI, S.   The problems of traditional music
in Tunisia   154
Report on the traditional music in Libanon 157
REINHARD, K.   Cultivation and encouragement
of traditional music in Turkey (discussion
170)   160
ADLER, I.   Report on Israeli activities in the field
of traditional music (discussion 181)   177
POP, M.   Collecting and diffusion of traditional
music in Rumania (discussion 194)   186
SANTORO, C.   Means of preservation and dif-
fusion of traditional music in Latin
America   199
CVETKO, D.   Research into the folk music of
Jugoslavia (discussion 207)   204

KRAUS, E.   The role of international organizations in creating a wider interest in traditional
music (discussion 219)   214
Round table (chairman CHAILLEY, J.)   227

67 BRN[1]   Bericht über die 2. Internationale Arbeitstagung der Study Group on Folk Musical
Instruments des International Folk Music Council in Brno 1967
Brno 23–5 May 1967
Study Group on Folk Musical Instruments of the International Folk Music Council
ed. E. Stockmann, Studia instrumentorum musicae popularis i (Stockholm: Musikhis-
toriska museet, 1969 = Musikhistoriska museets skrifter, ed. E. Emsheimer, 3)

ELSCHEK, O. and STOCKMANN, E.   Zur Typ-
ologie der Volksmusikinstrumente   11
ELSCHEK, O.   Typologische Arbeitsverfahren bei
Volksmusikinstrumenten   23
MOECK, H.   Typen europäischer Kern-
spaltflöten   41

SEVÅG, R.   Die Spaltflöten Norwegens   74
DEVIĆ, D.   Zur Typologie der serbischen
Kernspaltflöten   82
EMSHEIMER, E.   Zur Typologie der schwedi-
schen Holztrompeten   87
van der MEER, J. H.   Beitrag zur Typologie der

westeuropäischen Sackpfeifen   98
MAČÁK,   I.   Typologie   der   slowakischen
  Sackpfeifen   113
MARKL,   J.   Typologie   der   tschechischen
  Sackpfeifen   128
VERTKOV, K. A.   Beiträge zur Geschichte der
  russischen Guslitypen   134
KAČULEV, I.   Zweistimmige Volksmusikinstru-
  mente in Bulgarien   142

GRAF, W.   Zur klanglichen Dokumentation von
  Volksmusikinstrumenten   159
HOLÝ, D.   Zur akustischen Messung der Rhyth-
  mik in der Volksmusik   165
LENG, L.   Technische   Probleme   bei   der
  Schallaufzeichnung   mehrstimmiger   Volks-
  musik   171
HΛBENICHT, G.   Methoden zur Erforschung der
  rumänischen Volksmusikinstrumente 176

67 BRN^2   Musica antiqua colloquium Brno 1967: On the Interpretation of Old Music: Colloquia on the History and Theory of Music at the International Musical Festival in Brno 2/Zur Interpretation der alten Musik: Musikwissenschaftliche Kolloquien der Internationalen Musikfestivale in Brno 2
Brno 2–4 October 1967
Mezinárodní hudební festival [International Music Festival], Brno
ed. R. Pečman (Brno: International Musical Festival, 1968)

RACEK, J.   Tschechische Musik und Ihre Stellung in der europäischen Musikkultur   9

General problems

ZICH, J.   Die Interpretationsauffassung und ihre
  Wandlungen   17
KOLNEDER, W.   Intuition und Wissen in der
  Aufführungspraxis alter Musik   25
HRADECKÝ, E.   Heuristische Probleme bei der
  Interpretation der alten Musik   30
HARNONCOURT, N.   Das Musizieren mit alten
  Instrumenten – Einflüsse der Spieltechnik auf
  die Interpretation   34

Vocal and instrumental music of the 14th – 18th
centuries

FHEODOROFF, N.   Interpretationsprobleme in
  der gotischen Musik   39
BADURA-SKODA, E.   Probleme der Aufführungspraxis der Musik des 14. Jahrhunderts   47
COSMA, V.   Mentions historiques roumaines au
  sujet de l'interprétation dans la musique byzan-
  tine (XIVe-XVIIIe siècles)   53
ERISMANN, G.   L'interprétation de la musique
  polyphonique française de la Renaissance et
  notamment les rapports de la poésie et de la
  musique à cette époque   61
VENHODA,   M.   Die   Anforderungen   der
  Renaissance-Komponisten an die menschliche
  Stimme   69
CVETKO, D.   Contribution à la question de la
  technique d'exécution des compositions de
  Jacobus Gallus   73
ŠAFAŘÍK, J.   The question of dynamics in the
  interpretation of the vocal polyphony of the
  Renaissance   79
SZWEYKOWSKI, Z. M.   The choice of means of
  performance   in   seventeenth-century   Polish
  vocal-instrumental music   82
MUNCLINGER, M.   Old music on the concert
  platform   88
GINSBURG, L. S.   Zur Interpretation der Musik

des 18. Jahrhunderts für Streichinstrumente 92
SCHENK, E.   Zur Aufführungspraxis des Tremolo
  in der Instrumentalmusik des 17. und 18.
  Jahrhunderts   101
RYBARIČ, R.   Zur Frage der Tabulatur-Partitur
  im 17. Jahrhundert   106
BĚLSKÝ, V.   Zur Frage der Generalbasstechnik
  im 17. und 18. Jahrhundert   113
FUKAČ, J.   Zur Entwicklung der Generalbass-
  kenntnis im Gebiete von Mähren   116
SEHNAL, J.   Das Orgelspiel in Mähren im 17. und
  18. Jahrhundert   123
JEANS, S.   English ornamentation of the 16th to
  18th centuries (keyboard music)   128
BUCHNER, A.   Interpretationsprobleme der spät-
  barocken Musik im Lichte der Automato-
  phone   137
ŠTĚDROŇ, M.   Die Versionen der Violinsonate in
  A-Dur von František Benda   142
VOLEK,   T.   Mozarts   Kompositionen   auf
  tschechischen Kirchenchören (zur Frage ihrer
  Kompositions-   und   Interpretationsgest-
  altung)   147

The opera

ANDREJEW, A.   Neue Erkenntnisse über den Ur-
  sprung und die Anfänge des Operntheaters 153
WASSERBAUER, M.   An approach to the pro-
  duction of Baroque opera   155
NĚMCOVÁ, A.   Zur Frage der Interpretation des
  Vokalparts   in   Monteverdis   'Lamento
  d'Arianna'   159
SIEGMUND-SCHULTZE, W.   Probleme bei der In-
  terpretation Händelscher Opern   164
PEČMAN, R.   Die Oper der Neapolitanischen
  Schule als Inszenierungsproblem   171
SCHWALBE, G.   Wiedergewinnung von Opern
  und Intermezzi des 18. Jahrhunderts durch
  Bearbeitung der Libretti   176
NOSEK, V.   Tamerlan, opéra de Mysliveček (re-
  marques sur la réalisation scénique)   183

67 BUC Naţional şi universal în muzică: lucrările sesiunii ştiinţifice a cadrelor didactice [National and universal in music: 2nd conference of teaching staff]
Bucharest 10–12 May 1967
Conservatorul de muzică 'Ciprian Porumbescu', Bucharest
(Bucharest: Conservatorul de muzică 'Ciprian Porumbescu', 1967)

[all papers have résumés in French, English, German and Russian]

VANCEA, Z. Legătura dintre tradiţie şi inovaţie, văzută în lumina dezvoltării creaţiei muzicale româneşti [The relationship between tradition and innovation in the light of the development of Romanian music] 21

VARGA, O. Relaţia naţional-universal în muzica europeană [The relationship between national and universal in European music] 33

COSMA, V. Citeva aspecte ale fundamentării teoretice privind raportul dintre naţional şi universal în muzica românească [Theoretical aspects of the relationship between national and universal in Romanian music] 49

CIOBANU, G. Naţional şi universal în folclorul muzical românesc [The national and the universal in Romanian folk music] 60

COMISEL, E. Contribuţia etnomuzicologiei contemporane la definirea raportului dintre naţional şi universal în muzica folclorică [The contribution of contemporary ethnomusicology to the definition of the relationship between national and universal in folk music] 69

BÎRSAN, M. Există un specific naţional în violonistica noastră? [Do specifically national traits exist in the Romanian school of violin playing? 80

PASCU, G. Naţional şi universal în creaţia clasicilor ieşeni ai muzicii corale [The national and universal aspects in Classical choral works from Jassy] 86

ŞTEFĂNESCU, I. Naţional şi universal în concepţia lui George Breazul [The national and the universal in Breazul's conception] 96

GIULEANU, V. Muzicologia contemporană şi ideea de ritm [Contemporary musicology and the concept of rhythm] 107

RAŢIU, A. Limbajul armonic şi specificul naţional [Specifically national aspects of harmonic technique] 117

HERMAN, V. Importanţa universală a limbajului modal [The universal importance of modal language] 127

STROE, A. Implicaţii componistice actuale ale unei melodii populare româneşti [The implications for contemporary composition of a Romanian folk tune] 137

MARBE, M. and CONSTANTINESCU, D. Evoluţia mijloacelor de expresie muzicală în lumina relaţiei dintre naţional şi universal [The evolution of the means of expression in the light of the relationship between national and universal] 149

POP, D. Interdependenţa dintre naţional şi universal în procesul educaţiei artistice [The interdependence of national and universal features in the process of artistic education] 155

NEGREANU, R. Începuturile muzicii de cameră şi aspecte contemporane româneşti ale acesteia, în lumina relaţiei national–universal [The beginnings of chamber music and some contemporary Romanian aspects in the light of national–universal relations] 162

VICOL, I. D. Naţional şi universal în arta dirijatului de cor [National and universal sides to the art of conducting a choir] 171

JELESCU, P. Ce înseamnă a prelucra folclorul? [How does one use folklore in art music composition?] 181

NICULESCU, Ş. Naţional şi universal în creaţia lui George Enescu [National and universal traits in Enesco's works] 193

MANOLIU, G. Particularităţi stilistice enesciene în violonistica mondială [Stylistic traits of Enesco in international violin playing] 202

COSMA, O. L. 'Oedip' şi unele aspecte ale conceptului naţional în muzica enesciană ['Oedipe', and some aspects of national character in Enesco's music] 211

COBAN, L. Specificul naţional în creaţia pianistică a lui George Enescu [Specifically national traits in Enesco's piano works] 222

BUGHICI, D. Particularităţi naţionale ale formelor muzicale în sonatele lui George Enescu [National traits in the forms of Enesco's sonatas] 235

67 CER L'ars nova italiana del trecento: convegni di studio 1961–1967, ed. F. A. Gallo (Certaldo: Centro di studi sull'ars nova italiana del trecento, 1962) [This is not a congress report but an edited symposium.]

67 FLOR   La lezione di Toscanini: Atti del convegno di studi toscaniniani al XXX Maggio musicale
fiorentino
Florence 6–11 June 1967
XXX Maggio musicale fiorentino
ed. F. D'Amico and R. Paumgartner (Florence: Vallecchi, 1970 = La cultura e il
tempo 29)

TURCHI, G.   Lineamenti di una biografia   10
FREEMAN, J. W.   Di fronte alla critica   23
GUALERZI, G.   A Torino (discussion 75)   41
RADIUS, E.   A Milano   55
LABROCA, M.   L'organizzatore   64
BUZZATI, D.   Toscanini specchio delle folle (discussion 77)   69
KOLODIN, I.   Negli Stati Uniti (discussion 100)   83
LENDVAI, E.   Di fronte a Beethoven   102
ANSERMET, E.   Ricordo di Toscanini   121
LEIBOWITZ, R.   La lezione dei suoi dischi   128
SERPA, F.   Il repertorio   137
MORINI, M.   I rapporti con la Giovane . Scuola   152
SACCHI, F.   La messinscena (discussion 187)   175
Round table (chairman GUALERZI, G.; panel DAL MONTE, T., FAVERO, M., PAMPANINI, R., PASERO, T., STABILE, M.)   191

VOTTO, A.   Come concertava l'opera lirica (discussion 235)   231
CARNER, M.   In Inghilterra   237
PUGLIESE, G.   L'interpretazione del II atto dell'"Orfeo' di Gluck (discussion 261)   249
CROLL, G.   A Salisburgo e a Vienna   273
SELDEN-GOTH, G.   In Israele   285
SANTI, P.   Per noi del dopoguerra   289
GAVAZZENI, G.   Toscanini, il testo e la tradizione nel melodramma dell'ottocento (discussion 298)   293
Conclusions (D'AMICO, F., TOSCANINI, W., SACCHI, F., PAONE, R.)   300

Appendix
LAURI-VOLPI, G.   Con Toscanini   311
SERPA, F.   I cosiddetti schiaffi di Bologna   319
SERPA, F. and GUALERZI, G.   Elenco cronologico degli spettacolo d'opera   337
VEGETO, R.   Discografia   347

67 GRA   Symposion für Musikkritik
Graz 12–14 October 1967
Institut für Wertungsforschung an der Akademie für Musik und darstellende Kunst in
Graz
ed. H. Kaufmann (Graz: Institut für Wertungsforschung an der Akademie für Musik
und darstellende Kunst, 1968 = Studien zur Wertungsforschung 1)

ADORNO, T. W.   Reflexion über Musikkritik   7
KAISER, J.   Zur Praxis der Musikkritik   22
KAUFMANN, H.   Thesen über Wertungsforschung   39
SCHUH, W.   Die Schweiz   49
ROGNONI, L.   Italien   57

ECKSTEIN, P.   Tschechoslowakei   66
REICHING, A.   Jugoslawien   71
FÁBIÁN, I.   Ungarn   77
FIECHTNER, H. A.   Österreich   81
METZGER, H.-K.   Einige Voraussetzungen   91
RAZUMOVSKY, A.   Ost und West   96
Round table   101

67 KAS   Alte Musik in unserer Zeit: Referate und Diskussionen der Kasseler Tagung 1967
Kassel 11–13 October 1967
Arbeitskreis für Haus- und Jugendmusik, Kiel; Gesellschaft für Musikforschung;
Hamburger Telemann-Gesellschaft; Internationale Heinrich-Schütz-Gesellschaft
(Kassel and Basle: Bärenreiter, 1968 = Musikalische Zeitfragen, ed. W. Wiora, 13)

GREBE, K.   Die Alte Musik als ein Phänomen im Musikleben unserer Zeit   9
FINSCHER, L.   Historisch getreue Interpretation – Möglichkeiten und Probleme   25
WENZINGER, A.   Der Ausdruck in der Barockmusik und seine Interpretation   35
EWERHART, R.   Wiederbelebung des originalen

Klangbildes: gelöste und ungelöste Fragen   47
BLAUKOPF, K.   Probleme der Raumakustik und des Hörverhaltens   61
GÖNNENWEIN, W.   Historisch-getreue oder gegenwartsnahe Interpretation – das Dilemma der Alten Musik in unserer Zeit   73

67 LJU   Report of the Tenth Congress Ljubljana 1967
Ljubljana 3–8 September 1967
International Musicological Society
ed. D. Cvetko (Kassel and Basle: Bärenreiter/Ljubljana: University of Ljubljana,
1970)

BLUME, F.   Historische Musikforschung in der Gegenwart   13
CVETKO, D.   South Slav music in the history of European music   26

Symposia
Critical years in European musical history 1400–1430 (chairman von FISCHER, K.)
GÜNTHER, U.   Frankreich und Italien 1400–1430   43
GÖLLNER, T.   Deutschland 1400–1430   60
HARRISON, F. Ll.   Contexts and styles in music in Great Britain c. 1400 to c. 1430   69
Critical years in European musical history 1500–1530 (chairman VERCHALY, A.)
BROWN, H. M.   The transformation of the chanson at the end of the fifteenth century   78
D'ACCONE, F.   Bernardo Pisano and the early madrigal   96
PERZ, M.   Der niederländische Stil in Polen 107
Critical years in European musical history 1640–1660 (chairman TAGLIAVINI, L. F.)
BRAUN, W.   Die Entstehung der deutschen Kantate   116
BUŽGA, J.   Die Gattungen des Musiktheaters in den böhmischen Landern des 17. Jahrhunderts   126
JACQUOT, J.   Luth et clavecin français vers 1650   134
MATHIEU-ARTH, F.   Du masque à l'opéra anglais   149
Critical years in European musical history 1740–1760 (chairman GEIRINGER, K.)
HEARTZ, D.   Opera and the periodization of eighteenth-century music   160
CROLL, G.   Ballett und Pantomime um 1750   168
PETROBELLI, P.   Tartini and folk music   176
VOLEK, T.   Tschechische Musik in der Zeit von 1740–1760   181
Critical years in European musical history 1800–1820 (chairman WESTRUP, J.)
GOSSETT, P.   Rossini's operas and their printed librettos   194
KELDYSH, G.   Das russische Lied vor Glinka   202
SÝKORA, V. J.   Tschechische Musik der Beethovenzeit   209

Critical years in European musical history 1915–1925 (chairman von FISCHER, K.)
AUSTIN, W. W.   Music in Paris around 1920   216
STEVENS, H.   Stravinsky: a critical decade   221
RUBELI, A.   Paul Hindemith um 1920   233
ŠTĚDROŇ, B.   Zu Leoš Janáčeks Oper Jenufa in den Jahren 1916–1918   241

Round Tables
Musical style changes and general history (chairman KNEPLER, G.; panelists LANG, P. H., LISSA, Z., NOSKE, F., SUESS, J. G.)   251
Liturgical and secular elements in medieval liturgical drama (chairman SMITS van WAESBERGHE, J.; panelists BIEGANSKI, K., FALVY, Z., LIPPHARDT, W., SMOLDON, W. L., WAGENAAR-NOLTHENIUS, H.)   271
The English carol (chairman STEVENS, J. E.; panelists BENT, M., BROWN, H. M., GREENE, R. L., HARRISON, F. Ll., HOPE ROBBINS, R., TROWELL, B.)   284
The Baroque in Slav music (chairman RACEK, J.; panelists FUKAČ, J., RIJAVEC, A., SEHNAL, J., STRAKOVÁ, T., SZWEYKOWSKI, Z., WIRSTA, A.)   310
The problem of historicity in European folksong (chairman SUPPAN, W.; panelists BEZIĆ, J., ELSCHEK, O., RAJECZKY, B., STESZEWSKI, J., STOCKMANN, E.)   329
Traditional recitation forms of the epic chants (chairman RIHTMAN, C.; panelists COMISEL, E., EMSHEIMER, E., VALAVANIS, T.)   359
The problem of value in music of the nineteenth century (chairman DAHLHAUS, C.; panelists KAUFMANN, H., LIPPMANN, E. A., LISSA, Z., RICHTER, L., STEPHAN, R.)   380
Sociology in music: results and perspectives of current research (chairman SUPIČIĆ, I.; panelists BEYLIN, P., BROOK, B. S., FELLERER, K. G., MARCEL-DUBOIS, C., UGOLINI, G.)   405
Computers aids to musicology (chairman LARUE, J.; panelists BENGTSSON, I., CZEKANOWSKA-KUKLINSKA, A., HECKMANN, H., JACKSON, R., KLUGE, R., LOCKWOOD, L., MEYLAN, R., REINECKE, H. P.)   424

67 MAG   Georg Philipp Telemann, ein bedeutender Meister der Aufklärungsepoche: Konferenzbericht
          der III. Magdeburger Telemann-Festtage
          Magdeburg 22–6 June 1967
          Arbeitskreis 'Georg Philipp Telemann' im Deutschen Kulturbund Magdeburg
          ed. G. Fleischhauer and W. Siegmund-Schultze (Magdeburg: Rat der Stadt
          Magdeburg/Arbeitskreis 'Georg Philipp Telemann' im Deutschen Kulturbund
          Magdeburg, 1969)

Vol. i (1969)
SIEGMUND-SCHULTZE, W.   Telemann – Meister
  kunstvoller Popularität   32

RUHNKE, M.   Beziehungen zwischen dem Leben
  und dem Schaffen G. Ph. Telemanns   50
HOBOHM, W.   Zum Stil einiger Jugendwerke
  Telemanns   61
BASELT, B.   Zum Typ der komischen Oper bei G.
  Ph. Telemann   73
PEČMAN, R.   Zur Interpretation der Opern des
  18. Jahrhunderts unter besonderer Berück-
  sichtigung von Telemanns 'Pimpinone'   88
LITT, D. H.   Einige Erfahrungen mit der 'opera
  buffa' G. Ph. Telemanns   92
COSMA, V.   Die Musik G. Ph. Telemanns in
  Rumänien   101
MAERTENS, W.   Georg Philipp Telemanns Ham-

burger 'Admiralitätsmusik' 1723   106

Vol. ii (1969)
PETZOLDT, R.   Zur sozialen Stellung Telemanns
  und seiner Zeitgenossen   5
NOACK, E.   Telemanns Beziehungen zu Darm-
  städter Musikern   13
ELLER, R.   Telemann, der 'Vielschreiber'   18
KROSS, S.   Zu Telemanns Konzertschaffen   26
WOLFF, H. C.   Das Tempo bei Telemann   32
FLEISCHHAUER, G.   Einige Gedanken zur In-
  strumentation Telemanns   40
BECKER, H.   Das Chalumeau bei Telemann   68
BERGMANN, W.   Der Generalbass in Telemanns
  Werken   77
JUNG, H. R.   Telemann und die Mizlersche 'Soci-
  etät der musikalischen Wissenschaften'   87

67 NAN   Dramaturgie et société: Rapports entre l'oeuvre théâtrale, son interprétation et son public aux
          XVIᵉ et XVIIᵉ siècles
          Nancy 14–21 April 1967
          Centre national de la recherche scientifique: sciences humaines
          ed. J. Jacquot (Paris: Centre national de la recherche scientifique, 1968)

Domaine d'expression allemande
DIETRICH, M.   Le livret d'opéra et ses aspects
  sociaux à la cour de Léopold Iᵉʳ   203

France
ROBERT, J.   La clientèle aristocratique des com-

édiens et des musiciens dans le Midi méditerranéen (1610–1720)   267

Angleterre
JACQUOT, J.   Le répertoire des compagnies
  d'enfants à Londres (1600–1610): essai
  d'interprétation socio-dramatique   729

67 PAR   Acoustique et electroacoustique musicale: facture instrumentale: Conférences des journées
          d'études: Festival international du son haute fidélité stéréophonie facture musicale
          Paris 1967
          Syndicat des industries electroniques de reproduction et d'enregistrement, Paris
          (Paris: Chiron, 1967)

BURGEAT, M.   Perspectives nouvelles dans
  l'exploration de la fonction auditive   3
CASTELLENGO   Instruments de musique tradi-
  tionels: instruments de musique électronique 7
DACOS, F.   Essai de théorie électroacoustique
  des instruments à cordes   18
MEYER, J.   Effet directionnel des instruments à

cordes: son influence sur leur répartition spa-
  tiale dans l'orchestre   36
CHAILLEY   Expériences de corrélation entre
  musique et parole   44
FERRIEU   Parole et machines   53
PIEPLOW, H.   Les tendances actuelles dans la
  conception des magnétophones   60

ERMANN La cartouche pour bandes magnétiques: situation actuelle et avenir 71
WALTON, J. Distorsion phonographique et détérioration du disque 81
de LAMARE Interprétation de la courbe de réponse d'un haut-parleur 97

PUJOLLE Procédés de réverbération artificielle 111
LEIPP La transparence musicale des appartements 117

67 PARM   Atti del VI° congresso internazionale stendhaliano
Parma 22–4 May 1967
Aurea Parma li/2–3 (Parma, 1967)

2 Le teorie estetiche di Stendhal
GUICHARD, L. Berlioz et Stendhal 180
MAGNANI, L. Le teorie estetiche di Stendhal:

arti figurative, musica 195
TINTORI, G. La musique dans La Chartreuse de Parme de Stendhal 206

67 PRA   Proceedings of the Sixth International Congress of Phonetic Sciences
Prague 7–13 September 1967
International Society of Phonetic Sciences
ed. B. Hála, M. Romportl and P. Janota (Prague: Academia, 1970)

GROBBEN, L. M. Transient phenomena in music and speech 399
KURKA, E. and STOCK, E. Zur Beeinflussung der Prosodie in der Sprache von Stotterern

durch simultane Musikperzeption 511
WEIHS, H. Der stimmliche Ausdruck in Sprechstimme und Musik 1005

67 RAD   Analyse und Klassifikation von Volksmelodien: Bericht über die III. Arbeitstagung der Study Group of Folk Music Systematization beim International Folk Music Council
Radziejowice 24–8 October 1967
Study Group of Folk Music Systematization of the Internàtional Folk Music Council
ed. D. Stockmann and J. Stęszewski (Warsaw: Polskie wydawnictwo muzyczne, 1973)

Allgemeine Beiträge zur Thematik der Studiengruppe
STOCKMANN, D. Zur Arbeit der study Group of Folk Music Systematization des IFMC 9
BIELAWSKI, L. Formale Aspekte der Ordnungsmethoden bei Volksliedweisen 31
SUPPAN, W. Zur Verwendung der Begriffe Gestalt, Struktur, Modell und Typus in der Musikethnologie 41

Beispielsammlung, Analyse und Klassifikation nichtstrophischer, ein- und zweizeiliger Melodien
BIELAWSKI, L. Polnische Volksgesänge ohne Strophenbau und primitive Strophenformen 53
KVĚTOVÁ, R. Tschechische Liedauswahl (böhmische Region) 73
GELNAR, J. Mährische Liedauswahl 79

ELSCHEKOVÁ, A. Slowakische Liedauswahl 85
VODUŠEK, V. Jugoslawische Liedauswahl 91
RAJECZKY, B. Vorstrophische Formen in Ungarn 93
DEUTSCH, W. Musikalische Kleinformen im österreichischen Volksliedgut 101
ANDRASCHKE, P. Ein- und zweizeilige Melodien im deutschsprachigen Volkslied 109
HJELMSTRÖM-DAHL, B. and JERSILD, M. Schwedische (und norwegische) Liedauswahl 125
ELSCHEKOVÁ, A. Motiv-, Zeilen- und Strophenform – Begriffsklärung, Analyse und Klassifikation 131
GELNAR, J. Zur Frage der zweizeiligen Melodien 171
BIELAWSKI, L. Versuch einer Klassifikation des in Radziejowice vorgelegten Materials 179

67 SIE   Atti del convegno di studi dedicato a Claudio Monteverdi
Siena 28–30 April 1967
Società italiana di musicologia
Rivista italiana di musicologia ii/2 (Florence: Leo S. Olschki, 1967)

BLUME, F.   Saluto al convegno: conquiste e prospettive monteverdiane   203

ABERT, A. A.   Monteverdi e lo sviluppo dell'opera   207

BARBLAN, G.   Un ignoto 'Lamento d'Arianna' mantovano   217

BUSSI, F.   La produzione sacra di Cavalli e i suoi rapporti con quella di Monteverdi   229

DELLA CORTE, A.   Aspetti del 'comico' nella vocalità teatrale di Monteverdi   255

FANO, F.   Il Monteverdi sacro, la 'prima prattica' e la scuola veneziana   264

FELLERER, K. G.   Claudio Monteverdi e la musica del suo tempo   270

GALLICO, C.   Strutture strumentali nella musica da camera di Monteverdi   282

KAST, P.   Tracce monteverdiane e influssi romani nella musica sacra del Kapsberger   288

MONDOLFI BOSSARELLI, A.   Ancora intorno al Codice napoletano della 'Incoronazione di Poppea'   294

OSTHOFF, W.   Unità liturgica e artistica nei 'Vespri' del 1610   314

REDLICH, H. F.   Problemi monteverdiani   328

SALVETTI, G.   Alcuni criteri nella rielaborazione ed orchestrazione dell''Incoronazione'   332

SÖRENSEN, S.   L'eredità monteverdiana nella musica sacra del Nord   341

STROHM, R.   Osservazioni su 'Tempro la cetra'   357

TAGLIAVINI, L. F.   Registrazioni organistiche nei 'Vespri'   365

WITZENMANN, W.   Stile antico e stile nuovo nella musica sacra di Claudio Monteverdi   372

WOLFF, H. C.   L'influsso di Monteverdi sull'opera veneziana   382

67 VAN   Proceedings of the Centennial Workshop on Ethnomusicology
Vancouver 19–23 June 1967
Canadian Folk Music Society; Simon Fraser University; Department of University Extension, University of British Columbia
ed. P. Crossley-Holland (Vancouver: Government of the Province of British Columbia, 1968, 3/Victoria: Aural History, Provincial Archive, 1975)

CARLSON, R.   Culture of the B.C. Coast Indians (discussion 21)   16

HALPERN, I.   Music of the B.C. Northwest Coast Indians (discussion 41)   23

LIST, G.   The Hopi as composer and poet (discussion 52)   43

ROVSING-OLSEN, P.   Intervals and rhythm in the music of the Eskimos of East Greenland (discussion 59)   54

TANIMOTO, K.   Music of the Ainu (discussion 66)   60

ADRIAANSZ, W.   On the evolution of the classic repertoire of the Koto (discussion 77)   68

CROSSLEY-HOLLAND, P.   The religious music of Tibet and its cultural background (discussion 92)   79

SMITH, B.   Music of Polynesia (discussion 100)   94

WATERMAN, R. A.   Aboriginal songs of Groote Eylandt, Australia (discussion 113)   102

67 ZAG   IMZ Report: Records – Disques – Schallplatten: Die Schallplatte in der Musikkultur der Gegenwart: Generalbericht über den 6. internationalen Kongress des IMZ
Zagreb 10–13 May 1967
International Music Centre (IMZ), Vienna
ed. K. Blaukopf, *IMZ: Bulletin 1968/1–2 des Internationalen Musikzentrums* (Vienna: IMZ, 1968)

[all papers printed in German, English and French]

BLAUKOPF, K.   Soziologische Aspekte   14

DEWÈVRE, J.   Schallplatte und Publizistik   17

Discussion I 20

van der VOSSEN, E. T. Nationale und internationale Aspekte des klassischen Repertoires 21

HICKMANN, H. Der Beitrag der Musikwissenschaft zur Gestaltung des Schallplattenrepertoires 22

Discussion II 26

BREH, K. Die Schallplatte – ein unbekannter Fortschritt 27

Discussion III 29

URBANSKI, J. Die Tonaufnahme als Problem künstlerischer Interpretation 30

HELM, E. Gesichtspunkte und Probleme der Schallplattenkritik 33

KRUK, P. Die Schallplatte im polnischen Musikleben 36

BECK, L. Die Rolle der Phonographie in Ungarn: von der Volksliedforschung Bartóks und Kodálys bis zur Schallplattenindustrie von heute 37

Discussion IV 40

HENNEBERG, I. Der Komponist und die Schallplatte: Rechtliche und wirtschaftliche Probleme 41

KÖHLER, S. Musikgeschichte auf Schallplatten 44

Round table: Produktion, Repertoire und Vertrieb (chairman SCHEIB, W.) 46

GRAF, W. Sonagraphie als musikwissenschaftliche Grundlage 50

SELJAN, V. Schallplatte, Rundfunk und Fernsehen 51

PARAMOR, N. Musik und Musiker 54

HOFFMAN, A. Die Situation der Schallplatte in Rumänien 56

PROWAZNIK, B. Jugend und Schallplatte 57

Round table (chairman BORNOFF, J.) Schallplatte und andere technische Medien: Probleme der Kooperation und Koproduktion 59

68 BRN   Colloquium Leoš Janáček et musica europaea Brno 1968: Colloquia on the History and Theory of Music at the International Musical Festival in Brno 3/Musikwissenschaftliche Kolloquien der Internationalen Musikfestivale in Brno 3 [cancelled; scheduled for Brno 29 September – 3 October 1968]
    Mezinárodní hudební festival [International Musical Festival], Brno
    ed. R. Pečman (Brno: International Musical Festival, 1970)

RACEK, J.   Leoš Janáček et musica europaea 11

General problems
RACEK, J.   Zur Frage von Leoš Janáčeks Stellung in der tschechischen Musik und in der Weltmusik   23
JIRÁNEK, J.   Das Werk Leoš Janáčeks als Stilmikrokosmos der tschechischen Musik des XX. Jahrhunderts   31
FUKAČ, J.   The continuity of Janáček's style and Czech music   57
STRAKOVÁ, T.   Janáček und der Verismus   67
HOLLANDER, H.   Der Natur-Impressionismus in Janáčeks Musik   81
von GOERTZ, H.   Der historische Zeitgenosse 85
FIRCA, C. L.   Principes et perspectives de l'architectonique musicale chez Leoš Janáček   89
FIRCA, G.   Leoš Janáček – promoteur de la pensée modale contemporaine   99
ŠTĚDROŇ, M.   The tectonic montage of Janáček   119

The stage works of Leoš Janáček
PEČMAN, R.   Leoš Janáček und einige Strömungen des modernen Theaters (eine Handvoll Bemerkungen und Glossen)   131
TYRRELL, J.   Janáček's three types of prose-opera   141
ŠTĚDROŇ, B.   Zu Janáčeks Oper Jenufa in den Jahren 1916–1918   145
KNEIF, T.   Apologie des Fahnenflüchtigen (kritische Bemerkungen zu 'Brouček')   153
WÖRNER, K. H.   Natur, Liebe und Tod bei Janáček   159

The orchestral and chamber music of Leoš Janáček
WEHNERT, M.   Zur Ästhetik der motivisch-thematischen Gestaltung der Sinfonietta von Leoš Janáček   171
GERLACH, R.   Les quatuors á cordes de Leoš Janáček (leurs rapports avec la tradition européenne et la musique nouvelle de leur époque)   181

Leoš Janáček and the European music
HELMAN, Z.   Zur Modalität im Schaffen Szymanowskis und Janáčeks   201
SIEGMUND-SCHULTZE, W.   Janáček und Berg   213
DRUSKIN, M.   Leoš Janáčeks und Sergej Prokofjews Opernschaffen (Thesen eines Vortrages)   219
NOVÁČEK, O.   Leoš Janáček et Olivier Messiaen   221
ŽUPANOVIĆ, L.   Leoš Janáček et la musique croate   227

Leoš Janáček and the folk music
VETTERL, K.   Janáček's creative relationship to folk music   235
TROJAN, J.   Leoš Janáček – Entdecker und Theoretiker der harmonischen Struktur im mährischen Volkslied   243
VYSLOUŽIL, J.   Janáček's marginalia in 'Moravian National Songs' of 1835 (a contribution to our knowledge of the master's relationship to 'the idea of Slavonic music')   251

Leoš Janáček's works abroad
HONOLKA, K.   Leoš Janáček auf der deutschen Bühne   263
FRELIH, E.   Janáčeks Opern in Jugoslawien 271
PEJOVIĆ, R.   The works of Leoš Janáček in the light of Czech music performed in Belgrade between the two wars   277

European music at the time of Leoš Janáček
SALMEN, W.   Die soziale Verpflichtung von Komponisten im 19. Jahrhundert   289
WOLFF, H. C.   Realistische und expressive Sprachmelodie zur Zeit Janáčeks   297
MIES, P.   Zu Stil und Auffassung bei Richard Strauss und Max Reger   303
TAWASTSTJERNA, E.   Jean Sibelius und Claude Debussy (eine Begegnung in London 1909) 307
COLLAER, P.   Erik Satie et 'Les Six' en fonction des événements de 1914–1918   321
RUBELI, A.   Die Überwindung der Spätromantik in den vor 1939 entstandenen Werken Paul Hindemiths   325
KÁRPÁTI, J.   Bartók – Schönberg – Stravinsky   331
RICHTER, L.   Schönbergs Harmonielehre und die 'freie Atonalität'   339

BURDE, W.   Anton von Weberns instrumentale
Miniaturen (zum Begriff des musikalischen Ex-
pressionismus)   355

Miscellanea
STEPHAN, R.   Aus der Geschichte des musikalischen Folklorismus   365

68 EVA   **Expanding Horizons in African Studies: Proceedings of the Twentieth Anniversary Conference, 1968**
Evanston, Illinois 10–13 September 1968
Program of African Studies, Northwestern University, Evanston
ed. G. M. Carter and A. Paden (Evanston: Northwestern University Press, 1969)

WACHSMANN, K.   Ethnomusicology in African
studies: the next twenty years (discussion
NKETIA, J. K. H.   143)   131

68 FUS   **Studi corelliani: Atti del primo congresso internazionale**
Fusignano 5–8 September 1968
ed. A. Cavicchi, O. Mischiati, P. Petrobelli (Florence: Leo S. Olschki, 1972 = Quaderni della rivista italiana di musicologia, ed. Società italiana di musicologia, 3)

PINCHERLE, M.   Corelli et la France   13

Problemi e rapporti stilistici: le origini dello stile corelliano (chairman GALLICO, C.)
MISCHIATI, O.   Aspetti dei rapporti tra Corelli e
la scuola bolognese   23
CAVICCHI, A.   Corelli e il violinismo bolognese   33

Fonti corelliane (chairman TAGLIAVINI, L. F.)
MARX, H. J.   Unveröffentlichte Kompositionen
A. Corellis   53

Problemi e rapporti stilistici: la diffusione dello stile corelliano (chairman PINCHERLE, M.)
FINSCHER, L.   Corelli und die 'Corellisierenden'

Sonaten Telemanns   75
PETROBELLI, P.   Tartini e Corelli – preliminari
per l'impostazione di un problema   99

Problemi di prassi esecutiva (chairman
TAGLIAVINI, L. F.)
Discussion by TAGLIAVINI, L. F., MISCHIATI, O.,
CAVICCHI, A., FINSCHER, L., MARX, H. J.,
GOTTI, T., PETROBELLI, P., and GALL-
ICO, C.   113

Notizie biografiche e conclusione dei lavori
(chairman ZECCHI, A.)
CAVICCHI, A.   Notizie biografiche su Arcangelo
Corelli   131
GALLICO, C.   Conclusions   141

68 GRA   **Das romanische Element am Balkan: III. Grazer Balkanologen-Tagung 1968**
Graz 8–11 May 1968
Akademie für Musik und darstellende Kunst in Graz
(Munich: Dr Dr Rudolf Trofenik, 1968; Beiträge zur Kenntnis Südosteuropas und des Nahen Orients, ed. H.-G. Beck and others, 7)

POP, M.   Beziehungen zwischen der rumänischen
und der südslawischen Epik   53
WÜNSCH, W.   Die Volksmusik des Ostens und

Südostens und der französische Im-
pressionismus als Inspirationsquelle der neuen
Musik des 20. Jahrhunderts   80

68 LIÈ   **Annales du congrès de Liège: quarantième session**
Liège 6–12 September 1968
Fédération archéologique et historique de Belgique
ed. J. Pieyns (Liège: Wagelmans, 1969–71)

Vol. i (1969)

Musicologie
BARTHELEMY, M.   Aperçus et réflexions sur la

carrière de Thomas-Louis Bourgeois (Fontaine-
l'Evêque 1679 – Paris 1750)   33
de MEEUS, F. La structure grégorienne à la
lumière des travaux d'un érudit liégeois: l'abbé
Joseph Vos (1875–1945)   217
MERCIER, P. Recherches récentes concernant la
vie et l'oeuvre du compositeur liégeois Antoine-
Frédéric Gresnick (1755–1799)   225
PAHAUT, R. Le musicologue et la dis-
cothèque de prêt   235
PIETZSCH, G. Archivalische Forschungen zur
Musikgeschichte um 1400   241

POHI, R. Johannes Mangon (v. 1525–v.
1578)   271
QUAEDVLIEG, G. M. I. Traditie en vernieuwing
in het 19ᵉ eeuwse muziekleven te Maes-
tricht   285
QUITIN, J. La musique à Liège sous le règne de
Georges d'Autriche (1544–1557)   293
SENNY, E. Pierre Froidebise et la mouvement
dodécaphoniste à Liège   323
vander LINDEN, A. Les instruments de musique
figurés sur les marques typographiques (XVᵉ–
XVIIIᵉ siècle)   353

68 MIL   Il Duomo di Milano: congresso internazionale
Milan 8–12 September 1968
Veneranda fabbrica del Duomo; Istituto per la storia dell'arte lombardia
ed. M. L. Gatti Perer (Milan: La Rete, 1969 = Monografie di arte lombarda: I
monumenti 3)

Vol. ii (1969)
La Cappella musicale
CAGLIO, E. M. Il canto nel Duomo prima della
costituzione della Cappella musicale   3
FANO, F. La Cappella musicale del Duomo dalle
origini all'età barocca nello svolgimento della
civiltà musicale in Europa   11
LOWINSKY, E. E. Josquin des Prez and Ascanio
Sforza   17

LOCKWOOD, L. Vincenzo Ruffo and two patrons
of music at Milan: Alfonso d'Avalos and Car-
dinal Carlo Borromeo   23
DE FLORENTIS, G. Inediti sulla Cappella musicale del Duomo al tempo dei Borromei   35
MIGLIAVACCA, L. Contributo per la conoscenza
del maestro di Cappella Giovanni Antonio
Grossi   38

68 MTA   Montauban 1968: Actes des journées internationales d'étude du Baroque III: Analyse
spectrale et fonction du poème Baroque
Montauban 19–21 September 1968
Baroque iii (Montauban: Centre international de synthèse du Baroque, 1969)

Fonctions poétiques
VERCHALY, A. La poésie française Baroque et la
musique (1580–1645)   127

68 NEWY   Music and Communication: International Music Congress
New York and Washington 6–15 September 1968
International Music Council (6th congress); International Association of Music
Libraries (8th congress); US National Commission for UNESCO
[Washington: US National Commission for UNESCO, 1970]

Panel discussions
The sounds of things to come (chairman
COPLAND, A.)   25
The impact of communication media on music
(chairman BABBITT, M.)   35
The interaction of vernacular and formal music:
1 Directions of oriental and occidental music
(chairman DANIÉLOU, A.)   49

2 Light music – serious music and future audi-
ence (chairman CONOVER, W.)   57
New directions in musical notation (chairman
STONE, K.)   62
Examples of communication of music through
television and film (chairmen BOXER, H.,
ENGLANDER, R.)   69
Technology (chairman LIEBERSON, G.)   74

1 The evolution of néw techniques in electronic amplification and sound reinforcement
2 Examples of sound recording
The sound recording as communication (chairman SPIVACKE, H.)   84
1 Documentation

2 Preservation: a) Publication b) Education c) Broadcasting
Copyright and communication (chairman CARY, G.)   95
The patronage of music (chairman STEVENS, R.)   108

68 PARM   Atti del convegno sul settecento parmense nel 2⁰ centenario della morte di C. I. Frugoni
Parma 10–12 May 1968
Deputazione di storia patria per le province parmensi
(Parma: Deputazione di storia patria per le province parmensi, 1969 = Fonti e studi 2/5)

Il teatro musicale
GALLICO, C. Note sul melodramma settecentesco: poetica e morfologia   259
HEARTZ, D. Operatic reform at Parma: 'Ippolito ed Aricia'   271

MARCHESI, G. Due momenti iniziali della librettistica di Frugoni: 'Il trionfo di Camilla' (1725) – 'Medo' (1728)   301

68 STRS   L'expressionnisme dans le théâtre européen
Strasbourg 27 November – 1 December 1968
Centre d'études germaniques de l'Université de Strasbourg; Équipe de recherches théâtrales et musicologiques du CNRS
ed. D. Bablet and J. Jacquot (Paris: Centre national de la recherche scientifique, 1971)

CURJEL, H. Le théâtre lyrique expressionniste et sa mise en scène: aspects et problèmes 221
LEIBOWITZ, R. Théâtre lyrique et expressionnisme   237

JACQUOT, J. Les musiciens et l'expressionnisme, I: Schoenberg et le 'Blaue Reiter'; II: 'Lulu': de Wedekind et Kraus à Alban Berg   245

68 SVE   Papers of the Yugoslav–American Seminar on Music
Sveti Stefan 6–14 July 1968
Union of Yugoslav Composers; Indiana University
ed. M. H. Brown (Bloomington: Indiana University, 1970)

KOSTIĆ, V. Financing music in Yugoslavia   1
HANKS, N. Support for music in the United States   9
CIPRA, M. Schooling the young composer in Yugoslavia   20
WUORINEN, C. The schooling of young composers in the United States   26
MILOŠEVIĆ, P. The scope of music studies in Yugoslav music institutions   35
BAIN, W. C. The scope of music studies in American music institutions   43
JOSIF, F. Contemporary trends in Yugoslav music   52
FOSS, L. Notes on American music in the 1960's   58

SUPIČIĆ, I. Music and the mass audience in Yugoslavia today   62
TAUBMAN, H. Music today and the mass audience in the United States   67
CVETKO, D. Musicological studies in Yugoslavia   73
VELIMIROVIĆ, M. Musicological studies in the United States   80
KLEMENČIĆ, I. Problems of music bibliography in Yugoslavia   86
WATERS, E. N. Problems of music bibliography in the United States   95
KOERBLER, M. Light and popular music in Yugoslavia   113
RIJAVEC, A. Applications of modern technology

in musicology and music theory in Yugoslavia   119
USSACHEVSKY, V.   Applications of modern technology in musicology, music theory, and composition in the United States   123
RIHTMAN, C.   The philosophy of folk and traditional music study in Yugoslavia   143
KRADER, B.   The philosophy of folk and traditional music study in the United States   149
PETROVIĆ, R.   The place of ethnomusicology in
Yugoslav music study   164

NETTL, B.   Ethnomusicology in American music
education   173
KUČUKALIĆ, Z.   Folk music as an influence on
art music in Yugoslavia   179
ORREGO-SALAS, J.   Folk and popular music as
sources in the development of national schools
of composition in the Americas   185
KOVAČEVIĆ, K.   Nationalism in textbooks, articles, and general studies in the history of music
in Yugoslavia   194
HITCHCOCK, H. W.   Nationalism and anti-
nationalism in American music histories   199

68 THU   Orgel und Orgelmusik heute: Versuch einer Analyse: Bericht über das erste Colloquium der
Walcker-Stiftung für orgelwissenschaftliche Forschung
Thurner im Schwarzwald 25–7 January 1968
Walcker-Stiftung für orgelwissenschaftliche Forschung
ed. H. H. Eggebrecht (Stuttgart: Musikwissenschaftliche Verlags-Gesellschaft,
1968 = Veröffentlichungen der Walcker-Stiftung für orgelwissenschaftliche Forschung, ed. H. H. Eggebrecht, 2)

SACHS, K.-J.   Bericht über die Arbeiten an den
Pfeifenmensurtraktaten des Mittelalters (discussion 34)   18
DAHLHAUS, C.   Moderne Orgelmusik und das
19. Jahrhundert (discussion 54)   37
BILLETER, B.   Das orgelmusikalische Schaffen
der Gegenwart (discussion 79)   64
ZACHER, G.   Zur Orgelmusik seit 1960 (discussion 92)   86
STROUX, C.   Zur Entwicklung der Vorstellungen
über die Orgel seit Albert Schweitzer   96
KLOTZ, H.   Bauliche Beschreibung der heute
anzutreffenden Orgeltypen: eine Bestandsauf-
nahme   105

RÖSSLER, E. K.   Orgeltypen heute   112
HASELBÖCK, H.   Zur Situation des Orgelbaus
und Orgelspiels nach dem Zweiten Vatikani-
schen Konzil   120
HUCKE, H.   Zur Situation der Orgel in der
katholischen Kirche   130
WIDMANN, J.   Die Orgel in der evangelischen
Kirche (discussion 141)   139
WELIN, K.-E.   Bemerkungen zu Komposition,
Notation und Interpretation heute   158
LIGETI, G.   Was erwartet der Komponist der
Gegenwart von der Orgel? (discussion 183) 168

68 TOK¹   Reports of the 6th International Congress on Acoustics
Tokyo 21–8 August 1968
International Commission on Acoustics, International Union of Pure and Applied
Physics
ed. Y. Kohasi (Tokyo: Maruzen/Amsterdam: Elsevier, [1968])

Vol. iii [1968]
E Architectural acoustics
MARSHALL, A. H.   Concert hall shapes for mini-
mum masking of lateral reflections   49
MÜLLER, L.   Zur Klangfärbung durch
Kurzzeitreflexionen bei Rauschen, Sprache und
Musik   61

Vol. vi [1968]
N Musical acoustics
MIYAWAKI, K. and KITAMURA, O.   Training
machine of pianoforte   1

SHIRASUNA, S.   A study of the setting-technique
of string on the musical instrument 'Koto'
relating to the string properties   5
CREMER, L. and LAZARUS, H.   Der Einfluss des
Bogendruckes beim Anstreichen einer Saite   9
KUNI, A. and KONDO, M.   An experimental
study of a bowed string   13
CREMER, L. and ISING, H.   Messung und Be-
rechnung der Wellenbewegung des Windbandes
bei einer Labialpfeife   17
ANDO, Y.   Influence of air beam direction upon
acoustical properties of flute tones   21

CASTELLENGO, M.   Rôle du musicien dans les signaux rayonnés par la flûte traversière   25
SLAWSON, A. W.   Phonetic notation for timbre in computer synthesized music   29

NÖSSELT, V.   Probleme einer programmierten elektroakustische Musikrealisation mittels elektron. Digital-Datenverarbeitungsanlagen 33

68 TOK²   Proceedings: VIIIth International Congress of Anthropological and Ethnological Sciences
Tokyo and Kyoto 3–10 September 1968
International Union of Anthropological and Ethnological Sciences
ed. B. Endo, H. Hoshi, S. Masuda (Tokyo: Science Council of Japan, 1968–9)

Vol.ii Ethnology (1968)
B-7 Arts
VIRSALADZÉ, H.   Le problème de la classification des oeuvres lyriques populaires   334
MARCEL-DUBOIS, C.   Musiques cérémonielles et sociétés rurales en France   340
UCHIDA, R.   The musical character of rice planting song in 'Tokunoshima' Island – compare

the rice planting song in 'Chugoku' district in mainland Japan and one in 'Tokunoshima' Island   340
HEYMAN, A. C.   The music and dance of the Koréan Buddhist ceremony   345
ROUGET, G.   Les instruments à cordes chez les Malinké (Afrique Occidentale), accords et techniques d'accord   348

68 UPP   Actes du sixième congrès international d'esthétique Uppsala 1968
Uppsala 15–20 August 1968
International Congress of Aesthetics
ed. R. Zeitler (Uppsala; 1972 = Figura, Uppsala Studies in the History of Art, ed. R. Zeitler, new series 10)

1 Social and cultural background of the arts and their theories
SUPIČIĆ, I.   Art in society as a subject of study   115

2 Position of the arts and situation of the artist in ancient and contemporary societies
MAHLING, C.-H.   Zur sozialen Stellung von musikalischem Kunstwerk und Musiker im Wandel vom 18. zum 19. Jahrhundert – eine Skizze   215
BALAN, G.   Le concept d'antimusique et la crise de la société contemporaine   223
VOLEK, J.   Der Einfluss der gesellschaftlichen Situation des 20. Jahrhunderts auf die Ent-

wicklung der Kunst   251

12 Special categories and concepts in aesthetics
FUBINI, E.   Musica, linguaggio et struttura 621
UJFALUSSY, J.   Bemerkung zur Methodologie einer musikalischen Gattungstheorie   633
LASZLO, E.   Why is there music?   635

16 Studies in musicology
DALE, R. A.   The rise and fall of the scale 811
KRAFFT de BOËRIO, C.   D'Olympie à Bayreuth   823
DERI, O.   A Jungian interpretation of the musical experience   825
TIRRO, F.   Jazz interpretation   827

68 VEN   Congresso internazionale sul tema Claudio Monteverdi e il suo tempo: relazioni e comunicazioni
Venice, Mantua and Cremona 3–7 May 1968
ed. R. Monterosso (Verona: Comitato per le celebrazioni nazionali del IV centenario della nascita di Claudio Monteverdi, 1969)

MONTEROSSO, R.   Claudio Monteverdi e il suo tempo   17
ABERT, A. A.   Die Opernästhetik Claudio Mon-

teverdis   35
PIRROTTA, N.   Teatro, scene e musica nelle opere di Monteverdi   45

COLLAER, P. Notes concernant l'instrumentation de l''Orfeo' de Claudio Monteverdi 69

von FISCHER, K. Eine wenig beachtete Quelle su Busenellos 'L'Incoronazione di Poppea' 75

DEGRADA, F. Gian Francesco Busenello e il libretto della 'Incoronazione di Poppea' 81

WOLFF, H. C. Bühnenbild und Inszenierung der italienischen Oper 1600–1700 109

MONTEROSSO VACCHELLI, A. M. Elementi stilistici nell''Euridice' di Jacopo Peri in rapporto all''Orfeo' di Monteverdi 117

MARTINOTTI, S. Teatralità e teatro a Venezia nell'età di Monteverdi 129

CAVICCHI, A. Teatro monteverdiano e tradizione teatrale ferrarese 139

ALLORTO, R. Il prologo dell''Orfeo': note sulla formazione del recitativo monteverdiano 157

APEL, W. Probleme der Alternierung in der liturgischen Orgelmusik bis 1600 171

ARNOLD, D. Formal design in Monteverdi's church music 187

FERRARI BARASSI, E. Il madrigale spirituale nel cinquecento e la raccolta monteverdiana del 1583 217

HUCKE, H. Palestrina als Autorität und Vorbild im 17. Jahrhundert 253

JÜRGENS, J. Urtext und Aufführungspraxis bei Monteverdis 'Orfeo' und 'Marien-Vesper' 269

GHISI, F. Alcuni aspetti stilistici della musica sacra monteverdiana in Giacomo Carissimi 305

JEPPESEN, K. Monteverdi, Kapellmeister an S.ta Barbara? 313

HERMELINK, S. Das rhythmische Gefüge in Monteverdis Ciaccona 'Zefiro torna' 323

BIANCONI, L. Struttura poetica e struttura musicale nei madrigali di Monteverdi 335

PESTELLI, G. Le poesie per la musica monteverdiana: il gusto poetico di Monteverdi 349

PETROBELLI, P. 'Ah, dolente partita': Marenzio, Wert, Monteverdi 361

VECCHI, G. L'opera didattico-teorica di A. Banchieri in rapporto alla 'nuova prattica' 385

MASSERA, G. Dalle 'imperfezioni' alle 'perfezioni' della moderna musica 397

LEDDA, P. Giovanni Battista Doni: il 'De praestantia musicae veteris' 409

STEVENS, D. Claudio Monteverdi: 'Selva morale e spirituale' 423

FEDERHOFER, H. Die Dissonanzbehandlung in Monteverdis kirchenmusikalischen Werken und die Figurenlehre von Christoph Bernhard 435

SPINELLI, G. Confronto fra le registrazioni organistiche dei 'Vespri' di Monteverdi e quelle de 'L'arte organica' di Antegnati 479

WESTRUP, J. A. The continuo in Monteverdi 497

GALLICO, C. Per la nuova edizione nazionale di tutte le opere di Claudio Monteverdi 505

UBERTI, M. and SCHINDLER, O. Contributo alla ricerca di una nuova vocalità monteverdiana: il 'colore' 519

RIGHINI, P. Contributo per le ricerche sul linguaggio musicale originario dell'epoca monteverdiana 539

CÈ, N. Saggio di discografia monteverdiana 543

RASTELLI, D. Tancredi e Clorinda 'al paragone' 557

GALLENI LUISI, L. Il 'Lamento d'Arianna' di Severo Bonini (1613) 573

CORTELLAZZO, A. T. Il melodramma di Marco da Gagliano 583

DELFRATI, C. Vecchio e nuovo nei madrigali di Adriano Banchieri 599

69 BIN The Medieval Drama: Papers of the Third Annual Conference of the Center for Medieval and Early Renaissance Studies
Binghamton, New York State 3–4 May 1969
Center for Medieval and Early Renaissance Studies, State University of New York at Binghamton
ed. S. Sticca (Albany: State University of New York Press, 1972)

SMOLDON, W. L. The origins of the 'quem quaeritis' trope and the Easter sepulchre music- dramas, as demonstrated by their musical settings 121

69 BRN Music and Word Colloquium Brno 1969: Colloquia on the History and Theory of Music at the International Musical Festival in Brno 4 / Musik and Wort Kolloquium Brno 1969: Musikwissenschaftliche Kolloquien der Internationalen Musikfestivale in Brno 4
Brno 29–30 September 1969
Mezinárodní hudební festival [International Musical Festival], Brno
ed. R. Pečman (Brno: International Musical Festival, 1973)

VYSLOUŽIL, J. Zur Frage der Sprachvertonung in der tschechischen Musik 11
RACEK, J. Das Wort-Ton-Problem in der geschichtlichen Entwicklung der abendländischen Musik 15

General problems
RACEK, J. Zum Wort-Ton-Problem in der Vokalmusik am Ende des 16. und am Anfang des 17. Jahrhunderts (mit besonderer Hinsicht auf die italienische begleitete Monodie) 27
STAHMER, K. Vier Thesen zum Grundsatzproblem 'Musik und Sprache' 35
GOSTUŠKI, D. Quelques analogies entre le langage poetique et langage musical 45
BAJER, J. The relation between music and speech in musical theatre 53
PILKOVÁ, Z. The differences in the relationship between the music and the word in melodrama, recitative and aria in the second half of the eighteenth century 59

Czech music
VYSLOUŽIL, J. Zur Vers- und Prosavertonung in der tschechischen Musik 67
HRADECKÝ, E. Nationalsprache im lateinischen Schulspiel aus der ersten Hälfte des 18. Jahrhunderts 77
SEHNAL, J. Renaissanceerbe und neues Denken in den Kirchenmelodien von Adam Michna mit Bezug auf die dichterisch-metrische Vorlage 81
VOLEK, T. Zur Funktion des Wortes in der tschechischen Kirchenmusik des 18. Jahrhunderts 87

SMOLKA, J. Das Wort und die Musik in der Vokalfuge 91
FUKAČ, J. Der Vokaltyp der tschechischen Wiedergeburt 95
JIRÁNEK, J. Das Problem der Beziehung von Musik und Wort im Schaffen Bedřich Smetanas 107
ČERNÝ, M. Zum Wort-Ton-Problem im Vokalwerk Antonín Dvořáks 139
JIRÁNEK, J. Die Beziehung von Musik und Wort im Schaffen Zdeněk Fibichs 159
ŠTĚDROŇ, B. Janáčeks Sprechmotive 171
TYRRELL, J. Janáček's speech-melody theory: claims and conclusions 175
JIČÍNSKÝ, B. Zu den Bühnenaspekten der Wort-Ton-Problematik (E. F. Burians Voiceband) 183
NĚMCOVÁ, A. Musik und Wort in der Komposition 'Übungen für Gydli' von Jan Kapr 205

World music
WELLESZ, E. Die Bedeutung der byzantinischen Musik für das Gesamtgebiet der Musikgeschichte 209
CIOBANU, G. Rapport entre mélodie et texte dans la musique roumaine 215
PEČMAN, R. Zur Frage der 'Literarisierung' der Musik des 17. und 18. Jahrhunderts 219
von HARNONCOURT, N. Das quasi Wort-Ton-Verhältnis in der instrumentalen Barockmusik 225
GEORGIADES, T. G. Der Chor 'Triumph, Triumph, du edles Paar' aus dem 2. Finale der

Zauberflöte   229
SCHENK, E.   Zur musikalischen Rhetorik des
  'Fidelio'   239
EGGEBRECHT, H. H.   Der 'Ton' als ein Prinzip
  des Schubert-Liedes   243
MOSUSOVA, N.   Opernwerke Petar Konjović im

lichte von Janáčeks dramatischen Prinzipien
  und der Sprechgesangtheorie   259
GERLACH, R.   Die Funktion des Textes in Liedern Anton Weberns   263
PEČMAN, R.   Musik und Wort im Vokalschaffen
  des Abendlandes   287

69 BYD   Musica antiqua II: acta scientifica
Bydgoszcz 4–9 September 1969
Bydgoskie towarzystwo naukowe [Bydgoszcz Scientific Society]; Filharmonia po-
morska imienia Ignacego Paderewskiego [Paderewski Pomeranian Philharmonia]
(Bydgoszcz: Bydgoskie towarzystwo naukowe, 1969)

[Polish résumés given for those papers not in
Polish; French résumés for those in Russian or
Polish]
DINEV, P.   Tserkovnoye penie v Bolgarii vo
vremya I i II gosudarstva (865–1396 g.)[Church
chant in Bulgaria during the first and second
states (865–1396)]   9
SNIŽKOVÁ, J.   Le motet tchèque 1570–1620   33
SIVEC, J.   Stilistische Orientierung der Musik des
Protestantismus in Slowenien   47
STEFANOVIĆ, D.   Some aspects of the form and
  expression of Serbian medieval chant   61
ŽUPANOVIĆ, L.   La musique croate du XVIᵉ
siècle   79
SIEGMUND-SCHULTZE, W.   Zum Problem der
Entwicklung   einer   Selbständingen   In-
strumentalmusik in Deutschland im 17. Jahr-
hundert   127
HŁAWICZKA, K.   Sprawa Kancjonału Arto-
miusza z roku 1578 [The Artomiusz Cantionale
of 1578]   141
MALINOWSKI, W.   Prolegomena do pojecia dimi-
nucji [Introductory remarks on the concept of
diminution]   175
PERZ, M.   Cechy socjologiczne polskiej kultury
muzycznej XVI stulecia [Sociological traits of
Polish musical culture of the 16th century]197
SZWEYKOWSKI, Z. M.   Problem przełomu stylis-
tycznego między renesansem i barokiem w
muzyce polskiej [The problem of the break in
style between the Renaissance and the Baroque
in Polish music]   209
COSMA, V.   La culture musicale roumaine à
l'époque de la Renaissance   221
FIRCA, G.   Principes et traits de style communs à
la littérature, aux arts plastiques et à la musique

pendant la Renaissance roumaine   241
GHENEA, C. C.   Documents rélatifs à la vie
musicale sur le territoire de la Roumaine pen-
dant la Renaissance   267
PAPP, G.   Die Haupttypen des ungarischen
Liedes im XVI–XVII Jahrhundert   283
SZABOLCSI, B.   Einige Thesen zum Problem der
Tanzmusik der Renaissance-Zeit   315
ATAJAN, R.   Les chants de maîtres armeniens du
moyen-âge   321
TSADAY-YAKIMENKO, A.   Muzïkal'no-teo-
reticheskaya mïsl' na Ukraine v XVII stoletii i
trudï Nikolaya Diletskovo [Thoughts on music
theory in the Ukraine in the 17th century and
the works of Nicolas Diletsky]   347
GERASIMOVA-PERSIDSKAYA, N.   Kharakternï
kompozitsionnïe   chertï   mnogogolosiya
partesnïkh   kontsertov   XVII–XVIII   st.
[Characteristic compositional traits in polyphonic concerts in the 17th and 18th cen-
turies]   369
GVAKHARIYA, V. A.   Muzïkal'naya kul'tura
Gruzii XI–XII v. v. [The musical character of
Georgia in the 11th and 12th centuries]   401
GRITSA, S. I.   Dumï–vïdayushcheyesya dost-
royaniye ukrainskoy kul'turï [Dumy–a re-
markable product of Ukrainian culture]   413
KELDÏSH, Yu.   Ob isotoricheskikh kornyakh
kanta [The historical sources of the 'kanty'
chants]   437
USPENSKIY, N.   Problema metodologii obuch-
eniya ispolnitel'skomu masterstvu v drev-
nerusskom pevcheskom iskusstve [Metho-
dological problems in teaching the performance
of ancient Russian vocal music]   467

69 CAS   Quarto congresso di antichità è d'arte
Casale Monferrato 20–24 April 1969
Società piemontese di archeologia e belle arti
(Turin: Marietti, 1974)

Documenti: dal gotico al manierismo

MARTINOTTI, S.   Notizie sulla musica a Casale
nell'età cortese   315

69 CER   L'ars nova italiana del trecento: secondo convegno internazionale
Certaldo and Florence 17–22 July 1969
Centro di studi sull'ars nova italiana del trecento, Certaldo; International Musicological Society
ed. F. A. Gallo (Certaldo: Centro di studi sull'ars nova italiana del trecento, 1970)

von FISCHER, K.   Musica e società nel trecento
italiano   11
MONTEROSSO, R.   La tradizione melismatica
sino all'ars nova   29
SEAY, A.   The beginnings of the coniuncta and
Lorenzo Masini's 'L'Antefana'   51
TOGUCHI, K.   Sulla struttura e l'esecuzione di
alcune cacce italiane   67
GHISI, F.   Danza e strumenti musicali nella pit-
tura senese del trecento   83
BRIDGMAN, N.   Les illustrations musicales des
oeuvres de Boccaccio dans les collections de la
Bibliothèque nationale de Paris   105
THIBAULT, G.   Emblèmes et devises des Visconti
dans les oeuvres musicales du trecento   131
PLAMENAC, D.   Alcune osservazioni sulla strut-
tura del codice 117 della Biblioteca comunale di
Faenza   161
GÖLLNER, T.   Die Trecento-Notation und der
Tactus in den ältesten deutschen Orgel-
quellen   176
MARTINEZ-GÖLLNER. M. L.   Marchettus of
Padua and chromaticism   187
VECCHI, G.   Teoresi e prassi del canto a due voci
in Italia nel duecento e nel primo trecento 203
GALLO, F. A.   Mottetti del primo trecento in un
messale di Biella (Codice Lowe)   215

von FISCHER, K.   Quelques remarques sur les
relations entre les Laudesi et les compositeurs
florentins du trecento   247
D'ACCONE, F. A.   Le compagnie dei Laudesi in
Firenze durante l'ars nova   253
CATTIN, G.   Uno sconosciuto codice quat-
trocentesco dell'Archivio capitolare di Vicenza
e le lamentazioni di Johannes de Quadris 281
STRUNK, O.   Church polyphony a propos of a
new fragment at Grottaferrata   305
GÜNTHER. U.   Quelques remarques sur des
feuillets récemment découverts à Grottaferrata   315
WAGENAAR-NOLTHENIUS, H.   Estampie/Stan-
tipes/Stampita   399
MARROCCO. T.   Integrative devices in the music
of the Italian trecento   411
PIRROTTA, N.   Tradizione orale e tradizione
scritta nella musica   431
REANEY, G.   The Italian contribution to the
Manuscript Oxford, Bodleian Library, Canonici Misc. 213   443
PERZ, M.   Die Einflüsse der ausgehenden
italienischen Ars nova in Polen   465
VECCHI, G.   Letteratura e musica nel
trecento   485

69 EXE   Hacia Calderón: coloquio anglogermano Exeter 1969
Exeter 31 March – 2 April 1969
Association of Hispanists of Great Britain and Ireland
ed. H. Flasche (Berlin: Walter de Gruyter & Co., 1970 = Hamburger Romanististische
Studien: B Ibero-Amerikanische Reihe, ed. H. Flasche and R. Grossmann, 35 = Cal-
deroniana, ed. H. Flasche, 6)

SAGE, J.   Texto y realización de 'La estatua de
Prometeo' y otros dramas musicales de Calderón (music examples 123)   37

69 JER   **Proceedings of the Fifth World Congress of Jewish Studies**
Jerusalem 3–11 August 1969
World Union of Jewish Studies
ed. A. Shinan (Jerusalem: World Union of Jewish Studies, 1972–3)

Vol. iv (1973) [Full Hebrew versions of all articles printed elsewhere in this volume]
KATZ, I.   The 'myth' of the Sephardic musical legacy from Spain   237
SPECTOR, J.   Jewish song from Cochin, India   245
HOFMAN, S.   The cantillation of the Bible by the Karaites [English résumé]   278
SMOIRA, M.   Ne'ima – an attempt at elucidation of the term [English résumé]   282
AVENARY, H.   'Science of music' and the Jews of the 13th and 14th centuries [English résumé]   283

LAUFER, A.   Chironomy and head movement in reciting the Hebrew scriptures [English résumé]   290
SHILOAH, A.   Two commentaries on the 'Canon of Avicenna' (the section on the analogy of the pulse action to the elements of music) [English résumé]   292
KATZ, R. and COHEN, D.   Attempts to define the style of the Hebrew song with the aid of the computer [English résumé]   300

69 KUA   **Traditional Drama and Music of Southeast Asia: Papers presented at the International Conference on Traditional Drama and Music of Southeast Asia**
Kuala Lumpur 27–30 August 1969
Malaysian Society for Asian Studies
ed. M. T. Osman (Kuala Lumpur: Dewan Bahasa dan Pustaka, 1974)

C Music and musical instruments in southeast Asia
MORTON, D.   Instruments and instrumental functions in the ensembles of southeast Asia: a cross-cultural comparison   187
ROYAL UNIVERSITY OF FINE ARTS, CAMBODIA   Pinpeat and Mohori music   196
BRUNET, J.   The origins of Cambodian music   208
BRUNET, J.   The orchestra and the musical accompaniment of the 'Nang Sbek'   216
BRUNET, J.   Music and rituals in traditional Cambodia   219
BRUNET, J.   The mouth-organ among the Samre of the Cardamom Mountains
ROYAL UNIVERSITY OF FINE ARTS, CAMBODIA   Characteristic aspects in the interpretation of Cambodian classical music   225
THAI DELEGATION   Thai traditional music   234

MACEDA, J.   Drone and melody in Philippine musical instruments   246
TRIMILLOS, R. D.   Vocal music among the Tausug of Sulu, Philippines   274
SUWANDONO   Gamelan orchestra in Wayang Kulit   290
BRUNEI DELEGATION   A short survey of Brunei Gulintangan orchestra   298
OSMAN, M. T.   Some observations on the socio-cultural context of traditional Malay music 309
SANDIN, B.   The Iban music   320
ONGKILI, J. P.   The traditional musical instruments of Sabah   327
MALM, W. P.   The music of the Malaysian 'Ma'yong'   336
FRANCILLON, G.   Sociological interpretation of differences in musical styles of the southern Tetun (Timor)   345

69 MARB   **Probleme interdisziplinärer Afrikanistik: die erste Jahrestagung der Vereinigung von Afrikanisten in Deutschland (VAD) 1969**
Marburg 18–20 July 1969
Vereinigung von Afrikanisten in Deutschland
(Hamburg: Helmut Buske, 1970)

SIMON, A.   Ein Krankenheilungsritus der Digo aus musikethnologischer Sicht   107

69 NUR   Studia musico-museologica: Bericht über das Symposium. Die Bedeutung, die optische und akustische Darbietung und die Aufgaben einer Musikinstrumentensammlung
Nuremberg 6–8 May 1969
     Germanisches Nationalmuseum, Nuremberg
     (Nuremberg: Germanisches Nationalmuseum/Stockholm: Musikhistoriskt Archiv, [1970])

WINTERNITZ, E. Über Musikinstrumentensammlungen des Frühbarock   6
EMSHEIMER, E. Entwurf zu einem Musikinstrumentenmuseum   19
van der MEER, J. H. Die Musikinstrumentensammlung des Germanischen Nationalmuseums und ihre Darbietung   32
LAMBRECHTS-DOUILLEZ, J. How to look at a collection of musical instruments with historical ears   48
HRADECKÝ, E. Die Darbietungsprobleme einer Musikinstrumentensammlung in historischen Ausstellungsräumen   55
CERVELLI, L. Museographische Kriterien und Arbeitsplanung, dargestellt anhand der Instrumentenmuseen von Rom und Neapel   64
GAI, V. Einige Aspekte der graphischen und photographischen Darstellung von Musikinstrumenten in Museumskatalogen   68

BERNER, A. Das 19. Jahrhundert im Musikinstrumententen-Museum   80
MAČÁK, I. Zur theoretischen Zielsetzung einer Instrumentendokumentation   90
MARCEL-DUBOIS, C. The objectives of music and musical instrument collections in a national ethnological museum   98
HELLWIG, F. Aufgabenstellung und Methode bei der Restaurierung von Musikinstrumenten   103
de CHAMBURE, Mme H. The restoration of harpsichords at the Paris 'Musée instrumental du Conservatoire national supérieur de musique'   113
BARNES, J. Some restoration problems in the Russell Collection discussed in the light of 'Provisional recommendations' by Mme. de Chambure, Prof. Berner and Dr. van der Meer   117

69 PAR   L'interprétation de la musique française aux XVIIème et XVIIIème siècles
Paris 20–26 October 1969
     Centre national de la recherche scientifique
     ed. E. Weber (Paris: Centre national de la recherche scientifique, 1974)

1 Problèmes généraux
SCHMITZ, H.-P. Les possibilités d'instrumentation 'ad libitum' dans la musique de chambre française, dans la première moitié du XVIIIe siècle, en tenant particulièrement compte de la flûte et de sa littérature   25
CHAILLEY, J. Apport du vocal et du verbal dans l'interprétation de la musique française classique   43
BOULAY, L. Du goût dans l'interprétation de la musique française du temps de Couperin et de Rameau   59
SAINT-ARROMAN, J. Les inégalités   67
GEOFFROY-DECHAUME, A. Du problème actuel de l'appogiature ancienne   87
SOURIS, A. Apport du répertoire du luth à l'étude des problèmes d'interprétation   107
THOENE, W. L'interprétation de la musique française des XVIIe et XVIIIe siècles sur les instruments à claviers et à cordes   121
WIRSTA, A. La pratique de l'art violonistique, d'après les ouvrages didactiques et la littérature du violon du XVIIe siècle jusqu'au début de XIXe siècle   131
COSSART-COTTE, F. 'Documents sonores' de la

fin du XVIIIe siècle: leurs enseignements pour l'interprétation   139

2 Problèmes particuliers à l'orgue et au clavecin
KLOTZ, H. Les critères de l'interprétation française sont-ils applicables à la musique d'orgue de J.-S. Bach?   155
DOUGLASS, F. Dom Bedos joue Le Bègue   173
DARASSE, X. Les enseignements d'André Raison   183
THIBAULT, G. L'interprétation, sur les clavecins anciens, de la musique française des XVIIe et XVIIIe siècles   197
GILBERT, K. Le clavecin français et la registration   203
DART, T. Quelques précisions sur la notation des pièces de clavecin de François Couperin   213

Discussions
Le clavecin: interprétation et facture   223
Le clavecin: les liaisons et leur notation   229
Le clavecin: les nuances   231
Le changement de registration et de clavier au clavecin   233

L'influence des doigtés anciens sur l'inégali-
sation   235
Le 'rallentando' à la fin des pièces   237
Les divergences entre Nicolas Le Bègue et Dom
Bedos   238

La date de l'apparition du gros nasard   239
Le tempérament inégal de François Couperin 239

Synthèse et conclusions I   243
CHAILLEY, J. Synthèse et conclusions II   247

69 PARM   **Primo incontro con la musica italiana in Polonia: dal Rinascimento al Barocco**
Parma 11–13 June 1969; Bydgoszcz 11–12 September 1969
Istituto di studi musicali e teatrali, Università di Bologna; Instytut muzykologii
Universytetu warszawskiego
(Bologna: Antiquae musicae italicae studiosi, 1974 = Miscellanee saggi convegni 7)

Presenza e funzione della musica italiana in Polonia
VECCHI, G. Momenti di storia musicale italiána e sue presenze in Polonia tra i secoli XV e XVII   11
PERZ, W. Le funzioni dell'Italia nella formazione della cultura musicale polacca   21

Nel campo della teoria
GALLO, F. A. L'Europa orientale e l'Italia tra il XIV e il XV secolo   29
GALLO, F. A. Lo studio della 'Musica speculativa' di Johannes de Muris in Polonia e in Italia: le glosse dell'Università di Cracovia e i 'Glossemata' di Franchino Gaffurio   39

Il Rinascimento e la pratica delle variazioni
BRISTIGER, M. Appunti sulla forma delle variazioni strumentali nel Rinascimento   57
BRISTIGER, M. Premesse teoriche per l'analisi della forma di variazioni strumentali nel Rinascimento   71

Verso il Barocco: lo stile concertante
SZWEYKOWSKI, Z. M. Concertato style in Polish vocal–instrumental music   89
MALINOWSKI, W. La gorgia nella musica polacca: Mikołaj Zieleński   101

CHODKOWSKI, A. L'aspetto stilistico della musica strumentale polacca del XVII secolo   121

Musici italiani in Polonia
SANDELEWSKI, W. Giulio Cesare Gabussi in Polonia   133
SZWEYKOWSKA, A. I musici italiani in Polonia nel sec. XVII   137
VECCHI, G. La 'Docta schola' di Asprilio Pacelli   153
GIBELLI, V. La musica strumentale lombarda in Polonia e Tarquinio Merula   163
MARTINOTTI, S. Promordi del melodramma in Polonia   173
STĘSZEWSKA, Z. Danze italiane in Polonia e danze polacche in Italia nel XVI e nel XVII secolo   181

Sul 'Cribrum musicum' della Scacchi
MASSERA, G. Precisazioni teoriche nel 'Cribrum' di Marco Scacchi   201
MASSERA, G. Marco Scacchi: dalla polemica antisifertina allo schema formale degli stili musicali   209

DE FLORENTIIS, G. Necessità di un catalogo completo dei manoscritti italiani in Polonia 223

69 PER   **Risultati e prospettive della ricerca sul movimento dei Disciplinati: Convegno internazionale di studio**
Perugia 5–7 December 1969
Centro di documentazione sul movimento dei disciplinati: Deputazione di storia patria per l'Umbria
(Perugia: Arte grafiche, Città di Castello, 1972)

MONTEROSSO, R. L'oratorio musicale in Bologna nel secolo XVIII   99

69 ROM   Colloquium 'Verdi–Wagner' Rom 1969: Bericht
           Rome 6–9 October 1969
           Musikgeschichtliche Abteilung des Deutschen historischen Instituts in Rom
           ed. F. Lippmann, *Analecta musicologica* no. 11 (Cologne and Vienna: Böhlau, 1972)

ABERT, A. A.   Verdi und Wagner   1

ZIINO, A.   Rassegna della letteratura wagneriana
in Italia (discussion 136)   14

HORTSCHANSKY, K.   Die Herausbildung eines
deutschsprachigen   Verdi-Repertoires   (discussion 183)   140

KÄMPER, D.   Das deutsche Verdi-Schrifttum
(discussion 198)   185

LIPPMANN, F.   Wagner und Italien (discussion
248)   200

ZANETTI, E.   Palestrina e Verdi   250

FINSCHER, L.   Wort und Ton in den Opern
Verdis (discussion 271)   255

D'AMICO, F.   Note sulla drammaturgia verdiana
(discussion 288)   272

DAHLHAUS, C.   Wagners dramatisch-musikal-
ischer Formbegriff (discussion 302)   290

WITZENMANN,   W.   Grundzüge   der   Instrumentation in den Opern Verdis und Wagners (discussion 327)   304

CELLETTI, R.   Lo stile vocale di Verdi e di Wagner
(discussion 342)   328

69 STOC   **Bericht über die 3. Internationale Arbeitstagung der Study Group on Folk Musical
           Instruments des International Folk Musik Council in Stockholm 1969**
           Stockholm 9–13 June 1969
           Study Group on Folk Musical Instruments of the International Folk Music Council
           ed. E. Stockmann, *Studia instrumentorum musicae popularis* ii (Stockholm: Musik-
           historiska museet, 1972 = Musikhistoriska museets skrifter, ed. E. Emsheimer, 4)

STOCKMANN,   E.   Internationale   und   in-
terdisziplinäre Zusammenarbeit in der Volks-
musikinstrumentenforschung   11

REINECKE, H.-P.   Methodische Probleme der
akustischen   Forschung   an   Volksmusikinstrumenten   24

GRAF, W.   Aspekte   musikalischer   Schall-
forschung   47

BENGTSSON, I., TOVE, P.-A. and THORSÉN, S.-M.
Sound analysis equipment and rhythm research
ideas at the Institute of Musicology in Uppsala   53

TJERNLUND, P., SUNDBERG, J. and FRANSSON, F.
Ein   statistische   Methode   für   Grund-
frequenzmessungen an schwedischen Kernspaltflöten   77

DROYSEN, D.   Zur Analyse akustischer Eigenschaften nicht stationär klingender Musikinstrumente   97

MEYER, J.   Akustische   Untersuchungen   an
Klarinetten   103

JOST,   E.   Akustische   Messmethoden   als
Transkriptionshilfe   112

SÁROSI, B.   Instrumentalensembles   in   Ungarn   116

MAČÁK, I.   Streichinstrumentensembles in der
Slowakei   137

MARKL,   J.   Instrumentalensembles   in
Böhmen   146

TODOROV, M.   Instrumentalensembles in Bulgarien   152

STRAJNAR, J.   Ein slowenisches Instrumentalensemble in Resia   158

RAVNIKAR, B.   Zur höheren Stimmung der
Geigen in Resia   163

KUMER, Z.   Schriftzeugnisse und Bildquellen
von Instrumentalensembles in Slowenien 165

MARCEL-DUBOIS, C.   The type and nature of
French instrumental ensembles   173

BECKER, H.   Historische und systematische Aspekte der Instrumentenkunde   184

69 VER   Atti del II° congresso internazionale di studi verdiani: Don Carlos/Don Carlo
Verona, Parma, Busseto 30 July – 5 August 1969
Istituto di studi verdiani, Parma
ed. M. Medici (Parma: Istituto di studi verdiani, 1971)

Introduzione ai lavori del congresso
PUGLIESE, G.   Gli studi verdiani e il 'Don Carlos' oggi   2

Indagini storiche – aspetti religiosi – libretto
ALONSO, M. R.   El tema de Don Carlos en la literatura: sus orígenes y desarrollo   16
BEARD, H. R.   'Don Carlos' on the London stage: 1676 to 1969   59
KÜHNER, H.   Don Carlos: storia – idea – scena   70

AMMANNATI, L. F.   Nota sulla religiosità nel 'Don Carlos' di Verdi   76
LÓPEZ-CALO, J.   Il conflitto tra Chiesa e Stato nel 'Don Carlos/Don Carlo'   80

GÜNTHER, U.   Le livret français de 'Don Carlos': le premier acte et sa révision par Verdi   90
MARTIN, G.   Verdi, la Chiesa e il 'Don Carlo'   141
VECCHI, G.   Per il libretto del 'Don Carlos'   148

Schiller – Verdi
CHUSID, M.   Schiller revisited: some observations on the revision of 'Don Carlos'   156
CUSATELLI, G.   'Don Carlos' di Schiller tradotto da Andrea Maffei   170
DONÀ, M.   Verdi e il romanticismo tedesco   180
GERHARTZ, L. K.   Il sogno di Fontainebleau: alcune riflessioni sulla tecnica dell'introduzione nel dramma schilleriano e nell'opera verdiana   186
GRÄWE, K. D.   Dialogo e duetto come attività intermediarie di personaggi drammatici: struttura e modi della funzione del dialogo in 'Don Carlo' – dramma di Schiller e opera di Verdi   193
QVAMME, B.   Les deux princesses d'Eboli: historique et dramatique   204
SANTI, P.   Etica verdiana ed etica schilleriana   209
STRINGHAM, S.   Schiller and Verdi: some notes on Verdi's dramaturgy   234

Don Carlos/Don Carlo di Verdi
CONATI, M.   Verdi, il grand opéra e il 'Don Carlos'   242
LUDWIG, H.   'Quel feroce sovrano . . .': 'Don Carlos' dramma musicale? – dramma per musica!   280
MARTINOTTI, S.   L'ambiente operistico attorno al 'Don Carlo'   289

BUCKLEY, J.   Drama through tonality   302
BUDDEN, J.   L'influenza della tradizione del grand opéra francese sulla struttura ritmica di 'Don Carlo'   311
CAULA, G. A.   Forme di vita e linguaggio musicale nel 'Don Carlo' verdiano   319
EŐSZE, L.   Mondo ideale ed espressione musicale nel 'Don Carlos'   323
FREEMAN, J. W.   The ambivalence of personal relationships in 'Don Carlo'   331
GALLICO, C.   'Scena ed Aria'   336
GHISI, F.   Sogno e realtà nell'introduzione al terzo atto del 'Don Carlo'   343
OSBORNE, C.   'Don Carlo': the extra dimension – music?   348
PORTER, A.   Verdi's ballet music, and 'La Pérégrina'   355
ROSEN, D.   Le quattro stesure del duetto Filippo-Posa   368
SHAWE-TAYLOR, D.   The extended formal arias in 'Don Carlo'   389
UGOLINI, G.   Verifiche e confronti della vocalità del 'Don Carlos' anno 1867 e del 'Don Carlo' anno 1884   394
VÁRNAI, P. P.   Unità musicale e drammaturgica nel 'Don Carlo'   402

BARBLAN, G.   Il personaggio dell'Infante nel 'Don Carlos' verdiano   412
GUGLIELMI, E.   Elisabetta di Valois: caratteri di un grande personaggio verdiano   430
MICHELONI, S.   Il Marchese di Posa: un girondino mancato alla corte di Filippo II   434
NICASTRO, A.   Carlos, Infante di Spagna: ovvero il mito dell'antieroe nella drammaturgia verdiana   440
PESTELLI, G.   Il personaggio di Filippo dalla versione parigina a quella del 1884   449
VIOZZI, G.   Note sul Grande Inquisitore   455

ADAMS, J. C.   'Don Carlo': problemi di rappresentazione e interpretazione   461
CELLETTI, R.   La vocalità nel 'Don Carlo'   475
DAVIS, P. G.   Le incisioni complete del 'Don Carlo'   484
GUALERZI, G.   Un secolo di 'Don Carlos'   494
SGUERZI, A.   Indirizzi nell'interpretazione vocale del dopoguerra   505

BELLO, J.   Verdi a New York   509
CAVICCHI, A.   Le prime scenografie del 'Don Carlo': con alcune considerazioni fra spettacolarità e musica   516
CVETKO, D.   'Don Carlos' nella luce della critica contemporanea slovena   525
DE BELLIS, F. V. and GHISI, F.   Alcune lettere inedite sul 'Don Carlos' dal carteggio Verdi – Mazzucato   531

FARINA, E.   Il finale del terzo atto nella parafrasi pianistica di Liszt   542
MARTINOV, I.   'Don Carlos' de Verdi et le théâtre russe (Chaliapine et Verdi)   546
ROSENTHAL, H.   The rediscovery of 'Don Carlos' in our day   550

Verdiana
FUKUHARA, N.   Verdi in Giappone   560
GOURY, J.   Verdi et la France   565
MARINOV, I.   Die Musikform in Schaffen Gius-
eppe Verdis und einige Probleme ihrer Bühnengestaltung   573
MATZ, M. J.   Verdi e la lotta contro la ragione   583
SHTARBANOV, P.   Il problema scenico nell'interpretazione di Verdi   588

ADAMS, J. C.   Giovanni Martinelli and the joy of singing: 1885–1969   593
MEDICI, M.   Ricordo di Harry R. Beard   600

69 WAR   Opera w dawnej Polsce na dworze Władysława IV i królów saskich: studia i materiały [Opera in old Poland at the court of Władysław IV and Saxon kings: studies and documents] Warsaw 26–9 November 1969

   Polska akademia nauk: Instytut badań literackich [Polish Academy of Sciences: Institute of literary research]

   ed. J. Lewański (Wrocław, Warsaw, Kraków, Gdańsk: Ossolineum, 1973 = Studia staropolskie, ed. C. Hernas and others, 35)

TOMKIEWICZ, W.   Opera Władysławowska w powiązaniu ze zjawiskami kultury artystycznej w Polsce [Opera of the Władysław period in relation to cultural events in Poland]   5
MIKS-RUDKOWSKA, N.   Niektóre projekty dekoracji scenograficznych Giovanniego Battisty Gisleniego na dworze Wazów [Some plans for stage sets by Giovanni Battista Gisleni at the Waza court]   9
LEWAŃSKI, J.   Świadkowie i świadectwa opery Władysławowskiej [Witnesses and reports of the Władysław opera]   25
PERZ, M.   Materiały do dziejów muzyki i opery na dworze Stanisława Mateusza Rzewuskiego [Documents on the history of music and opera at the court of Stanisław Mateusz Rzewuski]   61
WOLFF, H. C.   Typologie der Musik der italienischen Oper 1600–1750 (Polish résumé 82)   69

REICH, W.   Die gesellschaftlichen und musikalischen Grundlagen der Dresdner Opernkultur vor Johann Adolph Hasse (Polish résumé 95)   87
RUDLOFF-HILLE, G.   Dresdener Opernhäuser und Opernaufführungen im 17. und 18. Jahrhundert (Polish résumé 125)   99
VIERTEL, K.-H.   Probleme der Operndramaturgie der Metastasio-Epoche, unter besonderer Berücksichtigung der Affektenheuristik (Polish résumé 146)   131
CHODKOWSKI, A.   Repertuar muzyczny teatru saskiego w Warszawie [The music repertory of the Saxon theatre in Warsaw]   151
KRÓL-KACZOROWSKA, B.   Dekoracje w operze Augusta III. Warszawa 1748–1763 [Stage decor in the opera of August III in Warsaw 1748–1763]   169

70 ANT Colloquium Restauratieproblemen van Antwerpse klavecimbels
Antwerp 10–12 May 1970
Ruckers-Genootschap, Antwerp
(Antwerp: Ruckers-Genootschap, 1971)

BROECKX, J. L. Over de muziekhistorische en estetische betekenis van muziekuitvoeringen op oude instrumenten 7
RIPIN, E. M. Antwerp harpsichord-building: the current state of research 12
SCHÜTZE, R. Die akustischen und klanglichen Veränderungen von Ruckers' Cembali durch die späteren Erweiterungen im Tonumfang (Ravalement) 23
SKOWRONECK, M. Zu welchem Zweck und Ziel, mit welcher Absicht werden historische Musikinstrumente restauriert? 28
BARNES, J. The Flemish instruments of the Russell collection Edinburgh 35
HRADECKÝ, E. Flämische Instrumente in Prag 39
BÉDARD, H. Report on the restoration of the virginal by J. Couchet, 1650 41
LAMBRECHTS-DOUILLEZ, J. The Ruckers–Couchet instruments in the museum Vleeshuis: restoration or copy? 44
LUITHLEN, V. Die Entwicklungsreihe des Klaviers in der Sammlung alter Musikinstrumente des Kunsthistorischen Museums in Wien 49
BERNER, A. Der Ruckers-Bestand des Berliner Musikinstrumenten-Museums: Bemerkungen zu den Konstruktionen 53
van der MEER, J. H. Flämische Kielklaviere im Germanischen Nationalmuseum, Nürnberg 63
THIBAULT-de CHAMBURE, G. Les clavecins et épinettes des Ruckers au musée instrumental du Conservatoire national supérieur de musique 77

70 BERL¹ Über Musiktheorie: Referate der Arbeitstagung 1970 in Berlin
Berlin 10–11 July 1970
Staatliches Institut für Musikforschung Preussischer Kulturbesitz
ed. F. Zaminer (Cologne: Arno Volk/Hans Gerig, 1970 = Veröffentlichungen des Staatlichen Instituts für Musikforschung Preussischer Kulturbesitz, ed. H.-P. Reinecke, 5)

ZAMINER, F. Griechische Musiktheorie und das Problem ihrer Rezeption 9
EGGEBRECHT, H. H. Gedanken über die Aufgabe, die Geschichte der Musiktheorie des hohen und späten Mittelalters zu schreiben 15
NIEMÖLLER, K. W. Zur Musiktheorie im enzyklopädischen Wissenschaftssystem des 16./17. Jahrhunderts 23
BRAUN, W. Musiktheorie im 17./18. Jahrhundert als 'öffentliche' Angelegenheit 37
DAHLHAUS, C. Hermann von Helmholtz und der Wissenschaftscharakter der Musiktheorie 49
REINECKE, H.-P. Über Zusammenhänge zwischen naturwissenschaftlicher und musikalischer Theorienbildung 59

70 BERL² Bericht über den internationalen Beethoven-Kongress 10.–12. Dezember 1970 in Berlin
Berlin 10–12 December 1970
ed. H. A. Brockhaus and K. Niemann (Berlin: Neue Musik, 1971)

Das Beethoven-Bild in Geschichte und Gegenwart
KNEPLER, G. Das Beethoven-Bild in Geschichte und Gegenwart 23
GOLDSCHMIDT, H. Der späte Beethoven – Versuch einer Standortbestimmung 41
HRABUSSAY, Z. Beethoven und Hummel: ihre künstlerischen und persönlichen Beziehungen 59

LAUX, K. Das Beethoven-Bild Carl Maria von Webers 65

BALLOVÁ, L. Über Beethovens Musik in Pressburg zu Lebzeiten des Komponisten 71

TARANTOVÁ, M. Ludwig van Beethoven und die tschechische Wiedergeburt 75

FUKAČ, J. Soziale Bedingtheit der ersten Kontakte Beethovens mit Böhmen 79

PROCHÁZKA, J. Die Rezeption von Beethovens Schaffen in Böhmen 85

KONEN, V. Zum Problem: Beethoven und seine Nachfolger 93

BESSER, J. Frühe Spuren eines realistischen Beethoven-Bildes im Schumann-Brendel-Kreis 99

SIEGMUND-SCHULTZE, W. Beethovens Nachwirkung bei bedeutenden Komponisten des 19. Jahrhunderts 107

OLIAS, G. Zum Beethoven-Bild in der russischen Literatur der ersten Hälfte des 19. Jahrhunderts 115

ČERNÝ, M. K. Die Problematik des geschichtlichen und gegenwärtigen Beethoven-Bildes 121

ŠTĚDROŇ, B. Leoš Janáček und Ludwig van Beethoven 125

JAKUBCOVÁ, D. Die Musik Ludwig van Beethovens in Bratislava seit dem Jahre 1918 131

TOMESCU, V. Bedeutung und Werte der Musik Beethovens in der rumänischen Musikkultur 135

FELIX, W. Zur Tradition der Beethoven-Pflege des Gewandhausorchesters 141

NESTJEW, I. Musik Beethovens in Sowjetrussland 147

LAMMEL, I. Zur Beethoven-Rezeption in der deutschen Arbeiterbewegung 155

ELSNER, J. Zur Beethoven-Rezeption Hanns Eislers 165

NIEMANN, K. Beethoven-Ehrung 1927 und ihre Probleme 171

SCHNEIDER, F. Zur Kritik der spätbürgerlichen Beethoven-Deutung 177

PLESSKE, H.-M. Das Beethoven-Bild in der erzählenden Literatur 183

MICHEL, P. Das Beethoven-Bild der deutschen Musikerziehung in Vergangenheit und Gegenwart – ein Beitrag zur Geschichte der Beethoven-Rezeption und der Schulmusik 189

KEIL, W. Beethoven in der Schule 201

HÜTTEL, W. Beethovens Bedeutung für das kulturelle Leben einer ländlichen Schrittmachergemeinde in der DDR 203

CZERNY, P. Die Beethoven-Gesamtausgabe des VEB Deutsche Schallplatten: Ergebnisse, Erkenntnisse und Probleme einer umfassenden Klasskeredition auf Schallplatten 207

Der klassische Realismus Ludwig van Beethovens
Colloquium: Beethovens Stellung im gesellschaftlichen Leben seiner Zeit 215

BROCKHAUS, H. A. Konflikthaftigkeit und Idealität im klassischen Realismus Ludwig van Beethovens 235

RUDOLPH, J. Realismus und Antizipation in Werken Ludwig van Beethovens: zur Wechselwirkung der Künste am Beispiel der 'Egmont'-Musik und des 'Fidelio'-Problems in Shakespeares 'Cymbeline' 249

JARUSTOWSKI, B. Zum Problem der Entstehung des 'Fidelio' 269

PISCHNER, H. Zur Interpretation des 'Fidelio' 275

KRAFT, G. Quellenstudien zur thematischen Konzeption des 'Fidelio' 283

VIERTEL, K.-H. Beethovens Oper 'Leonore' 291

RIENÄCKER, G. Zur Dialektik in der dramaturgischen Gestaltung der Beethovenschen Bühnenmusik zu Goethes 'Egmont' 301

MAINKA, J. Beethovens Bonner Kantaten 315

SCHNEIDER, A. Bemerkungen zur Konzeption des Liederkreises op. 98 'An die ferne Geliebte' 327

CHRISTOFF, D. Einige Gedanken zur Fuge der Klaviersonate op. 106 333

RHYSHKIN, I. Probleme des Ideals in der 9. Sinfonie von Beethoven und Besonderheiten ihrer musikalisch-dramaturgischen Entwicklung 337

NIKOLAJEWA, N. Die Gegenwartsbeziehungen der 9. Sinfonie Beethovens 343

GÜLKE, P. Beethovens Bestimmung des Sinfonischen als Ausdruck seines Realismus 349

MARKIEWICZ, L. Formkreuzungen bei Beethoven 359

ORDSHONIKIDZE, G. Zur Dialektik der Idee des Kampfes in Beethovens Musik 365

SÓLYOM, G. Beethovens Spätwerke und die klassische zyklische Form 373

ZUKKERMAN, V. Die Beethovensche Dynamik in ihren strukturellen und formbildenden Erscheinungen 379

PROTOPOPOW, W. Die Rolle der Polyphonie im Prozess der Entwicklung von Beethovens Werken 387

CHODKOWSKI, A. Die Koda in der Sonatenform Beethovens 391

SCHRAMOWSKI, H. Bemerkungen zu zwei Funktionsarten der Klavierimprovisation im Schaffen Beethovens 395

WEHNERT, M. Bemerkungen zur semiotischen Werkbetrachtung bei Beethoven 405

KROSS, S. Neue Fragestellungen in der Beethoven-Skizzenforschung 417

FISCHMAN, N. Realistische Tendenzen im Schaffensprozess Beethovens 427

KREMLJOW, J. Der unvergängliche Wert Beethovens 433

USZKOREIT, H.-G. Über Beethovens Verhältnis zur musikalischen Volkskultur 437

RICHTER, L. Beethoven und die Gassenhauer seiner Zeit 443

LISSA, Z. Bearbeitungen polnischer Volkslieder

von Beethoven 447

PEČMAN, R. Ludwig van Beethoven und Jiří Antonín Benda 453

FLEISCHHAUER, G. Beethoven und die Antike 465

KÖHLER, K.-H. Beethovens literarische Kontakte – ein Beitrag zum Weltbild des Komponisten 483

HERRE, G. Aus der Arbeit an Beethovens Konversationsheften: zu speziellen Untersuchungsergebnissen 489

NOVÁČEK, Z. Angaben über Beethovens Schaffen in den Archiven von Bratislava 495

HIRSCH, F. Ludwig van Beethoven und seine Verleger: im besonderen dargestellt an seinen Beziehungen zum Leipziger Musikverlag Breitkopf & Härtel 499

ZSCHOCH, F. Zum gegenwärtigen Stand der Beethoven-Editionen 507

Probleme der Beethoven-Interpretation

GÜLKE, P. Zum Verhältnis von Intention und

Realisierung bei Beethoven 517

REBLING, E. Der Künstler und unser heutiges Publikum 533

Discussion (panel PISCHNER, H., GÜLKE, P., REBLING, E., ZECHLIN, D., SCHREIER, P.) 537

GOLDSCHMIDT, H. Beethovens Anweisungen zum Spiel der Cramer-Etüden 545

SASSE, K. Bemerkungen zur Berücksichtigung des Klanges historischer Hammerflügel für die Interpretation Beethovenscher Klavierwerke auf modernen Instrumenten 559

PONIATOWSKA, I. Zur Frage der Interpretation von Beethovens Klavierwerken 565

FRIEGE, B. Der Wandel im Interpretationsideal der Klaviersonaten Ludwig van Beethovens 569

SCHOLLUM, R. Zu Form und Wiedergabe von Liedern Beethovens 575

MEYER, E. H. Das Werk Ludwig van Beethovens und seine Bedeutung für das sozialistisch-realistische Gegenwartsschaffen 581

70 BOL   Secondo incontro con la musica italiana e polacca: Musica strumentale e vocale strumentale dal Rinascimento al Barocco

Bologna 29–30 September 1970
Istituto di studi musicali e teatrali, Università di Bologna; Instytut muzykologii Universytetu warszawskiego
(Bologna: Antiquae musicae italicae studiosi, 1974 = Miscellanee saggi convegni 8)

BRISTIGER, M. Precisazioni teoriche sul 'Tratado de glosas sobre clausulas' di Diego Ortiz 9

DE GIORGI, G. Voci e strumenti nelle villanelle di Giovanni Girolamo Kapsberger 23

PERZ, M. Trasformazioni dello stile e della pratica dell'organo nei secoli XVI e XVII in Polonia 33

CHINI, T. Giovanni Cavaccio e i 'Sudori musicali' 47

GIBELLI, V. La musica strumentale di Biagio Marini 55

CHODKOWSKI, A. Trascrizioni strumentali delle opere dei maestri italiani eseguite da Adam Jarzębski 67

OSOSTOWICZ-SUTKOWSKA, A. The Pelpin Tabulature as a source to the history of Polish-Italian musical ties 75

CARAPEZZA, E. La musica strumentale didattica della scuola polifonica siciliana 81

CAFFAGNI, M. Il chitarrone come strumento per il basso continuo ed esempi del ms. M. 127 della Biblioteca Estense di Modena 117

CAPACCIOLI, E. Sull'opera di Barnaba Milleville e sul suo soggiorno in Polonia 153

MARTINOTTI, S. Notizie su Vincenzo Scapitta valenzano 173

SZWEYKOWSKI, Z. M. Marco Scacchi's opinions on art of music 181

GHISI, F. Cronistoria delle visite a Firenze nel 1624 e 1634 dei principi di Polonia Ladislao Sigismondo e Alessandro 191

RIGHETTI, S. Una rappresentazione a Roma in onore del principe Alessandro Carlo di Polonia: Il S. Alessio 199

FERRARI BARASSI, E. 'La Luciata' di Francesco Manelli 211

GLUSZCZ-ZWOLINSKA, E. Musici italiani alla corte reale degli Jagelloni 243

SEHNAL, I. [J] La musica alla corte dei vescovi di Olomouc dal sec. XIII alla metà del sec. XVII 251

Bononiensia

GIBELLI, V. Scheda critico-bibliografica per Adriano Banchieri 269

DUCKLES, V. General plan for a history of music by Doctor Charles Burney with a catalogue of his musical library 279

70 BON **Bericht über den internationalen musikwissenschaftlichen Kongress Bonn 1970**
Bonn 7–12 September 1970
Gesellschaft für Musikforschung
ed. C. Dahlhaus, H. J. Marx, M. Marx-Weber, G. Massenkeil (Kassel and Basle:
Bärenreiter, 1972); pp. 619–98 published separately as *Reflexionen über Musikwiss-
enschaft heute: Bericht über das Symposium im Rahmen des internationalen musik-
wissenschaftlichen Kongresses der Gesellschaft für Musikforschung, Bonn 1970*, ed. H.
H. Eggebrecht (Kassel and Basle: Bärenreiter, 1972)

von FISCHER, K. Versuch über das Neue bei Beethoven 3

SCHMIDT-GÖRG, J. Missa solemnis: Beethoven in seinem Werk 13

I.1 Rhythmisch-metrische Fragen bei Beethoven

BOCKHOLDT, R. Eigenschaften des Rhythmus im instrumentalen Satz bei Beethoven und Berlioz 29

FEIL, A. 'Abmessung (und Art) der Einschnitte': Rhythmus in Beethovens Satzbau 33

GEORGIADES, T. G. Zu den Satzschlüssen der Missa solemnis 37

NEWMAN, W. S. On the rhythmic significance of Beethoven's annotations in Cramer's études 43

DIETZ, H.-B. Relations between rhythm and dynamics in works of Beethoven 47

VOLEK, T. Das Verhältnis von Rhythmus und Metrum bei J. W. Stamitz 53

Discussion 55

I.2 Haydn und Beethoven

BLUME, F. Haydn und Beethoven – Bemerkungen zum Stand der Forschung 61

FEDER, G. Stilelemente Haydns in Beethovens Werken 65

MANN, A. Haydns Kontrapunktlehre und Beethovens Studien 70

SCHWARZ, B. Beethovens op. 18 und Haydns Streichquartette 75

WALTER, H. Die biographischen Beziehungen zwischen Haydn und Beethoven 79

Discussion 84

I.3 Probleme der Skizzen Beethovens

KROSS, S. Schaffenspsychologische Aspekte der Skizzenforschung 87

UNVERRICHT, H. Skizze – Brouillon – Fassung: Definitions- und Bestimmungsschwierigkeiten bei den Skizzen Beethovens 95

CZESLA, W. Skizzen als Instrument der Quellenkritik 101

FISCHMAN, N. Das Skizzenbuch Beethovens aus den Jahren 1802–1803 aus dem Familienarchiv Wielhorski und die ersten Skizzen zur 'Eroica' 104

BRANDENBURG, S. Beethovens 'erste Entwürfe' zu Variationszyklen 108

STADLEN, P. Possibilities of an aesthetic evaluation of Beethoven's sketches 111

Discussion 118

I.4 Beethoven und Osteuropa

BÓNIS, F. Beethoven und die ungarische Musik 121

CERNÝ, M. Zum Beethoven-Bild in der tschechischen Musikliteratur 128

BALLOVÁ, L. Beethoven und die Slowakei 130

CVETKO, D. Beethovens Beziehungen zu der Laibacher Philharmonischen Gesellschaft 132

GINSBURG, L. S. Zur Geschichte der Aufführung der Streichquartette Beethovens in Russland 135

MARTINOV, I. Glinka und Beethoven 140

STANTSCHEWA-BRASCHOWANOWA, L. Bulgarische Musikliteratur über Beethoven 144

Discussion 146

II.1 Opernkomponist und Textbuch

ABERT, A. A. Opernkomponist und Textbuch (discussion 154) 151

BECKER, H. Giacomo Meyerbeers Mitarbeit an den Libretti seiner Opern (discussion 161) 155

LIPPMANN, F. Zum Verhältnis von Libretto und Musik in der italienischen Opera Seria der ersten Hälfte des 19. Jahrhunderts (discussion 168) 162

SCHUH, W. Richard Strauss und seine Libretti (discussion 174) 169

II.2 Die Opernszene und ihre musikalischen Typen

GÖLLNER, T. Falsobordone-Anklänge in Prologen und Auftritten der frühen Oper 179

HÜCKE, H. Die szenische Ausprägung des Komischen im neapolitanischen Intermezzo und in der Commedia musicale 183

BIANCONI, L. Die pastorale Szene in Metastasios 'Olimpiade' 185

OSTHOFF, W. Beethovens 'Leonoren'-Arie 191

KUNZE, S. Naturszenen in Wagners Musikdrama 199

CAHN, P. Naturszenenaufbau in Debussys 'Pelléas et Mélisande' 207

Discussion 212

II.3 Oper und Gesellschaft

FINSCHER, L. Einführung 217

BRAUN, W. Oper und Konzert – Gegensatz und Ergänzung 220

HORTSCHANSKY, K. Die Anfänge des Opern-Repertoires und der Repertoire-Oper 225

MAHLING, C.-H. Selbstdarstellung und Kritik

der Gesellschaft in der Oper? Bemerkungen zu Opern von Mozart bis Dessau   232

RINGER, A. L.   The political uses of opera in revolutionary France   237

STEINBECK, D.   Soziologische Aspekte der Opern-inszenierung   242

Discussion   247

III.1 Musikalischer Neoklassizismus

GOJOWY, D.   Formentwicklungen bei sowjetischen Neoklassizisten   257

KÄMPER, D.   Zur Frage des Neomadrigalismus   261

WAELTNER, E. L.   Aspekte zum Neoklassizismus Strawinskys: Schlussrhythmus, Thema und Grundriss im Finale des Bläser-Oktetts 1923   265

Discussion   275

III.2 Der gegenwärtige Stand der Schönberg-Forschung

STEPHAN, R.   Zur Gesamtausgabe der musikalischen Werke Arnold Schönbergs   279

BRINKMANN, R.   Zur Entstehung der Zwölftontechnik   284

REXROTH, D.   Zum Theoretiker Schönberg – Anmerkungen zur Harmonielehre von 1911   288

Discussion   293

III.3 Aussenseiter der Neuen Musik

DAHLHAUS, C.   Aussenseiter der Neuen Musik: Charles Ives und Edgard Varèse [résumé]   299

AUSTIN, W. W.   Ives and histories   299

BUDDE, E.   Anmerkungen zum Streichquartett Nr. 2 von Charles E. Ives   303

BOEHMER, K.   Über Edgard Varèse   307

BRINKMANN, R.   Anmerkungen zu Varèse   313

Discussion   317

ALBERSHEIM, G.   Die Wesensverschiedenheit von Fugen- und Sonaten-Thema als Beispiel für den Stilunterschied zwischen Barock und Klassik   323

ANGERMÜLLER, R.   Beaumarchais und Salieri   325

BABITZ, S.   Modern errors in Beethoven performance   327

BADURA-SKODA, E.   Probleme einer Dokumentar-Biographie Beethovens   331

BARON, J. H.   First report on the use of computer programing to study the secular solo songs in France from 1600 to 1660   333

BARTELS, I.   Zum Problem des instrumentalstückes in der frühvenezianischen Oper   336

BECK, H.   Zur Struktur des Beethovenschen Themas   339

BECKMANN, K.   Echtheitsprobleme bei D. Buxtehudes freien Orgelwerken   341

BELLO, J.   The origins of the knowledge of Beethoven and his music in America reconsidered   343

BOETTICHER, W.   Die älteren Lautentabulaturen und das Problem ihrer Klassifizierung   345

BOLLERT, W.   Auber, Verdi und der 'Maskenball'-Stoff   349

BOSONNET, F. R.   Die Bedeutung des Begriffs 'Empfindsamkeit' für die Deutsche Musik des 18. Jahrhunderts   352

BRANDENBURG, S.   Beethovens Skizzen zum zweiten Satz der 7. Symphonie op. 92   355

BUSCH, H. J.   Wertkategorien in der Kritik Neuer Musik   358

CARNER, M.   Beethoven's deafness and the heroic element in his music   360

CHODKOWSKI, A.   Zu Problemen der Reprise in der Sonatenform bei Beethoven   362

CLARO, S.   The scope of musicology in Latin American countries   365

COSMA, V.   Rumänien, eines der ersten Länder im Südosten Europas, in dem die Musik Beethovens Verbreitung fand   367

CZESLA, W.   Eine kritische Stelle in Beethovens IX. Symphonie   370

DAHLHAUS, C.   Schönbergs Orchesterstück op. 16, 3 und der Begriff der 'Klangfarbenmelodie'   372

DERR, E. S.   Elaboration: a prime musical and dramatic ingredient in the performance of operas of the Classical period   374

DUPONT, W.   Reflexionen zur lokalen Musikforschung   378

ELVERS, R.   Felix Mendelssohns Beethoven-Autographe   380

FELLINGER, I.   Friedrich August Kanne als Kritiker Beethovens   383

FIRCA, C.   Transfigurations de certaines modalités musicales de tradition européenne à travers la musique de Georges Enesco   386

FIRCA, G.   Der Beitrag des Tritonus zur Entwicklung konstruktiver Prinzipien   388

FLINDELL, E. F.   Randformen in der Polyphonie des Mittelalters   392

FORCHERT, A.   Rhythmische Probleme in Beethovens späten Streichquartetten   394

FRICKE, J.   Die Relativität optimaler Intervallgrössen   397

GEIRINGER, K.   Zu Glucks Oper 'Il Telemaco'   400

GERSON-KIWI, E.   Beethoven's sacred drama – a revaluation   402

GMEINWIESER, S.   Girolamo Chiti (1679–1759) und die Kirchenmusik Roms in der ersten Hälfte des 18. Jahrhunderts   406

GÖLLER, G.   Liturgische Aspekte der Rezeption kirchenmusikalischer Werke Beethovens und Haydns in der Domkapelle zu Köln unter Carl Leibl   408

GÜNTHER, R.   Gedanken und Initiativen in der Erforschung der Äthiopisch-Orthodoxen Kirchenmusik   410

GÜNTHER, U.   Die Pariser Skizzen zu Verdis 'Don Carlos'   412

HAACK, H. Das Phrasierungsproblem 415
HAMMERSTEIN, R. Die Musik im mittelalterlichen Totentanz 417
HARDECK, E. Debussys 'Jeux': Struktur – Stellung im Gesamtwerk 424
HARRAN, D. Cyclical processes in Beethoven's early quartets 426
HEARTZ, D. Sturm und Drang im Musikdrama 432
HERMELINK, S. Die Gegenquintsprungkadenz, ein Ausdrucksmittel der Satzkunst Lassos 435
HOFFMANN-ERBRECHT, L. Skrjabins 'Klangzentrenharmonik' und die Atonalität 438
HOFMAN, S. Trends in the music of emerging Israel 441
HOLSCHNEIDER, A. Unbekannte Skizzen Beethovens zur Cello-Sonate op. 5 II–WoO 36, WoO 37 und Hess Nr. 13 sind nicht im Autograph überliefert 444
JANTARSKI, G. N. Beethoven und Bulgarien 447
KARBUSICKÝ, V. Beethoven und Smetana: Stilanalytische und soziologische Notizen 450
KIRBY, F. E. Beethovens Gebrauch von charakteristischen Stilen: ein Beitrag zum Problem der Einheit in der Mehrsätzigkeit 452
KLEIN, R. Forschungsbericht zur Beethoven-Topographie 455
KNAUS, J. Leoš Janáček – Aussenseiter der Neuen Musik 458
KÖHLER, V. Rezitativ, Szene und Melodrama in Heinrich Marschners Opern 461
KÖRNER, F. Jazzforschung – ein neues Anliegen der Musikwissenschaft 464
KOHRS, K. H. Zur Stilistik der sogenannten aparallelen Sequenzen 467
KOJIMA, S. A. Die drei Solovioline-Fassungen von Beethovens Violinkonzert op. 61 in morphologischem Vergleich 472
KOS, K. Darstellungen der Musikinstrumente in den mittelalterlichen bildenden Künsten von Dalmatien und Istrien 474
KROPFINGER, K. Der musikalische Strukturbegriff bei E. T. A. Hoffmann 480
KRUMMACHER, F. Über Autographe Mendelssohns und seine Kompositionsweise 482
KÜMMERLING, H. Beethovens Akademien am 8. und 12. Dezember 1813 und ihre Vorgeschichte 486
LANGE, H. K. H. Die Orgelstimmung Gottfried Silbermanns: ein Beitrag zur Aufführungspraxis alter Musik 487
LIEBE, A. Zum Problem der Beethoven-Kritik 489
LISSA, Z. Beethovens Polonika 491
LIVINGSTONE, E. F. Das Formproblem des 4. Satzes in Beethovens 9. Symphonie 494
LONGYEAR, R. M. The ecology of 19th-century opera 497
MAEGAARD, J. Arnold Schönberg: op. 16 Nr. 3 499
McCREDIE, A. D. Mecklenburgische Quellen

einer Gesamthistoriographie der Epoche Ludwig van Beethovens 507
MOHR, W. Beethovens Klavierfassung seines Violinkonzerts op. 61 509
MORCHE, G. Zum Problem der parallelen Quinten bei Marc-Antoine Charpentier 512
MOSUSOWA, N. Die Vielseitigkeit der Ausdrucksmittel schauspielerischer und gesanglicher Art in den russischen Opern des 19. Jahrhunderts 515
MUSIOL, K. August Kahlert und Beethoven: ein Beitrag zur Ästhetik und Musikkritik der ersten Hälfte des 19. Jahrhunderts 517
NIEMÖLLER, K. W. Die musikalische Festschrift für den Direktor der Prager Hofkapelle Kaiser Rudolfs II. 1602 520
NITSCHKE, W. Zu Paul Sieferts Psalmen 522
NOMURA, Y. Beethoven and Japanese musicology 524
NOVÁČEK, Z. Beethovens Schülerin Babette Keglevich aus der Slowakei und ihre Familie 526
von OPPEN, J. Beethovens Klavierfantasie op. 77 in neuer Sicht 528
PILKOVÁ, Z. Charakteristische Züge im Klavierschaffen der tschechischen Komponisten an der Wende des 18. zum 19. Jahrhundert 531
PLATEN, E. Beethovens Autographen als Ausgangspunkt morphologischer Untersuchungen 534
PONIATOWSKA, I. Der Klaviersatz bei Beethoven 536
POOS, H. Der dritte Tristan-Akkord: zur Harmoniestruktur der Takte 1–16 der Einleitung von 'Tristan und Isolde' 539
PROTOPOPOV, V. V. Synthetische Qualitäten der Sonatenform von Beethoven 542
REXROTH, D. Zum Spätwerk Franz Liszts – Material und Form in dem Klavierstück 'Unstern' 544
RIJAVEC, A. Slavko Osterc und die stilistische Situation seiner Zeit 547
RÖNNAU, K. Der repetierende Bass im Orchestersatz des 18. Jahrhunderts 550
RUMMENHÖLLER, P. Die Funktion der langsamen Einleitung in Beethovens op. 13: ein Beitrag zum Problem der inneren und äusseren Form bei Beethoven 553
SCHMIDT, H. Ein wiederaufgefundenes 'Fidelio'-Libretto 555
SCHMITT-THOMAS, R. Über ein wenig bekanntes Beethoven-Bildnis (Der Beethoven II von Joseph Karl Stieler) 557
SCHWARZ, B. Zur Uraufführung von Beethovens 'Missa solemnis' in St. Petersburg 559
SCHUHMACHER, G. Josef Matthias Hauers Kantate 'Der Menschen Weg' op. 67 561
SEEBASS, T. Über die sakrale und profane Bedeutung der Musikinstrumente im Mittelalter 564

SEIDEL, W. Heinrich Christoph Kochs Begriff des musikalischen Metrums   570

SMITH, J. The relation between Baroque figures and Classical motives in Beethoven   573

SMITS van WAESBERGHE, J. Rhythmus, Metrum, Tempo und Struktur im biologischen Rhythmus der Musik   575

SORDO, C. Beethoven's projection in Mexico   577

STAJIĆ, P. J. S. Bachs Fantasie-Satz und sein Einfluss auf Beethovens Schaffen   579

STERNFELD, F. W. Goethe and Beethoven 587

STOCKMANN, B. Die Interpretationsausgaben der Klaviersonaten Beethovens   590

TARR, E. H. Monteverdi, Bach und die Trompetenmusik ihrer Zeit   592

THOMPSON, D. Facilities for musical research in the Caribbean   597

THÜRMER, H. Zum Deklamationsproblem in den Liedern Beethovens   598

VOSS, E. Beethovens 'Eroica' und die Gattung der Sinfonie   600

VYSLOUŽIL, J. Zur Frage der mährischen und slawischen Volksidiome im Schaffen von Leoš Janáček   603

WATANABE, M. Die Bühnenmusik des 'Kabuki'-Theaters   605

WEISS, N. Titel moderner absoluter Musik 607

WOLFF, C. Arten der Mensuralnotation im 15. Jahrhundert und die Anfänge der Orgeltabulatur   609

Reflexionen über Musikwissenschaft heute, 10 September 1970 (chairman EGGEBRECHT, H. H.)

DAHLHAUS, C. Über historische und systematische Musikwissenschaft   621

BRISTIGER, M. Strukturelle und genetische Perspektive   626

LISSA, Z. Tradition in der Musik   630

HEISTER, H.-W. Musikwissenschaft als Sozialwissenschaft   639

EGGEBRECHT, H. H. Konzeptionen   648

von FISCHER, K. Über die Verantwortung des Musikwissenschaftlers   659

GOTTWALD, C. Musikwissenschaft und Kirchenmusik   663

ABRAHAM, L. U. Musikgeschichte bestimmt Musikpädagogik   672

REINECKE, H.-P. Studiengänge der Musikwissenschaft   677

HECKMANN, H. Wissenschaftliche und ausserwissenschaftliche Bereiche in der Musikologie   680

BOEHMER, K. 'Musikwissenschaft' – Voraussetzungen ihrer Zukunft   689

70 BRN   **Colloquium musica bohemica et Europaea Brno 1970: Colloquia on the History and Theory of Music at the International Musical Festival in Brno 5 / Musikwissenschaftliche Kolloquien der Internationalen Musikfestivale in Brno 5**
Brno 28–30 September 1970
        Mezinárodní hudební festival [International Musical Festival], Brno
        ed. R. Pečman (Brno: Mezinárodní hudební festival, 1972)

VYSLOUŽIL, J. Musica bohemica et Europaea 15

1 Kinds and types of late Gothic and Reformation compositions in the Czech lands (chairman von FISCHER, K.)

POKORNÝ, F. Der tschechische Beitrag zum liturgischen Drama Europas   27

LIPPHARDT, W. Das erste in Böhmen gedruckte katholische Gesangbuch Prag 1581 und sein Verfasser Christoph Hecyrus aus Budweis 33

PLOCEK, V. Zur Problematik der Osterspiele in Böhmen   47

von FISCHER, K. Zum Repertoire der böhmischen Mehrstimmigkeit vom 14. bis zum 16. Jahrhundert: die Verbreitung des böhmischen Repertoires ausserhalb Böhmens   55

TICHOTA, J. Intabulationen und tschechischer Gemeinschaftsgesang an der Wende des 16. Jahrhunderts   63

ČERNÝ, J. Die mehrtextige Motette des 14. und 15. Jahrhunderts in Böhmen   71

SNÍŽKOVÁ, J. Die kalixtinische Messe gegen Ende des 16. Jahrhunderts   89

2 Mannerism in the music of the 16th and 17th centuries (chairman RACEK, J.)

RACEK, J. Zum Problem des Manierismus in der europäischen Musik des 16. und 17. Jahrhunderts unter Berücksichtigung der tschechischen Musikkultur   101

VÁLKA, J. Manierismus als Kulturepoche 113

NOSKE, F. Manierismus als Desintegrationserscheinung musikgeschichtlicher Perioden   121

FINSCHER, L. Gesualdos 'Atonalität' und das Problem des musikalischen Manierismus 127

PASS, W. Die originelle Ansicht des Unendlichen: die Madrigali spirituali von Philippo de Monte und der Manierismus   145

STRAKOVÁ, T. Manierismus und die tschechische Renaissancemusik   159

PREISS, P. Farbe und Klang in der Theorie und Praxis des Manierismus   163

WOLFF, H. C.   Die Malerei des Manierismus und
die frühe Oper   171

**3 The music of the Czech lands and the Mannheim
school** (chairman EGGEBRECHT, H. H.)
EGGEBRECHT,   H.   H.   Mannheimer   Stil –
Technik und Gehalt   205
FUKAČ, J.   Biographische und quellenkundliche
Gegebenheiten in der Musikgeschichte der böh-
mischen Länder in Beziehung zur Mannheimer
Schule   219
ANDRASCHKE, P.   Formbildung in den An-
fangssätzen der späten Symphonie von Johann
Stamitz   235
RIETHMULLER,   A.   Mannheimer   Kompo-
sitionsstil und zeitgenössische Ästhetik   243
VYSLOUŽIL, J.   Vorklassische Phänomene in der
Musik der böhmischen Länder und die Mann-
heimer Schule   255
Discussion   266

**4 On the relationships of the Czech musical
tradition to the non-Czech development in the
18th century** (chairman LARSEN, J. P.)
VOLEK, T.   Musikalische Zentren in Böhmen im
18. Jahrhundert   281
PEČMAN, R.   Böhmen und Italien: ein offenes
Kapitel aus der Geschichte der Musik Böhmens
im 18. Jahrhundert   289
BADURA-SKODA, E.   Wien und die böhmische
Musiktradition im 18. Jahrhundert   299
SEHNAL, J.   Die Kirchenmusik der böhmischen
Länder im 18. Jahrhundert   309
PILKOVÁ, Z.   Dramatic music   317
HATTING, C. E.   Klaviermusik   325
LARSEN, J. P.   Kammermusik und Sinfonie   349
JEANS, S.   Einige Bemerkungen über böhmische

Orgel- und Cembalokonzerte in England   359
Discussion   362

5 Czech music in the 19th and 20th centuries
(chairman JIRÁNEK, J.)
JIRÁNEK, J.   Die moderne tschechische Musik
seit Smetana, ihre Spezifik und ihre Interaktion
mit   der   Musik   anderer   europäischer
Völker   365
CVETKO, D.   Der Einfluss der tschechischen mo-
dernen Musik auf die Entwicklung der Tonkunst im südslawischen Raum   373
VAJDA, I.   Randbemerkungen zur Genese der
klassischen slowakischen Musikmoderne   377
BEK, J.   Prag als Zentrum der tschechischen und
deutschen Musikkultur zwischen den beiden
Weltkriegen   381
ČERNÝ, M. K.   Ad vocem Dreigestirn Wagner –
Brahms – Mahler   in   der   Beziehung   zur
tschechischen Musik   389
STRÖBEL, D.   Auf der Suche nach Janáčeks
musikgeschichtlichem Ort   397
STEPHAN, R.   Hába und Schönberg (die Wiener
Schule und die tschechische Musik des 20.
Jahrhunderts)   407
BAJER, J.   Das tschechische Musiktheater im 20.
Jahrhundert und das europäische Drama   419
STUCKENSCHMIDT, H. H.   Gedanken über tsche-
chische Musik des 20. Jahrhunderts   423
Discussion   426

6 Miscellanea
ŘEHÁNEK,   F.   Janáčeks   Beitrag   zur   Har-
monielehre   435
ZENKL, L.   Beitrag zur Theorie der temperierten
Stimmung   443

70 GRA   **Der junge Haydn: Wandel von Musikauffassung und Musikaufführung in der österreichischen
Musik zwischen Barock und Klassik: Bericht der internationalen Arbeitstagung des Instituts
für Aufführungspraxis der Hochschule für Musik und darstellende Kunst in Graz**
Graz 29 June – 2 July 1970
Institut für Aufführungspraxis der Hochschule für Musik und darstellende Kunst in
Graz
ed. V. Schwarz (Graz: Akademische Druck- und Verlagsanstalt, 1972 = Beiträge zur
Aufführungspraxis, ed. V. Schwarz, 1)

LARSEN, J. P.   Der Stilwandel in der österreichischen Musik zwischen Barock und Wiener
Klassik   18
PEČMAN, R.   Der junge Haydn und die tschechische Musik des 18. Jahrhunderts   31
WÜNSCH, W.   Das Volkslied als Thema der Zeit
von Joseph Haydn   38
MAYEDA, A.   Nicola Antonio Porpora und der
junge Haydn   41
BADURA-SKODA, E.   'Teutsche Comoedie-Arien'
und Joseph Haydn   59

BECKER-GLAUCH, I.   Die Kirchenmusik des jun-
gen Haydn   74
SOMFAI, L.   Zur Aufführungspraxis der frühen
Streichquartett-Divertimenti Haydns   86
MAHLING, C.-H.   Orchester, Orchesterpraxis
und Orchestermusiker zur Zeit des jungen
Haydn (1740–1770)   98
THEMELIS, D.   Violintechnik in Österreich und
Italien um die Mitte des 18. Jahrhunderts   114
HELLWIG, F.   Der Wandel des Streichinstrumen-
tariums zwischen Barock und Klassik   126

GARTNER, J. Die Gesangsschule G. B. Mancinis   141
MELKUS, E. Die Entwicklung der freien Auszierung im 18. Jahrhundert   147
GRUBER, G. Musikalische Rhetorik und barocke Bildlichkeit in Kompositionen des jungen Haydn   168
FEDER, G. Die beiden Pole im Instrumentalschaffen des jungen Haydn   192
van der MEER, J. H. Die Verwendung der Blas-

instrumente im Orchester bei Haydn und seinen Zeitgenossen   202
FITZPATRICK, H. Waldhorntechnik um die Jahrhundertmitte   221
KLEBEL, B. Oboe und Oboespiel zur Zeit des jungen Haydn   231
WALTER, H. Das Tasteninstrument beim jungen Haydn   237
SCHWARZ, V. Die Rolle des Cembalos in Österreich nach 1760   249

70 HAMM   La tradition artistique face aux moyens audio-visuels/Artistic Tradition and Audio-Visual Media / Kunsttradition und audio-visuelle Medien: Colloquium in Hammamet 1970

Hammamet 21–7 April 1970

        Tunisian Ministry of Cultural Affairs, International Institute for Music, Dance and Theatre in the Audio-Visual Media

        ed. K. Blaukopf (Vienna: Universal, 1972)

DANIÉLOU, A. L'influence de l'écriture et de l'enregistrement sur la création musicale (English 15, German 18)   12
SCHEIB, W. Comment la télévision peut-elle

contribuer à l'évolution esthétique de traditions populaires dans le domaine de la musique et de la danse? (English 49, German 53)   45

70 LAW   Gilbert and Sullivan: Papers presented at the International Conference held at the University of Kansas in May 1970

Lawrence, Kansas May 1970

        International Theatre Studies Center

        ed. J. Helyar (Lawrence, Kansas: University of Kansas Libraries, 1971 = University of Kansas Publications Library Series 37)

ASHLEY, L. R. N. Gilbert and Melodrama   1
BARGAINNIER, E. F. 'Ruddigore': Gilbert's burlesque of melodrama   7
BOOTH, M. R. Research opportunities in nineteenth-century drama and theatre   17
COLE, D. W. The policy of contentiousness: some non-literary factors contributing to Gilbert's theatrical success   25
COTTIS, E. F. Gilbert and the British tar   33
ELLIS, J. D. Bab Ballads lost and found   43
FARNSWORTH, D. B. W. S. Gilbert and 'That Topic of the Age'   53
HARGREAVES, H. A. Sir William Schwenck Gilbert and the lure of the fairies   63
HARRIS, R. The artistry and authenticity of the Savoy overtures   71
HEAD, T. G. Rank and value in the plays of W. S. Gilbert   77
JONES, J. B. 'Bab' and *Punch*: Gilbert's contributions identified   85

McELROY, G. Meilhac and Halevy – and Gilbert: comic converses   91
MANHEIM, L. Strephon's 'Tipsy Lout': to cut or not to cut   107
PRESTIGE, C. D'Oyly Carte and the Pirates: the original New York productions of Gilbert and Sullivan   113
REES, T. W. S. Gilbert and the London pantomime season of 1866   149
ROGAL, S. J. The hymn tunes of Arthur Seymour Sullivan   175
STEDMAN, J. W. Gilbert's stagecraft: little blocks of wood   195
SUGDEN, J. G. The production of Gilbert and Sullivan operas in schools   213
SUTTON, M. K. The significance of 'The Grand Duke'   221

70 LIM   Actas y memorias del XXXIX congreso internacional de Americanistas
Lima 2–9 August 1970
International Congress of Americanists
(Lima: Instituto de estudios peruanos, 1972)

Vol. vi (1972)
4 Danzas, canciones y romances

CAMPBELL, R.   Remoto origen de la música
primitiva de Rapanui   189

70 MTA   Montauban 1970: Actes des journées internationales d'étude du Baroque [IV]: Contribution à
l'étude des origines de l'opéra et de l'alliance des arts dans la fête théâtrale et musicale
Montauban 24–6 September 1970
Baroque v (Montauban, 1972)

JACQUOT, J.   Presentation [survey]   9
HEARTZ, D.   Un ballet turc à la cour d'Henri II:
les Branles de Malte   17
STERNFELD, F. W.   Les intermèdes de Florence
et la genèse de l'opéra   25
SIMON, R.   Les rapports de la musique et de la
poésie dans le madrigal italien   31
JACQUOT, J.   Sur la forme du masque jaco-
béen   35
McGOWAN, M. M.   Deux fêtes en Savoie en 1644
et 1645   49
CHRISTOUT, M.-F.   'Les noces de Pelée et Thétis',
comédie italienne en musique entremêlée d'un
ballet dansé par le Roi (1654)   59
PURKIS, H.   Les intermèdes musicaux de 'George
Dandin'   63

MATHIEU-ARTH, F.   Les adaptations de 'La tem-
pête' de Shakespeare sous la Restauration anglaise   71
SHERGOLD, N.-D.   La musique et le thème litté-
raire dans l' 'Auto Sacramental' de Calderón,
'No Hay mas fortuna que Dios'   97
SAGE, J.   Nouvelles lumières sur la genèse de
l'opéra et la zarzuela en Espagne   107
DECROISETTE, F.   Le passage des jeux guerriers à
l'opéra dans 'L'Hipermestra' de Giovan Andrea
Moniglia   115
SCHONE, G.   Les grandes fêtes de Münich en
1662   121
HILMERA, J.   Mise en scène de l'opéra solennel
'Costanza e fortezza' au château de Prague en
1723   129

70 PIE   Feiern zum 200. Jahrestag der Geburt Ludwig van Beethovens in der ČSSR: Tagungsbericht
des II. internationalen musikologischen Symposiums
Piešt'any and Moravany, Slovakia, 27 June – 1 July 1970
ed. L'. Ballová (Bratislava: Slowakisches Nationalmuseum, 1970)

SZABOLCSI, B.   Beethoven und Osteuropa   11
SMOLKA, J.   Die Parallelen zwischen Antonín
Rejchas Fugenreform und den Fugen aus
Beethovens letzter Schaffensperiode   13
SÝKORA, V. J.   Die Vorahnungen des Beethoven-
Stils in den Klaviersonaten von Georg
Benda   27
TARANTOVÁ, M.   L. v. Beethoven und Josef
Dessauer   33
ČERNÝ, M. K.   Beethoven als Inspirator in der
tschechischen Musik der zweiten Hälfte des 19.
Jahrhunderts, besonders des jungen Dvořák 67
HULÁ, M.   Beethoven und Reichenberg   71
LISSA, Z.   Beethovens Stilelemente im Schaffen
Fryderyk Chopins   75
HRABUSSAY, Z.   Beethoven und Liszt (ihre per-

sönlichen und künstlerischen Beziehungen) 101
NOVÁČEK, Z.   Die Hauskapelle F. Eszterházys in
Bernolákovo und ihre Beziehung zu den Wiener
Komponisten   113
PROCHÁZKA, J.   Die Beziehungen Dr. Ján Theo-
bald Helds zu Beethoven   119
PONIATOWSKA, I.   Über die Zusammenhänge
von Beethovens Klaviersatz und den Klavieren
seiner Zeit   129
UNVERRICHT, H.   Bemerkungen zur Umgangs-
musik der Klassik   143
KRESÁNEK, I.   À cause de Schöner   155
ALBRECHT, J.   Zum Weg Beethovens aus seiner
Zeit   163
MARX, H. J.   Beethoven als politischer
Mensch   173

Judenič, N.　Beethoven und die Volksmusik (dargestellt an seinen Streichquartetten)　191

Richter, L.　Beethoven und die Gassenhauer seiner Zeit　217

70 STGE　Actes du colloque de Saint-Germain-en-Laye: Études sur la musique du XIXᵉ siècle / Papers of the Colloque at Saint-Germain-en-Laye: Studies on 19th-Century Music / Berichte über das Kolloquium von Saint-Germain-en-Laye: Studien zur Musik des 19. Jahrhunderts
St Germain-en-Laye 1–5 September 1970
International Musicological Society (1st symposium)
Acta musicologica xlii/1–2 and xliii (Kassel and Basle: Bärenreiter, 1970 and 1971)

[Preliminary papers in xlii/1–2 (1970)]
Wangermée, R.　Tradition et innovation dans la virtuosité romantique (discussion xliii, 114) 5

Problèmes de création musicale au XIXe siècle
Lockwood, L.　On Beethoven's sketches and autographs: some problems of definition and interpretation [see also xliii, 283]　32
Gossett, P.　Gioachino Rossini and the conventions of composition　48
Petrobelli, P.　Osservazioni sul processo com-positivo in Verdi (preliminary paper and discussion xliii, 125, 142)

Fédorov, V.　Čajkovskij, musicien type du XIXe siècle (discussion xliii, 205)　59
Meylan, R.　À propos du développement de l'instrumentation au début du dix-neuvième siècle (discussion xliii, 236)　70
Duckles, V.　Patterns in the historiography of 19th-century music (discussion xliii, 248)　75

70 STOC　Music and Technology
Stockholm 8–12 June 1970
UNESCO
ed. W. Skyvington (Paris: La revue musicale, Editions Richard-Masse, 1971); also published in French, ed. W. Skyvington, in *La revue musicale* nos. 239–40 (Paris: Éditions Richard-Masse, 1971)

Kaegi, W.　Music and technology in the Europe of 1970　11
Richard, A.　Interrogatory of a musician　33
Lesche, C.　Weltanschauung, science, technology and art　39
Schaeffer, P.　Music and computers　57
Koenig, G.　The use of computer programmes in creating music　93
Risset, J.-C.　Synthesis of sound by computer and problems concerning timbre　117
Mathews, M.　The electronic sound studio of the 1970's　129

Ciamaga, G.　The training of the composer in the use of new technological means　143
Szlifirski, K.　New technology and the training of composers in experimental music　151
Blaukopf, K.　Space in electronic music　157
Shibata, M.　Music and technology in Japan　173
Brün, H.　Technology and the composer　181
Helm, E.　UNESCO report on the Stockholm Meeting 1970　193

70 TRČ Súčasný stav etnomuzikologického bádania na Slovensku: 1. Etnomuzikologický seminár / Die gegenwärtige ethnomusikologische Forschung in der Slowakei
Trenčín, Slovakia 18–21 November 1970
Slovenská akadémie vied: Ústav hudobnej vedy [Slovak Academy of Sciences: Institute of Musicology]
ed. O. Elschek (Bratislava: Ústav hudobnej vedy, Slovenská akadémia vied, 1973 = Seminarium ethnomusicologicum 1)

[All papers in Slovak are printed with German résumés]

BURLAS, L. Minulost' a súčasnost' [Past and present] 5

ELSCHEK, O. Stav a perspektívy etnomuzikologického bádania na Slovensku [The state of and prospects for ethnomusicological research in Slovakia] 11

ELSCHEKOVÁ, A. Etnomuzikologické bádanie v oblasti l'udových piesni [Ethnomusicological research on folksongs] 33

BURLASOVÁ, S. Súčasny stav bádania o l'udovej piesni zo stanoviska slovesného [The present state of folksong research from a literary angle] 49

POTÚČEK, J. Annotierte Bibliographie der gedruckten Sammlungen von slowakischen Volksliedmelodien 61

ONDREJKA, K. K situácii v štúdiu l'udových tancov [The situation on the study of folk dances] 67

ONDREJKA, K. Aus dem Schrifttum über das Studium der slowakischen (ethnisch und territorial) Volkstänze und Spiele (bis 1965) 77

JELÍNKOVÁ, Z. K výzkumu lidového tance na Slovensku [Research into folk dance in Slovakia] 93

LENG, L. Stav bádania v l'udovej inštrumentálnej hudbe [The state of research into instrumental folk music] 99

MAČÁK, I. Stav dokumentácie slovenských l'udových hudobných nástrojov [The state of documentation of Slovak folk musical instruments] 109

MATÚŠ, F. Informácia o stave etnoorganologického bádania na východnom Slovensku [The state of ethno-organological research in east Slovakia] 115

HORVÁTHOVÁ, E. Stav bádania v oblasti zvykoslovia [The state of research into folk customs] 119

DÚŽEK, S. K výskumu a dokumentácii zvykov v slovenskej etnomuzikologii [Research into and documentation of customs in Slovak ethnomusicology] 127

ŠVEHLÁK, S. Dokumentácia l'udovej kultúry v archíve Národopisného ústavu SAV s prihliadnutím na stav rukopisných a zvukopisných folklórnych fondov [The documentation of folk culture in the archive of the Folksong Institute of the Slovak Academy of Sciences with a survey of the state of folklore collections of manuscripts and sound archives] 133

SULITKA, A. Fotodokumentácia v Národopisnom ústave SAV vzhl'adom k etnomuzikologickým dokumentom [Photographic documentation in the Folksong Institute of the Slovak Academy of Sciences with a view to ethnomusicological documentation] 145

MÓŽI, A. Spôsoby využívania zvukovej techniky pri výskume hudobného folklóru v minulosti a dnes [Ways of using sound technique in folk music research, past and present] 151

RUTTKAY, M. Využitie filmu v hudobno- a tanečnofolklórnej dokumentácii [The use of film in the documentation of folk music and dance] 161

Round table: Katalogizácia a spolupráca v etnomuzikológii [Cataloguing and cooperation in ethnomusicology] (chairman ELSCHEK, O.)

Katalogizácia textov [The cataloguing of texts]

SIROVÁTKA, O. Katalogizácia textov lyrických piesni [The cataloguing of texts of lyrical songs] 165

HRABALOVÁ, O. K evidencii a katalogisaci písňových fondů v brnenském UEF [The cataloguing of song collections in Brno Institute of Ethnography] 167

BURLASOVÁ, S. Žánrová klasifikácia l'udových piesni [Classification of folksongs by genre] 169

Katalogizácia tancov [The cataloguing of dances]

LAUDOVÁ, H. Dokumentace, anylýza a katalógy lidových tanců [Documentation, analysis and catalogues of folk dances] 172

ONDREJKA, K. O motivickom katalógu slovenských l'udových tancov [A catalogue of Slovak folk dance motifs] 177

Katalogizácia a samočinné počítače [Cataloguing and computers]

FILIP, M. Využitie samočinných počítačov v dokumentácii [The use of computers in documentation] 181

HOLÝ, D. Návrh realizácie projektu spracovania l'udových piesni na SP [A sketch for a project of working on folksongs with a computer] 184

MARKL, J. Aplikace tzv. taktového systému při katalogizace českých lidových písní [The application of the so-called bar system of cataloguing Czech folksongs] 187

70 VEN   Italia Venezia e Polonia tra illuminismo e romaniticismo: Atti del III convegno di studi
Venice 15–17 October 1970
  Fondazione Giorgio Cini, Venice; Polish Academy of Sciences
  ed. V. Branca (Florence: Leo S. Olschki, 1973)

MAMCZARZ, I.   Gli intermezzi comici italiani in   STARZYŃSKI, J.   Le portrait de Chopin par De-
Polonia nella seconda metà del settecento 175   lacroix   323
                                                        BELOTTI, G.   Chopin, l'Italia e Venezia   333

70 VIE   **Beethoven-Symposion Wien 1970: Bericht**
Vienna 7 October 1970
  Österreichische Akademie der Wissenschaften; Gesellschaft zur Herausgabe von
  Denkmälern der Tonkunst in Österreich
  *Österreichische Akademie der Wissenschaften: Philosophisch-historische Klasse Sit-
  zungsberichte* 271 (Vienna: Hermann Böhlaus Nachf./Kommissionsverlag der Österrei-
  chischen Akademie der Wissenschaften, 1971 = Veröffentlichungen der Kommission
  für Musikforschung, ed. E. Schenk, 12)

BRAUBACH, M.   Beethovens Abschied von Bonn: LISSA, Z.   Beethovens Einfluss auf den Klavier-
das rheinische Erbe   25   satz Chopins   175
EGGEBRECHT, H. H.   Beethoven und der Begriff   MAGNANI, L.   Beethoven, das philosophische
der Klassik   43   Denken und die Ästhetik seiner Zeit
FELLERER, K. G.   Beethoven und die liturgische   von der OSTEN, G.   Théodore Géricault – ein
Musik seiner Zeit   61   Pariser Maler der Beethoven-Zeit   213
von FISCHER, K.   Beethoven – Klassiker oder   RACEK, J.   Beethoven auf Schloss Grätz
Romantiker   77   (Hradec) bei Troppau in den Jahren 1806 und
GOLDSCHMIDT, H.   Vers und Strophe in   . 1811: ein Beitrag zur Frage Beethoven und die
Beethovens Instrumentalmusik   97   böhmischen Länder   215
KIRKENDALE, W.   Beethovens Missa solemnis   SCHMIDT-GÖRG, J.   Entwicklung und Aufgaben
und die rhetorische Tradition   121   der Beethoven-Forschung   237
KÖHLER, K.-H.   Beethovens Gespräche –   STAIGER, E.   Das Geburtsjahr 1770 – Hölderlin,
biographische Aspekte zu einem modernen   Hegel und Beethoven   253
Beethovenbild: Bemerkungen zur Edition der   SZABOLCSI, B.   Maqam und Modell bei Mozart
noch unveröffentlichten Konversationshefte 159   und Beethoven   267

70 WÜR   **Beiträge zur weltlichen und geistlichen Lyrik des 13. bis 15. Jahrhunderts: Würzburger
Colloquium 1970**
Würzburg 17–20 March 1970
  Institut für Ältere Deutsche Philologie der Philipps-Universität, Marburg
  ed. K. Ruh and W. Schröder (Berlin: Erich Schmidt, 1973)

MERTENS, V.   Ein neumiertes Minnelied des 14.   STEER, G.   'Dat dagelyt von der heiligen passien':
Jahrhunderts aus Kremsmünster   68   die sogenannte 'Grosse Tageweise' Graf Peters
KESTING, P.   'Martine Christi famule': zum Mar-   von Arberg   112
tinskanon des 'Mönchs von Salzburg'   98

70 YAO   La musique africaine: réunion de Yaoundé
Yaoundé 23–7 February 1970
UNESCO
La revue musicale nos. 288–9 (Paris: Éditions Richard-Masse, 1972)

NKETIA, J. H. Les langages musicaux de l'Afrique subsaharienne 7

NKETIA, J. H. Les sources de documentation historique sur les traditions musicales de l'Afrique 43

DANIÉLOU, A. Les langages musicaux de l'Afrique noire 49

SOWANDE, F. Le rôle de la musique dans la société africaine traditionnelle 57

ENO BELINGA, S. La musique traditionnelle de l'Afrique occidentale: genres, styles et influences 69

KAKOMA, G. W. Les traditions musicales de l'Afrique orientale 75

ISMAIL, M. Les traditions musicales du Soudan 87

DUVELLE, C. La musique orientale en Afrique noire 95

EUBA, A. Évolution et diffusion de la musique africaine traditionnelle 117

MENSAH, A. A. Le contact de l'Africain moderne avec la musique: l'expérience de la Zambie 125

KEBEDE, A. La musique africaine dans l'hémisphère occidental: la musique noire des Amériques 129

ALMEIDA, R. L'influence de la musique africaine au Brésil 135

COLLINS, E. Les traditions musicales au Liberia 141

71 ANN   **Chinese and Japanese Music-Dramas**
Ann Arbor 1–4 October 1971
Association for Asian Studies; Center for Japanese Studies, Center for Chinese Studies,
School of Music and Speech Department of the University of Michigan
ed. J. I. Crump and W. P. Malm (Ann Arbor: Center for Chinese Studies, University of
Michigan, 1975 = Michigan papers in Chinese studies 19)

CRUMP, J. I.   Giants in the earth: Yüan drama
as seen by Ming critics (discussion 39)   1
RULAN CHAO PIAN   Aria structural patterns in
the Peking opera (discussion 90)   65
MALM, W. P.   The musical characteristics and
practice of the Japanese Noh drama in an East

Asian context (discussion 133)   99
SESAR, C.   China vs. Japan: the Noh play 'Haku
Rakuten' (discussion 171)   143
TEELE, R. E.   The structure of the Japanese Noh
play (discussion 215)   189
Glossary   235

71 BLE   **Bericht über die 5. Sitzung der Studiengruppe für die Systematisierung von Volksweisen**
Bled, Yugoslavia 13–18 April 1971
Study Group of Folk Music Systematization of the International Folk Music Council
ed. W. Deutsch (Vienna, 1974)

Ceol Rince na hEireann (DEUTSCH, W. 6,
JERSILD, M.   10, STIEF, W.   12, discussion 21)
BRAUN, H.   Beitrag zum Problem der 'Zeile'
(discussion 25)   23
STESZEWSKI, J.   Die Benennungen, das Bewus-
stsein und die Dinge in der Ethnomusikologie
(discussion 30)   26
KATZAROVA, R. D.   Wie der bulgarische Volk-

sänger die Lieder systematisiert (discussion
47)   33
HOSCHOWSKYJ, W.   Die Melodie-Register als ein
Bestandteil der theoretisch-methodologischen
und analytischen Probleme der neuzeitlichen
Ethnomusikologie (discussion 55)   49
THEMELIS, D.   Bemerkungen zur Systematisie-
rung der neugriechischen Volkslieder   57

71 BRN   **Colloquium musica cameralis Brno 1971: Colloquia on the History and Theory of Music at the
International Musical Festival in Brno 6 / Musikwissenschaftliche Kolloquien der In-
ternationalen Musikfestspiel in Brno 6**
Brno 27–9 September 1971
Mezinárodní hudební festival [International Musical Festival], Brno
ed. R. Pečman (Brno: International Musical Festival, 1977)

VYSLOUŽIL, J.   Colloquium musica cameralis –
Brno 1971   9

1 Theoretica, aesthetica et sociologica
ZENGINOV, D.   Die Kammermusik und der
Mensch des XX. Jahrhunderts   17
GINZBURG, L.   Die Kammermusik in der moder-
nen Musikpraxis (nach den Erfahrungen der
sowjetischen Interpretationsschule)   23
SALMEN, W.   Neue Bildquellen zur Praxis von
Haus- und Kammermusik im 16. Jahr
hundert   37

van der MEER, J. H.   Einige Probleme bei der
Besetzung der Kammermusik für Streicher des
Barock   49
SCHWARZ, V.   Die Wertschätzung der Instru-
mente und die Rolle des Begleiters in der
Kammermusik des 18. Jahrhunderts   73
STAHMER, K.   Zur Frage der Interpretation von
Musik – eine   Musiksoziologische   Modell-
studie, dargestellt an dem 1. Satz von
Beethovens Streichquartett op. 130   81
HRADECKÝ, E.   Zum   Satzunterschied   der
klassischen Orchester- und Kammermusik 100

2 Musica cameralis bohemica

Vít, P.   Jan Zachs Quartettsinfonien   109
Lipphardt, W.   Das Generalbassbegleitete deutsche geistliche Lied in Böhmen 1650–1750   115
Krutová, A.   Les quintettes pour instruments à vent d'Antoine Reicha   127
Kyas, V.   Lyrische Klavierstücke der Zeit vor Smetana   131
Janeček, K.   Smetanas hastiger Abschied: Bemerkungen über den Finalsatz von Smetanas Zweitem Streichquartett   143
Clapham, J.   Indian influence in Dvořák's American chamber music   147
Gerlach, R.   War Schönberg von Dvořák beeinflusst? Bemerkungen zu Arnold Schönbergs Streichquartett D-Dur   157
Hudec, V.   Zum Stil von Z. Fibichs kammermusikalischem Schaffen   171
Wehnert, M.   Anmerkungen zur Semantik in den Streichquartetten Leoš Janáčeks   177

3 'Musica cameralis' – definitio termini (chairman Eggebrecht, H. H.; panel Bártová, J., Cvetko, D., Černý, M. K., Ghircoiaşiu, R., Ginsburg, L. S., Haack, H., Polák, P., Siegmund-Schultze, W., Stephan, R., Stŕitecký, J., Vysloužil, J., Zaminer, F.)

Minutes of the round table 'Begriff Kammermusik' (28.9.1971) prepared in the Cabinet for Music Lexicography, Brno University   201
Reimer, E.   Zur Geschichte des Begriffs Kammermusik   205
Haack, H.   Die Doppelbedeutung des Terminus Kammermusik bei Hindemith   231
Gülke, P.   Lutosławskis Streichquartett als Kammermusikwerk   243
Team of the Cabinet for Music Lexicography, Brno University: report   255
Bártová, J.   Zur Frage der Begriffsanalyse   285

4 Musica cameralis europaea saec. XVII, XVIII et XIX

Sehnal, J.   Zur Differenzierung der Sonata da chiesa und Sonata da camera in der zweiten Hälfte des 17. Jahrhunderts   303
Siegmund-Schultze, W.   Zur Idee der Kammermusik bei Mozart   311
Bose, F.   Pibroch, schottische Kammermusik für Dudelsack   325
Pečman, R.   Johann Sebastian Bach und der Stil der italienischen Triosonate   337
Fleischhauer, G.   Zur instrumentalen Kammermusik Georg Philipp Telemanns   345
Croll, G.   Klaviermusik von Michael Haydn?   361
Richter, L.   Beethovens Britische Volksliedbearbeitungen für Gesang und Klaviertrio 373
Pass, W.   Der Kammermusikkreis Gottfried van Swietens und das 'Kammermusikalische'   387
Riethmüller, A.   Bemerkungen zum Vorhalt bei Schubert: der 2. Satz der Klaviersonate A-Dur, op. 120, D 664   397

5 Musica cameralis saec. XX

Smirnov, M. A.   Vom nationalen Charakter der Klavierkompositionen Skrjabins   411
Štědroň, B.   Die Inspirationsquellen von Janáčeks Concertino   423
Wolff, H. C.   Die Kammermusik Paul Hindemiths   435
Kochlewska-Woźniak, J.   Smyčkovyje kvartety pol'skogo kompozitora Grażyny Bacewicz   447
Ochs, E.   Bemerkungen zum Streichquartett-Schaffen Dmitri Schostakowitschs   455
Cvetko, D.   Die slowenische Kammermusik in der ersten Periode der Moderne   471
Vetter, M.   Bemerkungen zum Kammermusikschaffen in der DDR   481
Němcová, A.   Die Rolle des Vokalparts in der modernen Kammermusik   491
Štědroň, M.   Das Zunehmen musikfremder Elemente in den Kammerkompositionen der Neuen Musik der 60. Jahre   497

71 BUD[1]   **International Musicological Conference in Commemoration of Béla Bartók 1971**
Budapest 24–7 March 1971
Association of Hungarian Musicians; Hungarian Music Council; Hungarian Section of the International Society for Contemporary Music
ed. J. Ujfalussy and J. Breuer (Budapest: Editio Musica, 1972)

Lukács, G.   Bartók und die ungarische Kultur   11
Zoltai, D.   Bartók in Sicht der Frankfurter Schule (English résumé 223)   13
Volek, J.   Bartók – determination of a period 19
Kovács, J.   'Heiliger Dankgesang in der lydischen Tonart' und 'Adagio religioso' (English résumé 224)   25
Kapst, E.   Zum Tonalitätsbegriff bei Bartók (English résumé 224)   31
Kárpáti, J.   Le désaccordage dans la technique de composition de Bartók (English résumé 225)   41

SOMFAI, L. A characteristic culmination point in Bartók's instrumental forms 53

STEVENS, H. The sources of Bartók's rhapsody for violoncello and piano 65

SCHOLLUM, R. Stilkundliche Bemerkungen zu Werken Bartóks und der 2. Wiener Schule (English résumé 225) 77

KRONES, H. Stilkundliche Betrachtungen auf soziologischer Basis insbesondere dargestellt am Beispiel Béla Bartók (English résumé 226) 83

SUCHOFF, B. Béla Bartók: man of letters 89

KROÓ, G. On the origin of the Wooden Prince 97

SZABOLCSI, B. Bartók and world literature 103

MARTYNOV, I. Quelques pensées sur Bartók (English résumé 226) 107

DEMÉNY, J. Ady-Gedichtbände in Bartóks Bibliothek (English résumé 226) 111

TAWASTSTJERNA, E. Sibelius und Bartók: einige Parallelen (English résumé 227) 121

NESTYEV, I. Prokofiev and Bartók: some parallels 137

BÓNIS, F. Bartók und der Verbunkos (English résumé 227) 145

UJFALUSSY, J. Gemeinsame Stilschicht in Bartóks und Kodálys Kunst (English résumé 228) 155

MOLNÁR, A. Die Bedeutung der neuen Osteuropäischen Musik (English résumé 228) 159

BREUER, J. Die zeitgenössische ungarische Musik auf dem Pfade Bartóks (English résumé 229) 163

SZELÉNYI, I. Bartók und Modalität (English résumé 229) 169

BURLAS, L. The influence of Slovakian folk music on Bartók's musical idiom 181

DJOUDJEFF, S. Bartók – promoteur de l'ethnomusicologie balkanique et sud-est européenne (English résumé 229) 189

ELSCHEK, O. Bartóks Beziehung zur Volksmusik und Volksmusikforschung (English résumé 230) 197

71 BUD² Proceedings of the 7th International Congress on Acoustics
Budapest 18–26 August 1971
International Commission on Acoustics, International Union of Pure and Applied Physics
(Budapest: Akadémiai kiadó, 1971)

Vol. i General Progress Papers/Round Table Conferences/Section E General Acoustics (1971)

LEIPP, E. Tour d'horizon sur l'acoustique musicale: le point de vue du laboratoire d'acoustique de la Faculté des sciences de Paris 253

Vol. iii Sections C-H-S (Subjective Acoustics) (1971)

LIEBER, E. Über Nichtlinearitaten von Saitenschwingungen 557

JANSSON, E. and others An investigation of a violin by hologram interferometry and electroacoustical measurements 561

MEINEL, H. F. Über Schwingungen von Geigenkörpern bei Eigenfrequencen 565

CASTELLENGO, M. and NAGAI, Y. Etude du déplacement continu d'un trou latéral dans un tuyau à embouchure de flute 569

KRÜGER, W. Stimmungsprobleme bei Metallblasinstrumenten und Möglichkeiten zur Verbesserung der Stimmung 573

MARTIN, D. W. Acoustics of an educational electropiano 577

HOJAN, E. and SZUBERT, B. Transient shapes of violin string sounds 581

GANEV, S. A. Das Spektrum von Instrumentengruppen eines Orchesters 585

AEBI, W. Die innere Akustik des Waldhornes I. 589

SUNDBERG, J. Voice source properties of bass singers 593

TOYAMA, F. M. Study of timbre of wet and dry Japanese bamboo pipe, shakuhachi 597

HUTCHINS, C. M. and STETSON, K. A. Hologram interferometry applied to violin plates and compared with an acoustical test method 601

AEBI, W. Die innere Akustik des Waldhornes II. 605

LEIPP, E. Un paradoxe en sensation de hauteur tonale 609

RISSET, J. C. Paradoxes de hauteur: le concept de hauteur sonore n'est pas le même pour tout le monde 613

LINDQUIST, J. and SUNDBERG, J. Perception of the octave interval 617

TERHARDT, E. Pitch shifts of harmonics, an explanation of the octave enlargement phenomenon 621

PRUS, S. Theory of the perception and discrimination of intensity with an interpretation of the divergences between loudness scales 625

NÖSSELT, V. Das Klingen: Determination einer musikalischen Empfindung, ihre akustischen Korrelate sowie deren Existenzbereich 629

EGGELING, H. Informationspsychologische An-

sätze zur Verarbeitung musikalischer Eindrücke in der Gegenwartsdauer 633

von BISMARCK, G. Timbre of steady sounds: scaling of sharpness 637

KUSSEV, A. J. Die mittlere kurze Notendauer für 5 typische Instrumentengruppen 641

MELKA, A. Beitrag zur Problematik der Hörbarkeit von Einschwingverzerrung bei der Musikübertragung 645

FILIP, M. Pitch period extraction in monophonic music and similar signals 649

SUNDBERG, J. and TJERNLUND, P. Real time notation of performed melodies by means of a computer 653

SHITOV, L. V. Statistics of music and speech signals in short time intervals 657

TARNÓCZY, T. and SZENDE, O. Experiments on the musical interval sense 685

SPELDA, A. Die Fluktuationen des fixierten Dynamikpegels und die wechselseitige Maskierung der Orchesterinstrumente 737

CARDOZO, B. L. and DOMBURG, G. Annoyance of dropouts in music 741

CALAME, B. Le 'calacoustic' et son emploi dans l'amélioration de la perception des sons chez les musiciens et les locuteurs 745

Vol. iv Sections A-N-V (Technical Acoustics) (1971)

MEYER, J. Über die Hallradien einiger Musikinstrumente in verschiedenen Konzertsälen 1

71 EIS   Joseph Haydn und seine Zeit

Eisenstadt 11–18 September 1971
Institut für österreichische Kulturgeschichte
ed. G. Mraz, *Jahrbuch für österreichische Kulturgeschichte* ii (Eisenstadt: Institut für österreichische Kulturgeschichte, 1972)

GUTKAS, K. Österreich und Europa zur Zeit Joseph Haydns 9

LARSEN, J. P. Das Echtheitsproblem in der Musik des 18. Jahrhunderts 25

FEUCHTMÜLLER, R. Farbe und Raum im Spätbarock 40

FEDER, G. Joseph Haydn als Mensch und Musiker 43

NOVÁČEK, Z. Haydns Kontakte zu der Stadt Pressburg 57

SOMFAI, L. Vom Barock zur Klassik: Umgestaltung der Proportionen und des Gleichgewichts in zyklischen Werken Joseph Haydns 64

THOMAS, G. Joseph Haydns Tanzmusik 73

WÜNSCH, W. Zum Thema 'Türkenoper und Allaturca-Stil' 86

MRAZ, G. Barocke Frömmigkeit im aufgeklärten Staat 92

MRAZ-KOLLER, G. Bildungsanspruch und Bildungsmöglichkeiten im aufgeklärten Österreich 105

ZEMAN, H. Die österreichische Lyrik der Haydn-Zeit 121

BAUER, W. M. Der Roman der josephinischen Aufklärung: Strukturen und literaturhistorische Bedeutung, gezeigt an Johann Pezzels 'Faustin' 147

HILGER, W. 'Kammermaler' des österreichischen Spätbarocks 153

71 FLOR   La musica occidentale e le civiltà musicali extraeuropee: Atti della tavola rotonda organizzata in occasione del XXXIV Maggio musicale fiorentino

Florence 18–19 May 1971
Teatro comunale, Florence; XXXIV Maggio musicale fiorentino
ed. S. Felici (Florence: Ente autonomo del Teatro comunale di Firenze, n.d. = Quaderno 2)

VLAD, R. Il XXXIV Maggio musicale fiorentino 11

GARIN, E. Le civiltà extraeuropee 27

DANIÉLOU, A. Le civiltà musicali dell'oriente 53

KÁRPÁTI, J. Influenze extraeuropee sulla musica occidentale (discussion NATALETTI, G. 131) 67

GOLÉA, A. Lavori di Jolivet 83

MARAINI, F. L'esotico inverso: Cina e Giappone guardano l'Europa 95

SANTI, P. Appunti sul rock e l'esotico 133

CARNER, M. L'elemento esotico in Puccini 141

CARPITELLA, D. Il mito del primitivo 147

HALFFTER, E. L'influenza orientale sulla musica europea: il 'Cante Jondo' 157

JOLIVET, A. Influssi della musica giapponese 167

GASLINI, G.   La nuova ondata del jazz del rock   SHILOAH, A.   Musiche contemporanee e tradi-
del folk   173   zionali del vicino oriente   197
LEVI, L.   Le liturgie tradizioni dell'oriente   183   Discussion   207

71 GRA   Der klangliche Aspekt beim Restaurieren von Saitenklavieren: Bericht der internationalen Tagung von Restauratoren für besaitete Tasteninstrumente am Institut für Aufführungspraxis der Hochschule für Musik und darstellende Kunst in Graz
Graz 13–16 September 1971
Institut für Aufführungspraxis der Hochschule für Musik und darstellende Kunst in Graz
ed. V. Schwarz (Graz: Akademische Druck- und Verlagsanstalt, 1973 = Beiträge zur Aufführungspraxis, ed. V. Schwarz, 2)

van der MEER, J. H.   Zielsetzung bei der Res-   WITTMAYER, K.   Bericht (Auszug) über die Restaurierung historischer Saitenklaviere   15   taurierungsarbeiten an einem Kirckman-
SCHÜTZE, R.   Der 'historische' Klang, Wunsch-   Cembalo   69
traum oder technoide Banalität?   25   STRADNER, G.   Bemerkungen zu den besaiteten
WILLIAMS, P.   The implications of correct res-   Tasteninstrumenten in Sebastian Virdungs
toration for performers   29   'Musica getutscht . . .'   79
BARNES, J.   The stringing of Italian harpsi-   SCHWARZ, V.   Johann Samuel Petris Anweisun-
chords   35   gen zum Beziehen, Bekielen und Stimmen besai-
LAMBRECHTS-DOUILLEZ, J.   Hans Ruckers and   teter Tasteninstrumente   87
his workshop   41   STRADNER, G.   Zur Ausstellung von Tasten-
MERTIN, J.   Cembalo-, Clavichord- und Orgel-   instrumenten   101
bau aus der Gemeinsamkeit der Erzeugung   SCHWARZ, V.   Josef Fischhof und das Wiener
historischer Tasteninstrumente   47   Klangideal um 1840   105
WATZEK, A.   Zusammenfassende Erfahrungen
an Klaviermechaniken   53   KUKELKA, P.   Konservierung und Denkmal-
HELLWIG, F.   Historische musikalische Tempe-   pflege an historischen Musikinstrumenten 119
raturen und ihre Einstimmung   57

71 HIN   Heutige Probleme der Volksmusik: Bericht über ein internationales Seminar der Deutschen UNESCO-Kommission
Hindelang, Allgäu 19–21 May 1971
Deutsche UNESCO-Kommission, Cologne
ed. H.-F. Meyer and H.-D. Dyroff (Cologne: Deutsche UNESCO-Kommission Pullach/Munich: Verlag Dokumentation, 1973 = Seminarbericht der Deutschen UNESCO-Kommission 19)

HOERBURGER, F.   Was ist Volksmusik?   11   ter Feldforschung zu Volkstanz und Volkslied
EIBNER, F.   Was ist Volksmusik? Gestalt-   in Bayern (discussion 98)   76
analytische Aspekte   27   DEUTSCH, W.   Stand der Volksmusik in Öster-
KLUSEN, E.   Zur Entideologisierung des Begriffs   reich   99
Volkslied (discussion 57)   47   KRINGS, A.   Bearbeitung von Volksmusik, ins-
KARLINGER, F.   Kunstlied oder Volkslied? (dis-   besondere bei Aufnahmen für den Funk (dis-
cussion 60)   59   cussion 118)   111
HIRSCH, H.   Urheberrecht und Volksmusik 62   LORENZ, K.   Die Metamorphose der Volks-
VODUŠEK, V.   Die Stellung der Volkskunst und   musik im Industriezeitalter   119
der Volksmusik in Recht und Gesetzgebung in   Discussion   127
Jugoslawien   69   SCHICKHAUS, K. H.   Instrumentalkunde am
ARTMEIER, A.   Die derzeitige Situation der   Beispiel der bayerisch-alpenländischen Volks-
Volksmusik im bayerischen Raum (discussion   musik   130
75)   71   GRAD, T.   Instrumentenkunde – Fragen der
MAYER, W. A.   Probleme und Ergebnisse neues-   Darbietung und Besetzung   140

SCHIEDE, H. Instrumentenkunde – die Zither 153
VÖLKEL, A. Instrumentenkunde – zwei Instrumente aus Nordbayern 155
CELLIER, M. Von der Tatra zum Schwarzen

Meer: Volks-Instrumental-Kuriositäten 156
DŽUDŽEV, S. Volksmusik in Bulgarien und Pro-
bleme der bulgarischen Volkskultur 163
BREDL, M. Volksmusikpflege in Schwaben 172

71 KAS   Dokumentation musikgeschichtlicher Objekte
Kassel 2–4 February 1971
Arbeitsgemeinschaft 'Dokumentation in den historischen Wissenschaften', Darmstadt
ed. F. Schulte-Tigges (Darmstadt: 1974 = Akten der Arbeitsgemeinschaft Dokumentation in den Historischen Wissenschaften, ed. R. Gundlach and F. Schulte-Tigges, 2)

BÖKER-HEIL, N. Automationsgerechte Darstellung der Weissen Mensuralnotation (mit
einem Anhang über computergenerierten
Mensuralnoten-Druck) 6
HECKMANN, H. Katalog 'Deutsches Tenorlied' 38
KINDERMANN-KORTHAUS, I, Erfahrungen bei
der Codierung (discussion 41) 40
BIRKNER, G. Datenverarbeitung in der Edition
'Das deutsche Kirchenlied (DKL)' (discussion
53) 48
van der MEER, J. H. Zur Erfassung von Musikinstrumenten in öffentlichem und privatem
Besitz (discussion 66) 56
BERNER, A. Dokumentation von Musikinstrumenten (Aufgaben/Prinzipien und bisher
geleistete Arbeiten) 69
OTTO, I. Die Instrumentenkunde geht am besten

vom real vorhandenen Objekt aus 77
KRICKEBERG, D. Bemerkungen zur Speicherung
von Daten von Musikinstrumenten (discussion
103) 93
SALMEN, W. Vorbemerkungen zu einem Repertorium der Musik-Ikonographie (discussion
114) 109
REINECKE, H.-P. Formale Gesichtspunkte zur
Kategorisierung von Bild- und Text-
dokumenten 115
DROYSEN, D. Das Problem der Selektion und
des funktionellen Zusammenhangs bei der
Dokumentation mittelalterlicher Buchmalerei – dargestellt in der Psalter-Illus-
tration (discussion 128) 123
SCHUG, A. Probleme der Erschliessung ikonographischer Sachverhalte (discussion 139) 131

71 MOS   Muzïkal'nïye kul'turï narodov: traditsii i sovremennost' [The musical cultures of nations:
traditions and the present day]
Moscow 6–9 October 1971
International Music Council (7th congress)
ed. B. Yarustovskiy (Moscow: Sovetskiy kompozitor, 1973)

YARUSTOVSKIY, B. Muzïkal'nïye kul'turï narodov: traditsii i sovremennost' [The musical
cultures of nations: traditions and the present
day] 10
MENON, N. Muzïkal'nïye kul'turï narodov:
traditsii i sovremennost' Razvivayushchiesya
stranï [The musical cultures of nations: traditions and the present day in developing count-
ries] 25
de LEUV, T. [de LEEUW, T.] Muzïkal'nïye
kul'turï narodov: traditsii i sovremennost' [The
musical cultures of nations: traditions and the
present day] 35

Traditsii i novatorstvo [Traditions and in-
novation]
LISSA, Z. Traditsii i novatorstvo v muzïke

[Traditions and innovations in music] 42
fon FISHER, K. [von FISCHER, K.] Priroda i
funktsii traditsii v evropeyskoy muzïke [The
nature and functions of tradition in European
music] 51
ORDZHONIKIDZE, G. O dinamike natsional'novo stilya [The dynamic of national
style] 59
EGGEBREKHT, G. G. [EGGEBRECHT, H. H.]
Traditsii, nóvatorstvo i universal'nost'
muzïkal'nïkh kul'tur [Traditions, innovation
and universality of musical cultures] 66
MAROTI, Ya. [MARÓTHY, J.] Rol' klassovïkh
traditsiy v muzïkal'noy kul'ture nashevo vrem-
eni [The role of class traditions in the musical
culture of our time] 72
OSTIN, Ui. [AUSTIN, W.] Natsional'nïye tradit-

sii i tekhnicheskiye priyemï avangarda [National traditions and technical methods of the avantgarde] 77

EL'SNER, Yu. [ELSNER, J.] Problema traditsii v muzïkal'nïkh kul'turakh neevropeyskikh stran [The problem of tradition in the musical cultures of non-European countries] 82

Traditsionnoye muzïkal'noye mïshleniye i sovremennaya muzïka [Traditional musical thinking and contemporary music]

DANIELU, A. [DANIÉLOU, A.] Traditsiya i novatorstvo v razlichnïkh muzïkal'nikh kul'turakh mira [Tradition and innovation in different musical cultures of the world] 86

MELLERS, Ui. [W.] Ispol'zovaniye narodnoy muzïki v proizvedeniyakh kompozitorov XX veka [The use of folk music by composers of the 20th century] 90

MENON, N. Traditsionnoye muzïkal'noye mïshleniye i sovremennaya muzïka [Traditional musical thought and contemporary music] 98

DANILEVICH, L. O natsional'nom i internatsional'nom v sovetskoy muzïke [National and international elements in Soviet music] 102

EUBA, A. Sozertsatel'nïy kharakter afrikanskoy traditsionnoy muzïki [The contemplative character of African traditional music] 108

DANIEL, O. Traditsiya: proshloye i budushcheye [Traditions: past and future] 115

KRÏSTEV, V. O svoyeobrazin bolgarskoy national'noy kompozitorskoy shkolï [The character of the Bulgarian national school of composition] 118

Discussion 276

Vklad razlichnïkh muzïkal'nïkh kul'tur v kul'turu sovremennovo mira [The contribution of different musical cultures to the culture of the present-day world]

MALIP'ERO, R. [MALIPIERO, R.] Vklad muzïkal'noy kul'turï Zapadnoy Evropï [The contribution of the musical culture of western Europe] 124

MARTÏNOV, I. Vklad muzïkal'noy kul'turï Vostochnoy i Yuzhnoy Evropï [The contribution of the musical culture of eastern and southern Europe] 133

ORREGO-SALAS, Kh. [J.] Vklad muzïkal'noy kul'turï Severnoy i Latinskoy Amerik [The contribution of the musical culture of southern and Latin America] 136

TRAN VAN KKHE [KHE] Vklad Azii v mirovuyu muzïkal'nuyu kul'turu [The contribution of Asia to world musical culture] 147

de LEUV, T. [de LEEUW, T.] Sintez (ili neytralizatsiya) vsekh vkladov v sovremennuyu muzïku [Synthesis (or neutralization) of all contributions to contemporary music] 156

Evolyutsiya natsional'nïkh traditsiy i opït sovetskikh Respublik [The evolution of national

traditions and experience of Soviet republics]

SHOSTAKOVICH, D. Natsional'nïye traditsii i zakonomernosti ikh razvitiya [National traditions and the regularity of their development] 166

TOMESCU, V. Vzaimodeystviye muzïkal'nïkh kul'tur Vostoka i Zapada [The interaction of musical cultures of the east and the west] 170

SHAKHNAZAROVA, N. Zapozhdeniye i razvitiye simfonizma i muzïkal'nostsenncheskikh zhanrov na osnove osvoyeniya natsional'nokhudozhestvennïkh traditsiy respublik Sovetskovo Bostoka [The origin and development of the symphony and music-theatre genres on the basis of mastering the national artistic traditions of the republics of the Soviet East] 178

EL' KHOLI, S. Traditsiya muzïkal'noy improvisatsii na Vostoke i professional'naya muzïka [Traditional music improvisation in the east and in professional music] 183

TAKTAKISHVILI, O. Pristal'no izuchat' muzïkal'nïye kul'turï narodov mira [The detailed study of the musical cultures of the nations of the world] 189

DZHABBAROV, A. Muzïka Vostoka i Zapada (evolyutsiya natsional'nikh traditsii na opïte uzbekskoy muzïki) [Music of the east and the west (the evolution of national traditions as seen in Uzbek music)] 192

KHLEBAROV, I. Zakonomernosti razvitiya simfonizma v Bolgarii na osnove natsional'nïkh khudozhestvennïkh traditsiy [The regularity of the evolution of symphonic style in Bulgaria on the basis of national artistic tradition] 196

Discussion 301

Vospitaniye molodïkh muzïkantov [The training of young musicians]

KABALEVSKIY, D. Obucheniye i vospitaniye molodïkh kompozitorov [The teaching and training of young composers] 202

PROTOPOPOV, V. Metodï analiza sovremennoy muzïki [Methods of analysing contemporary music] 210

AMELLER, A. Znachenie novovo muzïkal'novo yazïka [The meaning of the new musical language] 218

SAVAY, M. Natsional'nïye i internatsional'nïye elementï v vospitanii molodïkh muzïkantov [National and international elements in the education of young musicians] 220

SHAFER, M. [SCHAFER, M.] Mïsli po povodu muzïkal'novo vospitaniya [Thoughts on the occasion of musical education] 225

KHRISTOV, D. Ot natsional'novo k internatsional'nomu [From the national to the international] 232

LEMAN, A. O natsional'nom i internatsional'nom nachulakh v sovremennoy muzïkal'noy pedagogike [On the national and inter-

national bases of contemporary musical education] 235

Discussion 332

Problemï muzïkal'noy sotsiologii [Problems of musical sociology]

KNEPLER, G. Muzïkal'naya istoriografiya v izmenyayushchemsya mire [Musical historiography in a changing world] 242

SOKHOR, A. Funktsionirovaniye muzïki v izmenivshikhsya sotsial'nikh i tekhnicheskikh usloviyakh [The functioning of music in changing social and technical conditions] 249

BLAUKOPF, K. Muzïkal'nïye organizatsii v

menyayushchemsya mire [Musical organizations in a changing world] 254

MOKRY, L. [MOKRÝ, L.] Novïye formï muzïki v menyayushchemsya mire [New forms of music in a changing world] 261

BORRIS, Z. [S.] Vnutrinatsional'nïye i nadnatsional'nïye tendentsii v muzïke XX veka [Supranational and subnational tendencies in 20th-century music] 266

NIMAN, K. [NIEMANN, K.] Novïye formï muzïki v menyayushchemsya mire [New forms of music in a changing world] 271

Discussion 349

71 NEWY Josquin des Prez: Proceedings of the International Josquin Festival-Conference
New York 21–5 June 1971
American Musicological Society
ed. E. E. Lowinsky (London, New York and Toronto: Oxford University Press, 1976)

BLUME, F. Josquin des Prez: the man and the music 18

1 Biographical background and historical view

LOWINSKY, E. E. Ascanio Sforza's life: a key to Josquin's biography and an aid to the chronology of his works 31

NOBLE, J. New light on Josquin's benefices 76

LOCKWOOD, L. Josquin at Ferrara: new documents and letters 103

GATTI PERER, M. L. Art and architecture in Lombardy at the time of Josquin des Prez 138

HARRÁN, D. Burney and Ambros as editors of Josquin's music 145

2 Source studies

KELLMAN, H. Josquin and the courts of the Netherlands and France: the evidence of the sources 181

STEVENSON, R. Josquin in the music of Spain and Portugal 217

PICKER, M. Josquiniana in some manuscripts at Piacenza 247

KIRSCH, W. Josquin's motets in the German tradition 261

SNIŽKOVÁ, J. Josquin in Czech sources of the second half of the sixteenth century 279

HOFFMANN-ERBRECHT, L. Problems in the interdependence of Josquin sources 285

3 Style and analysis

MENDEL, A. Towards objective criteria for establishing chronology and authenticity: what help can the computer give? 297

WIORA, W. The structure of wide-spanned melodic lines in early and late works of Josquin 309

NOVACK, S. Tonal tendencies in Josquin's use of harmony 317

DAHLHAUS, C. On the treatment of dissonance

in the motets of Josquin des Prez 334

SPARKS, E. H. Problems of authenticity in Josquin's motets 345

MATTFELD, J. A. An unsolved riddle: the absence of Ambrosian melodies in Josquin's sacred music 360

4 Studies of genres

RUBSAMEN, W. H Unifying techniques in selected masses of Josquin and La Rue: a stylistic comparison 369

JEFFERY, B. The literary texts of Josquin's chansons 401

van BENTHEM, J. Josquin's three-part 'chansons rustiques': a critique of the readings in manuscripts and prints 421

GALLICO, C. Josquin's compositions on Italian texts and the frottola 446

THIBAULT, G. Instrumental transcriptions of Josquin's French chansons 455

BROWN, H. M. Accidentals and ornamentation in sixteenth-century intabulations of Josquin's motets 475

ELDERS, W. Plainchant in the motets, hymns, and Magnificat of Josquin des Prez 525

5 Individual works

ANTONOWYCZ, M. 'Illibata dei Virgo': a melodic self-portrait of Josquin des Prez 545

CALLAHAN, V. W. 'Ut Phoebi radiis': the riddle of the text resolved 560

HAAR, J. Some remarks on the 'Missa La sol fa re mi' 564

REESE, G. The polyphonic 'Missa de Beata Virgine' as a genre: the background of Josquin's Lady Mass 589

6 Performance practice

D'ACCONE, F. The performance of sacred music

in Italy during Josquin's time, c. 1475–
1525   601
LENAERTS, R. B. Musical structure and performance practice in masses and motets of Josquin and Obrecht   619
FINSCHER, L. Historical reconstruction versus structural interpretation in the performance of Josquin's motets   627
BRIDGMAN, N. On the discography of Josquin and the interpretation of his music in recordings   633

7 Workshops on performance and interpretation
Josquin's motets (chairmen FINSCHER, L., KIRSCH, W.)   645
Josquin's secular music (chairman BROWN, H. M.)   663
Josquin's masses (chairman MENDEL, A.)   687

8 Symposium on problems in editing the music of Josquin des Prez: a critique of the first edition and proposals for the second edition (chairman REESE, G.; panel ANTONOWYCZ, M., FINSCHER, L., LENAERTS, R. B., LOCKWOOD, L., LOWINSKY, E. E., MENDEL, A.)   721

71 STGA   **Neuvième congrès international des bibliothèques musicales St-Gall: actes du congrès**
St-Gall 22–8 August 1971
International Association of Music Libraries
ed. V. Fédorov, *Fontes artis musicae* xix (Kassel and Basle: Bärenreiter, 1972)

2 Réunions publiques
Organismes de la radiodiffusion: bibliothèques et archives sonores
I Radio and television music libraries (chairman DAVIES, J. H.; panel SALTER, L., ROUYER, L., KYHLBERG, B., ROSSER, W., DEAN, A., HOWGILL, P. A.)   113

II Structures and operation of broadcasting sound

archives (chairman LOTICHIUS, D.; panel WILD, E., BOLOGNA, P., JOHO, S., BREITWIESER, E., ECKERSLEY, T., van DALFSEN, J., LINDBERG, F., MANAL, G., KJAER, B., ADLER, W., CNATTINGIUS, C. M., LEWIS, D.)   126

von FISCHER, K. The interpretation of musical sources   148

71 STP   **Die Geige in der europäischen Volksmusik: Bericht über das I. Seminar für europäische Musikethnologie**
St Pölten 14–19 June 1971
Institut für Volksmusikforschung an der Hochschule für Musik und darstellende Kunst in Wien
ed. W. Deutsch and G. Haid (Vienna: A. Schendl, 1975 = Schriften zur Volksmusik 3)

DEUTSCH, W. Geige und Geigenmusik in Europa: einige Probleme ihrer Erforschung 10
STĘSZEWSKI, J. Geige und Geigenspiel in der polnischen Volksüberlieferung   16
DEVIĆ, D. Gusle und Lirica – zwei chordophone Bogeninstrumente in Jugoslawien 38
STRAJNAR, J. Geige und Geigenmusik in der slowenischen Volkstradition   48
SÁROSI, B. Geige und Zigeunermusikanten in Ungarn   60
BRANDL, R. Die Rolle der Violine in der Volksmusik des Dodekanes, anhand eigener Feldaufnahmen 1965–1969   71
BRUNE, J. A. Geige und Geigenmusik in Grossbritannien und Irland   81
SEVÅG, R. Geige und Geigenmusik in Norwegen   89

THIEL, H. Quellen und Nachrichten zur volkstümlichen Geigenmusik in Österreich 102
SCHMIDT, L. Die Sammlung alter Volksmusikinstrumente des Österreichischen Museums für Volkskunde   124
EIBNER, F. Geigenmusik in Wien   129
DERSCHMIDT, H. Landlergeigen – die Geige in der oberösterreichischen Volksmusik 161
HORAK, K. Die Geige als Volksmusikinstrument in Tirol   176

Aktuelle Fragen zur Streichermusik
FRANK-MITTENWALD, K. Die neue Fidel – ein altes Volksmusikinstrument?   180
SITTNER, H. Streichermusik in unserer Zeit 184

71 STU   **Bericht über den I. internationalen Kongress für Musiktheorie**
Stuttgart 18–20 November 1971
Hochschule für Musik und darstellende Kunst in Stuttgart
ed. P. Rummenhöller, F. C. Reininghaus, J. H. Traber (Stuttgart: Kongressleitung des
I. internationalen Kongresses für Musiktheorie, 1972)

1 Zu einer historischen und kritischen Theorie der Musik
LACHENMANN, H. Zum Verhältnis Kompositionstechnik – gesellschaftlicher Standort (discussion 35)   28
SIEGELE, U. Normative und historische Satzlehre (discussion 47)   40
von DADELSEN, G. Das Märchen von der grauen Theorie   49
BÖKER-HEIL, N. Ein algebraisches Modell des durmoll-tonalen Systems (discussion 105)   64
REININGHAUS, F. C. and TRABER, J. H. Über Theoriebildung und Theorie-Bildung (discussion 150)   108

2 Konkrete Ansätze
DAHLHAUS, C. Über einige theoretische Voraussetzungen der musikalischen Analyse (discussion 170)   153
ZILLHARDT, R. Spezielle Ansätze einer Analyse der Tonhöhen in Musikwerken verschiedener Epochen (discussion 202)   177
DOBROWOLSKI, A. Schwierigkeiten der Formenlehre neuer Musik: Überlegungen an einem praktischen Beispiel   204
MIDZIC-DABAC, S. Über musikalischen Professionalismus heute (discussion 217)   212
WELIN, K.-E. Musik über Musik: zwölf Aphorismen (discussion 225)   220

BÖCKL, R. Versuch über Metamusik: ein Beitrag zur Systematisierung musikalischer Analysemethoden (discussion 234)   227
BEUERLE, H.-M. Einige Anmerkungen zum Verhältnis von musikalischer Theorie und Praxis (discussion 243)   236

3 Musiktheorie und Pädagogik
GÜMBEL, M. and RUMMENHÖLLER, P. Dialog über Möglichkeit und Unmöglichkeit traditioneller Musiklehre (discussion 255)   247
KARKOSCHKA, E. Fragen an die Musiktheorie (discussion 269)   260
KOMMA, K. M. Musikgeschichte und Musiktheorie als pädagogische Disziplin (discussion 280)   272
NIELSEN, T. Bericht über den Versuch einer Neugestaltung der theoretischen Fächer für Instrumentalisten und Sänger an der Musikhochschule in Aarhus (discussion 296)   281
BRÖMSE, P. Tonsatzlehre als Analyse – Musiktheorie für Studierende im Nebenfach (discussion 306)   299
ABRAHAM, L. U. Musiktheorie in der Schule (discussion 316)   310
KELEMEN, M. Wie lässt sich neue Musik unterrichten? (discussion 324)   318

71 VAN   **Shakespeare 1971: Proceedings of the World Shakespeare Congress**
Vancouver 20–29 August 1971
University of British Columbia; Simon Fraser University
ed. C. Leech and J. M. R. Margeson (Toronto and Buffalo: University of Toronto Press, 1972)

Shakespeare and the other arts
JACQUOT, J. The last plays and the masque 156

INGRAM, R. W. Music as structural element in Shakespeare   174

71 VIC   **Atti dal primo e secondo seminario di studi e ricerche sul linguaggio musicale**
Vicenza September 1971; August – September 1972
Istituto musicale F. Canneti, Vicenza
ed. R. Shackelford (Padua: G. Zanibon, 1973)

1971
DANIÉLOU, A. Musical languages   131
TOULMIN, S. Language and technique in the fine

arts: the individual and the tradition   137

1972 [Italian and English texts in double columns]

DANIÉLOU, A. Le alternative al sistema temperato/The alternatives to the tempered system 9
CUMAR, R. L'armonia nei limiti dell'intonazione/Harmony in the limits of intonation 29
TRÂN-VAN-KHÊ Linguaggio della musica nella tradizione cinese/The language of music in the Chinese tradition 37
JUNIUS, M. Sull'emancipazione della musica classica indiana/On the emancipation of Indian

classical music 55
JUNIUS, M. L'arte dell'improvvisazione nella musica classica indiana/The art of improvisation in Indian classical music 71
NONO, L. La funzione della musica oggi/The function of music today [extracts of 3 meetings] 83
DALLA VECCHIA, W. L'evoluzione del linguaggio musicale nell'opera di Igor Strawinsky/Evolution in the musical language of Igor Stravinsky 105

71 WAR   **Pagine: Polsko-włoskie materiały muzyczne / Argomenti musicali polacco–italiani**
ed. M. Bristiger (Warsaw: Polskie centrum muzyczne, 1974)
III Sesja poświęcona muzyce polskiej i włoskiej/III° Incontro con la musica polacca e italiana
Warsaw 17–18 October 1971
Istituto di studi musicali e teatrali, Università di Bologna: Instytut muzykologii
Uniwersytetu warszawskiego

TATARKIEWICZ, W. Chi fu il teorico del manierismo? 11
VECCHI, G. Muzyka a przedstawienie: dramat klasyczny i manierystyczny w opowieściach teatralnych i w dziołach teoretycznych A. Ingegneriego [Music and performance: classical and mannerist drama in the theatrical librettos and theoretical works of A. Ingegneri] 27
MASSERA, G. Od Franchino Gaffuriusa do Stefana Monetariusa: termin 'practica musices' w tekstach metodologicznych renesansowej teorii muzyki [From Franchino Gaffurius to Stefan Monetarius: the term 'practica musices' in the methodological texts of Renaissance music theory] 41
PERZ, M. Wyznaczniki początków renesansu muzycznego w Polsce [Factors determining the beginnings of Renaissance music in Poland] 57
ZWOLIŃSKA, E. Muzycy włoscy na dworze królewskim Jagiellonów [Italian music at the royal court of the Jagiellons] 71
BRISTIGER, M. Pojęcie manieryzmu w muzyce [The concept of mannerism in music] 79
BUCHNER, A. Historia skowana: kilka uwag na temat pojęć 'renesans' i 'barok' w muzyce [Some

thoughts on the concept of 'Renaissance' and 'Baroque' in music] 91
MORAWSKA, K. Muzyka instrumentalna XV i XVI wieku jako kryterium periodyzacji [Instrumental music of the 15th and 16th centuries as a criterion for periodization] 111
SZWEYKOWSKA, A. Kilka uwag o manieryzmie na terenie wczesnego 'dramma musicale' [Some thoughts on mannerism in the field of early 'dramma musicale'] 123
MARTINOTTI, S. Kilka indywidualności nadpadańskiego baroku muzycznego: Bassani, Perti, Vallotti, Martini [Some individual figures in the decline of the musical Baroque] 131
BARASSI, F. Tarquinio Merula i jego dialog 'Satiro e Corisca' [Merula and his dialogue 'Satiro e Corisca'] 149
POZNIAK, P. Utwory lutniowe Hortensjusza Perli i Mikołaja z Padwy [The lute compositions of Hertensjusz Perlus and Nicholas of Padua] 177
STĘSZEWSKA, Z. Renesans i barok jako okres wykształcania się cech narodowych w tanecznej muzyce europejskiej [Renaissance and Baroque as a field for the crystalizing of national traits in European dance music] 191

IV Sesja poświęcona muzyce włoskiej i polskiej: Muzyka wokalna i wokalno-instrumentalna XVII wieku/IV° Incontro con la musica italiana e polaccha [sic]*: Musica vocale e vocostrumentale del seicento*
Bardolino 25–6 July 1972
Istituto di studi musicali e teatrali, Università di Bologna; Instytut muzykologii Uniwersytetu warszawskiego

[Polish papers only]

ZWOLIŃSKA, E. Twórczość kompozytorów włoskich z I połowy XVII wieku dla kapeli rorantystów wawelskich [Works by Italian composers from the first half of the 17th century for the choir of Wawel rorantists]   203

PERZ, M. Missarum quattuor vocibus liber primus Marci Scacchii Romani   217

BRISTIGER, M. O duetach Sigismondo d'India (1609–1615) [The duets of Sigismondo d'India]   239

CHODKOWSKI, A. Giovanni Alberto Ristori a Polska [Ristori and Poland]   253

STĘSZEWSKA, Z. Popularność pieśni włoskiej w Polsce w XVII wieku [The popularity of Italian song in Poland in the 17th century]   263

PERZ, M. Kilka uwag o źródłach i repertuarze polifonii retrospektywnej we Włoszech i Polsce [Some thoughts on the origins and repertory of backward-looking polyphony in Italy and Poland]   277

IV Sesja poświęcona muzyce włoskiej i polskiej: Muzyka wokalna i wokalno-instrumentalna XVII wieku / IV Incontro con la musica italiana e polaccha [sic]: Musica vocale e voco-strumentale del seicento
Bardolino 25–6 July 1972

see 71 WAR

72 BERN   Bericht über den III. internationalen Kongress für Kirchenmusik 1972 in Bern
           Berne 1–8 September 1972
               ed. M. Favre (Berne and Stuttgart: Paul Haupt, 1974 = Publikationen der
           Schweizerischen Musikforschenden Gesellschaft ii/26)

FREI, W.   Geistliche Musik inner- und ausserhalb des Gottesdienstes   9
BORNEFELD, H.   Kirchenlied? Versuch einer Analyse   24
SCHNEBEL, D.   Neue Möglichkeiten der Kirchenmusik   48
MERTENS, F.   Problèmes de l'interprétation   55
TAGLIAVINI, L. F.   Interpretationsfragen bei alter Musik   67

WULSTAN, D.   Stand der Kirchenmusik in der Church of England   74

GÖRANSSON, H.   Stand der Kirchenmusik in der lutherischen Staatskirche Schwedens   76
BORS, I. and JÁKI, T. S.   Die Kirchenmusik in Ungarn   81
STEFANOVIĆ, D.   Die serbische Kirchenmusik   84
EGLI, U. and GÄHWYLER, K.   Kirchenmusik in Kamerun   86
ZIMMERMANN, C.   Keimhafte Ansätze indonesischer Kirchenmusik   89

TAPPOLET, W.   Die Gottesdienste   98

72 BLA   Telemann-Renaissance – Werk und Wiedergabe: Bericht über die wissenschaftliche Arbeitstagung aus Anlass des 20. Jahrestages des Telemann-Kammerorchesters
          Blankenburg, Harz 30 June – 2 July 1972
          Arbeitskreis 'Georg Philipp Telemann' im Kulturbund der DDR
              ed. W. Maertens (Magdeburg: Arbeitskreis 'Georg Philipp Telemann' im Kulturbund
          der DDR, 1973 = Magdeburger Telemann-Studien 4)

SIEGMUND-SCHULTZE, W.   Gedanken zur Telemann-Forschung und Telemann-Pflege   11
FLEISCHHAUER, G.   Zum Konzertschaffen G. Ph. Telemanns   21
THOM, E.   Die Oboe d'amore in Telemanns Werken   41

HOBOHM, W.   G. Ph. Telemann als Herausgeber   47
YOUNG, P. M.   Telemann und England   62
MAERTENS, W.   Georg Philipp Telemann und seine Interpreten: Margaretha Susanna und Johann Kayser   68

72 BYD   Musica antiqua III: acta scientifica
          Bydgoszcz 10–16 September 1972
          Bydgoskie towarzystwo naukowe [Bydgoszcz Scientific Society]; Filharmonia pomorska imienia Ignacego Paderewskiego [Paderewski Pomeranian Philharmonia]
          (Bydgoszcz: Bydgoskie towarzystwo naukowe, 1972)

[Polish résumés given for those papers not in Polish; French résumés for those in Russian or Polish]
LISSA, Z.   Z zagadnień współczesnej periodyzacji historii kultur muzycnych świata [Some problems of the present-day periodization of the history of musical cultures of the world] (English résumé 28)   8

TONTSCHEVA, E. B.   Kompositions- und Strukturbesonderheiten des 'Bolgarski rosspew'   33
BALLOVÁ, L'.   Tänze aus dem 'Musikalisch-Türkischen Eulenspiegel'   69
MIKANOVÁ, E.   Musik an den tschechische Landschulen im 18. Jahrhundert   87
PILKOVÁ, Z.   On the periodization of Czech music   95

RYBARIČ, R. Samuel Capricornus in Bratislava (Pressburg)   107

SEHNAL, J. Die entwicklungstendenzen und stilschichten im tschechischen barocken Kirchenlied   127

SNIŽKOVÁ, J. Les formes de la musique tchèque à la fin de Renaissance et au début du Baroque   161

MARVIA, E. Die Instrumentalmusik in Finnland im 17. und 18. Jahrhundert   177

LAUNAY, D. L'art du compositeur de musique: essai sur la composition musicale en France au temps de Henri IV et de Louis XIII   209

ROSE, G. La musique à la cour de Lorraine sous le Roi Stanislas   247

KOS, K. Volkstümliche Züge in der Kirchenmusik Nordkroatiens im 17. und 18. Jahrhundert   267

PETROVIĆ, D. A liturgical anthology manuscript with the Russian 'hammer headed' notation from A.D. 1674   293

RIJAVEC, A. Gabriel Plavec und seine 'Flosculus vernalis' (1622)   323

ŽUPANOVIĆ, L. Formes de la musique croate professionelle aux XVIIe et XVIIIe siècle   337

VIERTEL, K.-H. J. S. Bach und die Oper seiner Zeit   387

FEIL, A. Das Erlöschen mündlicher musikalischer Traditionen im 18. Jahrhundert und die Komposition 'volkstümlicher' und 'leichter' Musik   415

KESSLER, F. Professionelle Musik des 17. und 18. Jahrhunderts in Gdańsk   429

WILKOWSKA-CHOMIŃSKA, K. Sonaty Chrysziana W. Podbielskiego [Podbielski's sonatas]   459

CIOBANU, G. La musique psaltique romaine aux XVIIe et XVIIIe siècles   487

COSMA, V. La culture musicale roumaine au cours des XVIIe–XVIIIe siècles (1600–1789)   507

GHIRCOIAŞIU, R. Démètre Cantemir – ethnographe et musicien   529

PORFETYE, A. Daniel Croner und die Orgelmusik in Siebenbürgen vom 15. bis zum 18. Jahrhundert   551

BOYDEN, D. D. The Corelli 'solo' sonatas and their ornamental additions by Corelli, Geminiani, Dubourg, Tartini, and the 'Walsh anonymous'   591

LEMONDS, W. W. Venetian polychoral music: old or new   609

MRACEK, J. Slavic musicology in the United States of America: some observations relating to research and the problems of bibliography, archives and sources   615

PAPP, G. Stilelemente des frühen Werbungstanzes in der Gebrauchsmusik des 18. Jahrhunderts   639

GHISI, F. Folklore et prefessionalisme dans la musique de l'Europe centrale aux XVIIe et XVIIIe siècle en relation aux chansons des vallées vaudoises du Piémont   683

VITOLIN, Ye. Muzïkal'naya kul'tura latvii XVII–XVIII vekov [The musical culture of Latvia in the 17th and 18th centuries]   701

GVAKHARIYA, V. A. Muzïkal'naya kul'tura Gruzii XVII–XVIII [The musical culture of Georgia in the 17th and 18th centuries]   727

GERASIMOVA PERSIDSKAYA, N. A. Narodnïye istoki partesnovo kontserta [National sources of the polyphonic concert]   769

KELDÏSH, Yu. Problema stiley v russkoy muzïke XVII–XVIII vekov [Problems of style in Russian music of the 17th and 18th centuries]   795

LEVASHEVA, O. Kozlovskiy i russkiy klassitsizm [Kozlovsky and Russian classicism]   825

PROTOPOPOV, V. Tvoreniya Vasiliya Titova vïdayushchegosya russkovo kompozitora vtoroy polovinï XVII – nachala XVIII veka [The works of Vasily Titov, an outstanding Russian composer of the second half of the 17th to the first half of the 18th century]   847

RYUYTEL', I. Estonskaya narodnaya muzïka v XVII i XVIII veke [Estonian folk music of the 17th and 18th centuries]   873

72 COP   **Report of the Eleventh Congress Copenhagen 1972**
Copenhagen 20–25 August 1972
International Musicological Society
ed. H. Glahn, S. Sørensen, P. Ryom (Copenhagen: Wilhelm Hansen, 1974)

LARSEN, J. P. Towards an understanding of the development of the Viennese Classical style   23

PLESSNER, H. Die Musikalisierung der Sinne: Grundsätzliches zu einem modernen Phänomen   32

Round tables

1 Current methods of stylistic analysis of music (chairman LOCKWOOD, L.)

BENT, I. D. Current methods in stylistic analysis: summary of remarks   43

BÖKER-HEIL, N. Musikalische Stilanalyse und Computer: einige grundsätzliche Erwägungen   45

CVETKO, D. Ein Versuch der Analyse (einige Ausgangspunkte für die Diskussion): V. Globokar, Concerto Grosso (Henry Litolff's Verlag 1970)   50

FINSCHER, L. Thesen zu Analyse und Interpretation (supplementary papers GALLICO, C. 56 and POWERS, H. 58)   54
TREITLER, L. Methods, style, analysis   61
WESTERGAARD, P. On the notion of style   71
WOLFF, C. Towards a methodology of dialectic style consideration: preliminary terminological and historical considerations   74
TREITLER, L. Contributions on Beethoven, Pianoforte Sonata, Op. 10 No. 3: Largo e mesto   80
FINSCHER, L. Zur Interpretation des langsamen Satzes aus Beethovens Klaviersonate Opus 10 Nr. 3   82
WOLFF, C. Contribution to the discussion of Beethoven, Op. 10/3   85
GALLICO, C. Observations on Palestrina 'Vestiva i colli'   86
POWERS, H. The modality of 'Vestiva i colli'   89
WESTERGAARD, P. Linear operations necessary to generate a Palestrina foreground   103
BÖKER-HEIL, N. Der Zustand polyphoner Strukturen: ein Beispiel automatischer Stilbeschreibung   108
Discussion   121

2 Musical instruments as objects of historical and anthropological research (chairman STOCKMANN, E.)
STOCKMANN, E. Das Musikinstrument als Gegenstand anthropologischer und historischer Forschung   131
WACHSMANN, K. P. Social roles for musical instruments and their interaction with musical form in Africa   135
ANING, B. A. Sociocultural systems and their relationships with musical instruments in Africa   137
ARETZ, I. Zur Erforschung lateinamerikanischer Musikinstrumente   138
ZAGIBA, F. Probleme und Methoden frühgeschichtlicher Instrumentenforschung   140
AVENARY, H. Die Diskrepanz der ikonographischen und literarischen Darstellungen altöstlicher Musikinstrumente   141
CHAMBURE, H. de The lesson of a restoration   145
JAKOB, F. Physiologische Grenzen der Instrumente und deren Überwindung   146
REINECKE, H.-P. Zur Funktion der Musikinstrumente im internationalen Kontext   147
EMSHEIMER, E. Die Darbietung von Musikinstrumenten als Gegenstand historischer und anthropologischer Forschung in Instrumentenmuseen   149
ELSCHEK, O. Tendenzen und Aufgaben der gegenwärtigen Instrumentenforschung   151
Discussion   152

3 Musicology today (chairman OESCH, H.)
BOEHMER, K. Musikwissenschaft heute – einige Vorwürfe   167
BROOK, B. S. On musicology today   172

DAHLHAUS, C. Das abstrakte historische Bewusstsein   174
FÉDOROV, V. La musicologie de demain   176
GOLDSCHMIDT, H. Musikwissenschaft heute   181
JARUSTOWSKY, B. M. Thesen des Referats   183
LISSA, Z. Über die polychrone Periodisierung der allgemeinen Musikgeschichte   185
MAEGAARD, J. Altes und neues Denken   187
OESCH, H. Unfruchtbarer Methodenstreit   189
RINGER, A. L. A question of commitment   191
STEPHAN, R. Flüchtige Bemerkungen zu den Problemen 'Aktualität und Tradition'   195
Discussion   197

Free research papers
ADKINS, C. New discoveries in the development of the trumpet marine   221
ALPHONCE, B. The invariance matrix as an analytical tool   228
BADURA-SKODA, E. An unknown Singspiel by Joseph Haydn?   236
BAILEY, R. The evolution of Wagner's compositional procedure after 'Lohengrin'   240
BARON, J. H. Paul Emile Johns of New Orleans: tycoon, musician, and friend of Chopin   246
BARTH-WEHRENALP, R. Der 'Trouvère' Adan de le Hale – ein französischer Meistersänger   250
BECKMANN, K. A. Vivaldi oder J. Meck? Zum Echtheitsproblem des Concerto P 217   253
BENT, M. A lost English choirbook of the fifteenth century   257
BERGSAGEL, J. Anglo-Scandinavian musical relations before 1700   263
BLANKENBURG, W. Neu aufgetauchte Textbücher von Rudolstädter Kantaten-Jahrgängen aus der ersten Hälfte des 18. Jahrhunderts   271
BOCKHOLDT, R. Zum vierstimmigen Choralsatz J. S. Bachs   277
BONTA, S. A formal convention in 17th-century Italian instrumental music   288
BOORMAN, S. Petrucci at Fossombrone: The 'Motetti de la Corona'   295
BROCKETT, C. W. 'Noeane' and 'Neuma': a theoretical and musical equation   301
BROCKHAUS, H. A. Bemerkungen zur Verbalisierung des Musikalischen im Prozess der Analyse   309
BROWN, A. P. Structure and style in the string quartets of Carlos d'Ordoñes (1734–1786)   314
CHUSID, M. Rigoletto and Monterone: a study in musical dramaturgy   325
COHEN, A. René Ouvrard (1624–1694) and the beginnings of French Baroque theory   336
DARBELLAY, É. Peut-on découvrir des indications d'articulation dans la graphie des tablatures de clavier de Claudio Merulo, Girolamo Frescobaldi et Michel-Angelo Rossi?   342
DEKAN, K. Auswertung von musikalischen Dynamikbereichen bei verschiedenen Blechblas-Instrumentenspielern und die Klangfar-

beänderungen bei Piano, Mezzo-forte und Forte 351

DI BENEDETTO, R. The sonate a quattro of Angelo Ragazzi (1736) 356

FEDER, G. Die Bedeutung der Assoziation und des Wertvergleiches für das Urteil in Echtheitsfragen 365

FLINDELL, E. F. Syllabic notation in isolated voices 378

GALLIVER, D. Vocal colour in singing in 17th century Italy: the contribution of Caccini 385

GALLO, F. A. Die Musik in der Einteilung der Wissenschaften bei Egidius Romanus und Johannes Dacus 388

GEIRINGER, K. From Guglielmi to Haydn: the transformation of an opera 391

GÜNTHER, U. Zur Entstehung der zweiten französischen Fassung von Verdis 'Don Carlos' 396

HAMMERSTEIN, R. Bemerkungen zur niederländischen Bildmotette 403

HANSELL, S. H. Stage deportment and scenographic design in the Italian opera seria of the settecento 415

HANSEN, F. E. Tonality in Gregorian chant based on an investigation of the melodies in Codex H 159, Montpellier 425

HARRAN, D. The theorist Giovanni del Lago: a new view of his writings 432

HENDERSON, C. W. Structural importance of borrowed music in the works of Charles Ives: a preliminary assessment 437

HUDSON, F. The study of watermarks as a research factor in undated manuscripts and prints: beta-radiography with carbon-14 sources 447

HUGHES, A. Viella: facere non possumus 453

HUNKEMÖLLER, J. Das lexikographische Stichwort 'Jazz' in der Musikwissenschaft 457

JACOBI, E. R. C. F. Zelters kritische Beleuchtung von J. N. Forkels Buch über J. S. Bach, aufgrund neu aufgefundener Manuskripte 462

JANSSON, E. On the acoustics of the violin 466

JENSEN, N. M. Solo sonata, duo sonata, trio sonata: some problems of terminology, texture, and genre in 17th century Italian instrumental music 478

KARP, T. Text underlay and rhythmic interpretation of 12th c. polyphony 482

KLUGE, R. Was kann die Kybernetik der Musikwissenschaft helfen? 486

KÖHLER, K.-H. Das dramatische Jugendwerk Felix Mendelssohn Bartholdys – Basis seiner Stil- und Persönlichkeitsentwicklung 495

KOS, K. Ost- und westeuropäische Impulse in der kroatischen Musik des 19. Jahrhunderts 499

KRICKEBERG, D. Einführungen zu Berliner Konzerten mit Musik des 20. Jahrhunderts seit 1947 507

KROPFINGER, K. Wagners 9. Symphonie – das ambivalente Werk 512

KRUMMACHER, F. Klassizismus als musikgeschichtliches Problem 518

KUNZE, S. Zur Kritik des Stilbegriffs in der Musik 527

LAZAREVICH, G. Humor in music: literary features of early eighteenth-century Italian musical theatre 531

MALMSTRÖM, D. Music and its development in a socially underdeveloped country 538

MARX, H. J. Zur Bedeutung des Begriffs 'Symphonia' im Mittelalter 541

van der MEER, J. H. Zur Frühgeschichte der Viola d'Amore 547

MORCHE, G. Règle de l'octave und Basse fondamentale 556

MOSUSOVA, N. Rhapsodische Inspiration als schöpferisches Prinzip in der instrumentalen Musik des 19. und 20. Jahrhunderts 561

MRÁČEK, J. An unjustly neglected source for the study and performance of seventeenth-century instrumental dance music 563

NEWCOMB, A. Alfonso Fontanelli and the 'Seconda pratica' in Ferrara: some newly uncovered music and letters 576

NEWMAN, W. S. Some articulation puzzles in Beethoven's autographs and earliest editions 580

NOWAK, A. Über das Verhältnis der Schichttheorie zur Geschichtlichkeit des Musikwerks 585

PERROT, J. Le positif à pied du IXe au XIIIe siècle 590

PERZ, M. Organum, Conductus und mittelalterliche Motette in Polen: Quellen und Probleme 593

RAKOWSKI, A. A scale for dissonance sensation in chords 597

RAVIZZA, V. Formprobleme des frühen Coro spezzato 604

RECKOW, F. Aspekte der Ausbildung einer lateinischen musikalischen Fachsprache im Mittelalter 612

ROMAN, Z. Bar form in Mahler's songs – omission and misconception 617

RUBSAMEN, W. H. Irish folk music in 'Midas', a ballad burlesque of the 18th century 623

RYOM, P. Un nouveau catalogue des oeuvres d'Antonio Vivaldi 633

SCHWAB, H. W. Formen der Virtuosenehrung und ihr sozialgeschichtlicher Hintergrund 637

SCHWARZ, B. Problems of chronology in the works of G. B. Viotti 644

SEIDEL, W. Über Figurationsmotive von Chopin und Liszt 647

SERWER, H. New linguistic theory and old music theory 652

SMITHER, H. E. What is an oratorio in midseventeenth-century Italy? 657

STAEHELIN, M. Eine wenig beachtete Gruppe von Chorbüchern aus der ersten Hälfte des 16. Jahrhunderts 664

STESZEWSKI, J. Sachen, Bewusstsein und Benennungen in ethnomusikologischen Untersuchungen 668
STRAINCHAMPS, E. N. A brief report on the madrigal style of Marco da Gagliano 675
SUNDBERG, J. Production and function of the 'singing formant' 679
TERÉNYI, E. Klangschichten-Strukturen in der Musik des 20. Jahrhunderts 686
TISCHLER, H. Musica ficta in the 13th century 695
VOGEL, M. Zur Etymologie von 'tromba marina' 696
VOLEK, T. Über die Notwendigkeit der musikalischen Anthropologie 702
WEBER, H. Schönbergs und Zemlinskys Vertonung der Ballade 'Jane Grey' von Heinrich Ammann: Untersuchungen zum Spätstadium der Tonalität 705
WOGRAM, K. Die Beeinflussung von Klang und Ansprache durch das 'Summenprinzip' bei Blechblasinstrumenten 715
ZASLAW, N. Mozart's tempo conventions 720

Musica byzantina

ADAMIS, M. An example of polyphony in Byzantine music of the late middle ages 737

CONOMOS, D. The treatise of Manuel Chrysaphes 748
DRAGOUMIS, M. P. A contribution to the study of the interpretation of late Byzantine notation 751
HUGLO, M. Comparison de la terminologie modale en orient et en occident 758
LEVY, K. The Trisagion in Byzantium and the West 761
PETROVIĆ, D. One aspect of the Slavonic oktoechos in four Chilandari music manuscripts 766
RAASTED, J. Modernization and conversion: two types of national change and their consequences for the transmission of Byzantine music 775
SCHIØDT, N. and SVEJGAARD, B. A method of indexing musical incipits of Byzantine hymns 777
STATHIS, G. Problems connected with the transcription of the old Byzantine notation into the Pentagram 778
THODBERG, C. The discussion of the Psaltikon tonality 782
VELIMIROVIĆ, M. The 'Bulgarian' musical pieces in Byzantine musical manuscripts 790
RAASTED, J. Résumé of the discussions 797

---

72 FRE/B   **Zur Terminologie der Musik des 20. Jahrhunderts: Bericht über das zweite Colloquium der Walcker-Stiftung**
Freiburg im Breisgau 9–10 March 1972
    Walcker–Stiftung
    ed. H. H. Eggebrecht (Stuttgart: Musikwissenschaftliche Verlags-Gesellschaft, 1974 = Veröffentlichungen der Walcker-Stiftung, ed. H. H. Eggebrecht, 5)

DAHLHAUS, C. Adornos Begriff des musikalischen Materials (discussion 17) 9
REINECKE, H.-P. Die Sprachebenen über Musik als Hierarchie relationaler Systeme: Überlegungen zu Wittgensteins 'Sprachspiel'-Modell 22
STROH, W. M. Mathematik und Musikterminologie (discussion 54) 33
ZAMINER, F. Rhythmus und Zeitdauern-Organisation 60
STEPHAN, R. Zum Terminus 'Grundgestalt' (discussion 76) 69
BREIG, W. Schönbergs Begriff des vagierenden Akkordes (discussion 114) 83

WAELTNER, E. L. Neue Musik, Terminologie und Analyse-Sprache: Reflexionen zur 'Exposition' von Schönbergs op. 16, 1 (discussion 151) 116
EGGEBRECHT, H. H. Punktuelle Musik (discussion 180) 162
KROPFINGER, K. Bemerkungen zur Geschichte des Begriffswortes 'Struktur' in der Musik (discussion 199) 188
BRINKMANN, R. Stockhausens 'Ordnung': Versuch, ein Modell einer terminologischen Untersuchung zu beschreiben (discussion 213) 205

72 GRA   Violinspiel und Violinmusik in Geschichte und Gegenwart: Bericht über den internationalen Kongress am Institut für Aufführungspraxis der Hochschule für Musik und darstellende Kunst in Graz

Graz 25 June – 2 July 1972

Institut für Aufführungpraxis der Hochschule für Musik und darstellende Kunst in Graz

ed. V. Schwarz (Vienna: Universal Edition, 1975 = Beiträge zur Aufführungspraxis, ed. V. Schwarz, 3)

1 Die Violinmusik in Geschichte und Gegenwart

ROSTAL, M.   Zur Interpretation der Werke von J. S. Bach   13

DOFLEIN, E.   Violinsonaten aus Paris aus den Jahren 1770–1785   20

PEČMAN, R.   František Bendas Kunst des Violinspiels in bezug auf sein kompositorisches Schaffen   27

SCHWARZ, B.   Viotti – eine Neubewertung seiner Werke   41

WIRSTA, A.   La musique romantique du violon   47

SCHWARZ, V.   Zur Programmgestaltung des Violinabends in Wien 1880–1920   52

WAGNER, M.   Zum Verlust der Solovioline in den Werken der Avantgarde   56

STEPHAN, R.   Die Violinmusik des Zwanzigsten Jahrhunderts   60

FINSCHER, L.   Zur Geschichte des Streichquartetts als musikalischer Gattungsgeschichte 80

Discussion: Zur Interpretation von Bachs Violinwerken   90

Discussion: Die Stellung der Kammermusik im Konzertleben unserer Zeit   97

2 Das Violinspiel in Geschichte und Gegenwart

GEISER, B.   Wie wurden die ersten Violinen gespielt?   109

MONOSOFF, S.   Biagio Marini, virtuoso of Brescia   120

THEMELIS, D.   Violintechnik und Methodik in der Violinetüde um 1800   123

SITTNER, H.   Zur Tradition der Wiener Geigerschule   133

KRATINA, J.   Otakar Ševčík, sein Leben, Werk und Vermächtnis für heute   142

GINSBURG, L.   Die russische klassische Geigenschule und die Entwicklung ihrer progressiven Tradition in der sowjetischen Geigenschule   149

GUTH, P.   Die moderne russische Violinschule und ihre Methodik   154

3 Pädagogische Probleme

KOLISCH, R.   Religion der Streicher   175

von HAUSEGGER, F.   Was ist ein Fehler?   181

KLEIN-VOGELBACH, S.   Das Violinspiel aus der Sicht des Physiotherapeuten   189

WAGNER, C.   Physiologische Voraussetzungen für das Geigenspiel   196

THOENE, H.   Neue Übungsmethoden in der Violinpädagogik   211

von der GOLTZ, C.   Technik und Spontaneität   214

MÜLLER-NISHIO, W.   Zur Typologie des Fingersatzes auf der Violine   221

von STUMPFF, K.-H.   Locker – oder gelöst?   226

STRADNER, G.   Untersuchungen über den Saitenwechsel   228

KROEMER, M.   Die Violinschule in Geschichte und Gegenwart   235

4 Der Streicherberuf

ROSTAL, M.   Problematik des Streicherberufes in Vergangenheit und Zukunft   259

MAHLING, C.-H.   Die Situation des Geigers im Orchester   263

HEIDER, M.   Aus der täglichen Praxis: Dirigent und Konzertmeister   270

ROSNER, F.   Wie verhalten sich der heutige Studiengang und die Berufserwartung der Violinstudenten zu den Realitäten des künstlerischen Berufslebens?   274

RASCHL, E.   Wunschdenken des Geigers und die Chancen beruflicher Realisierung in der Steiermark   277

Discussion: Die Situation des Geigers im Orchester   282

5 Geigenbau

BOYDEN, D. D.   Der Geigenbogen von Corelli bis Tourte   295

STRADNER, G.   Die Situation Geigenbauer – Musiker heute   311

STRADNER, G.   Eine Ausstellung: Zur Entwicklung der Geige   314

72 MALT   **Proceedings of the First Congress on Mediterranean Studies of Arabo-Berber Influence / Actes du premier congrès international des cultures méditerranéens d'influence arabo-berbère** [title also in Arabic]
Msida, Malta 3–6 April 1972
Royal University of Malta; École pratique des hautes-études, Paris
ed. M. Galley (Algiers: Société nationale d'édition et de diffusion, 1973)

CAMILLERI, C.   The growing awareness by mediterranean countries of their musical homogeneity due to Arabo-Berber culture   58

72 MIL   **Atti del III° congresso internazionale di studi verdiani: Il teatro e la musica di Giuseppe Verdi**
Milan 12–17 June 1972
Istituto di studi verdiani, Parma
ed. M. Medici (Parma: Istituto di studi verdiani, 1974)

Drammaturgia e librettistica
BARBLAN, G.   Il sentimento dell'onore nella drammaturgia verdiana   2

CANESSA, F.   Salvatore Cammarano e il 'libretto ideale' del 'Trovatore'   14
EŐSZE, L.   'Otello': dramma di Shakespeare e opera di Verdi   20
GRÄWE, K. D.   L'uno e gli altri: osservazioni sulla drammaturgia verdiana di conflitto interumano e della sua soluzione   27
KIMBELL, D. R. B.   'Il Trovatore': Cammarano and Garcia Gutiérrez   34
LAVAGETTO, M.   Ipotesi per un'analisi strutturale dei libretti verdiani   45

Indagini storiche, critiche e musicali
ABERT, A. A.   Leidenschaftsausbrüche zwischen Rezitativ und Arie   56
BUDDEN, J.   'La Battaglia di Legnano': its unique character with special reference to the finale of Act I   71
CELLETTI, R.   Caratteri della vocalità di Verdi   81
CHUSID, M.   Drama and the key of F major in 'La Traviata'   89
DEAN, W.   Some echoes of Donizetti in Verdi's operas   122
FREEMAN, J. W.   Berlioz and Verdi   148
GALLICO, C.   L'espressione armonica del 'Rigoletto'   166
GUALERZI, G.   Linee di sviluppo per una storia del teatro verdiano nel dopoguerra   172
KAUKO, O.   Themes and transformations   178
LAWTON, D. and ROSEN, D.   Verdi's non-definitive revisions: the early operas   189
LEIBOWITZ, R.   Tempo and character in the music of Verdi   238
LÓPEZ-CALO, J.   La Spagna in Verdi   244
MAGNANI, L.   L' 'ignoranza musicale' di Verdi e la biblioteca di Sant'Agata   250

MANCINI, R.   Y a t-il une renaissance-Verdi en France   258
MARCHESI, G.   Verdi e Manzoni   274
MARTINOTTI, S.   Verdi e lo strumentalismo italiano dell'ottocento   285
MARTYNOV, I.   Stanislavsky et Verdi   298
MATZ, M. J.   Verdi and the 'total theatre' of our time   303
MILA, M.   Fétis e Verdi, ovvero gli infortuni della critica   312
MINARDI, G. P.   Temporali e battaglie nell'opera verdiana   322
NICASTRO, A.   Il teatro francese nell'evoluzione del melodramma verdiano   338
NOSKE, F. R.   Verdi and the musical figure of death   349
PETROBELLI, P. L.   Per un'esegesi della struttura drammatica del 'Trovatore'   387
PINZAUTI, L.   'Aida' e 'Lohengrin' a confronto nella Firenze di cent'anni fa   401
QVAMME, B.   Verdi e il realismo   408
SABBETH, D.   Dramatic and musical organization in 'Falstaff'   415
SGUERZI, A.   O terra addio (gli interpreti vocali di 'Aida')   443
VÁRNAI, P. P.   Dramma e musica nel 'Nabucco'   453
VEINUS, A. and ADAMS, J. C.   'Rigoletto' as drama   464
VLAD, R.   Alcune osservazioni sulla struttura delle opere di Verdi   495
WEAVER, W.   Verdi and the drama of love   523

Lettere e documenti – bibliografia – discografia – medaglie
BUSCH, H.   Per una documentazione esauriente delle opere di Verdi   530
CELLA, F.   L'opera di Verdi nella corrispondenza col suo editore italiano   532
CONATI, M.   Bibliografia verdiana: aspetti, pro-

blemi, criteri per la sistemazione della letteratura verdiana   546
GÜNTHER, U.   Documents inconnus concernant
les relations de Verdi avec l'Opéra de
Paris   564
STRINGHAM, S.   The Verdi Catalog: an interim
report   584

TINTORI, G.   Le medaglie verdiane nelle collezioni del Museo teatrale alla Scala   587
ZANUSO MAURI, O.   L'editoria fonografica e
Verdi (con riferimento agli ultimi dieci
anni)   607

72 PAR   Actes du colloque l'Amiral de Coligny et son temps
Paris 24–8 October 1972
Société de l'histoire du protestantisme français
(Paris: Société de l'histoire du protestantisme français, 1974)

WEBER, E.   L'influence de la pédagogie et de la
musique humanistes sur le style du choral
luthérien et du psaume huguenot   251

72 ROM   Atti del XL congresso internazionale degli Americanisti
Rome and Genoa 3–10 September 1972
International Congress of Americanists
(Genoa: Tilgher, 1973–6)

Vol. ii (1974)
Problemi generali
TEKINER, R.   Trans-Pacific contact: the evidence
of thc panpipe   31

**72 SÁR   International Folk Music Council Studiengruppe zur Erforschung und Edition älterer
Volksmusikquellen: 3. Arbeitstagung in Sárospatak (Ungarn, 1972)**
Sárospatak, Hungary 18–23 September 1972
Studiengruppe zur Erforschung und Edition älterer Volksmusikquellen des In-
ternational Folk Music Council
Studia musicologica Academiae scientiarum hungaricae xv (Budapest: Akadémiai
kiadó, 1973)

BRAUN, H.   Volkskundlich-historische For-
schungen zu den Balladen- und Legendenauf-
nahmen von Künzig Werner   5
DOBSZAY, L.   Comparative research into an 'old
style' of Hungarian folk music   15
FALVY, Z.   Troubadourmelodien im mittel-
alterlichen Ungarn   79
KUBINYI, A.   Musikleben am Budaer Königshof:
Anfang des 16. Jahrhunderts   89
MARTIN, G.   Die Branles von Arbeau und die
osteuropäischen Kettentänze   101
PERKUHN, E.   Die arabische Theorie und die
Ursprungsfrage der Troubadourkunst   129
PESOVÁR, E.   Die geschichtlichen Probleme der
Paartänze im Spiegel der südosteuropäischen
Tanzüberlieferung   141
PETNEKI, A.   Die polnischen Kolenda-Lieder im
Mittelalter   165

PETNEKI, Á.   Ikonographie der musikalischen
Darstellungen des ungarischen Mittelalters 175
PETZSCH, C.   Neue Aspekte zum Liede des
Mittelalters   187
RAJECZKY, B.   Europäische Volksmusik und
Musik des Mittelalters   201
SCHNEIDER, A.   Die Megalithkulturen in West-
europa   205
SPECHTLER, F. V.   Zur Methode der Edition
mittelalterlicher Texte   225
STIEF, W.   Die Melodien des Minnesangs als
Spiegel verschollener Volkslieder?   245
STOCKMANN, D.   Deutsche Rechtsdenkmäler
des Mittelalters als volksmusikalische
Quelle   267
SZENDREI, J.   Tedeum als ungarischer Volks-
gesang im Mittelalter   303

72 TOD   Musica e arte figurativa nei secoli X–XII: Convegni del Centro di studi spiritualità medievale XIII
Todi 15–18 October 1972
Centro di studi sulla spiritualità medievale
(Todi: Accademia Tudertina, 1973)

HESBERT, R.-J.   La théologie du répertoire grégorien (la gloire de Dieu)   103
APEL, W.   Music and mathematics in the middle-ages   133
BRIDGMAN, N.   Les thèmes musicaux de

l'apocalypse, leur signification spirituelle et leur interprétation dans les miniatures   195
PIRROTTA, N.   Ars musica   223
CORBIN, S.   Quelques réflexions sur le lyrisme et la spiritualité dans la musique médiévale   265

72 TOU   Les fêtes de la Renaissance III: Quinzième colloque international d'études humanistes
Tours 10–22 July 1972
Centre d'études supérieures de la Renaissance, Université de Tours
ed. J. Jacquot and E. Konigson (Paris: Centre national de la recherche scientifique, 1975 = Le choeur des muses, ed. J. Jacquot)

2 Le théâtre et la fête
STERNFELD, F. W.   La technique du finale: des intermèdes à l'opéra   267

3 La fête chevaleresque
GUIOMAR, P.   La musique dans trois fêtes à la

cour ducale de Wurtemberg en 1609, 1616, 1617   393

5 La fête joyeuse et satirique
MARCEL-DUBOIS, C.   Fêtes villageoises et va-carmes cérémoniels   603

72 VEN   Venezia e il melodramma nel seicento [Convegno internazionale di studio]
Venice 14–16 September 1972
Istituto di lettere musica e teatro, Fondazione Giorgio Cini
ed. M. T. Muraro (Florence: Leo S. Olschki, 1976 = Studi di musica veneta 5)

WALKER, T.   Gli errori di 'Minerva al tavolino'   7
CAMMAROTA, L.   L'orchestrazione dell'"Orfeo' di Monteverdi   21
GALLICO, C.   'In modo dorico'   41
BRIZI, B.   Teoria e prassi melodrammatica di G. F. Busenello e 'L'Incoronazione di Poppea'   51
ROSAND, E.   Aria as drama in the early operas of Francesco Cavalli   75
MORELLI, G. and WALKER, T.   Tre controversie intorno al San Cassiano   97
LAWRENSON, T. E.   Les 'Noces de Pélée' et la Guerre des Bouffons   121
CHRISTOUT, M.-E.   L'influence vénitienne exercée par les artistes italiens sur les premiers spectacles à machines montés à la cour de France durant la Régence (1645–1650)   131
VIALE FERRERO, M.   Repliche a Torino di alcuni melodrammi veneziani e loro caratteristiche   145
OSTHOFF, W.   Filiberto Laurenzis Musik zu 'La

Finta savia' im Zusammenhang der frühvenezianischen Oper   173
HOLMES, W. C.   Yet another 'Orontea': further rapport between Venice and Vienna   199
POWERS, H. S.   Il 'Mutio' tramutato, part I: sources and libretto   227
BIANCONI, L.   'L'Ercole in Rialto'   259
PETROBELLI, P.   La partitura del 'Massimo Puppieno' di Carlo Pallavicino (Venezia 1684)   273
VECCHI, G.   Il 'Nerone fatto Cesare' di Giacomo Antonio Perti a Venezia   299
WOLFF, H. C.   Manierismus in den venezianischen Opernlibretti des 17. Jahrhunderts   319
PUPPI, L.   Il melodramma nel giardino   327
MAROTTI, F.   Lo spazio scenico del melodramma, esaminato sulla base della trattatistica teatrale italiana   349
CAVICCHI, A.   Scenotecnica e macchinistica teatrale in un trattato inedito di Fabrizio Carini Motta (Mantova 1688)   359

Secondo seminario di studi e ricerche sul linguaggio musicale
Vicenza August – September 1972

see 71 VIC

72 VIE¹   Webern-Kongress
Vienna 13–17 March 1972
Österreichische Gesellschaft für Musik; Webern Society, USA
Beiträge 1972/73 (Kassel and Basle: Bärenreiter, 1973)

1 Zur Biographie und Stilentwicklung
SWAROWSKY, H. Anton von Webern: Bemerkungen zu seiner Gestalt   14
ROBERTS, D. L. Music history from primary sources – the Moldenhauer archive   23
CLAYCOMBE, G. Personal recollections of Webern in Vienna 1929–1934   29
SZMOLYAN, W. Webern in Mödling und Maria Enzersdorf   36
BRINKMANN, R. Die George-Lieder 1908/9 und 1919/23 – ein Kapitel Webern-Philologie   40

2 Werkanalysen und Interpretation I
BUDDE, E. Metrisch-rhythmische Probleme im Vokalwerk Weberns   52
DEPPERT, H. Zu Weberns klanglichharmonischem Bewusstsein   61
DAHLHAUS, C. Rhythmische Strukturen in Weberns Orchesterstücken Opus 6   73
KARKOSCHKA, E. Weberns Opus 11 unter neuen analytischen Aspekten   81

3
MOLDENHAUER, H. Anton von Webern – neue Sichten: ein Gespräch mit Harald Goertz   93

4 Werkanalysen und Interpretation II
SOMFAI, L. Rhythmic continuity and articulation in Webern's instrumental works   100
GERLACH, R. Kompositionsniederschrift und Werkfassung am Beispiel des Liedes 'Am Ufer' (1908) von Webern   111
SCHOLLUM, R. Stilistische Elemente der frühen Webern-Lieder   127
STEPHAN, R. Zu einigen Liedern Anton Weberns   135

5 Webern und die Folgen
BRESGEN, C. Gibt es eine Webern-Nachfolge?   146
CHASE, G. Webern in America: the growth of an influence   153
KOLNEDER, W. Hat Webern seriell komponiert?   167
STADLEN, P. Das pointillistische Missverständnis   173
MCKENZIE, W. Webern's posthumous music   185

6 Round table: Quellenlage und Editionsfragen
(chairman EGGEBRECHT, H. H.; panel BRINKMANN, R., BUDDE, E., CERHA, F., FÜSSL, K. H., McKENZIE, W., MOLDENHAUER, H., ROBERTS, D. L., SOMFAI, L., STEPHAN, R.)   198

72 VIE²   New Patterns of Musical Behaviour of the Young Generation in Industrial Societies: Communications presented to the International Symposium Vienna 1972
Vienna 18–23 September 1972
International Institute for Music, Dance and Theatre in the Audio-Visual Media
ed. I. Bontinck (Vienna: Universal Edition, 1974)

BONTINCK, I. Foreword: Meeting on unexplored ground   9
BLAUKOPF, K. New patterns of musical behaviour of the young generation in industrial societies   13

Mass consumption and mass communication
VALKMAN, O. Some methodological aspects of preferences in pop music   33
NIEMANN, K. Mass media – new ways of approach to music and new patterns of musical behaviour   44
PHILIPPOT, M. P. Observations on sound volume and music listening   54
NUMMINEN, M. A. An inside view of pop music in Finland   60

New forms of youth music
VITÁNYI, I. The musical and social influence of beat music in Hungary   69

URBANSKI, J.   Sweet beat and other forms of youth music in Poland   80

BELZ, C.   Relationships between the popular and fine arts: recent developments   84

Musical interests and group activities

ALEKSEEV, E. Y. and GOLOVINSKY, G. I.   From the experience of the Moscow Youth Music Club: on the question of the socio-psychological determinants of musical taste   91

CÂMPEANU, P.   The implications of light music for a group of apprentices in Bucharest   103

WILLIS, P.   Youth groups in Birmingham and their specific relation to pop music   108

MALMROS, A.-L.   Organisational set-up and politico-cultural aspects of beat in Copenhagen   114

AMBROŽIC-PAIC, A.   Mass media and pop groups in Yugoslavia   119

MAURER, W.   Music of contrasts: report on the contests of Austrian beat groups   129

PAVLOV, E.   Musical interests of 5th to 8th-graders in Pleven   135

ŠIMEK, M.   Musical interests of the Czech youth in the light of research findings   140

ARVIDSON, P.   On interest, activity and taste in music   142

Music education and environment

PAYNTER, J.   Music education and the emotional needs of young people: towards a new type of research in Great Britain   159

HOFFER, C. R.   Youth, music education and the new sound environment   167

ROMAN, Z.   Higher music education in Canada: the challenge of a changing musical environment   178

MICHEL, P.   On physical and psychological acceleration: effects on the musical development during childhood and adolescence   183

TEINER, M.   The influence of the mass media on children between the age of six and eight: receptivity and listening preferences at elementary schools in Vienna   192

Youth sub-culture and cultural time budget

GEERTS, C.   The share of music in the time budget of young people in Belgium   201

DE CLERCQ, J.   The musical receptivity of young people   205

BEAUD, P.   Musical sub-cultures in France: latest investigations into the position held by sub-cultures within cultural life   212

SOKHOR, A. N.   Young people's leisure time and its use for musical-aesthetic education: a report based on Soviet experience   219

THOVERON, G.   Leisure time behaviour and cultural attitude of the youth: subjects of an international research project   226

BLAUKOPF, K.   Postscript: towards a new type of research   231

73 ANK   I. Uluslararası Türk Folklor Semineri/The First International Turkish Folklore Meeting/Bildirileri [Papers]
Ankara 8-14 October 1973
T. C. Başbakanlık Kültür Müsteşarlığı Millî Folklor Enstitüsü Müdürlüğü [Republic of Turkey Prime Minister's Directorate of the National Institute of Folklore]
(Ankara: Başbakanlık Basımevi, 1974 = Millî Folklor Araştırma Dairesi Yayınları 9)

ATTILÂ, O. Türkülerin Derlenmesinde Yeni Metodlar [New methods for collecting folksongs (Türkü)]   172
KAYA, A. K. Türk ve Batı Çalgıları Arasındaki İlişkiler [Relationships between Turkish and western musical instruments]   178
ORANSAY, G. Türkiye Yerel Musiki Anıtlarının Kataloglanması [Cataloguing local Turkish music (regional)]   184

REINHARD, K. Güney Türk Ağıtlarının Biçimleri [Types of Southern Turkish folksongs (Ağit)]   192
ÜNGÖR, E. R. Türk Davulu [The Turkish drum]   216
ATAMAN, S. Y. Anadolu Efe ve Yâren Dernekleri, Seymen Kuruluşları Oyun ve Musikileri [Anatolian dances and music]   315

73 BAL   Bericht über die 4. Internationale Arbeitstagung der Study Group on Folk Musical Instruments des International Folk Music Council in Balatonalmádi 1973
Balatonalmádi, Hungary 22-6 May 1973
Study Group on Folk Musical Instruments of the International Folk Music Council ed. E. Stockmann, *Studia instrumentorum musicae popularis* iv (Stockholm: Musikhistoriska museet, 1976 = Musikhistoriska museets skrifter, ed. E. Emsheimer, 6)

Methoden der historischen Forschung
ELSCHEK, O. Historische Quellentypen der Instrumentenkunde und die ihnen angemessenen quellenkritischen Methoden   10
BECKER, H. Das Volksmusikinstrument in der Rezeption des Musikhistorikers   30
KADEN, C. Methoden der graphischen Modellierung sozialhistorischer Prozesse als Hilfsmittel bei der Erforschung instrumentaler Volksmusik   39
NIXDORFF, H. Die Bestimmung historisch-genetisch relevanter Kriterien an Musikinstrumenten als Grundlage für ihre historische Erforschung   45

Ikonographische Quellen
MAČÁK, I. Zur Verifikation ikonographischer Informationen über Musikinstrumente   49
DROYSEN, D. Über Darstellung und Benennung von Musikinstrumenten in der mittelalterlichen Buchmalerei   51
SALMEN, W. Neue Wort- und Bildquellen zur Geschichte der 'musica instrumenta, quae amusa sunt'   55
GEISER, B. Der Codex 542 der Stiftsbibliothek St. Gallen als Beitrag zur Instrumentenkunde des 16. Jahrhunderts   60
MAHLING, C.-H. Der Dudelsack in west-

europäischer Plastik und Malerei   63
MÜLLER, M. Der himmlische Lobgesang in Rynkeby, eine dänische ikonographische Quelle des 16. Jahrhunderts   70
MØLLER, D. F. Folk music instruments in Danish iconographic sources   73
KUMER, Z. Volksmusikinstrumente in ikonographischen Quellen Sloweniens   77
DEVIĆ, D. Volksmusikinstrumente auf mittelalterlichen Fresken in Serbien und Mazedonien   78
ATANASSOV, V. Volksmusikinstrumente in ikonographischen Quellen Bulgariens   84
FALVY, Z. Volksmusikinstrumente in ikonographischen Quellen Ungarns   86

Archäologische, literarische und musikalische Quellen
SCHNEIDER, A. Möglichkeiten der paläoorganologischen Forschung   88
PERKUHN, E. Beispiele arabisch-spanischer Glossographie in instrumentenkundlicher Sicht   94
HARRISON, F. Towards a chronology of Celtic folk instruments   98
RIMMER, J. The instruments called chirimía in Latin America   101
MARKL, J. Historische Notierungen in-

strumentaler Volksmusik in Böhmen   110   PAPP, G.   Zur Geschichte der ungarischen Tanz-
                                                     musik, Probleme des Werbungstanzes   142
Ungarische Instrumentalmusik
SÁROSI, B.   Instrumentale Volksmusik in Un-
garn   115

73 BEL   Actes du 1ᵉʳ congrès international de semiotique musicale / Proceedings of the Ist International
           Congress on Semiotics of Music
           Belgrade 17–21 October 1973
               Centro internazionale di semiotica e di linguistica di Urbino
               ed. G. Stefani (Pesaro: Centro di iniziativa culturale, 1975)

STEFANI, G.   Situation de la sémiotique musicale   9
JIRÁNEK, J.   The development and present situation of the semiotics of music in Czechoslovakia   27
CARPITELLA, D.   Sistema metrico e sistema ritmico nei canti popolari   40
AROM, S.   La méthode distributionnelle en
ethnomusicologie   44
OSMOND-SMITH, D.   Iconic relations within formal transformation   45
KARKOSCHKA, E.   Ueber Exaktheit in Musikanalyse   56
NATTIEZ, J.-J.   From taxonomic analysis to stylistic characterization: Debussy's Syrinx   83
LINDBLOM, B. and SUNDBERG, J.   A generative
theory of Swedish nursery tunes   111
BARONI, M. and JACOBONI, C.   Analysis and
generation of Bach's choral melodies 125

LEVY, M.   On the problem of defining musical
units   135
DELIÈGE, C.   Théorie et pratique de l'analyse
musicale   151
PORENA, B.   Musica/società: una questione semiologica?   173
GASPAROV, B.   Some descriptive problems of
musical semantics   183
VITÁNYI, I.   Semiotics of standard musical language   197
KNEIF, T.   Once more 'meaning' in music 208
LASKE, O. E.   Musical semantics: a procedural
point of view   214
IMBERTY, M.   Sémantique musicale: approche
structurale, approche expérimentale   225
FOCHT, I.   Semiotics and aesthetics: some preliminary questions of methodology   245
SUPIČIĆ, I.   Signification et intelligibilité de la
musique   249

73 BUC   Enesciana I: La personnalité artistique de Georges Enesco: Travaux de la première session
           scientifique du Centre d'études 'Georges Enesco'
           Bucharest 19 September 1973
               Georges Enesco Research Centre, Romanian Academy of Social and Political Sciences
               ed. M. Voicana (Bucharest: Editura Academiei Republicii Socialiste România, 1976)

VOICANA, M.   Das Problem des Stils und die
Entfaltung der schöpferischen Persönlichkeiʲ
des Komponisten Enescu   13
COSMA, O.-L.   The thematic process in Enescu's
creation   19
ZOTTOVICEANU, E.   Concordances esthétiques
aux environs de 1900 à propos de la monodie
énescienne   25
FIRCA, G.   Die Giusto-Rhythmik und ihre Ein-
wirkungen auf die Musik Enescus   31
RAŢIU, A.   Sur certains aspects de la pensée
harmonique chez Georges Enesco   39
FIRCA, C.-L.   Enesco et la musique roumaine de
1900 à 1920   49
MANOLIU, G.   Enesco, le professeur   57
HOFFMAN, A.   Lettres de Georges Enesco ad-
ressées à des musiciens français (conservées à la
Bibliothéque nationale de Paris)   63
COSMA, V.   George Enescu – Förderer der
Konzert-Festspiele rumänischer Musik 71

VARGA, D.   La présence de la cellule B – A – C –
H dans le Quatuor à cordes op. 22 no. 2 de
Georges Enesco   83
MOISESCU, T.   Some remarks on the genuine
version of the String Quartet in G Major op. 22
no. 2 by George Enescu   93
VARGA, O.   Enescu's specific resonance 103
STAICOVICI, C.-I.   Echoes of Enescu's art in the
American press   109
DOLINESCU, E.   Une festivité en l'honneur de
Georges Enesco à New York   115
ŞIRLI, A.   Sources littéraires dans la création
vocale de chambre de Georges Enesco   121
POPESCU-DEVESELU, V.   'Les sept chansons sur
paroles de Clément Marot': notes d'inter-
prète   129
ALEXANDRESCU, L.-M.   Le timbre de la voix
humaine dans l'ensemble de l'expression musi-
cale énescienne ('Œdipe')   135
STIHI-BOOS, C.   A few aspects of the musical

transfiguration of the literary pretext in the symphonic poem 'Vox Maris' by George Enescu 141
JALOBEANU, A. Enesco: volonté et destin 151
MARBE, M. Georges Enesco, notre contemporain 155

NICULESCU, Ş. Pensées sur Georges Enesco 171
GHIRCOIAŞIU, R. Un humaniste: Georges Enesco 175

73 HAM **Deutsche Literatur des späten Mittelalters: Hamburger Colloquium 1973**
Hamburg 16–22 September 1973
Institute of Germanic Studies, University of London; Institut für Ältere Deutsche Philologie der Philipps-Universität, Marburg
ed. W. Harms and L. P. Johnson (Berlin: Erich Schmidt, 1975 = Publications of the Institute of Germanic Studies, University of London 22)

GÄRTNER, K. Zechparodien auf den Invitatoriumspsalm (Psalm 94) 164

73 MAG **Telemann und die Musikerziehung: Konferenzbericht der 5. Magdeburger Telemann-Festtage**
Magdeburg 19–27 May 1973
Arbeitskreis 'Georg Philipp Telemann' im Kulturbund der DDR
ed. G. Fleischhauer and W. Siegmund-Schultze (Magdeburg: Rat der Stadt Magdeburg/Arbeitskreis 'Georg Philipp Telemann' im Kulturbund der DDR, 1975)

SIEGMUND-SCHULTZE, W. Einige Gedanken zur Eröffnung der wissenschaftlichen Konferenz: 'Telemanns Beiträge zur Musikerziehung der Aufklärungsepoche und ihre Bedeutung für die Musikerziehung der Gegenwart' 14
KROSS, S. Telemanns Stellung in der Musikanschauung der Aufklärung 19
HOBOHM, W. Pädagogische Grundsätze und ästhetische Anschauungen Telemanns in der 'Kleinen Kammer-Musik' (1716) 30
FLEISCHHAUER, G. Telemanns Journal 'Der getreue Music-Meister' (1728–29) unter musikpädagogischen Aspekten 43
JUNG, H.-R. Zur Bedeutung der 'Methodischen Sonaten' (1728/1732) G. Ph. Telemanns für die Herausbildung des 'vermischten Geschmacks' und für die instrumentale Musikerziehung 60
ALLIHN, I. Telemanns methodisch-pädagog-ische Zielsetzung, dargelegt an den 'Trietti metodichi' (1731) 76
LÁSZLÓ, F. G. Ph. Telemanns '12 Fantasien für Querflöte ohne Bass' (1732–33) – eine hohe Schule der Komposition für Flöte allein 84
PEČMAN, R. Der Generalbass in der Auffassung G. Ph. Telemanns und Fr. X. Brixis 93
PETZOLDT, R. Die Musik in den protestantischen Lateinschulen der Telemann-Zeit 100
WITKOWSKI, L. Die Musikerziehung im Akademischen Gymnasium zu Toruń vom 16. bis zum 18. Jahrhundert 111
BUST, G. Telemanns Werke im Unterricht der Musikschule 125
VOIGT, H.-H. Telemann im Unterricht der allgemeinbildenden Schule 135

73 NEU/B **Oswald von Wolkenstein: Beiträge der philologisch-musikwissenschaftlichen Tagung in Neustift bei Brixen 1973**
Neustift bei Brixen 18–21 September 1973
Südtiroler Kulturinstitut
ed. E. Kühebacher (Innsbruck: Institut für deutsche Philologie der Universität Innsbruck, 1974 = Innsbrucker Beiträge zur Kulturwissenschaft, ed. E. Koller and others, Germanistische Reihe 1)

BEYSCHLAG, S. Oswalds von Wolkenstein Jagdlied 'Wolauff, gesell! Wer jagen well' Kl 52 37

BRESGEN, C. Untersuchungen zum Rhythmus bei Oswald von Wolkenstein 51

COSTA, O. Workshop anlässlich der Oswald-von-Wolkenstein-Tagung im September 1973 im Kloster Neustift bei Brixen 60

LOMNITZER, H. Wort-Ton-Probleme bei Oswald von Wolkenstein 68

RÖLL, W. Probleme der neuen Oswald-von-Wolkenstein-Ausgabe 219

SALMEN, W. Die Musik im Weltbilde Oswalds von Wolkenstein 237

SPECHTLER, F. V. Beiträge zum deutschen geistlichen Lied des Mittelalters II: Oswald von Wolkenstein 272

STÄBLEIN, B. Oswald von Wolkenstein und seine Vorbilder 285

TIMM, E. Ein Beitrag zur Frage: Wo und in welchem Umfang hat Oswald von Wolkenstein das Komponieren gelernt? 308

73 NUR   Max Reger 1873–1973: ein Symposion
Nuremberg 4–7 June 1973
Max-Reger-Institut (Elsa-Reger-Stiftung), Bonn-Bad Godesberg; Internationale Orgelwoche, Nuremberg
ed. K. Röhring (Wiesbaden: Breitkopf & Härtel, 1974)

WIRTH, H. Der Einfluss von Johann Sebastian Bach auf Max Regers Schaffen 3

STOCKMEIER, W. Karl Straube als Reger-Interpret 21

WALCKER-MAYER, W. Die Orgel der Reger-Zeit 31

SIEVERS, G. Die Harmonik im Werk Max Regers 55

BRINKMANN, R. Max Reger und die neue Musik 83

BLANKENBURG, W. Max Reger und das evangelische Kirchenlied 113

WALTER, R. Max Regers Beziehungen zur katholischen Kirchenmusik 123

von LEWINSKI, W.-E. Max Reger 1973 – zum Reger-Symposion in Nürnberg 149

73 PAR   Informatique musicale: Journées d'étude 1973: Textes des conférences
Paris 8–10 October 1973
E.R.A.T.T.O. (Équipe de recherche 152), Centre de recherches pluridisciplinaires, Ivry sur Seine
ed. H. Charnassé and H. Ducasse (Paris: Service de calcul sciences humaines and Centre de documentation sciences humaines, [1975] = Collection Calcul et sciences humaines)

MEYLAN, R. Limites de l'objectivité dans les écritures instrumentales de la Renaissance 1

JACQUOT, J. Problèmes d'édition des tablatures de luth 10

CHARNASSÉ, H. Transcription automatique de tablatures: intérêt, limites 25

DUCASSE, H. Un problème de saisie de l'information: le traitement des tablatures 48

LABUSSIÈRE, A. Codage des structures rythmomélodiques à partir de créations vocales 66

JANSEN, P. Emploi de l'ordinateur pour le dépouillement des périodiques littéraires 93

COUTURIER, M. L'emploi du langage FORCOD en collecte et traitement d'inventaires après décès 104

BERNARD, J. J. Sciences exactes et musicologie 115

Le classement par ordinateur des listes de répons liturgiques
HUGLO, M. Les problèmes musicologiques 125

OTTOSEN, K. Le traitement des données 135

L'apport de l'acoustique musicale à l'étude digitale des musiques ethniques
LEIPP, E. Une méthode d'étude des échelles musicales ethniques 144

MLOUKA, M. Traitement numérique de musiques ethniques 158

BARBAUD, P. Méthodes d'analyse de textes harmoniques 165

GREUSSAY, P. Structures de contrôle en description symbolique d'analyses musicales 177

Un périphérique d'ordinateur à l'usage des musiciens
MERMET, J. and FANTINO, Y. Composants technologiques du périphérique 204

JAEGER, D. Programmes d'utilisation 210

73 ROM¹   Atti del congresso internazionale sul tema 'Manierismo in arte e musica'
Rome 18–23 October 1973
Accademia nazionale di Santa Cecilia, Rome
ed. A. Ziino, *Studi musicali* iii, 1974 (Florence: Leo S. Olschki, 1977)

FUBINI, E. Il manierismo come categoria storiografica 3

STRINATI, C. M. Sulla storia del concetto di manierismo 13

FEDERHOFER, H. Der Manierismus-Begriff in der Musikgeschichte 37

WATKINS, G. Carlo Gesualdo and the delimitations of late mannerist style 55

FINSCHER, L. Zur Problematik des Manierismus-Begriffes in der Musikgeschichtsschreibung 75

LOCKWOOD, L. On 'mannerism' and 'Renaissance' as terms and concepts in music history 85

GALLICO, C. Aspetti musicale fra disposizione manieristica ed età del barocco 101

BIANCONI, L. 'Ah dolente partita': espressione ed artificio 105

LOWINSKY, E. E. The problem of mannerism in music: an attempt at a definition 131

HAAR, J. Self-consciousness about style, form and genre in 16th-century music 219

FABBRI, P. Tasso, Guarini e il 'divino Claudio': componenti manieristiche nella poetica di Monteverdi 233

HUCKE, H. H. L. Hasslers Neue Teutsche Gesang (1596) und das Problem des Manierismus in der Musik 255

MONTEROSSO, R. Strutture ritmiche nel madrigale cinquecentesco 287

PALISCA, C. Towards an intrinsically musical definition of mannerism in the sixteenth century 313

CARAPEZZA, P. E. 'O soave armonia': classicità, maniera e barocco nella scuola polifonica siciliana 347

73 ROM²   L'etnomusicologia in Italia: Primo convegno sugli studi etnomusicologici in Italia
Rome 29 November – 2 December 1973
Istituto di storia delle tradizioni popolari dell'Università di Roma; Istituto Accademico di Roma; Associazione italiana Museo vivo; International Folk Music Council (Comitato italiano)
ed. D. Carpitella (Palermo: S. F. Flaccovio, 1975 = Uomo e cultura – testi, ed. A. Buttita, 13, sezione etnologica)

CARPITELLA, D. Etnomusicologia e stato attuale della documentazione in Italia 17

CIRESE, A. M. Ricerca demologica e studi di folklore musicale 29

LEYDI, R. Etnomusicologia fra istituzione e problemi 41

RONCAGLIA, A. Etnomusicologia e filologia romanza 51

VANDOR, I. Sui compiti dell'etnomusicologia 69

NEILL, E. Problemi della documentazione etnomusicologica in Italia 77

VLAD, R. Tradizione orale e pratica musicale culta 85

PORENA, B. Musica – popolo – società 97

STEFANI, G. Sull'approccio funzionale alle pratiche musicali 105

BUTTITTA, A. Ricerche antropologiche e analisi semiologica nella musica di tradizione orale 115

LOMBARDI SATRIANI, L. M. Folk-music revival e profitto 121

RIGHINI, P. Possibilità e limiti dell'analisi temporizzata dei parametri del suono musicale e significato delle misure per ricerche etnicomusicali 141

DE SIMONE R. Testo verbale e strutture musicali nei canti popolari 151

GALLO, F. A. La tradizione orale della teoria musicale nel Medioevo 159

ZIINO, A. Aspetti della tradizione orale nella musica medioevale 167

GALLINI, C. Dinamiche di produzione, trasmissione, fruizione del canto sardo 189

SASSU, P. and SOLE, L. Un esempio d'integrazione nella analisi delle strutture musicali e verbali sarde 207

Sédute di ascolto

ARCANGELI, P. Registrazioni umbro-marchigiane 217

CONATI, M. Prime osservazioni sulla musica popolare in alcune zone della Valpolicella e della Lessinia in provincia di Verona 223

GUGGINO, E. Canti di lavoro in Sicilia 229

PORTELLI, A. Canti politici del Lazio 231

GHIDOLI, P., ROSALIO, R., SANGA, G. and SORDI, I. I canti del villaggio italiano di Štivor in

Bosnia   243
ROSSI, A. and DE SIMONE, R.   L'uso del videotape nella ricerca folklorica   251

Archivi e istituzioni
RECUPERO, J.   Attività di ricerca del Museo
nazionale delle arti e tradizioni popolari e
archivi di documentazione   257

COGGIOLA, F.   L'attività dell'Istituto Ernesto De
'Martino   265
GALTIERI, G.   L'Archivio etnico-linguistico-
musicale della Discoteca di Stato   271
PAGANO, G.   Attività del Folkstudio di
Palermo   277

73 SIE   **Atti del convegno internazionale di studi musicali: Gluck e la cultura italiana nella Vienna del suo tempo**
Siena 1–4 September 1973
    Accademia musicale Chigiana; Facoltà di lettere, Università di Siena; Istituto di storia
    della musica e dello spettacolo
    Chigiana xxix–xxx, new series 9–10, 1972–3 (Florence: Leo S. Olschki, 1975)

FUBINI, E.   Presupposti estetici e letterari della
riforma di Gluck   235
KLINGER, K.   Gluck e l'illuminismo aus-
triaco   247
FINSCHER, L.   Gluck e la tradizione dell'opera
seria   263
STERNFELD, F. W.   Gluck's operas and Italian
tradition   275
RUSHTON, J.   From Vienna to Paris: Gluck and
the French opera   283
GALLARATI, P.   Metastasio e Gluck: per una
collocazione storica della riforma   299
DEGRADA, F.   Aspetti gluckiani nell'ultimo
Hasse   309
MELONCELLI, R.   Un operista italiano alla corte
di Vienna: Giuseppe Bonno (1710–1788)   331
MARTINOTTI, S.   Traetta, o il musicista di
un'impossibile riforma   .   343
CARLI BALLOLA, G.   L'ultimo Calzabigi, Pais-
iello e l'"Elfrida"   357
ALLROGGEN, G.   La scena degli Elisi nell'"Or-
feo"   369
HEARTZ, D.   'Orfeo ed Euridice': some criti-
cisms, revisions, and stage-realization during
Gluck's lifetime   383

ROBINSON, M. F.   The 1774 S. Carlo version of
Gluck's 'Orfeo'   395
JOLY, J.   Deux fêtes théâtrales de Métastase: 'Le
Cinesi' et 'L'isola disabitata'   415
CARLI BALLOLA, G.   'Paride ed Elena'   465
DERRA de MORODA, F.   The ballet-masters
before, at the time of, and after Noverre   473
TOZZI, L.   La poetica angioliniana del balletto
pantomimo nei programmi viennesi   487
GRUBER, G.   I balli pantomimici viennesi di
Gluck e lo stile drammatico della sua mu-
sica   501
VIALE FERRERO, M.   Appunti di scenografia
settecentesca, in margine a rappresentazioni
di opere in musica di Gluck e balli di
Angiolini   513
TESTA, A.   Il binomio Gluck-Angiolini e la
realizzazione del balletto 'Don Juan'   535
TOZZI, L.   Attorno a 'Don Juan'   549
TOZZI, L.   'Sémiramis'   565
HORTSCHANSKY, K.   Gluck e la famiglia degli
Absburgo Lorena   571
BOSSARELLI MONDOLFI, A.   Gluck e i con-
temporanei attraverso i manoscritti donati da
Maria Carolina alla città di Napoli   585

73 STOC   **Papers presented at the Second Conference on Baltic Studies in Scandinavia**
Stockholm 8–11 June 1973
    Baltiska Institutet
    (Stockholm: Baltiska Institutet, 1973)

Vol. ii Literature and linguistics section (1973)
REYNOLDS, S.   The Baltic psaltery: bibliographi-
cal problems and desiderata   7
RŪĶE-DRAVIŅA, V.   Latvian folksongs as a

source for studies in lexical and syntactic syn-
onymy   44
DUNKELE, I.   Über das lettische Volkslied in
Jānis Mediņš Kompositionen   53

73 VEN   **Manzoni, Venezia e il Veneto: Atti della tavola-rotunda**
          Venice 10 November 1973
          Fondazione Giorgio Cini, Venice; Istituto veneto di scienze lettere ed arti
          ed. V. Branca, E. Caccia, C. Galimberti (Florence: Leo S. Olschki, 1976 = Civiltà
          veneziana saggi 20)

2 Presenza del Manzoni nella cultura triveneta
BELLINA, A. L.   Manzoni e il melodramma 127

73 WEIM   **Weimarer Tage für Musikbibliothekare: Berichte – Referate**
          Weimar 8–12 October 1973
          Ländergruppe DDR of the International Association of Music Libraries
          ed. K.-H. Köhler (Berlin: Ländergruppe DDR in der Internationalen Vereinigung
          der Musikbibliotheken = Bibliotheksverband der Deutschen Demokratischen Re-
          publik, 1974)

RUDOLPH, J.   Unsere Beziehungen zum musikal-
ischen Erbe   1
NIKOLAJEWA, L.   Die Entwicklung der bulgarischen Musik   21
MUSIOL, K.   Die Entwicklung der polnischen
Musik   30
KÖHLER, K.-H.   Max Reger – Grösse und Vermächtnis als Problem für unsere Zeit   48
PULKERT, O.   Zusammenarbeit und Organisation der Institutionen der tschechoslowaki-
schen Musikdokumentation   68
PROKOPOWICZ, M.   Polnische Musikbiblio-
theken in den Jahren 1964–1973   81

DVORAK, V.   Die sowjetische bibliothekarisch-
bibliographische Klassifikation – ihre Appli-
kation in der Universitäts-Bibliothek in Bratislava, Abteilung Musik   88
UNGER, I.   Einige Bemerkungen zur Bibliotheks-
arbeit mit Schallplatten und zu den Aufgaben
der Kommission Phonotheken   103
KITTEL, P.   Die neuen Regeln für die alphabet-
ische Katalogisierung   115
SCHULZE, H.   Zur Musikentwicklung in der
DDR und Fragen der kulturell-ästhetischen
Bildung und Erziehung der Jugend   118

74 BERL   Arnold Schönberg: Internationaler musikwissenschaftlicher Kongress
Berlin 23–7 September 1974
Gesellschaft für Musikforschung; Freie Universität, Berlin
(Berlin: Akademie der Künste, 1974)

RUFER, J.   Schönberg in Berlin   5
KROPFINGER, K.   Schönberg und Kandinsky   9
NITSCHE, P.   Schönbergs Orchesterwerke   15
DAHLHAUS,   C.   Schönberg und die Pro-
grammusik   21
MÖLLERS, C.   Schönbergs Kammermusik   26

BUDDE, E.   Schönbergs Klaviermusik   30
DÖHRING, S.   Schönbergs 'Erwartung'   35
KÜHN, H.   Botschaften aus dem Schädelinnern,
Bemerkungen zu Schönbergs Bericht 'Ein Über-
lebender aus Warschau'   41
BRINKMANN, R.   Schönbergs Lieder   44

74 BLA   Zu Fragen der Aufführungspraxis und Interpretation von Instrumentalmusik in der ersten Hälfte des 18. Jahrhunderts: Konferenzbericht der II. wissenschaftlichen Arbeitstagung
Blankenburg, Harz 13–14 July 1974
Telemann-Kammerorchester, Blankenburg
ed. E. Thom (Blankenburg: Telemann-Kammerorchester, 1975 = Studien zur Aufführungspraxis und Interpretation von Instrumentalmusik des 18. Jahrhunderts 1)

SIEGMUND-SCHULTZE, W.   Zu Fragen der Interpretation und Aufführungspraxis der Musik
der frühen Aufklärungsepoche   10
KOCH-REBLING, K.   Gedanken über eine zeit-
gemasse Interpretation von Violinwerken aus
der ersten Hälfte des 18. Jahrhunderts 17
REICHEL, F.   Zu einigen Fragen der Aufführungspraxis und Interpretation der Cembalo- bzw.
Klaviermusik in der Mitte des 18. Jahrhunderts   22
ZSCHOCH, F.   Zur Aufführungspraxis der Trom-

petenpartien in Werken Bachs, Händels und
Telemanns   29
VODÁK, Z.   Jan Dismas Zelenka und seine welt-
lichen Werke   35
YOUNG, P. M.   Thomas Augustine Arne und die
Interpretation von Werken der englischen Auf-
klärung   38
FLEISCHHAUER, G.   Zu den Einflüssen polni-
scher Musik im Instrumentalkonzertschaffen
G. Ph. Telemanns und ihrer Wiedergabe   43

74 BOL   Sesto incontro con la musica italiana e polacca: Settimana dedicata a Federico Chopin nel 125° anniversario della sua morte
Bologna 7–15 June 1974
Istituto di studi musicali e teatrali, Università di Bologna; Instytut muzykologii Universytetu warszawskiego
Bologna: Antiquae musicae italicae studiosi, 1976 = Miscellanee saggi convegni 10)

PONIATOWSKA, I.   Sur l'écriture pianistique de
M. Clementi   5
BRISTIGER, M.   Riflessi italiani e classici nel
pensiero musicale de Francesco Mirecki 21
IAROCIŃSKI, S.   Le Romantisme ou les Roman-
tismes?   39
COLOMBATI, C.   Aspetti di Chopin alla luce
dell'idea di poetica   55
FANO, F.   Integrità artistica di Chopin: sua tem-
pestiva liberazione da tendenze caduche osser-
vata specialmente attraverso i 'Notturni' 73

BELOTTI, G.   Il problema del testo autentico delle
opere di F. Chopin   89
CHECHLIŃSKA, Z.   L'edizione nazionale polacca
delle opere di Chopin e la prassi editoriale 119
KACZYŃSKI, T.   Chopin e la musica contemporanea polacca   129

[A further session of this congress, 'La musica italiana e polacca nella seconda metà del sette-cento e nel primo ottocento', took place in Bologna 12–15 October 1974.]

74 GRA[1]   Alexander Zemlinsky: Tradition im Umkreis der Wiener Schule
Graz 8–10 October 1974
Institut für Wertungsforschung an der Hochschule für Musik und darstellende Kunst in Graz
(Graz: Universal Edition für Institut für Wertungsforschung, 1976 = Studien zur Wertungsforschung, ed. O. Kolleritsch, 7)

WEBER, H.   Der retrospektive Komponist: Alexander Zemlinsky   7

MAHLER, A.   Alexander Zemlinsky: das Porträt eines grossen Musikers   13

KOLLERITSCH, O.   Motivationen zur Zemlinsky-Retrospektive   27

MAEGAARD, J.   Der geistige Einflussbereich von Schönberg und Zemlinsky in Wien um 1900   34

STAUDINGER, A.   Gesellschaft und Kultur im Österreich des beginnenden 20. Jahrhunderts   44

HILMAR, E.   Zemlinsky und Schönberg   55

PASS, W.   Zemlinskys Wiener Presse bis zum Jahre 1911   80

GRUBER, G.   Klangkomposition in den Opern Zemlinskys   93

LICHTENFELD, M.   Zemlinsky und Mahler   101

NEUWIRTH, G.   Alexander Zemlinskys 'Sechs Gesänge für eine mittlere Stimme nach Texten von Maurice Maeterlinck' op. 13 und Franz Schrekers 'Fünf Gesänge für eine tiefe Stimme' – ein Vergleich   111

STEPHAN, R.   Über Zemlinskys Streichquartette   120

KNEIF, T.   Zemlinsky als Harmoniker   137

GERLACH, R.   Zemlinsky und Berg: 'Lyrische Sinfonie' und 'Lyrische Suite'   145

74 GRA[2]   Bericht über die Erste internationale Fachtagung zur Erforschung der Blasmusik Graz 1974
Graz 25–9 November 1974
Gesellschaft zur Erforschung und Förderung der Blasmusik
ed. W. Suppan and E. Brixel (Tutzing: Hans Schneider, 1976 = Alta musica 1)

SUPPAN, W.   Das Blasorchester: Forschungsbericht und Forschungsaufgabe   9

MÜLLER-BLATTAU, W.   Venezianische Bläsermusik: Kompositionsstil und Aufführungspraxis   23

STOLLBERG, O.   Die Blasmusik, ihr Verhältnis zu den Schulkantoreien im Reformationszeitalter   31

ALTENBURG, D.   Zum Repertoire der Hoftrompeter im 17. und 18. Jahrhundert   47

FEDERHOFER, H.   Blasinstrumente und Bläsermusik in der Steiermark bis zum Ende des 18. Jahrhunderts   61

DÜRING, W. J.   Blasmusik am Dreikönigsgymnasium zu Köln   103

MAHLING, C.-H.   Die Rolle der Blasmusik im Saarländischen Industriegebiet im 19. und frühen 20. Jahrhundert   109

BIBER, W.   Aus der Geschichte der Blasmusik in der Schweiz   127

SCHNEIDER, E.   Die Entwicklung des Blasmusikwesens in Vorarlberg   145

ZAUBEK, O. K. M.   Blasmusikmuseum und Blasmusikarchiv in ihrer Bedeutung für die regionale Blasmusikkunde   175

BLANK, L.   Die Entwicklung des zivilen Blasmusikwesens in Nordwürttemberg   187

KARSTÄDT, G.   Die Verwendung der Hörner in der Jagdmusik   197

KÖRNER, F.   Instrumentenkundliche Untersuchungsmethoden in der Erforschung der Blechblasinstrumente   217

EPPELSHEIM, J.   Das 'Subkontrafagott'   233

BRIXEL, E.   Tongemälde und Schlachtenmusiken: ein militärmusikalisches Genre des 19. Jahrhunderts   273

SÁROSI, B.   Eine ungarische Bauernkapelle   291

MOOG, H.   Der Einsatz von Blechblasinstrumenten in der Sonderpädagogik   301

THELEN, F.   Willy Schneider: eine monographie   311

74 JER   Tenth International Congress of Music Libraries Jerusalem
Jerusalem 18–24 August 1974
International Association of Music Libraries
ed. I. Adler and B. Bayer, *Fontes artis musicae* xxii/1–2 (Kassel and Basle: Bärenreiter, 1975)

4 Public sessions
Round table: Libraries and non-western music (chairman RINGER, A.; panel BAYER, B., HERZOG, A., MARCEL-DUBOIS, C., AROM, S., LESURE, F.)   32

Historical text and pretext in the works of an Israeli composer (TAL, J., ELIRAZ, I.)   43

74 KRP   Methoden der ethnomusikologischen Analyse Vorbericht: 5. ethnomusikologisches Seminar; 6. Arbeitstagung der Study Group of Folk Music Systematisation, International Folk Music Council
Krpáčová, Slovakia, 23–7 September 1974
Slovenská akadémie vied [Slovak Academy of Sciences]; Study Group of Folk Music Systematization of the International Folk Music Council
ed. O. Elschek (Bratislava: Sekcia hudobnej vedy, Etnomuzikológia, Umenovedný ústav, Slovenská akadémia vied, 1975 = Seminarium ethnomusicologicum 5, Abstracts)

BURLAS, L.   Die Musikanalyse in der Entwicklung der europäischen Musikwissenschaft 5
CHALUPKA, L'. Kybernetik und EDV im Dienste der Musikanalyse   7
FUKAČ, J.   Typologie der Aussagen in der Musikanalyse   9
ADAMČIAK, M.   Die semiotische Systemanalyse des Musikwerkes   12
PEČMAN, R.   Die Auffassung der Musikanalyse bei O. Hostinský   13
BERGER, R.   Melos und Logos   14
CZEKANOWSKA, A.   Wirklichkeit und Möglichkeit einer modernen wissenschaftlichen Werkstatt   16
BOTUSCHAROFF, L.   Das Allgemeine und Besondere bei der ethnomusikologischen Analyse 18
ELSCHEKOVÁ, A.   Die Entwicklung der ethnomusikologischen Analyse   20
STOCKMANN, D.   Analytische Zugänge zu schriftlos überlieferter Musik   22
SCHNEIDER, A.   Ethnomusikologie und Tonalität   26
HOŠOVSKIJ, V.   Katalogisierungsanalyse: Algorythmus einer umfassenden formalisierten Beschreibung   28
DADAK, K.   Die Anwendung analytischer Daten beim Vergleich slawischer Erntelieder 30
HOLÝ, D. and BALLOVÁ, L'.   Die Bearbeitung der Ballade 'Vyletel vták' mit Hilfe traditioneller und mathematischer Methoden 31

BIELAWSKI, L.   Ähnlichkeiten und Zusammenhänge, System und Syntagma in der ethnomusikologischen Analyse   32
BAČINSKAJA, N. M.   Über die Bedeutung des Aspekts der Zeiteinheiten bei der Analyse von Melodien   34
PAWLAK, A.   Die Analyse und Klassifikation der Melodien aus der Region Kujawa 36
GALKO, L.   Die musikalische Liedanalyse für einen Inzipitenkatalog   38
BRAUN, H.   Das Problem der Zeilenbegrenzung   40
TROJANOWICZ, A.   Die Musik – und Tanzbewegung   42
VYSLOUŽIL, J.   Leoš Janáček als Analytiker des Volksliedes   43
VETTERL, K. and GELNÁR, J.   Zur Frage der Gliederung und Formgestaltung der Volksliedweisen   44
HRABALOVÁ, O.   Das Wort und die Musik im Volkslied   46
MUŠINKA, M.   Die thematische Gattungsanalyse der Musikfolklore   47
KRÖSCHLOVÁ, E. and LAUDOVÁ, H.   Grundlagen der Formanalyse des Volkstanzes 48
ZÁLEŠÁK, C.   Die Ordnung von Tanzmotiven nach ihrer Bewegungsstruktur   50
TOMEŠ, J.   Die Funktion der Volkstänze in den Volksbräuchen   51

74 LON   The Eighth International Congress on Acoustics
London 23–31 July 1974
International Commission on Acoustics, International Union of Pure and Applied
Physics
(privately distributed, [1974])

Vol. i Contributed Papers [1974]
Musical acoustics
SOM, A. K. Acoustics of a Malawian xylophone   333
McNULTY, P. J. Characteristics and tone quality of the Irish Uilleann pipes   334
HARAJDA, H. Les recherches sur l'étalon du son violon moderne   335
MEYER, J. Der Gitarrenkorpus als gekoppeltes System von Hohlraum- und Plattenresonanzen   336
CASTELLENGO, M. Spectrographie des transitoires d'attaque des instruments à embouchure de flûte   337
JANSSON, E. V. On the acoustics of the guitar   338
HUTCHINS, C. M. Acoustical development of eight new instruments of the violin family 339
FIRTH, I. The wolfnote in the cello   340
NÖSSELT, V. Über die Quantifizierung von audioqualitäten   im   Ton-Klingen-Geräusch-Kontinuum   341
HAINES, D. W. Fiber-reinforced plastics as substitutes for wood in stringed instruments 342
SEYMOUR, J. Glottal source spectra in singing voices   343

SUNDBERG, J. Formants in female singing 344
PISANI, R. Effect of a local temperature change in an organ pipe   345
KUNI, A. and KONDO, M. Force-velocity diagram of a string under bowing   346
BELDIE, J. P. Über die Eigenschwingungen des Geigenkörpers   347
WINCKEL, F. The hunting mechanism of the larynx control during the stressed phonation   348

Architectural acoustics
GOTTLOB, D. Comparative study of concert hall acoustics   604
ALLEN, W. A. and BICKERDIKE, J. The principal auditoria of the Royal Northern College of Music Manchester   607
KARSAI, M. The acoustical reconstruction of teaching studios at the Hungarian Academy of Music   612
WILKENS, H. Subjektive Beurteilung der raumakustischen Eigenschaften von Konzertsälen: Erfassung der Urteile und mehrdimensionale Auswertung   623

74 MANT   Mantova e i Gonzaga nella civiltà del Rinascimento: Atti del convegno
Mantua 6–8 October 1974
Accademia nazionale dei Lincei; Accademia virgiliana
(Milan: Città di Mantova/Arnoldo Mondadori, 1977)

5 La musica
PRIZER, W. La cappella di Francesco il Gonzaga e la musica sacra a Mantova nel primo ventennio del cinquecento   267

GALLICO, C. Guglielmo Gonzaga signore della musica   277
CAMPOGALLIANI, E. Nascita del melodrama alla reggia dei Gonzaga   285

74 NEWY[1]   An Ives Celebration: Papers and Panels of the Charles Ives Centennial Festival-Conference
New York 17–19 October, New Haven 20–21 October 1974
Institute for Studies in American Music at Brooklyn College, City University of
New York; School of Music, Yale University
ed. H. W. Hitchcock and V. Perlis (Urbana: University of Illinois Press,
1977 = Music in American Life)

1 Ives and American culture
CRUNDEN, R. M. Charles Ives's place in American culture   4

ROSSITER, F. R. Charles Ives: good American and isolated artist   16

BRUCE, N.   Ives and nineteenth-century American music   29

2 Ives viewed from abroad
(chairmen PERLIS, V. and BROWN, E.; panel
ANDRIESSEN, L., DICKINSON, P., JOLAS, B.,
BAGGIANI, G., USMANBAS, I., HOFFMAN, A.,
HELMS, H., IOANNIDIS, Y., DAYTON, D.,
CADIEU, M., RIJAVEC, A., RASMUSSEN, K. A.,
CLARKSON, A., BECKWITH, J., HARRISON, L.,
REYNOLDS, R., MANDEL, A.)   45

3 On editing Ives
Editors' experiences (chairman MANDEL, A.;
panel KIRKPATRICK, J., HARRISON, L.,
SINCLAIR, J.)   65
Three realizations of *Chromâtimelôdtune* (chair-
man KIRKPATRICK, J.; panel SCHULLER, G.,
SCHWARZ, G., SINGLETON, K.)   87

4 On conducting and performing Ives
Conductors' experiences (chairman MAUCERI, J.;
panel ENGEL, L., SCHULLER, G., SLONIMSKY,
N.,   WEISBERG,   A.,   SINCLAIR,   J.,
SMITH, G.)   113
On performing the violin sonatas (chairman
MANDEL, A.; panel MANDEL, N./MANDEL, A.,
STEPNER, D./KIRKPATRICK, J., GRATOVICH,
E./BENOIT, R.)   127

5 Ives and present-day musical thought
MORGAN, R. P.   Spatial form in Ives   145
FORTE, A.   Ives and atonality   159
Five composers' views (REYNOLDS, R., DODGE,
C., HARRISON, L., MARTIRANO, S., MUMMA,
G.)   187
BROOKS, W.   Ives today   209

74 NEWY[2]   Papers read at the Dufay Quincentenary Conference

New York 6–7 December 1974
Department of Music, School of Performing Arts at Brooklyn College, City
University of New York
ed. A. W. Atlas (New York: Department of Music, School of Performing Arts at
Brooklyn College of the City University of New York, 1976)

LOCKWOOD, L.   Dufay and Ferrara   1
PLANCHART, A. E.   Guillaume Dufay's masses: a
view of the manuscript traditions   26
POLK, K.   Ensemble performance in Dufay's
time   61
COBIN, M.   The compilation of the Aosta manu-
script: a working hypothesis   76
PERKINS, L. L.   Toward a rational approach to

text placement in the secular music of Dufay's
time   102
TREITLER, L.   Dufay the progressive   115
WARREN, C. W.   Punctus organi and cantus
coronatus in the music of Dufay   128
WRIGHT, C.   An example of musical inversion
from the circle of Dufay   144

74 ROM   Colloquium 'Mozart und Italien' in Rom

Rome 27–30 March 1974
Musikgeschichtliche Abteilung des Deutschen historischen Instituts in Rom
ed. F. Lippmann, *Analecta musicologica* no. 18 (Cologne: Arno Volk/Hans Gerig,
1978)

FELLERER, K. G. Mozart und Italien   1

1 Zur Mozart-Rezeption in Italien
BARBLAN, G.   La fortuna di Mozart a Milano
nell'ottocento   19
PETROBELLI, P.   'Don Giovanni' in Italia: la
fortuna dell'opera ed il suo influsso   30
BASSO, A.   Il 'Don Giovanni' sulle scene tori-
nesi nell'ottocento   52
WITZENMANN, W.   Zu einigen Handschriften des
'Flauto magico'   55
Discussion   96

2 Zur Oper
BOSSARELLI MONDOLFI, A.   Mozart e Napoli 101
LIPPMANN, F.   Mozart und der Vers   107
CARLI BALLOLA, G.   Mozart e l'opera seria di
Jommelli, De Majo e Traetta   138
HORTSCHANSKY, K.   Mozarts 'Ascanio in Alba'
und der Typus der Serenata   148
CROLL, G.   Bemerkungen zum 'Ballo primo'
(KV Anh. 109/135 a) in Mozarts Mailänder
'Lucio Silla'   160
KUNZE, S.   Mozarts 'Don Giovanni' und die
Tanzszene im ersten Finale: Grenzen des

klassischen Komponierens 166
PORENA, B. La parola intonata in 'Così fan tutte', ovvero L'esplorazione musicale di una lingua e del suo uso sociale 198
ABERT, A. A. Mozarts italianità in 'Idomeno' und 'Titus' 205

3 Zur Instrumentalmusik
STROHM, R. Merkmale italienischer Versver-

tonung in Mozarts Klavierkonzerten 219
ALLROGGEN, G. Zur Frage der Echtheit der Sinfonie KV Anh. 216 = 74 g 237
FINSCHER, L. Mozarts erstes Streichquartett: Lodi, 15. März 1770 246
SALVETTI, G. Mozart e il quartetto italiano 279
PESTELLI, G. Mozart e Rutini 290
SCHERLIESS, V. Clementis Kompositionen 'alla Mozart' 308

74 SIE   Atti del convegno internazionale di studi musicali: La fortuna musicale e spettacolare delle fiabe di Carlo Gozzi
Siena 30 August – 1 September 1974
Accademia musicale Chigiana; Facoltà di lettere, Università di Siena; Istituto di storia della musica e dello spettacolo
Chigiana xxxi, new series 11, 1974 (Florence: Leo S. Olschki, 1976)

ZORZI, L. Struttura→ fortuna della 'Fiaba' gozziana 25
LUCIANI, G. Musica e spettacolo negli scritti di Carlo Gozzi 41
MANGINI, N. Sulla struttura scenica delle 'Fiabe' gozziane 61
MARTINOTTI, S. Gozzi e i musicisti romantici tedeschi – 'Turandot' di Weber e 'Le fate' di Wagner 69
SARTORI, C. Da 'Turandot' a 'Turanda' 125
KRAISKI, G. La fortuna critica di Gozzi in Russia nel novecento 137
SANTI, P. Le 'Fiabe' di Carlo Gozzi nel teatro musicale contemporaneo 143

MELONCELLI, R. 'Turandot' di Busoni, con alcune note sulle 'possibilità dell'opera' 167
CASINI, C. La fiaba didattica e l'opera della crudeltà 187
ORSELLI, C. Puccini e il suo approdo alla favola 193
TOZZI, L. 'L'amore delle tre melarance', balletto di Sonzogno-Fokine (1936) 205
RIMINI, R. Gozzi secondo Simoni 225
ZORZI, E. G. Intorno ai manoscritti di Gozzi – la 'traccia' de 'Il Corvo' 238
[Further documentary material on Gozzi pp. 249–307]

74 SINZ   Orgel im Gottesdienst heute: Bericht über das dritte Colloquium der Walcker-Stiftung für orgelwissenschaftliche Forschung
Sinzig am Rhein 13–15 January 1974
Walcker-Stiftung für orgelwissenschaftliche Forschung
ed. H. H. Eggebrecht (Stuttgart: Musikwissenschaftliche Verlags-Gesellschaft, 1975 = Veröffentlichungen der Walcker-Stiftung, ed. H. H. Eggebrecht, 6)

EGGEBRECHT, H. H. Ansichten über gottesdienstliche Musik 17
WIDMANN, J. Die Orgel im gottesdienstlichen Handeln 33
RÖHRING, K. Die Funktion der Orgel im Gottesdienst: zwischen Wirklichkeitsprechung und Rezeptionsermöglichung 40
Discussion 52

MUSCH, H. Die liturgische Funktion der Orgel im katholischen Gottesdienst 64
Discussion: Das Konzert und der ökumenischen Gottesdienst 79

ZIEGLER, K. M. Möglichkeiten einer geistlichen Aussage in der Musik der Gegenwart 89
JACOB, W. Der Beitrag von Bengt Hambraeus zur Entwicklung der neuen Orgelmusik 97
Discussion 107

TAGLIAVINI, L. F. Heutige Orgel und überlieferte Orgelmusik (discussion 119) 109
HERBST, W. Zur gegenwärtigen Situation des evangelischen Kirchengesanges (discussion 130) 123

74 STN   XLIII° congres Sint-Niklaas-Waas 1974: annalen – annales
St Niklaas September 1974
Federatie van kringen voor oudheidkunde en geschiedenis van Belgie Vzw./Fédération
des cercles d'archéologie et d'histoire de Belgique Asbl.
ed. J. P. d'Hanens (St Niklaas: Rinda, n.d.)

Muziekgeschiedenis/Histoire de la musique
PINSART, G. Louis Brassin et la vie musicale à
Bruxelles de 1860 à 1880   457
TSERETELLI, E. Quelques aspects sur le chant
traditionnel de Géorgie   462

VANHULST, H. Le Guide Musical, les concerts
du conservatoire, les concerts populaires et
Beethoven (1883)   466

74 VEN   Petrarca, Venezia e il Veneto: Atti del convegno internazionale
Venice 30–31 October 1974
Fondazione Giorgio Cini, Venice; Istituto veneto di scienze lettere ed arti
ed. G. Padoan (Florence: Leo S. Olschki, 1976 = Civiltà veneziana saggi 21)

BELLINA, A. L. Presenze della 'Griselda' petrar-
chesca nel melodramma veneto del
'700   367

74 ZAG   Report of the Second Symposium of the International Musicological Society
Zagreb 23–7 June 1974
International Musicological Society; Yugoslav Academy
International Review of the Aesthetics and Sociology of Music v/1 and vi/1 (Zagreb:
Institute of Musicology, Zagreb Academy of Music, 1974 and 1975)

preliminary papers in v/1 (1974)

DAHLHAUS, C. Das musikalische Kunstwerk als
Gegenstand der Soziologie (discussion vi/1,
67)   11
DELIÈGE, C. Les techniques du rétrospectivisme
(discussion vi/1, 99)   27
ETZKORN, K. P. On music, social structure and
sociology (discussion vi/1, 79)   43
KNEIF, T. Some non-communicative aspects in
music (discussion vi/1, 51)   51
NATTIEZ, J.-J. Sur les relations entre sociologie
et sémiologie musicales (discussion vi/1, 90) 61
STEFANI, G. Sur l'approche fonctionnelle des
pratiques musicales   77
CIPRA, M. Die Analyse im Musikunterricht 85
WIORA, W. Der musikalische Ausdruck von
Ständen und Klassen in eigenen Stilen (dis-
cussion vi/1, 100)   91
LISSA, Z. Musik und Revolution   113
CVETKO, D. Die soziologischen und nationalen
Bedingungen für die Wandlungen in der mus-
ikalischen Situation bei den Südslawen im 19.
Jahrhundert (discussion vi/1, 111)   125
RINGER, A. L. Musical taste and the industrial
syndrome (discussion vi/1, 125)   139

BEAUD, P. Musique, masses, minorités, mar-
ginaux (discussion vi/1, 159)   155
FUBINI, E. Implicazioni sociologiche nella creazione e nella fruizione della musica
d'avanguardia (discussion vi/1, 142)   169
TRÂN VĂN KHÊ L'acculturation dans les traditions musicales de l'Asie (discussion vi/1,
146)   181
DIESEN, R., HOLEN, A. and SELVIK, R. M. Das
Musikleben in einer Landgemeinde (discussion
vi/1, 152)   191
BEZIĆ, J. Die Akkulturation als eine Fort-
bestandsmöglichkeit der Volksmusik (discussion vi/1, 172)   209
PETROVIĆ, R. Folk music of eastern Yugoslavia:
a process of acculturation (discussion vi/1,
167)   217

preliminary papers and discussions in vi/1(1975)

BROOK, B. S. The Symphonie Concertante: its
musical and sociological bases (discussion
114)   9
FINSCHER, L. Die 'Entstehung des Komponisten': zum Problem Komponisten-Individualität

75 AUS   Proceedings of a Symposium on Form in Performance, Hard-Core Ethnography
Austin, Texas 17–19 April 1975
University of Texas: College of Fine Arts, College of Social and Behavioral Sciences
and Office of the President
ed. M. Herndon and R. Brunyate (Austin: Office of the College of Fine Arts, [1976])

McCLEOD, N. Keynote address   1
The theoretical boundaries of performance
(ABRAHAMS, R. 18, BAUMAN, R. 28; dis-
cussion KING, A. 45, WACHSMANN, K. 49)
Round table: The effects of staging on performance
(panel GARVIE, P., NANCARROW, D., DAVIS,
R., HERNDON, M., SUPPAN, A.)   52

Musical ceremonies
DRAPER, D. Madri Gras Indians   88

HERNDON, M. Maltese song duels   126
SUPPAN, A. Form in performance (discussion
148)   139
Round table: The musical occasion (panel
BÉHAGUE, G., WACHSMANN, K., KING, A.,
DRAPER, D., McCLEOD, N.)   164
Summary discussion (McCLEOD, N., BÉHAGUE,
G., DRAPER, D., KING, A., WACHSMANN,
K.)   194

75 BLA   Zu Fragen des Instrumentariums, der Besetzung und der Improvisation in der ersten Hälfte des
18. Jahrhunderts: Konferenzbericht der 3. wissenschaftlichen Arbeitstagung
Blankenburg, Harz 28–9 June 1975
Telemann-Kammerorchester, Blankenburg
ed. E. Thom (Blankenburg: Telemann-Kammerorchester, 1976 = Studien zur Aufführungspraxis und Interpretation von Instrumentalmusik des 18. Jahrhunderts 2)

Vol. i (1976)
SIEGMUND-SCHULTZE, W. Die Erkenntnis der
Besetzung und des Instrumentariums der Musik
der frühen Aufklärungsepoche als Vorausset-
zung für eine historisch getreue und lebendige
heutige Interpretation: zur Frage der Ornamen-
tik und der Improvisation   9

Instrumentarium – Besetzungen
SCHULZE, H. J. Über die angemessene Beset-
zung einiger Konzerte Johann Sebastian
Bachs   21
BASELT, B. Instrumentarium und Besetzung bei
Georg Friedrich Händel, dargestellt an aus-
gewählten Beispielen aus seinen Werken   26
FLEISCHHAUER, G. Zu einigen Besetzungsfragen
im Instrumentalmusikschaffen Georg Philipp
Telemanns   33
PEČMAN, R. Zur Frage der Interpretation der
Violinsonaten František Bendas   38

PILKOVÁ, Z. Die Instrumentation der geistlichen
Kantaten der böhmischen Komponisten in der
ersten Hälfte des 18. Jahrhunderts   49
TZSCHÖCKELI, H. Über Probleme und Erfahrun-
gen bei der originalgetreuen Wiedergabe der
Viola-d'amore-Partien   56

Vol. ii (1976)
Zu Fragen der Improvisation
LIST, E. Bemerkungen zur Aufführungspraxis
der Musik der Bach-Handel-Zeit   64
BÖHME, R. Zu Fragen der Improvisation auf
Tasteninstrumenten   77
HELLER, K. Zu einigen Aspekten der solisti-
schen Improvisation im Instrumentalkonzert
des frühen 18. Jahrhunderts   80

Discussion (MAHLING, C.-H. 88, MAERTENS,
W. 98, PEČMAN, R. 103, OCHS, G. 106,
SIEGMUND-SCHULTZE, W. 107)

75 BRUN Bericht über die 5. Internationale Arbeitstagung der Study Group on Folk Musical Instruments des International Folk Music Council in Brunnen, Schweiz 1975
Brunnen, Switzerland 5–11 February 1975
Study Group on Folk Musical Instruments of the International Folk Music Council
ed. E. Stockmann, *Studia instrumentorum musicae popularis* v (Stockholm: Musikhistoriska museet, 1977 = Musikhistoriska museets skrifter, ed. E. Emsheimer, 7)

EMSHEIMER, E. Schwedische Schellenmagie 10
GEISER, B. Schellen und Glocken in Tierhaltung, Volksbrauch und Volksmusik der Schweiz 20
BAUMANN, M. P. Funktion und Symbol: zum Paradigma 'Alphorn' 27
MEYER, W. Von Maultrommeln, Flöten und Knochenschwirren: ein Beitrag der Mittelalter-Archäologie zur Geschichte volkstümlicher Musikinstrumente in der Schweiz 33
KJELLSTRÖM, B. Zur schwedischen Spilopipa 39
LEISIÖ, T. The taxomony and historical interpretation of the Finnish pastoral aerophones 45
KADEN, C. Utilitäres und Ästhetisches in der Struktur instrumentaler Arbeitssignale der Hirten 51
BROCKPÄHLER, R. 'Hirtenstücke' für Orgel im Weihnachtsbrauchtum von Westfalen 61
MAČÁK, I. Über die Möglichkeiten zur Erforschung der Geschichte der Hirtenmusikinstrumente in der Slowakei 71
DEVIC, D. Hirtentrompeten in Nordostserbien 76

ATANASSOV, V. Die historische Entwicklung der Hirteninstrumente in Bulgarien 81
BUCKLEY, A. Notes on the tiompán in Irish literature 84
BRÖCKER, M. Eine unbekannte Quelle zum Instrumentarium des 13. Jahrhunderts 91
ELSCHEKOVÁ, A. Slowakische Volksmusikinstrumente in den weihnachtlichen Hirtenliedern des 17.–19. Jahrhunderts 96
MAHLING, C.-H. Musikinstrumente in der deutschsprachigen Idylle und Schäferdichtung des 17. und 18. Jahrhunderts 106
SÁROSI, B. Angaben über die instrumentale Volksmusik Ungarns in den Gedichten von József Gvadányi und János Arany 114
HABENICHT, G. Der Informationswert von Franz Joseph Sulzers 'Geschichte des transalpinischen Daciens' (1781/1782) für die Erforschung der rumänischen Musikinstrumente 121
BAUD-BOVY, S. L'évolution parallèle de la construction, de la technique et du répertoire de la lyre crétoise 127
BRANDL, R. Musiksoziologische Aspekte der Volksmusikinstrumente auf Karpathos 131

75 BYD Musica antiqua IV: Acta scientifica
Bydgoszcz 16–19 September 1975
Bydgoskie towarzystwo naukowe [Bydgoszcz Scientific Society]; Filharmonia pomorska imienia Ignacego Paderewskiego [Paderewski Pomeranian Philharmonia]
(Bydgoszcz: Bydgoskie towarzystwo naukowe, 1975)

ARRO, E. Die Frage der Existenz einer lokalen Dialekt – Variante des gregorianischen Chorals im Baltikum des 13.–15. Jahrhunderts 7
BORISOWA-TONSCHEWA, E. Die Kirchenmusik in der Literarischen Schule Eftimis zu Tirnovo (14. Jahrhundert-Synodik des Zaren Boril) 45
PETROW, S. Einige neue Untersuchungen der Tätigkeit des Johannes Kukuzeles 59
BUCHNER, A. Die Guittara Latina und Morisca auf der Freske der Karlsteiner Apokalypse 79
ČERNÝ, J. Petrus Wilhelmi of Grudziądz – an unknown composer of the 'age of Dufay' 91
SNIŽKOVÁ, J. La tradition de Magister Johannes Hus dans la musique médiévale 105
HAAPALAINEN, T. I. Über die alten musikgeschichtlichen Denkmäler in Finnland 119
CARAPEZZA, P. E. Oposicione e sintesi dei due principi costituzionali di costruzione e discorso

nella musica dal XIII al XVI secolo 133
KOS, K. Tonart und Kadenz in den Madrigalen von A. Patricij und J. Skjavetić 145
MAKSIMOVIĆ, S. Some elements of melodic construction in Serbian chant of the fifteenth century 163
PETROVIĆ, D. Byzantine and Slavonic oktoechos until the 15th century 175
SIVEC, J. Neues zum Musikrepertoire Mitteleuropas im Zeitalter der Reformation 191
STEFANOVIĆ, D. Services for Slavonic saints in early Russian music manuscripts 211
LEHMANN, D. Der russische Skomoroch als Typ des europäischen mittalalterlichen Spielmanns 221
CHANIECKI, Z. Początki działalności cechów muzycznych w Polsce [The beginnings of the activities of musical guilds in Poland] 235

DOMAŃSKI, W.   Renesansowa teoria solmizacji Sebastiana z Felsztyna [The Renaissance theory of solmization of Sebastian z Felsztyna]   247

MACIEJEWSKI, T.   Kyriale i jego percepcja w Polsce do XVI wieku [The kyrial and its perception in Poland up to the 16th century] 261

PIKULIK, T.   Polistrukturalny charakter polskiej kultury muzyczne w średniowieczu na podstawie propium de tempore, sekwencji i ordinarium missae [The polystructural character of Polish musical culture in the middle ages on the basis of the proprium de tempore, the sequence and the ordinary of the mass]   273

ŠCIBOR, J.   Tonalo-modalny aspekt chorału cysterskiego [Tonal and modal aspects of the Cistercian chant]   287

FELLERER, K. G.   Musikalische Beziehungen zwischen Ost- und Mitteleuropa in der Zeit der Renaissance   301

FLOROS, C.   Über Zusammenhänge zwischen den Musikkulturen des Ostens und des Westens im Mittelalter   321

COMIŞEL, E.   Aspects du folklore roumain au moyen-âge (13–15 siècles)   343

COSMA, V.   Ein Mittelpunkt blühender Musikkultur im 16. Jahrhundert: Alba Julia   357

ZOTTOVICEANU, E.   Nouvelles données sur Giovanni Battista Mosto et ses relations avec la Transylvanie   369

von FISCHER, K.   Quellen mehrstimmiger Musik des 13. bis 15. Jahrhunderts aus slavischen Ländern   381

APEL, W.   Orgelmusik in Ost-Europa im 15. und 16. Jahrhundert   391

FALVY, Z.   Die arabische und die europäische Musik   407

ATAYAN, R.   Nerses Shnorali i nektorïye voprosï evo muzïkal'novo tvorchestva [Shnorali and some questions of his compositions]   421

GERASIMOVA-PERSIDSKAYA, N. A.   Rol' slova v znamennom raspeve i partesnom mnogogolosii [The role of words in Znamenny chant and in polyphony]   439

GINZBURG, L.   Russkiy narodnïy smïchkovïy instrument gudok i evo predshestvenniki [The Russian national instrument, the gudok, and its predecessors]   455

GVAKHARIYA, V.   Muzïkal'naya kul'tura Gruzii epokhi tsaritsï Tamarï i Shota Rustaveli [The musical culture of Georgia in the time of Tsarina Tamara and Shot Rustavel]   469

KARASTOYANOV, B. P.   K vosprosu rasshifrovki kryukovïkh pevcheskikh rukopisey znamennovo raspeva [On deciphering crook singing notation in Znammeny chant manuscripts]   487

KELDÏSH, Yu. V.   K probleme proiskhozhdeniya znamennovo raspeva [The problem of the origins of Znammeny chant]   505

KONOTOP, A.   Struktura suprasl'skovo irmologiona 1598–1601 gg. drevneyshevo pamyatnika ukrainskovo notolineynovo pis'ma [The structure of the Suprasl Hirmologion 1598–1601, the oldest document of Ukrainian staff notation]   521

KORABDEVA, K.   Drukhovnïye stikhi kak pamyatniki znamennovo pospeva (stikhi pokayannïye) [Religious poems as monuments of Znammeny chant (penitential poetry)]   535

NIKISHOV, G.   Sravnitel'naya paleografiya kondakarnovo pis'ma XI–XIV vekov [Comparative paleography of Kondakar notation from the 11th to the 14th century]   557

PROTOPOPOV, V.   Nikolay Diletzkiy i evo 'Muzïkal'naya grammatika' [Diletsky and his 'Musical grammar']   573

USPENSKIY, N. D.   K voprosu o proiskhozhdenii russkovo khorovo kontserta [The question of the origins of the Russian choral concert]   587

VLADISHEVSKAYA, T.   Tipografskiy Ustav – kak istochnik dlya izucheniya drevneyshikh form russkovo pevcheskovo iskusstva [Typographical rules as a basis for the study of the ancient forms of Russian singing]   607

REINHARD, K.   Über die Beziehungen zwischen byzantinischer und türkischer Musik   623

75 EIS   **Kongress-Bericht Eisenstadt 1975**
Eisenstadt 20–25 October 1975
European Liszt Centre
ed. W. Suppan (Graz: Akademische Druck- und Verlagsanstalt, 1977 = Liszt-Studien 1)

ALTENBURG, D.   Eine Theorie der Musik der Zukunft: zur funktion des Programms im symphonischen Werk von Franz Liszt   9

BARBAG-DREXLER, I.   Liszts Klavierbearbeitungen: ein Beitrag zum Thema 'Der vergessene Liszt'   27

BENARY, P.   Geschmack und Stil bei Franz Liszt   37

BORONKAY, A.   Frühe und endgültige Fassun-

gen von Liszt-Werken in der Neuen Liszt-Ausgabe   47

DONATH, A.   Franz Liszt und Polen   53

FALVY, Z.   Franz Liszt in den Schriften Béla Bartóks   65

GÁRDONYI, Z.   Hauptproblem der Neuen Liszt-Ausgabe   73

GRUBER, G.   Zum Formproblem in Liszts Orchesterwerken – exemplifiziert am ersten

Satz der Faust-Symphonie 81
GUT, S. Die historische Position der Modalität bei Franz Liszt 97
HEINEMANN, E. G. Kunstbegriff und Engagement bei Liszt 105
HILMAR, E. Kritische Betrachungen zu Liszts Transkriptionen von Liedern von Franz Schubert: Allgemeines und Spezielles zur Niederschrift des 'Schwanengesangs' 115
KAISER, M. Anmerkungen zur Kompositionstechnik Franz Liszts: am Beispiel der 'Hunnenschlacht' 125
KOLLERITSCH, O. Liszt in der Kritik Robert Schumanns 131
PRESSER, D. Liszts 'Années de pèlerinage. Pre-

mière année: Suisse' als Document der Romantik 137
RÜSCH, W. Franz Liszt in Bellagio 155
SEBESTYÉN, A. Franz Liszts Originalkompositionen für Violine und Klavier 163
SUPPAN, W. Blasorchesterbearbeitungen Liszt'scher Werke 179
SUTTER, M. Liszt and the Weimar organist-composers 203
SZELÉNYI, L. Liszts Opernpläne: ein wenig bekanntes Kapitel aus dem Schaffen des Komponisten 215
WAGNER, M. Liszt und Bruckner – oder ein Weg zur Restauration sakraler Musik 225

75 ESP Föredrag och diskussionsinlägg från nordiskt kollokvium III i latinsk liturgiforskning Espoo 22–4 May 1975
Institutionen för praktisk teologi vid Helsingfors Universitet: Allmänna sektionen för praktisk teologi
(Helsinki, 1976 = Helsingin yliopiston käytännöllisen teologian laitos käytännöllisen teologian julkaisuja A3)

ANDRÉN, Å. Botens sakrament i den svenska medeltida liturgin sedd i internationell belysning 6
BERGSAGEL, J. Liturgical relations between England and Scandinavia: as seen in selected musical fragments from the 12th and 13th centuries 11
HOHLER, C. Structures and patterns in surviving breviaries from Scandinavia 27
HUGLO, M. De monodiska handskrifternas fördelning i trå grupper, öst och väst 47
NYBERG, T. Iakttagelser rörande kung David i högmedeltida kalendarier 67
OTTOSEN, K. Udvalgte resultater af edb-behandlingen af det middelalderlige dødsofficium 79
PARVIO, M. Källorna till Missale Aboense 91
REIER, E. and REIER, W. The introit trope repertory at Revers 97

WEISS, G. Die 'Monumenta monodica medii aevi' 111

Trope research
JONSSON, R. Corpus troporum 123
BJÖRKVALL, G. Problem rörande handskrifterna 129
ODELMAN, E. Rubrikerna i trophandskrifterna 139
IVERSEN, G. Troperna til Agnus Dei 147
MARCUSSON, O. Prosula 151

Register of fragments in Scandinavia (Sweden: ODENIUS, O. 171; Norway: GJERLØW, L. 171; Denmark: JEXLEV, T. and RÅSTED, J. 173; Finland: LEHTINEN, A. I. 179)

Non-Scandinavian liturgy research
RASMUSSEN, N. K. Report 189
OTTOSEN, K. Edition principles: discussion 193

75 ROM Musica indigena: Einheimische Musik und ihre mögliche Verwendung in Liturgie und Verkündigung: Musikethnologisches Symposion / Symposium musico-ethnologicum
Rome 14–22 November 1975
Consociatio internationalis musicae sacrae, Rome
ed. J. Overath and J. Kuckertz (Rome: Sekretariat der CIMS, 1976 = Veröffentlichungen der Consociatio internationalis musicae sacrae)

NETTL, B. On method in the study of indigenous musics 13
KUCKERTZ, J. Fragen zur Übertragung einheimischer Musik in den Gottesdienst 26
WACHSMANN, K. P. African music 36

MBUNGA, S. Afrikanische Musik im Gottesdienst 51
OUEDRAOGO, R. La musique sacrée dans les missions du pays Mossi 72
KUCKERTZ, J. Indische Musik 87

ALBUQUERQUE, W. Indian music in divine service 97
McCREDIE, A. D. Transplanted and emergent indigenous liturgical musics in East Asia, Australasia and Oceania 117
Conclusions 141

FELLERER, K. G. Zum 450. Geburtstag des Princeps musicae, Pierluigie Sante da Palestrina: Festrede in Palestrina am 21. November 1975 147

---

75 SIE **Atti del convegno internazionale di studi musicali: La cultura musicale e teatrale italiana nella Parigi illuministica**
Siena 28–30 August 1975
Accademia musicale Chigiana; Facoltà di lettere, Università di Siena; Istituto di storia della musica e dello spettacolo
Chigiana xxxii, new series 12, 1975 (Florence: Leo S. Olschki, 1977)

PETRONIO, G. Venezia, Parigi, Amburgo: la nascita del teatro borghese 33
FUBINI, E. Il mito della musica italiana nel pensiero di Rousseau e di Diderot 45
ALBERTI, L. 'L'orchestre colore la scène' (Voltaire): note per l'individuazione di consonanze tra musica e mesinscene nella opera e nei balli del secondo settecento 57
VIALE FERRERO, M. In margine alla voce 'Ballet' dell'"Encyclopédie' 73
MANGINI, N. Tramonto di un mito: il 'Théâtre italien' a Parigi 87
JOLY, J. Du théâtre italien de Paris au théâtre de San Giovanni Grisostomo à Venise: 'Il genio buono e il genio cattivo' 'pièce à spectacle' de Goldoni 105

MARTINOTTI, S. Mozart e Anfossi: un appuntamento mancato a Parigi 141
DEGRADA, F. Due volti di Ifigenia 165
Appendix: Le due 'Ifigenie' e la querelle Gluck-Piccinni 185
TOZZI, L. Il 'Renaud' di Sacchini: genesi di una metamorfosi 225
CAGLI, B. 'La buona figliola' e la nascita dell'opera semiseria 265
JENKINS, N. The vocal music of G. B. Sammartini 277
MARTINOTTI, S. La Villanella di Bianchi rapita da Ferrari 311

---

75 STRS **Strasbourg au coeur religieux du XVIe siècle: Hommage à Lucien Febvre: Actes du Colloque international de Strasbourg**
Strasbourg 25–9 May 1975
Société savante d'Alsace et des régions de l'est
(Strasbourg: Istra, 1977 = Société savante d'Alsace et des régions de l'est: Grand publications xii)

WEBER, E. Musique et théâtre à Strasbourg à l'époque de la Reforme (1) 577

INDEX OF PLACES

Aix 58 AIX
Algiers 05 ALG, (39 ALG)
Amsterdam 32 AMS, 48 AMS, 64 AMS, 65 AMS
Ancona 51 IES
Ankara 73 ANK
Ann Arbor 71 ANN
Antwerp 30 ANT, 57 BRUS, 70 ANT
Arras 54 ARR, 55 ARR
Athens 30 ATH, 60 ATH, 64 ATH
Austin 75 AUS
Avignon 55 AVIG

Balatonalmádi 73 BAL
Bamberg 53 BAM
Bardolino 71 WAR
Basle 06 BAS, 24 BAS, 49 BAS
Bayreuth 38 BAY
Beaune 65 DIJ
Belgrade 27 BEL, 73 BEL
Berlin 12 BERL, 13 BERL, 24 BERL, 27 BERL, 64 BERL, 65 BERL[1], 65 BERL[2], 67 BERL, 70 BERL[1], 70 BERL[2], 74 BERL
Berne 52 BERN, 62 BERN, 72 BERN
Binghamton 69 BIN
Bissau 47 BIS
Blankenburg, Harz 72 BLA, 74 BLA, 75 BLA
Bled 71 BLE
Bloomington 65 BLM
Bologna 11 BOL, 70 BOL, 74 BOL
Bonn 27 BON, 30 BON, 64 BON, 70 BON
Bratislava 64 BRA, 65 BRA
Brno 58 BRN, 65 BRN, 66 BRN, 67 BRN[1], 67 BRN[2], (68 BRN), 69 BRN, 70 BRN, 71 BRN
Bruges 25 BRUG
Brunnen 75 BRUN
Brussels 23 BRUS, 35 BRUS[1], 35 BRUS[2], 48 BRUS, 53 BRUS, 55 BRUS, 57 BRUS
Bucharest 67 BUC, 73 BUC
Budapest 59 BUD, 61 BUD, 63 BUD, 71 BUD[1], 71 BUD[2]
Busseto 69 VER
Bydgoszcz 66 BYD, 69 BYD, 69 PARM, 72 BYD, 75 BYD

Cagliari 56 CAG
Cairo 32 CAIR
Cambridge 52 CAM, 54 CAM, 59 CAM
Cambridge, Massachusetts 56 CAM/M, 57 CAM/M, 61 CAM/M
Carbondale 65 CARB
Cartagena de Indias 63 CART
Casale Monferrato 69 CAS
Certaldo 59 CER, 69 CER
Chicago 66 CHIC
Chieti 57 CHIE
Cluny 49 CLU
Cologne 58 COL, 61 COL
Copenhagen 32 COP, 38 COP, 54 STAD, 59 KIE, 62 COP, 65 COP, 72 COP
Cremona 37 FLOR, 68 VEN

Dakar 45 DAK
Dijon 65 DIJ
Dinant 03 DIN

Edinburgh 48 EDIN
Eisenstadt 71 EIS, 75 EIS
Espoo 75 ESP
Evanston 68 EVA
Exeter 69 EXE

Fabriano 51 IES
Ferrara 54 FER
Fez 39 FEZ
Florence 29 FLOR, 33 FLOR, 37 FLOR, 38 FLOR, 39 FLOR, 48 FLOR, 49 FLOR, 50 FLOR, 56 FLOR, 61 FLOR, 67 FLOR, 69 CER, 71 FLOR
Frankfurt am Main 08 FRA, 38 FRA
Freiburg im Breisgau 26 FRE/B, 38 FRE/B, 72 FRE/B
Freiberg in Sachsen 27 FRE/S
Fusignano 68 FUS

Genoa 72 ROM
Geneva 09 GEN, 26 GEN, 65 GEN
Ghent 13 GHE, 38 GHE, 57 BRUS
Giessen 04 GHE
Göttingen 14 GÖT
Graz 64 GRA[1], 64 GRA[2], 66 GRA, 67 GRA, 68 GRA, 70 GRA, 71 GRA, 72 GRA, 74 GRA[1], 74 GRA[2]
Groningen 26 GRON

Halle 27 HAL, 59 HAL
Hamburg 02 HAM, 30 HAM[1], 30 HAM[2], 31 HAM, 56 HAM, 64 HAM, 73 HAM
Hammamet 70 HAMM
Hanover 54 STAD
Hindelang 71 HIN

Iesi 51 IES
Innsbruck 10 INN
Istanbul 55 IST

Jena 36 JEN
Jerusalem 61 JER, 65 JER, 69 JER, 74 JER

Kassel 62 KAS, 67 KAS, 71 KAS
Kiel 59 KIE, 63 KIE
Kielce 65 WAR
Kraków 65 WAR
Krpáčová 74 KRP
Kuala Lumpur 69 KUA
Kyoto 68 TOK[2]

La Plata 32 LAP
Lawrence 70 LAW
Leiden 31 LEID
Leipzig 23 LEIP, 25 LEIP, 33 LEIP, 50 LEIP, 66 LEIP
Liège 09 LIÈ, 30 LIÈ, 32 LIÈ, 57 BRUS, 65 LIÈ, 68 LIÈ
Lima 39 MEX, 70 LIM
Ljubljana 67 LJU
London 11 LON, 74 LON
Lüneburg 50 LÜN[1], 50 LÜN[2]
Luxeuil 50 LUX

Magdeburg 62 MAG, 67 MAG, 73 MAG
Maiolati 51 IES
Malines 11 MAL
Malmö 54 STAD
Malta 72 MALT
Manila 66 MANL
Mantua 61 FLOR, 68 VEN, 74 MANT
Marburg 65 MARB, 69 MARB
Marseilles 58 MARS
Merano 63 MER
Mexico City 39 MEX, 62 MEX
Milan 56 FLOR, 68 MIL, 72 MIL
Milwaukee 66 CHIC

Montauban 63 MTA, 66 MTA, 68 MTA, 70 MTA
Montserrat 65 MTS
Moravany 70 PIE
Morgantown 66 MOR
Moscow 64 MOS, 71 MOS
Msida 72 MALT
Munich 00 MUN, 25 MUN, 57 MUN

Namur 38 NAM
Nancy 67 NAN
Naples 24 NAP
Netherlands 53 NET
Neuilly-sur-Seine 57 NEU/S
Neustift bei Brixen 73 NEU/B
New Delhi 64 NEWD[1], 64 NEWD[2]
New Haven 29 NEWH, 65 NEWH, 74 NEWY[1]
New York 28 NEWY, 39 NEWY, 49 NEWY[1], 49 NEWY[2], 61 NEWY, 65 NEWY, 68 NEWY, 71 NEWY, 74 NEWY[1], 74 NEWY[2]
Nuoro 56 CAG
Nuremberg 69 NUR, 73 NUR

Ochsenhausen 51 OCH
Okhrida 61 OKH
Oslo 28 OSL
Oxford 66 OXF[1], 66 OXF[2]

Palermo 51 PAL, 54 PAL
Paris 00 PAR[1], 00 PAR[2], 00 PAR[3], 00 PAR[4], 00 PAR[5], 00 PAR[6], 21 PAR, 31 PAR, 37 PAR[1], 37 PAR[2], 37 PAR[3], 37 PAR[4], 47 PAR, 48 PAR[1], 48 PAR[2], 51 PAR, 53 PAR, 54 PAR[1], 54 PAR[2], 56 PAR, 57 PAR, 60 PAR[1], 60 PAR[2], 62 PAR, 67 PAR, 69 PAR, 72 PAR, 73 PAR
Parma 67 PARM, 68 PARM, 69 PARM, 69 VER

Perugia 69 PER
Philadelphia 56 PHIL
Piešt'any 70 PIE
Prague 28 PRA, 34 PRA, 47 PRA, 56 PRA, 63 PRA, 67 PRA

Quebec 06 QUE

Radziejowice 67 RAD
Ravenna 65 RAV
Rio de Janeiro 22 RIO
Rome 03 ROM, 05 ROM, 11 ROM, 26 ROM, 29 ROM, 36 ROM, 50 ROM, 60 ROM, 69 ROM, 72 ROM, 73 ROM[1], 73 ROM[2], 74 ROM, 75 ROM
Rouen 54 ROU
Royaumont 55 ROY, 59 ROY, 62 ROY, 63 ROY

Salzburg 31 SAL, 64 SAL
San José 58 SJOS
Santa Isabel 51 STIS
São Tomé 56 STOM
Santo Tirso 63 STT
Sárospatak 72 SÁR
Sassari 56 CAG
Siena 67 SIE, 73 SIE, 74 SIE, 75 SIE
Sinaia 62 SIN
Sinzig am Rhein 74 SINZ
Sofia 34 SOF, 66 SOF
Stade 54 STAD
Stavelot 65 STAV
St-Gall 71 STGA
St Germain-en-Laye 70 STGE
St Niklas 74 STN
Stockholm 51 STOC, 62 STOC, 69 STOC, 70 STOC, 73 STOC
St Pölten 71 STP
Strasbourg 05 STRS, 32 STRS, 68 STRS, 75 STRS
Stratford, Ontario 60 STRT
Stuttgart 04 STU, 59 STU, 71 STU

Sveti Stefan 68 SVE

Teheran 61 TEH
Thessaloniki 53 THE
Thurner im Schwarzwald 68 THU
Todi 57 TOD, 58 TOD, 61 TOD, 62 TOD, 63 TOD, 72 TOD
Tokyo 61 TOK, 68 TOK[1], 68 TOK[2]
Toruń 65 WAR, 66 BYD
Tours 72 TOU
Trenčín 70 TRČ
Trento 34 TRT
Tübingen 34 TÜB
Turin 21 TUR, 48 TUR

Udine 31 UDIN
Uppsala 62 STOC, 68 UPP
Utrecht 52 UTR

Vancouver 67 VAN, 71 VAN
Venice 29 ROM, 40 VEN, 56 VEN, 57 VEN[1], 57 VEN[2], 61 VEN, 63 VEN, 66 VEN, 68 VEN, 70 VEN, 72 VEN, 73 VEN, 74 VEN
Verona 69 VER
Vienna 08 VIE, 09 VIE, 27 VIE, 28 VIE, 52 VIE, 54 VIE, 56 VIE, 70 VIE, 72 VIE[1], 72 VIE[2]
Vicenza 71 VIC

Warsaw 60 WAR[1], 60 WAR[2], 62 WAR, 65 WAR, 69 WAR, 71 WAR
Washington 15 WAS, 58 WAS, 68 NEWY
Wégimont 54 WÉG, 55 WÉG, 56 WÉG, 57 WÉG, 58 WÉG
Weimar 73 WEIM
Würzburg 70 WÜR

Yaoundé 70 YAO

Zagreb 67 ZAG, 74 ZAG
Zurich 38 ZUR

INDEX OF TITLES, SERIES AND SPONSORS

in a series   * no report published
            – no musical papers

AIBM Association internationale des bibliothèques musicales
Académie de la République populaire roumaine 62 SIN, 73 BUC
Accademia musicale Chigiana 73 SIE, 74 SIE, 75 SIE
Accademia nazionale dei Lincei 60 ROM, 74 MANT
Accademia nazionale di Santa Cecilia, 73 ROM¹
Accademia polacca delle scienze see Polska akademia nauk
Accademia virgiliana 74 MANT
Acculturation in the Americas 49 NEWY
À Cluny 49 CLU
Acoustics 58 MARS, 67 PAR
  see also International Congress on Acoustics
Aesthetics see International Congress on Aesthetics and Kongress für Ästhetik und allgemeine Kunstwissenschaft
Africa 68 EVA, 70 YAO
Africanists 69 MARB
  see also International West African Conference
Akademie (Hochschule, from 1970) für Musik und darstellende Kunst in Graz
  Abteilung für Kirchenmusik 64 GRA¹
  Institut für Aufführungspraxis 70 GRA, 71 GRA, 72 GRA
  Institut für Wertungsforschung 67 GRA, 74 GRA¹
  see also (Grazer) Balkanologen-Tagung
Allgemeine Kunstwissenschaft see Kongress für Ästhetik und allgemeine Kunstwissenschaft
Allgemeiner Cäcilien-Verband für die Länder der deutschen Sprache 61 COL
Allmänna sektionen för praktisk teologi, Institutionen för praktisk teologi vid Helsingfors Universitet 75 ESP
Alte Musik in unserer Zeit 67 KAS
American Anthropological Association 49 NEWY²,
58 WAS
Americanists see International Congress of Americanists
American Musicological Society 39 NEWY, 71 NEWY
  Greater New York Chapter 65 NEWY
American-Yugoslav Seminar 68 SVE
Amiral de Coligny 72 PAR
Amis de Guillaume Apollinaire 65 STAV
Analyse spectrale et fonction du poème Baroque 68 MTA
Analyse und Klassifikation von Volksmelodien 67 RAD
Anfänge der slavischen Musik 64 BRA
Annales internationales d'histoire 00 PAR³
Anthropology see Congrès international d'anthropologie et d'archéologie préhistorique and International Congress of Anthropological and Ethnological Sciences

Antichità e arte 69 CAS
Apollinaire 65 STAV
Arab Music 32 CAIR, 72 MALT
Arbeitsgemeinschaft 'Dokumentation in den historischen Wissenschaften', Darmstadt 71 KAS
Arbeitskreis für Haus-und Jugendmusik, Kiel 67 KAS
Arbeitskreis 'Georg Philipp Telemann' im (Deutschen) Kulturbund Magdeburg (der DDR) 72 BLA
  see also Magdeburger Telemann-Festtage
Arbeiterliedforschung 64 BERL
Arbeitstagung der Studiengruppe zur Erforschung und Edition älterer Volksmusikquellen see International Folk Music Council
Arbeitstagung der Study Group of Folk Music Systematization see International Folk Music Council
Arbeit und Volksleben 65 MARB
Archéologie préhistorique see Congrès international d'anthropologie et d'archéologie préhistorique
Archeologique et historique de Belgique see Fédération archéologique et historique de Belgique
Argomenti musicali polacco-italiani 71 WAR
Ars nova 55 WÉG
Ars nova italiana del trecento
  I Certaldo, 1959 59 CER
  – Certaldo, 1967 67 CER
  II Certaldo, 1969 69 CER
Art 21 PAR, 55 ARR, 61 FLOR, 64 BON, 69 CAS, 72 TOD, 73 ROM¹
Arte neoclassica 57 VEN²
Arte pensiero e cultura a Mantova 61 FLOR
Artistic Tradition and Audio-Visual Media 70 HAMM
Artistic Values in Traditional Music 65 BERL²
Arts popularies 28 PRA see also Folk
Asia 59 ROY, 66 MANL, 69 KUA
Aspects sociologiques de la musique à la radio 54 PAR²
Association des Amis de St Colomban, Luxeuil 50 LUX
Association for Asian Studies 71 ANN
Association internationale des bibliothèques musicales see International Congress of Music Libraries
Association internationale des études byzantines see International Congress of Byzantine Studies
Association internationale des historiens de la Renaissance (et l'humanisme) 55 ROY, 57 BRUS
Association of Hispanists of Great Britain and Ireland 69 EXE
Association of Hungarian Musicians 71 BUD¹
Associazione italiana Museo vivo 73 ROM²
Ästhetik see International Congress on Aesthetics and Kongress für Ästhetik und allgemeine Kunstwissenschaft
Audio-Visual Media 70 HAMM

Aufführungspraxis und Interpretation von Instrumentalmusik 74 BLA

Bach 50 LEIP
Balkan 62 SIN, 66 SOF
see also (Grazer) Balkanologen-Tagung
Baltic Studies 73 STOC
Baltiska Institutet 73 STOC
Barock, seine Orgeln und seine Musik in Ober-
schwaben 51 OCH
Baroque 57 WÉG, 60 ROM
see also Journées internationales d'étude du Baroque
Bartók 61 BUD, 71 BUD[1]
Bedeutung, die optische und akustische Darbietung und
die Aufgaben einer Musikinstrumentensamm-
lung 69 NUR
Beethoven 27 VIE, 70 BERL[2], 70 BON, 70 PIE, 70 VIE
Beiträge 72/73 72 VIE[1]
Beiträge zu einem neuen Telemannbild 62 MAG
Beiträge zur weltlichen und geistlichen Lyrik des 13. bis
15. Jahrhunderts 70 WÜR
Belgique 35 BRUS[1]
see also Fédération archéologique et historique
Bibliotecari musicali 54 PAL
Biblioteche e bibliografia 29 ROM
Bibliothèques-musées des arts du spectacle 65 AMS
Blasmusik 74 GRA[2]
Bohemian Music 70 BRN
Bydgoskie towarzystwo naukowe *see* Musica antiqua
(Europae orientalis)
Bydgoszcz Scientific Society *see* Musica antiqua (Euro-
pae orientalis)
Byzantine Studies *see* International Congress of Byzan-
tine Studies

CIDEM Consejo interamericano de música
CIM Conseil international de la musique
CIMP Conseil international de la musique populaire
CIPSH Conseil international de la philosophie et
des studies humanistiques
CNRS Centre national de la recherche scientifique
Calderón 69 EXE
Cäcilien-Verband für die Länder der deutschen Sprache,
Allgemeiner 61 COL
Canadian Folk Music Society 67 VAN
Canadian League of Composers 60 STRT
Canneti, Istituto musicale, Vicenza 71 VIC
Cantus gregoriani studiosorum conventus 32 STRS
Catholic Scholars 00 MUN
Centennial Workshop on Ethnomusicology 67 VAN
Center for Japanese Studies, Center for Chinese Studies,
School of Music and Speech Department of the
University of Michigan 71 ANN
Center for Medieval and Early Renaissance Studies, State
University of New York at Binghamton 69
BIN
Centre d'études 'Georges Enesco' 73 BUC
Centre d'études germaniques de l'Université de Stras-
bourg 68 STRS
Centre d'études radiophoniques 54 PAR[2]
Centre d'études supérieures de la Renaissance,
Université de Tours 72 TOU
Centre national de la recherche scientifique (CNRS) 53
PAR, 54 ARR, 54 PAR[1], 56 PAR, 57 NEU/S,
58 MARS, 60 PAR[1], 62 PAR, 63 ROY, 67
NAN, 69 PAR
Équipe de recherches théâtrales et musicologiques du
CNRS 68 STRS
Groupe de recherches sur le théâtre (CNRS) 59
ROY, 62 ROY

see also 73 PAR
Centro di documentazione sul movimento dei disci-
plinati: Deputazione di storia patria per
l'Umbria 69 PER
Centro di studi sull'ars nova italiana del trecento,
Certaldo *see* Ars nova italiana del trecento
Centro di studi sulla spiritualità medievale *see* Convegni
del Centro di studi sulla spiritualità medievale
Centro etnografico Sardo, Cagliari 56 CAG
Centro internazionale di semiotica e di linguistica di
Urbino 73 BEL
Centro nazionale di studi sul Rinascimento, Flor-
ence 39 FLOR
Centro per la documentazione e la difesa del folklore
italiano, Gubbio 56 CAG
Cercle international d'études ethno-musicologiques *see*
Ethnomusicologie (Colloques de Wégimont)
Chamber Music 71 BRN
Chanson & Madrigal, 1480–1530 61 CAM/M
Charakter und Erziehung 38 BAY
Charles Quint 57 BRUS
Chiesa e riforma nella spiritualità del sec. XI 63 TOD
Chigiana 73 SIE, 74 SIE, 75 SIE
Chinese and Japanese Music-Dramas 71 ANN
Chopin 60 WAR[1], 74 BOL
Church Music 00 PAR[6], 27 BERL[1], 37 PAR[1], 49 CLU,
63 TOD, 64 GRA[1], 65 MTS, 72 PAR, 75 ROM,
75 STRS
see also International Church Music Congress and
Internationaler Kongress für Kirchenmusik in Bern
Cini *see* Fondazione Giorgio Cini
City University of New York
Department of Music, School of Performing Arts at
Brooklyn College 74 NEWY[2]
Institute for Studies in American Music at Brooklyn
College 74 NEWY[1]
Civilisations balkaniques 62 SIN
Classification *see* International Folk Music Council:
Study Group of Folk Music Systematization
Coligny 72 PAR
College of Social and Behavioral Sciences, University of
Texas 75 AUS
College of Fine Arts, University of Texas 75 AUS
Colloques de Wégimont (including Ethnomusicologie)
I Wégimont, 1954 54 WÉG
II Wégimont, 1955 55 WÉG
III Wégimont, 1956 56 WÉG
IV Wégimont, 1957 57 WÉG
V Wégimont, 1958, 1960 58 WÉG
Colloquia on the History and Theory of Music at the
International Musical Festival in Brno
I Brno, 1966 66 BRN
II Brno, 1967 67 BRN[2]
III Brno, 1968 68 BRN
IV Brno, 1969 69 BRN
V Brno, 1970 70 BRN
VI Brno, 1971 71 BRN
Colloquium der Walcker-Stiftung (für orgelwissenschaft-
liche Forschung)
I Thurner im Schwarzwald, 1968 68 THU
II Freiburg im Breisgau, 1972 72 FRE/B
III Sinzig am Rhein, 1974 74 SINZ
Colomban, St 50 LUX
Coloquio anglogermano 69 EXE
Comitato nazionale italiano per le arti popolari 34
TRT, 40 VEN
Comitato nazionale per le tradizioni popolari 29
FLOR, 31 UDIN
Comité international des musées et collections
d'instruments de musique 65 DIJ

Comité international d'histoire de l'art 64 BON
Commissione di musica sacra per l'Anno santo 50 ROM
Composers 47 PRA
  Inter-American 65 BLM
  Modern 60 STRT
Computer, Musicology and 65 NEWY
Computer Applications in Music 66 MOR
Computers for the Humanitites? 65 NEWH
Comune di Venezia 57 VEN¹
Conférence internationale des Africanistes de l'ouest *see* International West African Conference
Conferencia interamericana de etnomusicologia *see* Inter-American Conference on Ethnomusicology
Conferencia internacional de Africanistas occidentales *see* International West African Conference
Conferência internacional dos Africanistas ocidentais *see* International West African Conference
Congrès de la Société internationale de musique *see* Congress of the International Musical Society
Congrès international d'acoustique *see* International Congress on Acoustics
Congrès international d'anthropologie et d'archéologie préhistorique
  XV Paris etc. 1930-31 31 PAR
  XVI Brussels 1935 35 BRUS²
Congrès international de langue et littérature du midi de la France
  I Avignon, 1955 55 AVIG
  II Aix 1958 58 AIX
Congrès international de folklore 37 PAR⁴
Congrès international de musique 00 PAR¹
Congrès international de musique sacrée *see* International Church Music Congress
Congrès international de philosophie *see* International Congress of Philosophy
Congrès international de psychologie *see* International Congress of Psychology
Congrès international des Américanistes *see* International Congress of Americanists
Congrès international des bibliothèques musicales *see* International Congress of Music Libraries
Congrès international (d') des études byzantines *see* International Congress of Byzantine Studies
Congrès international des orientalistes *see* International Congress of Orientalists
Congrès international des sciences anthropologiques et ethnologiques *see* International Congress of Anthropological and Ethnological Sciences
Congrès international des sciences historiques
  Congresso internazionale di scienze storiche
  [I] Paris, 1900 00 PAR³
  [III] Rome, 1903 03 ROM
  V Brussels, 1923 23 BRUS
  VI Oslo, 1928 28 OSL
  VIII Zurich, 1938 38 ZUR
  see also Congrès international d'histoire des sciences
Congrès international d'esthétique (et de science de l'art) *see* International Congress on Aesthetics
Congrès international d'histoire de la musique 00 PAR²
Congrès international d'histoire des sciences
  VIII Florence, Milan, 1956 56 FLOR
  XI Warsaw etc., 1965 65 WAR
  see also Congrès international des sciences historiques
Congrès jubilaire 25 BRUG
Congreso internacional de Americanistas *see* International Congress of Americanists

Congress for Experimental Psychology *see* Kongress für experimentelle Psychologie and Kongress der Deutschen Gesellschaft für Psychologie
Congresso di musica *see* Congresso (internazionale) di musica
Congress of the International Musical Society
  Congrès de la Société international de musique– Kongress der Internationalen Musikgesellschaft
  I Leipzig, 1904 *
  II Basle, 1906 06 BAS
  III Vienna, 1909 09 VIE
  IV London, 1911 11 LON
  V Paris, 1912 *
Congresso internacional de Americanistas *see* International Congress of Americanists
Congresso internacional de etnografia 63 STT
Congresso internazionale degli Americanisti *see* International Congress of Americanists
Congresso internazionale di estetica *see* International Congress on Aesthetics
Congresso internazionale di filosofia *see* International Congress of Philosophy
Congresso (internazionale) di musica
  I Florence, 1933 33 FLOR
  II Florence etc., 1937 37 FLOR
  III Florence, 1938 38 FLOR
  IV Florence, 1939 *
  V Florence, 1948 48 FLOR
  VI Florence, 1949 49 FLOR
  see also 50 FLOR
Congresso internazionale di musica sacra *see* International Church Music Congress
Congresso internazionale di psicologia *see* International Congress of Psychology
Congresso internazionale di scienze storiche *see* Congrès international des sciences historiques
Congresso internazionale di studi bizantini *see* International Congress of Byzantine Studies
Congresso internazionale di studi verdiani
  I Venice, 1966 66 VEN
  II Verona etc., 1969 69 VER
  III Milan, 1972 72 MIL
Congresso italiano di musica 21 TUR
Congresso nazionale delle (di) tradizioni popolari (Congresso nazionale di arti e tradizioni popolari)
  I Florence, 1929 29 FLOR
  II Udine, 1931 31 UDIN
  III Trento, 1934 34 TRT
  IV Venice, 1940 40 VEN
  V Turin, 1948 48 TUR
  VI Cagliari, etc 1956 56 CAG
  VII Chieti 1957 57 CHIE
Congressus ethnographicus in Hungaria 63 BUD
Conseil international de la musique *see* International Music Council
Conseil international de la musique populaire *see* International Folk Music Council
Conséil international de la philosophie et des studies humanistiques 65 COP
Consejo interamericano de música *see* Inter-American Conference on Ethnomusicology
Conselho Cientifico para a Africa ao Sul do Sara 56 STOM
Conservatorul de muzică 'Ciprian Porumbescu', Bucharest 67 BUC
Consociatio internationalis musicae sacrae, Rome 66 CHIC, 75 ROM
Contemporary Music Theatre 64 HAM
Contribution à l'étude des origines de l'opera 70 MTA

Convegni del Centro di studi sulla spiritualità medievale
  I Todi, 1957   57 TOD
  II Todi, 1958   58 TOD
  IV Todi, 1961   61 TOD
  V Todi, 1962   62 TOD
  VI Todi, 1963   63 TOD
  XIII Todi, 1972   72 TOD
Convegno internazionale di studi musicali   73 SIE, 74 SIE, 75 SIE
Convegno (inter)nazionale di studi sul Rinascimento
  II Florence,   1939   39 FLOR
  VI Florence etc.,   1961   61 FLOR
Corelli   68 FUS
Couperin Conference   69 PAR
Creating a Wider Interest in Traditional Music   67 BERL
Critics   47 PRA, 67 GRA
Cultures méditerranéens d'influence arabo-berbère   72 MALT
Cultura musicale e teatrale italiana nella Parigi illuministica   75 SIE
Czech Music   70 BRN

Dante   65 RAV
Debussy   62 PAR
Department of Music, Harvard University   57 CAM/M, 61 CAM/M
Department of Music, School of Performing Arts at Brooklyn College, City University of New York   74 NEWY²
Department of University Extension, University of British Columbia   67 VAN
Deputazione di storia patria per le province parmensi   68 PARM
Deputazione di storia patria per l'Umbria, Centro di documentazione sul movimento dei disciplinati   69 PER
Deutsche Akademie der Künste, Berlin: Abteilung Arbeiterlied   64 BERL
Deutsche Gesellschaft für Psychologie *see* Kongress der Deutschen Gesellschaft für Psychologie
Deutsche Gesellschaft für Volkskunde, Leipzig   65 MARB
Deutsche Literatur des späten Mittelalters   73 HAM
Deutsche Musikgesellschaft   25 LEIP
Deutsche Orgelkunst   27 FRE/S
  see also Freiburger Tagung für deutsche Orgelkunst
Deutscher Kongress für Kirchenmusik   27 BERL
Deutscher Volkskundekongress   65 MARB
Deutsche UNESCO-Kommission, Cologne   71 HIN
Deutsches historische Institut in Rom: Musikgeschichtliche Abteilung   69 ROM, 74 ROM
Deutsch-italienisches Kulturinstitut in Süd-Tirol, Merano   63 MER
Disciplinati   69 PER
Disques   67 ZAG
Dokumentation in den historischen Wissenschaften   71 KAS
Dokumentation musikgeschichtlicher Objekte   71 KAS
Dolore e la morte nella spiritualità dei secoli XII e XIII   68 TOD
Don Carlos/Don Carlo   69 VER
Dramaturgie et société   67 NAN
Dufay   74 NEWY²
Duomo di Milano   68 MIL

East and West   61 TOK, 64 NEWD²
Échelles musicales   60 PAR¹
École pratique des hautes-études, Paris   72 MALT
Ecos del Magrib   39 FEZ
Editions: folk music *see* International Folk Music Council: Studiengruppe zur Erforschung und Edition älterer Volksmusikquellen
Einheimische Musik und ihre mögliche Verwendung in Liturgie und Verkündigung   75 ROM
Electro-Acoustics   53 NET, 67 PAR
Enesco   73 BUC
Équipe de recherches théâtrales et musicologiques *see* Centre nationale de la recherche scientifique
E.R.A.T.T.O., Centre de recherches pluridisciplinaires, Ivry sur Seine   73 PAR
Esthétique *see* International Congress on Aesthetics and Kongress für Ästhetik und allgemeine Kunstwissenschaft
Ethnology, Ethnography   63 BUD, 63 STT, 71 STP, 75 AUS
  see also International Congress of Anthropological and Ethnological Sciences
Ethnomusicologie (Colloques de Wégimont)
  I Wégimont, 1954   54 WÉG
  II Wégimont, 1956   56 WÉG
  III Wégimont, 1958   58 WÉG
  IV Wégimont, 1960   58 WÉG
Ethnomusicology   67 VAN, 73 ROM², 75 ROM
  see also Ethnomusicologie, Folk, Inter-American Conference on Ethnomusicology and Slovenská akadémie vied: Etnomuzikologický seminár
Etnografia   63 STT
Ethnomusicologia in Italia   73 ROM²
Etnomuzikologický seminár *see* Slovenská akadémie vied: Etnomuzikologický seminár
Étude du Baroque *see* Journées internationales d'étude du Baroque
Étude du XVIIIᵉᵐᵉ siècle en Belgique   35 BRUS¹
Études balkaniques   66 SOF
Études byzantines *see* International Congress of Byzantine Studies
Études humanistes   72 TOU
Études sur la musique du XIXᵉ siècle   70 STGE
Europa et Hungaria   63 BUD
European Liszt Centre   75 EIS
Expanding Horizons in African Studies   68 EVA
Experimental phonetics   30 BON
Experimental Psychology *see* Kongress für experimentelle Psychologie and Kongress der Deutschen Gesellschaft für Psychologie
Exposition internationale de Rome   11 ROM
Exposition internationale des arts et techniques de 1937, Paris   37 PAR¹
Exposition universelle de 1900   00 PAR¹, 00 PAR²
Expressionisme dans le théâtre européen   68 STRS

Fachtagung zur Erforschung der Blasmusik   74 GRA²
Facoltà di lettere, Università di Siena   73 SIE, 74 SIE, 75 SIE
Febvre   75 STRS
Federatie van kringen voor oudheidkunde en geschiedenis van Belgie Vzw.   74 STN
Fédération archéologique et historique de Belgique
  Congresses
  XVII Dinant,   1903   03 DIN
  XXI Liège,   1909   09 LIÈ
  XXII Malines,   1911   11 MAL
  XXIII Ghent,   1913   13 GHE
  XXVI Bruges,   1925   25 BRUG
  XXVII Antwerp,   1930   30 ANT
  XXIX Liège,   1932   32 LIÈ
  XXXI Namur,   1938   38 NAM
  XL Liège,   1968   68 LIÈ
  XLIII St Niklaas, 1974   74 STN
Fédération des cercles d'archéologie et d'histoire de Belgique Asbl.   74 STN

Feiern zum 200. Jahrestag der Geburt Ludwig van Beethovens 70 PIE
Festival de Montauban 63 MTA
Fêtes de la Renaissance
   I Royaumont, 1955 55 ROY
   II Brussels etc., 1957 57 BRUS
   III Tours, 1972 72 TOU
Fêtes et cérémonies de Charles Quint 57 BRUS
Filharmonia pomorska imienia Ignacego Paderewskiego *see* Musica antiqua (Europae orientalis)
Film 50 FLOR
Filosofia *see* International Congress of Philosophy
Folk 00 PAR⁵, 28 PRA, 37 PAR⁴, 54 PAL, 61 TEH, 65 BERL², 65 MARB, 71 HIN, 71 STP, 73 ANK
   see also Arts popularies, Congresso nazionale delle tradizioni popolari, Ethnology, Ethnomusicology, Ethnomusicologie (Colloques de Wégimont), (Grazer) Balkanologen-Tagung, International Congress for Folk-Narrative Research, International Folk Music Council, Traditional Music, Traditions popularies
Folk-narrative research *see* International Congress for Folk-Narrative Research
Fondazione Giorgio Cini, Venice 63 VEN, 70 VEN, 73 VEN, 74 VEN
   Istituto di lettere musica e teatro 57 VEN¹, 72 VEN
   Istituto di storia dell'arte 57 VEN²
Föredrag och diskussionsinlägg från nordiskt kollokvium III 75 ESP
Fortuna musicale e spettacolare della fiabe di Carlo Gozzi 74 SIE
Fragen der Aufführungspraxis und Interpretation von Instrumentalmusik 74 BLA
Fragen der Arbeiterliedforschung 64 BERL
Fragen des Instrumentariums, der Besetzung und der Improvisation 75 BLA
Freiburger Tagung für deutsche Orgelkunst
   I Freiburg im Breisgau, 1926 26 FRE/B
   II Freiburg im Breisgau, 1938 38 FRE/B
   see also 27 FRE/S
Freie Universität, Berlin 74 BERL
Frugoni 68 PARM

GFM Gesellschaft für Musikforschung
Galpin Society 59 CAM
Gefühl und Wille 36 JEN
Gegenwärtige ethnomusikologische Forschung in der Slowakei 70 TRČ
Geige in der europäischen Volksmusik 71 STP
Georges Enesco Research Centre, Romanian Academy of Social and Political Sciences 73 BUC
Georg Philipp Telemann, ein bedeutender Meister der Aufklärungsepoche 67 MAG
Germanisches Nationalmuseum, Nuremberg 69 NUR
Geschichtsbild in deutschen und italienischen Sprachraum 63 MER
Gesellschaft der Orgelfreunde 51 OCH, 54 STAD
Gesellschaft für Ästhetik und allgemeine Kunstwissenschaft *see* Kongress für Ästhetik und allgemeine Kunstwissenschaft
Gesellschaft für experimentelle Psychologie *see* Kongress für experimentelle Psychologie
Gesellschaft für Musikforschung 50 LEIP, 67 KAS, 74 BERL
   Congresses
   Lüneburg, 1950 50 LÜN¹
   Bamberg, 1953 53 BAM
   Hamburg, 1956 56 HAM
   Kassel, 1962 62 KAS
   Leipzig, 1966 66 LEIP
   Bonn, 1970 70 BON

Gesellschaft zur Erforschung und Förderung der Blasmusik 74 GRA²
Gesellschaft zur Herausgabe von Denkmälern der Tonkunst in Österreich 56 VIE, 70 VIE
Gilbert and Sullivan 70 LAW
Gluck 73 SIE
Goldoni 57 VEN¹
Gonzaga 74 MANT
Gozzi 74 SIE
(Grazer) Balkanologen-Tagung
   I Graz, 1964 64 GRA²
   II Graz, 1966 66 GRA
   III Graz, 1968 68 GRA
Gregorian chant 05 STRS
Groupe de recherches sur le théâtre *see* Centre national de la recherche scientifique

Hacia Calderón 69 EXE
Hamburger Telemann-Gesellschaft 67 KAS
Handel 59 HAL
Händel-Ehrung der Deutschen Demokratischen Republik 59 HAL
Hard-Core Ethnography 75 AUS
Harvard University: Department of Music 57 CAM/M, 61 CAM/M
Haydn 09 VIE, 59 BUD, 70 GRA, 71 EIS
Hebrew University of Jerusalem 61 JER
Helsingfors Universitet Institutionen för praktisk teologi 75 ESP
Heutige Probleme der Volksmusik 71 HIN
Histoire comparée 00 PAR², 00 PAR³
Histoire de l'art 21 PAR, 64 BON
Histoire des sciences *see* Congrès international d'histoire des sciences
Historical Science *see* Congrès international des sciences historiques
History of Science *see* Congrès international d'histoire des sciences
Hochschule für Musik und darstellende Kunst in Graz *see* Akademie für Musik und darstellende Kunst in Graz
Hochschule für Musik und darstellende Kunst in Stuttgart 71 STU
Hochschüle für Musik und darstellende Kunst in Wien: Institut für Volksmusikforschung 71 STP
Hudba národů 47 PRA
Humanities, Computers for 65 NEWH
Hungarian Academy of Sciences *see* Magyar tudományos akadémia
Hungarian Music Council 71 BUD¹
Hungarian Section of the International Society for Contemporary Music 71 BUD¹

IAML International Association of Music Libraries
IFMC International Folk Music Council
IMC International Music Council
IMDT International Institute for Music, Dance and Theatre in the Audio-Visual Media
IMS International Musicological Society
IMZ Internationales Musikzentrum
IVMB Internationale Vereinigung der Musikbibliotheken
Iacopone e il suo tempo 57 TOD
ICA-Congress *see* International Congress on Acoustics
Incontro con la musica (in Polonia) italiana e polacca
   I Parma etc., 1969 69 PARM
   II Bologna, 1970 70 BOL
   III Warsaw, 1971 71 WAR
   IV Bardolino, 1972 71 WAR
   V Bologna, Bydgoszcz, 1973 *
   VI Bologna, 1974 74 BOL

Indiana University 68 SVE
Indian Council for Cultural Relations 64 NEWD[2]
Indian Tribes of Aboriginal America 49 NEWY[1]
Influence étrangères dans l'oeuvre de W. A. Mozart 56 PAR
Informatique musicale 73 PAR
Institute of Literary Research, Polish Academy of Sciences 69 WAR
Institut de rythmique de Genève 26 GEN
Institute for Studies in American Music at Brooklyn College, City University of New York 74 NEWY[1]
Institute of Germanic Studies, University of London 66 OXF[2], 73 HAM
Institut français de Florence: Section d'histoire musicale 11 ROM
Institut für Ältere Deutsche Philologie der Philipps-Universität, Marburg 66 OXF[2], 70 WÜR, 73 HAM
Institut für Aufführungspraxis der Hochschule für Musik und darstellende Kunst in Graz 70 GRA, 71 GRA, 72 GRA
Institut für österreichische Kulturgeschichte 71 EIS
Institut für Volksmusikforschung an der Hochschule für Musik und darstellende Kunst in Wien 71 STP
Institut für Wertungsforschung an der Akademie (Hochschule, from 1970) für Musik und darstellende Kunst in Graz 67 GRA, 74 GRA[1]
Institut international d'anthropologie *see* Congrès international d'anthropologie et d'archéologie préhistorique
Institut international de cooperation intellectuelle 28 PRA
Institutionen för praktisk teologi vid Helsingfors Universitet: Allmänna sektionen för praktisk teologi 75 ESP
Institut Jaques-Dalcroze, Geneva 65 GEN
Instrumental Music 54 PAR[1], 57 CAM/M, 70 BOL, 74 BLA, 74 GRA[2]
Instrumentarium, Besetzung und Improvisation 75 BLA
Instruments 59 CAM, 67 PAR, 69 NUR, 70 ANT, 71 GRA, 72 GRA, 75 BLA
  see also International Folk Music Council: Study Group on Folk Musical Instruments
Instytut badań literackich, Polska akademia nauk 69 WAR
Instytut muzykologii, Uniwersytet warszawski *see* Incontro con la musica italiana e polacca
Inter-American Composers 65 BLM
Inter-American Conference on Ethnomusicology
  I Cartagena de Indias, 1963 63 CART
  II Bloomington,   1965 65 BLM
Inter-American Music Council (CIDEM) *see* Inter-American Conference on Ethnomusicology
International Association for (of) Byzantine Studies *see* International Congress of Byzantine Studies
International Association of Music Libraries 53 BAM, 73 WEIM
  see also International Congress of Music Libraries
International Association of South-East European Studies 66 SOF
International Center for Typographic Arts 65 CARB
International Church Music Congress
  Congrès international de musique sacrée – Congresso internazionale di musica sacra – Internationaler Kongress für Kirchenmusik
  I Rome,   1950 50 ROM
  II Vienna,   1954 54 VIE
  III Paris,   1957 57 PAR
  IV Cologne, 1961 61 COL
  V Chicago,   1966 66 CHIC
  see also Internationaler Kongress für Kirchenmusik in Bern
International Commission on Acoustics, International Union of Pure and Applied Physics *see* International Congress on Acoustics
International Congress for Folk-Narrative Research
  [I] Kiel, Copenhagen, 1959 59 KIE
  IV Athens,   1964 64 ATH
International Congress of Aesthetics *see* International Congress on Aesthetics
International Congress of Americanists
  Congrès international des Américanistes – Congreso (Congresso) internacional de Americanistas – Congresso internazionale degli Americanisti – Internationaler Amerikanisten-Kongress
  XII Paris,   1900 –
  XIII New York,   1902 –
  XIV Stuttgart,   1904 04 STU
  XV Quebec,   1906 06 QUE
  XVI Vienna,   1908 08 VIE
  XVII Buenos Aires,   1910 –
  XVIII London,   1912 –
  XIX Washington,   1915 15 WAS
  XX Rio de Janeiro,   1922 22 RIO
  XXI The Hague etc., 1924 –
  XXII Rome,   1926 26 ROM
  XXIII New York,   1928 28 NEWY
  XXIV Hamburg,   1930 30 HAM[1]
  XXV La Plata,   1932 32 LAP
  XXVI Seville,   1935 –
  XXVII Mexico, Lima, 1939 39 MEX
  XXVIII Paris,   1947 47 PAR
  XXIX New York,   1949 49 NEWY[1]
  XXX Cambridge,   1952 52 CAM
  XXXI São Paolo,   1954 –
  XXXII Copenhagen,   1956 –
  XXXIII San José,   1958 58 SJOS
  XXXIV Vienna,   1960 –
  XXXV Mexico,   1962 62 MEX
  XXXVI Spain,   1964 –
  XXXVII Mar del Plata, 1966 –
  XXXVIII Stuttgart etc., 1968 –
  XXXIX Lima,   1970 70 LIM
  XL Rome, Genoa,   1972 72 ROM
International Congress of Anthropological and Ethnological Sciences
  Congrès international des sciences anthropologiques et ethnologiques
  I London,   1934 –
  II Copenhagen,   1938 38 COP
  III Brussels,   1948 48 BRUS
  IV Vienna,   1952 52 VIE
  V Philadelphia, 1956 56 PHIL
  VI Paris,   1960 60 PAR[2]
  VII Moscow,   1964 64 MOS
  VIII Tokyo, Kyoto, 1968 68 TOK[2]
International Congress of Byzantine Studies
  Congrès international (d') des études byzantines – Congresso internazionale di studi bizantini
  I Bucharest,   1924 –
  II Belgrade,   1927 27 BEL
  III Athens,   1930 30 ATH
  IV Sofia,   1934 34 SOF
  V Rome,   1936 36 ROM
  (VI Algiers,   1939 39 ALG)
  VI Paris,   1948 48 PAR[2]

VII Brussels, 1948 –
VIII Palermo, 1951 51 PAL
IX Thessaloniki, 1953 53 THE
X Istanbul, 1955 55 IST
XI Munich, 1958 –
XII Okhrida, 1961 61 OKH
XIII Oxford, 1966 66 OXF[1]
International Congress of Music Libraries
Congrès international des bibliothèques musicales
I Florence, 1949 *
II Lüneburg, 1950 50 LÜN[2]
III Paris, 1951 51 PAR
IV Brussels, 1955 55 BRUS
V Cambridge, 1959 59 CAM
VI Stockholm etc., 1962 62 STOC
VII Dijon, 1965 65 DIJ
VIII New York, etc., 1968 68 NEWY
IX St-Gall, 1971 71 STGA
X Jerusalem 1974 74 JER
see also 53 BAM, 73 WEIM
International Congress of Musicology 39 NEWY
International Congress of Orientalists
Congrès international des orientalistes –
Internationaler Orientalisten-Kongress
XIII Hamburg, 1902 02 HAM
XIV Algiers, 1905 05 ALG
XVIII Leiden, 1931 31 LEID
XXI Paris, 1948 48 PAR[1]
XXIII Cambridge, 1954 54 CAM
XXIV Munich, 1957 57 MUN
XXVI New Delhi, 1964 64 NEWD[1]
International Congress of Philosophy
Congrès international de philosophie – Congresso internazionale di filosofia
IV Bologna, 1911 11 BOL
V Naples, 1924 24 NAP
VIII Prague, 1934 34 PRA
X Amsterdam, 1948 48 AMS
XI Brussels, 1953 53 BRUS
International Congress of Phonetic Sciences
I Amsterdam, 1932 32 AMS
III Ghent, 1938 38 GHE
VI Prague, 1967 67 PRA
International Congress of Psychology
Congrès international de psychologie – Congresso internazionale di psicologia
IV Paris, 1900 00 PAR[4]
V Rome, 1905 05 ROM
VI Geneva, 1909 09 GEN
VII Oxford, 1923 –
VIII Groningen, 1926 26 GRON
IX New Haven, 1929 29 NEWH
X Copenhagen, 1932 32 COP
XI Paris, 1937 37 PAR[2]
XII Edinburgh, 1948 48 EDIN
XIII Stockholm, 1951 51 STOC
International Congress on Acoustics (ICA-Congress)
Congrès international d'acoustique
I Netherlands, 1953 53 NET
II Cambridge, Mass., 1956 56 CAM/M
III Stuttgart, 1959 59 STU
IV Copenhagen, 1962 62 COP
V Liège, 1965 65 LIÈ
VI Tokyo, 1968 68 TOK[1]
VII Budapest, 1971 71 BUD[2]
VIII London, 1974 74 LON
International Congress on (of) Aesthetics
Congrès international d'esthétique – Congresso internazionale di estetica
I Berlin, 1913 13 BERL
II Paris, 1937 37 PAR[3]

III Venice, 1956 56 VEN
IV Athens, 1960 60 ATH
V Amsterdam, 1964 64 AMS
VI Uppsala 1968 68 UPP
International Council for Philosophy and Humanistic Studies 65 COP
Internationale Arbeitstagung der Study Group of Folk Musical Instruments *see* International Folk Music Council
Internationale Gesellschaft der Musikbibliotheken *see* International Congress of Music Libraries
Internationale Gesellschaft für experimentelle Phonetik 30 BON
Internationale Gesellschaft für Musikwissenschaft *see* International Musicological Society
Internationale Heinrich-Schütz-Gesellschaft 67 KAS
Internationale Musikgesellschaft *see* Congress of the International Musical Society
Internationale Musikwissenschaftliche Konferenz (59 BUD), 61 BUD
Internationale Orgelwoche, Nuremberg 73 NUR
Internationaler Amerikanisten-Kongress *see* International Congress of Americanists
Internationaler Kongress der Volkserzählungsforscher *see* International Congress for Folk-Narrative Research
Internationaler Kongress für (Katholische) Kirchenmusik *see* International Church Music Congress
Internationaler Kongress für Kirchenmusik in Bern
I Berne, 1952 52 BERN
II Berne, 1962 62 BERN
III Berne, 1972 72 BERN
Internationaler Kongress für Schubertforschung 28 VIE
Internationaler Musikrat *see* International Music Council
Internationaler Orientalisten-Kongress *see* International Congress of Orientalists
Internationales Institut für vergleichende Musikstudien und Dokumentation, Berlin 65 BERL[2], 67 BERL
Internationales Musikologische Symposium 70 PIE
Internationales musikzentrum 67 ZAG
Interationales Seminar marxistischer Musikwissenschaftler
I Prague, 1963 63 PRA
II Berlin, 1965 65 BERL[1]
Internationale Stiftung Mozarteum 31 SAL
Internationale Tagung von Restauratoren für besaitete Tasteninstrumente 71 GRA
Internationale Vereinigung der Musikbibliotheken *see* International Congress of Music Libraries
International Federation of Libraries Associations: International Section for Performing Arts Libraries and Museums 65 AMS
International Folk Music Council
Studiengruppe zur Erforschung und Edition älterer Volksmusikquellen (Study Group on Historical Sources of Folk Music)
I Freiburg im Breisgau, 1967 *
II Brno, 1970 *
III Sárospatak, 1972 72 SÁR
Study Group of Folk Music Systematization (Study Group on Analysis and Systematization of Folk Music)
I Bratislava, 1965 65 BRA
II Vienna, 1966 *
III Radziejowice, 1967 67 RAD
IV Stockholm, 1969 *
V Bled, 1971 71 BLE

VI Krpáčová, 1974 74 KRP
Study Group on Folk Musical Instruments
    I Budapest, 1964 *
    II Brno, 1967 67 BRN[1]
    III Stockholm, 1969 69 STOC
    IV Balatonalmádi, 1973 73 BAL
    V Brunnen, 1975 75 BRUN
Comitato italiano 73 ROM[2]
International Institute for Comparative Music Studies
    and Documentation, Berlin 65 BERL[2], 67
    BERL
International Institute for Music, Dance and Theatre in
    the Audio-Visual Media 70 HAMM, 72 VIE[2]
International Institute of Intellectual Co-operation 28
    PRA
International Musical Festival, Brno *see* Colloquia on
    the History and Theory of Music at the In-
    ternational Musical Festival in Brno
International Musical Society *see* Congress of the In-
    ternational Musical Society
International Music Centre (IMZ), Vienna 67 ZAG
International Music Council (Conseil international de
    musique, Internationaler Musikrat) 61 TEH,
    66 MANL, 67 BERL
    Congresses
    IV Hamburg, 1964 64 HAM
    VI New York, 1968 68 NEWY
    VII Moscow, 1971 71 MOS
International Musicological Society (International Soci-
    ety for Musical Research)
    Internationale Gesellschaft für Musikwissenschaft –
    Société internationale de musicologie
    Congresses
    I Liège, 1930 30 LIÈ
    II Cambridge, 1933 *
    III Barcelona, 1936 *
    IV Basle, 1949 49 BAS
    V Utrecht, 1952 52 UTR
    VI Oxford, 1955 *
    VII Cologne, 1958 58 COL
    VIII New York, 1961 61 NEWY
    IX Salzburg, 1964 64 SAL
    X Ljubljana, 1967 67 LJU
    XI Copenhagen, 1972 72 COP
    see also 39 NEWY
    Symposia
    I St Germain-en-Laye, 1970 70 STGE
    II Zagreb, 1974 74 ZAG
    see also Ars nova italiana del trecento
International Section for Performing Arts Libraries and
    Museums, Federation of Libraries Associ-
    ations 65 AMS
International Society for Contemporary Music: Hun-
    garian Section 71 BUD[1]
International Society for Folk-Narrative Research *see*
    International Congress for Folk-Narrative
    Research
International Society for Musical Research *see* Inter-
    national Musicological Society
International Society of Music Libraries *see* Inter
    national Congress of Music Libraries
International Society of Phonetic Sciences *see* Inter-
    national Congress of Phonetic Sciences
International Theatre Studies Center 70 LAW
International Union of Anthropological and Ethnologi
    cal Sciences *see* International Congress of
    Anthropological and Ethnological Sciences
International Union of Pure and Applied Physics: In-
    ternational Commission on Acoustics *see* In-
    ternational Congress on Acoustics

International West African Conference
    Conférence internationale des Africanistes de l'ouest –
    Conferencia internacional de Africanistas
    occidentales – Conferência internacional dos
    Africanistas ocidentais
    I Dakar, 1945 45 DAK
    II Bissau, 1947 47 BIS
    III Ibadan, 1949 –
    IV Santa Isabel, 1951 51 STIS
    V Abidjan, 1953 –
    VI São Tomé, 1956 56 STOM
Interprétation de la musique française 69 PAR
Isham Memorial Library 57 CAM/M, 61 CAM/M
Istituto Accademico di Roma 73 ROM[2]
Istituto culturale italo-tedesco in Alto Adige,
    Merano 63 MER
Istituto di lettere musica e teatro, Fondazione Giorgio
    Cini 57 VEN[1], 72 VEN
Istituto di storia della musica e dello spettacolo 73
    SIE, 74 SIE, 75 SIE
Istituto di storia dell'arte, Fondazione Giorgio Cini 57
    VEN[2]
Istituto di storia delle tradizioni popolari dell'Università
    di Roma 73 ROM[2]
Istituto di studi musicali e teatrali, Università di
    Bologna *see* Incontro con la musica italiana e
    polacca
Istituto di studi verdiani, Parma *see* Congresso inter-
    nazionale di studi verdiani
Istituto musicale F. Canneti, Vicenza 71 VIC
Istituto nazionale di studi sul Rinascimento, Flor-
    ence 61 FLOR
Istituto per la storia dell'arte lombardia 68 MIL
Istituto veneto di scienze lettere ed arti 57 VEN[1], 73
    VEN, 74 VEN
Italia Venezia e Polonia 70 VEN
Ives 74 NEWY[1]

Janáček 58 BRN, 65 BRN, 68 BRN
Japanese Music-Dramas 71 ANN
Jewish Studies *see* World Congress of Jewish Studies
Joseph Haydn und seine Zeit 71 EIS
Josquin des Prez 71 NEWY
Journées internationales d'étude du Baroque
    I Montauban, 1963 63 MTA
    II Montauban, 1966 66 MTA
    III Montauban, 1968 68 MTA
    IV Montauban, 1970 70 MTA
Jumièges 54 ROU
Junge Haydn 70 GRA

Katholische Gelehrter 00 MUN
Katholische Kirchenmusik 54 VIE
Kirchenmusik *see* Church Music
Kirchenmusik in ökumenischer Schau 62 BERN
Kirchenmusik und das II. Vatikanische Konzil 64
    GRA[1]
Klangliche Aspekt beim Restaurieren von Saitenklav-
    ieren 71 GRA
Klassifikation *see* International Folk Music Council:
    Study Group of Folk Music Systematization
Kongelige danske videnskabernes selskab 65 COP
Kongress der Deutschen Gesellschaft für Psychologie
    (continuation of Kongress für experimentelle
    Psychologie)
    XI Vienna, 1929 –
    XII Hamburg, 1931 31 HAM
    XIII Leipzig, 1933 33 LEIP
    XIV Tübingen, 1934 34 TÜB
    XV Jena, 1936 36 JEN
    XVI Bayreuth, 1938 38 BAY

Kongress der Internationalen Musikgesellschaft *see* Congress of the International Musical Society
Kongress für Ästhetik und allgemeine Kunstwissenschaft
  I Berlin,   1913 13 BERL
  II Berlin,   1924 24 BERL
  III Halle,   1927 27 HAL
  IV Hamburg, 1930 30 HAM²
Kongress für experimentelle Psychologie (continued as Kongress der Deutschen Gesellschaft für Psychologie)
  I Giessen,   1904 04 GIE
  II Würzburg,   1906 –
  III Frankfurt, 1908 08 FRA
  IV Innsbruck, 1910 10 INN
  V Berlin,   1912 12 BERL
  VI Göttingen, 1914 14 GÖT
  VII Marburg, 1921 –
  VIII Leipzig, 1923 23 LEIP
  IX Munich,   1925 25 MUN
  X Bonn,   1927 27 BON
Kunstgeschichte 64 BON
see also Art
Kunsttradition und audio-visuelle Medien 70 HAMM

Ländergruppe DDR of the International Association of Music Libraries 73 WEIM
Landeskundliche Abteilung des Musikwissenschaftlichen Instituts der Universität Kiel 63 KIE
Langue et littérature du midi de la France *see* Congrès international de langue et littérature du midi de la France
Leben und Werk W. A. Mozarts 56 PRA
Leoš Janáček a soudobá hudba 58 BRN
Lezione di Toscanini 67 FLOR
Libraries 29 ROM, 53 BAM, 54 PAL, 65 AMS, 73 WEIM
see also International Congress of Music Libraries
Libraries and Museums of the Performing Arts 65 AMS
Lieu théâtral à la Renaissance 63 ROY
Linguaggio musicale 71 VIC
Liszt 61 BUD, 75 EIS
Liturgy 65 MTS, 66 CHIC, 75 ROM
Luth et sa musique 57 NEU/S

Magdeburger Telemann-Festtage
  I Magdeburg, 1962 62 MAG
  II Magdeburg, 1965 (festival only)
  III Magdeburg, 1967 67 MAG
  IV Magdeburg, 1970 (festival only)
  V Magdeburg, 1973 73 MAG
see also 72 BLA
Maggio musicale fiorentino 50 FLOR, 67 FLOR, 71 FLOR
see also Congresso (internazionale) di musica
Magrib 39 FEZ
Magyar tudományos akadémia
  I Budapest, 1959 59 BUD
  II Budapest, 1961 61 BUD
Malaysian Society for Asian Studies 69 KUA
Manierismo, barocco, rococò 60 ROM
Manierismo in arte e musica 73 ROM¹
Mantova e i Gonzaga nella civiltà del Rinascimento 74 MANT
Manzoni, Venezia e il Veneto 73 VEN
Martinů 66 BRN
Marxist Musicologists *see* Internationales Seminar marxistischer Musikwissenschaftler
Max-Reger-Institut (Elsa-Reger-Stiftung), Bonn-Bad

Godesberg 73 NUR
Medieval 66 OXF², 70 WÜR, 73 HAM
see also Convegni del Centro di studi sulla spiritualità medievale
Medieval Drama 69 BIN
Mediterranean Studies of Arabo-Berber Influence 72 MALT
Mélanges colombaniens 50 LUX
Melodramma nel seicento 72 VEN
Mémoires de musicologie sacrée 00 PAR⁶
Men and Cultures 56 PHIL
Methoden der ethnomusikologischen Analyse 74 KRP
Methoden der Klassifikation von Volksliedweisen 65 BRA
Mezhdunarodniy kongress antropologicheskikh i etnograficheskikh nauk *see* International Congress of Anthropological and Ethnological Sciences
Mezinárodní hudební festival *see* Colloquia on the History and Theory of Music at the International Musical Festival in Brno
Mezinárodní sjezd skladatelů a hudebních kritiků 47 PRA
Milleterarasi Bizans Tetkikleri Kongresi Tebliğleri 55 IST
Modern Composer and his World 60 STRT
Monestir de Montserrat 65 MTS
Monteverdi 67 SIE, 68 VEN
Moravské Museum, Brno 65 BRN
Moroccan Music 39 FEZ
Mozart 31 SAL, 56 PAR, 56 PRA, 56 VIE, 74 ROM
Musica antiqua colloquium Brno 67 BRN²
Musica antiqua (Europae orientalis)
  I Bydgoszcz etc., 1966 66 BYD
  II Bydgoszcz,   1969 69 BYD
  III Bydgoszcz,   1972 72 BYD
  IV Bydgoszcz,   1975 75 BYD
Musica bohemica et Europaea 70 BRN
Musica cameralis 71 BRN
Musica e arte figurativa nei secoli X–XII 72 TOD
Musica indigena 75 ROM
Musica marroquí 39 FEZ
Music and Communication 68 NEWY¹
Music and Technology 70 STOC
Music and Word 69 BRN
Musica nel film 50 FLOR
Musica occidentale e le civiltà musicali extraeuropee 71 FLOR
Musica sacra *see* Church Music
Musica strumentale e vocale strumentale dal Rinascimento al Barocco 70 BOL
Musica vocale e voco-strumentale del seicento 71 WAR
Music East and West 61 TOK, 64 NEWD²
Musikethnologisches Symposion 75 ROM
Musiche popolari mediterranee 54 PAL
Music in the Americas 65 BLM
Music Libraries and Instruments 59 CAM
Musicologie sacrée 00 PAR⁶
Musicology and the Computer 65 NEWY
Musicology 1966–2000: A Practical Program 65 NEWY
Musics of Asia 66 MANL
Musikgeschichtliche Abteilung des Deutschen historischen Instituts in Rom 69 ROM, 74 ROM
Musikkritik 47 PRA, 67 GRA
Musiktheorie 70 BERL¹, 71 STU
Musik und Wort 69 BRN
Musikwissenschaftliche Kolloquien der Internationalen Musikfestivale in Brno *see* Colloquia on the History and Theory of Music at the International Musical Festival in Brno

Musikwissenschaftlicher Kongress der deutschen Musik-
gesellschaft 25 LEIP
Musikwissenschaftlicher Kongress in Basel 24 BAS
Musikwissenschaftliches Institut der Universität Frei-
burg im Breisgau *see* Freiburger Tagung für
deutsche Orgelkunst
Musique africaine 70 YAO
Musique contemporaine française 11 ROM
Musique des nations 47 PRA
Musique et poésie au XVIᵉ siècle 53 PAR
Musique instrumentale de la Renaissance 54 PAR¹
Musique populaire *see* Folk
Musique sacrée *see* Church Music
Musique sacrée, chant et orgue 37 PAR¹
Muzïkal'nïye kul'turi narodov 71 MOS
Muzyka wokalna i wokalno-instrumentalna XVII
wieku 71 WAR

National Music Council of the Philippines 66 MANL
National şi universal in muzică 67 BUC
Neue Schweizerische Musikgesellschaft: Ortsgruppe
Basel 24 BAS
New Patterns of Musical Behaviour 72 VIE²
Norddeutsche und nordeuropäische Musik 63 KIE
Nordiskt kollokvium I 75 ESP
Nord-Sud 65 COP
Northwestern University, Evanston: Program of African
Studies 68 EVA

Opera w dawnej Polsce 69 WAR
Operni dilo Leoše Janáčka 65 BRN
Organ 27 FRE/S, 32 STRS, 37 PAR¹, 51 OCH, 54
STAD
see also Colloquium der Walcker-Stiftung (für orgel-
wissenschaftliche Forschung) and Freiburger
Tagung für deutsche Orgelkunst
Orgel *see* Organ
Orgelbewegung und Historismus 54 STAD
Orgel im Gottesdienst heute 74 SINZ
Orgel und Orgelmusik heute 68 THU
Orgue *see* Organ
Orientalists *see* International Congress of Orientalists
Orientalische Elemente am Balkan 66 GRA
Österreichische Akademie der Wissenschaften 56 VIE,
70 VIE
Österreichische Gesellschaft für Musik 72 VIE¹
Oswald von Wolkenstein 73 NEU/B

Paderewski Pomeranian Philharmonia *see* Musica
antiqua (Europae orientalis)
Pagine 71 WAR
Pan-American Union: Music Division *see* Inter-
American Conference on Ethnomusicology
Parigi illuministica, Cultura musicale e teatrale italiana
nella 75 SIE
Parma/Parmense 68 PARM
Pellegrinaggi e culto dei santi in Europa 61 TOD
Pepragmena tou d' diethnous synedriou aisthētikēs 60
ATH
Pepragmena tou th' diethnous byzantinologikou syned-
riou 53 THE
Performing Arts 65 AMS
Personalité artistique de Georges Enesco 73 BUC
Petrarca, Venezia e il Veneto 74 VEN
Philipps-Universität, Marburg: Institut für Ältere De-
utsche Philologie 66 OXF², 70 WÜR, 73
HAM
Philosophy 65 COP
see also International Congress of Philosophy
Phonetics *see* International Congress of Phonetic
Sciences

experimental 30 BON
Il pianoforte 21 TUR
Plain-chant grégorien 32 STRS
Poetry, Poetics 53 PAR, 55 ARR, 60 WAR², 68 MTA
Polish Academy of Sciences *see* Polska akademia nauk
Polska akademia nauk 60 WAR², 63 VEN, 69 WAR,
70 VEN
see also Incontro con la musica italiana e polacca
Polsko-włoskie materiały muzyczne 71 WAR
Pontificio istituto di musica sacra 50 ROM
Preservation of Traditional Forms 61 TEH
Probleme interdisziplinärer Afrikanistik 69 MARB
Probleme mittelalterlicher Überlieferung und Text-
kritik 66 OXF²
Problèmes d'acoustique 65 LIÈ
Program of African Studies, Northwestern University,
Evanston 68 EVA
Psychologie des Gemeinschaftslebens 34 TÜB
Psychology *see* International Congress of Psychology
experimental *see* Kongress der Deutschen Gesell-
schaft für Psychologie and Kongress für expe-
rimentelle Psychologie

Radio, musique et société 54 PAR²
Rapport sur la musique contemporaine française 11
ROM
Reflexionen über Musikwissenschaft heute 70 BON
Records 67 ZAG
Recueil des travaux de congrès du musique arabe 32
CAIR
Reger 73 NUR
Renaissance 62 ROY, 63 ROY, 74 MANT
see also Convegno (inter)nazionale di studi sul Rinas-
cimento and Fêtes de la Renaissance
Renaissance dans les provinces du Nord 54 ARR
Résonance dans les échelles musicales 60 PAR¹
Restauratieproblemen van Antwerpse klavecimbels 70
ANT
Rhythm
I Geneva, 1926 26 GEN
II Geneva, 1965 65 GEN
Rinascimento *see* Renaissance
Risultati e prospettive della ricerca sul movimento dei
Disciplinati 69 PER
Rivista musicale italiana 21 TUR
Romanian Academy of Social and Political Sciences 62
SIN
Georges Enesco Research Centre 73 BUC
Romanian National Commission of UNESCO 62 SIN
Romanische Element am Balkan 68 GRA
Royal University of Malta 72 MALT
Ruckers-Genootschap, Antwerp 70 ANT

SIM Société internationale de musicologie
Sacred Music *see* Church Music
Sacred Music and Liturgy Reform after Vatican II 66
CHIC
Santa Cecilia 21 TUR
Schallplatten 67 ZAG
Schönberg 74 BERL
School of Music, Yale University 74 NEWY¹
Schubert 28 VIE
Schweizerische musikforschende Gesellschaft Orts-
gruppe Basel 49 BAS
Sciences historiques *see* Congrès international des
sciences historiques
Scientific Council of Africa South of the Sahara 56
STOM
Scola Cantorum 00 PAR⁶
Section d'histoire musicale de l'Institut français de

Florence 11 ROM
Seminario di studi ricerche sul linguaggio musicale 71 VIC
Semiotics of Music 73 BEL
Sesja poświęcona muzyce polskiej i włockiej 71 WAR
Settecento parmense 68 PARM
Shakespeare 1971 71 VAN
Simon Fraser University 67 VAN, 71 VAN
Singen und Sprechen 38 FRA
Situazione e prospettive degli studi verdiani nel mondo 66 VEN
Sitzung der Studiengruppe für die Systematisierung von Volksweisen *see* International Folk Music Council
Slavischen Musik, Anfänge der 64 BRA
Slovak Academy of Sciences *see* Slovenská akadémie vied
Slovenská akadémie vied
  Etnomuzikologický seminár
    I Trenčin 1970 70 TRČ
    V Krpáčová, 1974 74 KRP
  Symposia
    I Bratislava, 1964 64 BRA
    II Bratislava, 1965 65 BRA
Slowakische Akademie der Wissenschaften *see* Slovenská akadémie vied
Società di etnografia italiana, Rome 48 TUR, 56 CAG, 57 CHIE
Società di studi romagnoli 65 RAV
Società italiana di musicologia 67 SIE
Società piemontese di archeologia e belle arti 69 CAS
Société archéologique de Namur 03 DIN
Société de l'histoire de l'art français 21 PAR
Société de l'histoire du protestantisme français 72 PAR
Société des amis du Prince de Ligne 35 BRUS[2]
Société française de musicologie 65 DIJ
Société internationale de musicologie *see* International Musicological Society
Société internationale de musique *see* Congress of the International Musical Society
Société internationale des bibliothécaires musicaux *see* International Congress of Music Libraries
Société savante d'Alsace et des régions de l'est 75 STRS
Sound and Man 56 CAM/M
Sources: folk music *see* International Folk Music Council: Studiengruppe zur Erforschung und Edition älterer Volksmusikquellen
Southeast Asia 69 KUA
Spiritualità cluniacense 58 TOD
Spiritualità medievale *see* Convegni del Centro di studi sulla spiritualità medievale
Spontini 51 IES
Staatliche Akademie für Kirchen- und Schulmusik in Charlottenburg, Berlin 27 BERL
Staatliches Institut für Musikforschung Preussischer Kulturbesitz 70 BERL[1]
Stage Works of Bohuslav Martinů 66 BRN
State University of New York at Binghamton: Center for Medieval and Early Renaissance Studies 69 BIN
Stendhal 67 PARM
Stiftung Mozarteum 31 SAL
Stil and Überlieferung in der Kunst des Abendlandes 64 BON
Storiografia nel mondo italiano 63 MER
Strasbourg au coeur religieux du XVIᵉ siècle 75 STRS
Studia musico-museologica 69 NUR
Studi bizantini *see* International Congress of Byzantine

Studies
Studi corelliani 68 FUS
Studiengruppe für die Systematisierung von Volksweisen *see* International Folk Music Council
Studiengruppe zur Erforschung und Edition älterer Volksmusikquellen *see* International Folk Music Council
Studien zur Musik des 19. Jahrhunderts 70 STGE
Studi e ricerche sul linguaggio musicale 71 VIC
Studies on 19th-Century Music 70 STGE
Studi goldoniani 57 VEN[1]
Studi italo-tedeschi 63 MER
Study Group of Folk Music Systematization *see* International Folk Music Council
Study Group on Folk Musical Instruments *see* International Folk Music Council
Súčasný stav etnomuzikologického bádania na Slovensku 70 TRČ
Südtiroler Kulturinstitut 73 NEU/B
Svaz československých skladatelů 56 PRA, 65 BRN
  see also 47 PRA
Symposion für Musikkritik 67 GRA
Symposium musico-ethnologicum 75 ROM
Symposium on Cherokee and Iroquois Culture 58 WAS
Symposium on Form in Performance, Hard-Core Ethnography 75 AUS
Symposium on Local Diversity in Iroquois Culture 49 NEWY[2]
Syndicat des compositeurs tchèques 47 PRA
Syndicat des industries electroniques de reproduction et d'enregistrement, Paris 67 PAR
Syndikát českých skladatelů 47 PRA
Systematization, Systematisierung *see* International Folk Music Council
Szymanowski 62 WAR

Tagung für deutsche Orgelkunst 27 FRE/S
  see also Freiburger Tagung für deutsche Orgelkunst
Tasso 54 FER
Teatro communale, Florence 71 FLOR
Teatro e la musica di Giuseppe Verdi 72 MIL
Technology 70 STOC
Telemann 72 BLA
  see also Magdeburger Telemann-Festtage
Telemann-Kammerorchester, Blankenburg, Harz: Wissenschaftliche Arbeitstagung
  I Blankenburg, 1972 72 BLA
  II Blankenburg, 1974 74 BLA
  III Blankenburg, 1975 75 BLA
Telemann und die Musikerziehung 73 MAG
Terminologie der Musik des 20. Jahrhunderts 72 FRE/B
Theatre 59 ROY, 62 ROY, 63 ROY, 64 HAM, 67 NAN, 68 STRS
Théâtre musical contemporain 64 HAM
Théâtres d'Asie 59 ROY
Theory of Music 70 BERL[1], 71 STU
Torquato Tasso 54 FER
Toscanini 67 FLOR
Tradition artistique face aux moyens audio-visuels 70 HAMM
Traditional Drama and Music of Southeast Asia 69 KUA
Traditional Music 65 BERL[2], 67 BERL, 69 KUA
  see also Folk
Tradition im Umkreis der Wiener Schule 74 GRA[1]
Traditions populaires 00 PAR[5]
  see also Folk

Tradizioni popolare   *see* Folk and Congresso nazionale delle (di) tradizioni popolare
Tragédies de Sénèque   62 ROY
Trecento   *see* Ars nova italiana del trecento
Tunisian Ministry of Cultural Affairs   70 HAMM
Turkish Folklore Meeting   73 ANK

Über Musiktheorie   70 BERL[1]
Uluslararası Türk Folklor Semineri   73 ANK
UNESCO   70 STOC, 70 YAO
  Deutsche UNESCO-Kommission   71 HIN
  National Commission of the Philippines   66 MANL
  Romanian National Commission   62 SIN
  US National Commission   68 NEWY
  see also International Association of Music Libraries, International Folk Music Council, International Music Council, International Society for Contemporary Music: Hungarian Section
Union internationale des orientalistes   *see* International Congress of Orientalists
Union internationale des sciences anthropologiques et ethnologiques   *see* International Congress of Anthropological and Ethnological Sciences
Union internationale d'histoire et de philosophie des sciences   *see* Congrès international d'histoire des sciences
Union of Czechoslovak Composers   56 PRA, 65 BRN
  see also 47 PRA
Union of Yugoslav Composers   68 SVE
Università di Bologna: Istituto di studi musicali e teatrali   *see* Incontro con la musica italiana e polacca
Università di Roma: Istituto di storia delle tradizioni popolari   73 ROM[2]
Università di Siena: Facoltà di lettere   73 SIE, 74 SIE, 75 SIE
Universita J. E. Purkyně, Brno   65 BRN
Universität Freiburg im Breisgau: Musikwissenschaftliches Institut   *see* Freiburger Tagung für deutsche Orgelkunst
Universität Kiel: Landeskundliche Abteilung des Musikwissenschaftlichen Instituts   63 KIE
Université de Strasbourg   32 STRS
  see also Centre d'études germaniques   68 STRS
Université de Tours: Centre d'études supérieures de la Renaissance   72 TOU
University of British Columbia   71 VAN
  Department of University Extension   67 VAN
University of London: Institute of Germanic Studies   66 OXF[2], 73 HAM
University of Michigan: Center for Japanese Studies, Center for Chinese Studies, School of Music and Speech Department   71 ANN
University of Southern Illinois at Carbondale   65 CARB
University of Texas: College of Fine Arts, College of Social and Behavioral Sciences and Office of the President   75 AUS
Uniwersytet warszawski   62 WAR
  see also Incontro con la musica italiana e polacca
  see also City University of New York, Freie Universität, Berlin, Harvard University, Helsingfors Universitet, Indiana University, Northwestern University, Royal University of Malta, State University of New York at Binghamton, West Virginia University and Yale University
Veneranda fabbrica del Duomo   68 MIL
Venezia e il melodramma nel seicento   72 VEN
Venezia e la Polonia   63 VEN
Verdi   69 ROM
  see also Congresso internazionale di studi verdiani
Vereinigung von Afrikanisten in Deutschland   69 MARB
Violinspiel und Violinmusik in Geschichte und Gegenwart   72 GRA
Visages et perspectives de l'art moderne   55 ARR
Vision 65   65 CARB
Vita musicale dell'Italia d'oggi   21 TUR
Volkserzählungsforscher   *see* International Congress for Folk-Narrative Research
Volksmusik   *see* Folk
Volksmusik südosteuropas   64 GRA[2]

Wagner   69 ROM
Walcker-Stiftung   (für   orgelwissenschaftliche Forschung)   *see* Colloquium der Walcker-Stiftung (für orgelwissenschaftliche Forschung)
Warsaw University   62 WAR
  see also Incontro con la musica italiana e polacca
Webern   72 VIE[1]
Webern Society, USA   72 VIE[1]
Weimarer Tage für Musikbibliothekare   73 WEIM
Weltkongress der Musikbibliotheken   *see* International Congress of Music Libraries
West Africa   *see* International West African Conference
West Virginia University   66 MOR
Wiener Schule   74 GRA[1]
Wissenschaftliche Bachtagung   50 LEIP
Wolkenstein, Oswald von   73 NEU/B
World Congress of Jewish Studies
  III Jerusalem 1961   61 JER
  IV Jerusalem 1965   65 JER
  V Jerusalem 1969   69 JER
World Union of Jewish Studies   *see* World Congress of Jewish Studies

Yale University   65 NEWH
  School of Music   74 NEWY[1]
Yugoslav Academy   74 ZAG
Yugoslav-American seminar on Music   68 SVE

Zeitgenössisches Musiktheater   64 HAM
Zemlinsky   74 GRA[1]

INDEX OF AUTHORS AND EDITORS

codes in italics indicate editors of that congress
c = chairman   p = panel contribution   d = participation in discussion
a number in brackets indicates more than one paper given

Aarburg U   50 LÜN[1]
Aber A   25 LEIP
Abert A A   50 LÜN[1], 56 HAM, 61 NEWY, 62 KAS (c), 67 SIE, 68 VEN, 69 ROM, 70 BON, 72 MIL, 74 ROM
Abert H   06 BAS, 09 VIE, 24 BAS, 24 BERL
Abiuso V   40 VEN
Abraham G   *58 COL*, 60 WAR[1], 61 BUD, 61 NEWY (c), 64 SAL (c)
Abraham L U   64 SAL (p), 70 BON, 71 STU
Abrahams R   75 AUS
Acerenza E   55 BRUS
Achille T E   57 PAR
Adamčiak M   74 KRP
Adamis M   72 COP
Adams J C   66 VEN (2), 69 VER (2), 72 MIL
Adkins C   72 COP
Adler F   54 PAR[2]
Adler G   09 VIE, 11 LON, 24 BAS, 25 LEIP (1; c)
Adler I   65 JER, 67 BERL, *74 JER*
Adler J   81 JER
Adler W   71 STGA (p)
Adorno T W   67 GRA
Adriaansz W   67 VAN
Aebi W   71 BUD[2] (2)
van Aerde R   11 MAL, 13 GHE
Agustoni L   50 ROM, 57 PAR
Ahrens J   50 ROM, 57 PAR
Aikin W A   09 VIE
Akhobadze V V   63 BUD, 64 MOS
Alaleona D   21 TUR
Albersheim G L   64 SAL (2p), 70 BON
Alberti G   50 ROM
Alberti L   75 SIE
Albertini A M   57 CHIE
Albrecht H   49 BAS, *50 LÜN[1]*, *50 LÜN[2]*
Albrecht J   70 PIE
Albuquerque W   61 COL, 75 ROM
Alcini J   57 PAR

Aldrich P   58 COL
Alekseev A   60 WAR[1]
Alekseev E Y [Alekseev E Ye]   64 MOS, 72 VIE[2]
Alexandrescu L–M   73 BUC
Alfaiate Marvão A   63 STT
Alford V   28 PRA
Alisky M   54 PAR[2]
Allihn I   73 MAG
Allen W A   74 LON
Allende U   28 PRA
Allorto R   56 VIE, 66 VEN, 68 VEN
Allroggen G   73 SIE, 74 ROM
Almeida R   70 YAO
d'Almendra J   54 VIE, 62 PAR (2)
Alonso M R   69 VER
Alphonce B   72 COP
Altar C M   56 VIE
Altenburg D   74 GRA[2], 75 EIS
Alvares V   61 COL
Altisent M   50 ROM, 65 MTS
Altmann W   24 BAS, 25 LEIP, 27 VIE
Alvares V   61 COL
Amades J   54 PAL (3)
Amaradeva W D   66 MANL
Ambrožić-Paić A   72 VIE[2]
Ameller A   71 MOS
Amelli P   05 STRS
Ameln K   49 BAS, 53 BAM, 62 BERN
de Amezua G   57 PAR
Amfitheatrof D   50 FLOR
Ammannati L F   69 VER
Amon K   64 GRA[1]
Anderluh A   65 MARB
Andersen G P   54 STAD
Anderson K   59 CAM
Andersson O   09 VIE (2), 11 LON (2)
Ando Y   68 TOK[1]
Andoyer   05 STRS
Andraschke P   67 RAD, 70 BRN
Andrejev [Andrejew] A   58 BRN, 67 BRN[2]
Andrén Å   75 ESP
Andreychin L   60 WAR[2]

Andriessen L   74 NEWY[1] (p)
Angermüller R   70 BON
Anglas J   11 ROM
Anglès H [1]   24 BAS, 25 LEIP, 27 VIE, 30 LIÈ, 49 BAS (2), *50 ROM*, 52 UTR, 53 BAM, 54 PAL, 54 VIE, 56 VIE, 57 PAR, 58 COL, 61 NEWY, 62 BERN
Aning B A   72 COP
Annegarn A   62 STOC
Annen F   54 PAR[2]
Anschütz G   24 BERL, 50 LEIP (1; c)
Ansermet E   49 FLOR, 62 PAR (2), 65 GEN, 67 FLOR
Antcliffe H   09 VIE, 11 LON
Antoniadis S   30 ATH
Antonowycz [Antonowytch, Antonowytsch] M   52 UTR, 57 PAR, 61 NEWY, 64 SAL (p), 71 NEWY (1; p)
Apel W   55 WÉG, 60 WAR[1], 64 SAL (p), 68 VEN, 72 TOD, 75 BYD
Apfel E   62 KAS
Appia A   25 LEIP
Aramon y Serra R   28 PRA
Arcangeli P   73 ROM[2]
Archer W K   *61 TEH*, 61 TEH, 65 BERL[2]
del Arco y Garay R   28 PRA (2)
Aretz I   58 SJOS, 63 CART, 65 BLM, 72 COP
Arima D   61 TOK
Armstrong R G   64 SAL (p)
Arnella J   65 MTS
Arnheim A   09 VIE, 11 LON, 13 GHE
Arnold D   58 COL, 68 VEN
Arom S   67 BERL, 73 BEL, 74 JER (p)
Arrizabalaga J M   65 MTS
Arro E   64 BRA, 75 BYD
Artmeier A   71 HIN
Arvidson P   72 VIE[2]
Ashley L R N   70 LAW
Ashton R   *64 NEWD[2]*, 64 NEWD[2]

259

Asselbergs A 64 AMS
Ataman S Y 73 ANK
Atanassov V 73 BAL, 75 BRUN
Atayan [Atajan] R A 64 MOS, 69 BYD, 75 BYD
Atehortúa B 65 BLM
Atlas A W *74 NEWY*[2]
Attilâ O 73 ANK
von der Au H 50 LÜN[1]
Aubrun C V 63 ROY
Aubry P 00 PAR[2], 00 PAR[6] (2), 09 VIE
Auda A 30 LIÈ, 37 PAR[1]
Auler W 38 FRE/B
Auriol [Busser H] 37 PAR[1]
Austerlitz R 60 WAR[2]
Austin W W 61 NEWY, 62 PAR, 67 LJU, 70 BON, 71 MOS
Avenary H 61 JER, 64 SAL (p), 65 JER, 69 JER, 72 COP
Ayestarán L 63 CART, 65 BLM
de Azevedo L H C 54 PAL, 61 NEWY (1;c), 62 PAR, 64 SAL (p), 65 BLM

Babbitt M 61 NEWY, 64 SAL (c), 68 NEWY (c)
Babitz S 62 KAS, 70 BON
Bachmann W 56 HAM, 64 BRA
Bačinskaja N M 74 KRP
Badings H 60 STRT
Badura-Skoda E 58 COL, 67 BRN[2], 70 BON, 70 BRN, 70 GRA, 72 COP
Baensch O 27 HAL
Baggiani G 74 NEWY[1] (p)
Bahle J 32 COP, 33 LEIP, 34 TÜB, 36 JEN, 37 PAR[2]
Bailey R 72 COP
Baillie H 57 BRUS
Bain W C 68 SVE
Bainchi G 40 VEN
Baines A 59 CAM
Bajer J 69 BRN, 70 BRN
Bake A A 49 BAS, 50 LÜN[1], 53 BAM, 58 COL
Balan G 68 UPP
Balandier G 47 BIS
Ballarà J 65 MTS
Ballin E D H 61 COL
Ballmann W 25 LEIP
Ballová L' 70 BERL[2], 70 BON, *70 PIE*, 72 BYD, 74 KRP
Balthasar K 25 LEIP
Barassi F 71 WAR
Barbag-Drexler I 75 EIS
Barbaud P 73 PAR
Barbi M 34 TRT
Barblan G 50 ROM, 56 VIE, 66 VEN, 67 SIE, 69 VER, 72 MIL, 74 ROM
Barbour J M 64 SAL (p)
Bar-Dayan H 61 JER
Bardolet S 65 MTS
Barfüss F 60 WAR[1]
Bargainnier E F 70 LAW
Barini G 03 ROM (2), 11 LON (c)
Barkechil M 50 COL, 60 MARS (2), 60 PAR[1], 61 TEH, 67 BERL

Barnes J 69 NUR, 70 ANT, 71 GRA
Baron J H 70 BON, 72 COP
Baroni M 73 BEL
Barraqué J 62 PAR
Barros M 56 STOM
Bartels I 70 BON
Bartha D 50 LEIP, 56 PAR, 56 VIE, 58 COL, *59 BUD*, 59 BUD, 60 PAR[1], 62 PAR, 64 SAL (c)
Barthelemy M 68 LIÈ
Barth-Wehrenalp R 72 COP
Bartók B 28 PRA
Bártová J 65 BRN, 66 BRN, 71 BRN (1;p)
Baruch G W 50 LÜN[1]
Bas G 21 TUR
Baselt B 66 LEIP, 67 MAG, 75 BLA
Basile 57 PAR
Basso A 60 WAR[1], 74 ROM
Baud-Bovy S 54 PAL, 61 TEH, 75 BRUN
Baudin G 11 ROM
Baudot 00 PAR[1] (2)
Bauer M 25 LEIP, 27 HAL
Bauer W M 71 EIS
Bauer-Mengelberg S 65 NEWY
Bauman R 75 AUS
Baumann M P 75 BRUN
Bautier-Régnier A-M 54 ARR
Bayard S P 39 NEWY
Bayart 13 GHE
Bayer B 61 JER, *74 JER*, 74 JER
Beard H R 69 VER
Beatty R T 30 BON
Beaud P 72 VIE[2], 74 ZAG
Beaudouin E 37 PAR[3]
Becerra G 65 BLM
Becherini B 55 BRUS, 55 WÉG, 56 VIE, 57 TOD, 58 COL, *59 CER*, 59 CER (2), 60 WAR[1]
Beck C 37 FLOR
Beck H 56 VIE, 62 KAS, 70 BON
Beck L 67 ZAG
Becker H 62 KAS, 67 MAG, 69 STOC, 70 BON, 73 BAL
Becker-Glauch I 50 LÜN[2], 70 GRA
Becking G 24 BAS, 24 BERL, 25 LEIP, 32 AMS
Beckmann K 70 BON, 72 COP
Beckwith J *60 STRT*, 74 NEWY[1] (p)
Béclard d'Harcourt M 26 ROM, 57 PAR
Bédard H 70 ANT
Beerli C A 55 ROY
Béhague G 75 AUS (p;d)
Behrend W 09 VIE
Bek J 70 BRN
Bekker P 33 FLOR
Bekku S 61 TOK
Belardinelli A 51 IES (2)
Beldie J P 74 LON
Bellas J 65 STAV
Bellina A L 73 VEN, 74 VEN
Bello J 69 VER, 70 BON
Belotti G 70 VEN, 74 BOL

Bělský V 67 BRN[2]
Belvianes M 54 PAR[2]
Belyayev V M 64 BRA, 64 MOS (1;d)
Belz C 72 VIE[2]
Belza I 60 WAR[1] (2)
Benary P 62 KAS (2), 75 EIS
Benedetti-Michelangeli F 54 PAR[1]
Benedito R 28 PRA
Benet S 65 MTS
Benttson A F V 64 MOS (d)
Bengtsson I 47 PRA, 62 KAS, 63 KIE, 64 SAL (p), 67 LJU (p), 69 STOC
Bennedik F 25 LEIP
Benoit R 74 NEWY[1] (p)
Bent I D 72 COP
Bent M 67 LJU (p), 72 COP
Bente M 66 LEIP
van Benthem J 71 NEWY
Benton R 59 CAM, 62 STOC
Beranek L L 59 STU, 62 COP
Bérenger de Miramon 32 STRS
Berger R 66 VEN, 74 KRP
Bergmann R 62 KAS
Bergmann W 59 CAM, 67 MAG
Bergmans P 09 LIÈ (2), 11 MAL, 25 BRUG (1;c), 27 VIE
Bergsagel J 72 COP, 75 ESP
Berio L 60 STRT
Berlin I 66 VEN
Bernard J J 73 PAR
Berner A 50 LÜN[1], 53 BAM, 58 COL, 64 SAL (p), 69 NUR, 70 ANT, 71 KAS
Bernet Kempers K P 30 LIÈ, 32 AMS, 49 BAS, 56 VIE, 61 NEWY (c), 62 KAS (1;c), 64 AMS
Bernhardt K-F 56 HAM
Bernoulli E 06 BAS, 09 VIE (2), 11 LON, 21 PAR, 24 BAS
Bernzott P 65 NEWY
de Bertha A 11 LON
Berthier P 37 PAR[1]
Besseler H 26 FRE/B, 38 FLOR, 49 BAS, 50 LEIP, 50 LÜN[1], 50 ROM, 52 UTR, 53 BAM, 56 VIE, 59 BUD, 66 LEIP (p)
Besser J 70 BERL[2]
Beuerle H-M 71 STU
Bévenot L 50 ROM
Bewerunge H 11 LON
Beylin P 67 LJU (p)
Beyschlag S 73 NEU/B
Beythien J 66 LEIP
Bezić J 67 LJU (p), 74 ZAG
Bhatia V 61 TOK
Bianchi G 48 FLOR
Bianconi L 68 VEN, 70 BON, 72 VEN, 73 ROM[1]
Biber W 74 GRA[2]
Bickerdike J 74 LON
Biegański K 60 WAR[1], 67 LJU
Biehle H 24 NAP, 27 VIE, 30 LIÈ
Biehle J 11 LON, 37 PAR[3]
Bielawski L 60 WAR[1], 62 WAR, 65 BRA, 67 RAD (3), 74 KRP

Bienenfeld E   09 VIE
Bierl R   53 NET, 65 LIÈ
Biggs E P   56 CAM/M
Bihan J   57 PAR
Billeter B   68 THU
Bimberg S   56 HAM, 56 VIE, 65 BERL[1]
Binkley T E   57 NEU/S
Birembaut A   56 FLOR
Birkner G   60 WAR[1], 62 KAS, 71 KAS
Birsan M   67 BUC
Bismarck G   71 BUD[2]
Björkvall G   75 ESP
Bladier B   58 MARS
Blancafort G   65 MTS
Blank L   74 GRA[2]
Blankenburg W   50 LEIP, 52 BERN, 56 HAM, 58 COL, 62 BERN, 72 COP, 73 NUR
Blasetti A   50 FLOR
Blaukopf K   48 AMS, 59 STU, 67 KAS, *67 ZAG*, 67 ZAG, *70 HAMM*, 70 STOC, 71 MOS, 72 VIE (2)
Blémont E   00 PAR[5]
Blinowa M   64 SAL (p)
Blomdahl K-B   60 STRT, 64 HAM
Blum K   54 PAR[2]
Blume F   27 FRE/S, 51 PAR, 53 BAM, 55 BRUS, 60 ROM, 62 KAS, 67 LJU, 67 SIE, 70 BON, 71 NEWY
Bockholdt R   70 BON, 72 COP
Böckl R   71 STU
Bodky E   52 UTR
Bodnár G   61 BUD
Boehmer K   70 BON (2), 72 COP
Boepple P   24 BAS
Boetticher W   50 LÜN[1], 53 BAM, 56 HAM, 56 VIE, 57 NEU/S, 58 COL (1;c), 60 WAR[1], 61 NEWY, 62 KAS, 70 BON
Boghen F   21 PAR
Böhme E W   31 SAL
Böhme R   75 BLA
Böhringer H   51 OCH, 54 STAD
Böker-Heil N   71 KAS, 71 STU, 72 COP (2)
Bokesová Z   47 PRA
Boll A   64 HAM
Bollert W   56 VIE, 70 BON
Bollini G   40 VEN
Bologna P   71 STGA (p)
Bomm U   50 ROM, 62 BERN, 64 GRA[1], 66 CHIC
Bonal M D   65 MTS
Bonaventura A   00 PAR[2], 03 ROM, 29 FLOR, 29 ROM
Bonavia F   33 FLOR
Bondeville E   37 FLOR
Bonelli L   21 PAR
Bónis F   61 BUD, 66 BYD, 70 BON, 71 BUD[1]
Bonnerot J   28 OSL
Bonnet A   50 ROM
Bonnet J   37 PAR[1]
Bonta S   72 COP

Bontempelli M   38 FLOR
Bontinck I   *72 VIE[2]*, 72 VIE[2], 74 ZAG
Boorman S   72 COP
Booth M R   70 LAW
Boretz B   64 SAL (p)
Borghezio G   21 PAR, 25 BRUG
Borisowa-Tonschewa E   75 BYD
Bornefeld H   72 BERN
Bornoff J   61 TEH, 64 HAM, 67 ZAG (c)
Boronkay A   75 EIS
Borrel E   54 PAL
Borrelli E   48 FLOR, 49 FLOR
Borrelli N   28 PRA
van den Borren C   09 LIÈ, 11 MAL, 21 PAR, 23 BRUS, 24 BAS, 25 BRUG (2), 30 LIÈ, 32 LIÈ, 52 UTR, 54 ARR, 55 WÉG
Borris S   50 LEIP (1;c), 50 LÜN[1], 60 WAR[1], 62 KAS, 64 HAM, 66 LEIP (p), 71 MOS
Bors I   72 BERN
Boruttau   38 FRA
Bose F   53 BAM, 58 COL, 62 KAS, 67 BERL, 71 BRN
Böser F   26 FRE/B
Bösken F   51 OCH
Bosonnet F R   70 BON
Bossarelli Mondolfi A
   see Mondolfi-Bossarelli A
Boston N   59 CAM
Botuscharoff L   74 KRP
Boulay L   69 PAR
Bouman A   38 FRE/B
Bovet   26 GEN
Bowles E A   64 SAL (p), 65 NEWH
Boxer H   68 NEWY (c)
Boyden D D   58 COL, 72 BYD, 72 GRA
Bragard R   32 LIÈ, 61 TEH
Brǎiloiu C   37 PAR[4], 49 BAS, 54 PAL (2), 54 WÉG, 58 COL
Brandenburg S   70 BON (2)
Brandl R   71 STP, 75 BRUN
Brandsma E   09 VIE
Brata S   67 BERL
Braubach M   70 VIE
Braun H   71 BLE, 72 SÁR, 74 KRP
Braun W   59 HAL, 62 KAS, 63 KIE, 64 SAL (p), 66 LEIP, 67 LJU, 70 BERL[1], 70 BON
Bräutigam   38 FRA
Brazhnikov M   66 BYD
Breazul G   56 VIE
Brediceanu T   28 PRA
Bredl M   71 HIN
Brednich R W   64 ATH
Breh K   67 ZAG
Brehmer F   25 MUN
Breig W   63 KIE, 72 FRE/B
Breitweiser E   71 STGA (p)
Brelet G   54 PAR[2]
Brencher K-E   50 LÜN[1]
Brenet M   00 PAR[2], 11 ROM
Brenn F   37 PAR[3], 49 BAS (2), 58

COL, 62 KAS
Brennecke W   *53 BAM*, 54 PAR[1], 60 WAR[1]
Bresgen C   72 VIE[1], 73 NEU/B
Breton A C   08 VIE
Breuer J   *71 BUD[1]*, 71 BUD[1]
de Bricqueville E   11 ROM
Bridgman N   53 PAR, 54 ARR, 54 PAL, 57 BRUS, 59 CER, 61 CAM/M, 61 NEWY, 69 CER, 71 NEWY, 72 TOD
Brillouin J   37 FLOR, 58 MARS
Briner A   58 COL
Brinkman R   70 BON (2), 72 FRE/B, 72 VIE[1] (1;p), 73 NUR, 74 BERL
Briquet M   56 VIE, 58 COL
Bristiger M   54 PAR[2], 65 WAR, 69 PARM (2), 70 BOL, 70 BON, *71 WAR*, 71 WAR (2), 74 BOL
Britten V   55 BRUS
Britton A P   61 NEWY
Brixel E   *74 GRA[2]*, 74 GRA[2]
Brizi B   72 VEN
Brock H   59 HAL
Brockbernd B   57 PAR
Bröcker M   75 BRUN
Brockett C W   72 COP
Brockhaus H A   65 BERL[1], 66 LEIP, *70 BERL[2]*, 70 BERL[2], 72 COP
Brockhoff M E   49 BAS, 52 UTR
Brockpähler R   75 BRUN
Broder N   57 CAM/M (p), 61 NEWY (c)
Broeckx J L   70 ANT
Brömse P   71 STU
Bronzini G B   48 TUR
Brook B S   64 SAL (2p), 65 DIJ (3;p), *65 NEWY*, 65 NEWY (2), 66 MOR, 67 LJU (p), 72 COP, 74 ZAG
Brooks W   74 NEWY[1]
Brou L   50 ROM
Brown A P   72 COP
Brown E   74 NEWY[1] (c)
Brown H M   61 CAM/M, 67 LJU (1;p), 71 NEWY (1;c)
Brown M H   *68 SVE*
Bruce N   74 NEWY[1]
Bruger H D   25 LEIP
Brugnoli A   21 TUR
Brun   37 PAR[1]
Brün H   70 STOC
Brune J A   71 STP
Brunet   69 KUA (4)
Bruni M   66 VEN
Brunner A   62 BERN
Brunold P   21 PAR
Brunyate R   *75 AUS*
Bucchi V   49 FLOR
Buchanan A M   39 NEWY
Buchner A   61 BUD, 67 BRN[2], 71 WAR, 75 BYD
Bücken E   25 LEIP, 28 VIE, 38 FLOR
Buckley A   75 BRUN
Buckley J   69 VER

Budde E 70 BON, 72 VIE¹ (l;p), 74 BERL
Budden J 69 VER, 72 MIL
Bughici D 67 BUC
Bugiel V 31 PAR
Buhle E 06 BAS
Bukofzer M F 37 PAR³, 39 NEWY, 49 BAS, 52 UTR, 54 WÉG
Bundi G 24 BAS
Burchenal E 28 PRA
Burde W 68 BRN
Burgeat M 67 PAR
Burlas Ł 61 BUD, 64 SAL (p), 70 TRČ, 71 BUD¹, 74 KRP
Burlasová S 70 TRČ (2)
Burlingham Hill E 21 PAR
Burris-Meyer H 59 STU
Burssens A 38 GHE
Busch H J 70 BON, 72 MIL
Bush A 47 PRA, 59 HAL
Bush Jones J 70 LAW
Bussi F 67 SIE
Busser H see Auriol
Busson M 50 ROM
Bust G 73 MAG
Buttitta A 73 ROM²
Bužga J 62 KAS, 67 LJU
Buzzati D 67 FLOR

Cadieu M 66 VEN, 74 NEWY¹(p)
Caffagni M 70 BOL
Caffarelli F 51 IES (3)
Cagli B 75 SIE
Caglio E M 68 MIL
Cahn P 70 BON
Cairati 38 FRA
Calame B 71 BUD²
Callahan V W 71 NEWY
Calmus G 09 VIE
Calvocoressi M D 11 LON (1;c)
Cambissa G 63 MER
Cametti A 03 ROM
Camilleri C 72 MAL
Cammarota L 72 VEN
Campbell R 70 LIM
Campeanu P 72 VIE²
Campogalliani E 74 MANT
Campos R M 39 MEX
Camps G 65 MTS
Canac F 60 PAR¹, 61 TEH, 65 LIÈ
Canat de Chizy 00 PAR¹
Canessa F 72 MIL
Capaccioli E 70 BOL
Cape S 54 PAR¹
Capiow T 54 PAR²
Carapezza P E 70 BOL, 73 ROM¹, 75 BYD
Caravaglios C 34 TRT
Carceller P 65 MTS
Cardine E [J] 50 ROM, 54 VIE, 57 PAR
Cardozo B L 71 BUD²
Carducci-Agustini E 50 ROM, 54 VIE
Carillo J 00 PAR², 11 LON
Carli Ballola G 73 SIE (2), 74 ROM
Carlson R 67 VAN

Carner M 67 FLOR, 70 BON, 71 FLOR
Carpitella D 56 CAG, 57 CHIE, 60 PAR², 71 FLOR, 73 BEL, *73 ROM²*, 73 ROM²
Carraud G 11 ROM
Carraz P 50 ROM
Carrière 58 MARS
Carter E 61 TOK
Cary G 68 NEWY (c)
Casals J 65 MTS
Casella A 33 FLOR, 37 FLOR, 38 FLOR
Casini C 74 SIE
Castellà M C 65 MTS
Castellengo M 65 LIÈ, 67 PAR, 68 TOK¹, 71 BUD², 74 LON
Castrillo Hernandez G 28 PRA
Casulleras J 65 MTS
Cattaneo E 50 ROM
Cattin G 69 CER
Cauchie M 27 VIE, 30 LIÈ
Caula G A 66 VEN, 69 VER
Cavalcanti A 37 FLOR
Cavallini E 47 PRA
Cavazzuti E 50 FLOR
Cavicchi A 66 VEN, *68 FUS*, 68 FUS (2), 68 VEN, 69 VER, 72 VEN
Cè N 68 VEN
Cella F 72 MIL
Celletti R 66 VEN, 69 ROM, 69 VER, 72 MIL
Cellier A 32 STRS (2)
Cellier M 71 HIN
Cerha F 72 VIE¹ (p)
Černohorská M 58 BRN
Černý J 70 BRN, 75 BYD
Černý M K 65 BERL¹, 69 BRN, 70 BERL², 70 BON, 70 BRN, 70 PIE, 71 BRN (p)
Cervelli L 54 PAL, 58 COL, 69 NUR
Cervera J M 65 MTS
Cervera M 65 MTS
Cesari G 09 VIE, 21 TUR, 33 FLOR
Chailley J 52 UTR, 53 PAR, 54 PAR², 54 ROU, 54 VIE, 56 VIE, 57 PAR, 58 COL (1;c), 58 MARS (2), 58 WÉG, 60 PAR¹ (4), 60 WAR¹ (2), 61 NEWY (c), 61 TEH (1;c), 62 PAR, 67 BERL (c), 67 PAR, 69 PAR (2)
Chaillon P 54 ARR
Chainaye S 60 WAR¹
Chalupka L' 74 KRP
de Chambure Mme H see Thibault G
Chamrath G C 55 BRUS
Chaniecki Z 75 BYD
Chao Feng 61 BUD
Charles D 64 AMS
Charlier C 30 LIÈ, 32 LIÈ
Charnassé H *73 PAR*, 73 PAR
Charpentier J 61 TEH
Chase G 39 NEWY, 70 NEWY (c), 72 VIE¹

Chechlińska Z 60 WAR¹, 74 BOL
Cherbuliez A-E 24 BAS, 26 GEN (2), 31 SAL (3), 38 ZUR
Chérion 00 PAR¹
Chevais M 37 PAR⁴
Chevreuille P 64 HAM
Chiarini L *50 FLOR*
Chiarucci H 65 LIÈ
Chigi Saracini G 21 PAR
Chilesotti O 00 PAR², 03 ROM (2), 09 VIE
Chilkovsky N 56 PHIL
Chini T 70 BOL
Chkhikvadze G Z 64 MOS
Chlubna O 58 BRN
Chmara B 60 WAR¹
Chodkowski A 69 PARM, 69 WAR, 70 BERL², 70 BOL, 70 BON, 71 WAR
Chojak A 62 WAR
Chomiński J M 56 VIE, 60 WAR¹, 61 BUD, 62 WAR, 63 VEN, 66 BYD
Chottin A 37 PAR⁴
Chou Wen Chung 66 MANL
Chrennikov T 50 FLOR
Christensen D 58 COL
Christoff [Christov, Khristov] D 65 BERL¹, 70 BERL², 71 MOS
Christout M-F 70 MTA, 72 VEN
Chuang Pen-Li 66 MANL
Chubow W N 50 LEIP
Chusid M 66 VEN, 69 VER, 72 COP, 72 MIL
Chyurlionite Ya 64 MOS
Ciamaga G 70 STOC
Cicognini A 50 FLOR
Ciernak J 28 PRA
Ciobanu G 66 BYD, 66 SOF, 67 BUC, 69 BRN, 72 BYD
Cipra M 68 SVE; 74 ZAG
Cirese A M 57 CHIE, 73 ROM²
Civil F 65 MTS (2)
Clapham J 71 BRN
Clarkson A 74 NEWY¹ (p)
Claro S 70 BON
Claudius C 06 BAS
Claycombe G 72 VIE¹
Clemens W 66 LEIP
Clercx [Clercx-Lejeune] S 52 UTR, 53 PAR, 54 PAL, 54 PAR¹, 55 BRUS (2), 55 WÉG (3), 57 WÉG, *58 COL*, 59 CER
Clerval 00 PAR⁶
Closson E 23 BRUS, 27 VIE
Clough F F 55 BRUS
Cnattingius C M 71 STGA (p)
Coates E J 59 CAM
Coban 67 BUC
Cobin M 74 NEWY²
Coeuroy A 33 FLOR
Cogan R 65 BLM
Coggiola F 73 ROM²
Cogni G 56 VIE
Cohen A 72 COP
Cohen D 69 JER
Colazinski J 33 FLOR, 34 TRT
Cole D W 70 LAW

Cole E   54 PAR[1]
Collaer P   37 FLOR, 38 FLOR, 54 PAL, *54 WÉG*, 54 WÉG, *56 WÉG*, 56 WÉG (2), 57 WÉG, 58 COL (c), *58 WÉG*, 58 WÉG (2), 61 NEWY (c), 64 SAL, 68 BRN, 68 VEN
Collins E   70 YAO
Colombati C   74 BOL
Cols D   65 MTS (2)
Combarieu J   00 PAR[1] (2), *00 PAR[2]*, 00 PAR[2]
Comişel E   58 WÉG, 64 MOS, 67 BUC, 67 LJU (p), 75 BYD
Conati M   66 VEN, 69 VER, 72 MIL, 73 ROM[2]
Connick-McCollester R   64 SAL (p)
Conomos D   72 COP
Conover W   68 NEWY (c)
Conradin H   50 LÜN[1]
Consolo F   02 HAM
Constantinescu D   67 BUC
Cook C C   66 MOR
Copeau J   38 FLOR
Copland A   68 NEWY (c)
Coppola P   37 FLOR, 38 FLOR
Corbin [Corbin de Mangoux] S   50 ROM, 54 ROU, 61 NEWY, 64 SAL (2p), 72 TOD
Cordero R   65 BLM
Corio E   21 TUR (2)
Cornette A   23 BRUS
Corrêa de Azevedo L H   *see* de Azevedo L H C
Cortellazzo A T   68 VEN
Corver G M A   64 AMS
Cosma O L   67 BUC, 73 BUC
Cosma V   66 BRN, 66 BYD, 67 BRN[2], 67 BUC, 67 MAG, 69 BYD, 70 BON, 72 BYD, 73 BUC, 75 BYD
Cossart-Cotte F   69 PAR
Costa O   73 NEU/B
Costantini   57 PAR
Costarelli N   50 FLOR
Costère E   54 PAR[2], 60 PAR[1]
Cottis E F   70 LAW
Coupleux L   32 STRS
Cousin P   50 LUX
Couturier C   61 COL
Couturier M   73 PAR
Cowell H   61 TEH, 61 TOK
Crane F   64 SAL (p)
Cremer L   50 LÜN[1], 68 TOK[1] (2)
Cremer M   50 LÜN[2]
Croiza C   37 PAR[3]
Croll G   58 COL, 67 FLOR, 67 LJU, 71 BRN, 74 ROM
Crossley-Holland P   61 TEH, 61 TOK (2), 64 NEWD[2], *65 BERL[2]*, 65 BERL[2], 67 *VAN*, 67 VAN
Crump J I   *71 ANN*, 71 ANN
Crunden R M   74 NEWY[1]
Cuclin D   34 PRA
Cudworth C   52 UTR, 65 DIJ (2; p)

Cukkerman V   *see* Zukkerman, V
Cumar R   57 VEN[2], 71 VIC
Cuming G   55 BRUS
Cummings W H   11 LON
Curjel H   68 STRS
Cusatelli G   69 VER
Cutts J P   55 ROY
Cuvelier M   37 FLOR, 47 PRA
Cvetko D   56 VIE, 58 COL, 59 CAM, 60 WAR[1], 61 TEH, 61 TOK, 62 KAS, 64 NEWD[2], 64 SAL (3p), 65 BRN, 66 BYD, 66 VEN, 67 BERL, 67 BRN[2], *67 LJU*, 67 LJU, 68 SVE, 69 VER, 70 BON, 70 BRN, 71 BRN (1; p), 72 COP, 74 ZAG
Czekanowska   [Czekanowska-Kuklińska] A   60 PAR[2], 60 WAR[1], 67 LJU (p), 74 KRP
Czerny P   70 BERL[2]
Czesla W   70 BON (2)
Czyżowski S   62 WAR

Dabo-Peranić M   58 COL
D'Accone F   61 CAM/M (p), 67 LJU, 69 CER, 71 NEWY
Dacos F   67 PAR
Dadak K   74 KRP
von Dadelsen G   56 VIE, 61 NEWY, 62 KAS (1; c), 66 LEIP (p), 71 STU
Dahlhaus C   53 BAM, 56 HAM, 58 COL, 62 KAS (2), *63 KIE*, 63 KIE, *66 LEIP*, 66 LEIP, 67 LJU (c), 68 THU, 69 ROM, 70 BERL[1], *70 BON*, 70 BON (3), 71 NEWY, 71 STU, 72 COP, 72 FRE/B, 72 VIE[1], 74 BERL, 74 ZAG
Dale R A   68 UPP
van Dalfsen J   71 STGA (p)
Dalla Libera E   50 ROM
Dallapiccola L   49 FLOR, 64 HAM
Dalla Vecchia W   71 VIC
Dal Monte T   67 FLOR (p)
Damerini A   48 FLOR, 49 FLOR, 54 PAL
D'Amico F   48 FLOR, 49 FLOR, *67 FLOR*, 67 FLOR, 69 ROM
Damilano P   54 VIE
Danckert W   25 LEIP, 31 SAL
D'Angeli A   09 VIE, 36 ROM
Daniel O   71 MOS
Daniélou A   60 PAR[1], 61 TEH, 61 TOK (2), 64 HAM, 64 NEWD[2], 65 BERL[2], *67 BERL*, 67 BERL, 68 NEWY (c), 70 HAMM, 70 YAO, 71 FLOR, 71 VIC (2), 71 MOS
Danilevich L   71 MOS
Daniskas J   52 UTR
Dannemann M   65 BLM
Darasse X   69 PAR
Darbellay É   72 COP

Dart T   52 UTR, 53 PAR, 54 PAR[1] (2), 57 NEU/S (2), 61 NEWY, 69 PAR
Darwiche A   32 CAIR
Daubresse M   09 VIE
Dauriac L   00 PAR[2], 09 GEN, 09 VIE
Dave D   37 PAR[4]
David L   26 GEN
Davidsson Å   62 STOC
Davie D   60 WAR[2]
Davies J H   50 LÜN[2], 51 PAR, 55 BRUS, 62 STOC (c), 65 DIJ (1; p), 71 STGA (c)
Davies M   65 STAV
Davis P G   69 VER
Davis R   75 AUS (p)
Dayan L   50 ROM, 56 VIE, 57 PAR
Dayton D   74 NEWY[1] (p)
Dean A   50 ROM, 71 STGA (p)
Dean W   72 MIL
De Bellis F V   69 VER
Debes L H   62 KAS
De Bonis A   50 ROM
Debus   38 FRA
Décaudin M   *65 STAV*
Dechevrens A   06 BAS
De Clercq J   72 VIE[2]
Decroisette F   70 MTA
Decsey E   28 VIE
De Feo S   37 FLOR
De Florentiis G   69 PARM
De Florentis G   68 MIL
De Giorgi G   70 BOL
Degrada F   68 VEN, 73 SIE, 75 SIE
Dehnert M   50 LEIP
Deinhardt H   25 LEIP
Deininger H F   56 VIE
Dekan K   72 COP
Delacroix S   50 ROM
Delalande D   50 ROM, 57 PAR
Delarue P   37 PAR[4]
Delfrati C   68 VEN
Deliège C   73 BEL, 74 ZAG
Della Corte A   33 FLOR, 37 FLOR, 38 FLOR, 56 VEN, 56 VIE, 57 VEN[1], 60 ROM, 65 BRN, 67 SIE
Delporte J   30 LIÈ, 37 PAR[1]
De Luigi M   66 VEN
Demény J   61 BUD, 71 BUD[1]
Demuth N   54 PAR[2]
Denéréaz A   24 BAS, 25 BRUG, 26 GEN, 27 VIE
Denis P   57 PAR
Denis V   50 LÜN[2], 50 ROM, 51 PAR
Densmore F   22 RIO, 32 LAP
Dent E J   11 LON, 33 FLOR, 39 NEWY
Deodhar B R   64 NEWD[2]
De' Paoli D   57 VEN[1]
Deppert H   72 VIE[1]
Deri O   68 UPP
Derr E S   70 BON

Derra de Moroda F 73 SIE
Derschmidt H 71 STP
De Sanctis G B 57 VEN[1]
De Simone R 73 ROM[2] (2)
Desparmet J 05 ALG
Deutsch O E 27 VIE, 28 VIE, 29 ROM, 59 CAM (p), 62 KAS, 64 SAL (p)
Deutsch W 65 BRA, 67 RAD, *71 BLE*, 71 BLE, 71 HIN, *71 STP*, 71 STP
Dević D 67 BRN[1], 71 STP, 73 BAL, 75 BRUN
Dévigne R 37 PAR[4]
Devoto D 64 SAL (p)
Dewèvre J 67 ZAG
Dias M 64 MOS
Di Benedetto R 72 COP
Dickinson P 74 NEWY[1] (p)
Di Clemente R 56 VIE
Didier A 60 PAR[1]
Di Donato V 21 TUR
Diesen R 74 ZAG
Dietrich M 67 NAN
Dietz H-B 70 BON
van Dijk H 54 PAR[2]
Dille D 61 BUD
Dillenseger R P 32 STRS
D'Indy V 00 PAR[1] (5), 09 VIE (2)
Dinekov P 60 WAR[2]
Dinev P 69 BYD
Di Salvo B 50 ROM (2), 51 PAL, 54 PAL, 61 COL
Di San Martino E 37 FLOR
Disertori B 57 NEU/S (3)
Dittmer K 56 HAM
Dittmer L A 52 UTR, 64 SAL (p), 65 NEWY
Djoudjeff S 60 WAR[2], 71 BUD[1]
Djurić-Klajn S 56 VIE, 58 COL, 66 BYD
Dobiáš V 56 PAR, 60 STRT
Dobrahinović G 66 SOF
Dobrowolski A 71 STU
Dobrowolski J 60 WAR[1]
Dobszay L 72 SÁR
Dodge C 74 NEWY[1]
Doflein E 72 GRA
Döhring S 74 BERL
Dolinescu E 73 BUC
Domański W 75 BYD
Domburg G 71 BUD[2]
Dominguez Berrueta J 28 PRA
Domokos S 66 SOF
Dompé G 56 CAG
Donà M 64 SAL (p), 65 DIJ (p), 69 VER
Donath A 75 EIS
Donath G 56 VIE
Donington R 61 NEWY (c)
de Donostia J A 37 PAR[4], 50 ROM
van Doorslaer G 11 MAL (4), 25 BRUG, 30 ANT, 30 LIÈ
van Doren R 25 BRUG
Dorfmüller K 57 NEU/S, 62 STOC (2)
Dosse 54 PAR[2]
Douglass F 69 PAR
Douillez J 59 CAM

Dovaz R 54 PAR[2]
Downes E O D 57 CAM/M (p), 61 NEWY
Dräger H-H 50 LEIP, 53 BAM, 56 HAM, 61 NEWY (c), 61 TOK, 64 SAL (2p)
Dragoumis M P 72 COP
Draper D 75 AUS (1; p)
Dreimüller K 30 LIÈ, 56 VIE
Dreyer E-J 60 WAR[1]
Dreyfus S 60 PAR[2]
Droysen D 62 KAS, 64 SAL (p), 66 LEIP, 69 STOC, 71 KAS, 73 BAL
Druskin M 68 BRN
Drzewiecki Z 60 WAR[1], 62 WAR
Ducasse H *73 PAR*, 73 PAR
Duchemin G-J 45 DAK, 47 BIS
Duchow M 60 STRT
Duck L W 59 CAM, 62 STOC
Duckles V H 51 PAR, 55 BRUS (2), 58 COL, 59 CAM, 65 DIJ (p), 70 BOL, 70 STGE
Dufourcq N 32 STRS (2), 37 PAR[1], 54 PAR[1], 57 PAR, 59 CAM, 62 BERN
Duft J 50 LUX, 54 ROU
Dumont C 54 PAR[2], 57 PAR
Dunkele I 73 STOC
Dunning A 66 LEIP, 66 VEN
Dupont J 64 HAM
Dupont W 70 BON
Duran S M 28 PRA
Durant F 11 LON
Dureau T 00 PAR[1]
Düring W J 74 GRA[2]
Dürr A 50 LEIP, 50 LÜN[1], 56 HAM
Dürr J M 65 BRN
Dürr W 62 KAS, 66 LEIP
Dussaut R 58 MARS
Dutilleux H 60 STRT
Duvelle C 64 SAL (p), 70 YAO
Důžek S 70 TRČ
Dvorak V 73 WEIM
Dwelshauvers 09 LIÈ (2), 11 MAL
Dyker 57 PAR
Dyroff H-D *71 HIN*
Dzhabbarov A 71 MOS
Džudžev S 71 HIN

Ebel A 25 LEIP
Ebel B 61 COL
Ebenstein Y J 56 VIE
Ebert C 33 FLOR
Eccher C 50 ROM
Eckanove C A 54 PAR[2]
Eckardt H 50 LÜN[1]
Eckersley T 71 STGA (p)
Eckstein P *56 PRA*, 58 BRN, 67 GRA
Ecorcheville J 06 BAS (2c), 09 VIE (2), 11 LON (1; c)
Edwards E D 31 LEID
Eggebrecht H H 50 LEIP, 52 UTR, 53 BAM (p), 56 HAM, 58 COL, · 61 NEWY, *68 THU*, 69 BRN, 70 BERL[1], 70 BON (1; c),

70 BRN (1; c), 70 VIE, 71 BRN (c), 71 MOS, 72 VIE[1] (c), *72 FRE/B*, 72 FRE/B, *74 SINZ*, 74 SINZ
Eggeling H 71 BUD[2]
Egk W 64 HAM
Egli U 72 BERN
Ehmann W 38 FRE/B, 50 LÜN[1]
Ehrenhofer W E 09 VIE
Eibner F 54 VIE, 60 WAR[1], 71 HIN, 71 STP
Eickhoff P 25 LEIP (2)
Einstein A 27 VIE, 30 LIÈ, 33 FLOR, 39 NEWY
Eisenring C 00 MUN
Ekier J 60 WAR[1]
El'darova M 64 MOS (d)
Elders W 71 NEWY
El Garem A 32 CAIR
El Hefny M 56 PRA
El' Kholi S 71 MOS
Eliraz I 74 JER (p)
Eller R 50 LEIP, 53 BAM, 56 HAM, 56 VIE, 64 SAL (p), 67 MAG
Ellinwood L 39 NEWY
Elliott K 55 ROY
Ellis J D 70 LAW
El Mahdi S 60 PAR[1], 61 TEH, 67 BERL
Elschek O *65 BRA*, 67 BRN[1] (2), 67 LJU (p), *70 TRČ*, 70 TRČ (1; c), 71 BUD[1], 72 COP, 73 BAL, *74 KRP*
Elscheková A 64 BRA, 65 BRA, 67 RAD (2), 70 TRČ, 74 KRP, 75 BRUN
Elsner J 64 BERL, 66 LEIP (1;p), 70 BERL[2], 71 MOS
Elssner M 66 LEIP
Elvers R 59 CAM (p), 62 KAS, 70 BON
Emery W 61 NEWY
Emge 38 FRA
Emmanuel M 37 FLOR, 37 PAR[1], 37 PAR[3]
Emsheimer E 50 LÜN[1] (2), 67 BRN[1], 67 LJU (p), 69 NUR, 72 COP, 75 BRUN
Engel H 31 SAL (2), 49 BAS (2), 50 LÜN[1] (2; c), 51 IES, 52 UTR, 56 HAM, 58 COL, 61 NEWY, 62 KAS (1; c), 64 SAL (2p)
Engel L 74 NEWY[1] (p)
Engelbrecht C 56 HAM, 58 COL, 60 WAR[1]
Engelbrecht C 56 HAM, 58 COL, 60 WAR[1]
Engelmann H U 62 KAS
Engländer R ‚68 NEWY (c)
Engländer R 59 HAL, 64 SAL (p)
Eno Belinga S 70 YAO
Eösze L 66 VEN, 69 VER, 72 MIL
Eppelsheim J 74 GRA[2]
Eppstein H 63 KIE
Epstein P 25 LEIP
Erdmann H 56 HAM, 56 VIE
Ergo E 00 PAR[1], 11 LON
Erismann G 67 BRN[2]
d'Erlanger F R 32 CAIR
Ermann 67 PAR

Erpf H   24 BAS, 25 LEIP, 26 FRE/B
Espiau de la Maestre A   56 VIE
Espinosa G   *63 CART*
Espinosa L C   63 CART
Estrada G   64 SAL (p), *65 MTS*, 65 MTS (2)
Estreicher Z   58 WÉG
Etzkorn K P   74 ZAG
Euba A   70 YAO, 71 MOS
Evenari H   *see* Avenary H
Ewerhart R   67 KAS

Fabbri P   73 ROM[1]
Fábián I   67 GRA
Fábregues A   65 MTS
Fabro C   56 VEN
Fack H   56 HAM
Falcke W   60 WAR[1]
Faller R   65 GEN
Falvy Z   56 VIE, 64 SAL (p), 66 BYD, 67 LJU (p), 72 SÁR, 73 BAL, 75 BYD, 75 EIS
Fano F   59 CER, 60 WAR[1], 67 SIE, 68 MIL, 74 BOL
Fantino Y   73 PAR
Fara G   21 TUR, 29 FLOR, 34 TRT, 40 VEN, 48 TUR
Fara S   40 VEN
de la Farge   37 PAR[4]
Farina E   69 VER
Farnsworth D B   70 LAW
Favara A   03 ROM
Favero M   67 FLOR (p)
Favre M   *72 BERN*
Fedeli V   11 LON (1;c), 21 TUR (2)
Feder G   56 HAM, 61 NEWY, 62 KAS, 66 LEIP (1;p), 70 BON, 70 GRA, 71 EIS, 72 COP
Federhofer H   53 BAM, 54 VIE, 56 HAM, 56 VIE, *58 COL*, 60 WAR[1], 61 BUD, 62 KAS (2;c), 68 VEN, 73 ROM[1], 74 GRA[2]
Federhofer-Königs R   62 KAS
Fédorov V   50 LÜN[2] (2), *51 PAR*, 51 PAR, 54 PAL, *55 BRUS*, 58 COL, 62 PAR, 62 STOC, *65 DIJ*, 70 STGE, *71 STGA*, 72 COP
Fédorov Y   59 CAM (p)
Feicht H   56 VIE, 60 WAR[1], 64 SAL (3p), 66 BYD (2)
Feil A   62 KAS, 70 BON, 72 BYD
Feininger L   50 ROM (2), 58 COL, 62 KAS
Felber E   11 LON (2), 27 VIE (1;c)
Feldbrill V   60 STRT
Feldmann F   56 HAM
Felici S   *71 FLOR*
Felix W   56 VIE, 59 HAL, 61 BUD, 70 BERL[2]
Feller M   58 COL
Fellerer K G   27 VIE, 30 LIÈ, 31 SAL, 38 FRE/B, 50 LÜN[1], 50 ROM, 51 IES, 52 BERN, 52 UTR, 53 BAM (c), 54 PAL, 56 PAR, 56 VIE, 59 BUD, 59 CER, 61

NEWY (1;c), 62 KAS (c), 64 SAL (p), 66 CHIC, 67 LJU (p), 67 SIE, 70 VIE, 74 ROM, 75 BYD, 75 ROM
Fellinger I   62 KAS, 66 LEIP, 70 BON
Fellowes E H   30 LIÈ (2)
Felsenstein W   58 BRN (d)
Fenton W N   49 NEWY[2]
Ferand E T   49 BAS, 56 VIE, 57 CAM/M (p), 58 COL, 61 NEWY
Ferchault G   53 BAM
Ferrara F   :0 FLOR
Ferraria L E   21 TUR
Ferrari Barassi E   68 VEN, 70 BOL
Ferraz de Mesquita R   37 PAR[3]
Ferretti E   65 NEWH
Ferreyra B   65 LIÈ
Ferrieu   67 PAR
Feschotte J   58 BRN (2d)
Feuchtmüller R   71 EIS
Feuchtwanger E   32 AMS
Fheodoroff N   67 BRN[2]
von Ficker R   27 VIE (c), 49 BAS, 50 ROM, 52 UTR, 53 BAM (c)
Fiechtner H A   67 GRA
Filip M   70 TRČ, 71 BUD[2]
Finscher L   62 KAS, 64 SAL, 66 LEIP (1;p), 67 KAS, 68 FUS, 69 ROM, 70 BON, 70 BRN, 71 NEWY (1;c;p), 72 COP (2), 72 GRA, 73 ROM[1], 73 SIE, 74 ROM, 74 ZAG
Firca C L   68 BRN, 70 BON, 73 BUC
Firca G   68 BRN, 69 BYD, 70 BON, 73 BUC
Firth I   74 LON
von Fischer K   49 BAS, 50 LÜN[1], 52 UTR, 55 WÉG (3), 58 COL, 59 CER, 61 NEWY, 64 SAL (p), 65 COP, 67 LJU (2c), 68 VEN, 69 CER (2), 70 BON (2), 70 BRN (1;c), 70 VIE, 71 MOS, 71 STGA, 75 BYD
Fischer P   64 AMS
Fischer W   24 BAS, 25 LEIP (1;c), 26 FRE/B, 27 VIE (c), 31 SAL
Fischman N   70 BERL[2], 70 BON
Fitz   38 FRA
Fitzpatrick H   70 GRA
Flade E   26 FRE/B, 27 FRE/S, 50 LEIP
Flagel C   57 WÉG
Fleischer H   33 FLOR, 48 FLOR, 49 FLOR
Fleischhauer G   59 HAL, 62 MAG, 66 LEIP, *67 MAG*, 67 MAG, 70 BERL[2], 71 BRN, 72 BLA, *73 MAG*, 73 MAG, 74 BLA, 75 BLA
Fleury L   09 VIE
Flindell E F   70 BON, 72 COP
Flood W H G   11 LON, 25 BRUG

Floros C   61 OKH, 62 KAS, 64 SAL (p), 75 BYD
Flothuis M   58 BRN
Focht I   73 BEL
Fock G   54 STAD
Fokker A D   49 BAS, 52 UTR, 58 MARS, 64 SAL (2p)
Forchert A   70 BON
Forchhammer J   38 FRA
Foret R   57 PAR
Fortassier P   56 PAR
Forte A   65 NEWY, 66 MOR, 74 NEWY[1]
Fortner W   64 HAM
Foss L   68 SVE
Foucauld   05 STRS
Fourdouiev V   65 LIÈ
Frączkiewicz A   60 WAR[1]
Fraile G   57 PAR
Fraisse P   37 PAR[2]
Franca U   54 VIE
Francès R   55 ARR, 60 ATH
Francillon G   69 KUA
Franco J L   62 MEX
Frankenstein A   60 STRT, 61 TOK
Frank-Mittenwald K   71 STP
Fransson F   69 STOC
Frazzi V   48 FLOR
Freeman J W   67 FLOR, 69 VER, 72 MIL
Frei F   50 ROM
Frei W   72 BERN
Freitag W M   62 STOC
de Freitas-Branco L   21 PAR
Frelih E   68 BRN
Frémond   00 PAR[1]
Frere W H   11 LON
Freyse C   50 LEIP
Fricke J   70 BON
Friedlaender M   11 LON (1;c), 24 BAS, 28 VIE (2)
Friege B   70 BERL[2]
Froger J   50 ROM
Froidebise P   54 PAR[1], 57 WÉG
Frommel G   62 KAS
Frotscher G   25 LEIP (2), 26 FRE/B, 27 FRE/S, 38 FRE/B
Fryklund D   30 LIÈ
Fubini E   60 ATH, 64 AMS, 68 UPP, 73 ROM[1], 73 SIE, 74 ZAG, 75 SIE
Fujii K   28 PRA
Fukač J   64 BRA, 65 BRN, 66 BRN, 67 BRN[2], 67 LJU (p), 68 BRN, 69 BRN, 70 BERL[2], 70 BRN, 74 KRP
Fukuhara N   69 VER
Fulin A   64 AMS
Fuller Maitland J A   11 LON, 21 PAR
Fürst L   33 FLOR
Füssl K H   64 SAL (p), 72 VIE[1] (p)

Gabriel G   34 TRT, 56 CAG
Gagnebin H   24 BAS, 37 PAR[3]
Gagnon E   06 QUE
Gähwyler K   72 BERN
Gai V   69 NUR

Gaillard M F 50 FLOR
Gaillard P-A 49 BAS, 52 UTR, 60 WAR[1] (2)
Gaïsser [Gaisser] U A [H] 00 PAR[2] (2; d), 03 ROM, 09 VIE
Gajard 37 PAR[1]
Gajard J 50 ROM, 57 PAR
Galanti B 54 PAL
Galko L 65 BRA, 74 KRP
Gallarati P 73 SIE
Galleni Luisi L 68 VEN
Gallico C 61 FLOR, 63 MER, 66 VEN, 67 SIE, 68 FUS (1;c), 68 PARM, 68 VEN, 69 VER, 71 NEWY, 72 COP (2), 72 MIL, 72 VEN, 73 ROM[1], 74 MANT
Gallini C 73 ROM[2]
Galliver D 72 COP
Gallo F A 69 CER, 69 CER, 69 PARM (2), 72 COP, 73 ROM[2]
Galpin F W 11 LON
Galtieri G 73 ROM[2]
Gamble J I 49 NEWY[1]
Gamissans J 65 MTS
Gandillot M 09 VIE, 11 LON
Gandolfi R 09 VIE
Ganev S A 71 BUD[2]
Ganss 38 FRA
Gara E 66 VEN
Garces Bedregal M 39 MEX
García J A 65 MTS
García J M 65 MTS
García Matos M 54 PAL
García Morillo R 65 BLM
Gardavský Č 58 BRN, 61 BUD
von Gardner J 57 PAR, 64 SAL (p)
Gárdonyi Z 61 BUD, 61 BUD (2), 62 KAS, 75 EIS
Garfias R 61 TOK, 64 NEWD[2], 66 MANL, 67 BERL
Gariel É 00 PAR[2]
Garin E 71 FLOR
Garros M 58 COL
Gartner J 70 GRA
Gärtner K 73 HAM
Garvie P 75 AUS (p)
Gasco A 21 TUR (3)
Gaslini G 71 FLOR
Gasparov B 73 BEL
Gasperini G 29 ROM
Gastoué A 00 PAR[6], 05 STRS (2), 06 BAS, 21 PAR, 27 BEL, 37 PAR[1] (2)
Gatti G M 33 FLOR
Gatti Perer M L 68 MIL, 71 NEWY
Gaugusch F 54 VIE
Gaukstad Ö 50 LÜN[2]
Gaur G D 57 MUN
Gauthier-Villars M 37 PAR[4]
Gavazzeni G 37 FLOR, 38 FLOR, 67 FLOR
Gavazzi M 64 GRA[2]
Gazé A 50 ROM
Geering A 49 BAS, 64 SAL (2p)
Geerts C 72 VIE[2]

Gégou F 64 SAL (p)
Geiringer K 27 VIE, 57 CAM/M (p), 58 COL, 59 BUD, 64 SAL (3p), 67 LJU (c), 70 BON, 72 COP
Geiser B 72 GRA, 73 BAL, 75 BRUN
Geisler C 06 BAS, 09 VIE
Gelineau J 57 PAR, 62 BERN
Gelnar J 65 BRA, 67 RAD (2), 74 KRP
Geluk J J 53 NET
Gennrich D 27 BERL
Gentili A 21 PAR, 49 FLOR
Geoffroy-Dechaume A 69 PAR
George W H 53 NET
Georgiades T G 54 PAL, 56 VIE, 62 BERN, 64 SAL (c), 69 BRN, 70 BON
Gérar M 38 FRA
Gerasimova-Persidskaya N A 69 BYD, 72 BYD, 75 BYD
Gerber R 50 LÜN[1] (2;c)
Gerhard R 59 CAM
Gerhartz L K 66 VEN, 69 VER
Gerigk H 37 FLOR
Gerlach R 68 BRN, 69 BRN, 71 BRN, 72 VIE[1], 74 GRA[1]
German F 60 WAR[1]
Germani F 50 ROM
Gérold T 00 PAR[2], 32 STRS
Gerson-Kiwi E 54 PAL, 61 TEH, 61 JER, 64 SAL (p), 70 BON
Gerstenberg W 49 BAS, 50 LÜN[1] (1;c), 53 BAM, 56 HAM, 58 COL, 62 KAS (1;c), 64 SAL (c), 66 LEIP
Gervais F 62 PAR (2)
Gervasio R 50 FLOR
Geshuri M S 61 JER
Geyer J 27 FRE/S, 32 STRS (2)
Ghenea C C 69 BYD
Ghidoli P 73 ROM[2]
Ghircoiaşiu R 66 BYD, 71 BRN (p), 72 BYD, 73 BUC
Ghisi F 39 FLOR, 48 FLOR, 48 TUR, 49 BAS, 49 FLOR, 50 LÜN[1], 50 ROM, 53 PAR, 55 ROY, 56 WÉG, 56 VIE, 57 CHIE, 59 CER, 61 NEWY (c), 64 SAL (p), 66 VEN, 68 VEN, 69 CER, 69 VER (2), 70 BOL, 72 BYD
Ghislanzoni A 50 ROM, 51 IES (3), 54 PAL, 55 WÉG, 56 VIE
Giazotto R 48 FLOR
Gibelli V 69 PARM, 70 BOL (2)
Giegling F 49 BAS, 64 SAL, 64 SAL (p)
Giese F 26 GEN
Gil B 63 STT
Gilbert K 69 PAR
Gillis F 65 BLM
Gindele C 51 OCH
Ginsburg [Ginzburg] L S 67 BRN[2], 70 BON, 71 BRN (1;p), 72 GRA, 75 BYD

Giraldi R 34 TRT
Girardon R 51 PAR
Girod R 54 PAR[2]
Giuleanu V 67 BUC
Gjerløw L 75 ESP
Glahn H 52 UTR, 72 COP
von Gleich C C J 65 AMS
Gliński M 51 IES, 60 WAR[1]
Glowacki J 62 WAR
Gluszcz-Zwolinska E 70 BOL
Gmeinwieser S 70 BON
Goehr A 64 SAL (p)
von Goertz H 68 BRN
Goidànich P G 31 UDIN
Gojowy D 70 BON
Goldhammer O 61 BUD, 66 LEIP (p)
Goldschmidt H(arry) 58 BRN (d), 58 COL, 63 PRA, 64 SAL (p), 65 BERL[1], 66 LEIP, 70 BERL[2] (2), 70 VIE, 72 COP
Goldschmidt H(ugo) 09 VIE
Goléa A 56 PRA, 71 FLOR
Göller G 66 CHIC, 66 LEIP, 70 BON
Göllner T 64 SAL (2p), 67 LJU, 69 CER, 70 BON
Gołos J 64 SAL (p)
Golovinsky G I 72 VIE[2]
von der Goltz C 72 GRA
Gölz R 27 BERL
Gombosi O J 27 VIE, 39 NEWY, 49 BAS, 54 PAR[1]
Gönnenwein W 67 KAS
Gonzalez V 32 STRS
Gorali M 64 MOS
Göransson H 72 BERN
Gorczycka M 61 BUD, 62 WAR
Gordeychuk N M 64 MOS
Görner 38 FRA
Goslich S 38 FRA
Gossett P 67 LJU, 70 STGE
Gostuški D 69 BRN
Gotti T 68 FUS (d)
Gottlob D 74 LON
Gottron A 51 OCH, 54 VIE, 56 VIE
Gottwald C 70 BON
Götz J 09 VIE (2)
Gould M J 65 NEWY
Goury J 69 VER
Gouzou L 54 PAR[2]
Gow G C 09 VIE
Grad T 71 HIN
Gradenwitz P 56 VIE, 65 JER
Graeser W 24 BAS, 27 VIE
Graf E 06 BAS
Graf H 38 FLOR, 64 HAM, 66 VEN
Graf M 27 VIE (c)
Graf W 56 VIE, 66 GRA, 67 BRN[1], 67 ZAG, 69 STOC
Grafczyńska M 27 VIE
Grasberger F 55 BRUS, 56 VIE
Grases Gonzalez P 28 PRA
Grassi Landi B 00 PAR[2] (2)
Gratovich E 74 NEWY[1] (p)
Graupner F 50 LEIP

Gräwe K D   66 VEN, 69 VER, 72 MIL
Gray C   49 FLOR
Grebe K   67 KAS
Greene R L   67 LJU (p)
Gregor J   09 VIE, 56 VIE
Greni L   54 WÉG
Gress F-H   66 LEIP
Greussay P   73 PAR
Grimaud Y   56 WÉG, 58 WÉG, 60 PAR¹, 61 TOK
Gritsa S I   69 BYD
Griveau M   11 LON
Grobben L M   67 PRA
Grout D J   57 CAM/M (p), 58 COL (c), 64 SAL (p)
Gruber G   70 GRA, 73 SIE, 74 GRA¹, 75 EIS
Gruber R I   59 HAL
Grusnick B   63 KIE
Grüss H   66 LEIP
Grützmacher M   38 GHE, 53 NET, 58 MARS
Gualerzi G   66 VEN, 67 FLOR (2;c), 69 VER, 72 MIL
Gudewill K   50 LÜN¹, 53 BAM, 58 COL, 61 NEWY, 63 KIE
Guerrini G   48 FLOR, 49 FLOR
Guggino E   73 ROM²
Gugliemi E   66 VEN, 69 VER
Gui V   38 FLOR
Guichard L   61 NEWY, 67 PARM
Guiliante G   57 CHIE
Guillaume M   50 ROM
Guiomar P   72 TOU
Guittard   58 MARS
Gülke P   66 LEIP, 70 BERL² (2;p), 71 BRN
Gümel M   71 STU
Guntebrüch R   27 VIE
Günther F   28 VIE
Günther R   56 WÉG, 70 BON
Günther U   62 KAS, 64 SAL (p), 66 LEIP, 67 LJU, 69 CER, 69 VER, 70 BON, 72 COP, 72 MIL
Gurlitt W   24 BAS, 25 LEIP, 26 FRE/B, 26 FRE/B, 27 FRE/S, 27 VIE, 30 LIÈ (2), 49 BAS, 50 LEIP (2), 52 BERN, 52 UTR, 53 BAM (2)
Gurvin O   63 KIE
Gut S   75 EIS
Gutfleisch P   64 GRA¹
Guth P   72 GRA
Gutkas K   71 EIS
Güttler H   11 LON, 25 LEIP, 27 VIE, 30 LIÈ
Guttman N   59 STU
Guttmann A   13 BERL, 27 BON, 29 NEWH, 31 HAM
Gutzmann   38 FRA
Guzman A   28 PRA
Gvakhariya V A   69 BYD, 72 BYD, 75 BYD
Gysi F   24 BAS, 25 LEIP

Haack H   64 SAL (p), 70 BON, 71 BRN (1;p)
Haag H   38 FRE/B
Haapalainen T I   75 BYD
Haapanen T   24 BAS, 27 VIE, 30 LIÈ
Haar J   61 CAM/M, 71 NEWY, 73 ROM¹
Haas R   09 VIE, 25 LEIP, 27 VIE (2;c), 28 VIE, 31 SAL, 50 LÜN¹
Hába A   25 LEIP, 47 PRA, 56 PRA, 58 BRN (2)
Habenicht G   67 BRN¹, 75 BRUN
Haberl F   50 ROM
Haberl F X   00 MUN
Haböck F   09 VIE
Habunek V   64 HAM
Hacobian Z   61 TEH
Hadow J H   11 LON
Haenni G   37 PAR⁴
Haerpfer F   09 VIE
Hahn H   50 LEIP
Hahn K   56 HAM
Hahne G   63 KIE
Haid G   71 STP
Haines D W   74 LON
Hajtas   57 PAR
Halbreich H   66 BRN
Halffter E   71 FLOR
Halm H   50 LÜN², 53 BAM (1;c), 59 CAM (p)
Halpern I   67 VAN
Halski R C   60 WAR¹
Hamann F   62 KAS
Hamann H W   62 KAS, 64 SAL (p)
Hamel F   52 UTR, 56 HAM
Hamilton I   60 STRT
Hammerich A   06 BAS (1;2c), 09 VIE, 11 LON (1;c)
Hammerschlag J   49 BAS
Hammerstein R   64 SAL (p), 70 BON, 72 COP
Händchen   38 FRA
Handschin J   24 BAS, 25 LEIP, 27 FRE/S, 27 VIE, 30 LIÈ (2), 38 FLOR, 38 ZUR, 49 BAS (2), 52 BERN, 54 PAL
Hankiss J   38 ZUR
Hanks N   68 SVE
Hansell S H   72 COP
Hansen F E   72 COP
Harajda H   74 LON
Haraszti E   30 LIÈ, 54 PAR¹
Hardeck E   70 BON
Harding R   30 LIÈ
Hardouin P   54 PAR¹
Harewood   61 TOK, 64 HAM
Hargreaves H A   70 LAW
Harich-Schneider E   50 LÜN¹, 56 HAM, 58 COL
Harnoncourt N   67 BRN², 69 BRN
Harnoncourt P   64 GRA¹
Harrán D   70 BON, 71 NEWY, 72 COP
Harris R   70 LAW
Harrison F Ll   52 UTR, 61

NEWY, 64 SAL (2p), 67 LJU (1;p), 73 BAL
Harrison L   61 TOK, 74 NEWY¹ (1;2p)
Hartmann   38 FRA
Hartmann C V   08 VIE
Hartmann H   53 BRUS
Haselböck H   68 THU
Hasse K   25 LEIP, 26 FRE/B, 27 FRE/S, 27 VIE
Hatting C E   70 BRN
Hause H E   48 BRUS
von Hausegger F   72 GRA
Hausleithner A   28 VIE
Hausswald G   50 LEIP, 53 BAM
Haydon G   39 NEWY, 58 COL
Haywood C   65 BLM
Head T G   70 LAW
Heartz D   54 PAR¹, 57 BRUS, 57 NEU/S, 61 CAM/M, 64 SAL (p), 67 LJU, 68 PARM, 70 BON, 70 MTA, 73 SIE
Hecht T   54 VIE
Hecklinger D   62 KAS
Heckmann H   54 PAR¹, 56 HAM, 59 CAM, 62 KAS, 65 DIJ (c), 67 LJU (p), 70 BON, 71 KAS
Hedley A   60 WAR¹
Hedlund H J   59 CAM
Heider M   72 GRA
Heilmann I   59 CAM
Heineman E G   75 EIS
Heinitz W   25 LEIP (2;c), 27 VIE, 30 LIÈ, 56 HAM, 56 VIE, 59 HAL, 60 WAR¹, 62 KAS
Heinlein C P   29 NEWH
Heins E   64 SAL (p)
Heinz R   66 LEIP
Heiske W   37 PAR⁴
Heister H-W   70 BON
Helgason H   58 COL
Heller K   66 LEIP, 75 BLA
Hellouin F   00 PAR¹
Hellwig F   69 NUR, 70 GRA, 71 GRA
Helm E   58 BRN, 61 BUD, 64 HAM, 67 ZAG, 70 STOC
Helman Z   60 WAR¹, 62 WAR, 62 WAR, 68 BRN
Helms H   74 NEWY¹ (p)
Hélouin   00 PAR²
Helyar J   70 LAW
Henderson C W   72 COP
Hendrik K   30 BON
Henneberg I   67 ZAG
Hennerberg C F   09 VIE (2), 11 LON (1;c)
Hennig J   66 CHIC
Henze H W   64 HAM
Herbst W   74 SINZ
Herdieckerhoff U   62 KAS
Héricard J   64 HAM
Herman V   67 BUC
Hermelink S   56 VIE, 58 COL, 68 VEN, 70 BON
Hermet A   48 FLOR, 49 FLOR
Hernádi L   60 WAR¹

Herndon R 75 *AUS*, 75 AUS (1;p)
Herre G 70 BERL[2]
Herskovits M J 48 BRUS
Hertz O 57 PAR
Hertzmann E 30 LIÈ, 57 CAM/M (p), 61 CAM/M (p)
Herzog A 61 JER, 74 JER (p)
Herzog E 56 HAM, 58 COL
Herzog G 28 NEWY, 39 NEWY (1;c)
Hesbert R-J 49 CLU, 50 LUX, 50 ROM (2), 54 ROU (6), 54 VIE, 57 PAR, 72 TOD
Hess E 56 PAR, 64 SAL (p)
Hetschko A 56 VIE
Heuss A 09 VIE (2), 24 BAS, 25 LEIP
Heusz A 13 BERL
Heyde H 66 LEIP
Heyman A C 68 TOK[2]
Hiao-Tsiun M 59 ROY
Hickmann H 48 PAR[1], 49 BAS, 50 ROM, 52 UTR, 59 HAL, 60 PAR[1], 67 ZAG
Hiekel H O 62 KAS
Hilber J B 54 VIE
Hilger W 71 EIS
Hill E B *see* Burlingham Hill E
Hill R S 51 PAR(2)
Hiller L A 66 MOR
Hilmar E 74 GRA[1], 75 EIS
Hilmera J 70 MTA
Hindemith P 37 FLOR
Hirashima M 61 TOK
Hirsch F 70 BERL[2]
Hirsch H 71 HIN
Hitchcock H W 68 SVE, *74 NEWY*[1]
Hitzig W 27 VIE
Hjelmström-Dahl B 67 RAD
Hławiczka K 60 WAR[1] (2), 69 BYD
Hobohm W 66 LEIP, 67 MAG, 72 BLA, 73 MAG
Höchel L 66 LEIP
Hoebaer K 54 PAR[2]
Høeg (Höeg) C 30 ATH, 50 ROM, 53 THE
Hoerburger F 50 LÜN[1], 71 HIN
Hoffer C R 72 VIE[2]
Höffer P 37 FLOR
Hoffman A 60 WAR[1], 61 BUD, 67 ZAG, 73 BUC, 74 NEWY[1] (p)
Hoffmann-Erbrecht L 53 BAM, 56 HAM, 58 COL, 62 KAS, 70 BON, 71 NEWY
Hofman S 69 JER, 70 BON
Hohler C 75 ESP
Hojan E 71 BUD[2]
Hoke H G 66 LEIP
Holečková-Dolanská J 56 PRA, 58 BRN
Holen A 74 ZAG
Holland J B 59 CAM
Hollander H 58 BRN, 68 BRN
Hollinshead M T 29 NEWH
Holman H-J 64 SAL (p)
Holmboe V 60 STRT
Holmes W C 64 SAL (p), 72 VEN

Holschneider A 62 KAS, 70 BON
Holst I 49 BAS
Holý D 67 BRN[1], 70 TRČ, 74 KRP
Homs J 65 MTS
Honegger M 62 KAS
Honolka K 68 BRN
Hood M 59 CAM, 61 TOK, 63 CART, 65 BERL[2], 66 MANL
van Hoogenhouck-Tulleken 28 PRA
Hope Robbins R 67 LJU (p)
Hopkinson C 59 CAM (c), 66 VEN
Hoppe A 54 STAD
Hoppin R H 55 WÉG, 59 CER
Horák J 28 PRA
Horak K 71 STP
Hordyński W 60 WAR[1]
Hořejš A 56 PRA, 59 BUD
Horn P 05 STRS
von Hornbostel E M 06 BAS (1;c), 09 VIE, 10 INN, 24 BAS, 24 BERL
Horová E 65 BRN
van der Hoorst A 52 BERN
Hortschansky K 69 ROM, 70 BON, 73 SIE, 74 ROM
Horváthová E 70 TRČ
Hoschowskyj W [Hošovskij V] 65 BRA, 71 BLE, 74 KRP
Hostinský O 09 VIE
Houdard G 00 PAR[2] (2)
Hourlier J 50 ROM
Houston E 28 PRA
Höweler C 53 BAM
Howgill P A 71 STGA (p)
Hrabal F 58 BRN
Hrabalová O 70 TRČ, 74 KRP
Hrabussay Z 56 PRA, 61 BUD, 70 BERL[2], 70 PIE
Hradecký E 67 BRN[2], 69 BRN, 69 NUR, 70 ANT, 71 BRN
Hrovatin R 64 BERL
Hrušovský I 56 PRA
Hucke H 54 PAL, 54 VIE, 56 HAM, 57 PAR, 58 COL, 61 NEWY, 64 SAL (p), 68 THU, 68 VEN, 70 BON, 73 ROM[1]
Hudec V 61 BUD, 71 BRN
Hudson F 59 HAL, 72 COP
Hughes A 72 COP
Hughes D G *57 CAM/M*
Huglo M 50 ROM, 54 VIE, 64 SAL(c), 66 OXF[1], 72 COP, 73 PAR, 75 ESP
Hulá M 70 PIE
Humbert G 00 PAR[2]
Humbert-Sauvageot 37 PAR[3]
Hummel W 56 PRA
Hunkemöller J 72 COP
Huré J 11 ROM
Hüschen H 56 HAM, 58 COL, 61 NEWY, 62 KAS (c), 66 LEIP (p)
Husmann H 52 UTR, 53 BAM, 55 AVIG, *56 HAM*, 56 HAM, 56 PRA, 56 VIE, 60

WAR[1], 61 NEWY (c), 64 SAL (1;c;p)
Husson R 58 MARS
Hutchins C M 71 BUD[2], 74 LON
Hüttel W 70 BERL[2]
Huys B 65 DIJ (p)
Hye-Kerkdal K 60 PAR[2]

Iarociński S see Jarociński S
Idaszak D 60 WAR[1]
Iljine V 52 BERN
Imberty M 73 BEL
Ingegnieros J 05 ROM
Ingram R W 71 VAN
Innamorati L 37 FLOR
Ioannidis Y 74 NEWY[1] (p)
Ippel A 50 ROM
Irza-Nour 31 PAR
Irving E 50 FLOR
Isaacs L 54 PAR[2]
Ising H 65 LIÈ, 68 TOK[1]
Ismail M 67 BERL, 70 YAO
Iversen G 75 ESP
Iwanow-Boretzky M 27 VIE
Iwaszkiewicz J 60 WAR[1], 62 WAR
Iyer M S 64 NEWD[2]

Jachimecki Z 09 VIE
Jackson G P 39 NEWY
Jackson R 65 NEWY, 67 LJU (p)
Jacob G 37 PAR[1]
Jacob W 74 SINZ
Jacobi E R 72 COP
Jacobini C 73 BEL
Jacobs C 64 AMS
Jacoby H 24 BERL
Jacquot J *53 PAR*, 53 PAR, *54 PAR*[1], 54 PAR[1], 55 ARR, *55 ROY*, 55 ROY, 57 BRUS, *57 NEU/S*, 57 NEU/S (2), 59 CAM, *59 ROY*, 60 WAR[1], 61 NEWY, *62 ROY*, *63 ROY*, 63 ROY, 67 LJU, *67 NAN*, 67 NAN, *68 STRS*, 68 STRS, 70 MTA, 71 VAN, *72 TOU*, 73 PAR
Jaeger D 73 PAR
Jaenicke G 65 GEN
Jahnn H H 25 LEIP, 26 FRE/B, 27 FRE/S
Jáki T S 72 BERN
Jakob F 62 BERN, 72 COP
Jakubcová D 70 BERL[2]
Jakubowski J Z 60 WAR[1]
Jalobeanu A 73 BUC
Janeček K 58 BRN, 71 BRN
Janković D S 56 WÉG
Janković L S 56 WÉG
Jansen P 73 PAR
Jansky H 52 VIE
Janssens A J 37 PAR[3]
Jansson E V 71 BUD[2], 72 COP, 74 LON
Jantarski G N 70 BON
Jaques-Dalcroze E 26 GEN
Járdányi P 61 BUD, 65 BRA
Jargy S 50 ROM
Jarnach P 24 BERL

Jarociński S 62 PAR (2), 74 BOL
Járosy D 27 VIE
Jarustowski [Jarustowsky, Yarustowski, Yarustovskiy] B M 64 HAM, 70 BERL², 71 *MOS*, 72 COP
Jeans S 52 BERN, 54 STAD, 56 HAM, 59 CAM, 67 BRN², 70 BRN
Jeffery B 71 NEWY
Jelescu P 67 BUC
Jelínková Z 70 TRČ
Jenkins N 75 SIE
Jensen N M 72 COP
Jeppesen K 24 BAS, 25 LEIP, 27 VIE, 30 LIÈ, 38 FLOR, 39 NEWY, 49 BAS, 50 ROM, 68 VEN
Jersild M 67 RAD, 71 BLE
Jexlev T 75 ESP
Jičínský B 65 BRN, 69 BRN
Jilek F 65 BRN
Jiránek J 58 BRN, 58 COL, 60 ATH, 60 WAR¹, 61 BUD, 63 PRA, 64 SAL (p), 65 BERL¹, 68 BRN, 69 BRN (2), 70 BRN (1;c), 73 BEL
Jöde F 25 LEIP
Johansson C 62 *STOC*
Johner D 27 BERL
Johnson A 61 CAM/M (p)
Joho S 71 STGA (p)
Jolas B 74 NEWY¹ (p)
Jolivet A 71 FLOR
Joly J 73 SIE, 75 SIE
Jonas O 56 VIE, 62 KAS (2)
Jones J B *see* Bush Jones J
Jones S 30 BON
Jonsson R 75 ESP
Jordan V L 59 STU
Jorissenne G 11 MAL
Josif E 68 SVE
Jost E 66 LEIP, 69 STOC
Josz R 21 PAR
du Jourdin G M 56 PRA
Judenič N 70 PIE
Juhász A 23 LEIP
Jung H 26 FRE/B
Jung H R 67 MAG, 73 MAG
Jungmann J A 54 VIE
Junius M 64 NEWD², 71 VIC (2)
Jurisch H 62 KAS
Jürgens J 68 VEN
Jurres A 59 CAM, 62 STOC, 64 AMS, 65 DIJ (1;p)
Just M 62 *KAS*, 62 KAS, 66 LEIP
Juten G C A 30 ANT

Kabalevskiy D 71 MOS
Kačulev I 67 BRN¹
Kaczyński T 60 WAR¹, 62 WAR, 74 BOL
Kaden C 73 BAL, 74 ZAG, 75 BRUN
Kaegi W 70 STOC
Kaelin 57 PAR
Kaftangian G 50 ROM
Kahl W 27 VIE, 28 VIE, 52 UTR, 53 *BAM*, 53 BAM, 56 VIE

Kahmann B 56 HAM
Kaiser F 62 KAS
Kaiser J 67 GRA
Kaiser M 75 EIS
Kakoma G W 70 YAO
Kallenbach-Greller L 25 LEIP, 27 VIE
Kalomiris M 54 PAL, 56 VIE
Kamburov I 47 PRA
Kamiński L 27 VIE
Kamiński W 60 WAR¹, 64 BRA
Kämper D 66 LEIP, 69 ROM, 70 BON
Kański J 60 WAR¹
Kapst E 71 BUD¹
Kara Z I 53 THE
Karásek B 58 BRN
Karastoyanov B P 75 BYD
Karbusický V 64 BERL, 64 BRA, 70 BON
Karkoschka E 62 KAS, 71 STU, 72 VIE¹, 73 BEL
Karlinger F 63 MER, 71 HIN
Karlyle C E 11 LON
Karomatov F M 64 MOS
Karp T 72 COP
Kárpáti J 61 TEH, 64 NEWD², 68 BRN, 71 BUD¹, 71 FLOR
Karpélès M 37 PAR⁴
Karsai M 74 LON
Karstädt G 53 BAM, 58 COL, 62 KAS, 74 GRA²
Kasemets U 60 *STRT*
Kašlik V 64 HAM
Kassler M 65 NEWY
Kast P 56 VIE, 57 BRUS, 62 KAS, 67 SIE
Kastner M S 54 PAR¹ (2), 57 WÉG, 63 MTA
Katz D 14 GÖT
Katz I 69 JER
Katz R 69 JER
Katzarova R D 71 BLE
Kaufmann H(arald) 67 *GRA*, 67 GRA, 67 LJU (p)
Kaufmann H E 56 WÉG
Kaufmann N 66 SOF
Kaufmann P 27 VIE
Kauko O 66 VEN, 72 MIL
Kaul O 27 VIE, 31 SAL
Kaya A K 73 ANK
Kebede A 70 YAO
Keel F 11 LON
Keil W 70 BERL²
Keldish Yu [Keldish J, Keldysch J, Keldysh G, Keldish Yu V] 60 WAR¹, 64 SAL (c;p), 66 BYD, 67 LJU, 69 BYD, 72 BYD, 75 BYD
Kelemen M 61 TOK, 71 STU
Keller H 25 LEIP, 26 FRE/B, 27 FRE/S, 49 BAS, 50 ROM, 56 VIE
Kellman H 71 NEWY
Kennedy D 28 PRA (2)
Kenton E 57 CAM/M (p)
Kerényi G 61 BUD
Kessler F 72 BYD
Kestenberg L 25 LEIP (c)
Kesting P 70 WÜR

von Keussler G 24 BERL, 25 LEIP, 27 HAL
Khadzhimanov V 64 MOS (d)
Khan A 64 NEWD²
Khlebarov I 71 MOS
Khristov D *see* Christoff D
Kickton E 49 BAS
Kienle A 00 MUN
Kilian D 63 KIE
Kimbell D R B 72 MIL
Kindermann-Korthaus I 71 KAS
King A(rden) 75 AUS (p;2d)
King A(lec) H(yatt) 51 PAR, 56 VIE, 58 COL (c), 59 CAM, 65 DIJ (1;p)
Kinkeldey O 57 CAM/M
Kinsky G 25 LEIP, 28 VIE
Kirby F E 70 BON
Kirby P R 58 COL
Kirchmeyer H 66 LEIP (p)
Kirkendale W 70 VIE
Kirkpatrick J 74 NEWY¹ (c;2p)
Kirsch W 62 KAS, 66 LEIP, 71 NEWY (1;c)
Kishibe S 64 HAM, 67 BERL
Kitamura O 68 TOK¹
Kitazawa M 61 TOK
Kittel P 73 WEIM
Kjaer B 71 STGA (p)
Kjellström B 75 BRUN
Klatte W 25 LEIP
Klauder K 64 BERL
Klausmeier F 53 BAM (p)
Klebel B 70 GRA
Klein R 70 BON
Klein-Vogelbach S 72 GRA
Klemantarski L 13 GHE
Klemeničić I 68 SVE
Klemetti H 21 PAR
Klemm E 62 WAR
Klier K M 27 VIE
Klinger K 73 SIE
Klinkenberg H M 56 HAM
Klotz H 38 FRE/B, 49 BAS, 54 STAD, 54 VIE, 62 BERN, 68 THU, 69 PAR
Kluge R 66 *LEIP*, 66 LEIP, 67 LJU (p), 72 COP
Klusen E 50 LÜN¹, 58 COL, 62 KAS, 63 STT, 65 MARB, 71 HIN
Kluyver P 38 FRE/B
Kmicic-Mieleszyński W 60 WAR¹
Knaus J 70 BON
Kneif T 68 BRN, 73 BEL, 74 GRA¹, 74 ZAG
Knepler G 50 LEIP, 56 PRA, 58 COL, 59 HAL, 60 WAR¹, 63 PRA, 64 SAL (2p), 66 LEIP (p), 67 LJU (c), 70 BERL², 71 MOS
Knight F E 54 PAR²
Knudsen V O 62 COP
Kobylańska K 60 WAR¹
Koch F 56 HAM
Koch L 33 FLOR
Kochlewska-Woźniak J 71 BRN
Koch-Rebling K 74 BLA
Koczirz A 09 VIE
Kodera S 28 PRA

Kodera Y 28 PRA (2)
Koechlin C 11 ROM, 37 PAR[3]
Koelreutter H J 64 NEWD[2]
Koenig G M 65 CARB, 70 STOC
Koerbler M 68 SVE
Köhler F 28 VIE
Köhler K-H 58 COL, 59 CAM, 62 STOC, 64 SAL (p), 66 LEIP (p), 70 BERL[2], 70 VIE, 72 COP, *73 WEIM*, 73 WEIM
Köhler S 56 PRA, 58 BRN, 59 HAL, 65 BRN, 66 LEIP (p), 67 ZAG
Köhler V 70 BON
Köhler W 12 BERL
Kohler-Helffrich 38 FRA
Kohmann 38 FRA
Kohrs K H 70 BON
Koizumi F 61 TEH
Kojima S A 66 LEIP, 70 BON
Kok W 53 NET
Kolessa F [P] 09 VIE, 11 LON, 28 PRA
Kolisch R 72 GRA
Koller O 06 BAS
Kolleritsch O *74 GRA*[1], 74 GRA[1], 75 EIS
Kolneder W 52 UTR, 58 COL (c), 62 KAS, 67 BRN[2], 72 VIE[1]
Kolodin I 67 FLOR
Költzsch H 27 VIE, 28 VIE
Komma K M 53 BAM, 64 GRA[2], 71 STU
Kondo M 68 TOK[1], 74 LON
Konen V 70 BERL[2]
König R 54 PAR[2]
Konotop A 75 BYD
Konstantinović Z 66 SOF
Koole A J C 52 UTR, 64 SAL (3p)
Kopp R 51 OCH
Korabdeva K 75 BYD
Körner F 70 BON, 74 GRA[2]
Kornfeld F 54 VIE
Kos K 70 BON, 72 BYD, 72 COP, 75 BYD
Kosch F 27 VIE, 56 VIE, 57 PAR
Koschel H 50 LÜN[1]
Koschmieder E 64 BRA, 64 SAL
Koshikawa T 65 LIÈ
Kosten C W 65 LIÈ
Kostić V 68 SVE
Koszewski A 60 WAR[1]
Kotek G 27 VIE
Kötter E 66 LEIP
Kovačević K 66 BYD, 68 SVE
Kovács J 66 VEN, 71 BUD[1]
Kovalevsky M 62 BERN
Krader B 66 SOF, 68 SVE
Krafft C 64 AMS
Krafft de Boërio C 68 UPP
Kraft G 58 COL, 59 HAL, 60 WAR[1], 61 BUD, 64 BERL, 70 BERL[2]
Kragemo H 50 LÜN[2]
Kraiski O 74 SIE
Krǎstev [Krïstev] V 66 BYD, 71 MOS
Kratina J 72 GRA
Kratochvil J 56 PRA

Kraus A 11 LON
Kraus E 67 BERL
Krause E 58 BRN
Krautwurst F 58 COL
Kreichgauer 38 FRA
Kreidler W 50 LÜN[1], 53 BAM
Kremlev [Kremljew, Kremljow] J 59 BUD, 60 WAR[1] (2), 62 PAR (2), 70 BERL[2]
Krenek E 28 VIE, 37 FLOR, 60 STRT, 64 HAM
Kreps J 23 BRUS, 25 BRUG, 26 GEN, 54 ARR, 58 MARS
Kresánek J 58 BRN, 63 PRA, 70 PIE
Kretzenbacher L 64 GRA[2]
Krickeberg D 71 KAS, 72 COP
Krings A 61 COL, 71 HIN
Krïstev V *see* Krǎstev V
Kroemer M 72 GRA
Krohn I 00 PAR[2], 06 BAS (4), 09 VIE (2), 11 LON, 24 BAS, 27 VIE, 30 LIÈ, 52 BERN, 56 VIE
Krohn J 25 LEIP
Król-Kaczorowska B 69 WAR
Kroll E 27 VIE, 58 COL
Kromolicki J 25 LEIP
Krones H 71 BUD[1]
Kronsteiner H 64 GRA[1]
Kroó G 60 WAR[1], 61 BUD, 64 SAL (p), 71 BUD[1]
Kropfinger K 70 BON, 72 COP, 72 FRE/B, 74 BERL
Kröschlová E 74 KRP
Kross S 62 KAS, 66 LEIP, 67 MAG, 70 BERL[2], 70 BON, 73 MAG
Kroyer T 09 VIE, 24 BAS, 25 LEIP
Krueger F 00 PAR[4], 05 ROM, 09 VIE
Krüger H 58 COL
Krüger W 50 LÜN[1], 53 BAM, 56 HAM, 71 BUD[2]
Kruk P 67 ZAG
Krummacher F 70 BON, 72 COP
Krutová A 71 BRN
Kruttge E 25 LEIP
Ktano H 28 PRA
Kuba L 09 VIE, 28 PRA
Kubinyi A 72 SÁR
Kučera V 65 BERL[1]
Kuckertz J *75 ROM*, 75 ROM (2)
Kučukalić Z 68 SVE
Kühebacher E 73 NEU/B
Kuhl W 56 CAM/M
Kühn H 74 BERL
Kühn W 25 LEIP
Kühner H 66 VEN, 69 VER
Kukelka P 71 GRA
Kukharski V 60 STRT
Kumer Z 69 STOC, 73 BAL
Kümmerling H 63 KIE, 66 LEIP 70 BON
Kuna L 64 MOŠ (d)
Kundera L 58 BRN, 65 BRN
Kuni A 68 TOK[1], 74 LON
Kunst J 28 PRA, 50 LÜN[1], 52 UTR

Kunze S 70 BON, 72 COP, 74 ROM
Kurath G P 49 NEWY[1], 49 NEWY[2] (2), 56 PHIL, 58 WAS
Kurka E 67 PRA
Kurthen W 25 LEIP (2)
Kussev A J 71 BUD[2]
Kuthy-Terey 28 PRA
Kuttner F A 58 COL, 64 SAL (p)
Květ J 27 BEL
Květová R 65 BRA, 67 RAD
Kyas V 71 BRN
Kyhlberg B 71 STGA (p)

Laaff E 53 BAM (p), 62 KAS (2;c)
von Laban R 37 PAR[3]
Labarraque L 38 GHE
Labhardt F 49 BAS
Labroca M 54 PAR[2], 64 HAM, 66 VEN, 67 FLOR
Labussière A 73 PAR
Lacas P-P 63 MTA
Lach R 27 VIE (c), 28 VIE, 31 SAL
Lachenmann H 71 STU
Lachmann R 25 LEIP, 27 VIE, 32 CAIR
Ladmanová M 60 WAR[1]
Laily P-A 50 ROM
Lajtha L 28 PRA, 37 FLOR, 54 WÉG
Laker K 25 LEIP
de La Laurencie L 09 VIE, 11 LON, 23 BRUS
Lalo C 11 ROM, 37 PAR[2], 37 PAR[3]
Laloy L 00 PAR[2], 06 BAS
de Lamare P
Lambrechts-Douillez J 69 NUR, 70 ANT, 71 GRA
Lammel I 59 HAL, 64 BERL, 70 BERL[2]
Lamson R 39 NEWY
Landé F 25 LEIP
Landon H C R 56 PAR, 57 CAM/M, 59 BUD
Landormy P 00 PAR[2], 11 ROM
Landowski W L 54 PAR[2]
Lang P H 49 BAS, 61 NEWY (c), 66 CHIC, 67 LJU (p)
Lange F C 39 NEWY
Lange H K H 70 BON
de Lange P A 65 LIÈ
Laragnino F 50 FLOR
de Larrea Palacin A 60 PAR[2]
Larsen J P 49 BAS, 56 HAM, 58 COL (c), 59 HAL, 61 NEWY (c), 70 GRA, 70 BRN (1;c), 71 EIS, 72 COP
Larsen W S 29 NEWH
LaRue J 56 VIE, 57 CAM/M (p), 58 COL, 59 CAM, *61 NEWY*, 64 SAL (p), 65 NEWY, 66 LEIP, 67 LJU (c)
de Las Cuevas E 28 FRA
Laske O E 73 BEL
Laszlo E 68 UPP
László F 73 MAG
Laudová H 70 TRČ, 74 KRP

Laufer A   69 JER
Launay D   54 PAR[1], 57 WÉG, 64
　　SAL (p), 65 DIJ, 72 BYD
Launis A   09 VIE, 11 LON
Laurent   62 BERN
Lauri-Volpi G   67 FLOR
Laux K   50 LEIP, 70 BERL[2]
Lavagetto M   72 MIL
Lavoye L   09 LIÈ (2), 30 LIÈ, 35
　　BRUS[1]
Lawrenson T E   72 VEN
Lawton D   66 VEN, 72 MIL
Lazarevich G   72 COP
Lazarov S   64 BRA
Lazarus H   68 TOK[1]
Leach MacE   63 CART
Lebeau E   56 VIE, 57 WÉG, 65 DIJ
　　(1;p)
Lebedinskiy L N   64 MOS
Lebègue R   53 PAR, 55 ROY
Lébl V   58 BRN (1;d)
LeCaine H   60 STRT
Lechthaler J   25 LEIP, 27 BERL,
　　27 VIE
Le Cosquino de Bussy J R   55
　　BRUS (2)
Ledda P   68 VEN
Ledesma J   66 VEN
de Leeuw T   64 HAM, 66 MANL,
　　71 MOS (2)
Lefkoff G   66 MOR, 66 MOR
Le Flem P   37 PAR[3]
Legley V   60 STRT
Le Guennant A   37 PAR[1], 50
　　ROM, 54 VIE
Lehmann D   56 VIE, 60 WAR[1], 61
　　BUD, 66 LEIP, 75 BYD
Lehmann F   26 FRE/B
Lehtinen A I   75 ESP
Leibowitz R   66 VEN, 67 FLOR,
　　68 STRS, 72 MIL
Leichtentritt H   06 BAS, 09 VIE
Leipp E   62 COP, 65 LIÈ (2), 67
　　PAR, 71 BUD[2] (2), 73
　　PAR
Leisiö J   75 BRUN
Lemacher H   54 VIE
Leman A   71 MOS
Lemonds W W   72 BYD
Lenaerts R B M   30 ANT, 30 LIÈ,
　　49 BAS, 50 ROM, 52 UTR,
　　58 COL, 61 COL, 61
　　NEWY (c), 71 NEWY
　　(1;p)
Lendvai E   66 VEN, 67 FLOR
Leng L   67 BRN[1], 70 TRČ
Lenihan J M A   53 NET
Lenk A   27 FRE/S
Lennards J   50 ROM, 54 VIE, 66
　　CHIC
Leon Perez A   64 MOS
Lesche C   70 STOC
Lessoa M   37 FLOR
Lesure F   53 BAM, 53 PAR, *54
　　ARR*, 54 PAL, 55 BRUS
　　(2), 55 ROY, 56 VIE, 57
　　NEU/S, 57 PAR, 59 BUD,
　　61 CAM/M (p), 61 NEWY,
　　62 PAR, 62 STOC (c), 74
　　JER (p)

Lesznai L   61 BUD
Levasheva O   72 BYD
Levelt W J M   62 COP, 64 AMS
Levi L   57 PAR, 71 FLOR
Levi V   56 VIE, 66 VEN
Levy E   26 GEN
Levy K J   53 PAR, 61 OKH, 64
　　BRA, 72 COP
Levy M   73 BEL
Levysohn S   09 VIE
Lewański J   69 WAR, 69 WAR
Lewicki E   31 SAL
von Lewinski W-E   73 NUR
Lewis D   71 STGA (p)
Leydi R   73 ROM[2]
Liang Tsai Ping   66 MANL
Liberovici S   64 BERL
Lichtenfeld M   74 GRA[1]
Liebe A   50 LEIP, 56 HAM, 70
　　BON
Lieber E   71 BUD[2]
Liebermann R   54 PAR[2], 64 HAM
Lieberson G   68 NEWY (c)
Liebner J   62 KAS (2), 66 VEN
Lienard J S   65 LIÈ
Liess A   52 UTR, 54 VIE, 62 KAS
Lifar S   37 PAR[3], 56 VEN
Ligeti G   68 THU
Li Gotti E   54 PAL
Lillie H W R   50 ROM
Lim W S   56 VIE
Li Man Kuei   64 HAM
Lindberg F   55 BRUS, 59 CAM, *62
　　STOC*, 65 DIJ (1;p), 71
　　STGA (p)
Lindblom B   73 BEL
Lindegren E   64 HAM
van der Linden A   35 BRUS[1], 38
　　NAM, 52 UTR, 54 ARR,
　　59 CAM (p), 68 LIÈ
Lindgren A   00 PAR[2]
Lindlar H   60 WAR[1], 62 KAS
Lindquist J   71 BUD[2]
Lineff E   09 VIE, 11 LON
Linhardt W   56 HAM, 56 VIE
Link J D   65 BRN
Linton M   59 CAM
de Lioncourt G   37 PAR[1]
Lipphardt W   50 LÜN[1], 50 ROM,
　　58 COL, 64 GRA[1], 67 LJU
　　(p), 70 BRN, 71 BRN
Lippman E   65 NEWY
Lippmann E A   67 LJU (p)
Lippmann F   66 VEN, *69 ROM*, 69
　　ROM, 70 BON, *74 ROM*,
　　74 ROM
Lissa Z   54 PAR[1], 56 HAM, 56
　　VIE, 58 COL, *60 WAR[1]*,
　　60 WAR[1] (2), 62 WAR, 64
　　SAL (1;2p), 65 WAR, *66
　　BYD*, 66 BYD (2), 67 LJU
　　(2p), 70 BERL[2], 70 BON
　　(2), 70 PIE, 70 VIE, 71
　　MOS, 72 BYD, 72 COP, 74
　　ZAG
List E   75 BLA
List G   63 CART, *65 BLM*, 65
　　BLM, 67 VAN
Litaize G   54 VIE
Litt D H   67 MAG

Liuzzi F   34 TRT, 39 NEWY
Livingstone E F   70 BON
Livanova [Liwanowa] T N   56
　　VIE, 59 BUD
Łobaczewska S   47 PRA, 56 PRA,
　　56 VIE, 60 WAR[1], 62
　　WAR
Lockspeiser E   54 PAR[2], 62 PAR
Lockwood L   65 NEWY (2), 67
　　LJU (p), 68 MIL, 70
　　STGE, 71 NEWY (1;p), 72
　　COP (c), 73 ROM[1], 74
　　NEWY[2]
Loebell   38 FRA
Loewenbach J   58 BRN
Löffer H   27 FRE/S
Logemann G W   65 NEWY
Logotheti   21 PAR
Lombardi Satriani L M   73 ROM[2]
Lomnitzer H   66 OXF[2], 73 NEU/B
Longo A(chille)   50 FLOR
Longo A(lexandre)   00 PAR[2]
Longyear R M   64 SAL (p), 70
　　BON
López-Calo J   64 SAL (p), 69 VER,
　　72 MIL
López Godoy R J   54 VIE
Lorente M   65 LIÈ
Lorenz K   71 HIN
Loria A   37 FLOR, 38 FLOR
Lotichius D   71 STGA (c)
Lottermoser W   51 OCH, 53 BAM,
　　56 HAM, 56 VIE (2), 58
　　MARS
Loudon E   28 PRA
Loulová O   56 PRA
Lourié A   37 PAR[3]
Lowens I   61 NEWY (c), 62 KAS,
　　64 SAL (p)
Lowinsky E E   61 NEWY, 68 MIL,
　　71 NEWY, 71 NEWY
　　(1;p), 73 ROM[1]
Loyonnet P   37 PAR[3]
Lualdi A   33 FLOR, 48 FLOR, 49
　　FLOR
Luciani G   74 SIE
Luciani S A   37 FLOR, 48 FLOR
　　(2), 50 FLOR
Ludwig F   09 VIE, 25 LEIP
Ludwig H   69 VER
Luedtke H   26 FRE/B
Luening O   57 CAM/M (p)
Luin E J   56 VIE
Luithlen V   59 CAM, 70 ANT
Lukács G   71 BUD[1]
Lukacs M   59 STU
Lumsden D   54 PAR[1], 57 NEU/S
Lundgren B   58 COL
Lunelli R   34 TRT, 50 ROM
Lunghi F L   34 TRT, 50 FLOR
Lunssens M   35 BRUS[1]
Lupi R   48 FLOR
Luther W M   51 PAR
Lutze L   64 NEWD[2]
Lyon G   00 PAR[1], 09 VIE

Mačák I   67 BRN[1], 69 NUR, 69
　　STOC, 70 TRČ, 73 BAL,
　　75 BRUN
Mac Crea D   00 MUN

Maceda J   61 TOK, *66 MANL*, 66 MANL, 67 BERL, 69 KUA
MacGillivray J   59 CAM
Machabey A   33 FLOR, 60 PAR[1]
Machatius F-J   58 COL, 62 KAS
Maciejewski T   75 BYD
Mackenzie A   09 VIE
Mackerness E D   58 COL
Mackerras C   65 BRN
Maclean C   *11 LON*
Madsen C   57 PAR
Maegaard J   70 BON, 72 COP, 74 GRA[1]
Maertens W   62 MAG, 67 MAG, *72 BLA*, 72 BLA, 75 BLA (d)
Maffioletti M   34 TRT
Magnani L   67 PARM, 70 VIE, 72 MIL
Mahillon V   00 PAR[1]
Mahler A   74 GRA[1]
Mahling C-H   68 UPP, 70 BON, 70 GRA, 72 GRA, 73 BAL, 74 GRA[2], 75 BLA (d), 75 BRUN
Mahrenholz C   *27 FRE/S*, 27 FRE/S (2), 38 FRE/B
Maillet F   50 ROM, 57 PAR
Maine B   33 FLOR
Mainka J   66 LEIP (1; p), 70 BERL[2]
Maksimović S   75 BYD
Malcolm G   50 ROM
Maletzke G   54 PAR[2]
(de) Malherbe C   09 VIE (3), 11 ROM
Mali J   54 SAL (p)
Malinowski W   69 BYD, 69 PARM
Malipiero G F   37 FLOR, 37 PAR[3], 50 FLOR
Malipiero R   71 MOS
Mall G D   34 TÜB
Mallory V   59 STU
Malm W P   69 KUA, *71 ANN*, 71 ANN
Malmros A-L   72 VIE[2]
Malmström D   72 COP
Mamczarz I   70 VEN
Manal G   71 STGA (p)
Mancini R   72 MIL
Mandel A   74 NEWY[1] (2c;2p)
Mandel N   74 NEWY[1] (p)
Manganaro G   55 IST
Mangini N   74 SIE, 75 SIE
Manheim L   70 LAW
Manley D M J P   65 LIÈ
Mann A   62 KAS, 70 BON
Manoliu G   67 BUC, 73 BUC
Mantelli A   48 FLOR, 62 PAR
Mantuani J   09 VIE (3)
Manucci de Grandis I   38 FRA
Manzanares R   63 CART, 65 BLM
Maquet J N   54 WÉG
Maraini F   71 FLOR
Marangos N   50 ROM
Marbe M   67 BUC, 73 BUC
Marcel-Dubois C   37 PAR[3], 37

PAR[4], 54 PAL, 54 WÉG, 56 WÉG, 60 PAR[1], 61 NEWY, 64 SAL (2p), 65 DIJ (2), 67 BERL, 67 LJU (p), 68 TOK[2], 69 NUR, 69 STOC, 72 TOU, 74 JER (p)
Marchal A   32 STRS
Marchesi G   66 VEN, 68 PARM, 72 MIL
Marckhl E   64 GRA[1]
Marcuse I   37 PAR[2]
Marcusson O   75 ESP
de Maré R   37 PAR[3]
Marggraf W   66 LEIP
Marica P   57 CHIE
Marie J-E   54 PAR[2]
Marilier J   54 ROU
Marinov I   69 VER
Marinuzzi G   50 FLOR
Markevich I   37 FLOR
Markiewicz L   70 BERL[2]
Markl J   56 PRA, 58 BRN, 65 BRA, 67 BRN[1], 69 STOC, 70 TRČ, 73 BAL
Maróthy J   63 PRA, 65 BERL[1], 71 MOS
Marotti F   72 VEN
Marrocco W T   69 CER
Marschner F   06 BAS, 27 VIE
Marshall A H   68 TOK[1]
Martienssen-Lohmann F   38 FRA
Martin C   57 PAR
Martin D W   56 CAM/M, 62 COP, 71 BUD[2]
Martin F   26 GEN, 65 GEN
Martin G   63 BUD, 66 VEN, 69 VER, 72 SÁR
Martinelli G   66 VEN
Martinez-Göllner M L   69 CER
Martinez Torner E   28 PRA
Martin Gonzalez C   28 PRA
Martinotti S   66 VEN, 68 VEN, 69 CAS, 69 PARM, 69 VER, 70 BOL, 71 WAR, 72 MIL, 73 SIE, 74 SIE, 75 SIE (2)
Martinov [Martinov, Martynov] I   56 PRA, 64 SAL (p), 69 VER, 70 BON, 71 BUD[1], 71 MOS, 72 MIL
Martirano S   74 NEWY[1]
Martorell A   65 MTS
Martorell O   65 MTS (2)
Marvia E   72 BYD
Marx H(ans) J(oachim)   68 FUS (1;d), *70 BON*, 70 PIE, 72 COP
Marx J(osef)   27 VIE (c), 28 VIE
Marxer J   05 STRS
Marx-Weber M   *70 BON*
Marzi G   61 OKH
Masel L   65 BERL[1]
Masetti E   50 FLOR
Masoliver Martinez J R   28 PRA
Massarani R   66 VEN
Massenkeil G   57 WÉG, 58 COL, 62 KAS, 66 LEIP, *70 BON*
Massera G   68 VEN, 69 PARM (2), 71 WAR
Masson P-M   06 BAS, *11 ROM*, 11

ROM, 30 LIÈ, 37 PAR[3], 52 UTR
Mathé A   54 VIE
Matheu A   65 MTS
Mathews M V   59 STU, 70 STOC
Mathias F X   05 STRS (2), 09 VIE, 11 LON (1;c), 30 LIÈ, *32 STRS*, 32 STRS (6)
Mathiassen F   64 SAL (p)
Mathieu-Arth F   66 MTA, 67 LJU, 70 MTA
Mattfeld J A   71 NEWY
Matthay T   11 LON
Matúš F   70 TRČ
Matz M J   66 VEN, 69 VER, 72 MIL
Mauceri J   74 NEWY[1] (c)
Maurer W   72 VIE[2]
Maximowna I   64 HAM
Maxton W   53 BAM, 62 KAS
Mayeda A   70 GRA
Mayer G   63 PRA, 65 BERL[1], 66 LEIP (1;p)
Mayer J E   64 GRA[1]
Mayer M V   57 CHIE
Mayer W A   71 HIN
Mayer-Reinach A   11 LON
Mayor G   64 NEWD[2]
Mbunga S   75 ROM
McAllester D P   56 PHIL
McCleod N   75 AUS (1;p;d)
McCredie A D   70 BON, 75 ROM
McElroy G   70 LAW
McGlinchee C   64 AMS
McGowan M M   70 MTA
McKenzie W   72 VIE[1] (1;p)
McNaught W G   11 LON
McNeill S   53 NET
McNulty P J   74 LON
McPhee C   61 TOK
Medici M   *66 VEN*, 69 VER, 69 VER, *72 MIL*
van der Meer J H   62 KAS, 64 SAL (1;c), 67 BRN[1], 69 NUR, 70 ANT, 70 GRA, 71 BRN, 71 GRA, 71 KAS, 72 COP
Meerens   00 PAR[2]
de Meeus F   68 LIÈ
Mehl J G   38 FRE/B, 53 BAM
Mehner K   66 LEIP
Meier B   56 VIE, 62 KAS (2)
Meinel H F   53 NET, 71 BUD[2]
Melka A   71 BUD[2]
Melkus E   70 GRA
Mellers W   53 PAR, 71 MOS
Meloncelli R   73 SIE, 74 SIE
Ménard R   58 COL
Menchaca A   11 LON
Mendel A   *39 NEWY*, 57 CAM/M (p), 61 NEWY (1;c), 71 NEWY (1;c;p)
Mendelssohn A   27 FRE/S
Mensah A A   70 YAO
Menon N   47 PRA, 61 TEH, 64 HAM, 71 MOS (2)
Menuhin Y   65 BERL[1]
Mercer D M A   53 NET, 65 LIÈ
Mercier J   58 MARS
Mercier P   47 BIS, 68 LIÈ

Mercù P 66 VEN
Merian W *24 BAS*, 24 BAS, 27 VIE
Merlier Mme M 30 ATH
Mermet J 73 PAR
Merriam A P 58 SJOS, 65 BLM
Mersmann H 24 BAS, 24 BERL, 25 LEIP, 27 VIE, 28 PRA, 30 HAM[2], 61 NEWY (c)
Mertens F 72 BERN
Mertens V 70 WÜR
Mertin J 38 FRE/B, 54 VIE, 71 GRA
Metzger H-K 67 GRA
Metzler F 62 KAS, 66 LEIP
Meugé J 37 PAR[2]
Meyer E(rnst) H(ermann) *50 LEIP*, 54 PAR[1], 56 PRA, 56 VIE, 59 HAL, 62 MAG, 64 BERL, 64 NEWD[2], 64 SAL (p), *66 LEIP*, 66 LEIP (c), 70 BERL[2]
Meyer E(rwin) 56 CAM/M
Meyer H-F *71 HIN*
Meyer J 62 COP, 65 LIÈ, 67 PAR, 69 STOC, 71 BUD[2], 74 LON
Meyer K 25 LEIP, 27 VIE
Meyer W 75 BRUN
Meyer-Eppler W 53 NET
Meyers H 57 PAR
Meylan P 55 BRUS
Meylan R 65 DIJ (1;p), 67 LJU (p), 70 STGE, 73 PAR
Miazga T 60 WAR[1]
Michaelides S 64 GRA[2]
Michel P 61 BUD, 66 LEIP, 70 BERL[2], 72 VIE[2]
Micheloni S 69 VER
Michelson T 28 NEWY
Midzic-Dabac S 71 STU
Miederer 38 FRA
Mies P 25 LEIP (2), 27 VIE, 28 VIE, 49 BAS, 56 VIE, 58 BRN, 58 COL, 59 BUD, 59 HAL, 62 KAS, 68 BRN
Migliavacca L 68 MIL
Mihule J 66 BRN
Mikanová E 72 BYD
Miks-Rudkowska N 69 WAR
Mila M 33 FLOR, 48 FLOR, 49 FLOR, 64 HAM, 64 SAL (c), 66 VEN, 72 MIL
Mikulicz K L 27 VIE
Milhaud D 37 FLOR, 38 FLOR
Miller C K 55 BRUS
Miller D C 39 NEWY (1;c)
Miller P L 55 BRUS, 61 NEWY
Millet L 27 VIE
Milliet P 00 PAR[1]
Milojković-Djurić J 61 OKH
Milošević P 68 SVE
Milstein J 60 WAR[1]
Minardi G P 72 MIL
Miranda y Gómez M D 57 PAR, 66 CHIC
Miret H 65 MTS
Mischiati O *68 FUS*, 68 FUS
Missir N 61 BUD
Mitchell W S 65 NEWY

Miyagawa R 65 LIÈ
Miyagi M 61 TOK
Miyawaki K 68 TOK[1]
Mladenović Ž 66 SOF
Młodziejowski J 58 BRN
Mlouka M 73 PAR
Moberg C-A 30 LIÈ, 56 HAM
Moe L H 57 NEU/S
Moeck H 67 BRN[1]
Mohr W 56 HAM, 62 KAS, 66 LEIP, 70 BON
Moisescu T 73 BUC
Moissl F 09 VIE
Mokrý L 60 WAR[1], 63 PRA, *64 BRA*, 64 BRA, 64 SAL (p), 71 MOS
Moldenhauer H 56 VIE, 72 VIE[1] (1;p)
Moles A 53 NET, 54 PAR[2]
Moll 38 PRA
Moll X 65 MTS (2)
Møller D F 73 BAL
Möllers C 74 BERL
Moll Roqueta J 55 BRUS (2)
Molnár A 59 BUD, 60 WAR[1], 61 BUD, 71 BUD[1]
Mompellio F 54 PAL
Mondolfi-Bossarelli A 67 SIE, 73 SIE, 74 ROM
Moneta-Caglio E 57 PAR
Monk E 64 HAM
Monosoff S 72 GRA
Monterosso R 61 TOD, 62 TOD, 63 TOD, 64 SAL (p), 65 RAV, *68 VEN*, 68 VEN, 69 CER, 69 PER, 73 ROM[1]
Monterosso Vacchelli A M 68 VEN
Moog H 74 GRA[2]
Moos P 06 BAS, 09 VIE, 13 BERL, 25 LEIP, 27 HAL, 27 VIE, 50 LÜN[1]
Mooser R-A 33 FLOR, 37 FLOR
Moragas B 65 MTS
Morawska K 71 WAR
Morche G 70 BON, 72 COP
de Morcourt R 54 PAR[1]
Morelli G 72 VEN
Moretti C 54 VIE
Moreux S 54 PAR[2]
Morgan R P 74 NEWY[1]
Morilleau 57 PAR
Morin E 54 PAR[2]
Morin G 03 DIN, 56 VIE
Morini M 67 FLOR
Moroi M 61 TOK
Mortari V 48 FLOR
Mortensen A O 60 WAR[1]
Morton D 66 MANL, 69 KUA
Moser H J 24 BAS, 24 BERL, 25 LEIP, 27 BERL, 27 FRE/S, 27 VIE, 50 LÜN[1], 52 UTR, 53 BAM, 54 PAL, 56 HAM, 56 VIE, 60 WAR[1]
Moser J 00 MUN
Mosusova [Mosusowa] N 69 BRN, 70 BRN, 72 COP
da Motta e Albuquerque J B 50 ROM

de la Motte D 64 HAM
de la Motte-Haber H 66 LEIP
de Moura Reis Pequeño M 55 BRUS
Mourinho A 63 STT
Mousses K 50 ROM
Möži A 70 TRČ
Mráček J 72 BYD, 72 COP
Mraz G 71 EIS
Mraz-Koller G *71 EIS*, 71 EIS
Mueller von Asow E H 50 LÜN[2], 56 VIE
Mueller von Asow H 62 KAS
van der Mueren F 56 VIE, 57 WÉG
Mukharinskaya L S 64 MOS
Muller F 58 COL
Müller H 09 VIE, 11 LON (1;c), 25 LEIP (2), 27 BERL (2), 27 VIE (c;1)
Müller J 25 LEIP
Müller L 56 HAM, 68 TOK[1]
Müller M 73 BAL
Müller R F 28 VIE
Müller-Blattau J M 24 BAS, 25 LEIP (2), 26 FRE/B, 27 VIE, 38 FRA, *38 FRE/B*, 38 FRE/B, 53 BAM (p), 56 VIE, 58 COL, 59 HAL, 62 KAS (c)
Müller-Blattau W 66 LEIP, 74 GRA[2]
Müller-Nishio W 72 GRA
Müller-Paderborn H 25 LEIP (c)
Müller-Walt T 38 FRE/B
Müllmann B 62 KAS
Mumma G 74 NEWY[1]
Munclinger M 67 BRN[2]
Mund H 26 FRE/B, 27 FRE/S
Münnich R 25 LEIP
Muñoz M A 63 STT
Munro K 58 COL
Münzer G 06 BAS
Muraro M T 66 VEN, *72 VEN*
Muroi M 56 VIE
Murphy R M 57 NEU/S
Musch H 74 SINZ
Mušinka M 74 KRP
Musiol K 70 BON, 73 WEIM
Mycielski Z 60 STRT
Myers C 12 BERL
Myers C S 13 BERL
Myers K 51 PAR

Nadel S 27 VIE, 28 PRA
Nagai Y 71 BUD[2]
Nagel W 09 VIE, 27 VIE
Nakayama T 65 LIÈ
Nancarrow D 75 AUS (p)
Naselli C 54 PAL
Nataletti G 34 TRT (2), 54 PAL (2), 58 COL, 58 WÉG, 71 FLOR (d)
Nattiez J-J 73 BEL, 74 ZAG
Nef K 06 BAS (1;c), 21 PAR, 24 BAS, 30 LIÈ
Nef W 49 BAS
Negreanu R 67 BUC
Neighbour O W 59 CAM (p)
Neill E 73 ROM[2]

Němcová A 67 BRN², 69 BRN, 71 BRN
Němeček J 56 PRA
Nestler G 53 BAM, 56 VIE, 58 COL
Nest'yev [Nestjew, Nestyev, Niestiew] I V 61 BUD, 62 WAR, 70 BERL², 71 BUD¹
Nettl B 58 COL, 65 BLM, 68 SVE, 75 ROM
Nettl P 25 LEIP, 27 VIE, 31 SAL (2)
Neumann A 64 HAM
Neumann F 50 LÜN¹, 62 KAS, 64 SAL (p)
Neumann H J 51 OCH
Neumann P 50 ROM
Neumann V 49 FLOR
Neumann W 66 LEIP
Neupert H 53 BAM, 62 KAS
Neuwirth G 74 GRA¹
Newcomb A 72 COP
Newman S 56 VIE
Newman W S 70 BON, 72 COP
Nicastro A 66 VEN, 69 VER, 72 MIL
Nicewonger C 59 CAM
Nicewonger H 59 CAM
Nicol K L 65 DIJ (p)
Niculescu S 67 BUC, 73 BUC
Niedecken-Gebhard 38 FRA
Nielsen T 71 STU
Niemann K 66 LEIP, 70 BERL², 70 BERL², 71 MOS, 72 VIE²
Niemeyer A 66 LEIP
Niemöller K W 56 HAM, 62 KAS, 70 BERL¹, 70 BON
Niestiew I see Nest'yev I V
Nievergelt E 52 BERN
Nigmedzyanov M N 64 MOS
Nikiprowetzky T 67 BERL
Nikishov G 75 BYD
Niklaus H 64 GRA¹
Nikolajewa L 73 WEIM
Nikolajewa N 70 BERL²
Nitsche P 74 BERL
Nitschke W 70 BON
Nixdorff H 73 BAL
Nketia J H K 61 TEH, 65 BERL², 67 BERL, 70 YAO (2)
Noack E ̀ 67 MAG
Noack F 24 BAS, 25 LEIP, 27 VIE (2)
Noble J 54 PAR¹, 71 NEWY
Nobre M 65 BLM
Noll G 62 KAS
Nomura F Y 58 COL, 61 COL, 61 TOK, 64 AMS, 70 BON
Nomura K 61 TOK
Nono L 71 VIC
Nordio M 66 VEN
Norlind T 11 LON (2; c)
Nosek V 66 BRN, 67 BRN²
Noske F 57 NEU/S, 58 COL, 61 NEWY (c), 64 SAI (p), 67 LJU (p), 70 BRN, 72 MIL
Nösselt V 68 TOK¹, 71 BUD², 74 LON

Noto Soeroto 28 PRA
Notowicz N 66 LEIP (p)
Nováček O 68 BRN
Nováček Z 58 BRN, 61 BUD, 70 BERL², 70 BON, 70 PIE, 71 EIS
Novack S 71 NEWY
Nowacki K 62 WAR
Nowak A 72 COP
Nowak L 28 VIE, 50 LÜN², 56 VIE
Nowak-Romanowicz A 60 WAR¹, 66 BYD
van Nuffel J 50 ROM
Numminen M A 72 VIE²
Nyberg T 75 ESP
de Nys C 56 PAR, 57 PAR, 59 BUD, 60 WAR¹

Obama J 57 PAR (2)
Oberborbeck F 25 LEIP, 50 LEIP, 53 BAM (c; p), 62 KAS
Oberti E 56 VEN
Obrist A 06 BAS (3; c)
Očadlík M 56 PRA, 58 BRN, 60 WAR¹, 61 BUD
Ochs E 71 BRN
Ochs G 75 BLA (d)
Odelman E 75 ESP
Odenius O 75 ESP
Oesch H 72 COP (1;c)
Ohmann F 13 BERL
Oldham G 59 CAM, 59 CAM
Oldman C B 59 CAM
Olias G 66 LEIP, 70 BERL²
de Oliveira-Lima M 09 VIE
Ondrejka K 70 TRČ (3)
O'Neill C E 66 CHIC
Ongkili J P 69 KUA
Onnen F 62 PAR
Opienski H 11 LON, 26 GEN, 27 VIE
Oppel R 25 LEIP
von Oppen J 70 BON
Oransay G 73 ANK
Ordshonikidze [Ordzhonikidze] G 70 BERL², 71 MOS
Orel A 25 LEIP (2), 27 HAL, 27 VIE (1: 2c), 28 VIE, 31 SAL, 53 BAM, 62 KAS, 64 SAL
Orff C 64 HAM
Origuchi N 28 PRA (2)
Orlandini I 11 LON
Orlando S 65 BRN
Orrego-Salas J 65 BLM, 68 SVE, 71 MOS
Orselli C 74 SIE
Ortis Diaz D L 28 PRA
Ortmann O 39 NEWY
Osborne C 69 VER
Osman M T 69 KUA, 69 KUA
Osmond-Smith D 73 BEL
Osostowicz-Sutkowska A 70 BOL
Ossorguine M 37 PAR¹
von der Osten G 70 VIE
Osthoff H 38 FRA, 50 LÜN¹, 50 LÜN¹ (c), 51 IES, 52 UTR, 53 BAM (c), 56 VIE, 61 NEWY (1; c), 62 KAS

Osthoff W 54 PAL, 62 KAS, 67 SIE, 70 BON, 72 VEN
Ott A 50 LÜN², 55 BRUS, 59 CAM, 62 KAS, 62 STOC (1; c)
Ott K 05 STRS
Ottich M 60 WAR¹
Otto D 60 ATH
Otto I 58 COL, 59 CAM, 62 KAS, 71 KAS
Ottosen K 73 PAR, 75 ESP (2)
Ouedraog[h]o R 61 COL, 75ROM
Overath J 54 VIE, 57 PAR, 61 COL, 66 CHIC, 75 ROM

do Paço A 63 STT
Padrós J 65 MTS
Pagano G 73 ROM²
Paglicci-Brozzi A 03 ROM
Pahaut R 68 LIÈ
Pala F 58 BRN
Palikarova-Verdeil R 48 PAR², 50 ROM
Palisca C 61 CAM/M (p), 65 NEWY, 73 ROM¹
Palm A 62 KAS
Palyulis Z 64 MOS (d)
Pampanini R 67 FLOR (p)
van Panhuys L C 48 BRUS (2)
van Panhuys L V 30 HAM¹
Pannain G 33 FLOR, 37 FLOR, 38 FLOR, 48 FLOR, 49 FLOR
Paoli R 50 ROM
Paolone E 40 VEN
Paone R 67 FLOR
Papadimitriou A 30 ATH
Papineau-Couture J 60 STRT
Papp G 69 BYD, 72 BYD, 73 BAL
Parain-Vial J 56 VEN
Paramor N 67 ZAG
Pardo Tovar A 63 CART
Parent H 00 PAR²
Parente A 33 FLOR, 38 FLOR, 48 FLOR, 49 FLOR
Parisot J 00 PAR⁶
Paroissin R 57 PAR (2)
Parry C H H 11 LON
Partini R 34 TRT
Parvio M 75 ESP
Pascu G 67 BUC
Pasero T 67 FLOR (p)
Pasinetti F 37 FLOR
Pasqualini G 53 NET
Pass W 70 BRN, 71 BRN, 74 GRA¹
Patmagrian A 54 CAM
Pätzig G 62 KAS
Pauli F W 53 BAM, 55 BRUS
Paumgartner B 31 SAL, 64 SAL
Paumgartner R 67 FLOR
Pavarini M 66 VEN
Pavlov E 72 VIE²
Pawlak A 74 KRP
Pawliszyn S 60 WAR¹
Paynter J 72 VIE²
Peacock P E 64 SAL (p)
Pečman R 58 BRN, 65 BRN, 66

BRN, 66 BRN, *67 BRN²*, 67 BRN², 67 MAG, *68 BRN*, 68 BRN, *69 BRN*, 69 BRN, 70 BERL², *70 BRN*, 70 BRN, 70 GRA, *71 BRN*, 71 BRN, 72 GRA, 73 MAG, 74 KRP, 75 BLA (1;d)
Pedrell F   21 PAR
Peeters T   11 MAL
Pejović R   61 OKH, 68 BRN
Pemberton J   62 STOC
Penkert A   13 BERL
Pepper H   51 STIS
Pereira de Sampaio J   11 LON
Pérez Simó A   65 MTS
Pericoli M   57 TOD
Perkins L L   74 NEWY²
Perkuhn E   72 SÁR, 73 BAL
Perlis V   *74 NEWY¹*, 74 NEWY¹ (c)
Pernot H   28 PRA
Perrachio L   21 TUR
Perrot J   72 COP
Perroy E   55 WÉG·
Perz M   60 WAR¹, 67 LJU, 69 BYD, 69 CER, 69 WAR, 70 BOL, 71 WAR (3), 72 COP
Perz W   69 PARM
Pesovár E   72 SÁR
Pestelli G   68 VEN, 69 VER, 74 ROM
Petersen H   62 STOC
Peterson J   29 NEWH
Petiot A   58 AIX
Petneki A(nna)   72 SÁR
Petneki A(ron)   72 SÁR
Petrassi G   49 FLOR, 50 FLOR
Petrescu [Petressco] I D   34 SOF, 36 ROM
Petrobelli P   66 VEN, 67 LJU, *68 FUS*, 68 FUS, 68 VEN, 70 STGE, 72 MIL, 72 VEN, 74 ROM
Petronio G   75 SIE
Petrov [Petrow] S   61 BUD (2), 64 MOS, 66 SOF, 75 BYD
Petrović D   72 BYD, 72 COP, 75 BYD
Petrović R   68 SVE, 74 ZAG
Petzoldt R   58 COL, 67 MAG, 73 MAG
Petzsch C   72 SÁR
Peukert H   60 WAR²
Pfaff M   56 VIE
Pfannhauser K   56 VIE
Pfannkuch W   *58 COL*, 62 KAS, 64 SAL (p)
Pfrimmer A   *26 GEN*, 26 GEN
Pfrogner H   53 BAM, 56 VIE, 58 COL
Philippat M P   55 ARR, 72 VIE²
Pian Rulan Chao   *see* Rulan Chao Pian
Piazzano G   11 LON
Piccolotti D   57 CHIE
Pichler L   50 ROM, 54 VIE
Picker M   71 NEWY
Pidoux P   62 BERN
Piechler A   50 ROM

Pieplow H   67 PAR
Piera Gelabert M   28 PRA
Pietzsch   38 FRA
Pietzsch G   68 LIÈ
Pikler A G   62 COP
Pikulik J   75 BYD
Pilarczyk H   64 HAM
Pilková Z   56 PRA, 69 BRN, 70 BON, 70 BRN, 72 BYD, 75 BLA
Pimonow L   58 MARS
Pincherle M   21 PAR, 49 FLOR, 61 NEWY, 68 FUS (1; c)
Pinck L   37 PAR⁴
Pineau L   00 PAR⁵
Pinilla E   65 BLM
Pinsart G   74 STN
Pinzauti L   72 MIL
Pinzón Urrea J   63 CART
Piovesan A   48 FLOR, 49 FLOR
Pirro A   00 PARⁿ, 30 LIÈ, 32 STRS (2)
Pirrotta N [A]   50 ROM, 51 PAR, 53 PAR, 54 PAL, 55 WÉG, 59 CER, 61 CAM/M (p), 68 VEN, 69 CER, 72 TOD
Pisani R   74 LON
Pischner H   60 WAR¹, 70 BERL² (1; p)
Piston W   57 CAM/M
Pizot-Monnier Mme P   32 STRS
Pizzardo   57 PAR
Pizzetti I   21 TUR, *48 FLOR, 49 FLOR*, 50 FLOR
Plamenac D   25 BRUG, 39 NEWY, 52 UTR, 58 COL, 61 NEWY (c), 69 CER
Plana Sh   66 SOF
Planas J   65 MTS
Planchart A E   74 NEWY²
Platen E   70 BON
Plath J   27 BERL
Plath W   62 KAS, 64 SAL
Plavec J   58 BRN
Plesske H-M   59 CAM, 70 BERL²
Plessner H   24 BERL, 72 COP
Pletka V   64 BERL
Plocek V   70 BRN
Plomp R   62 COP, 64 AMS
Pociej B   60 WAR¹, 62 WAR
Podolski M   57 NEU/S
Pohl R   68 LIÈ
Poirée É   00 PAR²(2)
Pokorný F   70 BRN
Pokrovskaya L A   66 SOF
Polak A J   06 BAS
Polák J   71 BRN (p)
Poljakova L   65 BRN
Polk K   74 NEWY²
Pollak F   47 PRA
Pollak H W   09 VIE
Poloczek F   56 HAM, 65 BRA
Pommer J   09 VIE (2)
Poniatowska I   70 BERL², 70 BON, 70 PIE, 74 BOL
Pontzen T   54 PAR²
Poos H   70 BON
Pop D   67 BUC
Pop M   67 BERL, 68 GRA
Pope [Conant] I   53 PAR, 61

CAM/M (p), 61 NEWY (c)
Popelka I   66 BRN
Popescu-Deveselu V   73 BUC
Poppen H   27 FRE/S
Porcelijn C   64 AMS
Porena B   73 BEL, 73 ROM², 74 ROM
Porfetye A   72 BYD
Porrino E   54 PAL
Porte J   54 PAR²
Portelli A   73 ROM²
Porter A   69 VER
Pospišil F   30 HAM¹
Poštolka M   56 PRA, 59 BUD, 61 BUD
Pothier J   05 STRS
Potiron H   37 PAR¹, 50 ROM
Potúček J   70 TRČ
Pouilliart R   65 STAV
Poulton D   57 NEU/S
Powell M   65 BLM
Powers H S   64 SAL (p), 66 MANL, 72 COP (2), 72 VEN
Pozniak P   71 WAR
Pozzi Escot   65 BLM
Prat J   65 MTS
Pratt C C   29 NEWH
Preiss P   70 BRN
Press K T   08 VIE
Presser D   75 EIS
Prestige C   70 LAW
Přibáňová S   65 BRN
Prieto J I   57 PAR
Prim J   37 PAR¹, 50 ROM, 57 PAR
Prizer W   74 MANT
Procházka J   60 WAR¹, 65 BRN, 70 BERL², 70 PIE
Prod'homme J G   11 LON, 13 GHE (2), 27 VIE, 28 VIE
Prokopowicz M   60 WAR¹, 62 STOC, 73 WEIM
Prosnak A   60 WAR¹ (2)
Prota-Giurleo U   30 LIÈ
Protopopov V V [Protopopow W]   60 WAR¹, 70 BERL², 70 BON, 71 MOS, 72 BYD, 75 BYD
Prowaznik B   67 ZAG
Prunières H   11 LON, 21 PAR, 33 FLOR, 37 PAR³, 38 FLOR
Prus S   71 BUD²
Prusik K   27 VIE
Prynne M W   57 NEU/S
Psachos C-A   28 PRA, 30 ATH
Pucelle J   60 ATH, 64 AMS
Pugh R   25 BRUG
Pugliese G   67 FLOR, 69 VER
Puig i Matas Ll   65 MTS
Pujol D   30 LIÈ, 50 ROM
Pujol E   54 PAR¹
Pujol F   27 VIE
Pujolie   67 PAR
Pulkert O   73 WEIM
Puppi L   72 VEN
Purkis H   70 MTA

Quaedvlieg G M I   68 LIÈ
Quaranta F   56 VIE
Quellmalz A   56 VIE
Querol Gavaldá M   50 ROM, 53
  PAR, 55 ROY, 57 WÉG,
  64 SAL (p)
Quitin J   52 UTR, 68 LIÈ
Quittard H   00 PAR[6]
Quoika R   27 FRE/S, 50 ROM,
  51 OCH (2), 53 BAM, 54
  STAD, 54 VIE (2), 56 VIE
Qvamme B   69 VER, 72 MIL

Raad V   62 PAR
Raasted J   61 OKH, 72 COP (2)
Rabsch E   25 LEIP (2)
Racek J   47 PRA, 56 PRA, 56 VIE,
  58 BRN, 58 COL, 60
  WAR[1], 61 BUD, 64 SAL
  (p), 65 BRN (2), 66 BRN,
  67 BRN[2], 67 LJU (c), 68
  BRN (2), 69 BRN (2), 70
  BRN (1; c), 70 VIE
Rackwitz W   61 BUD
Radiciotti G   03 ROM
Radiguer   00 PAR[1]
Radius E   67 FLOR
Radole G   54 VIE, 56 VIE
Raeli V   29 ROM
Rahlfs V   64 SAL (p)
Rajeczky B   61 BUD, 65 BRA, 66
  BYD, 67 LJU (p), 67
  RAD, 72 SÁR
Räkel H-H S   66 OXF[2]
Rakowski A   72 COP
Ramachandran N S   64 NEWD[2]
Ramón y Rivera L F   58 SJOS (2),
  63 CART, 65 BLM
Ramorino F   03 ROM
Raschl E   72 GRA
Rasi L   03 ROM
Rasmussen K A   74 NEWY[1] (p)
Rasmussen N K   75 ESP
Råsted J   75 ESP
Rastelli D   68 VEN
Rațiu A   65 BERL[1], 67 BUC, 73
  BUC
Ratner L G   56 VIE
Rattay K   25 LEIP
Raugel F   21 PAR (2), 32 STRS, 37
  PAR[1]. 50 LÜN[2]. 51 OCH,
  52 BERN, 52 UTR, 53
  BAM, 56 VIE, 58 COL, 59
  HAL
Ravina M   60 PAR[2]
Ravizza V   72 COP
Ravnikar B   69 STOC
Rawp-Raupp J   56 HAM
Razumovsky A   67 GRA
Razzi G   37 FLOR
Reaney G   53 BAM, 55 WÉG, 56
  HAM, 58 COL, 62 KAS
  (2), 64 SAL (c), 69 CER
Rebling E   50 LEIP, 70 BERL[2]
  (1; p)
Reboulet A   57 PAR
Reckow F   72 COP
Reckziegel W   65 DIJ (1; p), 66
  LEIP
Recupero J   73 ROM[2]

Redlich H F   50 LÜN[1], 64 SAL
  (p), 67 SIE
Rees T   70 LAW
Reese G   39 NEWY, 39 NEWY
  (c), 57 CAM/M (p), 61
  NEWY(c), 71 NEWY (1;c)
Reeser E   64 SAL (c)
Refardt E   26 GEN
Regamey C   60 PAR[1], 60 STRT
Régnier H   28 PRA
Řehánek F   70 BRN
Rehm W   58 COL, 62 KAS, 64
  SAL (p)
Reibal G   65 LIÈ
Reich W   37 FLOR, 69 WAR
Reichel B   65 GEN
Reichel F   74 BLA
Reichert G   50 LÜN[1], 51 OCH, 61
  NEWY (c), 62 KAS, 62
  KAS (c)
Reiching A   67 GRA
Reichling A   62 KAS
Reier E   75 ESP
Reier W   75 ESP
Reimann M   63 KIE
Reimann W   27 BERL
Reimer E   71 BRN
Reinach T   00 PAR[2] (2)
Reinecke H-P   56 HAM, 58 COL,
  61 NEWY, 62 KAS (3), 64
  SAL (p), 66 LEIP (2), 67
  LJU (p), 69 STOC, 70
  BERL[1], 70 BON, 71 KAS,
  72 COP, 72 FRE/B
Reinhard K   56 HAM, 58 COL,
  59 CAM, 60 WAR[1], 61
  TEH, 64 SAL (p), 66
  GRA, 67 BERL, 73 ANK,
  75 BYD
Reininghaus F C   71 STU, 71
  STU
Reinhold H   55 BRUS
Reinold H   56 HAM
Rennert W   64 HAM (2)
Renondeau G   59 ROY
Renshaw R   64 NEWD[2]
Repp F   28 PRA
Reusch F   53 BAM
Reuter F   25 LEIP
Revault J   60 PAR[2]
Revault d'Allones O   60 ATH
Révész G   08 FRA, 10 INN, 14
  GÖT (2)
Rexroth D   70 BON (2)
Reynolds R   74 NEWY[1] (1; p)
Reynolds S   73 STOC
van Reysschoot D   11 LON
Rhodes W   49 NEWY[1], 56 PHIL,
  63 CART, 65 BERL[2]
Rhyshkin I   70 BERL[2]
Riabouchinsky Mme V   37 PAR[3]
Ribó   65 MTS
Richard A   70 STOC
Richardson E G   53 NET, 58
  MARS
Richet C   00 PAR[4]
Richter   38 FRA
Richter L   56 HAM, 66 LEIP, 67
  LJU (p), 68 BRN, 70
  BERL[2], 70 PIE, 71 BRN

Rieber K   38 FRE/B
Riedel F W   62 KAS, 63 KIE, 64
  SAL (p)
Riegler E   27 VIE
Riegler-Dinu E   28 PRA
Riemann H   13 BERL
Rienäcker G   70 BERL[2]
Riethmüller A   70 BRN, 71 BRN
Rietsch H   11 LON (c)
Riety P   58 MARS
Riezler W   30 HAM[2]
Righetti S   70 BOL
Righini P   68 VEN, 73 ROM[2]
Rihouët Y   24 BAS
Rihtman C   58 BRN, 64 MOS, 66
  GRA, 67 LJU (c), 68 SVE
Rijavec A   67 LJU (p), 68 SVE, 70
  BON, 72 BYD, 74 NEWY[1]
  (p)
de Rillé L   00 PAR[1]
Rimbault L   52 BERN
Rimini R   74 SIE
Rimmer J   73 BAL
Rimsky-Korsakov   A   V   58
  MARS
Rinaldi M   48 FLOR, 49 FLOR
Ringer A L   64 SAL (p), 70 BON,
  72 COP, 74 JER (c), 74
  ZAG
Ripin E M   70 ANT
Ripollès V   24 BAS
Risinger K   58 BRN
Risler J   26 GEN
Risset J-C   70 STOC, 71 BUD[2]
Rist S   65 LIÈ
Rius J   65 MTS
Robbins R H   see Hope Robbins R
Robert J   67 NAN
Roberts D L   72 VIE[1] (1; p)
Robinson M F   73 SIE
Roblot   37 PAR[1]
Rochberg G   60 STRT
Roche C   54 PAR[2]
Rochelle E   21 PAR
de Roda C   11 LON (1; c)
Rodríguez F de M   65 BLM
Roenneke   38 FRA
Rogal S J   70 LAW
Rognoni L   56 VEN, 67 GRA
Roguet 57 PAR
Rohr H   64 GRA[1]
Röhring K   73 NUR, 74 SINZ
Rohwer J   50 LÜN[1], 58 COL, 66
  LEIP (p)
Roig G   39 NEWY
Roiha E   51 STOC
Rojo C   05 STRS
Rokseth Y   see Rihouët Y
Rolandi U   51 IES
Roland-Manuel   37   FLOR,   37
  PAR[3], 62 PAR
Röll W   73 NEU/B
Rolland G H   59 CAM
Rolland R   00 PAR[2]
Roman Z   72 COP, 72 VIE[2]
Romanska T   66 SOF
Romanska Ž   63 BUD
Romita F   50 ROM, 57 PAR, 61
  COL
Ronan J E   50 ROM, 61 COL

Roncaglia A 73 ROM²
Ronga L 33 FLOR, 37 FLOR (2), 38 FLOR, 48 FLOR, 49 FLOR, 50 ROM, 54 FER, 60 ROM
Rönnau K 70 BON
Rootham C B 11 LON
Rosalio R 73 ROM²
Rosand E 72 VEN
Rosati G 50 FLOR
Rosbaud H 33 FLOR, 37 FLOR
Rose G 72 BYD
Rosen D 69 VER, 72 MIL
Rosenthal A 59 CAM (p)
Rosenthal F 09 VIE, 27 VIE
Rosenthal H 69 VER
Rosenthal K A 27 VIE
Rosner F 72 GRA
Rössel-Majdan K 54 PAR²
Rosseau N 54 PAR²
Rossei W 71 STGA (p)
Rossi A 73 ROM²
Rossi-Doria G 33 FLOR
Rossini C 50 ROM
Rossiter F R 74 NEWY¹
Rössler E K 54 STAD, 68 THU
Rostal M 72 GRA (2)
Rothe H-J 66 LEIP
Rougé G see Rouget G(ilbert)
Rouget G(abriel) 55 BRUS
Rouget G(ilbert) 47 BIS, 54 WÉG, 60 PAR¹, 60 PAR², 61 NEWY, 64 SAL (c), 68 TOK²
Roussel G 50 ROM, 57 PAR
Rousset J 55 ROY
Rouyer L 71 STGA (p)
Rövenstrunck B 65 MTS
Rovsing-Olsen P 58 WÉG, 62 PAR, 67 VAN
Roy R L 61 TOK, 64 NEWD²
Rozing P 57 PAR
Rubardt P 27 FRE/S
Rubeli A 67 LJU, 68 BRN
Rubin M 56 PRA
Rubio S 50 ROM
Rubsamen W H 58 COL, 61 CAM/M, 62 KAS, 64 SAL (2p), 71 NEWY, 72 COP
Ruckmick C A 29 NEWH
Rudloff-Hille G 69 WAR
Rudneva A V 64 MOS (d)
Rudolph J 59 HAL, 70 BERL², 73 WEIM
Rudziński W 60 WAR¹, 62 WAR
Ruelle E 00 PAR²
Rufer J 74 BERL
Rühl 38 FRA
Rühlmann 38 FRA
Ruhnke M 62 KAS, 67 MAG
Rūķe-Draviņa V 73 STOC
Rulan Chao Pian 66 MANL, 71 ANN
Rummenhöller P 66 LEIP, 70 BON, 71 STU, 71 STU
Runge P 06 BAS, 09 VIE
Rung-Keller P S 09 VIE
Rupp E 33 STRS
Rüsch W 75 EIS

Rushton J 73 SIE
Ruth 38 FRA
Ruttkay M 70 TRČ
Rybarič R 66 BYD, 67 BRN², 72 BYD
Ryom P 72 COP, 72 COP
Ryuytel' I 72 BYD

Sàbat A 65 MTS
Sabbeth D 72 MIL
Sacchetti L 00 PAR², 09 VIE
Sacchi F 67 FLOR (2)
Sachs C 24 BAS, 24 BERL, 25 LEIP (c), 39 NEWY
Sachs K-J 68 THU
Sachs M E 11 LON
Sadagopan V V 64 NEWD²
Sadokov R L 64 MOS (d)
Šafařík J 67 BRN²
Šafránek M 66 BRN (2)
Sage J 69 EXE, 70 MTA
Saint-Arroman J 69 PAR
Saint-Saëns C 00 PAR²
Sakka K 61 TOK
Sakva K 56 VIE
Salmen W 50 LÜN¹, 52 UTR, 53 BAM, 56 VIE, 56 WÉG, 58 COL (c), 60 WAR¹, 62 KAS (1; c), 66 LEIP (c), 68 BRN, 71 BRN, 71 KAS, 73 BAL, 73 NEU/B
Salter L 71 STGA (p)
Salvagnini F A 03 ROM
Salvetti G 67 SIE, 74 ROM
Salvini G 38 FLOR
Salzman E 64 SAL (p)
Sambamoorthy P 64 NEWD²
Sambeth H M 25 LEIP
Samson J 57 PAR
Sandberger A 09 VIE (2), 11 LON (c)
Sanborn H C 29 NEWH
Sánchez de Fuentes E 39 NEWY
Sandelewski W 60 WAR¹, 69 PARM
Sanden H 50 ROM
Sandi L 65 BLM
Sandin B 69 KUA
Sandvik O M 28 PRA
Sanga G 73 ROM²
Sangiorgio C 50 ROM
Sannemann F 09 VIE, 11 LON
de San Sebastian J A 28 PRA (2)
Santi P 67 FLOR, 69 VER, 71 FLOR, 74 SIE
Santoli V 29 FLOR
Santollino R 40 VEN
Santoro C 67 BERL
San Valero Aparisi J 63 STT
Sapper K 04 STU
Sárosi B 69 STOC, 71 STP, 73 BAL, 74 GRA², 75 BRUN
Sartori C 54 PAL, 54 PAR¹, 62 STOC, 74 SIE
Sasse K 59 HAL, 70 BERL²
Sassu P 73 ROM²
Sastre 57 PAR
Sauget H 62 PAR, 64 HAM
Saul P 59 CAM, 65 DIJ (1; p)
Saulnier V L 53 PAR

Savay M 71 MOS
Saygun A A 61 BUD, 61 TEH
Schaal R 50 LÜN¹
Schaefer H 50 LÜN¹, 66 LEIP
Schaeffer P 70 STOC
Schaeffner A 37 FLOR, 37 PAR³, 38 COP, 38 FLOR, 54 WÉG, 55 BRUS, 56 WÉG, 58 WÉG, 60 PAR¹, 60 PAR², 61 NEWY, 62 PAR
Schafer M 71 MOS
Schäfer O 25 LEIP
Schäffer B 62 KAS
Schahl A 51 OCH
Schanzlin H P 58 COL
Scheib W 67 ZAG (c), 70 HAMM
Scheit K 57 NEU/S
Schenk E 31 SAL, 31 SAL (2), 54 VIE, 56 PAR, 56 VIE, 64 SAL (c), 67 BRN², 69 BRN
Schering A 06 BAS (2), 09 VIE, 13 BERL, 24 BAS, 24 BERL, 25 LEIP (3;c), 26 FRE/B, 27 HAL, 27 VIE
Scherliess V 74 ROM
Schetelich H 59 CAM, 65 DIJ (p)
Scheurleer D F 11 LON (1; c)
Schickhaus K H 71 HIN
Schiede H 71 HIN
Schiedermair L 06 BAS (2; c), 09 VIE, 25 LEIP (1; c), 27 VIE, 31 SAL
Schiess E 52 BERN
Schindler O 68 VEN
Schiødt N 65 DIJ (1; p), 72 COP
Schiørring N 55 BRUS, 56 WÉG, 61 NEWY, 63 KIE
Schirò G 40 VEN, 55 IST, 66 OXF¹
Schlenger 38 FRA
de Schloezer B 33 FLOR, 37 FLOR, 38 FLOR, 49 FLOR
Schlötterer R 55 IST, 62 KAS, 64 SAL (p)
Schmaus A 64 GRA²
Schmid A 00 MUN
Schmid E F 56 PAR, 56 PRA, 59 BUD
Schmid H 58 COL, 62 KAS
Schmidt H 06 BAS
Schmidt H 70 BON
Schmidt I. 71 STP
Schmidt W 06 BAS, 09 VIE
Schmidt-Görg J 50 ROM, 56 VIE, 70 BON, 70 VIE
Schmidt-Phiseldeck J 27 VIE
Schmiedel P 56 HAM, 66 LEIP
Schmieder W 50 LEIP, 53 BAM 56 VIE, 62 KAS (2c)
Schmit J P 54 VIE, 57 PAR
Schmitt-Thomas R 70 BON
Schmitz A 25 LEIP, 50 LÜN¹, 53 BAM
Schmitz E 09 VIE, 50 LEIP
Schmitz H-P 69 PAR
Schmitz P 58 TOD
Schnabl K 09 VIE
Schnapp 38 FRA

Schnebel D 72 BERN
Schneider A(lbrecht) 72 SÁR, 73 BAL, 74 KRP
Schneider A(nneliese) 70 BERL[2]
Schneider C 27 VIE (2)
Schneider E 74 GRA[2]
Schneider F 70 BERL[2]
Schneider M(arius) 49 BAS, 53 BAM, 54 PAL, 54 WÉG, 56 HAM, 56 WÉG (2), 58 COL (c; 1), 60 PAR[1], 61 NEWY, 61 TEH, 64 SAL (2p)
Schneider M(ax) 30 HAM[2], 62 MAG
Schnerich A 09 VIE (3), 27 VIE
Schnorr von Carolsfeld E 27 FRE/S
Schoen M 29 NEWH
Schoenbaum C 56 VIE
Schole 38 FRA
Schole H 34 TÜB
Schollum R 70 BERL[2], 71 BUD[1], 72 VIE[1]
Scholz G 66 LEIP (p)
Schone G 70 MTA
Schönfelder G 66 LEIP
Schrade L 31 SAL, 52 UTR, 53 PAR, 55 ROY, 55 WÉG, 61 TOK
Schrammek W 56 HAM, 66 LEIP
Schramowski H 70 BERL[2]
Schreiber O 56 VIE
Schreier P 70 BERL[2] (p)
Schrems 38 FRA
Schrems T 50 ROM
Schröder A E 52 UTR
Schroth 38 FRA
Schueller H M 60 ATH
Schug A 71 KAS
Schuh W 56 VIE, 64 SAL (c), 67 GRA, 70 BON
Schuhmacher G 66 LEIP, 70 BON
Schuke K 38 FRE/B
Schuler M 66 LEIP
Schuller G 60 STRT (2), 74 NEWY[1] (2p)
Schulte-Tigges F 71 KAS
Schulz-Dornburg 38 FRA
Schulze E 61 COL
Schulze H(elmut) 73 WEIM
Schulze H-J 66 LEIP, 75 BLA
Schünemann G 24 BERL, 25 LEIP (c)
Schütze R 70 ANT, 71 GRA
Schwab H W 72 COP
Schwaiger 38 FRA
Schwake G 50 ROM
Schwalbe G 67 BRN[2]
Schwartz R 09 VIE, 25 LEIP, 27 VIE
Schwarz B 64 SAL (p), 70 BON (2), 72 COP, 72 GRA
Schwarz G 74 NEWY[1] (p)
Schwarz V 70 GRA, 70 GRA, 71 BRN, 71 GRA, 71 GRA (2), 72 GRA, 72 GRA
Schwarz W 03 KIE
Schweitzer A 09 VIE (2)

Schweizer J 62 BERN
Ščibor J 75 BYD
Scolari 38 FRA
Searle H 61 BUD
Seashore C E 29 NEWH (1; c), 32 COP
Seashore R H 29 NEWH
Seay A 59 CER, 69 CER
Sebestyén A 75 EIS
Seebass T 70 BON
Seefehlner E 61 TOK
Seeger C 39 NEWY, 52 UTR, 61 NEWY, 63 CART, 65 BLM
Seeger H 59 BUD, 59 HAL
Seemann E 50 LÜN[1]
Sefardi J N *see* Consolo F
Sehnal J 67 BRN[2], 67 LJU (p), 69 BRN, 70 BOL, 70 BRN, 71 BRN, 72 BYD
Seidel 38 FRA
Seidel E 66 LEIP
Seidel W 70 BON, 72 COP
Seidl A 06 BAS (1; c)
Seifert W 66 LEIP (p)
Seiffert M 06 BAS, 11 LON (2; c), 24 BAS
Selden-Goth G 67 FLOR
Seljan V 67 ZAG
Selmer E W 30 BON
Selner J C 50 ROM
Selvik R M 74 ZAG
Semmer G 64 BERL
Senn W 53 BAM, 56 HAM, 64 SAL (p)
Senny E 68 LIÈ
Serandrei M 50 FLOR
Serauky W 50 LEIP (1; c), 53 BAM, 56 VIE, 58 BRN, 58 COL, 59 HAL
Serpa F 67 FLOR (3)
Serra y Boldu V 28 PRA
Servier J H 52 VIE
Servolini L 51 IES
Serwer H 72 COP
Sesar C 71 ANN
Sessions R 33 FLOR
Sevåg R 67 BRN[1], 71 STP
Seymour J 74 LON
Sguerzi A 69 VER, 72 MIL
Shackelford R 71 VIC
Shakhnazarova N 71 MOS
Shankar R 64 NEWD[2]
Shawe-Taylor D 69 VER
Shedlock J 00 PAR[2]
Shepard B 62 STOC, 65 DIJ (p)
Shergold N-D 70 MTA
Sherrington U 59 CAM
Shiba S 61 TOK
Shibata M 70 STOC
Shiloah A 65 JER, 69 JER, 71 FLOR
Shirasuna S 68 TOK[1]
Shire H M 55 ROY
Shitov L V 71 BUD[2]
Shiloah A 65 JER
Shostakovich D 47 PRA, 71 MOS
Shreyer-Tkachenko A 66 BYD
Shmueli F 69 VEN
Shukla N N 64 NEWD[2]

Siebeck H 04 GIE
Sieber P 50 LÜN[2]
Siedentopf H 62 KAS
Sieffert R 59 ROY
Siegele U 62 KAS, 66 LEIP, 71 STU
Siegele W 51 OCH
Siegmund-Schultze W 56 HAM, 56 PRA, 56 VIE, 58 COL, 59 BUD, 59 HAL, 59 HAL (2), 60 WAR[1], 62 MAG, 64 SAL (p), 66 LEIP, 67 BRN[2], 67 MAG, 67 MAG, 68 BRN, 69 BYD, 70 BERL[2], 71 BRN (1; p), 72 BLA, 73 MAG, 73 MAG, 74 BLA, 75 BLA (1; p)
Sienkiewicz J 60 WAR[1]
Sievers E 13 BERL
Sievers G 73 NUR
Sievers H 50 LEIP, 50 LÜN[1]
Sihleanu S 11 LON
Silbermann A 60 WAR[1]
Silberstein L 37 PAR[3]
Silesu F 57 CHIE
Silva G 21 TUR
Simbriger H 56 VIE
Šimek M 72 VIE[2]
Simon A(licja) 09 VIE, 11 LON, 27 VIE, 30 LIÈ
Simon A(rtur) 69 MARB
Simon R 70 MTA
Simonides J 60 WAR[1]
Sincero D 21 TUR
Sinclair J 74 NEWY[1] (2p)
Singleton K 74 NEWY[1] (p)
Singh T J 61 TOK (3), 64 NEWD[2]
Sinicropi E 40 VEN
Siohan R 56 VEN, 60 ATH, 60 PAR[1]
Şirli A 73 BUC
Širola B 27 VIE
Sirovátka O 70 TRČ
Sittner H 64 HAM, 71 STP, 72 GRA
Sivec J 69 BYD, 75 BYD
Skeaping K 59 CAM
Skorupska Z 60 WAR[1]
Skowroneck M 70 ANT
Skrebkov S 60 WAR[1], 66 BYD
Skudrzyk E 53 NET
Skyvington W 70 STOC
Slavyunas Z I 64 MOS
Sławiński A 60 WAR[1]
Slawson A W 65 LIÈ, 68 TOK[1]
Slonimsky N 74 NEWY[1] (p)
Small A M 56 CAM/M
Smend J 25 LEIP (c), 27 BERL, 27 FRE/S
Smetana R 56 PRA
Smijers A 39 NEWY, 50 ROM
Smirnov B F 64 MOS (d)
Smirnov M A 71 BRN
Smith B 66 MANL, 67 VAN
Smith C A 15 WAS
Smith C S 39 NEWY (c), 47 PRA, 57 CAM/M (p), 61 NEWY (p)
Smith G 74 NEWY[1] (p)

Smith J   70 BON
Smith M B   58 SJOS
Smith W C   59 HAL
Smith W F   29 NEWH
Smither H E   72 COP
Smits van Waesberghe J   49 BAS, 50 LÜN[1], 50 ROM, 52 UTR, 53 BAM, 54 VIE, 56 HAM, 56 VIE, 57 PAR, 58 COL (c; 1), 61 COL, 64 AMS, 64 SAL (3p), 67 LJU (c), 70 BON
Smoira M   65 JER, 69 JER
Smoira-Roll M   64 SAL (p)
Smoldon W L   67 LJU (p), 69 BIN
Smolka J   58 BRN, 69 BRN, 70 PIE
Snižková J   60 WAR[1], 69 BYD, 70 BRN, 71 NEWY, 72 BYD, 75 BYD
Sobiesky B   58 BRN (d)
Sobieska J   60 WAR[1]
Sobieski M   60 WAR[1]
Sofer Z   59 KIE
Söhner L   30 LIÈ
Söhngen O   62 BERN
Sokhor A N   71 MOS, 72 VIE[2]
Solà J M   65 MTS
Sole L   73 ROM[2]
Sólyom G   70 BERL[2]
Som A K   74 LON
Somers H   65 BLM
Somfai L   61 BUD, 64 SAL (p), 70 GRA, 71 BUD[1], 71 EIS, 72 VIE[1] (1; p)
Somigli C   11 LON (1; c)
Sommer   38 FRA
Sondheimer R   24 BAS, 25 LEIP
Sonneck O G   06 BAS, 09 VIE, 11 LON (1; c)
Sordi I   73 ROM[2]
Sordo C   70 BON
Sørensen [Sörensen] S   56 HAM, 58 COL, 63 KIE, 64 SAL (C), 67 SIE, *72 COP*
Šostakovič D   *see* Shostakovich
Sőtér I   61 BUD
Souderes V   54 PAR[2]
Souris A   54 PAR[1], 55 ARR, 57 NEU/S, 62 PAR, 69 PAR
Sowa G   56 HAM
Sowande F   70 YAO
Sparks E H   71 NEWY
Spechtler F V   72 SÁR, 73 NEU/B
Spector J   61 JER, 64 SAL (p), 65 JER, 69 JER
Spelda A   71 BUD[2]
Spier R F G   58 SJOS
Spies L   58 BRN
Spina A   30 LIÈ
Spinelli G   68 VEN
Spira Y   61 TEH
Spiro F   11 LON
Spiro-Rombro A   11 LON
Spivacke H   59 CAM, 62 STOC, 65 DIJ (c), 68 NEWY (c)
Spörri O   51 OCH
Springer H   06 BAS (2; c), 09 VIE, 11 LON (1; c), 24 BAS, 25 LEIP, 27 VIE (2)

Squire W B   09 VIE, 11 LON, 21 PAR
Stabile M   67 FLOR (p)
Stäblein B   49 BAS, 50 LÜN[1], 50 LÜN[2], 50 ROM, 52 UTR, 54 PAL, 61 NEWY, 62 BERN, 62 KAS, 64 SAL (3p), 73 NEU/B
Stadlen P   70 BON, 72 VIE[1]
Stadnicki K   60 WAR[1]
Stádnik M   56 PRA
Staehelin M   72 COP
Stahmer K   69 BRN, 71 BRN
Staicovici C-I   73 BUC
Staiger E   70 VIE
Staiger R   06 BAS
Stajić P   70 BON
Stalmann J   62 KAS
Stam H   50 LÜN[2]
Stani-Ducourt M   37 PAR[3]
Stanislav J   47 PRA, 61 TEH
Stanley A A   09 VIE, 11 LON (2; c)
Stanton H M   29 NEWH
Stantschewa-Braschowanowa L   62 KAS, 70 BON
Starzyński J   60 WAR[1], 62 WAR, 70 VEN
Stathis G   72 COP
Stauder   38 FRA
Stauder W   64 SAL (p)
Staudinger A   74 GRA[1]
Stechow W   30 HAM[2]
Stedman J W   70 LAW
Štědroň B   56 PRA, 56 VIE, 58 BRN (2), 60 WAR[1], 61 BUD, 64 SAL (p), 65 BRN (2), 66 LEIP, 67 LJU, 68 BRN, 69 BRN, 70 BERL[2], 71 BRN
Štědroň M   65 BRN, 66 BRN, 67 BRN[2], 68 BRN, 71 BRN
Steer G   70 WÜR
Stefan P   28 VIE, 33 FLOR
Stefănescu I   67 BUC
Stefani G   *73 BEL*, 73 BEL, 73 ROM[2], 74 ZAG
Stefanović D   61 OKH, 64 BRA, 64 SAL (p), 66 BYD, 66 OXF[1], 69 BYD, 72 BERN, 75 BYD
Steglich R   25 LEIP, 27 VIE, 31 SAL, 49 BAS, 50 LÜN[1] (2), *53 BAM*, 53 BAM (c), 58 COL, 59 HAL
Stein F   11 LON, 58 COL
Steinbeck D   70 BON
Steinitz W   64 BERL
Stellan Mörner C-G   62 STOC
Stempel M   50 LEIP, 56 PRA
Stephan R   50 LÜN[1], 56 HAM, 58 COL, 67 LJU (p), 68 BRN, 70 BON, 70 BRN, 71 BRN (p), 72 COP, 72 FRE/B, 72 GRA, 72 VIE[1] (1; p), 74 GRA[1]
Stephani H   25 LEIP, 27 VIE
Stephenson K   56 VIE
Stepner D   74 NEWY[1] (p)
Stern P   37 PAR[4]
Sternfeld F W   55 ROY, 62 ROY,

70 BON, 70 MTA, 72 TOU, 73 SIE
Stesser-Péan G   47 PAR
Steszewska Z   60 WAR[1], 69 PARM, 71 WAR (2)
Steszewski J   58 COL, 60 WAR[1], 62 WAR, 65 BRA, 67 LJU (p), *67 RAD*, 67 RAD, 71 BLE, 71 STP, 72 COP
Stetson K A   71 BUD[2]
Stevens D   53 PAR, 54 PAR[1], 55 ROY, 57 WÉG, 58 COL, 61 NEWY, 64 SAL (p), 68 VEN
Stevens H   67 LJU, 71 BUD[1]
Stevens J E   67 LJU (c)
Stevens R   68 NEWY (c)
Stevenson R   71 NEWY
Stichtenoth   38 FRA
Stief W   71 BLE, 72 SÁR
Stihi-Boos C   73 BUC
Stirnimann H   62 BERN
Stock E   67 PRA
Stockmann B   66 LEIP, 70 BON
Stockmann D   58 WÉG, 64 MOS, *67 RAD*, 67 RAD, 72 SÁR, 74 KRP
Stockmann E   56 HAM, 56 VIE, 58 WÉG, 64 MOS, 65 MARB, *67 BRN[1]*, 67 BRN[1], 67 LJU (p), *69 STOC*, 69 STOC, 72 COP (1; c), *73 BAL*, *75 BRUN*
Stockmeier W   73 NUR
Stöhr A   09 VIE
Stoin E   64 MOS
Stollberg O   62 KAS, 74 GRA[2]
Stompor S   59 HAL
Stone K   68 NEWY (c)
Stradner G   71 GRA (2), 72 GRA (3)
van der Straeten E   28 VIE
Strainchamps E N   72 COP
Strajnar J   69 STOC, 71 STP
Straková T   58 BRN, *65 BRN*, 65 BRN, 67 LJU (p), 68 BRN, 70 BRN
Stránská D   28 PRA
Straram E   55 BRUS, 65 DIJ (c)
Streck   38 FRA
Streich R   50 LÜN[1]
Střelcová V   58 BRN
Streller F   66 LEIP
Strelnikov I D   28 NEWY
Strinati C M   73 ROM[1]
Stringham S   69 VER, 72 MIL
Střitecký J   71 BRN (p)
Ströbel D   70 BRN
Strobel H   49 FLOR
Stroe A   67 BUC
Stroh W M   72 FRE/B
Strohm R   66 VEN, 67 SIE, 74 ROM
Stroux C   68 THU
Strunk O   39 NEWY, 50 ROM, 53 THE, 55 IST, 57 CAM/M (p), 61 OKH, 64 BRA, 64 SAL (3p), 66 OXF[1], 66 VEN, 69 CER
Stuckenschmidt H H   54 PAR[2], 61

TOK (l; c), 62 KAS (l; c), 64 HAM, 64 NEWD², 65 BRN, 70 BRN
Stumpf C 10 INN, 14 GÖT
von Stumpff K-H 72 GRA
Sturtevant W C 58 WAS (d)
Subirá J 30 LIÈ
Suchoff B 71 BUD¹
Suess J G 64 SAL (2; p), 67 LJU (p)
Sugden J G 70 LAW
Sulitka A 70 TRČ
Summers J 11 LON
Sundberg J 69 STOC, 71 BUD² (3), 72 COP, 73 BEL, 74 LON
Suñol G 36 ROM
Supičić I 67 LJU (c), 68 SVE, 68 UPP, 73 BEL
Suppan A 75 AUS (1; p)
Suppan W 61 BUD, 62 KAS, 65 BRA, 65 MARB, 67 LJU (c), 67 RAD, *74 GRA²*, 74 GRA², *75 EIS*, 75 EIS
Supper W 38 FRE/B, *51 OCH, 54 STAD*, 54 STAD (3), 54 VIE
Sutermeister H 60 STRT
Sutkowski A 60 WAR¹
Sutter M 75 EIS
Sutton M K 70 LAW
Suwandono 69 KUA
Švehlák S 70 TRČ
Svejgaard B 72 COP
Swan A J 54 VIE, 64 BRA
Swarowsky H 72 VIE¹
Świerzewski S 62 WAR
Swing R 66 LEIP
Sychra A 47 PRA, 56 PAR, 56 VIE, 58 BRN, 58 COL, 59 BUD, 59 HAL, 60 ATH, 60 WAR¹, 63 PRA, 64 NEWD², 64 SAL (c; p), 65 BERL¹, 65 BRN
Sýkora V J 56 PRA, 60 WAR¹, 67 LJU, 70 PIE
Szabolcsi B 37 PAR⁴, 50 LEIP, 56 PRA, 56 VIE, 58 COL, *59 BUD,* 59 BUD, *61 BUD,* 61 BUD, 64 SAL, 69 BYD, 70 PIE, 70 VIE, 71 BUD¹
Szczepanska M 60 WAR¹
Szelényi I 61 BUD, 71 BUD¹
Szelényi L 75 EIS
Szende O 71 BUD²
Szendrei J 72 SÁR
Szlifirski K 70 STOC
Szmolyan W 72 VIE¹
Szubert B 71 BUD²
Szweykowska A 69 PARM, 71 WAR
Szweykowski Z M 60 WAR¹, 66 BYD, 67 BRN², 67 LJU (p), 69 BYD, 69 PARM, 70 BOL

Tack F 50 ROM, 56 VIE
Tagliavini L F 56 PAR, 57 PAR, 64 SAL, 67 LJU (c), 67 SIE, 68 FUS (2c), 72

BERN, 74 SINZ
Taktakishvili O 71 MOS
Tal J 54 PAR², 60 STRT, 74 JER
Tampere Kh T 64 MOS
Tanabe H 28 PRA
Tancredi G 40 VEN
Tani G 54 PAL, 55 ROY
Tanimoto K 67 VAN
Tanner R 58 MARS (2), 60 PAR¹
Tannery P 00 PAR³
Tanzberger E 50 LÜN¹
Tappolet W 56 VIE, 58 COL, 72 BERN
Tarantová M 56 PRA, 70 BERL², 70 PIE
Tarnóczy T 58 MARS, 71 BUD²
Tarr E H 70 BON
Tatarkiewicz W 60 WAR¹, 71 WAR
Taubert K-H 65 GEN
Taubman H 68 SVE
Tavares de Lima R 63 CART
Taylor D 39 NEWY
Tawaststjerna E 64 SAL (p), 68 BRN, 71 BUD¹
Tedeschi R 66 VEN
Teele R E 71 ANN
Teiner M 72 VIE²
Tekiner R 72 ROM
Telcová J 65 BRN
Teleu W 50 ROM
Temprano I 65 MTS
Temprement J 54 PAR²
Tenschert R 56 VIE
Terényi E 72 COP
Terenzio V 56 VIE, 59 CAM, 66 VEN
Terhardt E 71 BUD²
Tessier A 21 PAR, 30 LIÈ
Testa A 73 SIE
Tetzel E 27 VIE
Teuber V 52 UTR
Texier M 37 PAR⁴
Teyssèdre B 64 BON
Thelen F 74 GRA²
Thelwall W H 11 LON
Themelis D 70 GRA, 71 BLE, 72 GRA
Thibault G [de Chambure Mme H] 53 PAR, 54 ARR, 56 PAR¹, 57 NEU/S, 59 CAM, 61 CAM/M (p), 61 NEWY (2;c), 64 SAL (2p), 65 DIJ (2;c), 69 CER, 69 NUR, 69 PAR, 70 ANT, 71 NEWY, 72 COP
Thibaut R P 00 PAR² (2)
Thiel 38 FRA
Thiel C 25 LEIP (c)
Thiel H 71 STP
Thienhaus E 38 FRE/B, 50 LÜN¹ (2; c), 53 NET
Thodberg C 61 OKH, 72 COP
Thoene H 72 GRA
Thoene W 69 PAR
Thom E 72 BLA, *74 BLA,* 75 *BLA*
Thomas 38 FRA
Thomas E 64 HAM
Thomas G 71 EIS

Thomas N W 00 PAR⁵
Thomas P 49 CLU, 50 ROM
Thompson D 70 BON
Thomson V 61 TOK (1; c)
Thorsén S-M 69 STOC
Thoveron G 72 VIE²
Thuren H 09 VIE
Thürlings A 06 BAS (2)
Thürmer H 70 BON
Tibaldi Chiesa M 34 TRT, 54 PAL
Tiby O 50 LÜN¹, 52 UTR, 53 BAM, 54 PAL
Tichota J 70 BRN
Tiersot J 00 PAR² (2), 27 VIE
Tillyard H J W 36 ROM
Timm E 73 NEU/B
Ting Shan-Teh 60 WAR¹
Tintori G 66 VEN, 67 PARM, 72 MIL
Tirabassi A 23 BRUS, 24 BAS
Tirro F 68 UPP
Tischler H 72 COP
Tjernlund P 69 STOC, 71 BUD²
Toch E 24 BAS
Todorov M 69 STOC
Toguchi K 69 CER
Tomaszewski M 60 WAR¹, 62 WAR
Tomatis A 60 PAR¹
Tomek O 64 HAM
Tomeš J 74 KRP
Tomescu V 65 BERL¹, 70 BERL², 71 MOS
Tomkiewicz W 69 WAR
Tommasini V 50 FLOR
Tončeva [Tontscheva] E B 66 SOF, 72 BYD
Torii R 35 BRUS²
Torrefranca F 11 BOL, 11 LON (1; c), 24 BAS, 29 ROM, 31 SAL, 34 TRT, 37 FLOR (2), 48 FLOR, 49 BAS (2), 50 LÜN¹, 50 ROM, 51 IES, 52 UTR, 53 BAM, 54 PAL
Torrent M 65 MTS
Torri L 21 PAR
Toscanini W 67 FLOR
Toschi P 54 PAL
Toulmin S 71 VIC
Tournemire C 37 PAR¹
Tove P-A 69 STOC
Toyama F M 71 BUD²
Toyama K 61 TOK
Toztke I 61 COL
Tozzi L 73 SIE (3), 74 SIE, 75 SIE
Traber J H 71 *STU,* 71 STU
Traglia G 51 IES
Trân Van Khê 59 ROY, 60 PAR¹, 61 NEWY, 61 TEH, 61 TOK (2), 64 HAM, 64 NEWD², 65 BERL², 66 MANL, 67 BERL (2), 71 MOS, 71 VIC, 74 ZAG
Traversari-Salazar P P 03 ROM
Trautwein 38 FRA
Trautwein F 32 AMS, 53 NET
Travert A 59 ROY

Treitler L   64 SAL (p), 72 COP (2), 74 NEWY[2]
Trend J B   30 LIÈ
Trendelenburg W   38 FRA
Trimillos R D   69 KUA
Trinchieri R   57 CHIE
Trojan J   66 BRN, 68 BRN
Trojanowicz A   74 KRP
Trommer   38 FRA
Tron E   48 TUR (2)
Trost P   60 WAR[2]
Trowell B   67 LJU (p)
Tsaday-Yakimenko A   69 BYD
Tseretelli E   74 STN
Tsitovich G I   64 MOS
Tullot M T   65 MTS
Turchi G   49 FLOR, 67 FLOR
Turfo T D   60 WAR[1]
Tyrrell J   68 BRN, 69 BRN
Tzschöckell H   75 BLA

Úbeda J   65 MTS
Uberti M   68 VEN
Uchida R   68 TOK[2]
Ugolini G   64 SAL (p), 66 VEN, 67 LJU (p), 69 VER
Ujfalussy J   61 BUD, 63 PRA, 64 SAL (p), 65 BERL[1], 68 UPP, *71 BUD[1]*, 71 BUD[1]
Ukhikvadze G   63 BUD
Underwood L   64 SAL (p)
Unger I   73 WEIM
Unger M   24. BAS, 30 LIÈ
Üngör E R   73 ANK
Unverricht H   70 BON, 70 PIE
Urbański J   60 WAR[1], 67 ZAG, 72 VIE[2]
Ursprung O   24 BAS, 25 LEIP, 27 VIE (2)
Usmanbas I   74 NEWY[1] (p)
Uspenskiy N D   69 BYD, 75 BYD
Ussachevsky V   60 STRT, 68 SVE
Uszkoreit H-G   59 HAL, 70 BERL[2]
Utermöhlen R   54 STAD

Václavek B   28 PRA
Väisänen A O A   53 BAM, 56 HAM
Vajda I   65 BRN, 70 BRN
Valabrega C   54 PAL, 56 PAR, 56 PRA
Valavanis T   67 LJU (p)
Válek J   58 BRN
Valensi H   37 PAR[3], 56 VEN
Valentin E   50 LÜN[1], 56 PRA
Válka J   70 BRN
Valkman O   72 VIE[2]
Vancea Z   56 PRA, 56 VIE, 58 BRN, 59 BUD, 60 WAR[1], 61 BUD, 67 BUC
Vandor I   73 ROM[2]
Vanhulst H   74 STN
Vanický J   66 BYD
Varga D   73 BUC
Varga O   67 BUC, 73 BUC
Vargyas L   63 BUD
Várnai P P   66 VEN, 69 VER, 72 MIL
Vašica J   64 BRA
Vasina-Grossman V   60 WAR[1]

Vatielli F   21 TUR, 37 FLOR
Vatsyayan K   64 NEWD[1], 67 BERL
de Vaux-Phalipau   31 PAR
Vaziri A-N   61 TEH
Vecchi G   64 SAL (2; p), 68 VEN, 69 CER (2), 69 PARM (2), 69 VER, 71 WAR, 72 VEN
Vedova E   64 HAM
van der Veen J   58 COL
de la Vega A   60 STRT, 65 BLM
Vega C   32 LAP (2), 63 CART, 65 BLM
Vègeto R   67 FLOR
Veinus A   72 MIL
Veit E   66 LEIP
Vékovitch D   31 PAR
Velimirović M   64 BRA, 64 SAL (p), 66 OXF[1], 68 SVE, 72 COP
Venhoda M   67 BRN[2]
Venturini G   38 FLOR
Verchaly A   53 PAR, *56 PAR*, 57 NEU/S, 61 NEWY, 64 SAL (p), 65 DIJ, 67 LJU (c), 68 MTA
Verdone M   50 FLOR (2)
Veretti A   37 FLOR, 48 FLOR, 50 FLOR
Vernon P E   29 NEWH
Vertkov K A   64 MOS (d), 67 BRN[1]
Vessella A   03 ROM
Vetter M   71 BRN
Vetter W   *50 LEIP*, 50 LEIP, 56 PRA, 56 VIE, 58 COL
Vetterl K   58 BRN, 65 BRA, 68 BRN, 74 KRP
Viale Ferrero M   72 VEN, 73 SIE, 75 SIE
Vianna da Motta J   27 VIE
Vicol I D   67 BUC
Victori L1   65 MTS
Viderö F   54 STAD
Viertel K-H   69 WAR, 70 BERL[2], 72 BYD
Vige-Langevin   37 PAR[3]
Vilanova J   65 MTS
Villanis L A   03 ROM
Villetard H   00 PAR[6]
Vincent J   65 BLM
Vinogradov V S   61 TEH, 64 MOS (d)
Viozzi G   66 VEN, 69 VER
Virgili L1   65 MTS
Virsaladzé H   68 TOK[2]
Viswanathan T   61 TOK, 64 NEWD[2]
Vít P   71 BRN
Vitányi I   72 VIE[2], 73 BEL
Vitolin' Ya Ya [Vitolin Ye]   64 MOS, 72 BYD
Vitry D   09 LIÈ
Vivancos J M   65 MTS
Vivet A   37 PAR[1]
Vlad R   50 FLOR, 71 FLOR, 72 MIL, 73 ROM[2]
Vladishevskaya T   75 BYD
Vodák Z   74 BLA
Vodušek V   67 RAD, 71 HIN

Vogel J   65 BRN
Vogel M   56. HAM, 62 KAS, 66 LEIP (1; p), 72 COP
Voicana M   *73 BUC*, 73 BUC
Voigt H-H   73 MAG
Voisé W   60 WAR[1]
Vojtěch I   64 SAL (p)
Vokos G   56 PRA
Volbach W R   56 VIE
Volek J   58 BRN, 60 WAR[1], 61 BUD, 68 UPP, 71 BUD[1]
Volek T   64 SAL (2p), 66 BYD, 67 BRN[2], 67 LJU, 69 BRN, 70 BON, 70 BRN, 72 COP
Völkel A   71 HIN
Voss E   70 BON
van der Vossen E T   67 ZAG
Vötterle K   59 CAM
Votto A   67 FLOR
Voulétich-Voukassovitch   V   00 PAR[5]
Vrieslander O   38 VIE
Vuillermoz É   33 FLOR, 37 FLOR, 38 FLOR
Vysloužil J   58 BRN (2), 65 BRN, 66 BRN, 68 BRN, 69 BRN (2), 70 BON, 70 BRN (2), 71 BRN (1; p), 74 KRP
Vyverman J   57 PAR

Wachsmann K P   58 WÉG, 61 NEWY, 64 SAL (p), 67 BERL, 68 EVA, 72 COP, 75 AUS (p; 2d), 75 ROM
Waeltner E L   58 COL, 62 KAS, 70 BON, 72 FRE/B
Wagenaar-Nolthenius H   67 LJU (p), 69 CER
Wagner C   72 GRA
Wagner J   62 BERN
Wagner M   72 GRA, 75 EIS
Wagner P   05 STRS (4), 06 BAS (1; c), 09 VIE, 25 LEIP, 27 BERL, 27 VIE
Waite W G   61 NEWY
Walcha H   38 FRE/B
Walcker O   26 FRE/B
Walcker-Mayer W   73 NUR
Waldmann G   64 GRA[2]
Walin S   56 PAR
Walker D P   53 PAR, 55 ROY
Walker T   72 VEN (2)
Wallaschek R   08 VIE
Wallau R   50 LÜN[1]
Walleck O   38 FLOR
Wallerstein L   31 SAL
Wallin N L   53 BAM
Wallner B   62 KAS
Wallon S   56 VIE, 65 DIJ (p)
Walter F   64 HAM
Walter H   70 BON, 70 GRA
Walter R   50 ROM, 54 VIE, 73 NUR
von Waltershausen H W   27 HAL
Walton J   67 PAR
Wangermée R   54 PAR[2], 57 WEG, 70 STGE
Ward J   52 UTR, 54 PAR[1], 57 NEU/S
Warde   38 FRA

Warren C W   74 NEWY²
Wasserbauer M   58 BRN, 65 BRN, 67 BRN²
Watanabe M   70 BON
Waterman R A   49 NEWY¹, 67 VAN
Waters E N   68 SVE
Watkins G   73 ROM¹
Watson J M   64 SAL (p)
Watzek A   71 GRA
Weaver W   72 MIL
Weber E   *60 PAR¹, 62 PAR*, 62 PAR, *69 PAR*, 72 PAR, 75 STRS
Weber H   72 COP, 74 GRA¹
Wechner B   61 COL
Węcowski J   66 BYD
Wehnert M   66 LEIP, 68 BRN, 70 BERL², 71 BRN
Weihs H   67 PRA
Weil L   64 SAL (p)
Weinhold L   59 CAM (p), 62 KAS
Weinmann K   09 VIE, 11 LON, 25 LEIP, 27 VIE
Weisberg A   74 NEWY¹ (p)
Weise D   56 VIE
Weismann W   59 HAL
Weiss G   75 ESP
Weiss N   70 BON
Weissbach   38 FRA
Weissenbäck A   25 LEIP, 27 VIE
Weissmann J   61 BUD
Welin K-E   68 THU, 71 STU
Wellek A   34 TÜB, 38 BAY, 56 VIE, 58 BRN, 61 NEWY
Wellesz E   11 LON, 27 VIE (1;c), 36 ROM, 37 FLOR (2), 39 ALG, 50 ROM, 54 VIE, 55 IST, 57 PAR, 61 OKH, 69 BRN
Wendler J   62 KAS
Wenker J   65 NEWY
Wenzinger A   67 KAS
Werner A   25 LEIP
Werner E   50 ROM, 52 UTR, 54 VIE, 57 CAM/M, 57 PAR, 62 KAS (2), 64 SAL (c;2p), 65 JER, 66 CHIC
Werner T W   24 BAS, 25 LEIP (2)
Wessely O   56 VIE
Wessely-Kropik H   56 VIE
Westergaard P   72 COP (2)
Westrup J A   53 PAR, 59 CAM, 61 NEWY (c), 62 KAS, 64 SAL (c;p), 67 LJU (c), 68 VEN
Wethlo   38 FRA
Wetzel H   13 BERL
Wever E G   61 NEWY
Weyler W   62 KAS
Wicart   38 FRA
Wicke R   25 LEIP, 25 MUN
Widmann J   68 THU, 74 SINZ
Widmann W   09 VIE
Widstrand C   60 PAR²
Wiehmayer I   25 LEIP
Wild E   71 STGA (p)
Wilkens H   74 LON
Wilkowska-Chomińska   K   57 NEU/S, 60 WAR¹, 62

MAG, 72 BYD
Willfort E S   11 LON
Williams P   71 GRA
Willis P   72 VIE²
Willner A   27 VIE
Winckel F   54 PAR², 56 VIE, 58 COL, 58 MARS, 62 COP, 64 SAL (c), 65 BERL², 65 GEN, 74 LON
Wing H D   48 EDIN
Winternitz E   55 ROY, 56 VIE, 58 COL, 59 CAM, 61 NEWY (1;c), 64 SAL (p), 69 NUR
Wiora W   37 PAR³, 49 BAS, *50 LÜN¹*, 50 LÜN¹ (1; c), 52 UTR, 53 BAM, 54 PAL, 54 WÉG, 60 PAR¹ (2), 60 WAR¹, 61 NEWY (c), 62 KAS (1; c), *63 KIE*, 64 SAL, 65 BRA, *66 LEIP*, 66 LEIP (c; p), 71 NEWY, 74 ZAG
Wirsta A   58 COL, 64 SAL (p), 67 LJU (p), 69 PAR, 72 GRA
Wirth H R   56 PAR, 62 KAS, 73 NUR
Witasek S   06 BAS
Witkowski L   73 MAG
Witold J   56 PRA
Wittmayer K   71 GRA
Wittrock W   63 KIE
Witzenmann W   67 SIE, 69 ROM, 74 ROM
Wogram K   72 COP
Woitinek J   11 LON
Wolf J   06 BAS (1;2c), 09 VIE, 11 LON (2;c), 24 BAS, 25 LEIP (1;c), 27 BERL, 27 VIE, 28 VIE
Wolf R E   57 WÉG, 66 MTA
Wolff C   70 BON, 72 COP (2)
Wolff H C   49 BAS, 50 LEIP, 50 LÜN¹, 52 UTR, 53 BAM, 54 PAL, 56 HAM, 56 VIE, 57 PAR, 58 COL, 59 HAL, 62 MAG, 64 SAL (c), 65 AMS, 67 MAG, 67 SIE, 68 BRN, 68 VEN, 69 WAR, 70 BRN, 71 BRN, 72 VEN
Wolfram R   64 GRA²
Worbs H C   56 HAM, 56 VIE
Wörner K H   56 VIE, 58 BRN, 58 COL, 68 BRN
Wörsching J   27 FRE/S, 50 ROM
Wright C   74 NEWY²
Wulstan D   72 BERN
Wünsch W   38 FRA, 38 GHE, 53 BAM, 56 HAM, 56 VIE, 58 COL, 62 KAS, *64 GRA²*, 64 GRA², 64 SAL (2p), 66 GRA, 68 GRA, 70 GRA, 71 EIS
Wuorinen C   68 SVE
Wustmann R   09 VIE
Wynn Jones L   26 GRON

Xenakis I   61 TOK, 66 MANL

Yarustowski [Yarustovskiy] B *see* Jarustowski B

Yates F A   53 PAR
Yeomans W   52 CAM
Yönetken H B   47 PRA, 56 PRA, 62 SIN, 66 SOF
Yoshida T   65 LIÈ
Young P M   58 COL, 59 HAL, 62 KAS, 72 BLA, 74 BLA
Young R W   53 NET, 58 MARS, 62 COP
Yuize S   61 TEH, 61 TOK

Zabłocka J   62 WAR
Zachariassen S   52 BERN, 54 VIE
Zacher G   68 THU
Zafred M   49 FLOR
Zagiba F   52 UTR, 53 BAM, 54 VIE (3), 72 COP
Zaldivar J   28 PRA
Zálešák C   74 KRP
Zambiasi G   03 ROM
Zaminer F   *70 BERL¹*, 70 BERL¹, 71 BRN (p), 72 FRE/B
Zampieri G   09 VIE (3)
Zanetti E   69 ROM
Zanuso Mauri O   72 MIL
Zaslaw N   72 COP
Zaubek O K M   74 GRA²
Zauner F   64 GRA¹
Zecchi A   50 FLOR, 68 FUS (c)
Zechlin D   70 BERL² (p)
Zehntner H   50 LÜN², 51 PAR, 62 STOC (c), 65 DIJ (p)
Zehrer F   50 ROM
Zeman H   71 EIS
Zenck H   49 BAS
Zenginov D   71 BRN
Zenkl L   70 BRN
Žganec V   64 GRA²
Zhubanov A   64 MOS (d)
Zich J   58 COL, 67 BRN²
Zich O   28 PRA
Ziegler K M   74 SINZ
Zieliński T A   60 WAR¹, 62 WAR
Ziino A   66 VEN, 69 ROM, 73 ROM¹, 73 ROM²
Zillhardt R   72 STU
Zillinger E   27 FRE/S
Zimmerman F B   58 COL, 62 KAS, 64 SAL (p), 65 NEWY
Zimmermann C   72 BERN
Zimmermann H W   62 BERN
Živković M   56 VIE
Zobeley F   27 VIE
Zoder R   09 VIE
Zoltai [Zoltay] D   65 BERL¹, 71 BUD¹
Zorzi E G   74 SIE
Zorzi L   74 SIE
Zottoviceanu E   73 BUC, 75 BYD
von Zschinsky-Troxler E M   56 VIE
Zschoch F   59 HAL, 70 BERL², 74 BLA
Zukkerman [Cukkerman] V   60 WAR¹, 70 BERL²
Županović I   68 BRN, 69 BYD, 72 BYD
Zwirner E   38 FRA, 38 GHE
Zwolińska E   71 WAR (2)

SUBJECT INDEX

numbers following congress codes are the page numbers of the actual report
italicized congress codes indicate whole reports devoted to a given subject

Aarhus, Musikhochschule in, 71 STU 281
Åbo missal, 75 ESP 91
Aboriginal songs, 67 VAN 102
Abruzzo folksongs, 57 CHIE 160, 449, 473
Absolute music, 38 FLOR 186, 70 BON 607
Accentuation, 13 BERL 476, 25 LEIP 460
  Beethoven, 49 BAS 190
  Brahms, 62 KAS 215
  ictus in metrical Latin, 50 ROM 192
Accidentals
  in intabulations of Josquin's motets, 71 NEWY 475
  14th c, 55 WÉG 167
  15th c, 09 VIE 124
  16th c, 09 VIE 109, 112, 124, 126, 128
Accompaniment
  in Gregorian chant, see Gregorian chant: specific
    elements, accompaniment
  obbligato in Viennese Classics, 25 LEIP 35
  organ in 17th c music, 27 FRE/S 95
  primitive music, 58 COL 72
Accompanist, role in 18th c, 71 BRN 73
Accordion in Trentino, 34 TRT 352
Acculturation, 61 NEWY i, 139
  Asia, 74 ZAG 181
  folk music, 74 ZAG 209
  South America, 65 BLM 220
  Yugoslavia, 74 ZAG 217
Acoustics, *53 NET 56 CAM/M, 58 MARS, 59 STU, 62
  COP, 65 LIE, 67 PAR, 68 TOK[1], 71 BUD[2],
  74 LON*
  the ear, 58 COL 227
  fotonomo, 11 LON 332
  France, 11 ROM 127
  institutes, 58 MARS 169, 185
  measurements, 58 MARS 221
  musician's environment, 56 CAM/M 50
  non-stationary sound, 69 STOC 97
  performing practice, 67 KAS 61
  prehispanic Indian instruments, 62 MEX 369
  psychology, 66 LEIP 407
  reed, 58 MARS 203, 215
  vocabulary, 58 MARS 111
  see also Architectural acoustics; Instruments (es-
    pecially electro-acoustical); Pitch; Pipes; Scale; Sing-
    ing; Timbre; individual instruments
Actus musicus, 66 LEIP 230
Adorno, T. W., 72 FRE/B 9
Ady, Endve, 71 BUD[1] 111
Aesthetics *13 BERL, 24 BERL, 27 HAL, 30 HAM², 37
  PAR³, 56 VEN, 60 ATH, 64 AMS, 68 UPP,* 06
  BAS 86–129, 29 NEWH 379, 47 PRA 69, 49
  BAS 183, 53 BRUS 271
  theories of music, explanations, approaches

anti-aesthetical, 37 PAR³ ii, 464
  dialectical, 63 PRA 275, 65 BERL¹ 347, 363
  Ganzheit psychology, 56 VIE 678
  Hegel's, 37 PAR³ ii, 32
  as illusion, 25 LEIP 416
  as impression, 09 VIE 315
  information theory, *see* Information theory
  Jungian, 68 UPP 825
  Kierkegaard's, 56 VEN 706
  T. Lipps's, 06 BAS 87, 09 VIE 345
  Marxist, *63 PRA, 65 BERL¹*
  as microorganism in sound, 56 VEN 647
  non-Aristotelian, 65 BERL¹ 387
  origins, 00 PAR² 221, 13 BERL 430, 21 PAR 759
  Schicht theory, 72 COP 585
  Schopenhauer's, 29 NEWH 350
  semiological, 73 BEL 173
  semiotics, *see* Semiotics
  Siebeck's, 27 VIE 312
  Stendhal's, 69 PARM 206
  as study of higher emotions, 29 NEWH 372
  transcendental, 62 KAS 193
music and other arts, and disciplines
  abstract art, 56 VEN 638
  the arts, 24 BERL 425
  art, science and philosophy, 34 PRA 1073
  dance, 37 PAR³ i, 322, ii, 474; 56 VEN 664
  ideology, 65 BERL¹ 257
  literature in the 19th c, 61 NEWY i, 314, 323
  musicalization of the senses, 72 COP 32
  painting in 17th c France, 64 BON 206
  philosophy, 11 ROM 117, 49 BAS 166
  poetry, 64 AMS 745
  psychology, 64 AMS 760
  psychophysiology, 11 LON 224
  religion, 64 AMS 843
aesthetics of musical disciplines
  ethnomusicology, 10 INN 256
  music criticism, 33 FLOR 11, 18, 31, 60 STRT 8,
    67 GRA
  music education, 06 BAS 129, 25 LEIP 159
  music history, 24 BAS 311, 50 LÜN¹ 202
  musicology, *see* Musicology
  music sociology, 68 UPP 115–251, *74 ZAG*
aesthetics of particular composers and periods
  antiquity, meaning for middle ages, 06 BAS 128
  Chopin, 60 WAR¹ 433, 649–735
  Debussy, 62 PAR 133–99
  musical humanism from Diderot to Hanslick, 48
    AMS 534
  18th c opera reform, 09 VIE 196
  late 18th c and early 19th c, 56 VIE 579, 70 VIE 199
  19th c, 30 LIÈ 139, 67 LJU 380, 70 BON 517

283

20th c, 60 ATH 232, 432, 64 AMS 570, 61 TOK 152
  evaluation, 65 BERL¹ 325, 328
  ideology, 65 BERL¹ 257
  language, 56 VEN 651, 65 BERL¹ 278, 337
  relation to exotic and medieval, 24 BERL 411
  vocal and instrumental style, 53 BAM 266
concepts, aesthetics of particular aspects
  colour and tone, 50 LÜN¹ 187
  creation, 24 BAS 67
  description, 52 UTR 360
  essential traits, 49 BAS 75
  evaluation, 66 LEIP 482
  expression, 60 ATH 428
  genres, 68 UPP 633
  harmony, 60 ATH 353
  inheritance, 50 LÜN¹ 197
  interpretation, 60 ATH 555
  intuition, 11 BOL 513
  jazz, 68 UPP 827
  language, 52 UTR 100, 56 VEN 642, 651, 68 UPP 621
  meaning, 56 HAM 145, 60 ATH 435, 65 BERL¹ 343, 66 LEIP 391, 73 BEL 183–249, 74 ZAG v, 51, 61
  mind, 29 NEWH 383
  movement, 50 LÜN¹ 189
  nature and limits, 61 NEWY i, 386, 398
  the new, 61 NEWY i, 184, 195
  organ sound and playing, 37 PAR³ ii, 239
  performance, 29 NEWH 217, 70 ANT 7
  pleasure, 06 BAS 111
  programme music, 64 AMS 626
  relevance, 49 BAS 96
  sacred and secular, 24 BERL 397
  scale, 68 UPP 811
  sense, 11 LON 238
  structure, 68 UPP 621
  style, 61 TOK 144
  taste, 60 ATH 257
  thought, 00 PAR² 296
  ugliness, 11 LON 77
  'Umdeutung', 52 UTR 282
  the unfinished, 64 AMS 219, 256
  value, 06 BAS 86, 65 BERL²
  why is there music?, 68 UPP 635
Affektenlehre
  and Bach's melodies, 25 LEIP 436, 439
  and Mestastasian opera dramaturgy, 69 WAR 131
  and music conception of 19th c, 64 AMS 969
African music, 48 BRUS 105, 61 TEH 244, 70 YAO, 75 ROM 36
  in America, 70 YAO 129
  in Brazil, 70 YAO 135
  church music, 57 PAR 547, 567, 75 ROM 51, 72
  contemplative character, 71 MOS 108
  documentary sources, 70 YAO 43
  drum, 51 STIS 165, 58 WÉG 229
  East Africa, 70 YAO 75
  ethnomusicology in Africa, 68 EVA 131
  evolution of traditional music, 70 YAO 117
  French-speaking traditional music, 67 BERL 132
  funeral music, 64 SAL ii, 143
  harmonic sense, 58 COL 154
  influence on American Indian music, 39 NEWY 130
  influence on American music, 49 NEWY¹ 207
  influence on Panamanian music, 58 SJOS 639
  instruments, *see* Instruments
  modern African contact with music, 70 YAO 125
  musical languages, 70 YAO 49

musical thought, 51 STIS 165
oriental music in Africa, 70 YAO 95
ornamentation, 61 NEWY i, 427
sickness rite from Digo, 69 MARB 107
social status of professional musicians, 56 WÉG 23
  in society, 56 WÉG 33, 70 YAO 57
Southern African music, 57 PAR 567, 58 COL 154
stratification, 58 COL 334, 58 WÉG 19
Sub-Saharan, 70 YAO 7
West African music, 06 BAS 60, 68 TOK² 348, 70 YAO 69
Ağit folksongs, 73 ANK 192
Aglié, le comte d', 55 ROY 221
Agogic accent
  in Baroque music, 58 COL 343
  in Chopin and Field, 60 WAR¹ 275
  in performance, 58 COL 319
Ainu music, 67 VAN 60
Air de cour, 53 PAR 185, 211
Akathistos Hymnos, 55 IST 297
Akimenko, Theodore, 58 COL 302
Aksak usuller rhythms, 66 SOF ii, 1123
Alba Iulia (Karlsburg), 75 BYD 357
Albania
  folk music instruments, 56 VIE 612
  Greek-Albanian folksongs, 54 PAL 329
  Greek Albanian church modes, 09 VIE 83
  Italo-Albanian folk music, 40 VEN 410
  polyphony in folksong, 56 HAM 229, 58 WÉG 85
  Sicilian Italo-Albanian liturgical chant, 50 ROM 129
Aleatoric music, 60 ATH 432
  in the Renaissance, 49 BAS 103
Alessandro Carlo of Poland, 70 BOL 191, 199
Algerian traditional music (rhythms), 32 CAIR 521
Alla Turca, 71 EIS 86
Alleluia, 56 VIE 276
Allgemeine musikalische Zeitung, 52 UTR 293
Alphameric language for musical analysis, 65 NEWY 57
Alphorn, 75 BRUN 27
Alps
  folk instruments, 27 VIE 373
  polyphony in folksongs, 58 COL 316
  work songs, 65 MARB 325
Alsace
  Gregorian chant in, 05 STRS 19
  Silbermann organs, 25 BRUG 224
  organs, 14th c to 18th c, 32 STRS 177
Alta, 49 BAS 59
Alternatim, 68 VEN 171
Ambros, August Wilhelm, 71 NEWY 145
Ambrosian chant, 50 ROM 196
  compared with Byzantine chant, 36 ROM 540
  compared with Gregorian chant, 49 BAS 185, 57 PAR 218
America, continent of, 47 PRA 62
  African influence, 49 NEWY¹ 207
  choreographic research, 30 HAM¹ 212
  contemporary composer in, 65 BLM 158
  ethnomusicology, 63 CART, 65 BLM
  folk and popular sources for composition, 68 SVE 185
  history of indigenous and popular music, 03 ROM 117
  Latin *see* Latin America
  musical 'Americanism', 39 NEWY 273
  musicians' problems, 39 NEWY 289
  North American folk music in cities, 65 BLM 139
  North American traditions and the composer, 65 BLM 195

South American contribution to contemporary musical culture, 71 MOS 136
South American acculturation, 65 BLM 220
South American musical traditions, 65 BLM 220
survival of European traditions, 61 NEWY i, 356, 364
American Indian music, 06 QUE 179, 32 LAP 119
acculturation, 49 NEWY[1] 127
African influence, 39 NEWY 130
Christian hymnology, 56 PHIL 324
influence on Dvořák's American chamber music, 71 BRN 147
prehispanic musical instruments, 52 CAM 54, 62 MEX 369
ritual music, 60 PAR[2] 101
rhythm, 22 RIO 85
specific tribes, 04 STU 403, 08 VIE 489, 513, 28 NEWY 796, 29 PRA 168, 49 NEWY[1] 94, 123, 49 NEWY[2] 109, 139, 56 PHIL 468, 58 SJOS 611, 58 WAS 173, 63 CART 119, 131, 187, 65 BLM 129, 67 VAN 16, 23, 75 AUS 88
styles, 28 NEWY 455
America, United States of,
general, *68 SVE*
ballads surviving in, 15 WAS 457
black music in, 70 YAO 129
early music scholarship, 62 STOC 12
ethnomusicology in music education, 68 SVE 173
film music, 50 FLOR 118
financial support for music, 68 SVE 9
folk music, 28 PRA 166, 39 NEWY 77, 84, 122, 68 SVE 149
Gregorian chant in, 57 PAR 241
mass audience, 68 SVE 67
musical life in, 09 VIE 446, 21 PAR 935
music bibliography, 68 SVE 95
music studies, 68 SVE 43
musicology, 68 SVE 80, 120
nationalism in American music histories, 68 SVE 199
opera, 20th c, 33 FLOR 188
piano (early), 59 CAM 179
singing school movement, 61 NEWY i, 89
Slav musicology in, 72 BYD 615
training composers, 68 SVE 26
19th c music, 62 KAS 74, 74 NEWY[1] 4, 16, 29
music of the 1960s, 68 SVE 58
and individuals
Beethoven, 27 VIE 26, 70 BON 343
Debussy, 62 PAR 215
Enesco, 73 BUC 109, 115
Ives, 74 NEWY[1] 4, 16, 29
Mozart, 56 VIE 285
Toscanini, 67 FLOR 83
Webern, 72 VIE[1] 153
see also Libraries and manuscripts: America
d'Amerval, Eloy, 00 PAR[2] 165
Analysis, 54 PAR[1] 347, 62 KAS 291, 71 STU 153, 73 BEL 56, 135, 151, 73 PAR 177
Bach chorale melodies, 73 BEL 125
Beethoven, 72 COP 80, 82, 85
computers (use of), *see* Computers
contemporary music, 71 MOS 210, 72 COP 50
ethnomusicological, 74 KRP 18, 20
folk music, *see* Folk music: classification
harmonic texts, 73 PAR 165
hermeneutic, 13 BERL 490
Hostinský's conception of, 74 KRP 13
invariancé matrix (use of), 72 COP 228
methods, 11 LON 250, 71 STU 227, 72 COP 43, 54, 56, 58, 61

in musicology, 56 VIE 373, 65 WAR 285, 74 KRP 5
oral traditional music, 74 KRP 22
Palestrina, 72 COP 86, 89, 103, 108
rhythmic, 26 GEN 70
semiotic, 74 KRP 12
sketches (importance of), 56 VIE 616
structure, 64 SAL ii, 261, 66 MOR 29, 72 COP 103
style, 65 NEWY 19, 194, 66 MOR 43, 72 COP 43–121
taxonomic, 73 BEL 83
in teaching, 74 ZAG 85
verbalization of the musical, 72 COP 309
Anatolia, (songs and dances) 73 ANK 315
Ancient world
and Beethoven, 70 BERL[2] 465
and Handel, 59 HAL 87
meaning for Western music, 56 HAM 24
polyphony, 58 COL 290
structural role of intervals, 60 PAR[1] 103
Andalusia, 63 STT 85
Andante, 62 KAS 156
André, Johann Anton 56 VIE 324
Anfossi, Pasquale, 75 SIE 141
Angiolini, Gasparo (ballets), 73 SIE 487, 513, 535
Anglican church music, 52 BERN 57, 72 BERN 74
Anna von Köln Liederbuch, 52 UTR 340
Antegnati, Costanzo, *L'arte organica*, 68 VEN 479
Anthem, Restoration, 62 KAS 27
Antiphon melodies, 11 LON 54
Antiphonary
of Fons Avellana, 54 VIE 129
of Presbyter de Gimedia, 54 ROU 925
Roman, 50 ROM 248
of Sedlec, 27 BEL 155
Visigothic and Gregorian, 50 ROM 183
Antwerp, instruments, 59 CAM 128, *70 ANT*
Apache music, 56 PHIL 468
Apocalypse (musical themes), 72 TOD 195
Apollinaire, Guillaume
and music, *65 STAV*
and musicians, 65 STAV 59, 99
Petite musique, 65 STAV 43
poems set to music (bibliography), 65 STAV 103
and Poulenc, 65 STAV 49, 59
Apollo, Second hymn to, 00 PAR[2] 70
Appoggiatura, 58 COL 58, 69 PAR 87
Appreciation, musical, 29 NEWH 372
Aptitude tests, 29 NEWH 284, 406, 48 EDIN 129
Arab
Arabo-Berber influence on Mediterranean music, 72 MALT 58
Arabo-Spanish glossary (instruments), 73 BAL 94
Arabo-Spanish music, 60 PAR[2] 107
influence in Spanish music, 53 BAM 175
music, 05 ALG 437, *32 CAIR*
music and European music, 75 BYD 407
theory, 72 SÁR 129
Aragon
folk dance, 28 PRA 189
jota, 28 PRA 187
musicians at 14th c court, 24 BAS 56
Arany, János, 75 BRUN 114
Arbeau, Thoinot (branles), 72 SÁR 101
Archeological research into folk instruments, 73 BAL 88
Architectural acoustics
audience, seat absorbtion, 59 STU 913
of churches, 11 LON 286
design, 56 CAM/M 53
and the listener in early music, 67 KAS 61

measurements and hearing conditions, 56 CAM/M 59
the musician's environment, 56 CAM/M 50
in musicology, 59 STU 983
objective evaluation, 65 LIÈ ii, 41
performing practice, 58 COL 295
reverberation time and tempo, 59 STU 979
in 17th c Roman polychoral music, 58 COL 100
of theatres, opera houses, concert halls and music rooms, 38 FRA 319, 59 STU 922, 967; 62 COP i, M37, ii, 15; 65 LIÈ i, G13, M51; 71 BUD² iv, 1
see also Concert halls
Archives *see* Libraries
Aria
  Aria di maggio, 53 PAR 265
  compared with recitative and melodrama in 18th c, 69 BRN 59
  and Lied, 38 FRA 17
Aristotle 37 PAR³ ii, 18
Armenia
  chant, 50 ROM 149, 152, 54 CAM 173, 57 PAR 324, 69 BYD 321
  folksongs, 64 MOS 329
  polychromaticism, 56 VIE 112
Arne, Thomas Augustine, 74 BLA 38
Arpichord, 58 COL 76
d'Arras, Jean, 21 PAR 829
Ars mensurablis, 09 VIE 108
Ars nova, 55 *WÉG*, 59 *CER*, 69 *CER*
  end, 62 KAS 108
  .in France, 55 WÉG 37, 59 CER 83
  in Italy, 55 WÉG 93, 59 CER 40
    influence in Poland, 69 CER 465
    instruments, 59 CER 40
  melismatic tradition, 69 CER 29
  see also Italy, trecento
Art
  in Lombardy in Josquin's time, 71 NEWY 138
  musical tendencies of painting, 37 PAR³ ii, 402
  in relation to music, 34 PRA 1073
  and sacred music, 50 ROM 411
Articulation
  marks in Beethoven autographs and early prints, 72 COP 580
  marks in 17th c keyboard tablature, 72 COP 342
  marks in Mozart autographs and early prints, 56 VIE 304
  in Webern, 72 VIE¹ 100
Artomiusz Cantionale, 69 BYD 141
Arts
  liberal arts, decline of, 56 HAM 129
  liberal arts, music as 56 HAM 46, 60, 64, 117
  and music, 24 BAS 310, 37 PAR³ i, 358, 56 VIE 653
Asaf'yev, Boris Vladimirovich, 58 COL 99
Ashkenazi *see* Jewish music
Asia
  acculturation, 74 ZAG 181
  Chinese music, in 66 MANL 191
  church music, 57 PAR 559
  contribution to contemporary musical culture, 71 MOS 147
  East Asia indigenous liturgical music, 75 ROM 117
  musics, 66 *MANL*
  South-East Asia music and instruments, 69 *KUA*
Assam folksongs, 56 WÉG 187
d'Astorga, Emanuele, 52 UTR 398
Atonality
  contemporary problems, 62 KAS 257
  definition, 58 COL 212

  and Ives, 74 NEWY¹ 159
  and Skryabin, 70 BON 438
  structure of atonal music, 65 NEWY 10
Auber, Daniel François Esprit, 70 BON 349
Audi tellus, 60 WAR¹ 565
Aulos, performing practice, 62 KAS 300
Aurelianus Reomensis, *Musica disciplina*, 58 COL 293
Australasian indigenous liturgical music, 75 ROM 117
Australian aborginal songs, 67 VAN 102
Austria
  Austro-Italian schools of composition in 17th c and 18th c, 64 SAL ii, 226
  Baroque organ, 50 ROM 371, 51 OCH 59
  courts (Italian musicians at), 37 FLOR 299
  Dukes (musicians in service of), 56 VIE 544
  Enlightenment, 71 EIS 92, 105, 147, 73 SIE 247
  folksong, 09 VIE 266, 27 VIE 326, 331, 67 RAD 101, 71 HIN 99
  harpsichord (after 1760), 70 GRA 249
  influence of Debussy, 62 PAR 241
  influence of Passau organ building, 54 VIE 246
  Ländler, beat in, 09 VIE 228
  lyrics in Haydn's time, 71 EIS 121
  music (Baroque), 71 EIS 153
    in Haydn's time, 71 EIS 9
    1830–1914, 62 KAS 54
  music bibliography, 27 VIE 265
  music criticism, 67 GRA 81
  place in European music, 56 VIE 421, 64 SAL ii, 7
  research into Gregorian chant, 54 VIE 149
  romantic crisis (1770), 56 PAR 27
  society and culture c1900, 74 GRA¹ 44
  violin technique in 18th c, 70 GRA 114
  violin and violin music (folk), 71 STP 102, 161
  yodelling, 09 VIE 248, 27 VIE 338
  youth music, 72 VIE² 129
Authenticity, 72 COP 365
  in 18th c music, 57 CAM/M 31, 71 EIS 25
Automatophones and performance of late Baroque music, 67 BRN² 137
d'Avalos, Alfonso, 68 MIL 23
Avant garde, *see* Twentieth-century music
Avignon flute players at Siena in 15th c, 21 PAR 802
Ayre, dance echoes in English, 53 PAR 203

Babinga, 56 WÉG 105
Babylonian notation, 39 NEWY 161
Bacewicz, Grażny (string quartets), 71 BRN 447
Bach, Carl Philipp Emanuel
  autographs, 56 VIE 412
  piano works (dynamics in), 62 KAS 178
  research, 27 VIE 211
  unknown portrait, 50 LEIP 349
  variation works, 52 UTR 189
Bach, Johann Christian, English environment, 62 KAS 32
Bach, Johann Sebastian, 50 *LEIP*, 52 UTR 218
  attitude to keyboard music of his time, 50 LEIP 405
  as Baroque composer, 50 LÜN¹ 195
  biographical, 50 LEIP 193
  derivation (problem of), 61 NEWY 236, 249
  and folk music, 50 LEIP 411, 416
  Forkel biography, 72 COP 462
  and the middle ages, 50 LEIP 201, 210
  as music teacher, 50 LEIP 201,210
  and opera of his time, 72 BYD 387
  and organs of his time, 27 FRE/S 122
  psychology, 25 LEIP 359
  and rationalism, 50 LEIP 420

sociological portrait, 50 LÜN¹ 223
bibliographical
  manuscript of B Minor Mass, 50 LEIP 231
  research, 50 LEIP 295
  source studies, 50 LEIP 219, 66 LEIP 269
and places
  Eastern Europe, 50 LEIP 411
  works in England (1750–1850), 50 LÜN¹ 131
  Germany, 50 LEIP 158
  Sweden, 50 LEIP 367
  Vienna, 50 LÜN² 129
and others
  Beethoven, 70 BON 579
  Bruckner, 50 LEIP 355
  Chopin, 60 WAR¹ 73
  Leibniz, 50 LEIP 431
  Mozart, 56 PRA 61
  Odeyevsky, 66 LEIP 287
  Purcell, 00 PAR² 210
  Reger, 73 NUR 3
  Vivaldi, 56 HAM 80
style
  articulation in instrumental works, 25 LEIP 251
  and authenticity in cantatas, 50 LEIP 259
  canon, 50 LEIP 250
  character theme, 50 LÜN¹ 7
  church, significance of the, 50 LÜN¹ 107
  dance rhythms in vocal music, 62 KAS 167
  form, 50 LEIP 270, 50 LÜN¹ 111
  instrumental elements in vocal music, 66 LEIP 265
  and Italian trio sonata, 71 BRN 337
  keyboard writing, 62 KAS 170
  in light of style changes, 25 LEIP 245
  linking prelude and fugue, 50 LÜN¹ 126
  melodic and architectural principles, 25 LEIP 250, 73 BEL 125
  ostinato technique, 50 LEIP 240
  phrase technique, 50 LÜN¹ 124
  real answer in fugues, 62 KAS 364
  siciliano, 54 PAL 301
  symmetry, 50 LEIP 277
  themes, and effect of *Affektenlehre*, 25 LEIP 436–9
  trumpet (use of), 70 BON 592
works (general)
  arias, 50 LÜN¹ 111
  arrangements, 49 BAS 160, 56 HAM 95
  of own works, 56 HAM 75
  cantatas, 50 LEIP 259, 50 LÜN¹ 120
  chorales, 72 COP 277, 73 BEL 125
  concertos, 75 BLA 21
  fugues, 37 PAR³ ii 243
  keyboard suites, 50 LÜN¹ 124
  keyboard suites (chronology), 24 BAS 127
  keyboard works (interpretation), 52 UTR 73
  oratorio works, 50 LÜN¹ 33
  polonaises, 50 LEIP 416
  preludes and fugues, 60 WAR¹ 73, 62 KAS 164
  vocal works, 62 KAS 167
works (specific)
  B Minor Mass, 50 LEIP 231, 320
  chorale on *Vater unser im Himmelreich*, 50 ROM 359
  fantasia movement, 70 BON 579
  Klavierübung III, 50 ROM 354
  Kunst der Fuge, 24 BAS 151
  St Matthew Passion, 50 LEIP 331
  Vor deinem Thron tret ich hiemit, 50 LEIP 285

performing practice
  concertos, forces in, 75 BLA 21
  motets, 50 LÜN¹ 121
  organ works, in French 17th–18th c, 49 BAS 172
  organ works, phrasing in, 50 ROM 363
  violin works, interpretation of, 72 GRA 13, 90
Bach sons, influence on Mozart, 56 PAR 91
Bach successors, works of in American collections, 58 COL 110
Bach, Wilhelm Friedemann
  polonaises, 60 WAR¹ 578
  unknown portrait, 50 LEIP 349
Badings, Henk (electronic ballet music), 60 STRT 106
Baga ritual music, 60 PAR² 123
Bagpipes
  Czech, 67 BRN¹ 128
  Highland, 53 NET 231
  Pibroch, 71 BRN 325
  Slovak, 67 BRN¹ 113
  West European, 67 BRN¹ 98
  in West European painting and sculpture, 73 BAL 63
Bahrain (folk music) 58 WÉG 137
Baillon, Pierre, 59 CAM 196
Bakala, Břetislav, 58 BRN 250
Bali music today, 61 TOK 60
Balkans
  dances, 72 SÁR 141
  epic, ballad and dance song compared with Western forms, 53 BAM 200
  epic, connections with Romanian, 68 GRA 53
  epics on disc, 62 KAS 317
  ethnomusicology, 71 BUD¹ 189
  folk music, 64 GRA², 66 SOF ii
  haiduks, 66 SOF vii, 903
  music history, folk music, instruments, 66 GRA 106
  oriental element, 66 GRA
  polyphony in folk music, 66 SOF ii, 1067
  primitive instruments, 64 GRA² 50
  revolutionary songs, 66 SOF vii, 777
  . as source of inspiration for 20th c music, 68 GRA 80
Ballad
  American, 15 WAS 457
  central European, 66 SOF vii, 903
  collecting techniques, 63 CART 177
  English broadside in 16th and 17th c, 39 NEWY 112
  Hungarian, 63 BUD 325
  of Künzig-Werner, 72 SÁR 5
  Romanian folk, 58 WÉG 39
  romantic, as copy of Wagnerian music drama, 62 KAS 233
  Southern European, 53 BAM 200
Ballade, piano before Chopin, 60 WAR¹ 519
Ballad opera
  burlesque in Ireland (*Midas*), 72 COP 623
  The Jovial Crew, 58 COL 240
Ballet, 61 TOK 30
  article in *Encyclopédie*, 75 SIE 73
  18th c ballet master, 73 SIE 473
  de cour, 55 ROY 221, 235
  electronic, 60 STRT 106
  evolution from 1900, 37 PAR³ ii 466
  in Italian play with music, 70 MTA 59
  and pantomime, 67 LJU 168
  Turkish, at court of Henri II, 70 MTA 17
  18th c Viennese ballet-pantomime, 73 SIE 487, 501
  volume of ballet music by Michel Henry, 55 ROY 205
  see also Dance
Baltic, *73 STOC*
  local variants of Gregorian chant, 75 BYD 7

psaltery, 73 STOC 7
Banat
    Liszt's tours in, 61 BUD 107
    music culture of the Banat Bulgarians, 64 MOS 272
Banchieri, Adriano, 70 BOL 269
    madrigals, 68 VEN 599
    theoretical works, 68 VEN 385
Band music
    collecting old Italian, 03 ROM 51
    evolution of band score, 03 ROM 43
    and Spontini, 51 IES 70
Bantu, concept of harmony, 58 COL 154
Barcelona, 17th c carnival, 55 ROY 371
Bar form, 50 LÜN¹ 65
    in Mahler's songs, 72 COP 617
Baroque, *57 WEG, 63 MTA, 66 MTA, 68 MTA, 70 MTA*, 60 ROM 361, 377, 71 WAR 91
    chamber performance, composition of orchestra, 71 BRN 49
    cheerfulness, 71 EIS 92
    colour and space in late Baroque, 71 EIS 40
    compared with Classical, 70 BON 323, 71 EIS 64
    decline of, 71 WAR 131
    dissonance treatment, 57 WÉG 151
    dynamics and agogics, 58 COL 343
    figures compared with classicals motifs in Beethoven, 70 BON 573
    form, hearing, 25 LEIP 430
    French poetry, 68 MTA 127
    French theory, 72 COP 366
    geographical limits, 57 WÉG 83
    instrumental music and Chopin, 60 WAR¹ 271
    interpretation, 57 WÉG 223
    lyricism and popular tradition, 57 WÉG 109
    and mannerism, 57 WÉG 35, 73 ROM¹ 101
    meaning of word 'Baroque' and application to music, 57 WÉG 17
    organ, 50 ROM 348, 371
    in organology, 63 MTA 25
    relation between opera/oratorio and instrumental music, 64 SAL ii, 212
    relation of word and music, 56 HAM 95, 69 BRN 225
    and Renaissance and mannerism, 57 WÉG 35
    in Slav music, 67 LJU 310
    Spanish and Portuguese, 63 MTA 85
    stylistic break with Renaissance in Poland, 69 BYD 209
    theatre music, 66 MTA 119
    theatrical and literary combination with music, *70 MTA*
    vocal improvisation, 53 BAM 252
Bartók, Béla, 61 BUD 339–587, *71 BUD¹*
    Ady poetry, in library 71 BUD¹ 111
    Balkan ethnomusicology (promoter of), 71 BUD¹ 189
    biography, 61 BUD 587
    and folk music, 61 BUD 435, 441, 549
    folk-music research, 71 BUD¹ 197
    man and nature in works, 61 BUD 525
    and the Nyugat movement, 61 BUD 347
    research on, 61 BUD 415, 587
    and 20th c music, 61 BUD 403
    bibliographical
        letters, 71 BUD¹ 89
        in world literature, 71 BUD¹ 103
    and places
        the Balkans, 71 BUD¹ 189
        Bulgaria, 61 BUD 491
        China, 61 BUD 393
        the East, 64 NEWD² 90
        England, 61 BUD 339
        Hungary, 71 BUD¹ 11, 163
        Russia, 61 BUD 481
        Slovakia, 71 BUD¹ 181
    and others
        Brăiloiu, 61 BUD 549
        Frankfurt school, 71 BUD¹ 13
        Janáček, 58 BRN 330, 61 BUD 501
        Kodály, 66 VEN 97, 71 BUD¹ 155
        Liszt, 75 EIS 65
        Prokofiev, 71 BUD¹ 137
        Schoenberg and Stravinsky, 68 BRN 331
        Sibelius, 71 BUD¹ 121
        Verdi, 66 VEN 97
        2nd Viennese School, 71 BUD¹ 77
    style 71 BUD¹ 83
        content, 61 BUD 541
        discords, 71 BUD¹ 41
        dramaturgy, 61 BUD 449
        form, 61 BUD 383, 541, 71 BUD¹ 53
        harmony, 58 COL 63
        Kodály, compared, 71 BUD¹ 155
        language, 66 LEIP 362
        modality, 71 BUD¹ 169
        monothematicism, 61 BUD 449
        motifs, 61 BUD 557
        orchestration, 61 BUD 557
        quotations, 61 BUD 355
        realism, 61 BUD 469
        resonance, 60 PAR¹ 279
        timbre, 61 BUD 425
        tonality, 71 BUD¹ 31
        Slovak folk music, influence of, 71 BUD¹ 181
        verbunkos, 71 BUD¹ 145
    works (general)
        instrumental, 71 BUD¹ 53
        stage, 61 BUD 449
        string quartets, 61 BUD 425
    works (specific)
        Concerto for Orchestra, 61 BUD 557
        lost work, 62 KAS 315
        Rhapsody for cello and piano, 71 BUD¹ 65
        The Wooden Prince, 71 BUD¹ 97
Barzelette, 39 NEWY 193
Bashkir drawling songs, 64 MOS 309
Basle collections of symphonies, 24 BAS 321
Basque
    folk dances, 28 PRA 177, 193
    folksongs, 28 PRA 155, 37 PAR⁴ 290
    liturgy, 65 MTS 151
Bassani, Orazio, 71 WAR 131
Basse danse
    15th c repertory, 65 DIJ 128
Basutoland, *see* Botswana
Battle music, 19th c, 74 GRA² 273
Bavaria
    chamber organ in Upper Bavaria, 38 FRE/B 136
    folk music, 71 HIN 71, 76, 130, 155
Bayreuth, 64 AMS 570, 68 UPP 823
Beard, Harry R., 69 VER 600
Beat
    in Beethoven, 27 VIE 97, 104
    in Greek-Roman metric system, 25 LEIP 203
    reform of indication, 09 VIE 386
    in Upper Austrian Ländler, 09 VIE 228
Beatrice d'Aragon, musicians of, 54 PAR¹ 35
Beaumarchais, Pierre Augustin Caron de, 70 BON 325
Bedos, Dom, 69 PAR 173, 238

Beethoven, Ludwig van
  general, *27 VIE, 70 BERL², 70 PIE, 70 VIE,* 70 BON
    3–146
  and the antique world, 70 BERL² 465
  1927 celebrations, 70 BERL² 171
  'classical realism', 70 BERL² 235, 249, 349, 427
  classicism, 70 VIE 43, 77
  in contemporary life in the DDR, 70 BERL²
    155, 177, 189, 203, 207, 581
  and criticism, 27 VIE 32, 70 BON 489
  and Croatian folk music, 27 VIE 111
  in German music education, 70 BERL² 189, 201
  and Leipzig Gewandhaus, 70 BERL² 141
  literary contacts, 70 BERL² 483
  literature, 70 BERL² 115, 183
  and liturgical music of his day, 70 VIE 61
  position in the society of his time, 70 BERL² 215
  and his publishers, 70 BERL² 499
  as Romantic, 27 VIE 40, 70 VIE 77
  semiotic view, 70 BERL² 405
 bibliographical
  American editions, 27 VIE 26
  autograph scores in Paris Conservatoire, 27 VIE
    25
  Bratislava, works in, 70 BERL² 495
  Bulgarian literature, 70 BON 144
  catalogues of works, 53 BAM 299
  conversation books, 70 BERL² 489, 70 VIE 159
  critical collected edition, 56 VIE 548
  in Czech literature, 70 BON 128
  documentary biography, 70 BON 331
  editions, present state, 70 BERL² 507
  Gesamtausgabe of sketches, necessity for, 27 VIE
    95
  letters, collected edition of, 56 VIE 673
  manuscripts, 24 BAS 363, 70 BON 380, 534, 70
    STGE 32
  Moscow sketchbook, 27 VIE 88
  portrait by J. K. Stieler, 70 BON 557
  research, 70 VIE 237
  sketchbook (1802–3) from Wielhorski archive, 70
    BON 104
 biographical
  Akademien, 70 BON 486
  confessional element, 27 VIE 107
  conversations, 70 VIE 159
  deafness, 70 BON 360
  documentary biography, 70 BON 331
  farewell from Bonn, 70 VIE 25
  Flemish characteristics, 27 VIE 16
  heroic element, 70 BON 360
  his times, 70 BON 507
  as political person, 70 PIE 173
  religiosity, 25 LEIP 274, 27 VIE 19
  Rhenish inheritance, 70 VIE 25
  in Schloss Grätz (Hradec) in 1806, 1811, 70 VIE
    215
  topography, 70 BON 455
 and places
  America, 70 BON 343
  Bohemia, 70 BERL² 75, 79, 85, 70 PIE 63, 70 VIE
    215
  Bonn, 27 VIE 11
  Bratislava, 70 BERL² 71, 131
  Bulgaria, 70 BON 447
  Eastern Europe, 70 BON 121–46, 70 PIE 11
  France, 27 VIE 116
  Hungary, 70 BON 121
  Japan, 70 BON 524
  Leipzig, 70 BERL² 141

  Ljubljana, 70 BON 132
  Mexico, 70 BON 577
  Poland, 70 BON 491
  Portugal, 27 VIE 132
  Rheinland, 27 VIE 7, 70 VIE 25
  Liberec, 70 PIE 71
  Romania, 70 BERL² 135, 70 BON 367
  Russia, 70 BERL² 147, 70 BON 135
  Slovakia, 70 BON 130
 and others
  J. A. Benda, 70 BERL² 453, 70 PIE 27
  Chopin, 27 VIE 138, 70 PIE 75, 70 VIE 175
  Dessauer, 70 PIE 33
  Dvořák, 70 PIE 63
  Eisler, 70 BERL² 165
  Glinka, 70 BON 140
  Goethe, 70 BON 587
  Haydn, 27 VIE 111, 70 BON 61–84
  J. T. Helds, 70 PIE 119
  E. T. A. Hoffmann, 27 VIE 128
  Hummel, 70 BERL² 59
  Janáček, 70 BERL² 125
  A. Kahlert, 70 BON 517
  F. A. Kanne, 70 BON 383
  B. Keglevich, 70 BON 526
  Liszt, 70 PIE 101
  Odeyevsky, 66 LEIP 287
  Rameau, 30 LIÈ 174
  Reicha, 70 PIE 13
  Schumann, 27 VIE 91, 70 BERL² 99
  Smetana, 70 BON 450
  successors, 70 BERL² 93
  Toscanini, 67 FLOR 102
  Wagner, 72 COP 512
  Weber, 70 BERL² 65
  19th c composers, 70 BERL² 107
 style
  accentuation, 49 BAS 190
  articulation in autographs and early editions, 72
    COP 580
  beat, 27 VIE 97, 104
  character styles, use of, 70 BON 452
  classical motif compared to Baroque figure, 70
    BON 573
  'classical realism' 70 BERL² 235, 249, 349, 427
  classicism 70 VIE 43, 77
  codas 70 BERL² 391
  cosmic rhythms 27 VIE 45
  creative process 70 BERL² 427
  cyclic principle, 27 VIE 52, 70 BERL² 373, 70 BON
    426
  dynamics, 27 VIE 75, 70 BERL² 379, 70 BON 47
  enharmonics, 27 VIE 83
  expression, 27 VIE 100
  folk music, relation to, 70 BERL² 437–43, 70 PIE
    191
  form, 70 BERL² 359, 70 BON 494, 553
  Haydn style in, 70 BON 65–75
  influenced by Bach's Fantasia, 70 BON 579
  late, 70 BERL² 41, 373
  in light of style changes, 25 LEIP 245
  melody, 70 VIE 267
  metre, tempo, 27 VIE 100
  musical language, 27 VIE 35, 37 PAR³ ii 247
  'new style' in variation works, 70 BON 487
  orchestral crescendo, 24 BAS 201
  polyphony, 27 VIE 79, 70 BERL² 387
  popular song, relation to, 70 BERL² 443, 70 PIE
    217
  rhythm, 27 VIE 45, 70 BON 29–55, 394

sonata form, 70 BON 542
structure of themes, 70 BON 339
verse/strophe in instrumental music, 70 VIE 97
works (general)
  Bonn cantatas, 70 BERL² 315
  church music, 27 VIE 123, 70 BON 408
  contrapuntal studies, 70 BON 70
  fugues, late, 70 PIE 13
  instrumental works, 70 VIE 97
  piano improvisations, 70 BERL² 395
  piano sonatas, 70 BERL² 569, 70 BON 590
  piano works, 70 BERL² 565, 70 BON 536, 70 PIE
    129
  Polish folksong arrangements, 70 BERL² 447
  Polonaise, development of, 27 VIE 66
  sketches, 24 BAS 244, 27 VIE 88, 91, 95, 59 BUD
    147, 70 BERL² 417, 70 BON 87–118, 355, 444,
    70 STGE 32
  sonata works, 70 BON 362
  songs, 70 BERL² 575, 70 BON 598
  string quartets, 70 BON 394, 426
  symphonic works, 70 BERL² 349
  variation works, 27 VIE 55, 49 BAS 111, 70 BON
    108
works (specific)
  An die ferne Geliebte, 70 BERL² 327
  British folksong arrangements, 71 BRN 373
  Cello sonata op.5, 70 BON 444
  Christus am Ölberg, 70 BON 402
  Egmont music, 70 BERL² 249, 301
  Fidelio, 27 VIE 48, 136, 69 BRN 239, 70 BERL²
    249, 269, 275, 283, 291, 70 BON 191, 555
  Jena Symphony, *see* Witt, Friedrich
  Leonore, 70 BERL² 291
  Missa solemnis, 27 VIE 229, 70 BON 13, 37, 559,
    70 VIE 121
  'Moonlight Sonata', 27 VIE 58
  Mozart Variations, 56 VIE 434
  Piano Fantasy op.77, 70 BON 528
  Piano Sonata op.10 no.3, 72 COP 80–85
  Piano Sonata op.13, 70 BON 553
  Piano Sonata op.106, 70 BERL² 333
  String Quartets op.18, 70. BON 75
  String Quartet op.130, 71 BRN 81
  3rd Symphony, 27 VIE 95, 70 BON 104, 600
  5th Symphony, 27 VIE 95
  7th Symphony, 70 BON 355
  9th Symphony, 59 BUD 147, 70 BERL² 337, 343,
    70 BON 370, 494
  Violin Concerto op.61, 58 COL 193, 62 KAS 196,
    70 BON 472, 509
performing practice (general), 70 BERL² 517–81
  Cramer studies (Beethoven's instructions), 70
    BERL² 545, 70 BON 43
  errors in, 70 BON 327
  instruments, old and modern, 70 BERL² 559
  piano sonatas, change in interpreting of, 70
    BERL² 569
  piano sonatas, interpretative editions of, 70 BON
    590
  piano works, 70 BERL² 565
  reprise in sonata form, 70 BON 362
  songs, 70 BERL² 575, 70 BON 598
Béjart, Maurice, *La reine verte*, 64 HAM 82
Bel canto 59 HAL 95
  in Chopin, 60 WAR¹ 220
  instrumental traits in 18th c, 53 BAM 256
Belgium
  carillons, 27 VIE 382
  church music in 18th c, 50 ROM 311

17th c and 18th c composers, and relations to Germany, 13 GHE 262
influenced by Debussy, 62 PAR 291
influenced by Ireland, 25 BRUG 228
17th c and 18th c organ contracts, 13 GHE 243
radio music, 54 PAR² 494
Renaissance music, 09 LIÈ 953
role in music history, 30 LIÈ 17
youth leisure music, 72 VIE² 201
see also Flanders, Netherlands
Bellagio, Liszt in, 75 EIS 155
Bellini, Vincenzo (and Verdi), 66 VEN 184
Bells
  acoustics of, 65 LIÈ i, M61, 58 MARS 239
  festive, 50 ROM 28
  Japanese gong bells, 35 BRUS² 990
  sleighbells, 75 BRUN 10, 20
  testing, 50 LÜN¹ 236
  timbre, 53 NET 226
Belorussian
  folksong, 64 MOS 253
  partisan songs and composers, 64 MOS 268
Benda, František
  interpretation of violin sonatas, 75 BLA 38
  technique in violin sonatas, 72 GRA 27
  violin sonata in A major, 67 BRN² 142
Benda, Jiří Antonín
  and Beethoven, 70 BERL² 453, 70 PIE 27
  melodramas, 56 PRA 85
  piano sonatas, 70 PIE 27
Benedictus (composer), 11 LON 152
Benedictus de Opitiis, 25 BRUG 223
Benevoli, Orazio, 50 ROM 298
Bentinck, Count of, 52 UTR 127
Berber
  Arabo-Berber influence on Mediterranean music, 72
    MALT 58
  folk music, 37 PAR⁴ 154
Berg, Alban
  film scenario, 50 FLOR 135
  and Janáček, 68 BRN 213
  Lulu, 68 STRS 245
  Lyric Suite, 74 GRA¹ 145
  and Zemlinsky, 74 GRA¹ 145
Berlin
  Biedermeier dance music 66 LEIP 293
  concerts of 20th c music since 1947, 72 COP 507
  and Schoenberg, 74 BERL 5
Berlioz, Hector
  rhythm, 70 BON 29
  and Stendhal, 67 PARM 180
  and Verdi, 72 MIL 148
Bernolákovo, 70 PIE 113
Berne, 55 ROY 347
Bernhard, Christoph
  Figurenlehre, 53 BAM 132, 135, 68 VEN 435
Bertali, Antonio, 53 BAM 140
Besard, Jean-Baptiste, 00 PAR³ 179
  Thesaurus harmonicus, 03 ROM 131
Beuron, 51 OCH 84
Bharata modes, 50 LÜN¹ 158
Bianchi, Francesco, *La villanella rapita*, 75 SIE 311
Bianchini, Domenico (lute tablatures), 54 PAR¹ 177
Bible (music in medieval exegesis), 65 JER 209
Bibliography/bibliographies, 06 BAS 1–7, 25 LEIP 54,
  27 VIE 263–96, 53 BAM 286, 56 VIE 143
  general
    abstracting of music periodicals, 50 LÜN² 49, 51
      PAR 62
    by computer 73 PAR 93

autographs, 27 VIE 290
and computers, 65 NEWY 229, 66 MOR 9
and data storing, 65 DIJ 123
dating music, 27 VIE 279
definition of terms, 59 CAM 147
and film music, 50 FLOR 139
graphological methods, 09 VIE 526
historical development of cataloguing musical manuscripts, 25 LEIP 49
international bibliography of music literature, 24 BAS 51, 27 VIE 296
inventory of works with scarce performing parts, 55 BRUS 112
Italian manuscript catalogues as basis for critical edition, 03 ROM 7
librettos, 29 ROM iv, 155
limits and aims of musical documentation, 56 VIE 551
microfilming autographs, 51 PAR 48
musical inventory (1620), 58 COL 84
music theory, 29 ROM iii, 105
opera texts, 25 LEIP 59
operatic documents, 65 AMS 29
original editions, 27 VIE 268, 29 ROM ii, 332
in public libraries, 29 ROM iv, 241
Quellenlexikon, new, 49 BAS 37, 51 PAR 20–32, 55 BRUS 44, 49, 144 see also *Répertoire internationale des sources musicales*
register of early music literature, 09 VIE 428
Repertorium musicae universale, 58 COL 221
Scriptores musici latini, critical edition, 03 ROM 3
Society for, 27 VIE 263
sources for new musical history, 25 LEIP 51
thematic catalogues, 06 BAS 194, 27 VIE 283, 28 VIE 183, 50 LÜN² 52, 65 NEWY 216
union catalogue of musicians' letters, 50 LÜN² 35
use of publishers' archives, 27 VIE 292
and different countries
America, United States of, 68 SVE 95
Austria, 27 VIE 265
Germany, 71 KAS 38
Ireland, 11 LON 359
Italy, 29 ROM ii, 188
Yugoslavia, 68 SVE 86
see also Cataloguing; Libraries
Biedermeier dance music in Berlin, 66 LEIP 293
Biella missal (motets), 69 CER 215
Binche (divertissement for Charles V), 57 BRUS 329
Birmingham youth music, 72 VIE² 108
Blahoslav, Jan, *Musica*, 53 BAM 128
Blaue Reiter, Der and Schoenberg, 68 STRS 245
Blida (Arab music at), 05 ALG 437
Bloch, Ernest, 54 PAL 295
Blomdahl, Karl Birger, *Aniara*, 60 STRT 102
Bochiman !Kung
folk dance, 56 WÉG 171
vocal music, 56 WÉG 105
Bohemia, see Czechoslovakia
Boïeldieu, François Adrien (letters), 13 GHE 339
Bologna
oratorio in 18th c, 69 PER 99
school and Corelli, 68 FUS 23, 33
and Toscanini, 67 FLOR 319
Bone whirring, 75 BRUN 33
Bonini, Severo, *Lamento d'Arianna*, 68 VEN 573
Bonn
Beethoven's farewell, 70 VIE 25
in Beethoven's time, 27 VIE 11
Bonno, Giuseppe, 73 SIE 331
Boril, Czar, 66 SOF ii, 1055

Borromeo family, 68 MIL 23, 35
Bosnia
Italian folk music in, 73 ROM² 243
oriental element in traditional music, 66 GRA 97
Boston and Verdi, 66 VEN 378
Botocudo music, 28 NEWY 796
Botswana (music and instruments), 52 UTR 263
Bourgeois, Thomas-Louis, 49 BAS 115, 68 LIÈ 33
Bow
French Guinea, 47 BIS 127
Saloum, 45 DAK 248
violin, Corelli to Tourte, 72 GRA 295
Boxberg, Christian Ludwig (cantatas), 58 COL 254
Brabançon organ of 1500, 62 BERN 91
Brahms, Johannes
accent signs, 62 KAS 215
and Chopin, 60 WAR¹ 388
correspondence (unpublished), 58 COL 88
creative process, 62 KAS 212
and Czech music, 70 BRN 389
forms, 66 LEIP 322
Lieder, 56 HAM 97
and Liszt and Reményi 61 BUD 89
private collection, 62 KAS 212
Rhapsody op.79 no.2, 66 LEIP 322
rhythm, 62 KAS 217
tempo, 62 KAS 219
Violin Sonata op. 78, 66 LEIP 325
Violin Sonata op.108, 66 LEIP 322
and Wolf, 50 LÜN¹ 140
word-setting, 56 HAM 97, 62 KAS 217
Brăiloiu, Constantin, 61 BUD 549
Branle
de Malte, 70 MTA 17
of Arbeau, 72 SÁR 101
Brassin, Louis, 74 STN 457
Bratislava (Pressburg)
and Beethoven, 70 BERL² 71, 131, 495
and Haydn, 71 EIS 57
and Liszt, 61 BUD 233
Mozart documents, 56 PRA 253
and Samuel Capricornus, 72 BYD 107
Brazil
African music (influence), 70 YAO 135
church music, 50 ROM 66
folk instruments, 63 CART 203
folk music, 28 PRA 162, 63 CART 203
music, 09 VIE 443
negro work songs, 65 BLM 64
Breazul, George 67 BUC 96
Brecht, Bertolt, influence on contemporary music theatre, 64 HAM 70
Breitkopf & Härtel, and Beethoven, 70 BERL² 499
Bremen, musical life in 17th c, 09 VIE 135
Breviaries, Scandinavian, 75 ESP 27
British Columbia, Indian music, 67 VAN 16, 23
Brixi, František Xavier, figured bass, 73 MAG 93
Brod, Max, and Janáček, 65 BRN 105, 109
Bruckner, Anton
and Bach, 50 LEIP 355
final and revised versions, 56 VIE 448
and Liszt, 25 LEIP 340, 75 EIS 225
masses, 25 LEIP 340
organs, 32 STRS 195
symphonies, 56 VIE 313
Brudieu, Jean, 21 PAR 823
Brunei, Gulintangan orchestra, 69 KUA 298
Brunswick tablatures, 50 LÜN¹ 97
Brussels
musical life, 1860–80, 74 STN 457

patronage at court, 1430–1559, 54 ARR 169
Bucharest, youth music 72 VIE² 103
Bückeburger Forschungsinstitut, 24 BAS 317
Budapest, musical life at royal court at Buda in 16th
   c, 72 SÁR 89
Buddhist
   influence on Noh, 59 ROY 163
   music and ceremony, 28 PRA 194, 68 TOK² 345
Buini, Guiseppe Maria, 11 LON 106
Bulgaria
   Banat Bulgarian music, 64 MOS 272
   and Bartók, 61 BUD 491
   and Beethoven, 70 BON 144, 447
   Byzantine music, 48 PAR² 321, 72 COP 790
   chant, 50 ROM 158, 64 BRA 49, 69 BYD 9, 72 BYD
     33
   folk instruments, 67 BRN¹ 142
     iconographical sources, 73 BAL 84
   folk music, 47 PRA 37, 54 PAL 71, 60 WAR² 501,
     537, 63 BUD 333, 64 MOS 248, 66 SOF ii, 1041,
     66 SOF vii, 885, 71 BLE 33, 71 HIN 163
   haiduk, 66 SOF vii, 755, 903
   instrumental ensembles, 69 STOC 152
   and Janáček, 58 BRN 75
   and Liszt, 61 BUD 249
   music, medieval, 66 SOF ii, 1055
     12th c–18th c, 66 BYD 45
     1830–1914, 62 KAS 85
     evolution, 73 WEIM 21
   national school, 71 MOS 118
   rhythmic traits, 47 PRA 37
   shepherd instruments, 75 BRUN 81
   symphonic tradition (evolution), 71 MOS 196
   wedding songs, 66 SOF ii, 1088
Bull, John, unpublished works, 54 PAR¹ 241
Buona figliola, La, 75 SIE 265
Burgundian, chanson, 24 BAS 153
   school, composition technique, 52 UTR 132
Burian, E.F., 69 BRN 183
Burney, Charles, 70 BOL 279, 71 NEWY 145
Burwell, Mary, lute method, 57 NEU/S 121
Busenello, Giano Francesco, 68 VEN 75, 81, 72 VEN
   51
Bushman concept of harmony, 58 COL 154
Busoni, Ferruccio Benvenuto, *Turandot*, 74 SIE 167
Buxheimer organ book as German song book, 56
   HAM 211
Buxtehude, Diderik, 54 STAD 97
   authenticity of organ works, 70 BON 341
   cantata, newly found, 56 HAM 221
   Membra, 63 KIE 32
   research, 58 COL 152
Bylina, roots of Russian, 64 BRA 165
Byrd, William, partsongs, 58 COL 322
Byzantine music, 27 BEL, 30 ATH, 34 SOF, 36 ROM,
   39 ALG, 48 PAR², 50 ROM 100–34, 51 PAL, 53
   THE, 55 IST, 61 OKH, 66 OXF¹, 72 COP 737–
   97
   Akathistos hymnos, 55 IST 297
   Ambrosian chant, relation to 36 ROM 540
   Bulgarian, 48 PAR² 321, 72 COP 790
   chromatic alternation in Sticherarium, 61 OKH ii,
     607
   communion cycle, 61 OKH ii, 571
   compared with Italo-Albanian chant, 50
     ROM 129
   'Cretan', 30 ATH 268
   data processing techniques, 65 DIJ 122
   Échoi, 00 PAR² 77, 93
   Greco-Byzantine chant, 50 ROM 155

   Gregorian chant, relation to, 36 ROM 479, 39 ALG
     113
   indexing, incipits, 72 COP 777
   instruments, 60 OKH ii, 589, 64 BRA 125
   Kanon, 50 ROM 131
   Kontakion, 50 ROM 131, 61 OKH ii, 563
   manuscripts, 10th to 12th c, 36 ROM 507
     at El Escorial, 50 ROM 119
     production of, 61 OKH ii, 601
   Martyria, 61 OKH ii, 575
   medieval Latin documents on chant, 27 BEL 157
   melody, 61 OKH i, 135
   modes, evolution of, 51 PAL 405
     'chromatique oriental', origin of, 00 PAR³ 93
   Monumenta musicae byzantinae, 57 PAR 294
   national variants, 72 COP 775
   notation, 00 PAR² 86, 36 ROM, 542, 50 ROM 108,
     111, 114, 123, 72 COP 751, 778
   Oktoechos, 50 ROM 107, 72 COP 766, 75 BYD 175
   Orient, relations with, 54 PAL 229, 66 OXF¹ 267
   performing practice, 67 BRN² 53
   polyphony in middle ages, 72 COP 737
   principles of chant, 34 SOF 242
   psaltikon, 72 COP 782
   research, present state of, 30 ATH 263, 36 ROM 546,
     66 OXF¹ 245
   Romanian, 66 BYD 419
   Russian, 48 PAR² 321, 53 THE 120
   Serbian, 61 OKH ii, 583
   significance of music history, 69 BRN 209
   Slavonic church music, elements in early, 64 SAL ii,
     167
   Slavonic music, influence on, 66 OXF¹ 119, 141
   Stichera, 55 IST 294
   terminology, 72 COP 758
   theory, 55 IST 287
   tonality, 72 COP 782
   transcription, 53 THE 140
   transmission, 72 COP 775
   Trisagion, 72 COP 761
   Turkish music, relations with, 75 BYD 623

Cabezón, Antonio de, 54 PAR¹ 217
Caccia, structure and execution, 69 CER 67
Caccini, Guilio, 09 VIE 208
   contribution to vocal colour in singing, 72 COP 385
   style, 58 COL 102
Cadence
   in Josquin, 52 UTR 86
   in Lassus, 70 BON 435
   in madrigals by Patricij and Skjavetić, 75 BYD 145
   as ornamentum musicae, 53 BAM 114
   16th c, 58 COL 133
   17th c Italian instrumental music, 72 COP 288
Cadenza, in 18th c concerto, 06 BAS 204
Caffi, Francesco, 03 ROM 55
Cage, John, 64 AMS 219
Calabria, Greek-Albanian folksongs of, 54 PAL 329
Calderón de la Barca, Pedro
   La estatua de Prometeo, 69 EXE 37
   No hay mas fortuna que Dios, 70 MTA 97
Calliphonic style in 13th c oriental chant, 57 PAR 326
Calzabigi, Ranieri da, *L'Elfrida*, 73 SIE 357
Cambodia
   interpretation of music, 69 KUA 225
   music, 06 BAS 61, 69 KUA 219
   origins of music, 69 KUA 208
Cambrai, Charles V's entry, 1540, 57 BRUS 235
Camerata, 58 COL 102
   comedy and tragedy, 53 PAR 287

Cameroons
  church music, 72 BERN 86
  Gregorian chant, 57 PAR 260
Cammarano, Salvatore, 72 MIL 14, 34
Campania, tarantella in, 28 PRA 175
Campori collection, 62 KAS 226
Canada
  folksong, 28 PRA 105
  higher music education, 72 VIE² 178
Canon
  improvisation in 16th c and 17th c, 58 COL 68
  meaning of in Bach's works, 50 LEIP 250
  medieval Liedkanon, 50 LÜN¹ 71
Canon of Avicenna, two commentaries on, 69 JER 292
Cantar d'affetto, 66 LEIP 208
Cantata
  Bohemian 18th c secular, 75 BLA 49
  by Boxberg, 58 COL 254
  decorated parody cantatas in early 18th c, 56 VIE 203
  German, 1640–60, 67 LJU 116
  librettos, in Rudolstadt, 72 COP 271
Cantemir, Dimitrie, 72 BYD 529
  history of Turkish music, 62 SIN 145
Cantillation see Jewish music
Cantio rhythm, 58 COL 281
Cantor, meaning of term, 49 BAS 134
Cantus coronatus in Dufay, 74 NEWY² 128
Canzoni a ballo, 39 NEWY 193
Cappello, Bianco, marriage festivities, 55 ROY 107
Capricornus, Samuel, 72 BYD 107
Caput masses and their plainsong, 49 BAS 82
Caravaglios, Cesare
  scheme for collecting folksong, 34 TRT 360
Caribbean, facilities for musical research, 70 BON 597
Carillon
  Belgian, 27 VIE 382
  origin and development, 11 MAL 353
Carissimi, Giacomo
  influence of Monteverdi's sacred works, 68 VEN 305
  and 17th c Italy, 00 PAR⁶ 75
  masses, 62 KAS 152
  oratorios, 50 LÜN¹ 103
Carlos, Don, in literature, 69 VER 16
Carol, English, 67 LJU 284
Carpathian
  folk dances, 64 GRA² 109
  folk music instruments, 75 BRUN 131
Casale Monferrato, music in Cortese period, 69 CAS 315
Castille folksongs, 28 PRA 151
Cataloguing and classification
  alphabetical, new rules for, 73 WEIM 115
  arrangement of music and music books in libraries, 03 ROM 19
  books on music, 53 BAM 282
  British music classification, 59 CAM 156
  Catholic liturgical texts, 09 VIE 437
  and computers, 70 TRČ 181–7
  folk dances, 70 TRČ 172–177
  folk texts, 70 TRČ 165–169
  general and specialized, 55 BRUS 76
  German songs, 09 VIE 434
  history of cataloguing MSS 25 LEIP 49
  microfilms, 59 CAM 169, 173
  music in cathedrals and parish archives, 50 ROM 295
  practical music, code for, 51 PAR 37
  records, 59 CAM 116–26, 73 WEIM 103
  Soviet classification system, 73 WEIM 88
  see also Folk music: classification
Catalonia
  Cobla and Alta dance orchestra, 49 BAS 59

exchanges with France in Middle Ages, 21 PAR 823
folk dance, 28 PRA 190, 54 PAL 123
folksong, 27 VIE 351, 355, 28 PRA 155, 54 PAL 47
instruments 54 PAL 115
liturgy, 65 MTS 138, 156
musicians in service of Catalan kings in 14th c, 24 BAS 56
Caucasus
  polyphony, 56 HAM 229
  psalms and religious songs of Russian sectarians, 11 LON 187
Cavaccio, Giovanni, *Sudori musicali*, 70 BOL 47
Cavalli, Francesco, 72 VEN 7, 97, 227
  relations with Monteverdi, 67 SIE 229
Cello
  acoustics, 65 LIÈ i, M54, 58 MARS 193, 74 LON 340
  Platti's style, 49 BAS 203
Celtic folk music instruments, chronology, 73 BAL 98
Central African Republic, music in, 67 BERL 135
Ceol Rince na hEireann, 71 BLE 6–21
Cesti, Antonio, *Orontea*, 72 VEN 199
Ceylon see Sri Lanka
Chaldean liturgical music, 50 ROM 164
Chaliapine see Shalyapin
Chalumeau, in Telemann, 67 MAG ii, 68
Chamber music, *71 BRN*
  accompanist's role in 18th c, 71 BRN 73
  Baroque string chamber orchestra, 71 BRN 49
  concept in Hindemith, 71 BRN 231
  in Mozart, 71 BRN 311
  history of, 71 BRN 205, 285
  contemporary Soviet performing practice, 71 BRN 23
  in England, origins and sources, 54 PAR¹ 177
  foreign elements in the 1960s, 71 BRN 497
  France, 19th c, 11 ROM 103
  iconographical sources for 16th c performances, 71 BRN 37
  in Monteverdi, 09 VIE 153
  music compared with that for classical orchestra, 71 BRN 100
  in Romania, 67 BUC 162
  in Slovakia, 71 BRN 471
  string quartet, social history, 62 KAS 37
  van Swieten's chamber music circle, 71 BRN 387
  vocal parts in 20th c, 71 BRN 491
  in 20th c, 71 BRN 17, 72 GRA 97
Chanson
  Burgundian, and German 15th c song, 24 BAS 153
  Clereau's, 27 VIE 175
  forces in 15th c, 52 UTR 65
  French and Walloon in first half of the 16th c, 30 LIÈ 76
  influence on German 15th c song, 24 BAS 153
  instrumental, by Lombardy musicians, 54 PAR¹ 305
  Josquin's, 71 NEWY 401, 421, 455
  and the madrigal, 61 CAM/M 88
  medieval polyphonic, 21 PAR 784
  Netherlands polyphonic in 15th and 16th c, 30 LIÈ 168
  Paris, 1500–30, 61 CAM/M 1
  popular elements in early 16th c French, 53 PAR 169
  style, genesis of, 61 CAM/M 1
  text underlay in 15th c, 27 VIE 155
  transformation at end of the 15th c, 67 LJU 78
  Willaert and its development, 30 LIÈ 154
Chanson de Rolland, 03 DIN 565
Chant
  general
    calliphonic style in oriental, 57 PAR 326

common ground of Christian and Jewish, 50 ROM 134

in Dead Sea Scrolls, 57 PAR 305

Germanic and Romance elements of early medieval, 25 LEIP 21

proto-Christian, notation, 57 PAR 329

Roman, role of St Gall Abbey in its diffusion, 25 BRUG 225

Slavonic Psalter of 18th c, 57 PAR 346

as symbol in medieval polyphony, 50 ROM 303

types

Ambrosian, *see* Ambrosian chant

Armenia, *see* Armenia: chant

Bulgaria, *see* Bulgaria: chant

Byzantine, *see* Byzantine music

Chaldean, 50 ROM 164

Cistercian, *see* Cistercian: chant

Eastern ecclesiastical, 02 HAM 214

epic, 67 LJU 359

Frankish, 58 COL 179

Gallican, 58 COL 217

Greco-Byzantine, 50 ROM 155

Gregorian, *see* Gregorian chant

Greek, 00 PAR² 15–70

Italo-Albanian, 50 ROM 129

Jewish, Ashkenazi, 61 JER 366

Karaites, 69 JER 278

Oriental, 61 JER 366, 371

Samaritan, 65 JER 153

'Kanty', 69 BYD 437

Mozarabic, 27 VIE 234

Oriental, 57 PAR 287, 326

Oriental Christian, 61 JER 371

Roman (new), 50 LÜN¹ 53

Roman (old), 50 LÜN¹ 53, 50 ROM 276, 54 PAL 245, 58 COL 358

Russian, 00 PAR² 134, 50 ROM 158, 52 BERN 38, 53 THE 120, 64 BRA 101, 66 BYD 455

Serbian, 61 OKH ii, 583, 64 BRA 55, 66 BYD 140, 69 BYD 61, 75 BYD 163

Slavonic, *64 BRA*

Spanish, old, 27 VIE 234

Syrian, 50 ROM 166

Ukrainian, 57 PAR 319

see also Liturgy; Znamenny chant

Charles Auchester and Mendelssohn, 58 COL 188

Charles V

at Binche, 57 BRUS 329

at Cambrai, 57 BRUS 235

musical exchanges between Spain and the Netherlands during his reign, 54 ARR 51

Charpentier, Marc-Antoine

as composer of masses, 66 LEIP 237

parallel 5ths in, 70 BON 512

Cherokee music, 58 WAS 173

Cherubini, Luigi, unpublished letters, 13 GHE 339

Chiavette, 56 VIE 264

Chicago, Verdi in, 66 VEN 336

Chilandar MSS, 61 OKH ii, 583, 64 BRA 65, 72 COP 766

Chile folk music, 28 PRA 118, 65 BLM 68

China

ancient musical instruments, 66 MANL 185

and Bartók, 61 BUD 393

Catholic church music in, 54 VIE 203

and Chopin, 60 WAR¹ 399

dance in ancient China, 60 PAR² 105

melody, 66 LEIP 561

musical language, 71 VIC 37

music in Asia, 66 MANL 191

music theatre, 64 HAM 121, 130, *71 ANN*

and Pythagorean tone system, 58 COL 174

Sino-Japanese musical traditions in 20th c, 61 TOK 54

T'ang dynasty, secular music in, 31 LEID 121

and western music, 71 FLOR 95

Chirimia, 73 BAL 101

Chironomy, use of in ancient Egypt, 52 UTR 233

Chitarrone, as continuo instrument, 70 BOL 117

Chiti, Girolamo, 70 BON 406

Choir

in liturgical music, 65 MTS 169–176

training, 38 FRA 178–196, 52 BERN 40

see also Church music: education

Chopin, Frédéric

general, *60 WAR¹, 74 BOL*

aesthetics, 60 WAR¹ 649–735

authenticity, sources, 60 WAR¹ 463–88

authentic text, establishing of, 74 BOL 89

and contemporary Polish music, 74 BOL 129

ideology, 60 WAR¹ 713

inner meaning of works, 60 WAR¹ 732

in light of memoirs, 60 WAR¹ 662

performing practice, 60 WAR¹ 421–55

personality, 60 WAR¹ 701

philosophical currents in his time, 60 WAR¹ 735

Polish national edition, 74 BOL 119

portrait by Delacroix, 70 VEN 323

sociological changes in idolatry of, 60 WAR¹ 604

letters

literary style of, 60 WAR¹ 679

to P. Michałowski, 60 WAR¹ 718

to D. Potocka, 60 WAR¹ 669

translations of, 60 WAR¹ 721

to T. Wodzińska, 60 WAR¹ 675

and places

China, 60 WAR¹ 359

Gdansk, 60 WAR¹ 559

Germany, 60 WAR¹ 334

Italy and Venice, 70 VEN 333

Mallorca, 60 WAR¹ 288

Palma and Valldemosa, 60 WAR¹ 288

Slovenia, 60 WAR¹ 281

and others

Bach, 60 WAR¹ 73

Beethoven, 27 VIE 138, 70 PIE 75, 70 VIE 175

Brahms, 60 WAR¹ 388

Delacroix, 60 WAR¹ 725, 64 AMS 187

J. L. Dusik, 60 WAR¹ 396

following generation, 60 WAR¹ 350

V. Hanka, 60 WAR¹ 365

Janáček, 60 WAR¹ 383

P. E. Johns, 72 COP 246

Liszt, 60 WAR¹ 319, 341

P. Michałowski, 60 WAR¹ 718

Mickiewicz, 60 WAR¹ 659

'mighty handful', 60 WAR¹ 413

C. Mikuli, 60 WAR¹ 410

C. Norwid, 60 WAR¹ 684

Schumann, 60 WAR¹ 329, 363

Skryabin, 60 WAR¹ 335

Smetana, 60 WAR¹ 304, 324, 347

Szymanowski, 60 WAR¹ 300, 415

style (general), 60 WAR¹ 23–415, 707

agogic accent, 60 WAR¹ 275

Bach, influence of, 60 WAR¹ 73

Baroque traits, 60 WAR¹ 271

Bel canto element, 60 WAR¹ 230

chromaticism, 60 WAR¹ 107, 122

evolution, 60 WAR¹ 44
figuration motif in, 72 COP 647
form, 60 WAR¹ 207, 213, 415
French Bergerette, influence of, 60 WAR¹ 374
genres, 60 WAR¹ 114
harmony, 60 WAR¹ 30, 202, 213, 241, 255, 259, 335
late works, 60 WAR¹ 104
lyricism, 60 WAR¹ 297
melody, 60 WAR¹ 132, 176, 355
modality, 60 WAR¹ 122
national style, 56 VIE 355, 60 WAR¹ 23
orchestration, 60 WAR¹ 85
ornamentation, 60 WAR¹ 255, 61 BUD 49
part writing, 60 WAR¹ 145
periodic form, 60 WAR¹ 415
piano writing, 60 WAR¹ 168, 304, 341
Polish folk influence, 60 WAR¹ 95, 100, 176, 247, 404
rhythm, 60 WAR¹ 185, 241
Styrian waltz, 60 WAR¹ 374
tempo, 60 WAR¹ 449
tempo rubato, 60 WAR¹ 247
thematic development, 60 WAR¹ 236
timbre, 60 WAR¹ 127
tonality, 60 WAR¹ 88
Ukrainian folk influence, 60 WAR¹ 355, 374
variation technique, 60 WAR¹ 219, 224
waltz element, 60 WAR¹ 196
works
  Album Leaf for Émile Gaillard, 60 WAR¹ 111
  concertos, 60 WAR¹ 293
  études, 60 WAR¹ 219
  Krakowiak, 60 WAR¹ 100
  mazurkas, 60 WAR¹ 95, 415
  nocturnes, 60 WAR¹ 275, 74 BOL 73
  piano sonatas, 27 VIE 138
  polonaises, 60 WAR¹ 241
  Prague Mazurka in G, 60 WAR¹ 365
  preludes, 60 WAR¹ 425
  songs, 60 WAR¹ 313, 404
Chorales
  by Bach, 72 COP 277
  and Gregorian chant, 58 COL 157
  influenced by Humanism, 72 PAR 251
  and the organ, 27 FRE/S 83
  rhythm of, 25 LEIP 365
Chords
  pure tuning, 58 MARS 49
  technique in West African string instruments, 68 TOK² 348
  theory, 50 LÜN¹ 217
Choreography
  research in America, 30 HAM¹ 212
  20th c, 37 PAR³ ii, 478
Choreology, jazz, 56 PHIL 152
Choruses, unaccompanied male, 25 LEIP 286
Chrismann, F. X., organ-building school, 54 VIE 249
Chromatic alteration in the Sticherarium, 61 OKH ii, 607
Chromatic step in polyphony in 16th c, 62 KAS 136
Chromaticism
  in Armenian music, 56 VIE 112
  in Chopin 60 WAR¹ 107
  and Marchettus of Padua 69 CER 187
  Renaissance (spirit and technique), 53 PAR 225
Chryasaphes, Manuel, treatise 72 COP 748
Chukchansi music 58 SJOS 611
Church music, *37 PAR¹, 50 ROM, 54 VIE, 57 PAR, 61*

  COL, 66 CHIC, 52 BERN, 62 BERN, 72 BERN, 74 SINZ, 11 LON 286–312, *27 BERL,* 61 TOK 26, 47
  general
    Les archives sonores de la musique sacrée, 57 PAR 656
    building from standpoint of church musician, 11 LON 286
    as career, 54 VIE 282–8, 64 GRA¹ 167
    care of treasures, 09 VIE 546
    characteristics of, 09 VIE 531
    fostering, 50 ROM 69
    indigenous, *75 ROM*
    influence of Romanticism, 50 ROM 392
    language divisions, 62 BERN 24
    in light of encyclical 'Musicae sacrae disciplina', 57 PAR
    and musicology, 70 BON 663
    negro spirituals in, 57 PAR 530
    new possibilities, 72 BERN 48
    old and new, 09 VIE 537, 62 BERN 9
    stile antico in 18th c, 27 VIE 244
    style, 25 LEIP 321, 27 VIE 232, 257
  and places, 61 COL 236, *75 ROM*
    Africa, 57 PAR 526, 547, 75 ROM 51, 72
      South, 57 PAR 567
    Asia, 57 PAR 559
      East, 75 ROM 117
    Australasia, 75 ROM 117
    Belgium, 50 ROM 311
    Bohemia, 69 BRN 87, 70 BRN 309
    Brazil, 50 ROM 66
    Cameroons, 72 BERN 86
    Canada, Catholic University of Ottawa, 50 ROM 304
    China, 54 VIE 265
    Croatia, North, 72 BYD 267
    Denmark, 63 KIE 11, 22
    England, 11 LON 61, 61 NEWY i, 346
      Westminster Cathedral, 50 ROM 62
    Ethiopa, 70 BON 410
    Far East, 57 PAR 564
    Finland, 52 BERN 41
    France, 11 ROM 63, 37 PAR¹ 130, 147; 52 BERN 55, 54 VIE 162, 57 PAR 171, 178
    Germany, 50 ROM 96, 66 LEIP 347
      Dresden, 50 LEIP 320
    Hungary, 27 VIE 247, 72 BERN 81
    India, 61 COL 287, 304; 75 ROM 97
    Indonesia, 57 PAR 552, 72 BERN 89
    Italy, 21 TUR 209
    Japan, 61 COL 247
    mission countries, 57 PAR 523–67
    Mossi, 61 COL 251, 75 ROM 72
    Oceania, 75 ROM 117
    Rome–Regensburg connections, 50 ROM 90
    Russia, 37 PAR¹ 122
      sects in Caucasus, 11 LON 187
    Serbia, 72 BERN 84
    Spain, 50 ROM 291, 323; 57 PAR 447
    Sweden, 30 LIÈ 184
  specific periods
    15th c use of organ, 26 FRE/B 87
    17th c, influence of ornamentation, 58 COL 57
    17th and 18th c, history of, 11 LON 312
    1600–1800, Catholic, in Rome, 62 KAS 147
    19th c, restoration, 75 EIS 225
    19th c revival of old church music, 00 MUN 331
    20th c, 50 ROM 395, 401, 405, 409, 411; 54 VIE 260–79, 57 PAR 437, 447

postwar, 27 VIE 257
and people
Beethoven, 27 VIE 123
the clergy, 37 PAR¹ 135
Liszt's plans for church music reform, 25 LEIP 341
Mendelssohn, 62 KAS 207
Reger, 73 NUR 123
Spontini, 51 IES 59
Protestant, 09 VIE 576, 27 BERL 41, 55
Anglican, 52 BERN 57, 72 BERN 74
contemporary, 52 BERN 50, 74 SINZ 123
developing traits in 16th c, 52 UTR 199
in Germany, origins, 62 BERN 47
since 1945, 66 LEIP 347
hymn and Reger, 73 NUR 113
national aspects, 50 ROM 53
and new liturgy, 25 LEIP 353, 52 BERN 42, 62 BERN 64, 68
rhythm of German hymns, 25 LEIP 360
Slovenian, 69 BYD 47
Swedish Lutheran, 72 BERN 76
Swiss, 62 BERN 43
Catholic
lexicon of, 57 PAR 650
principles of, 11 LON 303
and Reger, 73 NUR 123
in Rome 1600–1800, 62 KAS 147
subjectivity and objectivity in, 11 LON 303
and 2nd Vatican Council, *64 GRA²*
ecclesiastical aspects
ecumenical, 62 BERN 21
liturgy, 25 LEIP 329, 27 BERL 32, 62; 62 BERN 60
the mass, 61 COL 202
theology, 62 BERN 15
worship, 61 COL 163
organization, 54 VIE 320, 57 PAR 599, 635–56
Associations of St Cecilia and St Gregory, 50 ROM 87
cataloguing in cathedral and parish archives, 50 ROM 295
and copyright, 61 COL 87–102
editing classical church music, 25 LEIP 322
financial and legal basis, 50 ROM 73
writings on church music in 20th c Germany, 50 ROM 93
hymns etc.
analysis of hymns, 72 BERN 24
German hymns, prehistory, 09 VIE 532
hymns (general), 37 PAR¹ 158, 163
psalters, note against note in 16th c, 49 BAS 115
vernacular, church songs, 57 PAR 469–515
French, 57 PAR 494, 509
Hungarian, 57 PAR 515
performance, 72 BERN 55
accompanied, not suitable for liturgical use, 50 ROM 398
congregational singing, 66 CHIC 135, 148
early, 09 VIE 557, 61 COL 127, 72 BERN 67
instrumental, 54 VIE 174, 188
education, 54 VIE 296–316, 57 PAR 577–630, 61 COL 312–28, 64 GRA¹
children, 50 ROM 57, 54 VIE 296, 57 PAR 623
choirboys, 11 LON 307
choir schools, 00 PAR¹ 46, 82; 57 PAR 618, 61 COL 328
church choirs, 50 ROM 49, 65 MTS 169–76
clergy, 50 ROM 59, 61 COL 312
congregations, 26 FRE/B 110, 50 ROM 37, 41; 64 GRA¹ 173

diocesan, 50 ROM 80
higher institute of sacred music, 57 PAR 626
musicians, 27 BERL 11, 50 ROM 30, 61 COL 319
musicology in, 27 BERL 48
schools for renewal in spirit of Pius X, 61 COL 132
in seminaries, 50 ROM 77, 54 VIE 303, 57 PAR 577, 580
study of Gregorian chant, 50 ROM 220
use of radio, 57 PAR 630
Ciampi, Vincenzo Legrenzio, *Bertoldo, Bertoldino e Cacasenno*, 11 LON 71
Ciconia, Johannes, 50 ROM 280, 52 UTR 107
chronology of MSS, 55 WÉG 110
first stay in Italy, 54 PAL 223
masses, 59 CER 97
Ciociaria folk music, 34 ΓRT 289
Cistercian
chant, 00 MUN 328
reform of, 63 TOD 191
tonal and modal aspects, 75 BYD 287
traditions, 50 ROM 199
chủrch at Kaisheim, organ (1778), 50 ROM 384
Cittern, 59 CAM 209
Clarinet, acoustic research, 66 LEIP 407, 69 STOC 103
Clarsech, origin of 11 LON 317
Classical period, Classicism
and Baroque, 70 BON 323, 71 EIS 64
concept, 27 VIE 29, 66 LEIP 103–139
motifs in Beethoven, compared to Baroque figures, 70 BON 573
as music-history problem, 72 COP 518
and Romantic, 25 LEIP 292
and Schubert, 28 VIE 47
sources of style, 61 NEWY i, 285
stylistic elements, 49 BAS 22
symphony, inner unity of, 27 VIE 43
Class traditions in musical culture 71 MOS 72
Clausula, interrelations with conductus, 52 UTR 96
Clavicytherium, history of, 62 KAS 305
Clef, reforms, 06 BAS 55
Clementi, Muzio
compositions 'alla Mozart', 74 ROM 308
and Mozart, 56 VIE 1
writing for piano, 74 BOL 5
Clereau, Pierre, chansons, 27 VIE 175
Cloth of Gold, Field of the, 57 BRUS 135, 147
Cluny
liturgy, 58 TOD 83
music, *49 CLU*
reform of Gregorian chant, 63 TOD 191
Cobla, Catalan, 49 BAS 59
Cochin (India), Jewish song from, 69 JER 245
Codex *see* Libraries and manuscripts
Colinda *see* Kolenda
Collections
books, 59 CAM 131
historical music, 58 COL 162
instruments *see* Instruments: collections
Cologne
Cathedral, performances of Beethoven and Haydn, 70 BON 408
Jesuit Library, 52 UTR 252
Columbia folk music, 65 BLM 115
Communication media and music, *68 NEWY*
Composers, Composition
of aleatoric music in Renaissance, 49 BAS 103
computers, use of, *see* Computers
concept in 15th and 16th c, 58 COL 104
and electronic music, 53 NET 256, 55 ARR 183
and folk music, 67 BUC 137, 181

how does one compose?, 37 PAR³ ii, 236
individual styles of composing, origins, 74 ZAG vi, 29
inter-American composers, 65 BLM
Latin American composers in 20th c, 65 BLM 158
and libretto, 70 BON 151–69
modern composers, 60 STRT
and the performer, 60 STRT 35–43
and the public, 37 FLOR 9, 90–108, 60 STRT 3, 5
and the publisher, 1500–1850, 58 COL 340
rhapsody as source of composers' inspiration in 19th c and 20th c, 72 COP 561
technique, 71 STU 28
   Niedt's treatise, 53 BAM 152
   at time of Trent codices, 25 LEIP 219
and technology, 70 HAMM 12, 70 STOC 18J
training in 16th c and 17th c Germany, 53 BAM 103–152
in 20th c, 11 LON 355, 49 FLOR 33–74, 116, 125, 130, 60 STRT 17–32, 65 BLM 51, 78, 84, 164, 68 SVE 20, 26, 70 STOC 143, 151, 71 MOS 202
women, 56 HAM 55, 62 KAS 239
world of the composer, 61 TEH 99
Computers
in analysis, 70 BON 333, 74 KRP 7
   of authenticity and chronology, 71 NEWY 297
   of 15th c basse danse repertory, 65 DIJ 128
   of folksong, 66 LEIP 460
   of liturgical responses, 73 PAR 125, 135
   of medieval office for the dead, 75 ESP 79
   of musical structure, 65 NEWY 10, 66 MOR 29, 73 PAR 66
   of musical style, 65 NEWY 19, 66 MOR 43, 69 JER 300, 72 COP 45
in bibliography, 65 NEWY 229, 66 MOR 9
capabilities, 66 MOR 89
in cataloguing, 70 TRČ 181–187, 71 KAS 48
in composition, 65 NEWH 107, 66 MOR 63, 70 STOC 57, 93, 73 PAR 204, 210
in documentation, 65 NEWY 28, 70 TRČ 181–7
FORCOD, use of, 73 PAR 104
input languages, 65 NEWY 48–176
music generated by digital computer, 59 STU 253, 68 TOK¹ vi, 33
in musicology, 65 NEWH 103, 65 NEWY, 66 LEIP 466, 67 LJU 424, 72 COP 486
music reading machine, 65 NEWY 151
notation, 65 NEWY 91, 68 TOK¹ vi, 29, 71 BUD² iii, 653, 71 KAS 6
and periodical abstracts, 73 PAR 93
in synthesis of sound, 70 STOC 117
see also Documentation
Concepts, historical dictionary of musical, 52 UTR 211
Concert
instrumental, in 15 c, 54 PAR¹ 23
instrumental in Flemish art in 15th c, 54 ARR 197
programmes, 50 LÜN² 31
Concertare
and conserere, 66 LEIP 216
sense and essence, 49 BAS 129
Concert halls
boosting of weak instruments, 53 NET 253
comparative studies, 74 LON 604
evaluation, 74 LON 623
Hungarian Academy of Music, 74 LON 612
resonance of instruments in different concert halls, 71 BUD² iv, 1
Rotterdam, 65 LIÈ i, G43
Royal Northern College of music, 74 LON 607
shapes, 68 TOK¹ iii, 49

see also Architectural acoustics
Concertato style in Polish music, 69 PARM 89
Concerto
cadenza in 18th c instrumental, 06 BAS 204
concertare and conserere, 66 LEIP 216
Melchior Franck and the sacred concerto, 58 COL 120
improvisation in 18th c instrumental, 75 BLA 80
Romantic, 60 WAR¹ 293
solo, early history, 62 KAS 149
Concrète, concrète see Musique concrète
Conducting
choir, 67 BUC 171
film music, 50 FLOR 78
Spontini as conductor, 51 IES 86
Toscanini as conductor, see Toscanini
Conductus
and clausula, 52 UTR 96
Notre Dame, 25 LEIP 209
Polish sources, 72 COP 593
rhythm, 58 COL 219
Congo, ethnomusicological research, 47 BIS 193
Coniuncta, beginnings of, 69 CER 51
Consonance, 00 PAR⁴ 455, 53 NET 249, 58 MARS 21, 62 COP i, P55
in contemporary music, 58 BRN 261
experiments in, 26 GRON 448
hearing of, 58 COL 227
physical basis, 58 MARS 61, 65 LIÈ i, M64
psychological basis, 09 VIE 330, 58 MARS 61
in scales, 60 PAR¹ 199
theory of, 58 BRN 387
Contemporary music see Twentieth-century music
Contrafactum in early Minnesang, 66 OXF² 96
Copenhagen
folk music collection, 09 VIE 303
Johan Lorentz in, 58 COL 183
youth music, 72 VIE² 114
Coptic
liturgical music, 50 ROM 100
memorization and oral tradition, 58 COL 191
Copyright, 68 NEWY 95
composer's in Italy, 21 TUR 198
and church music, 61 COL 87, 102
and folk music, 71 HIN 62
Cora music, 08 VIE 489
Corelli, Arcangelo, 68 FUS
biographical, 68 FUS 131
and Bologna school, 68 FUS 23, 33
performing practice, 68 FUS 113
solo sonatas and additions, 72 BYD 591
and Tartini, 68 FUS 99
and Telemann, 68 FUS 75
unpublished compositions, 68 FUS 53
Cornet, Severin, 25 BRUG 229
Cornett, performing on, 53 BAM 93
Coro spezzato, form problems in early, 72 COP 604
Corpus des Troubadours, 64 SAL ii, 269
Corvin, Mathias, musicians of, 54 PAR¹ 35
Cosimo, Piero di, instruments in paintings, 55 ROY 379
Cossack songs, melody and rhythm, 09 VIE 276
Costa, Lorenzo, instruments in paintings, 55 ROY 379
Costanza e fortezza, in Prague 1723, 70 MTA 129
Couchet, Jan, harpsichords, 70 ANT 41, 44
Counterpoint
Evora school, 21 PAR 846
Fux and modern theory, 25 LEIP 187
Haydn's teaching, 70 BON 70
Palestrina's 24 BAS 211, 62 KAS 361

rhythmic counterpoint on Ceylonese drum, 58 COL 60
teaching, 25 LEIP 189
teaching in 17th c Germany, 25 LEIP 280
theory in Poglietti and Bertali, 53 BAM 140
Couperin, François, 69 PAR 213, 239
Couperin, Louis, pieces for five-part shawm band, 59 CAM 233
Craig, Gordon, and eastern music theatre, 59 ROY 271
Cramer, Johann Baptist, Beethoven's directions for playing his studies, 70 BERL² 545, 70 BON 43
Creative process
in Beethoven, 70 BERL² 427
in Brahms, 62 KAS 212
in Janáček, 58 BRN 98
in Liszt, 75 EIS 125
in Mendelssohn, 70 BON 482
in Mozart, 39 NEWY 145
in Rossini, 70 STGE 48
in Verdi, 70 STGE 125
in Webern, 72 VIE¹ 111
Crescendo, orchestral, in Beethoven, 24 BAS 201
Crete, folk music, 54 PAL 53
Lyre, 75 BRUN 127
Criticism
general, 33 FLOR 11, 18, 31, 60 STRT 8, 67 GRA
aesthetics, 47 PRA 69, 56 VEN 660
and composers
Beethoven, 27 VIE 32, 70 BON 489
Chopin, 60 WAR¹ 334
Szymanowski, 62 WAR 294
composers as critics
Janáček, 58 BRN 377
Mozart, 25 LEIP 266
the critic as educator, 37 FLOR 185
the critic's profession, 62 KAS 327
the critic's responsibilities, 37 FLOR 180
the critic's use of radio, 33 FLOR 61
evaluation, 67 GRA 39
and film music, 50 FLOR 86–94
method, 00 PAR¹ 15, 09 VIE 364
and modern music, 47 PRA 41
and musicology, 09 VIE 422
and omissions, neglect, 58 BRN 176
in places
Austria, 67 GRA 81
Czechoslovakia, 67 GRA 66
East and West, 67 GRA 96
Hungary, 67 GRA 77
Italy, 21 TUR 139, 67 GRA 57
Switzerland, 67 GRA 49
Yugoslavia, 67 GRA 71
and popular literature, 09 VIE 422
and Toscanini, 67 FLOR 23
and records, 67 ZAG 33
of singing, in daily press, 38 FRA 322
in 19th c, first half, 70 BON 517
Croatia
East and West European tendencies in 19th c, 72 COP 499
folk music and Beethoven and Haydn, 27 VIE 111
folk traits in church music, 72 BYD 267
and Janáček, 68 BRN 227
music
in 16th c, 69 BYD 79
in 17th and 18th c, 66 BYD 200, 72 BYD 337
1830–1914, 62 KAS 80
Croner, Daniel, 72 BYD 551
Crotch, William, 65 DIJ 196
Cuba, folk music, 39 NEWY 284, 64 MOS 283

Cunas del Darien, folk music, 63 CART 119
Cuozola, Moresca in, 00 PAR⁵ 77
Curaçao, folk music, 48 BRUS 266
Cursus, in antiphonal melodies of the mass, 11 LON 54
Cyclic form
in Beethoven, 27 VIE 52, 70 BERL² 373, 70 BON 426
in J. M. Kraus, 62 KAS 190
in Schubert's dance music, 56 VIE 408
Cyprien le Mage, 55 IST 284
Czechoslovakia, Bohemia and Moravia
general
, periodization, 72 BYD 95
word setting, 69 BRN, 67
folk music, 09 VIE 266, 28 PRA 146, 148, 184, 58 BRN 217, 65 BRA 145, 67 RAD 73
bagpipes, 67 BRN¹ 128
instrumental ensembles, 69 STOC 146
and Janáček, 58 BRN 217
and Mahler, 62 KAS 246
and Mozart, 56 PAR 189, 56 PRA 127
musicians, 64 GRA² 140
notation of instrumental folk music, 73 BAL 110
and Vaňhal, 56 PRA 70
and other places
and European music, 67 BRN² 9, 70 BRN 15
influence of modern Czech music on south Slavonic, 68 BRN 277, 70 BRN 373
polyphonic repertory abroad, 70 BRN 55
and individuals
Beethoven, 70 BON 128, 70 BERL² 75, 79, 85, 70 PIE 63, 70 VIE 215
Haydn, 59 BUD 69, 70 GRA 31
Janáček, 68 BRN 31, 57
Mozart, 56 PAR 183, 189, 56 PRA 175, 202, 236, 272, 67 BRN² 147
Wagner, Brahms and Mahler, 70 BRN 389
up to 1600
Calixtin mass at end of 16th c, 70 BRN 89
community song at turn of 16th c, 70 BRN 63
first printed song book (1581), 70 BRN 33
forms at end of Renaissance, 72 BYD 161
intabulation at turn of 16th c, 70 BRN 63
liturgical drama 70 BRN 27, 47
medieval and renaissance, 66 BYD 69
motet 14th c to 15th c, 70 BRN 71
motet 1570–1620, 69 BYD 33
Polish connections in 16th and 17th c, 60 WAR¹ 608
polyphonic repertory 14th to 16th c, 70 BRN 55
Renaissance and mannerism, 70 BRN 159
17th c
Baroque style, origins of, 47 PRA 51
church song, 72 BYD 127
music theatre, 67 LJU 126
secular song (1650–1750), 71 BRN 115
social position of Czech musician in Baroque period, 62 KAS 28
18th c, 66 BYD 80
chamber music and symphonies, 70 BRN 349
church music, 69 BRN 87, 70 BRN 309
dramatic music, 70 BRN 317
and Italy, 70 BRN 289
Mannheim school, relation to, 70 BRN 219
Mozartian style in Czech preclassical music, 56 PRA 34, 56 VIE 493
music 1740–60, 67 LJU 181
music at schools, 72 BYD 87
musical centres, 70 BRN 281
orchestration of secular cantatas, 75 BLA 49
organ and harp concerts in England, 70 BRN 359

preclassical elements, 70 BRN 255
and Vienna, 70 BRN 299
17th and 18th c, 66 BYD 80
19th c
  characteristics of piano music c1800, 70 BON 531
  Liszt's Czech teachers, 61 BUD 69
  Liszt, unpublished correspondence with Czech musicians, 61 BUD 255
  lyrical piano pieces before Smetana, 71 BRN 131
  music of Beethoven's time (1800–20), 67 LJU 209
  music since Smetana, 70 BRN 365
  national revival, 56 PRA 282, 69 BRN 95
20th c
  criticism, 57 GRA 66
  folk basis of compositional style, 53 BAM 203
  music, 49 FLOR 121, 70 BRN 423
  musical semiotics, 73 BEL 27
  music documentation in libraries, 73 WEIM 68
  music theatre and European drama, 70 BRN 419
  Second Viennese School, influence, 70 BRN 407
  youth music, 72 VIE² 140
see also Moravia; Slovakia

Dacus, Johannes, 72 COP 388
Dahomey, vodu music, 60 PAR² 121
Dalmatia
  instruments in medieval art, 70 BON 474
  Istrian-Dalmatian folksong, 09 VIE 271
  moresca, 00 PAR⁵ 77
  music in 16th and 17th c, 39 NEWY 21
Dance
general
  aesthetics, 37 PAR³ ii, 474, 56 VEN 664
  at Berne in 16th-c, 55 ROY 347
  Biedermeier dance music in Berlin, 66 LEIP 293
  classical dance and rhythm, 65 GEN 154
  elements in English ayre, 53 PAR 203
  in German organ tablature, 24 BAS 243
  history in 16th c, 24 BAS 72
  from *Musikalische-Türkischer Eulenspiegel*, 72 BYD 69
  national traits, 71 WAR 191
  Renaissance dance music, 69 BYD 315
  Renaissance and medieval dance music, 54 PAR¹163
  Schubert as dance musician, 28 VIE 233
  in 13th c Sienese painting, 69 CER 83
  source for 17th c instrumental, 72 COP 563
  synthesis with music, 37 PAR³ ii 251
  16th c tablature dances, 27 VIE 189
  15th c tunes, 57 CAM/M 3
folk
  aesthetics, technique, 37 PAR³ i, 322
  analysis, 74 KRP 48, 50
  classifying and cataloguing, 63 STT 179, 70 TRČ 172–7
  early forms, 50 LÜN¹ 178
  function, 74 KRP 51
  movement and music, 74 KRP 42
  pair dances, historical, 72 SÁR 141
  reconstructing lost folk dances, 65 BLM 183
  see also individual regions, countries and towns
Dandrieu, Jean-François, keyboard music, 21 PAR 918
Dante, Alighieri, music in *De vulgari eloquentia*, 65 RAV 83
Danzig, *see* Gdansk
Darmstadt
  composers and Telemann, 67 MAG ii, 13
  Graupner's operas in, 25 LEIP 252
  history of opera in, 09 VIE 184
  and Italian composers, 63 MER 679

Dastgah, integration with maqam, 61 TEH 146
Dattilapero, 11 LON 332
Day, Alfred, and harmonic theory, 39 NEWY 233
Dead Sea Scrolls, chant in, 57 PAR 305
Debussy, Claude
general, *62 PAR*
  aesthetics, 62 PAR 133–99
  influence in individual countries, 62 PAR 215–315
  letters, 62 PAR 341
  painting, relations with, 62 PAR 151
  psychology, 62 PAR 141
  and Russian music, 62 KAS 241
and others
  R. Godet, 62 PAR 339
  Russians, 62 PAR 199
  Schoenberg, 62 PAR 319
  Stravinsky, 62 KAS 252
  Varèse, 62 PAR 333
  Webern, 62 PAR 319
style
  impressionistic feeling for space, 62 KAS 244
  innovatory, 62 PAR 23
  language, 62 PAR 33–109
  modal element, 62 PAR 109
  nature depiction, 70 BON 207
  tonality, 62 PAR 97
  traditional elements, 62 PAR 27
works
  Jeux, 70 BON 424
  Pelléas et Mélisande, 70 BON 207
  Syrinx, 73 BEL 83
Declamation in accompanied art song, 38 FRA 27
Delacroix, Eugène, and Chopin, 60 WAR¹ 725, 64 AMS 187, 70 VEN 323
Della Ciaia, Azzolino Bernadino, 21 PAR 895
Del Lago, Giovanni, writings, 72 COP 432
Delphic Hymn, 00 PAR² 63, 65
Denkmäler Deutscher Tonkunst, mistakes, 62 KAS 295
Denmark
  and England in 17th c, 11 LON 129
  ethnomusicology and folk music, 56 WÉG 51
  Haydn cult in, 09 VIE 529
  iconographical sources of folk music instruments, 73 BAL 70, 73
  liturgical fragments, 75 ESP 173
  Labwasser Psalter, influence, 63 KIE 22
  musical topography, 09 VIE 484
  Polish dance in, 60 WAR¹ 572
  Protestant church music, 63 KIE 11
  and Schleswig-Holstein in 17th c, 63 KIE 48
Descartes, René, *Compendium musicae*, 58 COL 188
Dessauer, Josef, and Beethoven, 70 PIE 33
Deutsche Kirchenlied, Das, use of computer in editing, 71 KAS 48
Diderot, Denis
  aesthetics of musical humanism, 48 AMS 534
  view of Italian music, 75 SIE 45
Diepenbrock, Alphons, in Dutch music history, 64 AMS 201
Dies, Albert Christoph, Haydn biography, 59 BUD 131
Digo sickness rite, 69 MARB 107
Dijon rhymed office, 54 ROU 335
Diletsky, Nikolay Pavlovich, 69 BYD 347, 75 BYD 573
Diminution, 27 VIE 195, 69 BYD 175
Discant style, 24 BAS 364
Discography
  Josquin, 71 NEWY 633
  sacred music, 57 PAR 454
  Toscanini's recordings, 67 FLOR 347
Dissonance, 00 PAR² 455, 25 LEIP 181

chordal, 62 KAS 272
in composers
    Bartók, 71 BUD¹ 41
    G. Gabrieli, 66 LEIP 201
    Josquin, 71 NEWY 334
    Monteverdi, 68 VEN 435
    Schütz, 53 BAM 132
concept in Middle Ages, 58 COL 87
intervallic, 62 KAS 272
physiological basis, 58 MARS 61
psychological basis, 09 VIE 330, 58 MARS 61
scale of, 72 COP 597
theory, 58 BRN 387
treatment in 17th c, 57 WÉG 151
in 20th c music, 58 BRN 261
Dittersdorf, Karl Ditters von, autographs, 56 VIE 412
Documentary biographies, 62 KAS 337
Documentation, 62 KAS 334–345, *65 DIJ, 71 KAS*
of African music sources, 70 YAO 43
audio-visual means, 65 DIJ 147–152
centres of musical documentation, 65 DIJ 100–106
computers, use of in musical documentation, 65 NEWY 28, 70 TRČ 181–187
data processing in musical documentation, 65 DIJ 112–128
in editing and cataloguing, 71 KAS 6–48
in iconography, 71 KAS 109–131
of musical instruments, 67 BRN¹ 159, 71 KAS 56–93
and the music librarian and bibliographer, 65 DIJ 147–152
phonetic documentation and musicology, 53 BAM 295
of Slovak folk music, 70 TRČ 127–161
of 16th and 17th c sources, 62 KAS 342
Dodecanes, violin in folk music, 71 STP 71
Dodmenus Foundation, 50 LÜN² 56
Doni, Giovanni Battista, *De praestantia musicae veteris*, 68 VEN 409
Donizetti, Gaetano, and Verdi, 72 MIL 122
Donne, John, settings by contemporaries, 58 COL 91
Drama *see* Liturgical drama; Theatre
Dreikönigsgymnasium, Cologne, wind music, 74 GRA² 103
Dresden
    Catholic church music, 50 LEIP 320
    opera before Hasse, 69 WAR 87
    performance and opera houses in 17th and 18th c, 69 WAR 99
Drogon de St Winnoc, 13 GHE 280
Drum
    African, 58 WÉG 229
    Afro-Uruguay, 65 BLM 23
    Ceylonese frame drum, 58 COL 60
    friction, 56 WÉG 91
    language, 38 GHE 503, 51 STIS 165
    transcription of drum music, 58 SJOS 603
    Turkish, 73 ANK 216
Dubensammlung, dating, 63 KIE 27
Dufay, Guillaume, *74 NEWY²*
    Cantus coronatus, 74 NEWY² 128
    expression and technique, 11 MAL 899
    and Ferrara, 74 NEWY² 1
    progressive elements, 74 NEWY² 115
    punctus organi, 74 NEWY² 128
    works, 09 LIE 865
        Aosta MS, 74 NEWY² 16
        masses, 74 NEWY² 26
Dufay circle
    ensemble performances, 74 NEWY² 61
    musical inversion, 74 NEWY² 144

text underlay in secular music, 74 NEWY² 102
Duma, 69 BYD 413
Du Mont, Henri, tomb, 09 LIE 917
Duration, experiments with short, 34 TÜB 309
Dušek, František Xaver, 56 PRA 159
Dusik, Jan Ladislav
    as forerunner of Chopin, 60 WAR² 396
    in Malines, 11 MAL 735
Dutch Guiana, *see* Surinam
Dvořák, Antonin
    chamber music influenced by American–Indian music 71 BRN 147
    influence on Schoenberg, 71 BRN 157
    influenced by Beethoven, 70 PIE 63
    word-setting, 69 BRN 139
Dynamics
    and agogics in Baroque music, 58 COL 343
    in C.P.E. Bach's works, 62 KAS 178
    in Beethoven, 27 VIE 75, 49 BAS 190, 70 BERL² 379, 70 BON 47
    in brass instruments, 72 COP 351
    historical approach, 09 VIE 144
    and masking of orchestral instruments, 71 BUD² iii, 737

Ear
    acoustic functions, 58 COL 227
    relative auditory perception, 54 WÉG 37
    see also Hearing
Early music
    editing, *see* Editing
    performing practice, *see* Performing practice
    revival, 37 FLOR 40, 147, 195, 38 FLOR 7, 16, 21, 58, 81, 89, 147, 67 KAS 9
Easter plays, *see* Liturgical drama
Eastman School of Music, psychological tests for admission, 29 NEWH 406
Eboli, Princess, historical and operatic character, 69 VER 204
Echo, L', Liège period in 18th c, 30 LIÈ 87
Ecuador, Indian music, 63 CART 131
Editing
    general, 09 VIE 137
    early music, 49 BAS 109, 54 PAR¹ 287, 61 NEWY i, 150
    liturgical music, 75 ESP 193
    medieval texts, 72 SÁR 225
    Ives, 74 NEWY¹ 65, 87
    Josquin, 71 NEWY 721
    as profession for musicologist, 62 KAS 327
    Webern, 72 VIE¹ 198
    15th to 17th c vocal music, 11 LON 365
    17th c music, 63 KIE 83
    18th c music, 58 COL 349
Education
    general, 25 LEIP 142, 62 KAS 284, 286
        aesthetics, 06 BAS 129, 25 LEIP 159
        in America, 68 SVE 43, 173
        Arab music, 32 CAIR 605
        in Austria in 18th c, 71 EIS 105
        in France, 00 PAR² 289, 09 VIE 507, 11 ROM 139
        in Germany (DDR), 56 VIE 272, 73 WEIM 118
        institution, music studies in, 68 SVE 35, 43
        in Italy, 21 TUR, 58, 91, 96, 178
        new experiments, 14 GÖT 305
        organization, 25 LEIP 150
        as part of general education, 61 TOK 107–23
        as profession for musicologist, 62 KAS 331
        qualities of school, 37 FLOR 172
        scientific basis, 00 PAR² 281, 66 LEIP 375

seminar music teaching, 62 KAS 290
in 20th c Sweden, 63 KIE 56
theory, 25 LEIP 134
traditional instruction, 61 TEH 203, 279
and Telemann, *73 MAG*
the young, 71 MOS 202–35, 72 VIE² 159–92
in Yugoslavia, 68 SVE 35
applications, means
folk music, 37 PAR⁴ 382–403
liturgy, 65 MTS 179–200
musicology, 25 LEIP 165, 53 BAM 27–50, 70
    BON 672, 677
piano, popularization through, 00 PAR² 289
public lecture, 55 BRUS 35, 138
public library, 55 BRUS 37, 140, 62 STOC 63
radio music, 37 FLOR 135, 54 PAR² 391, 396, 401,
    458
record library, 55 BRUS 41
records, 37 FLOR 166, 67 ZAG 17
sound recording, 68 NEWY 84
of professions
composers, *see* Composers: training
music librarians, *see* Libraries and librarianship
opera singers, 38 FRA 116, 147, 178, 184, 211,
    64 HAM 140–51, 65 GEN 22
specific aspects of music
composition, 11 LON 355
counterpoint and fugue, 25 LEIP 189
Gregorian chant, 05 STRS 100, 50 LÜN¹ 136
harmony, 00 PAR¹ 56
history of music, *see* History of music
melody, 25 LEIP 190
orchestration, 00 PAR¹ 14
piano, 11 LON 326, 346
polyphony, 25 LEIP 127
rhythm, 26 GEN 92, 179, 65 GEN 22, 136
theory, *see* Theory
violin, 11 LON 337
voice training, 11 LON 62, 72 GRA 175–235
see also Church music: education
Eftimis, 14th c church music, 75 BYD 45
Egidius Romanus, 72 COP 388
Egypt
composition, 32 CAIR 166
harp and chironomy in ancient Egypt, 52 UTR
    233
maqamates, 32 CAIR 529
and Mozart, 56 PRA 200
musicological research, 48 PAR¹ 71, 49 BAS 150
rhythm, 32 CAIR 399
see also Coptic
Eisler, Hans
influenced by workers' songs, 64 BERL 301
view of Beethoven, 70 BERL² 165
Eitner, Robert, *Quellen-Lexicon*, 06 BAS 7
Eitz, Karl, Tonwort method, 14 GOT 86, 141
Electro-acoustics, *see* Instruments: electro-acoustical
Electronic music, 53 NET 256, 55 ARR 183, 59 CAM
    30, 61 TOK 130, 65 CARB 169, 65 LIE i, M65,
    68 TOK¹ vi, 33, 70 STOC 157
in ballet, 60 STRT 106
in opera, 64 HAM 108
Elizabethan *see* England: 16th c
Elsner, Józef, ideology, 60 WAR¹ 713
Emotion in composition, 36 JEN 194
Empathy, musical, 04 GIE 93
Empfindsamkeit, 70 BON 352
Encyclical 'Musicae sacrae disciplina', 56 VIE 309
church music in light of, *57 PAR*
Encylopédie entry on ballet, 75 SIE 73

Enesco, Georges
general, 67 BUC 193, *73 BUC*
aesthetics, 73 BUC 25, 103
in America, 73 BUC 109, 115
and Janáček, 58 BRN 330
letters to French musicians, 73 BUC 63
literary sources of works, 73 BUC 121, 141
and Romanian music 1900–1920, 73 BUC 49
Romanian music festivals, promoter of, 73 BUC
    71
as teacher, 73 BUC 57
style
development, 70 BON 386
harmony, 73 BUC 39
monodic elements, 73 BUC 25
national traits, 67 BUC 193–235
rhythmic, 73 BUC 31
thematic process, 73 BUC 19
violin playing and influence, 67 BUC 202
works, general
chamber vocal works, 73 BUC 121
piano works, 67 BUC 222
sonatas, 67 BUC 235
works, specific
Œdipe, 67 BUC 211, 73 BUC 135
Sept chansons, 73 BUC 129
String Quartet op. 22 no. 2, 73 BUC 83, 93
Vox maris, 73 BUC 141
England
general 09 VIE 489
church music, influence of secular idiom, 11 LON
    61
church musicians, social position of, 61 NEWY i,
    346
comic opera, influence by Théâtre de la Foire, 09
    VIE 193
Flemish music in England, 13 GHE 254
folk dance revival, 37 PAR⁴ 382
folk music, 28 PRA 124, 164
folk tunes, relation of American and British, 39
    NEWY 84, 122
influence on the evolution of music, 11 LON 83
keyboard music, sources of, 54 PAR¹ 225
lute music, foreign elements, 54 PAR¹ 197
lute sources, 57 NEU/S 297
lute technique, 57 NEU/S 107
poetry, relation of music and syntax, 60 WAR²
    203
virginal music, new edition of, 11 LON 369
and individuals
Bach, 50 LÜN¹ 131
Bartók, 61 BUD 339
Debussy, 62 PAR 239
Handel, 59 HAL 73, 81
Telemann, 72 BLA 62
Toscanini, 67 FLOR 237
up to 1500
carol, 67 LJU 284
liturgical relations with Scandinavia in 12th and 13th
    c, 75 ESP 11
lost choirbook of 15th c, 72 COP 257
role in 14th c music, 64 SAL ii, 188
Scandinavian relations before 1700, 72 COP 263
song before the madrigalists, 53 PAR 121
16th c
broadside ballads of the 16th and 17th c, 39
    NEWY 112
influence of Italian music on madrigal, 53 PAR 129
madrigal in 16th c, 27 VIE 186, 30 LIÈ 33
music in Elizabethan tragedies, 62 ROY 139

organs and organ building in 16th to 18th c, 54 STAD 97

ornamentation of keyboard music 16th to 18th c, 67 BRN² 128

Tudor theatre pieces and pageants, 55 ROY 259

17th c
chamber music (1500–30) sources and origins, 54 PAR¹ 77
collections in Germany, 11 LON 93
and Denmark, 11 LON 129
Holland, English music and musicians in, 52 UTR 139
instrumental repertory 1550–85, 54 PAR¹ 91
lute music, 11 LON 331
madrigal, and melancholy, early 17th c, 53 PAR 153
from masque to opera, 65 MTA 53, 67 LJU 149
social background of Restoration anthem, 62 KAS 27
suite composers, 11 LON 93
voluntary for double organ, 56 HAM 123

18th c
J. C. Bach, English environment of, 62 KAS 32
Czech organ and harpsichord concerts, 70 BRN 359
meaning of 'vivace', 65 DIJ 194
organs and organ building in 16th to 18th c, 54 STAD 97

19th and 20th c
film music, 50 FLOR 114
music (1830–1914), 62 KAS 51
opera, 33 FLOR 183

Engramelle brothers, 56 FLOR 149

Enharmonics in Beethoven, 27 VIE 83

Enlightenment
Austrian, 71 EIS 92, 105, 121, 73 SIE 247
and Telemann, 73 MAG 19
and Mozart, 56 PRA 98
and Paris, 75 SIE

Epic
Balkan
compared with early Western forms, 53 BAM 200
on records (1900–30), 62 KAS 317
relations with Romanian, 68 GRA 53
research, 64 GRA² 7, 14
Montenegrin, 32 AMS 144
recitation forms in epic chants, 67 LJU 359
Russian, 64 BRA 165
Serbo-Croat, 56 HAM 241
Sorbian, 56 HAM 175
Turkish, 66 GRA 83

Equiton, 62 KAS 275

Eskimo
intervals and rhythm, 67 VAN 54
pentatonic system of Copper-Eskimos, 26 ROM 15

Estampie, 69 CER 399

Esterhazy orchestra, and Viennese composers, 70 PIE 113

Estonia
melodic style of runes, 64 MOS 334
17th and 18th c folk music, 72 BYD 873

Ethiopian church music, 70 BON 410

Ethnomusicology
general, 37 PAR³ i, 308, 56 HAM 66, 61 NEWY i, 376, 380, 72 COP 668, 702 *see also* Ethnomusicology in *Index of Titles, Series and Sponsors*
acculturation, 61 NEWY i, 139
analysis, 74 KRP
artistic values in traditional music, 65 BERL²

and church music, 75 ROM
and classical harmony, 58 WÉG 249
community musical life, 74 ZAG v, 191
comparative musicology, 06 BAS 56, 64 SAL i, 3
concepts, 67 RAD 41
content of music, 56 VIE 242
creating a wider interest in traditional music, 67 BERL
distributional method, 73 BEL 44
in education, 68 SVE 164, 173
equipment of expeditions, 09 VIE 224
families of music, 61 TEH 132
and Fétis, 63 CART 13
as guide to national psychology, 52 VIE ii, 79
historical aspects, 58 COL 200
method, 58 WÉG 24, 75 ROM 13
musical stratigraphy, 58 WÉG 13
and musicology, 53 BAM 159–212, 58 COL 17
myths of origin of music, 50 LÜN¹ 151
national and universal in folk music, 67 BUC 69
numerical treatment of non-western music, 73 PAR 158
and organology, 25 LEIP 98
scales, non-western, 73 PAR 144
significance of research for aesthetics and psychology, 10 INN 256
subjective-motoric elements in primitive music, 30 LIÈ 148
tonality, 74 KRP 26
village music, 13 GHE 285
and different places
Africa, 58 WÉG 19, 68 EVA 131
inter-American, 63 CART, 65 BLM
Balkan, 71 BUD¹ 189
Hamburg, 56 HAM 109
Italy, 58 COL 198, 73 ROM²
see also Folk music

Eton College Choirbook (MS 178), 52 UTR 224

Euler, Leonard, musical genres with 7th harmonic, 49 BAS 113

Europe
continent
and Arab music, 75 BYD 407
as seen by China and Japan, 71 FLOR 95
folk music and the middle ages, 72 SÁR 201
influence of antique world and the orient, 56 HAM 24
influenced by non-European music, 71 FLOR 67, 157
ornamentation in folk music, 61 NEWY i, 439
violin and violin music, 71 STP
central
folksong and Mozart, 56 PAR 157
folksong and professionalism in 17th and 18th c, 72 BYD 683
music in Reformation, 75 BYD 191
relation with East in Renaissance, 75 BYD 301
Eastern
and Bach, 50 LEIP 411
and Beethoven, 70 BON 121–46, 70 PIE 11
and Central Europe in Renaissance, 75 BYD 301
chain dance, 72 SÁR 101
folk music and J. F. Reichardt, 60 WAR¹ 601
and Hungarian dance types, 63 BUD 469
and Italy in 14th and 15th c, 69 PARM 29
organ music in 15th and 16th c, 75 BYD 391
and Western Europe in Renaissance, 75 BYD 321
20th c music, 71 BUD¹ 159, 71 MOS 133
Northern
influenced by Monteverdi, 67 SIE 341

and German music, *63 KIE*
and South in 14th to 16th c music, 65 COP 31
Southern
and North in 14th to 16th c music, 65 COP 31
20th c music, 71 MOS 133
South-East *see* Balkans
Western
and Eastern Europe in Renaissance, 75 BYD 321
megalithic culture, 72 SÁR 205
and Poland in 15th to 17th c, 66 BYD 383
20th c music, 71 MOS 124
Evolution in music, 64 NEWD² 11–38
Evora, school of, 21 PAR 846
Exchanges, musical, 33 FLOR 223, 226, 233, 239
Exoticism, 71 FLOR 95, 133
ambience created by, 37 PAR³ i, 315
and new music, 24 BERL 411
polyrhythms, 26 GEN 71
Puccini, 71 FLOR 141
Expression
in Beethoven, 27 VIE 100
on organ, 32 STRS 146
research into musical expression, 60 ATH 428
self-expression, 49 FLOR 9–27, 78–108, 138–73
sorrow and death in music of the 12th and 13th c, 62
TOD 261
in speech melody, 05 ROM 245
Expressionism in opera, 68 STRS 221–45

Faburden/Fauxbourdon (meaning of term), 53 BAM
120
Falaquera, sources for his chapter on music, 65 JER 207
Falsobordone, echoes in early opera, 70 BON 179
Fantasia in France up to 17th c, 54 PAR¹ 327
Far East
church music, 57 PAR 564
modal music, 61 TEH 171
music traditions and new rhythms, 64 NEWD² 146
preservations of musical traditions, 65 BERL² 23
Fawcett system, 62 KAS 275
Felsztynski, Sebastian, 75 BYD 247
Ferdinand, Archduke, musical relations with Sigismund
III of Poland, 60 WAR¹ 522
Ferrara
and Dufay, 74 NEWY¹ 1
and Josquin, 71 NEWY 103
and seconda prattica, 72 COP 576
theatrical traditions in 17th c, 68 VEN 139
Ferrari, Gaudenzio, angel chorus in Saronno as iconog-
raphical source, 27 VIE 378
Festa, Sebastian and early madrigal, 62 KAS 122
Festivals
contemporary music at, 64 HAM 132
music theatre at, 64 HAM 134
Fêtes
Barcelona, 17th c, 55 ROY 371
Berne, 16th c, 55 ROY 347
Binche, 57 BRUS 329
Cambrai, entry of Charles V, 57 BRUS 235
Field of the Cloth of Gold, 57 BRUS 135, 147
Florence (1589), 55 ROY 133, 145
folk, 37 PAR⁴ 387, 389, 399
marriage of the Duc de Joyeuse, 53 PAR 241
marriage of Francesco di Medici, 55 ROY 107
Munich (1662), 70 MTA 121
of the Renaissance, *55 ROY, 57 BRUS, 72 TOU*
Savoy (1644, 1645), 70 MTA 49
Scotland, 55 ROY 335
village, 72 TOU 603
Württemberg (1609–1617), 72 TOU 393

Fétis, François Joseph
as librarian at Paris Conservatoire, 13 GHE 347
precursor of ethnomusicology, 63 CART 13
role in history of musicology, 30 LIÈ 35
Swedish collection of his correspondence, 30 LIÈ 113
and Verdi, 72 MIL 312
Fibich, Zdeněk
chamber-music style, 71 BRN 171
word-setting, 69 BRN 159
Ficinio, Marsilio, chant orphique, 53 PAR 17
Field, John, nocturnes, 60 WAR¹ 275
Field of the Cloth of Gold, music at, 57 BRUS 135, 147
Fiesta de San Juan, 63 CART 153
Figured bass
in Brixi, 73 MAG 93
chitarrone as continuo instrument, 70 BOL 117
German secular song with figured bass accompaniment
in Bohemia, 1650–1750, 71 BRN 115
improvisation, according to Seger, 56 VIE 490
and Italian musical instruments, 58 COL 76
by Merulo, 49 BAS 154
in Moravia in 17th and 18th c, 67 BRN² 116
Niedt's treatise, 53 BAM 152
and règle de l'octave, 72 COP 556
suspension of, in Italian opera, 11 LON 282
technique in 17th and 18th c, 67 BRN² 113
in Telemann, 67 MAG ii, 77, 73 MAG 93
Werckmeister's treatise, 53 BAM 149
c 1600, 64 SAL ii, 201
Film and music, *50 FLOR*
Berg scenario, 50 FLOR 135
bibliography, 50 FLOR 139
cartoon, 50 FLOR 63
communication of music through film, 68 NEWY 69
and the concert hall, 37 FLOR 245
and conducting, 50 FLOR 78
criticism, 50 FLOR 86–94
documentary films, 50 FLOR 69, 72
in England, 50 FLOR 114
in folk music research, 34 TRT 392, 70 TRČ 145, 161
in France, 50 FLOR 107
influence on music theatre, 64 HAM 108
music in film, 33 FLOR 216, 37 FLOR 219, 228, 232,
239, 253, *50 FLOR*
new possibilities, 33 FLOR 43
rhythm, 33 FLOR 209, 37 PAR³ ii, 364
as source for song and speech research, 38 FRA 30
in the Soviet Union, 50 FLOR 129
in the USA, 50 FLOR 118
and Verdi and Wagner, 37 FLOR 257
Finck, Heinrich, in Poland, 62 KAS 119
Finland
church music, 52 BERN 41
early music documents, 75 BYD 119
five-beat bars, 00 PAR² 241
folk melodies, characteristics of, 09 VIE 230
Gregorian chant, 24 BAS 184
history of music, 21 PAR 922
instrumental music in 17th and 18th c, 72 BYD 177
introit collection (1605), 30 LIÈ 132
liturgical fragments, 75 ESP 179
modes, 09 VIE 259
orchestral music, introduction into Finland, 11 LON
90
pastoral aerophones, 75 BRUN 45
pop music, 72 VIE² 60
and Verdi, 66 VEN 361
Finta Monacella, songs of the, 48 TUR 83, 57 CHIE
442
Fischer, Friedrich Theodore, on content and form, 66

LEIP 391
Fischhof, Josef, 71 GRA 105
Flanders
  Beethoven's Flemish traits, 27 VIE 16
  influence on Spanish polyphony, 52 UTR 47
  instrumental concert in 15th c art, 54 ARR 197
  music (concept), 62 KAS 229
  musicians in England, 13 GHE 254
  Renaissance, *54 ARR*
  songs in 14th and 15th c, 24 BAS 376
  see also Belgium; Netherlands
Flathead Indian music, 65 BLM 129
Florence
  composers in 14th c, 69 CER 247
  intermezzi, 55 ROY 133, 145, 70 MTA 25
  laude, 57 TOD 105
  laudesi, 69 CER 247, 253
  Maggio musicale, 71 FLOR 11
  visits by Polish princes in 1624 and 1634, 70 BOL 191
Flute
  acoustical aspects, 68 TOK¹ vi, 21, 25, 71 BUD² iii,
    569, 74 LON 337
  Avignon flute players in 15th c, 21 PAR 802
  in 18th c French music, 69 PAR 25
  Kernspaltflöte
    European, 67 BRN¹ 41
    Norwegian, 67 BRN¹ 74
    Serbian, 67 BRN¹ 82
    Swedish, 69 STOC 77
  medieval, 75 BRUN 33
  patent voice flute, 59 CAM 239
  of Pau andina, 32 LAP 333
  prehistoric Georgian bone flute, 63 BUD 451
  Telemann's 12 Fantasias as school for solo flute, 73
    MAG 84
  transverse Alpine flute, 27 VIE 373
Folia, 52 UTR 415
  16th c instrumental ensemble arrangements, 66 LEIP
    190
Folk music
  general *see* 'Folk' in *Index of Titles, Series and
    Sponsors*
  aims, 28 PRA 97
  in 12th c Armenian liturgical chant, 54 CAM 173
  arrangements, 71 HIN 111
  atlas of German, value for music history 53
    BAM 209
  audio-visual media, relation to, 70 HAMM 12, 45
  and Baroque lyricism, 57 WÉG 109
  collecting, 34 TRT 360, 37 PAR⁴ 286–90, 63
    CART 177
  contribution to music history, 53 BAM 159–212
  and copyright, 71 HIN 62
  cultivation of by musicology, 56 VIE 758
  decline, reasons for, 37 PAR³ 318
  difference between research and cultivation, 63
    STT 133
  different periods, different style, 64 MOS 221
  divergence of verbal and melodic stress, 58 BRN
    265
  editing of, 64 GRA² 29
  in education, 37 PAR⁴ 382–403
  European, and medieval music, 72 SÁR 201
  false intonation, 54 WÉG 145
  'folk', 71 FLOR 173
  form, 54 WÉG 132, 58 COL 257
  function of formulas in folksongs, 60 WAR² 525
  historicity in European, 67 LJU 329
  history, 68 BRN 365
  identification of folkloristic genres, 60 WAR² 505
  improvisation in, 58 COL 257

and industrial age, 71 HIN 119
magic chant, 54 WÉG 56
measuring rhythm, 67 BRN¹ 165
melody, *see* Melody: folk
methods, research, 11 LON 185, 28 PRA 97
in middle ages, 50 LÜN¹ 174
Minnesang melodies reflect forgotten folksong, 72
  SÁR 245
in myths and fairy tales, 11 LON 167, 178
national and universal aspects, 67 BUC 60, 69
nature/concept, 71 HIN 11–59
poetics of contemporary, 60 WAR² 487
polyphony, *see* Polyphony: folk
prenuptial, 54 PAL 163
present problems, *71 HIN*
recording, *see* Records, recording
relation between folksong and folk tale, 54 WÉG
  120, 59 KIE 406, 64 ATH 42
relation with opera in 17th c, 24 BAS 326
rhythm and metric systems, *see* Rhythm
scales in European, 60 PAR¹ 143
  in primitive, 60 PAR¹ 129
social history aspects, 73 BAL 39, 73 ROM² 97
and sociology of music, 31 SAL 304
sources, *72 SÁR*
in teaching, 28 PRA 101, 102
tonality in, 58 BRN 182
'Umsingen', 50 LÜN¹ 181
wandering melodies, 64 MOS 291
classification, *65 BRA, 67 RAD, 71 BLE, 74 KRP,* 68
  TOK² 334
and analysis, 66 LEIP 460, *74 KRP*
by Bartók, 61 BUD 435
cataloguing, 50 LÜN² 38, 73 ANK 184
comparative melody research, 65 BRA 31
by computer, 66 LEIP 460
Czech, 65 BRA 145
Deutsche Volksliedarchiv, 65 BRA 17
form, 65 BRA 57, 81
German, 62 KAS 345
Greek, 71 BLE 57
Hungarian, 65 BRA 123
by incipits, 65 BRA 141, 145
lexicographical, 06 BAS 66
melodic systems, 65 BRA 93–135
melody, 65 BRA 81
Monumenta monodica medii aevi, 65 BRA 135
non-strophic, 1- to 2-line melodies, 67 RAD 53–
  179
Polish, 65 BRA 47
rhythmic metric systems, 65 BRA 47–81
Slovak, 65 BRA 57, *70 TRČ*
tonality, 65 BRA 141
verse structure, 65 BRA 73
and individual composers
  Bach, 50 LEIP 411, 416
  Bartók, 61 BUD 435, 441, 549, 71 BUD¹ 181, 197
  Beethoven, 70 BERL² 437, 443, 447, 70 PIE 191
  Chopin, 60 WAR¹ 95, 100, 176, 247
  Janáček, *see* Janáček
  Schubert, 28 VIE 57
  Sibelius, 53 BAM 207
  Tartini, 67 LJU 176
folk-music institutes
  L'Archivio etnico-linguistico-musicale della Dis-
    coteca di stato, *73 ROM²* 271
  Folkstudio di Palermo, 73 ROM² 277
  Institute of Ethnomusicology, University of Califor-
    nia at Los Angeles, 65 BERL² 108
  International Institute for Comparative Music Stud-
    ies, Berlin, 65 BERL² 115

Istituto Ernesto De Martino, 73 ROM² 265
Museo nazionale delle arti e tradizion: popolari e
    archivi di documentazione, 73 ROM² 257
Národopisný ústav Slovenskiej akadémie vied, 70
    TRČ 133, 145
see also individual regions, countries and towns;
    Dance: folk; Ethnomusicology; Instruments: folk
Folk tales, relations with folk music, 54 WÉG 120, 59
    KIE 406, 64 ATH 42
Folk theatre, and Mozart, 56 VIE 623
Fontanelli, Alfredo, 72 COP 576
Ford-Columbia input language, 65 NEWY 48
Forkel, Johann Nikolaus, Bach biography, 72 COP 462
Forli and Spontini, 51 IES 50
Form
    in art and folk music, 58 COL 257
    bar form in Mahler's songs, 72 COP 617
    Baroque, 25 LEIP 430
    in Coro spezzato, 72 COP 604
    Italian instrumental music in 17th c (conventions of
        form), 72 COP 288
    musical organism, 62 KAS 271
    operatic form in 20th c, 64 HAM 66–82
    in oral traditions, 54 WÉG 132
    in performance, *75 AUS*
    pre-existing structures, 62 KAS 263
    Renaissance, 54 PAR¹ 165
    spatial form and Ives, 74 NEWY¹ 145
    and symphonic poem, 11 LON 206
    through timbre layers, 72 COP 686
    traditional forms in new musical idioms, 61 NEWY
        i, 100
    of 13th to 16th c music, 75 BYD 133
    of 20th c music, 60 STRT 134–145
    see also individual composers
Fossombrone, Petrucci at, 72 COP 295
Fotonomo, 11 LON 332
France
    general
        Bergerettes, influence on Chopin, 60 WAR¹ 374
        church music, *see* Church music
        libraries, *see* Libraries and manuscripts
        lute and women, 23 BRUS 366
        lute technique, 57 NEU/S 107
        the metronome, 00 PAR² 264
        sacred music in royal chapel, 52 BERN 55
        suite, influence on development of, 21 PAR 853
        vernacular songs, 57 PAR 494
            in Louisiana, 57 PAR 509
    folk music, 54 WÉG 97
        ceremonial music in rural areas, 68 TOK² 340
        folk dance, 28 PRA 169, 54 PAL 161
        instruments, 37 PAR⁴ 377
        instrumental ensembles, 69 STOC 173
    and individuals
        Beethoven, 27 VIE 116
        Enesco, 73 BUC 63
        Haydn, 59 BUD 79
        Josquin, 71 NEWY 181
        Mozart, 56 VIE 156, 170, 344
        Schubert, 28 VIE 87
        Verdi, 69 VER 565, 72 MIL 258, 338
    up to 1600
        Ars nova in, 55 WÉG 37, 59 CER 83
        Catalonia, exchanges with in middle ages, 21 PAR
            823
        chanson, *see* Chanson
        church music in 15th to 16th c, 37 PAR¹ 130
        Fantaisie, up to mid 17th c, 54 PAR¹ 327
        French and Walloon song in first half of 16th c, 30
            LIÈ 76

humanism, 16th c, 06 BAS 170
influence on Italian trecento manuscripts, 55 WÉG
    27
lute players, 16th c, 00 PAR² 179
music and poetry to the 16th c, 53 PAR 79
music history 1400–30, 67 LJU 43
musicians in 14th c, 55 WÉG 63
Renaissance, 12th c, 39 NEWY 200
    Northern provinces, *54 ARR*
    polyphonic performances, 67 BRN² 61
    polyphony and poetry, 67 BRN² 61
17th c
    Baroque poetry and music, 68 MTA 127
    chanson, early 17th c, 53 PAR 169
    church music, 57 PAR 171
    compared with Italian music 1704–6, 66 LEIP
        238
    composition, 72 BYD 209
    interpretation of, *69 PAR*
    Italian influence on stage design, 72 VEN 131
    lute, and keyboard c 1650, 67 LJU 134
    music, sources of, 30 LIÈ 217
    players, Parisian, 57 NEU/S 209
    and voice, volumes for (1603–43), 57 NEU/S
        155
    organists and organ registration, 49 BAS 172
    organs, *see* Organs and organ building
    origins of French overture (1640–60), 11 LON 149
    painting and music, 64 BON 206
    pastorales in music, influence on opera, 11 LON
        139
    secular solo song, 70 BON 333
    tempo, 65 DIJ 162–204
    theatre, musicians and public in, 67 NAN 267
18th c
    ad lib instrumental chamber music, 69 PAR 25
    church music, 57 PAR 171
    comic opera, Théâtre de la Foire, 09 VIE 193
    interpretation of, *69 PAR*
    opera and Gluck, 73 SIE 283
    organists and organ registration, 49 BAS 172
    political use of revolutionary opera, 70 BON 237
    tempo, 65 DIJ 162–204
19th c .
    acoustics, 11 ROM 127
    chamber music, 11 ROM 103
    church music after the Revolution, 37 PAR¹ 147
    educational, 00 PAR² 289, 09 VIE 507, 11
        ROM 139
    Grand opera, influence on Verdi, 69 VER 311
    instrument making, 11 ROM 151
    legislation, 11 ROM 157
    modal elements c 1890, 56 VIE 78
    music 1830–1914, 62 KAS 66
    music 1860–1910, 11 ROM 5
    musicology, 11 ROM 15
    opera, 11 ROM 21
    philosophy, 11 ROM 117
    religious, choral, 11 ROM 63
    symphonic, 11 ROM 77
20th c
    economic position of orchestral musicians, 09 VIE
        515
    film music, 50 FLOR 107
    impressionism as inspiration, 68 GRA 80
    influence of Debussy in, 62 PAR 269
    instrumental ensembles, 69 STOC 173
    and liturgical music, 65 MTS 144
    musical subcultures, 72 VIE² 212
    music in Paris c 1920, 67 LJU 216
    music teaching, 09 VIE 507

opera, 33 FLOR 139
organ building, 37 PAR¹ 171
sacred music, 54 VIE 162
society for protection and development of music, 00 PAR² 246
trends, 60 STRT 77
Francesco da Milano, 54 PAR¹ 165
Francis I's musicians at Field of the Cloth of Gold, 57 BRUS 135
Franck, César, 50 LÜN¹ 143
Franck, Melchior, 58 COL 120
Frankfurt School, view of Bartók, 71 BUD¹ 13
Frescobaldi, Girolamo
keyboard tablatures, 72 COP 342
in Malines: documents, 11 MAL 733
Froidebise, Pierre, 68 LIÈ 323
Frottola
and Josquin, 71 NEWY 446
transition to madrigal, 53 PAR 63, 61 CAM/M 51
Frugoni, Carlo Innocenzo, *68 PARM*
Ippolito ed Aricia, 68 PARM 271
Medo, 68 PARM 301
Il trionfo di Camilla, 68 PARM 301
Fulda, Adam of, 30 LIÈ 125
Fugues
academic, 09 VIE 108
Bach's, real answer in, 62 KAS 364
Handel's treatise, 62 KAS 172
Mozart's fugal fragments, 56 VIE 743
problems in teaching, 25 LEIP 189
Reicha's 70 PIE 13
themes, 70 BON 323
history of, 25 LEIP 246
word and music in, 69 BRN 91
Fux, Johann Joseph
and modern contrapuntal theory, 25 LEIP 187
new sources for research, 62 KAS 158

Gabela, music in, 58 COL 79
Gabler, Joseph, 51 OCH 78, 82
Gabrieli, Andrea, *Edipo Tiranno*, 53 PAR 275
Gabrieli, Giovanni
dissonance treatment, 66 LEIP 201
Sonata con voce, 56 HAM 88
Gabussi, Giulio Cesare, in Poland, 69 PARM 133
Gagaku, 50 LÜN¹ 168, 61 TOK 9, 66 MANL 107
Gagliano, Marco da
madrigal style, 72 COP 675
opera, 68 VEN 583
sacred music, 49 BAS 125
Gaillard, Émile, Album leaf for, 60 WAR¹ 111
Galilei, Vincenzo, transcription by, 03 ROM 135
Gamba, La, 66 LEIP 190
Gamelan, 52 UTR 271
Javanese, 66 MANL 16
orchestra of the Wayang Kulit, 69 KUA 290
Gargano folksongs and dances, 40 VEN 428
Gdansk
Chopin's stay in, 60 WAR¹ 559
professional music in 17th and 18th c, 72 BYD 429
18th c organ book, 25 LEIP 284
Gebrauchsmusik, 18th c influenced by verbunkos, 72 BYD 639
Gelineau, Joseph, 65 MTS 80
Geminiani, Francesco Saverio
additions to Corelli solo sonatas, 72 BYD 591
Geneva, Mozart and, 56 VIE 637
Geniza, Piyyut melody from, 61 JER 362
Genre
in Chopin, 60 WAR¹ 114

17th c Italian sonata types, 72 COP 478
Georgia
music 11th to 12th c, 69 BYD 401
music 17th to 18th c, 72 BYD 727
music at time of Tsarina Tamara, 75 BYD 469
'nadi' collective work, 63 BUD 459
'naduri' songs, 63 BUD 459, 64 MOS 287
polyphony, 50 LÜN¹ 172, 64 MOS 232
prehistoric bone flute, 63 BUD 451
traditional song, 74 STN 462
Géricault, Théodore, 70 VIE 213
Germany
general
cataloguing songs, 09 VIE 434
East Germany, music and musicians in, 63 KIE 120
influence by Italian music, 24 NAP 110
libraries, *see* Libraries and manuscripts
musicality, 34 TÜB 130
North German music history, 63 KIE 63–120
Norwegian music, relations with, 63 KIE 37
prelude, beginnings of, 60 WAR¹ 495
Scandinavian music, historical connections with, 63 KIE 11–56
shepherd idylls in 17th and 18th c, 75 BRUN 106
singing, difference between German and Italian, 38 FRA 161
and individuals
Bach, 50 LEIP 158
Chopin, 60 WAR¹ 334
Debussy, 62 PAR 241
Janáček, 68 BRN 263
Mozart, 31 SAL 1, 56 VIE 47, 156
Reger, 26 FRE/B 122, 130
Spontini, 51 IES 129
Verdi, 66 VEN 364
Vivaldi, 66 LEIP 247
music in other places
figured-bass accompanied song in Bohemia 1651–1750, 71 BRN 115
folksongs in Spiz, Slovakia, 28 PRA 150
folksongs in Yugoslavia, 38 FRA 336
oldest written sacred songs in Styria, 54 VIE 208
church music *see also* Organs
Catholic hymns, 09 VIE 532, 25 LEIP 353, 27 BERL 110
Protestant hymns, 25 LEIP 360, 52 BERN 42
folk music, 11 LON 59, 53 BAM 209, 67 RAD 109
cataloguing, 62 KAS 345
changes from 19th c to the present, 64 MOS 238
element in instrumental dances, 54 PAR¹ 139
manuscript collection, 11 LON 205
relation with folk tales, 64 ATH 42
to 1700
beginnings of German Passion, 49 BAS 39
Buxheimer organ book as German songbook, 56 HAM 211
dances of organ tablature, 24 BAS 243
earliest organ music, 69 CER 176
East Germany at time of Reformation, 25 LEIP 393
Gregorian chant, 30 LIÈ 208, 64 GRA¹ 121
lute tabulature, 57 NEU/S 245
medieval lyric, 66 OXF² 96, 118, 70 WUR 68, 98, 112, 73 HAM 164, 73 NEU/B 272
medieval polyphony, 50 LÜN¹ 68
Minnesang, 24 BAS 259, 66 OXF² 96

music history 1400–1430, 67 LJU 60
organ music 1450–1500, 27 FRE/S 133
parallels to melodies of Souterliedekens, 52 UTR
  438
15th c polyphonic songs, 58 COL 214
role in 14th c music, 64 SAL ii, 188
singing style of early German opera, 38 FRA 11
16th c song and Burgundian chanson, 24 BAS 153
16th c song influenced by chanson, 27 VIE 152
17th c
  Belgian composers in 17th to 18th c, relation to, 13
    GHE 262
  cantata, origins of, 67 LJU 116
  Central Germany history *c* 1700, 66 LEIP 230
  16th to 17th c composition teaching, 53 BAM
    103–52
  contrapuntal teaching, 25 LEIP 280
  evolution of independent instrumental music, 69
    BYD 127
  keyboard music, strict and free style, 63 KIE 63
  musical relations with Netherlands, 52 UTR 181
  organs, *see* Organs and organ building
  singing style of early opera, 38 FRA 11
18th c
  comic opera, 09 VIE 193
  Empfindsamkeit, 70 BON 352
  instruments in German dictionaries, 58 COL 207
  lute music, 25 LEIP 237
  Reichstil in music history, 62 KAS 34
  Swabian towns, bearer of 18th c German cul-
    ture, 25 LEIP 391
19th c
  criticism of Chopin, 60 WAR¹ 334
  Renaissance revival, 53 BAM 289
  romantic movement, 63 KIE 42
20th c
  chamber music in DDR, 71 BRN 481
  culture, music education in DDR, 56 VIE 272
  Darmstadt influence on Italian composers, 63
    MER 679
  development of music, training and education in
    DDR, 73 WEIM 118
  influence of Debussy, 62 PAR 241
  liturgical music, 65 MTS 141
  national and international language, 63 MER 409
  opera, 33 FLOR 169
  organ building and playing, 50 ROM 380
  organ music, 26 FRE/B 122, 130
  Protestant church music after 1945, 66 LEIP 347
  radio, 33 FLOR 118
  social position of church musician, 50 ROM 96
  writing on church music, 50 ROM 93
Gesualdo, Carlo, mannerism, 70 BRN 127, 73 ROM¹
  55
Gevaert, François Auguste, 30 LIÈ 158
Ghana, traditional music in, 67 BERL 120
Gibbons, Orlando, madrigals, 53 PAR 139
Gilbert, Sir William Schenck
  Savoy operas and their sources, 70 LAW
Gildes de Sainte-Cecile, 37 PAR¹ 94
'Gimedia, Presbyter de', 54 ROU 925
Giordano, Umberto, system of notating orchestral
  score, 09 VIE 382
Gisleni, Giovanni Battista, stage sets, 69 WAR 9
Glareanus, Henricus
  correspondence with Jan Laski, 60 WAR¹ 638
  Dodecachordon, 60 WAR¹ 638
  Isagoge in musicen, 56 VIE 397
Glinka, Mikhail Ivanovich, and Beethoven, 70 BON
  140
Globokar, Vinko, Concerto Grosso, analysis of, 72

COP 50
Glogauer Liederbuch, 53 BAM 248
Gluck, Christoph Willibald
  general
    and Austrian Enlightenment, 73 SIE 247
    as Baroque composer, 50 LÜN¹ 195
    and contemporaries, 73 SIE 585
    and French opera, 73 SIE 283
    and Hapsburg Lorena family, 73 SIE 571
    influence on Hasse, 73 SIE 309
    and Italian culture in Vienna, *73 SIE*
    and Italian tradition, 73 SIE 275
    and Metastasio, 73 SIE 299
    opera reforms, 73 SIE 235, 299
    opera seria, 73 SIE 263
  works
    Don Juan, 73 SIE 535, 549
    Ifigenia operas, 75 SIE 165, 185
    Orfeo, 67 FLOR 249, 73 SIE 369, 383, 395
    Paride ed Elena, 73 SIE 465
    Semiramide riconosciuta, 73 SIE 565
    Il Telemaco, 70 BON 400
    unknown instrumental works, 50 LÜN¹ 140
Godet, Robert, and Debussy, 62 PAR 339
Goertz, Harald, 72 VIE¹ 93
Goethe, Johann Wolfgang von
  and Beethoven, 70 BON 587
  poetry and music, 66 LEIP 3
Goigs, 28 PRA 155
Goldoni, Carlo, *57 VEN¹*
  Il genio buono e il genio cattivo, 75 SIE 105
  as librettist, 57 VEN¹ 567, 571
  opera buffa elements, 57 VEN¹ 593
Gomidas, as collector of Armenian folksongs, 64 MOS
  329
Gonzaga, court and music, *74 MANT*
  Francesco, 74 MANT 267
  Guglielmo, 74 MANT 277
  opera, 74 MANT 285
  sacred music, 74 MANT 267
Gorzanis, Giacomo, 56 VIE 525
Gossec, François Joseph, 23 BRUS 369
Gozos, 28 PRA 155
Gozzi, Carlo, *74 SIE*
  L'amore delle tre melarance, 74 SIE 205
  and Busoni, 74 SIE 167
  Il corvo, 74 SIE 238
  and German Romantics, 74 SIE 69
  music and spectacle in his writings, 74 SIE 41
  in 19th c Russia, 74 SIE 137
  structure of tales, 74 SIE 25, 61
  and 20th c theatre, 74 SIE 143
  Turandot, 74 SIE 125, 167
Gradual
  critical edition, 50 ROM 187
  Roman, 50 ROM 207
  use in small churches, 50 ROM 34
Graupner, Christoph, operas in Darmstadt, 25 LEIP
  252
Great Britain
  composers in 20th c, 47 PRA 22
  folksong, 11 LON 179
  folk violin and violin music, 71 STP 81
  music education research, 72 VIE² 159
  music history 1400–1430, 67 LJU 69
  see also England; Ireland; Scotland
Greece
  Ancient, 00 PAR² 15–70
    art and folk music, 54 PAL 91
    and Byzantine music, 36 ROM 479
    chant, 00 PAR² 15, 28

First Delphic Hymn, 00 PAR² 63, 65
Second Hymn to Apollo, 00 PAR² 70
harmonic sense, 58 COL 85
harmony, 00 PAR² 60
lyre from Mycenae period, 09 VIE 99
modes/scales, 00 PAR² 39, 57, 09 VIE 83, 60 PAR¹ 109
music, 39 NEWY 168
Roman-Greek metrical system, 25 LEIP 203
rhythm, 00 PAR² 70
state of research, 06 BAS 154
theory, 70 BERL¹ 9
tragedy and the Renaissance, 53 PAR 275
folksong, 21 PAR 929, 28 PRA 126, 30 ATH 267, 54 PAL 95, 64 GRA² 153
Greek-Albanian folksong, 54 PAL 329
systematization, 71 BLE 57
violin in folk music in Dodecanese, 71 STP 71
miscellaneous
history of music, 54 PAL 75
Italo-Greek church song, 03 ROM 107
musical tradition of Magna Grecia, 53 THE 274
and Mozart, 56 VIE 294
polyphony, 50 ROM 330, 54 PAL 243
Greenland–Eskimo, 67 VAN 54
Gregorian chant
general, 00 MUN 327–30, *05 STRS*, 09 VIE 550, 37 PAR¹ 55–79, 50 ROM 172–276, 54 VIE 98–149, 57 PAR 187–277
aesthetics, 27 BERL 71
and Ambrosian, *see* Ambrosian chant
Antiphonary, 8th c Gregorian and Visigothic, 50 ROM 183
and Byzantine, 36 ROM 479, 39 ALG 113
Cistercian, *see* Cistercian chant
and early Protestant chorale, 58 COL 157
fragments, research, 00 PAR⁶ 29
Gevaert's place in, 30 LIÈ 158
Gradual, 50 ROM 187, 207
hymns, 37 PAR¹ 184
in Josquin, 71 NEWY 525
in Klosterneuburg MSS, 54 VIE 124
and liturgical singing in vernacular, 66 CHIC 163
and liturgy, *65 MTS*
medieval treatises on, 05 STRS 80
neumatic notation, relation to, 00 PAR² 124
and the organ, 27 FRE/S 78, 50 ROM 344, 54 VIE 254
origin, 00 PAR⁶ 1, 52 BERN 38
in pastoral work of Pius X, 54 VIE 98
in Pro defunctis mass, 50 ROM 223
and the public, 50 ROM 265
reforms, 63 TOD 191
research, 54 VIE 149, 57 PAR 206, 64 SAL ii, 156
romance and Germanic traditions in, 27 VIE 237
sources, 50 ROM 212
teaching of in 18th c, 50 LÜN¹ 136
theology of repertory, 72 TOD 103
tradition, 58 COL 358
as song of worship, 62 BERN 38
in different places
Alsace, 05 STRS 19
America, 57 PAR 241
Baltic, 75 BYD 7
Cameroons, 57 PAR 260
Finland, 24 BAS 184
France, 50 ROM 245
Fons Avellana, 54 VIE 129
Germany, 30 LIÈ 208, 64 GRA¹ 121
Italy, northern, 54 VIE 142

Mediterranean, 54 PAL 237
Milan, 05 STRS 55
Portugal, 54 VIE 127
Rome, Schola Cantorum, 54 VIE 111, 120
St Gall, 05 STRS 123
Spain, 05 STRS 63
specific elements
accent, ictus in metrical Latin, 50 ROM 192
accompaniment, 05 STRS 117, 133, 27 FRE/S 78, 37 PAR¹ 66, 50 ROM 344, 54 VIE 254
melody, 50 ROM 177
in Liszt, 25 LEIP 341
use of oriental, 00 PAR⁶ 39
modes, 37 PAR¹ 79, 140, 49 BAS 72, 50 ROM 255
notation, 50 ROM 172, 202
ornamentation, 61 NEWY i, 428
performance, 05 STRS 40, 71, 27 BERL 81, 37 PAR¹ 109, 50 ROM 179, 54 VIE 105, 56 VIE 633
rhythm, 00 PAR⁶ 19, 05 STRS 29, 88, 06 BAS 17, 26 GEN 10, 15, 27 VIE 240, 54 VIE 146, 57 PAR 264, 58 COL 141
structure, 68 LIÈ 217
tonality, 72 COP 425
Gregory I, Pope, 50 ROM 248
Greith, Karl, 00 MUN 338
Gresnick, Antoine-Frédéric, 68 LIÈ 225
Grétry, André Ernest Modeste, in Warsaw, 30 LIÈ 201
Griepenkerl, Friedrich Conrad
and new MS of Bach's B minor Mass, 50 LEIP 231
Grillparzer, Franz, view of Mozart, 31 SAL 39
Grimache, *L'Alarme*, 21 PAR 784
Gros nasard, 69 PAR 239
Grossi, Giovanni Antonio, 68 MIL 38
Grottaferrata MSS, 55 IST 286, 69 CER 305, 315
Grudziądz, Petrus Wilhelmi of, 75 BYD 91
Guarini, Giovanni Battista, 73 ROM¹ 233
Gudok, and its predecessors, 75 BYD 455
Guglielmi, Pietro Alessandro, *Le pazzie d'Orlando*, 72 COP 391
Guide musical, 74 STN 466
Guido of Arezzo, 50 LÜN¹ 60
notation system, 05 STRS 141, 50 ROM 202
as teacher and theoretician, 53 BAM 44
theory of hexachord, 50 ROM 276
Guilds, beginnings in Poland, 75 BYD 235
Guilelmus Monachus, 49 BAS 145
Guinea (French), bows, 47 BIS 127
Guitar
acoustics, 58 MARS 203, 74 LON 336, 338
music in 16th and 17th c, 54 PAR¹ 205
tablature, 11 LON 354, 58 COL 329
Guittara Latina in Karlštejn frescoes, 75 BYD 79
Gulingtangan orchestra, 69 KUA 298
Gusle, in Yugoslavia, 71 STP 38
Gusli, history, 67 BRN¹ 134
Gutiérrez, Garcia, and Verdi, 72 MIL 34
Gvadányi, József, 75 BRUN 114
Gypsy
dance from Vallés, 28 PRA 192
Hungarian problem in music history, 30 LIÈ 140
musicians, 71 STP 60

Hába, Alois, and Schoenberg, 70 BRN 407
Hagenau organs and organists 1491–1525, 32 STRS 182
Haiduk
Bulgarian, 66 SOF vii, 755, 903
Halévy, Fromental, 70 LAW 91
Halle, Adam de la, 72 COP 250

Halleluia, in Jewish and Christian Chant,   61 JER 371
Hamal, Jean-Noël, op. 1,   09 LIÈ 722
Hambraeus, Bengt, new organ music,   74 SINZ 97
Hamburg
   birth of bourgeois theatre,   75 SIE 33
   ethnomusicology,   56 HAM 109
   opera and Telemann,   62 MAG 38
   opera house, reconstruction of,   56 HAM 235
   organists and Württemberg,   51 OCH 70
Handel, George Frideric
   general,   09 VIE 67, *59 HAL*
      and the ancient world,   59 HAL 87
      and England,   59 HAL, 73, 81
      languages, use of,   59 HAL 101
      and Liszt,   61 BUD 267
      and Mendelssohn,   59 HAL 215
      and R. Rolland,   59 HAL 219
      and school music,   59 HAL 223
      and social problems,   59 HAL 81
      spiritual world of in youth,   59 HAL 45
      and Weissenfels,   59 HAL 53
   bibliographical
      authenticity of early vocal works,   59 HAL 61
      dating of early vocal works,   59 HAL 61
      facsimile editions,   59 HAL 187
      research   50 LEIP 295, 58 COL 318
      watermarks,   59 HAL 193
   style
      as Baroque composer,   50 LÜN¹ 195
      biblical element,   59 HAL 181
      use of choral quotation,   59 HAL 173
      melody,   59 HAL 165
      polyphony,   59 HAL 22
      recitative,   59 HAL 135
      siciliano,   54 PAL 301
      tempo,   59 HAL 141
      thematic development,   59 HAL 155
   works, general
      French songs,   59 HAL 115
      Italian cantatas,   59 HAL 109
      operas,   59 HAL 165
      oratorios,   59 HAL 127, 155, 165, 173, 181
      vocal works, early,   59 HAL 61
   works, specific
      Agrippina,   59 HAL 241
      Athalia,   59 HAL 127
      Deborah,   59 HAL 127
      Esther,   59 HAL 127
      Messiah,   49 BAS 178, 59 HAL 141
      Requiem,   56 HAM 15
      Saul,   59 HAL 131
      treatise on fugue,   62 KAS 172
   performing practice,   59 HAL 207
      instrumental forces,   75 BLA 26
      operas,   59 HAL 235, 67 BRN² 164
      oratorios,   59 HAL 229, 245
         scenic performances of,   59 HAL 257
      in the Soviet Union,   59 HAL 261
      Saul,   59 HAL 131
      on Swedish stage,   59 HAL 251
Handl, Jacob, performing practice,   67 BRN² 73
Handwriting, musical in Reformation,   58 COL 166
Hanka, Václav, and Chopin,   60 WAR¹ 365
Hanslick, Eduard, aesthetics,   48 AMS 534
Harmonics
   inharmonicity of piano strings,   53 NET 259
   non-harmonic components in organ sound,   62 COP
      i, P53
   7th,   49 BAS 113, 58 MARS 47
Harmonium
   acoustical,   06 BAS 75

tessaradecatonic,   11 LON 333
Harmony
   analysis,   73 PAR 165
   classical,   49 BAS 23
   classical and ethnomusicology,   58 WÉG 249
   of colours in French 17th c,   64 BON 206
   concept – in ancient and medieval writings,   58 COL
      143
   in southern Africa,   58 COL 154
   new, breakdown,   48 FLOR 89
   conflict, between old and new theory,   50 LÜN¹ 211
   Day's theory,   39 NEWY 233
   describing complicated procedures in tonal music,   66
      LEIP 451
   enharmonic theory in Mozart's time,   56 VIE 471
   French Baroque theory,   72 COP 336
   Greek sense of,   58 COL 85
   harmonic information,   60 ATH 353
   harmonic rhythm,   58 COL 176
   harmonization, history of 1600–1750,   24 BAS
      328
   harmonization of Japanese melodies,   06 BAS 83
      of Znamenny chant,   64 BRA 117
   Italian trecento,   59 CER 32
   and limits of intonation,   71 VIC 29
   in Middle Ages and Renaissance,   56 VIE 92
   modern,   24 BAS 118, 251, 37 PAR³ ii, 458, 47 PRA
      25
   theories of,   60 PAR¹ 251
   Moravian folksong,   68 BRN 243
   national aspects,   67 BUC 117
   origin of harmonic functions   50 LUŇ¹ 209
   perception, changes in,   58 COL 176
   problems,   09 VIE 322
   psychological basis of consonance and dissonance,
      09 VIE 330
   relation to human life,   66 LEIP 469
   Riemann's theory of harmonic functions,   00 PAR¹
      56, 56 VIE 183
   of the spheres,   00 PAR² 60, 25 BRUG 221
   teaching,   00 PAR¹ 56
   Western, and Oriental music,   61 TEH 83
   see also Bartók, Chopin, Enesco, Janáček, Josquin,
      Mozart, Reger, Schoenberg, Schubert, Skry-
      abin, Szymanowski, Telemann, Wagner,
      Webern, Verdi, Zemlinsky
Harp,   64 AMS 518
   in ancient Egypt,   52 UTR 233
   history,   21 PAR 742
   Irish,   11 LON 317
Harpsichord
   in Austrian music after 1760,   70 GRA 249
   by Couchet,   70 ANT 41, 44
   Flemish,   70 ANT 35, 39, 63
   by Jobernadi,   54 PAR¹ 293
   by Kirckman,   71 GRA 69
   performance of French 17th and 18th c music,
      69 PAR 155–239
   pitch   71 BUD² iii, 621
   registration   69 PAR 203, 233
   restoration of Antwerp harpsichords,   *70 ANT*
   by Ruckers,   70 ANT 23, 44, 53, 77, 71 GRA 41
   stringing of Italian harpsichords,   71 GRA 35
   in first half of 17th c,   54 PAR¹ 269
Hasse, Johann Adolf, Gluckian aspects of late
      works,   73 SIE 309
Hasselt Collegium musicum in 16th c,   09 LIÈ 517
Hassler, Hans Leo, *Neue Teutsche Gesang*,   73 ROM¹
      255
Hauer, Josef Matthias, *Der Menschen Weg*,   70 BON
      561

Hauptmann, Moritz, music theory, 66 LEIP 387
Haydn, Franz Joseph
  general, 09 VIE 45, *59 BUD, 70 GRA, 71 EIS*
    contrapuntal teaching, 70 BON 70
    Croat folk music, relation to, 27 VIE 111
    Dies biography of, 59 BUD 131
    manuscripts in Sweden, 09 VIE 429
    as opera conductor, 59 BUD 17
    and orchestral music in his youth, 70 GRA 98
    performance of early string quartets, and diverti-
      menti, 70 GRA 86
  and places
    Bratislava, 71 EIS 57
    Czechoslovakia, 59 BUD 69, 70 GRA 31
    Denmark, 09 VIE 529
    France, 59 BUD 79
    Russia, 59 BUD 61, 85
  and others
    Beethoven, 70 BON 61–84
    Koželuh, 59 BUD 109
    Momigny, 62 KAS 187
    Mozart, 56 PAR 49, 59 BUD 95, 137
    Porpora, 70 GRA 41
    19th c Romanian composers, 59 BUD 177
  style, 66 LEIP 275
    brass instruments, use of in orchestra, 70 GRA
      202
    classical style, development of in instrumental
      works, 61 NEWY i, 305
    harpsichord, role of, 70 GRA 249
    and Hungarian music, 59 BUD 159
    proportions, 71 EIS 64
    rhetoric and Baroque pictorialism, 70 GRA
      168
    vocal ornamentation, 59 BUD 117
  works (general)
    church music, 59 BUD 49, 70 BON 408, 70 GRA
      74
    cyclic works, 71 EIS 64
    dance music, 59 BUD 25, 71 EIS 73
    instrumental works, 70 GRA 192, 61 NEWY i,
      305
    masses, 09 VIE 542, 59 BUD 41
    operas, 59 BUD 17
    piano sonatas (ascribed), 62 KAS 181
    string quartets, 70 BON 75, 70 GRA 86
    vocal canons, 59 BUD 93
  works (specific)
    Concerto for 2 horns and orchestra in E flat
      major, 59 BUD 103
    Orlando Paladino, 72 COP 391
    Singspiel, unknown, 72 COP 236
    Symphony no. 96 in D, 58 COL 197
    Tobias, 59 BUD 117
Haydn, Michael, piano music of, 71 BRN 361
Hearing and listening, 13 BERL 533, 61 TOK
  183
  changes, and interpretation 66 LEIP 487
  chords and timbre 58 COL 227
  deficiencies, 50 LÜN[1] 231
  and information theory, 56 HAM 91
  and interpretation, 66 LEIP 487
  music of another civilization, 64 NEWD[2] 103, 112
  physiological aspects, 61 NEWY i, 133
  psychological aspects, 38 FRA 305, 64 NEWD[2] 118–
    25, 61 BAL i, 11
  radio music, 54 PAR[2] 379
  research, 67 PAR 3
  variations in hearing, 56 HAM 58
Hebrew music, *see* Jewish music

Hecyrus, Christoph, 70 BRN 33
Hegel, Georg Friedrich, 70 VIE 253
  on content and form, 66 LEIP 391
    Moritz Hauptmann's music theory, 66 LEIP
      387
  music aesthetic, 37 PAR[3] ii, 32
Held, Ján Theobald, and Beethoven, 70 PIE 119
Helfer, Charles d', Mass, 57 WÉG 177
Helmholtz, Hermann von, music theory, 70 BERL[1]
  49
Henri II, ballet at court, 70 MTA 17
Henry VIII court musicians at Field of the Cloth of
  Gold, 57 BRUS 147
Henry, Michel, Receuil de ballets, 55 ROY 205
Herbst, Johann Andreas
  Musica poetica, 56 HAM 77
  relation of word and music, 56 HAM 77
  sacred works 25 LEIP 363
's Hertogenbosch, music of the Illustrious Confraternity
  of Our Lady 1330–1600, 39 NEWY 184
Herzogovina
  music, 58 COL 79
  traditional music, 66 GRA 97
Hessen-Darmstadt, Landgraf Ernst Ludwig as composer, 27 VIE 205
Heterophony in American–Indian music, 63 CART
  119
Hexachord, 50 ROM 276
Hijar (folk dance), 28 PRA 188
Hindemith, Paul
  chamber music, 71 BRN 231, 435
  music *c* 1920, 67 LJU 233
  and late Romanticism, 68 BRN 325
Hindustani
  classical music, 64 NEWD[2] 158
  evolution of music, 64 NEWD[2] 32
Historiography
  and the changing world, 71 MOS 242
  of 19th c music, 70 STGE 75
History of music
  aesthetics, 24 BAS 311, 63 PRA 291, 299
  compared to that of other arts, 56 VIE 653
  and ethnomusicology, 53 BAM 159–212, 61 NEWY
    i, 376, 380
  and musicology, 65 WAR 279
  through ornamentation, 61 NEWY i, 463
  in sound, 50 ROM 55
  sources
    archival for music *c* 1400, 68 LIÈ 241
    for later music, 25 LEIP 51
    oral traditions and writing, 53 BAM 159
  teaching
    at schools and colleges, 03 ROM 11, 09 VIE 306,
      381
    at university, 25 BRUG 223
Hoffmann, Ernst Theodor Amadeus
  and Beethoven, 27 VIE 128
  conception of musical structure, 70 BON 480
  and music criticism, 58 COL 169
Hofhaimer, Paul (as organ composer), 27 VIE 181
Hölderlin, Johann Christian Friedrich, 70 VIE 253
Holland
  and *Allgemeine musikalische Zeitung*, 52 UTR 293
  and the chamber organ, 38 FRE/B 125
  composers in mid 19th c, 64 AMS 15
  Debussy's influence, 62 PAR 291
  and Diepenbrock, 64 AMS 201
  English music and musicians in 17th c Holland, 52
    UTR 139
  and Janáček, 58 BRN 94

radio music, 54 PAR² 425
see also Netherlands
Homme armé, L', 25 BRUG 229
Homophony in 16th c, 52 UTR 384
Honduras
  ethnomusicology, 63 CART 197
  folk music instruments, 65 BLM 123
Hook, James, and patent voice flute, 59 CAM 239
Hopi, the, as composer and poet, 67 VAN 43
Hora, 28 PRA 140
Horn
  French horn, acoustics, 58 MARS 245, 71 BUD² iii,
    589, 605
  in hunting music, 74 GRA² 197
  natural horn, performing on, 53 BAM 93
  technique c1750, 70 GRA 221
Hostinský, Otakar, conception of music analysis, 74
  KRP 13
Hottentot concept of harmony, 58 COL 154
Hradec, near Opava (Beethoven at), 70 VIE 215
Huastec Indian dances, 47 PRA 335
Huguenot Psalter, 37 PAR³ ii, 510, 52 BERN 52, 62
  BERN 51
  influenced by Humanist teaching and music, 72 PAR
    251
Humanism
  in 16th c France, 06 BAS 170
  influence on Lutheran chorale and Huguenot Psal-
    ter, 72 PAR 251
  musical, 61 NEWY ii, 31
Hummel, Johann Nepomuk, and Beethoven, 70
  BERL² 59
Humour
  comic element in music, 58 COL 181
  in 18th c Italian music theatre, 72 COP 531
  and wit in music, 13 BERL 482
Hungary
  general
    ballads, 63 BUD 325
    Bulgarian and Macedonian songs about Hun-
      garians, 63 BUD 335
    church music, 27 VIE 247, 72 BERN 81
    East-European relations of Hungarian dance
      types, 63 BUD 469
    gramophone, role from Bartók to gramophone
      industry today, 67 ZAG 37
    gypsy music, 30 LIÈ 140, 71 STP 69
    instrumental ensembles, 69 STOC 116
    music criticism, 67 GRA 77
    pop music, music and social influence, 72 VIE² 69
    vernacular church songs, 57 PAR 515
  specific periods
    iconography, depiction of music in the middle
      ages, 72 SÁR 175
    medieval palaeography, 56 VIE 176
    medieval polyphony, 66 BYD 223
    Troubadour melodies in middle ages, 72 SÁR 79
    up to the 16th c, 66 BYD 237
    songs in the 16th and 17th c, 69 BYD 283
    17th to 18th c, 66 BYD 258
    music, 1830–1914, 62 KAS 91
    musicology, 1946–56, 56 VIE 22
    contemporary music influenced by Bartók, 71
      BUD¹ 163
  and individuals
    Bartók, 71 BUD¹ 11, 163
    Beethoven, 70 BON 121
    Debussy, 62 PAR 273
    Haydn, 59 BUD 159
  folk music, 28 PRA 127, 61 BUD 515, 65 BRA 123,

67 RAD 93, 72 SÁR 303, 74 GRA² 291
  folk dance, 28 PRA 172, 73 BAL 142
  iconographical sources of instruments, 73 BAL 86
  instrumental, 73 BAL 115, 75 BRUN 114
  old style of, 72 SÁR 15
  violin and violin players, 71 STP 60
Hunting music, use of horns, 74 GRA² 197
Hus, Jan, tradition in medieval music, 75 BYD 105
Hussite song research, 58 COL 150
Hymns
  evolution of Czech Baroque, 72 BYD 127
  late medieval polyphonic, 50 LÜN¹ 75
  North American Indian, 56 PHIL 324
  Sullivan hymn tunes, 70 LAW 175
  see also Church music

Iban music, 69 KUA 320
Ibiza folk music instruments, 54 PAL 133
Iceland peasant organum, 58 COL 132
Iconography
  general, 06 BAS 230, 21 PAR 731, 59 CAM 253–61,
    61 NEWY i, 109
  in Boccaccio works, 69 CER 105
  book decorations as sources, 59 CAM 256
  documentation of, 71 KAS 109, 115, 123, 131
  in English churches, 59 CAM 253
  Heavenly chorus in Rynkeby, 73 BAL 70
  Hungarian medieval, 72 SÁR 175
  Karlštejn frescoes, 75 BYD 79
  Repertorium of iconography, 71 KAS 109
  sources for 16th c performing practice of
    chamber music, 71 BRN 37
  Stimmer's women musicians, 59 CAM 261
  instruments, 11 LON 334
    bagpipe in West-European painting and sculp-
      ture, 73 BAL 63
    in Dalmatian and Istrian art, 70 BON 474
    in Flemish art of 15th and 16th c, 54 ARR 197
    folk music instruments, 73 BAL 49–86
    14th c Intarsien as source, 58 COL 300
    in medieval book paintings, 62 KAS 302, 73 BAL
      51
    in Serbian-Macedonian MSS, 61 OKH ii, 589
    in Sienese 13th c painting, 69 CER 83
    sources, 27 VIE 378, 73 BAL 55, 60
    sources and discrepancies, 72 COP 141
    strange instruments in Renaissance paintings, 55
      ROY 379
    15th to 18th c typographical marks as sources, 68
      LIÈ 353
Ictus in metrical Latin, 50 ROM 192
Iguna folksongs, 28 PRA 159
Ileborg Collection, 62 KAS 109
Impressionism in East and West, 58 COL 302, 68 GRA
  80
Improvisation, 58 COL 287
  in art and folk music, 58 COL 257
  Baroque vocal, 53 BAM 252
  canonic, in 16th and 17th c, 58 COL 68
  figured bass improvisation according to Josef
    Seger, 56 VIE 490
  group improvisation on Javanese gamelan, 66
    MANL 16
  in Indian classical music, 71 VIC 71
  in 18th c keyboard instrumental music, 75 BLA 77
  in the liturgy, 54 VIE 241
  obligatory improvisation of ornaments, 58 COL 55
  on organ, 32 STRS 141
  on organ and lute in Netherlands in 16th and 17th
    c, 58 COL 177

oriental influence on 16th and 17th c improvisation, 58 COL 308
and rhythm, 65 GEN 148
in Schola Cantorum, Rome, 54 PAL 259
18th c solo improvisation in concertos, 75 BLA 80
in 16th c vocal music, 58 COL 195
in Western music, 64 NEWD² 57
in the 18th c, 75 BLA 9
India
general, 61 TOK 1, 5, 64 NEWD² 73
Bharata scales, 50 LÜN¹ 158
church music, 61 COL 287, 304, 75 ROM 97
classical and traditional music, 61 TEH 190, 61 TOK 64, 67, 67 BERL 141, 71 VIC 55, 71, 75 ROM 87
dance and music in medieval period, 64 NEWD¹ 792
dance drama, 64 HAM 126
evolution, 64 NEWD² 16
improvisation in Indian classical music, 71 VIC 71
Jewish song from India, 69 JER 245
listening to Indian music, 64 NEWD² 112
music and industrial civilization, 64 NEWD² 137–92
'Nāda', 49 BAS 55
patronage, 61 TOK 159
rhythm, 64 NEWD² 77
South Indian traditional music, 64 NEWD² 166, 186
structure, 64 NEWD² 66
synaesthesia, 66 LEIP 165
Western music, differences and similarities, 64 NEWD¹ 43–97
Western music in India, 61 TOK 82
India, Sigismondo d'
duets, 71 WAR 239
music for one/two voices, 54 PAL 267
Indonesia
church music, 57 PAR 552, 72 BERN 89
music, 61 TOK 23, 67 BERL 94
Industrial music
and creative art, 61 TOK 178, 181
and folk music, 71 HIN 119
in Japan, 65 LIÈ i, M56
and taste, 74 ZAG v, 139
and traditional music, 64 NEWD² 137–92
Information theory
in analysis of structure, 64 SAL ii, 261
in comparative music studies, 65 BERL² 124
in Marxist music aesthetics, 65 BERL¹ 402
in problems of hearing, 56 HAM 91
in psychology of sound, 62 KAS 279
Ingegneri, Marc Antonio (writings), 71 WAR 27
In nomine sources, 54 PAR¹ 85
Inspiration
musical, 09 VIE 402
psychology, 32 COP 7, 37 PAR² 285, 293
rhapsody as source of inspiration in 19th and 20th c music, 72 COP 561
Instrumental music, *see* Index of Titles, Series and Sponsors
analysis of, 25 LEIP 428,429
Baroque instrumental music, relation with opera and oratorio, 64 SAL ii, 212
early instrumental music, research, 06 BAS 195
English instrumental repertory, 1550–85, 54 PAR¹ 91
ensembles in various countries, 69 STOC 116–73
evolution of German instrumental music in 17th c, 69 BYD 127
national style in Polish instrumental music of Renaissance, 54 PAR¹ 149
national traits in European instrumental styles, 53 BAM 259

in Renaissance, *54 PAR¹*
style in European instrumental music, 53 BAM 219–66
style in primitive instrumental music, 53 BAM 212
traits in 18th c Bel canto, 53 BAM 256
and vocal music in 17th c, 66 LEIP 221
Instruments
general, 06 BAS 217–42, 11 LON 313–54 *see also* Index of Titles, Series and Sponsors
Byzantine, 61 OKH ii, 589, 64 BRA 125
chromatic, 00 PAR¹ 31
documentation of, 67 BRN¹ 159, 71 KAS 56–93
duration of tone, 71 BUD² iii, 641
evolution and invention, 37 FLOR 283, 324, 64 NEWD² 28
historical and systematic aspects, 69 STOC 184
historical and anthropological research, 72 COP 131–52
iconographical sources, 06 BAS 230, 11 LON 334, 27 VIE 378, 54 ARR 197, 55 ROY 379, 58 COL 300, 61 OKH ii, 589, 69 CER 83, 70 BON 474, 72 COP 141, 73 BAL 55
obselete, 23 BRUS 371
organology, 25 LEIP 78, 98, 53 BAM 57–96, 63 MTA 25
photographing for scientific purposes, 62 KAS 309
physiological, 72 COP 146
research into non-stationary sound, 69 STOC 97
restoration, *see* Restoration
specific periods
early, 06 BAS 234, 58 COL 66, 67 BRN² 34
Poland early medieval, 60 WAR¹ 551;
sacred and secular meaning of medieval, 70 BON 564
Slavonic medieval, 64 BRA 139;
European 9th c to 11th c, 64 SAL ii, 176
source for 13th c, 75 BRUN 91
Spain 13th c, 11 LON 332
14th c of Italian Ars nova, 59 CER 40
of musique figuré in 15th to 18th c, 68 LIÈ 353
Italian in figured bass period, 58 COL 76
evaluation of in 18th c, 71 BRN 73
in 18th c German dictionaries, 58 COL 207
collections, 59 CAM 131
aims, 69 NUR 90, 98
Antwerp, 59 CAM 128, 70 ANT 44
Baroque, early, 69 NUR 6
Berlin musical instrument museum, 70 ANT 53
contents of, 66 LEIP 434
display in catalogues, 69 NUR 68
Edinburgh, Russell Collection, 69 NUR 117, 70 ANT 35
ethnological, 65 DIJ 207
historical approach, 69 NUR 48
importance to universities, 11 LON 341
Naples, 69 NUR 64
nineteenth c, 69 NUR 80
Nuremberg, Germanisches Museum, 69 NUR 32, 70 ANT 63
Österreiches Museum für Volkskunde, 71 STP 124
Paris, Conservatoire, 65 DIJ 209, 69 NUR 113, 70 ANT 77
Musée des arts et traditions populaires, 70 BERL 72
performance, 69 NUR 55
planning, 69 NUR 19, 64, 90
Prague, 70 ANT 39
as preservation of traditional forms of music, 61 TEH 63
problems, 53 BAM 82

restoration, 69 NUR 103, 113, 117, *70 ANT*
Rome, 69 NUR 64
Vienna, Kunsthistorisches Museum, 59 CAM 244, 70 ANT 49
violin fittings, Karl Schreinzer collection, 59 CAM 251
manufacture
  Baillon, Pierre, 59 CAM 196
  Engramelle brothers, 56 FLOR 149
  in France in 19th c, 11 ROM 151
  in Italy, 21 TUR 217, 226, 230
  as popular art, 34 TRT 350
  professional prospects, 62 KAS 323
  Tuerlinckx family, 13 GHE 311
electro-acoustical instruments and devices, 53 NET 212, 239; 67 PAR 7, 18
  and acoustical research, 50 LÜN¹ 233
  boosting in concert hall by electronic means, 53 NET 253
  chords, 53 NET 249
  in composition, 53 NET 256, 55 ARR 183
    electronic instruments, use of, 53 NET 239, 71 BUD² iii, 577
    and the liturgy, 51 OCH 155, 54 VIE 230, 65 MTS 223–6
  electronic organs, 57 PAR 380, 389–412
  electronic tuners, 53 NET 229
  pipe organ, synthesis of, 58 MARS 145
  pitch, 53 NET 220
  recording level, 53 NET 241
  soundbox in string instruments, 53 NET 244
  sound production compared with mechanical, 53 NET 218
  timbre, 53 NET 226, 241, 256, 259
  tone quality, 53 NET 224, 237, 58 MARS 119
  tuning, 53 NET 220, 229, 233
wind, *74 GRA²*
  and the mouth cavity, 62 COP i, P51
  museums, 74 GRA² 175
  in Styria to end of 18th c, 74 GRA² 61
  wind orchestra, 74 GRA² 9
  see also Wind music
brass
  arrangements of Liszt's works, 75 EIS 179
  combination of sound and speech in brass instruments, 72 COP 715
  evaluation of dynamics, change of tone colour, 72 COP 351
  omnitonic with 6 pistons, 11 LON 314
  orchestral use in Haydn's time, 70 GRA 202
  research, 74 GRA² 217
  in teaching, 74 GRA² 301
  tuning problems, 71 BUD² iii, 573
string
  acoustics, of bowing, 68 TOK¹ vi, 9, 13
    of string vibration, 71 BUD² iii, 557, 561, 565, 581, 601
  change between Classical and Baroque, 70 GRA 126
  composition of Baroque chamber orchestra, 71 BRN 49
  depicted in medieval book illustrations, 62 KAS 302
  directional effect, 67 PAR 36
  early Northern, 09 VIE 252
  electro-acoustical studies, 53 NET 244, 67 PAR 18
  history of string quartets, 72 GRA 80
  interpretation of French 17th and 18th c music, 69 PAR 121
  of the Malinké (West Africa), 68 TOK² 348

manufacture, 21 TUR 226, 74 LON 342
origins, 06 BAS 225
performance of 18th c compositions, 67 BRN² 92
Schubert's use of, 28 VIE 131
keyboard
  acoustics of, 66 LEIP 416
  Bach's writing for, 62 KAS 170
  conservation, 71 GRA 119
  display, 71 GRA 101
  early music, research, 06 BAS 200
  Elizabethan, 54 PAR¹ 241
  English music, sources of, 54 PAR¹ 225
  in figured bass, 53 BAM 149
  French *c* 1650, 67 LJU 134
  French 17th to 18th c, 69 PAR 121, 155–247
  historical, manufacture of, 71 GRA 47
  historical temperatures and tuning, 71 GRA 57
  improvisation on 18th c, 75 BLA 77
  Italian inventions for, 11 LON 324
  mechanism, 71 GRA 53
  music for 17th c German, 63 KIE 63
  music in first half of 17th c, 54 PAR¹ 269
  music of Bach's time, 50 LEIP 405
  performing practice of mid 18th c, 74 BLA 22
  principles of editing early music, 54 PAR¹ 287
  reconstructing old, 53 BAM 85
  restoration of stringed, *71 GRA*
  Vienna sound ideal *c*1840, 71 GRA 105
  and young Haydn, 70 GRA 237
folk music, *67 BRN¹, 69 STOC, 73 BAL, 75 BRUN,* 64 MOS 383–449, 71 HIN 130–56
  acoustical research, 69 STOC 24, 47, 53
  anthropological research, 72 COP 131–52
  archeological research, 72 COP 131, 149, 73 BAL 88
  historical and systematic aspects, 69 STOC 184, 73 BAL 10–45
  iconographical sources, 73 BAL 49–86
  international research, 69 STOC 11
  nomenclature, 59 CAM 204
  sound documentation, 67 BRN¹ 159
  sources for research, 73 BAL 10
  typology, 67 BRN¹ 11, 23
  and work, 65 MARB 331
  Africa, 38 COP 268, 72 COP 135, 137
    Basuto, 52 UTR 263
    names in Sudanic languages, 48 BRUS 103
    Tunisia, 60 PAR² 113
  Asia
    Brunei, 69 KUA 298
    China, 66 MANL 185
    Japan, 28 PRA 130
    Nang Shek, 69 KUA 216
    Philippine, 66 MANL 24, 69 KUA 246
    Sabah, 69 KUA 327
    South East Asia, *69 KUA*
    Wayang Kulit, 69 KUA 290
  America
    Brazil, 63 CART 203
    continent, 03 ROM 117
    Honduras, 65 BLM 123
    Latin, 72 COP 138
    prehispanic, 52 CAM 54, 62 MEX 369
  Europe
    Albania, 56 VIE 612
    Arab-Spanish glossary, 73 BAL 94
    Bavaria, 71 HIN 130, 155
    Bulgaria, 67 BRN¹ 142
    Carpathian, 75 BRUN 131

Catalan, 54 PAL 115
Celtic, 73 BAL 98
France, 37 PAR⁴ 377
German, 75 BRUN 106
Ibiza, 54 PAL 133
Italy, 58 WÉG 75
Romania, 27 VIE 340, 67 BRN¹ 176, 75 BRUN 121
Slavonic, 64 GRA² 34
Slovakia, 70 TRČ 99–115
South-East Europe, 64 GRA² 50, 66 GRA 106
Swiss, 75 BRUN 33
Turkey, 73 ANK 178
Valencia, 63 STT 337
Oceania, 38 COP 268
see also individual instruments
Intabulation
and Czech community song of the 16th c, 69 BRN 63
of Josquin's motets, 71 NEWY 475
Intermezzo, Intermedio
Florentine, 55 ROY 133, 145, 70 MTA 25
'George Dandin', 70 MTA 63
Neapolitan, 70 BON 183
and opera, 72 TOU 267
International influences in music, 21 PAR 735
Internationalism in music, 09 VIE 56, 11 LON 76, 24 BAS 36
Interpretation
aesthetics, 37 PAR³ ii, 254, 256, 60 ATH 555
and changes in musical hearing, 66 LEIP 487
jazz interpretation, 68 UPP 827
Jungian interpretation, 68 UPP 825
of music, 33 FLOR 250–68
of musical sources, 71 STGA 148
and records, 67 ZAG 30
Sievers's theories, 24 BAS 110
see also Performing practice
Intervals
acoustical study, 66 LEIP 477
dissonance, 62 KAS 272
in Eskimo music, 67 VAN 54
optimal sizes, 70 BON 397
perception of, 64 AMS 901, 71 BUD² iii, 617, 685
quarter-tone, *see* Quarter tone
tritone, 70 BON 388
structural role of 4ths, 5ths and 8ves, 60 PAR¹ 103–49
4ths, threnody implications in mensural music, 24 BAS 231
5ths
circle of, in Mozart's works, 56 VIE 640
scales from cycle of 5ths, 60 PAR¹ 161, 173
parallel 5ths in M.-A. Charpentier, 70 BON 512
1/5 tones, 52 UTR 191, 58 MARS 29
Intonation
in contemporary music, 57 CAM/M 70
'false' in folk music, 54 WÉG 145
hearing intonation in polyphony, 66 LEIP 529
limits of, and harmony, 71 VIC 29
measuring, 30 BON 49
research in unaccompanied single part singing, 66 LEIP 424
theory *see* Aesthetics
Introit, collection in Finnish (1605), 30 LIÈ 132
trope repertory at Revers, 75 ESP 97
Intuition, musical, 11 BOL 513
Iran
rhythms, 58 COL 61
tesnifs, 64 MOS 340
traditional music, 67 BERL 150

Iraq, rhythm of traditional music, 32 CAIR 516
Ireland
folk music in *Midas*, 72 COP 623
folk violin, and violin music, 71 STP 81
influence on Belgian music, 25 BRUG 228
musical bibliography, 11 LON 359
Iroquois music, 49 NEWY¹ 123, 49 NEWY² 109, 139, 58 WAS 173
Isaac, Heinrich, 62 KAS 112
Choralis Constantinus, 62 KAS 114
Isidor of Seville
meaning of 'musicus' and 'cantor', 49 BAS 134
Isorhythmic motet, 55 WÉG 139
Israel
and the composer, 74 JER 43
folksong in Salonika, 54 PAL 57
music, 56 VIE 148, 61 TEH 240, 70 BON 441
new folk music, 54 PAL 153, 60 PAR² 109
radio music, 54 PAR² 419
Sephardic mode, 61 JER 369
and Toscanini, 67 FLOR 285
traditional music, 67 BERL 177
see also Jewish music
Istria, instruments in medieval art, 70 BON 474
Italy
general
Austro-Italian schools of composition, 64 SAL ii, 226
catalogues of manuscripts as basis for critical edition, 03 ROM 7
difference between German and Italian singing, 38 FRA 161
museums of Italian opera, 03 ROM 17, 139
oral and written traditions, 69 CER 431
Polish manuscripts in Italy, necessity for catalogue of 69 PARM 223
and *RISM*, 62 STOC 28
music abroad
Austrian court, musicians at, 38 FLOR 299
English madrigal, influence on, 53 PAR 129
German music, influence on, 24 NAP 110
at Jagiellon court, 70 BOL 243, 71 WAR 71
17th c Poland, song in, 71 WAR 263
Wawel Rorantists, 71 WAR 203
and individuals
Chopin, 70 VEN 333
Ciconia, 54 PAL 223
Diderot and Rousseau, 75 SIE 45
Janáček, 65 BRN 86
Mozart, 74 ROM, *see also* 18th c Italy
Wagner, 69 ROM 200
forms/genres
ballet de cour, 55 ROY 221
band music, 03 ROM 51
cacce, 69 CER 67
Gregorian chant repertory in Northern Italy, 54 VIE 142
Italo-Albanian liturgical chant, 50 ROM 129
Italo-Greek church songs, 03 ROM 107
madrigal, 52 UTR 166
and poetry, 70 MTA 31
passacaglia, earliest Italian form of, 54 PAL 275
play with music and ballet, 70 MTA 59
polyphony, 71 WAR 277
prosody, 56 HAM 85
sequence in archaic Italy unknown, 54 PAL 289
folk music, ethnomusicology, 21 TUR 43, 29 FLOR, 31 UDIN, 34 TRT, 40 VEN, 48 TUR, 56 CAG, 57 CHIE, 58 COL 198, 73 ROM²
analysis, 73 ROM² 115, 141, 151, 207

anthropological research, 73 ROM² 115
documentation, 73 ROM² 77, 251, 257, 265, 271, 277
folk dance origins, 54 PAL 183
folksong revival, 73 ROM² 121
institutes, 73 ROM² 41, 257, 265, 271, 277
instruments, distribution, 58 WÉG 75
instrument making as popular art, 34 TRT 350
Italo-Albanian folk music, 40 VEN 410
oral tradition in medieval music, 73 ROM² 159, 167
philology, 73 ROM² 51
political songs, 73 ROM² 237
popular songs of Risorgimento, 34 TRT 368
research, methods in, 34 TRT 76
and society, 73 ROM² 97
verbal texts, 73 ROM² 151, 207
video tape, use of, 73 ROM² 251
trecento/14th c, *59 CER, 69 CER*
chronology, 55 WÉG 93
of manuscripts, 55 WÉG 110
composition for three parts, 59 CER 18
dances and instruments in Sienese painting, 69 CER 83
and Eastern Europe, 69 PARM 29
Florentine composers, 69 CER 247
forces in vocal music, 55 WÉG 232
harmony, 59 CER 32
influence on Poland, 69 CER 465
instruments, 59 CER 40
integrative devices, 69 CER 411
literary and musical forms, 55 WÉG 149
literature and music, 55 WÉG 239, 69 CER 485
monodic element in polyphony, 55 WÉG 217
motets, 69 CER 215
musical impressionism, 59 CER 57
music and society, 69 CER 11
notation and tactus, 69 CER 176
two-part songs, 69 CER 203
15th c
and Eastern Europe, 69 PARM 29
evolution of lute 15th to 16th c, 57 NEU/S 19
music history 1400–1430, 67 LJU 43
performing practice of sacred music, 1475–1525, 71 NEWY 601
16th c
Italian music in Poland, Renaissance to Baroque, *69 PARM, 70 BOL*
manuscripts for lute, 57 NEU/S 43
Polish dances in Italy/Italian dances in Poland, 69 PARM 181
polyphonic lauda, 30 LIÈ 155
secular vocal music, 61 CAM/M 51
17th c
and Carissimi, 00 PAR⁶ 75
harpsichord sonata in 1st half of 17th c, 11 LON 158
instrumental music, 72 COP 288, 478
instruments in figured bass period, 58 COL 76
Italian music and French music 1704–6, 67 LEIP 238
musicians in Paris under Mazarin, 00 PAR² 191
musicians in Poland, 69 PARM 133–81
opera, staging, 68 VEN 109, 72 COP 415
opera typology 1600–1750, 69 WAR 69
oratorio, 72 COP 657
Polish and Italian Baroque, *69 PARM, 70 BOL*
Polish dances in Italy/Italian dances in Poland, 69 PARM 181
vocal colour in 17th c singing, 72 COP 385

18th c
church music, 70 BON 406
comic intermezzos (in Poland), 70 VEN 175
culture and cult of Mozart, 56 VIE 128
culture in Vienna, *73 SIE*
early music theatre, 72 COP 531
influence of Italian musicians on Mozart, 24 BAS 336
opera and young Mozart, 56 PAR 125
opera tradition and Gluck, 73 SIE 275
quartet and Mozart, 74 ROM 271
reception of Mozart, 74 ROM 19–96
reform of 18th c opera, 09 VIE 196
taste, Mozart and, 56 PAR 117
violin concertos, technique, 56 VIE 765
violin technique, 70 GRA 114
19th c
instrumental music and Verdi, 72 MIL 285
relation of music to libretto in opera seria, 70 BON 162
revival of instrumental music, 66 VEN 126
20th c
authors' rights, 21 TUR 198
church music, 21 TUR 209
criticism, 21 TUR 139, 67 GRA 57
and Darmstadt, 63 MER 679
economic organization, 21 TUR 114
education, 21 TUR 58, 91, 96, 178
influence of Debussy, 62 PAR 289
institutions, 21 TUR 78
instrument making, 21 TUR 226, 230
musical life today, *21 TUR*
national and international language, 63 MER 409
opera, 21 TUR 184, 204, 33 FLOR 125
piano manufacture, 21 TUR 217
publishing, 21 TUR 49
recent experiments, 63 MER 679
scene design, 21 TUR 204
singing, 21 TUR 211
social security, 21 TUR 126
Viennese influence, 63 MER 447
writing new political songs, 64 BERL 337
see also Libraries and manuscripts
Ivanovich, Cristoforo, *Minerva al tavolino*, 72 VEN 7
Ives, Charles, *74 NEWY¹*
in American culture, 74 NEWY¹ 4, 16, 29
and atonality, 74 NEWY¹ 159
Chromâtimelôdtune, 74 NEWY¹ 87
conducting problems in his music, 74 NEWY¹ 113
editing problems, 74 NEWY¹ 65
and music histories, 70 BON 299
performing practice in his violin sonatas, 74 NEWY¹ 127
Second String Quartet, 70 BON 303
and spatial form, 74 NEWY¹ 145
structural importance of borrowed music in his works, 72 COP 437
today, 74 NEWY¹ 209
viewed by composers, 74 NEWY¹ 187
viewed from abroad, 74 NEWY¹ 45

Jacapone da Todi, laude, 57 TOD 105, 133
Jagiellon
Italian music at court, 70 BOL 243, 71 WAR 71
polyphony at court, 27 VIE 164
Janáček, Leoš
general, *58 BRN, 65 BRN, 68 BRN*, 70 BRN 397
Brod translations of, 65 BRN 105, 109
contribution to harmony teaching, 70 BRN 435
as critic, 58 BRN 377
edition problems, 65 BRN 94

interpretation, 58 BRN 189, 65 BRN 141, 145
nature impressionism, 58 BRN 281, 68 BRN 81
and new music, 70 BON 458
performed by Bakala, 58 BRN 250
relation to Czech culture, 58 BRN 37, 155, 198
and the theatre, 58 BRN 244
theoretical views, 58 BRN 352
and places
Bulgaria, 58 BRN 75
Croatia, 68 BRN 227
Germany, 68 BRN 263
Holland, 58 BRN 94
Italy, 65 BRN 86
Ljubljana, 65 BRN 80
Poland, 58 BRN 226, 60 WAR¹ 618
Romania, 66 BRN 207
Russia, 65 BRN 72
Slovakia, 65 BRN 68
Yugoslavia, 68 BRN 271, 277
and others
Bartók, 58 BRN 330, 61 BUD 501
Beethoven, 70 BERL² 125
Berg, 68 BRN 213
Chopin, 60 WAR¹ 383
contemporaries, 68 BRN 85
Enesco, 58 BRN 330
Kodály, 58 BRN 330
Liszt, 61 BUD 295
Martinů, 65 BRN 60, 65, 66 BRN 115
Messiaen, 68 BRN 221
Musorgsky, 58 BRN 205
Orff, 58 BRN 236
Prokofiev, 68 BRN 219
Schoenberg, 58 BRN 236
Stravinsky, 58 BRN 240
Verismo composers, 68 BRN 67
2nd Vienna School, 65 BRN 55
style, 58 BRN 117, 68 BRN 57
creative process, 58 BRN 98
folk element in, 70 BON 603
harmony and key, 58 BRN 121, 58 COL 136
melody, 58 BRN 275
modal elements, 65 BRN 32, 68 BRN 99, 201
modernism, 58 BRN 123, 169
monothematicism, 58 BRN 129
orchestration, 65 BRN 97, 102
relation of word and music, 58 BRN 298
speech melodies, 58 BRN 77, 217, 267, 281, 65
BRN 43, 46, 49, 66 LEIP 339, 69 BRN 171, 175
thematic development, 58 BRN 275, 65 BRN 28
operas, general, 65 BRN 16, 37, 65, 88
critical realism, 58 BRN 162
and folk music, 65 BRN 60
interpretation, 65 BRN 145, 148
and modern theatre, 68 BRN 131
singing, 58 BRN 124, 294
speech melody, significance for, 58 BRN 77
staging, 58 BRN 81, 381, 65 BRN 145, 148, 152
structure, 68 BRN 141
style, 58 BRN 140
Janáček's views on, 58 BRN 140
operas, specific
Fate, 58 BRN 289
Jenůfa, 58 BRN 317, 65 BRN 23, 131, 67 LJU 241,
68 BRN 145
Kát'a Kabanová, 58 BRN 392, 65 BRN 125, 68
BRN 159
Liška Bystrouška, 65 BRN 152
Mr Brouček's Excursions, 58 BRN 132, 65 BRN
114, 117, 123, 68 BRN 153

other works, general,
choral works, 58 BRN 254
orchestral works, 58 BRN 323
string quartets, 68 BRN 181, 71 BRN 177
other works, specific
Concertino, 71 BRN 423
Glagolitic Mass, 58 BRN 129
Jealousy overture, 65 BRN 131
Sinfonietta, 68 BRN 171
2nd String Quartet, 58 BRN 315
folk music, 68 BRN 235
analysis of folksong, 74 KRP 43
and Czech folksong, 58 BRN 217
folk theory, 58 BRN 361
Moravian music, research on, 68 BRN 243
Moravské národni písně, marginalia, 68 BRN 251
Jannequin, Clément, psalms, 30 LIE 86
Janssens, Jean François Joseph
letters from Boieldieu, Cherubini, Lesueur, 13 GHE
339
Japan
changing social values, 61 TOK 18
church music, 61 COL 247
composer today, 61 TOK 91, 99
concerts, 61 TOK 36
court music, 50 LÜN¹ 168, 61 TOK 9, 66 MANL
107
folk dance, 28 PRA 185, 50 LÜN¹ 170
folk music, 28 PRA 129, 194, 66 LEIP 547
gong-bells, 35 BRUS² 990
guilds of blind musicians, 56 HAM 107
harmonizing Japanese melodies, 06 BAS 83
industrial music, 65 LIÈ i, M56
influences of Japanese music, 71 FLOR 167
instruments, 28 PRA 130
melismatic song forms, 50 LÜN¹ 170
music, 56 VIE 440, 61 TOK 15
music and technology, 70 STOC 173
music theatre, 59 ROY 133, 163, *71 ANN*
musicology, 58 COL 201, 70 BON 524
observing European music, 71 FLOR 95
rice-planting song, comparisons, 68 TOK² 340
Sino-Japanese music traditions today, 61 TOK 54
sources of Japanese music, 58 COL 123
traditional music, 67 BERL 74
and Verdi, 69 VER 560
Western music in Japan, 61 TOK 77
Western style in 20th c music, 61 TEH 184
Jaques-Dalcroze, Émile 21 TUR 96, 26 GEN 92, 179
Jaqui Psalter, 49 BAS 115
Jarnović, Ivan-Marie, 56 VIE 134
Jarzębski, Adam, transcription of Italian works, 70
BOL 67
Jassy choral works, 67 BUC 86
Java
evolution of tone system, 39 NEWY 241
folk dance, 28 PRA 181
gamelan, 66 MANL 16
rebab, 59 CAM 220
20th c music, 28 PRA 107
Jazz
choreology, 56 PHIL 152
interpretation, 68 UPP 825
in 20th c musical life, 62 KAS 260
in musicological dictionaries, 72 COP 457
new wave, 71 FLOR 173
research, 70 BON 464
Jena Symphony, 11 LON 158, 58 COL 279
Jesuit, old library in Cologne, 52 UTR 252
Jesu Christe rex superne, 60 WAR¹ 510

Jeunesses musicales, 47 PRA 28
Jewish music, *61 JER, 65 JER, 69 JER*
and Bloch, 54 PAL 295
Canon of Avicenna, 69 JER 292
cantillation
Ashkenazi, 61 JER 366
Karaites, 69 JER 278
oriental, 61 JER 366, 371
Samaritan, 65 JER 153
fragment of Obadiah the Norman, 65 JER 209
Halleluia and Jubilus in Jewish chant, 61 JER 371
liturgy, 61 TEH 146
musical ethos, 65 JER 207
ne'ima, definition, 69 JER 282
reciting scriptures, 69 JER 290
research, 65 JER 157
science of music in 13th and 14th c 69 JER 283
Sephardic legacy from Spain, 69 JER 237
song from Cochin, India, 69 JER 245
style analysis of Jewish song, 69 JER 300
Tora readings to sephardic mode, 61 JER 369
Vilna Jewry, music of, 61 JER 360
Western and non-Western traditions, 61 JER 365
see also Israel
Jew's harp, 27 VIE 373, 75 BRUN 33
Jibaro music, 63 CART 131
Jihlava, fiddle music of, 09 VIE 227
Johannes de Quadris, Lamentations, 69 CER 281
John XXII, Pope 'Constitutio docta Sanctorum Patrum'
and music of his period, 59 CER 9
Johns, Paul Emile, 72 COP 246
Johnson, Ben, masques, 55 ROY 285
Jolivet, André, 71 FLOR 83
Jommelli, Niccolò (and Mozart), 74 ROM 138
Jongleur, 00 PAR⁶ 57
legend, 00 PAR² 155
Joseph the Hymnographer, canons at Grottaferrata, 55
IST 286
Josquin Desprez
general, *71 NEWY*
analysis by computer, 65 NEWY 19, 71 NEWY
297
authenticity and chronology, 52 UTR 303, 71
NEWY 297, 345
benefices, 71 NEWY 76
Burney and Ambros as editors, 71 NEWY 145
discography, 71 NEWY 633
editing problems, 71 NEWY 721
research, current state of, 61 NEWY i,53
and A. Sforza, 68 MIL 17, 71 NEWY 31
and places
Collegiale de Saint-Quentin, 21 PAR 807
Ferrara, 71 NEWY 103
French court, 71 NEWY 181
Netherlands court, 71 NEWY 181
source studies, general, 71 NEWY 285
Bohemia, 71 NEWY 279
France, 71 NEWY 181
Germany, 71 NEWY 261
Netherlands, 71 NEWY 181
Piacenza, 71 NEWY 247
Spain and Portugal, 71 NEWY 217
style
cadence, 52 UTR 86
dissonance, 71 NEWY 334
La Rue, compared with, 71 NEWY 369
plainchant, use of, 71 NEWY 360, 525
tonal tendencies in harmony, 71 NEWY 317
wide-spanned melodic lines, 71 NEWY 309

works, general
chansons, 71 NEWY 401, 421, 455
frottole, 71 NEWY 446
hymns, 71 NEWY 525
Italian texts, compositions on, 71 NEWY 446
masses, 52 UTR 79, 65 NEWY 19, 71 NEWY 369
motets, 24 BAS 375, 71 NEWY 261, 345, 475, 525
psalm motets, 56 VIE 452
works, specific
Illibata dei Virgo, 71 NEWY 545
Magnificat, 71 NEWY 525
Missa de Beata Virgine, 71 NEWY 589
Missa La sol fa re mi, 71 NEWY 564
Ut Phoebi radiis, 71 NEWY 560
performing practice, general, 71 NEWY 601–87
masses, 71 NEWY 619, 687
motets, 71 NEWY 619, 627, 645
sacred music, 71 NEWY 601
secular music, 71 NEWY 663
Jota, 28 PRA 187
Jouy, Etienne de, 51 IES 81
Joyeuse, Duc de, 53 PAR 241
Jubilus in oriental chant, 61 JER 371
Jumentier, Bernard, unpublished works, 53 BAM
279
Jumièges, *54 ROU*
influence, 54 ROU 335, 343
liturgy, 54 ROU 855–977
manuscripts, 54 ROU 855, 901
notation, 54 ROU 913
office, 54 ROU 335, 977
sequences, 54 ROU 937, 943
tropes, 54 ROU 959

Kaa-Ihwua music, 28 NEWY 796
Kabuki stage music, 70 BON 605
Kabyle poetry and African music, 52 VIE iii, 19
Kafka, Franz, 65 BRN 109
Kagura folk music, 28 PRA 194
Kahlert, August (and Beethoven), 60 BON 517
Kaisheim Cistercian organ, (1778), 50 ROM 384
Kandinsky, Wassily (and Schoenberg), 74 BERL 9
Kanne, Friedrich August, 70 BON 383
Kanon, Byzantine, 50 ROM 131
Kant, Immanuel, and his musical circle, 27 VIE
217
Kantor, medieval history of, 66 LEIP 169
Kapr, Jan, *Cvičeni pro Gvdli*, 69 BRN 205
Kapsberger, Giovanni Girolamo
sacred music, 67 SIE 288
villanelle, 70 BOL 23
Karadžić, Vuk, 66 SOF vii, 885, 887
Karaites, cantillation of the, 69 JER 278
Kayser, Johann and Margaretha Susanna, 72 BLA 68
Keglivich, Babette (and Beethoven), 70 BON 526
Keuroghlou, 31 PAR 725
Key
character, characteristics, 30 LIÈ 230, 49 BAS 181
in madrigals by Patricij and Skjavetić, 75 BYD 145
in medieval song, 50 LÜN¹ 62
and mode and species, 49 BAS 133
relationships in early medieval music, 11 LON 114
see also Tonality
Keyboard instruments *see* Instruments: keyboard
Khachaturian, Aram Ilyich, 66 LEIP 362
Kiel, music at University of, 63 KIE 95
Kierkegaard, Søren, on Mozart, 56 VEN 706
Kilpenen, Yrjö, Kanteletar songs, 56 HAM 231
Kiowa Indian music, 49 NEWY¹ 94

Kirckman harpsichord, 71 GRA 69
Kithara, 59 CAM 209
Klosterneuburg, Gregorian MSS at, 54 VIE 124
Koch, Heinrich Christoph, 70 BON 570
Kodály, Zoltán
    and Bartók, 66 VEN 97, 71 BUD¹ 155
    and Janáček, 58 BRN 330
    and Verdi, 66 VEN 97
Kolenda, Koleda, Colinda
    Bartók's collection, 61 BUD 549
    songs in middle ages, 72 SÁR 165
Komitas see Gomidas
Kondakarion notation, 64 BRA 77, 75 BYD 557
Königsberg, music in 17th c, 63 KIE 113
Konjović, Petar, operas, 69 BRN 259
Kontakion
    and Kanon, 50 ROM 131
    music and metrical construction, 61 OKH ii, 563
Korea
    music, 56 VIE 350, 66 MANL 132
    music of Buddhist ceremony, 68 TOK² 345
Koto
    acoustical aspects of string settings, 68 TOK¹ vi, 5
    classical repertory, 67 VAN 68
Koželuh, Leopold, 56 PRA 135, 59 BUD 109
Kozłovsky, Józef, 72 BYD 825
Kraus, Joseph Martin, string quartets, 62 KAS 190
Kraus, *Lulu*, 68 STRS 245
Kremsmünster, Minnelied from, 70 WÜR 68
Krkonoš folksongs, 28 PRA 148
Kuhnau, Johann, *Fundamenta compositionis*, 56 HAM 103
Kujawa folk melody, 74 KRP 36
Kukuzeles, Johannes, 75 BYD 59
Künzig-Werner, ballads about, 72 SÁR 5
Kurpian folk music, 58 COL 283
    and Szymanowski, 62 WAR 274
Kuru Pradesh folksongs, 57 MUN 573
Kuwait folk music, 58 WÉG 137
Kyrial in Poland up to 16th c, 75 BYD 261

Ladislav Sigismund of Poland, 70 BOL 191
Lahm, Baroque organ at, 53 BAM 78
Lalande, Michel de
    place in French church music, 57 PAR 171
    Te Deum, 65 DIJ 162
Ländler
    beat in Upper Austria, 09 VIE 228
    fiddles, 71 STP 161
Language, musical, 11 LON 228, *71 VIC*
    of children, 64 AMS 885
    of China, 71 VIC 37
    and the composer, 48 FLOR 11
    disturbance in hysterical subjects, 05 ROM 476
    meaning of new, 71 MOS 218
    poetical and musical, 69 BRN 45
    and structure, 68 UPP 621
    and tempered scale, 48 FLOR 39
    20th c, *48 FLOR*, 66 LEIP 362
    see also Style; individual composers
Lantins, Hugo and Arnold de, 32 LIÈ 263
Lapland
    pentatonic melodies, 09 VIE 244
    Skolt Lapp songs, 60 PAR² 127
    songs of worship, 50 LÜN¹ 153
La Rue, Pierre de
    dating works, 50 LÜN¹ 80
    masses, 71 NEWY 369
Laski, Jan, correspondence with Glareanus, 60 WAR¹ 638
Lassus, Orlande de

cadence, 70 BON 435
chronology of works, 50 LÜN¹ 82
expression, 70 BON 435
French chansons, 56 VIE 60
Gesamtausgabe, 56 VIE 216
late style, 58 COL 69
little-known volumes, 21 PAR 833
Magnificat settings, 56 HAM 62
parody problem, 61 NEWY i, 214
and teaching of music in 16th and 17th c, 53 BAM 124
transcription for lute of his works, 57 NEU/S 143
Latin
    accent and ictus in metrical Latin, 50 ROM 192
    liturgy, relation to Byzantine, 36 ROM 540
    modes, 00 PAR² 77
    schools, music in 16th c, 62 KAS 133
        music at Protestant in 18th, 73 MAG 100
    school plays, use of national vernacular, 69 BRN 77
    scientific language of music, development of in middle ages, 72 COP 612
Latin America
    influence of Debussy, 62 PAR 233
    folk music and ethnomusicology, 48 BRUS 266, 63 CART, 65 BLM, 67 BERL 199
    instruments, 72 COP 138
    music in college curriculum, 65 BLM 105
    musicology, 70 BON 365
    nationalism among composers, 65 BLM 192
    20th c music, 71 MOS 136
Latvia
    folk music, 64 MOS 226, 325, 73 STOC 44, 53
    music in 17th and 18th c, 72 BYD 701
Lauda
    15th c Italian, 57 TOD 105
    16th c Italian polyphonic, 30 LIÈ 155
    at Todi, 57 TOD 133
Laudes, 56 VIE 457
Laudesi
    Florentine, 69 CER 253
    relations with Florentine composers, 69 CER 247
Laudi Filippine, 54 VIE 184
Laurenzi, Filiberto, *La finta savia*, 72 VEN 173
Lazio folk music, 73 ROM² 237
Lebanon traditional music, 67 BERL 157
Le Bégue, Nicolas, 69 PAR 173, 238
Le Cerf de la Viéville, 66 LEIP 238
Leeuw, Ton de, *Alceste*, 64 HAM 114
Leibl, Carl, 70 BON 408
Leibnitz, Gottfried (and Bach), 75 LEIP 431
Leipzig Gewandhaus and Beethoven, 70 BERL² 141
Léon folksong, 28 PRA 158
Leopold I, opera libretto at his court, 67 NAN 203
Lesage, Théâtre de la Foire, 09 VIE 193
Lessinia folk music, 73 ROM² 223
Lesueur, Jean François, letters, 13 GHE 339
Letters, musicians', 50 LÜN¹ 35, 56 VIE 430
Lexicon musicum latinum, 62 KAS 349–51
Liberal Arts, music in, 56 HAM 46
Liberia, musical traditions, 70 YAO 141
Liberec (and Beethoven), 70 PIE 71
Libraries and Librarianship, *50 LÜN², 51 PAR*, 53 BAM 273–99, 54 PAL 331–69, *55 BRUS*, 59 CAM 25–173, *62 STOC, 65 DIJ, 68 NEWY, 71 STGA, 73 WEIM, 74 JER*
    arrangement of music and books in, 03 ROM 19
    broadcasting, radio music library, 50 LÜN² 15, 51 PAR 65, 55 BRUS 62, 109, 148, 153, 65 DIJ 106, 71 STGA 113
    sound archives, 71 STGA 126
    television music library, 71 STGA 113

building up, 06 BAS 6, 62 STOC 34–49
conservatory, 50 LÜN² 4
collaboration between, 50 LÜN² 57, 51 PAR 56, 54
   PAL 331–69, 55 BRUS 68, 70
folk, 50 LÜN² 24
international aspects, 62 STOC 60–62
non-Western music, 74 JER 32
professional prospects, 62 KAS 323
and the public, 62 STOC 63–70
public, in education, 55 BRUS 37, 140, 62 STOC 63
record, 50 LÜN² 46, 55 BRUS 39, 41, 84, 95, 146, 59
   CAM 99–126, 68 LIÈ 235, 73 WEIM 103
training of music librarian, 55 BRUS 51, 57, 74, 84,
   155, 62 STOC 51–7
un-catalogued sources, 51 PAR 46
university music library, gramophone in, 51 PAR 65
Libraries and manuscripts
Union catalogue of manuscripts, 09 VIE 433
America
   collections, works of Bach successors, 58 COL 110
   records, in public libraries, 51 PAR 71, 55 BRUS
      146
   research libraries, 59 CAM 47
   role of public libraries in music education, 55
      BRUS 140
   Washington, Library of Congress, Verdiana, 66
      VEN 452
   Washington, Moldenhauer Archive, 72 VIE¹ 23
Austria
   Vienna, Österreichische Nationalbibliothek Cod.
      (series nova) 12875 (formerly Fideikom-
      missionbibliothek Cod. 7970), 53 BAM 187
Czechoslovakia
   Prague, Universitni knihovna (Antiphonary of Sed-
      lec, 27 BEL 155
France
   Aix en Provence, Bibliothèque de la maîtrise de la
      cathèdrale, 50 LÜN² 33
   Ivrée, Bibliothèque capitulaire (MS with French and
      Latin poetry), 21 PAR 790
   Montpellier, Faculté de Médecin H 159, 72 COP
      425
   Paris, Biliothèque du Conservatoire, Beethoven
      MSS, 27 VIE 25
   Paris, Bibliothèque nationale
      Boccaccio works, 69 CER 105
      catalogue of early music, 09 VIE 432
      Enesco letters to French musicians, 73 BUC 63
      MS Vm¹, 61 JER 360
   Paris, Silbermann Archives, 30 LIÈ 182
   Strasbourg, Bibliothèque municipale (formerly Bib-
      liothèque de la Ville) MS. 222. c 22, 24 BAS 88
Germany
   Berlin, Arbeiterliedarchiv, 64 BERL 255
   Berlin, Deutsche Staatsbibliothek (formerly
      Preussische Staatsbibliothek; Königliche Bib-
      liothek etc.)
      fate of collection, 50 LÜN² 55
      lute music collection, 09 VIE 212
      music department, 62 STOC 49
      Schubert manuscripts, 28 VIE 147
   Berlin-Tübingen, Staatsbibliothek der Stiftung
      Preussische Kulturbesitz (formerly Preussi-
      scher Staatsbibliothek), Ms germ 8° 190, 52
      UTR 241, 53 BAM 187
   Bonn, Beethoven-Archiv, Beethoven letters, 56
      VIE 673
   Cologne, old Jesuit library, 52 UTR 252
   Darmstadt, Hesse Landesbibliothek, tabla-
      tures, 24 BAS 276
   Deutsches Volksliedarchiv, 65 BRA 17

English libraries in Germany, 50 LÜN² 20
Erlangen, Universitätsbibliothek MS 554, 62 KAS
   109
Heidelberg, Kapellkatalog, Senfl's music, 66 LEIP
   186
Jena, Universitätsbibliothek Chorbuch 34, 58
   COL 97
Munich, Bayerische Staatsbibliothek, music col-
   lection, 62 STOC 34
Munich, Universitätsbibliothek, organ book Cod
   MS 153, 25 LEIP 339
and music publishing, 59 CAM 67
public libraries, medium-size, 59 CAM 79
radio libraries, 55 BRUS 153
Regensburg, MS A.R. 940/41, 54 PAR¹ 127
Great Britain and Ireland
   Dublin, Trinity College (MS for virginal), 54
      PAR¹ 237
   general catalogue of early music in English public
      and private libraries, 11 LON 369
   Glasgow, Mitchell Library, 59 CAM 95
   Liverpool, Public Music Libraries, 59 CAM 60
   London, British Library, 59 CAM 62
      Mozart Bicentenary Exhibition, 56 VIE 305
   Oxford, Bodleian Library, Canonici Misc. 213, 69
      CER 443
   Tenbury, Ouseley Library, 30 LIÈ 112
   Scotland, 59 CAM 88
Italy
   Casale Monferrato, Archivio Capitolare (choir
      books), 72 COP 664
   Faenza, Biblioteca Comunale, Codex 117, 52
      UTR 310, 69 CER 161
   Florence, Biblioteca Medicea Laurenziana Palatino
      87, 58 COL 65, 59 CER 141
   Lucca, Archivio di Stato Ms 184 (Mancini), 55
      WÉG 110
   Modena, Biblioteca estense
      Campori collection, 62 KAS 226
      α M.5. 24 (formerly 568), 66 LEIP 175, 55 WÉG
         110
      MS M 127, 70 BOL 117
   Naples, Biblioteca del Conservatorio di Napoli
      (MSS donated by Maria Carolina), 73 SIE
      585
   Naples, Biblioteca nazionale MS. VI: E. 40, 25
      BRUG 229
   Piacenza, Archivio del duomo: Josquin MSS,
      71 NEWY 247
   Rome, Vatican Codice, 25 BRUG 231
      Archivio musicale Laterense 61, 58 COL 126
   Turin, Biblioteca nazionale
      J.11.9, 59 CER 75
      16th c MSS, 03 ROM 319
   Vicenza, Archivio capitolare (14th c codex), 69
      CER 281
Poland
   Kórnik, Biblioteka Polskiej akademii nauk, 60
      WAR¹ 488
   music libraries 1964–73, 73 WEIM 81
   Poznań, Miejska biblioteka publiczna im. Edwarda
      Raczyńskiego, MS 1361, 60 WAR¹ 588
Scandinavia, 59 CAM 83
   Århus, Statsbiblioteket, 59 CAM 86
   radio libraries, 55 BRUS 109
   Swedish collections of early music, 62 STOC 21
   Uppsala Universitetsbiblioteket, MS 409, 72 COP
      563
Spain
   El Escorial, Biblioteca del Monasterio: Byzantine
      manuscripts, 50 ROM 119

Montserrat, Biblioteca del Monasterio: Netherland manuscripts, 30 LIÈ 198, 50 ROM 319
Toledo, Biblioteca capitolar: polyphonic manuscripts, 52 UTR 276
Switzerland
  manuscript bequests to libraries, 50 LÜN² 41
  St Gall, Stiftsbibliothek: Codex 542, 73 BAL 60
  Zurich, Bibliothek der Allgemeinen Musikgesellschaft, 50 LÜN² 7
  see also Music, miscellaneous
Libretto
  bibliography, 29 ROM iv, 155
  and the composer, 70 BON 151-69
  in Italian opera seria in 19th c (first half), 70 BON 162
  Mannerism in 17th c Venetian librettos, 72 VEN 319
  Meyerbeer's contributions, 70 BON 155
  reconstructions of 18th c operas and intermezzi through their librettos, 67 BRN² 176
  of Rossini operas, 67 LJU 194
  of Rudolstadt cantata cycles, 72 COP 271
  social aspects of opera librettos at the court of Leopold I, 67 NAN 203
  of R. Strauss operas, 70 BON 169
  of Verdi operas, *see* Verdi: librettos
  of 20th c opera, 64 HAM 43-63
Lied
  and aria, 38 FRA 17
  declamation and instrumental symbolism, 38 FRA 27
  Germany polyphonic Lied in 15th c, 58 COL 214
Liedkanon, medieval, 50 LÜN¹ 71
Liège
  dodecaphonic movement, 68 LIÈ 323
  music 10th to 12th c, 09 LIÈ 746
  music 1544-57, 68 LIÈ 293
  music theatre in 18th c, 35 BRUS¹ ii, 212
  organ builders, 11 MAL 885
  research into music, 09 LIÈ 643, 11 MAL 891
Ligatures in Montpellier MS, 52 UTR 146
Light music
  and future audience, 68 NEWY 57
  and the radio, 54 PAR² 559
  in Yugoslavia, 68 SVE 113
  in the 18th c, 72 BYD 415
Ligne, Prince du
  music to his *Colette et Lucas*, 35 BRUS¹ i, 306
Linguistics *see* Theory
Lioghenniti, Song of, 55 IST 284
Lipatti, Dinu, 60 WAR¹ 436
Lippi, Filippino, strange instruments in his paintings, 55 ROY 379
Lipps, Theodor, aesthetics (of rhythm), 06 BAS 87, 09 VIE 345
Lirica, 71 STP 38
Lisa, Gerard de, 25 BRUG 222
Listening *see* Hearing
Liszt, Franz
  general, 61 BUD 27-333, 75 EIS
  church music, plans to reform, 25 LEIP 341
  compositional technique, 75 EIS 125
  concept of art, 75 EIS 105
  early and definitive versions in Neue Liszt-Ausgabe, 75 EIS 47
  new manuscript, 61 BUD 101
  political engagement, 75 EIS 105
  problems of new edition, 75 EIS 73
  as radical democrat, 61 BUD 241
  the Romantic, 23 BRUS 368
  as teacher, 61 BUD 217
  and 20th c music, 61 BUD 277
and places
  Banat, Transylvania, 61 BUD 107
  Bellagio, 75 EIS 155
  Bohemia, unpublished correspondence, 61 BUD 255
  Bratislava, 61 BUD 233
  Bulgaria, 61 BUD 249
  Poland, 75 EIS 53
  Prague, 61 BUD 27
  Russia, 1840s and 1850s, 61 BUD 211
  Styria, 61 BUD 301
  Weimar, works in, 61 BUD 193
and others
  Bartók, 75 EIS 65
  Beethoven, 70 PIE 101
  Brahms and Reményi, 61 BUD 89
  Bruckner, 25 LEIP 340, 75 EIS 225
  Chopin, 60 WAR¹ 319, 341
  Czech teachers, 61 BUD 69
  Handel, 61 BUD 267
  Janáček, 61 BUD 295
  Schumann, 75 EIS 131
  Slovak musicians, correspondence with, 61 BUD 125
  Smetana, 61 BUD 131, 139, 241
  Weimar organist composers, 75 EIS 203
style
  form, 75 EIS 81
  Gregorian chant, use of, 25 LEIP 341
  modality, 75 EIS 97
  motif, use of, 72 COP 647
  national themes, 61 BUD 77
  ornamentation, 61 BUD 49
  piano writing, 60 WAR¹ 341
  programmatic element, 61 BUD 59, 75 EIS 9
  relation between music and literature, 61 NEWY i, 314, 323
  taste and style, 75 EIS 37
  timbre, 61 BUD 37
works, general
  brass arrangements of, 75 EIS 179
  masses, 25 LEIP 340
  opera plans, 75 EIS 215
  piano arrangements, 75 EIS 27
  piano works, 61 BUD 49
  Schubert song transcriptions, 75 EIS 115
  symphonic works, 75 EIS 9
  transcriptions and paraphrases, 61 BUD 227
  unknown works, 61 BUD 311
  violin and piano works, 75 EIS 163
  in 1848, 61 BUD 59
works, specific
  Années de pèlerinage, 75 EIS 137
  Don Carlos, paraphrase of, 69 VER 542
  Faust Symphony, 61 BUD 283, 75 EIS 81
  Hungarian Rhapsodies, 11 LON 210, 62 KAS 210
  Hunnenschlacht, 75 EIS 125
  Schwanengesang, transcription of, 75 EIS 115
  Unstern, 70 BON 544
Litany, history in 17th c, 58 COL 259
Literary sciences, music in, 37 PAR³ ii, 213
Lithuania, folksongs, 60 WAR² 119, 64 MOS 278
Liturgy, liturgical
  general
    cataloguing of texts, 09 VIE 437
    and choir training 65 MTS 169-76
    and church music 66 CHIC
    computer use in listing responses 73 PAR 125, 135
    cult of saints in liturgical medieval music 61 TOD 181

and editions, 65 MTS 212, 75 ESP 193
essence of music, 25 LEIP 343
and folksong, 54 VIE 194–208
improvisation in, 54 VIE 241
instruments, use of, 65 MTS 219–233
and laity, 50 ROM 41
monodic manuscripts, distribution of, 75 ESP 47
music, 61 TOK 47
and organs, 26 FRE/B 92, 27 FRE/S 58, 57 PAR 355–85, 65 MTS 219, 222, 226–33
and teaching, 65 MTS 179–200
drama
  Czech contribution, 70 BRN 27
  Easter plays
    in Bohemia, 70 BRN 47
    Maastricht, 49 BAS 184
    in the Netherlands, 52 UTR 371
    sepulchre music dramas, 69 BIN 121
  medieval, 27 VIE 145, 67 LJU 271
specific types, periods
  Cluny, 58 TOD 83
  Coptic, 50 ROM 100
  East Asia, Australasia, Oceania, indigenous music, 75 ROM 117
  English–Scandinavian, 12th to 13th c, 75 ESP 11
  Jewish, 61 TEH 146
  Jumièges, 54 ROU 855–977
  Latin, research, 75 ESP
  music of Beethoven's day, 70 VIE 61
  movement in second half of 19th c, 62 KAS 236
  organ music to 1600, 68 VEN 171
  oriental traditions, 54 PAL 229, 61 COL 155, 61 TEH 146, 71 FLOR 183
  Petrus liturgy, 64 BRA 23
  16th c practice, and motet style, 66 LEIP 196
  prose in 13th c, 09 VIE 108
  Russian orthodox, 62 BERN 32
  9th c Slav liturgical song origins, East and West rite, 52 UTR 456
  Swedish medieval, 75 ESP 6
  after 2nd Vatican council, 64 GRA[1] 13, 33, 77
  vernacular, adapting to, 65 MTS
    Basque, 65 MTS 151
    in Catalonia, 65 MTS 138, 156
    in France, 65 MTS 144
    in Germany, 65 MTS 141
    vocal polyphony (meaning of in Roman), 54 VIE 154
see also Chant; Office
Ljubljana
  and Beethoven, 70 BON 132
  and Janáček, 65 BRN 80
  and Verdi, 66 VEN 346
Lobwasser Psalter in Denmark, 63 KIE 22
Locke, Matthew, 11 LON 100
Lombardy
  art and architecture in Josquin's time, 71 NEWY 138
  folksongs, 40 VEN 369
  instrumental music in 17th c Poland, 69 PARM 163
  musicians, practice of playing chansons, 54 PAR[1] 305
  orchestra in Mozart's time, 56 VIE 18
London
  Don Carlos on London stage, 69 VER 59
  influence of Italian musicians in London on Mozart, 24 BAS 336
  repertory of children's companies (1600–1610), 67 NAN 729
Lorena Hapsburgs, 73 SIE 571
Lorentz, Johan, in Copenhagen, 58 COL 183
Lorenzani, Paolo, 21 PAR 867

Lorraine
  folk music, 37 PAR[4] 145
  music under King Stanislav, 72 BYD 247
  organs and organists 14th to 18th c, 32 STRS 177
Louis XII, Northern musicians at his court, 54 ARR 63
Louis, Jean, Pseaulmes cinquantes, 52 UTR 193
Louisiana, French church songs, 57 PAR 509
Luba drum signals, 38 GHE 503
Lures, Northern bronze, 62 KAS 298
Lusatian Sorbs, folksongs, 31 PAR 715
Lute
  general, 57 NEU/S
    catalogue of sources, 57 NEU/S 297, 59 CAM 214
    evolution 15th–16th c, 57 NEU/S 19
    international commission, 09 VIE 211
    music, 09 VIE 212, 37 FLOR 292, 57 NEU/S 171, 61 NEWY i, 75
    pitch, 57 NEU/S 171
    size, 57 NEU/S 239
    soprano, 57 NEU/S 231
    tablature, 09 VIE 220, 54 PAR[1] 177, 57 NEU/S 127, 143, 155, 245, 259, 285, 58 COL 329, 70 BON 345, 73 PAR 10
    technique, 57 NEU/S 25, 107
    transcriptions, 09 VIE 220, 57 NEU/S 37, 143, 259, 277, 285, 73 PAR 25
    tutors, 57 NEU/S 77, 93, 121
    and women in France, 23 BRUS 366
  in different countries
    England, 11 LON 331, 54 PAR[1] 197, 57 NEU/S 107, 121, 297
    France, 00 PAR[2] 179, 23 BRUS 366, 30 LIÈ 217, 57 NEU/S 107, 155, 209, 67 LJU 134, 69 PAR 107
    Germany, 25 LEIP 237, 57 NEU/S 245
    Italy, 57 NEU/S 19, 43
    Netherlands, 57 NEU/S 179, 58 COL 177
    Poland, 57 NEU/S 193, 60 WAR[1] 547, 630, 71 WAR 177
Lutoslawski, Witold, String Quartet, 71 BRN 243
Lyre
  Cretan, 75 BRUN 127
  Greek, from Mycenae period, 09 VIE 99

Maastricht
  Easter play, 49 BAS 184
  musical life in 19th c, 68 LIÈ 285
McClure organ, 50 ROM 342
Macedonia
  folksongs, 63 BUD 333
  iconographical sources for instruments, 61 OKH ii, 589, 73 BAL 78
Machaut, Guillaume de
  musica ficta in, 55 WÉG 196
  voices and instruments in music, 53 BAM 245
Mâcon, hymns, 54 ROU 343
Madrigal
  compared with chanson, 61 CAM/M 88
  early (1500–1530), 67 LJU 96
  early and Sebastian Festa, 62 KAS 122
  English in 16th c, 27 VIE 186, 30 LIÈ 33
  English in 17th c, 53 PAR 153
  essence and worth, 58 COL 39
  Gibbons's, 55 PAR 139
  Italian influence on English, 53 PAR 129
  Italian and the Netherlanders, 52 UTR 166
  Italian and poetry, 68 MTA 31
  key and cadence in, by Patricij and Skjavetić, 75 BYD 145
  16th c madrigal spirituale, 68 VEN 217

Marco da Gagliano, style of, 72 COP 675
Monte, 30 LIÈ 102, 70 BRN 145
neomadrigalism, 70 BON 261
plan for thematic catalogue, 06 BAS 194
16th c rhythmic structure, 73 ROM¹ 287
Spanish, 30 LIÈ 225
transition from frottola, 53 PAR 63, 61 CAM/M51
F. Tregian's anthology of, 54 PAR¹ 115
Mardi Gras music, 75 AUS 88
Magdeburg, Telemann tasks, 66 LEIP 251
Maqemates
in Egypt, 32 CAIR 529
in Tunisia, 32 CAIR 583
Mahler, Gustav
bar form in songs, 72 COP 617
Czech music, relation to, 62 KAS 246, 70 BRN 389
and W. Mengelberg, 56 VIE 41
and Zemlinsky, 74 GRA¹ 101
Mainz
and J. Gabler, 51 OCH 78, 82
music history and Mozart, 56 VIE 230
Major
algebraic model of major/minor system, 71 STU 64
in tonality, 00 PAR² 175, 13 BERL 501
Malaysia
and *Ma'yong* music, 69 KUA 336
socio-cultural context, 69 KUA 309
Malines
Dusik in, 11 MAL 735
Frescobaldi in, 11 MAL 733
instrumental makers in 18th and 19th c 13 GHE 311
minstrels and instrumentalists (1311–1790) 11 MAL 507
organ builders, 11 MAL 605
vocal music, performing practice in 15th c, 30 ANT 465
Mallorca, and Chopin, 60 WAR¹ 288
Malta, song duels, 75 AUS 126
Mancini, Giambattista, singing school, 70 GRA 141
Manécanteries, 50 ROM 60
Manelli, Francesco, *La luciata*, 70 BOL 211
Mangon, Johannes, 68 LIÈ 271
Mannerism, *73 ROM¹*
concept of, 71 WAR 11, 79, 73 ROM¹ 13, 37, 75, 85, 131, 313
as cultural epoch, 70 BRN 113
and Czech Renaissance music, 70 BRN 159
drama, 71 WAR 27
in early opera, 70 BRN 171, 71 WAR 123
and Gesualdo, 70 BRN 127, 73 ROM¹ 55
and Monte, 70 BRN 145
periodization, as breakdown of, 70 BRN 121
in relation to Baroque and Renaissance, 57 WÉG 35, 73 ROM¹ 3, 85, 101
sound and colour in its theory and practice, 70 BRN 163
in Venetian 17th c opera librettos, 72 VEN 319
in 16th and 17th c, 70 BRN 101, 127
Mannheim school, 70 BRN 205–71
and contemporary aesthetics, 70 BRN 243
influence on Mozart, 56 PAR 85
preclassical elements, 70 BRN 255
prehistory, 58 COL 82
relation to Czech music, 70 BRN 219
style, 70 BRN 205
Mantua, music in *c* 1500, 61 FLOR 243
sacred music in 16th c, 74 MANT 267
Manuscripts, *see* Libraries and manuscripts
Manzoni, Alessandro
and opera, 73 VEN 127

and Verdi, 72 MIL 274
Maqam, 28 PRA 140, 66 LEIP 535
in Beethoven and Mozart, 70 VIE 267
integration and dastagh, 61 TEH 146
Maque, Jean, 30 LIE 191
Marchettus of Padua, and chromaticism, 69 CER 187
Maremare, 58 SJOS 649
Marenzio, Luca
Ah dolente partita, 68 VEN 361
compared with Monteverdi and Wert, 68 VEN 361
Maria Carolina, manuscripts donated to Naples, 73 SIE 585
Marie Enzerdorf, Webern in, 72 VIE¹ 36
Marieklage, Nibelungmelodies in Trier, 49 BAS 118
Marie-Thérèse of France, music for the death of, 57 WÉG 200
Marini, Biagio, 72 GRA 120
Marschner, Heinrich, recitative, *scena* and melodrama in operas, 70 BON 461
Martinelli, Giovanni, 66 VEN 323; 69 VER 593
Martini, Giovanni Battista, 71 WAR 131
Martinů, Bohuslav, *66 BRN*
Ariadne, 66 BRN 183
development, 66 BRN 19
Greek Passion, 66 BRN 183
and Janáček, 65 BRN 60, 65, 66 BRN 115
Juliette, 66 BRN 173
minute operas, 66 BRN 127
operas, 65 BRN 60, 66 BRN 39, 57, 75, 97, 221
reminiscences of, 66 BRN 25
in Romania, 66 BRN 207
Voice of the Forest, 66 BRN 159
Martyria, 61 OKH ii, 575
Marxist musicology, *63 PRA*, 65 *BERL¹*
Masini, Lorenzo, *L'Antefana*, 69 CER 51
Mason, C., 65 DIJ 196
Masque, 66 MTA 53, 71 VAN 156
form of Jacobean, 70 MTA 35
from masque to English opera, 67 LJU 149
role of music in Ben Johnson's, 55 ROY 285
Mass, masses
a cappella in 17th and 18th c, 57 WÉG 177
Calixtin, 70 BRN 89
Caput and their plainsong, 49 BAS 82
messe unitaire 14th c, 59 CER 97
parody, 49 BAS 179, 50 ROM 315
polyphonic in 14th c, 25 LEIP 218
Pro defunctis, Gregorian chant in, 50 ROM 223
thematic catalogue of 15th to 16th c, plan for, 06 BAS 194
Venetian 16th c, 56 VIE 35
see also individual composers
Mathematics, and music in the middle ages, 72 TOD 133
Mattheson, Johann, and rhetoric, 56 HAM 99
Ma'yong, music of, 69 KUA 336
Mazarin, Louis, and Italian musicians in Paris, 00 PAR² 191
Mazatec music, 63 CART 187
Mazurka
genesis and chronology of rhythm, 60 WAR¹ 624
in Polish music of the 18th c, 60 WAR¹ 538
Meaning *see* Aesthetics
Mechanized music, 33 FLOR 68, 84, 93
see also Film; Radio; Records
Meck, Joseph, or Vivaldi, composer of Concerto P217?, 72 COP 253
Mecklenburg, sources for general history of Beethoven's time, 70 BON 507
Medici, music at court of, intermède 1589, 55 ROY 133, 145

Medici, Francesco di, marriage festivities, 55 ROY 107

Mediņš, Jānis, compositions, 73 STOC 53

Mediterranean
aural and written traditions, 64 SAL ii, 121
dance, 54 PAL 101, 127, 181
early Christian chant, 54 PAL 237
folk music, 40 VEN 106, 54 PAL 37–329
melody, 54 PAL 59
musical homogeneity, 72 MALT 58

Meilhac, Henri, 70 LAW 91

Meistersingers
manuscripts with rhythmic notation of melodies, 11 LON 99
notation of song, 06 BAS 17–35, 09 VIE 84

Melisma
in polyphony, 61 NEWY i, 178
text underlay, 61 NEWY i, 12

Melodrama
Benda's 56 PRA 85
compared with recitative and aria in 2nd half of 18th c, 69 BRN 59
and Gilbert and Sullivan, 70 LAW 1, 7
in Marschner, 70 BON 461

Melody
general
and accent, experimental studies, 13 BERL 476
antiphon melodies, 11 LON 54
Baroque figure compared with classical motif in Beethoven, 70 BON 573
Byzantine chant, 61 OKH i, 135
comparative research in old Netherlands manuscripts, 53 BAM 187
in Chinese music, 66 LEIP 561
concept, relation to human life, 66 LEIP 469
conception, children's, 62 KAS 286
in 18th c German music theory, 62 KAS 362
Gregorian chant, *see* Gregorian chant: specific elements
in Japanese court music, 66 MANL 107
Japanese, 06 BAS 83, 66 MANL 107
Mediterranean, 54 PAL 59
medieval, early, 27 VIE 145
lyric, 61 NEWY i, 3
'night melodies' in Poland, 60 PAR² 97
perception of children, 25 MUN 140
personal melodic style, 25 LEIP 108
and stratigraphy, 58 WÉG 13
teaching, 25 LEIP 190
theory, 24 BAS 334
see also Bach, Beethoven, Chopin, Handel, Janáček, Josquin, Liszt, Musorgsky
folk, 24 BAS 131
Anglo-American folk music (structure in), 39 NEWY 84
Estonian, 64 MOS 334
Finnish, 09 VIE 230
Latvian, 64 MOS 325
Lapp, 09 VIE 244
1 to 2 line melodies in folksong, 67 RAD 53–179
relations of British and American folk tunes, 39 NEWY 122
research, 65 BRA 31
Ukrainian reciting songs, construction in, 09 VIE 276
see also Folk music: classification

Memory
in Coptic music, 58 COL 191
knowledge of musical, 54 WÉG 37

Mendelssohn, Felix, 09 VIE 60

autograph manuscripts, 70 BON 482
Beethoven autograph manuscripts, 70 BON 380
and *Charles Auchester*, 58 COL 188
church music, 62 KAS 207
compositional process, 70 BON 482
and Handel, 59 HAL 215
and Spontini, 51 IES 95
youthful works, 72 COP 495

Mengelberg, Willem and Mahler, 56 VIE 41

Mensural, threnodic, meaning of 4th in music, 24 BAS 231
see also Notation, mensural

Mersenne, Père, letters from to P. Trichet, 00 PAR³ 311

Merula, Tarquinio
and instrumental music in Poland, 69 PARM 163
Satiro e Corsica, 71 WAR 149

Merulo, Claudio
current state of research, 62 KAS 138
double-choir work with figured bass, 49 BAS 154
keyboard tablatures, 72 COP 342

Messiaen, Olivier, and Janáček, 68 BRN 221

Metastasio, Pietro
and Gluck, 73 SIE 299
Le cinesi, 73 SIE 415
L'isola disabilata, 73 SIE 415
pastoral scene in *Olimpiade*, 70 BON 185
reform drama, 50 LÜN¹ 138

Metre
ancient metre in Bulgarian folksongs, 60 WAR² 537
basic questions, 25 LEIP 445, 460
4-beat metre in Greek – Roman system, 25 LEIP 203
5-beat bars in Finnish music, 00 PAR² 241
in Beethoven, 27 VIE 100
in biological rhythm, 70 BON 575
classification of in folk music, 65 BRA 47–81
concept of, 53 BAM 47
of folksongs, 73 BEL 40
H. C. Koch's conception, 70 BON 570
of Lithuanian folksongs, 60 WAR² 119
and musical rhythm in time of Humanism, 61 NEWY i, 66
psychology of, 51 STOC 210
relations between ternary and binary in French 17th c, 65 DIJ 166
and rhythm, 26 GEN 76
of Russian Bylina, 64 BRA 165
of J. V. Stamic, 70 BON 53
in Webern, 72 VIE¹ 52

Metronome
history in France, 00 PAR² 264
regularization, 00 PAR¹ 31, 34, 38

Meyerbeer, Giacomo, and his own librettos, 70 BON 155

Mexico, 72 COP 538
and Beethoven, 70 BON 577
ceremonial dances, 08 VIE 513
20th c folk music, 39 MEX 441
Indian music, 08 VIE 513
radio music, 54 PAR² 446
Verdi and, 66 VEN 375

Miari, Antonio, 57 VEN² 105

Michna, Adam, hymn settings, 69 BRN 81

Mickiewicz, Adam, judgement on Chopin, 60 WAR¹ 659

Middle Ages
Ars musica, 72 TOD 223
Bulgarian music, history of, 66 SOF ii, 1055
Christian pre-1400 research, 65 NEWY 190
Church music in early, 56 VIE 199

dissonance, concept of, 58 COL 87
early and late, 27 VIE 149
editing problems, 49 BAS 109
folk music sources, *72 SÁR*
folksong, 50 LÜN¹ 174
German polyphony, 50 LÜN¹ 68
Greek influence on music, 25 LEIP 206
harmony, 56 VIE 92, 58 COL 143
Liedkanon, 50 LÜN¹ 71
lyrics, 49 BAS 45, 56 VIE 7, 61 NEWY i, 3, 66 OXF²
    118
lyricism, spirituality, 72 TOD 265
melody, 27 VIE 145
music and mathematics, 72 TOD 133
musician in society, 58 COL 354
relation of new music to early, 24 BERL 411
research, 06 BAS 161
song *c*1200, 50 LÜN¹ 62
'symphonia', concept of, 72 COP 541
theory, 70 BERL¹ 15
treatises on organ pipe measurements, 68 THU 18
Middle East, modal music, 61 TEH 222
Mikuli, Carl, and Chopin, 60 WAR¹ 410
Milan
    Conservatory, 09 VIE 374, 381
    Duomo, Cappella musicale, 68 MIL 3–38
    Gregorian chant in, 05 STRS 55
    in 18th c and Mozart, 74 ROM 19
    patrons, 68 MIL 17, 23, 35
    Toscanini in, 67 FLOR 55
Military music, 00 PAR¹ 62, 74 GRA² 273
    raising artistic level, 11 LON 313
Milleville, Barnaba
    in Poland, 70 BOL 153
    works, 70 BOL 153
Minas Gerais, negro work songs, 65 BLM 64
Ming Huang, establishment of schools of secular
    music, 31 LEID 121
Minnesang
    contrafacta in, 66 OXF² 96
    German, 24 BAS 259, 70 WÜR 68, 98, 112
    melodies, 72 SÁR 245
Minor, role of in tonality, 00 PAR² 175
Minstrels
    in Malines (1311–1790) 11 MAL 507
    Russian Skoromoch as, 75 BYD 221
Mirecki, Francesco, 74 BOL 21
Mizlersche Societät der musikalischen Wissenschaft-
    en, 67 MAG ii, 87
Mode, modes, modality
    Arab, 32 CAIR 131
    in Bartók, 71 BUD¹ 169
    Byzantine, 51 PAL 405
        relation to Greek and Roman, 00 PAR² 77
    in Chopin, 60 WAR¹ 122
    chromatic oriental, 00 PAR² 93
    church, 24 BAS 220
    Debussy and 20th c modal movement, 62 PAR 109
    in French music before 1890, 56 VIE 78
    in Greek–Albanian tradition, 09 VIE 83
    origin of, 62 KAS 101
    in folk music, 09 VIE 259
        Anglo-American, 39 NEWY 84
    Gregorian, 37 PAR¹ 79, 140, 49 BAS 72, 50 ROM
        255
    history, 53 BAM 184
    Indian, 50 LÜN¹ 158
    in Janáček, 65 BRN 32, 68 BRN 99, 201
    in Japanese court music, 66 MANL 107
    key and species, 49 BAS 133
    in Liszt, 75 EIS 97

major and minor, opposition of, 25 MUN 240
modal music in Far East, 61 TEH 171
    in Middle East, 61 TEH 222
polymodes, 37 PAR³ ii, 462
theory, 50 LÜN¹ 213
tonal-modal aspects of Cistercian chant, 75 BYD 287
transformation of, to 17th c, 00 PAR² 175
universal modal language, 67 BUC 127
see also Scale; Tone systems
Modern music
    see Twentieth century
Mödling, Webern in, 72 VIE¹ 36
Mohori music, 69 KUA 196
Moldavia, folksongs, 66 SOF vii, 731
Molise, Greek – Albanian folksongs of, 54 PAL 329
Momigny, Jérôme de, view of Mozart and Haydn, 62
    KAS 187
Moniglia, Giovan Andrea, 72 VEN 259
    L'Hipermestra, passage on opera, 70 MTA 115
Moniuszko, Stanisław
    birth of style, 60 WAR¹ 598
    songs, 60 WAR¹ 313
Monk of Salzburg, *Martine Christi famule*, 70 WÜR 98
Monochord, 49 BAS 182
Monody
    accompanied, Italian, 69 BRN 27
    church *c* 1600, 50 ROM 299
    medieval, mensural notation of, 58 COL 56
        Polish, 66 BYD 277
        rhythm of, 52 UTR 377
    performance of, 66 LEIP 208
    in 14th to 15th c polyphony, 55 WÉG 217
    thematic catalogue, 50 LÜN² 52
Monothematicism, in Bartók, 61 BUD 449
Monte, Philippe de
    as madrigal composer, 30 LIÈ 102
    Madrigali spirituali, 70 BRN 145
Montéclair, Michel de, two motets, 58 COL 75
Montenegro, folk epic, 32 AMS 144
Monterealese, folksong, 57 CHIE 267
Monteverdi, Claudio
    general, *67 SIE, 68 VEN*, 72 VEN 7, 41
    influence on sacred music of the north, 67 SIE 341
    influence on Venetian opera, 67 SIE 382
    inspired by 16th c Spain, 53 PAR 329
    musical language of his time, 68 VEN 539
    performing practice, 57 WÉG 241
    relation to Peri's *Euridice*, 68 VEN 117
    at Santa Barbara, 68 VEN 313
    texts, 68 VEN 349
    theatre in his time, 68 VEN 109, 129, 139
    and his time, 67 SIE 270, 68 VEN 17
    bibliographical
        discography, 68 VEN 543
        new edition of works, 68 VEN 505
        new research, 09 VIE 208
    and others
        Antegnati, 68 VEN 479
        C. Bernard, 68 VEN 435
        Carissimi, 68 VEN 305
        Cavalli, 67 SIE 229
        Kapsberger, 67 SIE 288
        Marenzio and Wert, 68 VEN 361
    style
        comic in vocal theatre, 67 SIE 255
        continuo, 68 VEN 497
        dissonance, handling of, 68 VEN 435
        formal design, 68 VEN 187, 335
        mannerist traits, 73 ROM¹ 233
        orchestration, 68 VEN 69, 72 VEN 21
        organ registration, 67 SIE 365, 68 VEN 479

ornamentation, 58 COL 284
recitative, 68 VEN 157
relation to words, 68 VEN 335, 349
rhythmic, 68 VEN 323
stilo antico, stile nuove, 67 SIE 372
trumpet, use of, 70 BON 592
vocal colour, 68 VEN 519
works, general
chamber music, 09 VIE 153, 67 SIE 282
church music, 67 SIE 264, 372, 68 VEN 187, 435
madrigals, 68 VEN 217, 335
opera, 67 SIE 207, 68 VEN 35, 45
shorter dramatic works, 58 COL 284
works, specific
Incoronazione di Poppea, 67 SIE 294, 332, 68 VEN 75, 81, 72 VEN 51
Lamento d' Arianna, 67 BRN² 159, 67 SIE 217
Orfeo, 68 VEN 69, 157, 269, 72 VEN 21
Selva morale e spirituale, 68 VEN 423
Tancredi e Clorinda, 68 VEN 557
Tempro la cetra, 67 SIE 357
Vespers, 67 SIE 314, 365, 68 VEN 269, 479
Zefira torna, 68 VEN 323
Montpellier, ligatures in manuscript, 52 UTR 146
.*Monumenta monodica medii aevi*, 65 BRA 135, 75 ESP 111
Monumenta musicae byzantinae, 57 PAR 294
Moorish theories of music, 47 BIS 135
Moravia
character of greater Moravian Empire, 64 BRA 43
folk idiom in Janáček, 70 BON 603
folksong, 67 RAD 79
harmonic structure, 68 BRN 243
Moravské národní písně, 68 BRN 251
research, 09 VIE 226
knowledge of figured bass in 17th and 18th c, 67 BRN² 116
and Mozart, 56 PRA 51, 56 VIE 603
organ playing in 17th and 18th c, 67 BRN² 123
Moresca, 00 PAR⁵ 77
in Karlštejn frescoes, 75 BYD 79
Morocco, *39 FEZ*
folk, 61 TEH 163
collection, 39 FEZ 68–90
maqamates, 32 CAIR 583
orchestras, 39 FEZ 40, 44, 48
popular music, 39 FEZ 50
rhythm, 32 CAIR 521
technique, 39 FEZ 58
traditional, 61 TEH 163
Moscow
Beethoven sketchbook, 27 VIE 88
youth music club, 72 VIE² 91
Mossi, church music, 61 COL 251, 75 ROM 72
Mosto, Giovanni Battista, 75 BYD 369
Motet, motets
Czech 1570–1620, 69 BYD 33
isorhythmic, 55 WÉG 139
social background, 62 KAS 25
Josquin's, *see* Josquin
medieval in Poland, 72 COP 593
Montéclair's, 58 COL 75
motet style and liturgical practice in 16th c, 66 LEIP 196
Netherlands picture motet, 72 COP 403
Nivers's, 58 COL 108
origins, 24 BAS 189
plan for thematic catalogue, 06 BAS 194
polytextual in 14th to 15th c Bohemia, 70 BRN 71
types in 16th c, 39 NEWY 155
in 14th c, 69 CER 215

Motetti de la Corona, Petrucci printing, 72 COP 295
Motta, Fabrizio Carini, 72 VEN 359
Motu proprio, 22 November 1903, on church music, 09 VIE 567, 27 VIE 229
Moulu, Pierre, Motet and transcription for organ, 24 BAS 286
Mount Horeb, 61 JER 362
Mouth organ, among the Samre, 69 KUA 223
Moutons, Jean, biography and work, 56 VIE 300
Mozart, Wolfgang Amadeus
general, *31 SAL, 56 PAR, 56 PRA, 56 VIE, 74 ROM*
and aesthetics of late 18th and early 19th c, 56 VIE 579
bicentenary, 56 VIE 69
bicentenary exhibition at British Museum, 56 VIE 305
as critic, 25 LEIP 266
cult in 18th c Italy, 56 VIE 128
and Enlightenment, 56 PRA 98
and folk theatre, 56 VIE 623
freemasonry, 31 SAL 142
and French Revolution, 56 PRA 156
his Hammerflügel, 64 SAL ii, 273
handwriting and creative process, 39 NEWY 145
humanism, 56 PRA 230
influence, 56 PRA 56
internationalism, 56 PAR 9
life's work, 56 PRA 15
and modern French literature, 56 VIE 170
and modern music, 56 PRA 225
and pre-romanticism, 56 VIE 643
and the Romantics, 31 SAL 22
spirituality, influence of, 56 VIE 132
biography
as a child, 56 PRA 196
genealogy, 56 VIE 116
maternal family, 31 SAL 45
Swabian heritage, 56 PAR 59
bibliography
Archive, 31 SAL 298
authenticity of K216/Anh 74g, 74 ROM 237
authenticity of K331a/Anh 8, 56 PAR 227
autographs, 56 VIE 412
Czech choir lofts, works in, 67 BRN² 147
documents in Bratislava, 56 PRA 253
Gesamtausgabe in Austria, 56 VIE 462
in literature, 31 SAL 179
manuscripts in America, 56 VIE 285
manuscripts of *Die Zauberflöte*, 74 ROM 55
memorials in Salzburg, 56 PRA 167
Passau manuscript vocal scores, 31 SAL 150
research, 31 SAL 298, 302, 64 SAL i, 47
in Bohemia, 56 PRA 175, 236
sketches of Requiem, 62 KAS 184
three unknown manuscripts, 58 COL 216
and places
Austria, 56 PAR 17
Austrian-Turkish relations, 56 VIE 5
Czechoslovakia, 56 PRA 202, 282
Egypt, 56 PRA 200
France, 56 VIE 344
Geneva, 56 VIE 637
Germany, 31 SAL 1, 56 VIE 156
Greece, 56 VIE 294
Italy, 56 VIE, 348, 74 ROM 1–96
Mainz, 56 VIE 230
Milan, 74 ROM 19
Moravia, 56 PRA 51, 56 VIE 603
Naples, 74 ROM 101
Paris, 56 PRA 26, 56 VIE 75, 535
Poland, 56 VIE 191

Romania, 56 PRA 112
Russia, 56 PRA 106, 56 VIE 365
Scandinavia, 56 VIE 387
Sweden, 56 PRA 189, 56 VIE 416
Turin, 74 ROM 52
and music of different places
central Europe, folk music, 56 PAR 157
Czechoslovakia, 56 PAR 183
Czechoslovakia, folksong of, 56 PAR 189, 56 PRA 127
German classics, 56 VIE 47
Italy, 56 PAR 117, 125, 56 PRA 44
Turkey, 56 PRA 118
and others
Anfossi, 75 SIE 141
Bach, 56 PRA 61
Bach sons, 56 PAR 91
Benda, 56 PRA 85
Clementi, 56 VIE 1
Grillparzer, 31 SAL 3
Haydn, 56 PAR 49, 59 BUD 95
Jommelli, Traetta, De Majo, 74 ROM 138
Kierkegaard, 56 VEN 706
Mannheim School, 56 PAR 85
Momigny, 62 KAS 187
Reicha, 56 PRA 79
the Romantics, 31 SAL 22
Serov, 56 VIE 328
Tchaikovsky, 56 VIE 537
Wagner, 56 VIE 657
style, 56 VIE 586
aesthetics of, 56 PRA 193
articulation marks, 56 VIE 304
chamber music, concept of, 71 BRN 311
circle of 5ths in, 56 VIE 640
exoticism, 56 PRA 181
feeling for space, 56 VIE 736
French Romance and vaudeville elements, 56 VIE 666
harmony, 31 SAL 103
Italian musicians, influence of, 24 BAS 336
Italianness, 74 ROM 205
and the Italian quartet, 31 SAL 79, 74 ROM 271
melody, 70 VIE 267
orchestration, 31 SAL 167, 56 PRA 121
polyphony, 56 PRA 210
pulse, 56 VIE 261
recitative in instrumental writing, 56 PAR 199
and the serenade, 74 ROM 148
sonata form, develop.nent of, 56 PRA 241
stability, 31 SAL 69
tempo, 31 SAL 172, 72 COP 720
and verse, 74 ROM 107
vocal character, 31 SAL 158
operas, general
in Italy, 56 VIE 348, 74 ROM 1–205
music theatre, 64 SAL ii, 3
orchestration of, 56 PRA 121
reflection of contemporary social conflicts, 56 VIE 195
in Scandinavia, 56 VIE 387
synchronization of action and music, 56 VIE 661
translation problems, 25 LEIP 270
operas, specific
Ascanio in Alba, 74 ROM 148
La clemenza di Tito, 74 ROM 205
Cosi fan tutte, 74 ROM 198
Don Giovanni, 31 SAL 150, 74 ROM 30, 166
Die Entführung, 56 VIE 78
Idomeneo, 31 SAL 158, 161, 74 ROM 205

Lucio Silla, 74 ROM 160
Le nozze di Figaro, 31 SAL 150
Die Zauberflöte, 56 VIE 249, 69 BRN 229
MSS, librettos, prints, 31 SAL 150, 56 VIE 571, 74 ROM 155
other works, general
concertos, 31 SAL 120
conflict elements in instrumental works, 56 VIE 402
contredanses, 31 SAL 133
fugue fragments, 56 VIE 743
'Haydn' quartets, 59 BUD 137
litanies, 31 SAL 136
minuets, 31 SAL 129
relations between vocal and instrumental works, 56 PRA 146
sonatas, contemporary performance, 56 VIE 28
symphonies, 31 SAL 72
variations for piano and violin, 56 VIE 666
violin concertos, playing technique compared with contemporary Italian, 56 VIE 765
other works, specific
Clarinet Concerto K622, 56 PRA 262
Clarinet Quintet K581, 56 PRA 262
Overture K311a/Anh.8, 56 PAR 227
Piano Concerto in F major, K459, 56 VIE 66
Piano Sonata in F major, K.533, 56 PRA 95
Requiem, 62 KAS 184
1st String Quartet, 74 ROM 246
String Quartet in C major, K465, 31 SAL 103
String Quintet in G minor K516, 56 VIE 447
Symphony K74g/Anh.216, 74 ROM 237
Symphony in G minor K183/173dB, 31 SAL 112, 56 PAR 27
Symphony in G minor K550, 31 SAL 112, 56 VIE 447
Munich, fête (1662), 70 MTA 121
Muris, Johannes de, *Musica speculativa* study in Poland and Italy, 69 PARM 39
Museums, instrument
see Instruments, collections
Mushroom, Mazatec ceremony, 63 CART 187
Music, miscellaneous
group of choirbooks 1st half of 16th c, 72 COP 664
lost English choirbook of 15th c, 72 COP 257
newly-found manuscript with text and notes (1544), 56 HAM 223
unknown manuscript from beginning of 18th c, 56 HAM 239
see also Libraries and manuscripts
Musica enchiriadis, Cologne manuscript, 58 COL 262
Musica ficta
in 13th c, 72 COP 695
in Machaut, 55 WÉG 196
Musicality
of Germans, 34 TÜB 130
nature of, 37 PAR[3] ii, 227
Musicology, 25 LEIP 113, 27 VIE 301, 59 CAM 25, 37, 67 LJU 13, 70 BON 621–89, 72 COP 167–97
general
and acoustics of rooms, 59 STU 983
aesthetics, relation to, 25 LEIP 405–14, 37 PAR[3] ii, 213, 223, 60 ATH 422
analysis in, 56 VIE 373, 65 WAR 285, 74 KRP 5
applied musicology and government, 39 NEWY 11
approach to jazz, 72 COP 457
and Catholic universities, 50 ROM 287
and church music, 70 BON 663

comparative *see* Ethnomusicology
and computers, 65 NEWH 103, *65 NEWY*, 66
LEIP 466, 67 LJU 424, 72 COP 486
and contemporary 'art', 25 LEIP 9
cultivation of folk music, 56 VIE 758
education, 25 LEIP 165, 53 BAM 27–50, 70 BON
672
and ethnomusicology, 58 COL 17
and exact sciences, 73 PAR 115
Fétis's rôle, 30 LIÈ 35
and geography, 54 ARR 19
historical, 70 BON 621
history of music, 65 WAR 279
influence on modern music, 56 VIE 227
international tasks, 52 UTR 11
lack of unity in various branches, 11 LON 227
local, 25 LEIP 381, 70 BON 378
method, 64 SAL i, 19
and music, 48 FLOR 157, 49 BAS 9, 53 BAM 7
principles, 03 ROM 27
and psychology, 61 NEWY i, 121
and quarter-tone music, 25 LEIP 304
and records, 61 NEWY i, 404, 418, 67 ZAG 22, 50
relation to popular literature and music criticism, 09 VIE 422
Russian, 58 COL 99
and sociology, 56 HAM 193, 70 BON 639
spiritual problems today, 58 COL 160
structural, 70 BON 626
systematic, 70 BON 621
theory of, 66 LEIP 372
universal history of music, 65 WAR 279
in different countries
America, 62 STOC 12, 68 SVE 80, 123
Czech, and Mozart, 56 PRA 175, 236
Caribbean, 70 BON 597
France, 11 ROM 15
Hungarian 1946–56, 56 VIE 22
Japan, 58 COL 201, 70 BON 524
Latin America, 70 BON 365
Slav in America, 72 BYD 615
Yugoslavia, 68 SVE 73, 119
Musicus, meaning, 49 BAS 134
Musikalische-Türkischer Eulenspiegel, 72 BYD 69
Musique concrète, 59 CAM 30, 60 ATH 232, 62 KAS
388
Musique figurée, 68 LIÈ 353
Musique mésurée, 06 BAS 170
tempo, 65 DIJ 202
Musorgsky, Modest Petrovich
and Janáček, 58 BRN 205
melody style, 53 BAM 262
Mysliveček, Josef, *Tamerlano*, 67 BRN² 183
Mythology, musical and sociology, 56 WÉG 13

Naduri songs, 63 BUD 459, 64 MOS 278
Naga-Bergen folksongs, 56 WÉG 187
Naġarah, Israel, 65 JER 208
Nang Sbek, orchestral and musical accompaniment
of, 69 KUA 216
Naples, Neapolitan
folksongs, 40 VEN 409
intermezzo, 70 BON 183
and Mozart, 74 ROM 101
opera, 06 BAS 217, 61 NEWY i, 253, 277
Spanish music at court of, in 15th c, 53 PAR 35
staging of Neapolitan opera, 67 BRN² 171
Nationalism
aesthetics of tradition, 65 BERL¹ 359
aspects of European instrumental styles, 53 BAM
259

in Chopin, 60 WAR¹ 23
cultures, development of, 66 LEIP 305
internationalism in music, 09 VIE 56, 11 LON 76, 24
BAS 36
16th c Italy, components in, 64 SAL i, 37
and Latin American composers, 65 BLM 192
in Liszt, 61 BUD 77
in music, 00 PAR² 226
in music histories, American, 68 SVE 199
Yugoslav, 68 SVE 194
opera in 19th c, beginnings of, 64 SAL i, 57
overcoming national style in late 19th c, 50 LÜN¹
143
in Polish Renaissance instrumental music, 54 PAR¹
149
of Renaissance artists of French northern provinces, 54 ARR 11
in Renaissance and Baroque dance music, 71 WAR
191
role of nations in history of music, 30 LIÈ 138
Romantic movements in German and Scandinavian
music, 62 KAS 60, 63 KIE 42
20th c and National styles, *71 MOS*
tendencies in music, 71 MOS 266
and the universal, *67 BUC*
Negro songs at the Fiesta de San Juan, 63 CART 153
Negro spirituals, 57 PAR 530
Ne'ima, definition, 69 JER 282
Nejedlý, Zdeněk, research on Hussite song, 58 COL
150
Neoclassicism, 48 FLOR 146, 70 BON 257–75
Neri, St Filippo, oratorio and Palestrina, 25 LEIP 323
Netherlands
Anna von Köln's Liederbuch, 52 UTR 340
character in dance, speech and song, 64 AMS 534
Easter play, 52 UTR 371
in European musical geography, 52 UTR 296
folksongs, Dutch, 48 BRUS 265
Germany in 17th c, relations with, 52 UTR 181
improvisation on lute and organ in 16th and 17th
c, 58 COL 177
Josquin and courts of, 71 NEWY 181
lute players (1580–1620), 57 NEU/S 179
mid-Netherlands songs of Berlin MS GERM. 8° 190,
52 UTR 241
music in Montserrat Monastery library, 50 ROM 319
18th c music and dance, 35 BRUS¹ ii, 197
musicians and Italian madrigal, 52 UTR 166
old manuscripts, comparative melody research, 53
BAM 187
parody mass in 16th c, 49 BAS 179
picture motets, 72 COP 403
Poland (1500–1530), style in, 67 LJU 107
polyphonic chanson 15th to 16th c, 30 LIÈ 168
polyphonic lamentations, origin, 52 UTR 352
polyphonic songs 15th to 16th c, 30 ANT 453
Renaissance, concept of, in early music, 52 UTR 450
Renaissance, relations with Spain in, 54 ARR 51
'topical' music in Netherlands period, 66 LEIP 181
works in old Cologne Jesuit library, 52 UTR 252
see also Belgium; Flanders; Holland
Neumes
development of, 23 BRUS 366
in German chant notation, 66 LEIP 173
without lines, 50 ROM 259
manuscripts from Chilandar, 61 OKH ii, 583
melodic significance of neumatic groups, 50 ROM 229
in Minnesang, 70 WÜR 68
and noeane, 72 COP 301
new finds from former Benedictine Abbey, München-
Gladbach, 30 LIÈ 100

printing of, 50 ROM 172
and rhythm, 57 PAR 264
texts in the Palausov, 66 SOF ii, 1055
see also Notation
New York
Enesco festival, 73 BUC 115
and Verdi's *Don Carlos*, 69 VER 509
Nibelung, melody in the Trier Marienklage, 49 BAS 118
Nicephorus Phocas, Emperor, stichera on death of, 55 IST 294
Nicholas of Cracow, 60 WAR¹ 640
Nicholas of Padua, 71 WAR 177
Niedt, Friedrich, *Musikalische Handleitung*, 53 BAM 152
Nineteenth century, 62 KAS 40–91, *70 STGE*
aesthetics, 30 LIÈ 139, 70 BON 517
Beethoven's influence on composers, 70 BERL² 107
convention of composition, 70 STGE 48
development of orchestration at beginning, 70 STGE 70
historiography, 70 STGE 75
motivation for research, 66 LEIP 385
musical conception of and Affektenlehre, 64 AMS 969
relation to modern organ music, 68 THU 37
social commitment of composers, 68 BRN 289
state of Western music *c* 1900, 25 LEIP 289
Tchaikovsky as 19th c musician, 70 STGE 59
value in music of the, 67 LJU 380
virtuosity, 70 STGE 5
Nivers, Guillaume Gabriel, unaccompanied motets, 58 COL 108
Noces de Pelée et Thétis, Les, 70 MTA 59
Noeane, and neume, 72 COP 301
Noh
Buddhist influence on, 59 ROY 163
music, 64 HAM 124, 71 ANN 99–189
music and manuscripts of, 25 LEIP 80
Nomenclature
of instruments, 59 CAM 204
of sounds, 00 PAR² 276
using numbers in chromatic scale, 00 PAR¹ 39
Nono, Luigi, *Intolleranza 60*, 64 HAM 103
Nonstrophic, melodies, 67 RAD 53–179
Normandy, alphabetical notation, 54 ROU 913
North, extreme, songs in, 56 WÉG 127
Norway
flute, 67 BRN¹ 74
folk music, 28 PRA 130, 54 WÉG 154, 67 RAD 125
folk violins and violin music, 71 STP 89
German music, connections with, 63 KIE 37
liturgical fragments, 75 ESP 171
Norwid, Cyprian, and Chopin, 60 WAR¹ 684
Notation
general, 06 BAS 8–55
computer, *see* Computers: notation
phonetic notation for timbre, 68 TOK¹ vi, 29
real-time notation of melodies, 71 BUD² iii, 653
use of for white mensural notation, 71 KAS 6
graphology, 09 VIE 371
influence of musical creation, 70 HAMM 12
new directions, 68 NEWY 62
non-transposing, usefulness of, 00 PAR¹ 44
notation instrument musical applications, 38 GHE 105
orchestral score according to Giordano system, 09 VIE 382
'popular' orchestral scores, reforms in, 11 LON 366

reform of, 00 PAR¹ 38, 00 PAR² 261, 27 VIE 317
rhythm, 21 PAR 810, 26 GEN 82, 52 UTR 377
and school singing, 09 VIE 368
simpler clefs, plea for, 06 BAS 55
tempered 19-tone system, 11 LON 279
transcription of implied accents, 55 WÉG 167
transposing voice parts, 00 PAR¹ 42
types
alphabetic, at Jumièges and Normandy, 54 ROU 913
Babylonian, 39 NEWY 161
Byzantine, *see* Byzantine music
crook, in Znamenny chant manuscripts, 75 BYD 487
10th c European, 25 BRUG 226
13th c German organ sources, 69 CER 176
11th to 14th c Kondakarny, 64 BRA 77, 75 BYD 557
Guidonian, *see* Guido of Arezzo
mensural, 23 BRUS 370
15th c, 70 BON 609
of medieval monody, 58 COL 56
old Spanish, 56 VIE 7
Tegernsee 15th c plainsong, 52 UTR 377
neumatic, 00 PAR² 103, 116, 124, 50 ROM 172, 56 VIE 599, 57 PAR 264, 277
of proto-Christian chant, 57 PAR 329
Rhine-Mosel, 56 VIE 599
oriental, 27 VIE 317
'Plaine and easie code' system for, 65 DIJ 156, 65 NEWY 53
17th c Russian hammer-headed, 72 BYD 293
syllabic, in isolated voices, 72 COP 378
trecento, French influence on, 55 WÉG 27
Ukrainian staff notation, 75 BYD 521
notation of genres, forms and styles
contemporary music, 65 BLM 148, 66 LEIP 332
Couperin harpsichord music, 69 PAR 213
Czech folk music, historic, 73 BAL 110
German chant, 66 LEIP 173
Greek music, ancient, 00 PAR² 63–70
the mass, 50 ROM 236
Meistersinger songs, 06 BAS 17–35, 09 VIE 84
20th c organ music, 68 THU 158
psalms and recitative chants, 06 BAS 47
traditional music, 61 TEH 251
vocal music, 06 BAS 48
see also Monody; Neumes; Tablature; Transcription
Note relationships in old and new music, 09 VIE 353
Notes inégales, 69 PAR 67, 235
Notre Dame conductus, 25 LEIP 209
organum, 56 HAM 135
Novak, Johann Baptist, 56 VIE 103
Nuova prattica, 68 VEN 385, 397
Nuremberg, Paumann circle, 50 LÜN¹ 91
Nyckelharpa, Swedish, 06 BAS 242
Nyiregyházy, Erwin, 10 INN 224
Nyugat movement, and Bartók, 61 BUD 347

Obadiah the Norman, and Jewish music research, 65 JER 209
Obbligato, accompaniment in Viennese Classical school, 25 LEIP 35
Oboe, and oboe playing *c* 1750, 70 GRA 231
Oboe d'amore, 72 BLA 41
Oberengadin, 24 BAS 106
Obrecht, Jacob, 30 ANT 441
masses, structure and performing practice, 71 NEWY 619

Oceania
  instruments, 38 COP 268
  liturgical music, 75 ROM 117
  music, 06 BAS 60
Odeyevsky, Vladimir Fyodorovich, view of Bach and
  Beethoven, 66 LEIP 287
Office
  11th to 12th c composers of, 13 GHE 280
  for the dead, computer analysed, 75 ESP 79
  Gaude, mater Ecclesia, 50 ROM 284
  rhymed, of St Philibert, 54 ROU 335, 977
  St Aycadre, 54 ROU 977
Okeghem, Johannes, spiritual rhythm of, 58 COL 73
Oktoechos, 50 ROM 107, 72 COP 766
  Byzantine and Slavonic to 15th c, 75 BYD 175
  history of early, 52 UTR 428
Olomouc, music at 13th to 17th c, 70 BOL 251
Ondes martenot, 30 ATH 265
Opera
  general, 61 TOK 30
    beginnings of opera repertory and repertory
      opera, 70 BON 225
    bibliography, 25 LEIP 59, 65 AMS 29
    classification of history, 58 COL 338
    compared with concert, 70 BON 220
    of cruelty, 74 SIE 187
    dialogue in, 38 FRA 225
    as Festspiel, 38 FLOR 161
    historic dramaturgy, 09 VIE 208
    history, 00 PAR¹ 19, 06 BAS 212, 24 BAS 22
    Italian museum of, 03 ROM 17, 139
    oratorio, relation with, 09 VIE 207
    and society, 70 BON 217–47
    speech and song in, 38 FRA 218
  types
    opera buffa, 70 BON 183
      development, 09 VIE 193
      elements in Goldoni, 57 VEN¹ 593
    opera seria
      18th c and Gluck, 73 SIE 263
      Italian 17th c deportment and scenographic de-
        sign, 72 COP 415
    opera semiseria, birth of, 75 SIE 265
  staging, production, 33 FLOR 105, 38 FLOR 94, 114
    Baroque, 67 BRN² 155, 176
    contemporary opera, 56 VIE 253, 64 HAM 86–103
    Costanza e Fortezza in Prague (1723), 70 MTA
      129
    early, 37 FLOR 210, 219, 38 FLOR 108, 67 MAG
      i, 88
    expressionist opera, 68 STRS 221
    Italian, 17th c, 68 VEN 109, 72 COP 415
    Janáček operas, 58 BRN 81, 381, 65 BRN 145, 148,
      152
    Mysliveček's *Tamerlano*, 67 BRN² 183
    Neapolitan opera, 67 BRN² 171
    Nono's *Intolleranza 60*, 64 HAM 103
    organization of opera theatre, 33 FLOR 194
    origins of opera houses, 67 BRN² 153
    at Polish court in 17th and 18th c, *69 WAR*
    on radio, 37 FLOR 118, 38 FRA 202, 64 HAM 109
    at Saxon courts in 17th and 18th c, *69 WAR*
    sociological aspects, 70 BON 242
    training of singers, 38 FRA 116, 147, 178, 184, 211,
      64 HAM 140–51, 65 GEN 22
    in Wagner, 25 LEIP 312–14
    see also Stage design
  to 1700
    Baroque literary account of, 70 MTA 115
    relation with oratorio and instrumental

  music, 64 SAL ii, 212
  in Dresden, 69 WAR 87, 99
  early, and mannerism, 70 BRN 171, 71 WAR 123
  falsobordone echoes in prologues of early, 70
    BON 179
  folk music, relation with, 24 BAS 326
  French pastorales, influence on, 11 LON 139
  from intermèdes to operas, 72 TOU 267
  Italian 1600–1750, 69 WAR 69
  in Mantua, 74 MANT 285
  from masque to English opera, 67 LJU 149
  origins, *70 MTA*
  17th c 'poetica e morfologia', 68 PARM 259
  Polish, 11 LON 146, 69 PARM 173
  in Salzburg to 1650, 27 VIE 196
  singing style of early German, 38 FRA 11
  Venetian, 70 BON 336, *72 VEN*
  18th c, 75 SIE 57
    arrangements of libretto, 67 BRN² 176
    and Bach, 72 BYD 387
    dramaturgy in Metastasio era, 69 WAR 131
    elaboration in, 70 BON 374
    German 1765–1830, 37 FLOR 205
    Italian, connection with musical aesthetics, 09 VIE
      196
    Neapolitan, 06 BAS 217, 61 NEWY i, 253–77
    and periodization of music, 67 LJU 160
    political use in Revolutionary France, 70 BON 237
    Russian, 66 BYD 489
    Spanish, 30 LIÈ 214
    and Toscanini, 67 FLOR 293
  19th c, 70 BON 497
    France, 11 ROM 21
    national, beginnings of, 64 SAL i, 57
    Polish historical opera in Chopin's youth, 60
      WAR¹ 503
    relation of music to words/libretto in Italian opera
      seria, 70 BON 162
    Russian, 70 BON 515
  20th c *64 HAM*
    America, 33 FLOR 188
    composer, theatre and public, 64 SAL ii, 255
    England, 33 FLOR 183
    expressionist, 68 STRS 221–45
    France, 33 FLOR 139
    Germany, 33 FLOR 169
    Italy, 21 TUR 184, 204, 33 FLOR 125
    see also Libretto
Oral tradition
  disappearance in 18th c, 72 BYD 415
  statistical laws on, 62 KAS 318
Oratorio
  in Bologna in 18th c, 69 PER 99
  in mid-17th c Italy, 72 COP 657
  origins, 06 BAS 216
  relation with opera, 09 VIE 207
    and instrumental music in the Baroque, 64 SAL ii,
      212
  20th c, 50 ROM 405
'L'Oratorio di Via Belsiana' 38 FLOR 102
Orchestra
  forces in 2nd half of 18th c, 09 VIE 159
  in Lombardy, at time of Mozart, 56 VIE 18
  Moroccan, 39 FEZ 40–48
  musicians, economic position in France, 09 VIE 515
  repeating bass in 18th c, 70 BON 550
  use of concertizing organ in 18th c, 26 FRE/B 68
Orchestral music
  1740–70, 70 GRA 98
  difference from chamber music, 71 BRN 100

Orchestration
  general
    of fanfares, 00 PAR¹ 11
    further development, 06 BAS 211
    teaching, 00 PAR¹ 14
    in 18th c music, 75 BLA 9–33, 49
    early 19th c, 70 STGE 70
  in individual composers
    Bartók, 61 BUD 557
    Chopin, 60 WAR¹ 85
    Janáček, 65 BRN 97, 102
    Monteverdi, 68 VEN 69, 72 VEN 21
    Mozart, 31 SAL 167, 56 PRA 121
    Telemann, 67 MAG ii, 40
    Verdi, 69 ROM 304
    Wagner, 69 ROM 304
Ordinary of the mass
  in 15th c, 50 ROM 308
  in medieval Poland, 75 BYD 273
Ordoñez, Carlos d', string quartets, 72 COP 314
Orff, Carl, and Janáček, 58 BRN 236
Organ
  general, 50 ROM 342–84, 54 VIE 214–54, 57 PAR
    355–423, *see also Index of Titles, Series and*
    Sponsors
    aesthetics of sound and playing, 37 PAR³ ii, 239
    and the chorale, 27 FRE/S 83
    definition, 54 VIE 243
    historical, 37 PAR¹ 182
    profession of organist, 27 FRE/S 87
    tablature, *see* Tablature
  use
    in Catholic church, 32 STRS 157, 162, 68 THU
      130, 74 SINZ 64
    in church music, in 15th c, 26 FRE/B 87
    contemporary, 74 SINZ 89
    concert in 18th c orchestra, 26 FRE/B 68
    as ecumenical instrument, 74 SINZ 79
    ecumenical and universal use, of pipe, 66 LEIP 424
    and folk song, 38 FRE/B 88
    and Gregorian chant, 27 FRE/S 78, 50 ROM 344,
      54 VIE 254
    in the liturgy, 26 FRE/B 92, 27 FRE/S 58, 50 ROM
      367, 57 PAR 355–85, 65 MTS 219–33
    older music and contemporary organ, 74 SINZ
      109
    in Protestant church, 27 FRE/S 102, 32 STRS 148,
      151
    as sacred instrument, 27 BERL 112, 27 FRE/S 43,
      72, 52 BERN 23, 57 PAR 355–423, 74 SINZ 33,
      40
    as secular instrument, 27 BERL 112, 27 FRE/S 43,
      38 FRE/B 78
    traditional, 50 ROM 356
  chamber organ, 38 FRE/B 118
    in domestic music making, 38 FRE/B 63
    and early positive organ, 38 FRE/B 37, 64
    in Holland, 38 FRE/B 125
    3-manual practice organ, 38 FRE/B 110
    portative for school singing, 51 OCH 141
    secular music on positive organ, 38 FRE/B 55
    sound and building, 38 FRE/B 88
    in Switzerland, 51 OCH 144
    in worship, 38 FRE/B 63
  organ building, 09 VIE 581–636, 32 STRS 114–39,
    51 OCH 59, 67, 76–155, 52 BERN 62, 65, 54
    STAD, 62 BERN 96
    acoustics, 38 FRE/B 104, 56 VIE 378, 62 COP i,
      P53, 65 LIE i, M52
    Catholic, 51 OCH 148
    and church space, 54 STAD 75

    electric, electronic, 51 OCH 155, 54 VIE 230, 57
      PAR 380, 389–412
    historicism, 54 STAD 25, 89
    international regulation, 09 VIE 636
    measurements, 25 LEIP 71, 26 FRE 43, 50, 68
      THU 18, 68 TOK¹ vi, 17
    Orgelhaus, 26 FRE/B 114, 54 STAD 58
    preservation, 38 FRE/B 20, 54 STAD 56
    reform of, 09 VIE 581, 621
    relation with organ music, 38 FRE/B 98
    restoration of historical, 65 MTS 233
    small organ, 38 FRE/B 8, 37
    sound, difference between old and new, 53 BAM
      75
      change of ideals, 26 FRE/B 11
    spectrum, 58 MARS 135
    synthesizing a pipe organ, 58 MARS 145
    timbre, 53 NET 226, 54 STAD 82
  organs and organ building in countries, towns etc.
    Alsace and Lorraine, 14th to 18th c, 32 STRS 177
    Austria, 51 OCH 59
    Belgium, 17th to 18th c, 13 GHE 243
    Brabant, 1500–1700, 62 BERN 91
    Chapelle de l'école Royale militaire, 32 STRS 187
    England, 16th to 18th c, 59 STAD 97
    France, old, 52 UTR 335
      Baroque, 51 OCH 87
      under Louis XIV, 62 BERN 88
      contemporary, 37 PAR¹ 171
    Germany, 50 ROM 380
      1500–1700, 30 LIE 208
      North Baroque, 54 STAD 15, 36, 48
      South Baroque, 51 OCH 76–84, 54 STAD 15
    Hagenau, 1491–1525, 32 STRS 182
    Italian-Austrian Baroque, 50 ROM 371
    Italy, 21 TUR 230
    Kaisheim, Cistercian Church (1778), 50 ROM 384
    Lahm, Baroque organ, 53 BAM 78
    Liège, builders in, 11 MAL 891
    Lorraine, 32 STRS 177
    Malines, builders in, 11 MAL 605
    Middle Rhine school, 51 OCH 78
    northern and southern Baroque organs, 53 BAM
      78
    Paris c1600, 54 PAR¹ 259
    Passau school influence in Austria, 54 VIE 246
    Protestant Saxony churches, 27 FRE/S 102
    Strasbourg, 32 STRS 172
    Swedish middle ages, 09 VIE 91
    Upper Bavaria, 38 FRE/B 136
    Upper Swabia, 51 OCH 59, 119
  specific period and types
    of Bach's time, 27 FRE/S 122
    Baroque, 50 ROM 348
    Bruckner's, 32 STRS 195
    of F. X. Chrisman, 54 VIE 249
    of Christian antiquity, 32 STRS 166
    McClure, and unequal temperament, 50 ROM 342
    Oskalyd as trial organ, 26 FRE/B 139
    of Reger's time, 73 NUR 31
    Silbermann, 26 FRE/B 59, 27 FRE/S 103
    Toggenburger Bauernorgel, 38 FRE/B 132
    J. Wagner, 27 FRE/S 139
    Water organ, 59 CAM 189
    from the year 228, 32 STRS 164
    in 1st half of 17th c, 54 PAR¹ 269
    18th c, in light of Silbermann Archives, Paris, 30
      LIE 182
    18th c, registration, 26 FRE/B 70
    20th c, 54 VIE 214–30, 251, 57 PAR 423, 68 THU
      120

20th c, installation, 09 VIE 611
20th c, tuning, 09 VIE 611, 27 FRE/S 206
20th c, types, 62 BERN 96, 68 THU 105, 112
individual parts
  flue pipes, 25 LEIP 71, 68 TOK¹ vi, 17
    voicing of, 53 NET 237
  Gros nasard, 69 PAR 239
  keyboard, 09 VIE 607, 26 FRE/B 76, 27 FRE/S
    182, 197
  pedals, 09 VIE 607
  pipes, adjustments, 65 LIÈ i, M52
    effect of temperature change, 74 LON 345
    theories of mechanism, 65 LIÈ i, M52
    tone formation, 65 LIÈ i, M55
  positif à pied, 9th to 13th c, 72 COP 590
  reed pipe, 27 FRE/B 189
  swell, 27 FRE/B 204
  tracking, mechanical action, 54 STAD 59
  systems, 56 HAM 142, 56 VIE 352
organ music (general)
  alternation in liturgical, 68 VEN 171
  dances in German tablature, 24 BAS 243
  and Gregorian chant, 50 ROM 344
  Munich University Library Cod. MS 153, 25
    LEIP 339
  Reger and German, 26 FRE/B 122
  secular music on positive, 38 FRE/B 55
  'Shepherd' Christmas music in Westphalia, 75
    BRUN 61
  for small organ, 38 FRE/B 43
organ music (specific periods)
  earliest German, tactus and notation in, 69 CER
    176
  early editions of, 54 PAR¹ 277
  earliest Italian, 50 ROM 351
  late medieval, 26 FRE/B 141
  1450–1500 German, 27 FRE/S 133
  15th to 16th c, East Europe, 75 BYD 391
  15th to 17th c, Spanish, 25 LEIP 227
  15th to 18th c, Transylvania, 72 BYD 551
  17th c accompaniment in, 27 FRE/S 95
  17th c north German chorale arrangements, 63
    KIE 71
  under Louis XIV, 62 BERN 88
  of Bach's time, 50 LEIP 405
  18th c Danzig organ book, 25 LEIP 284
  since Bach, 27 FRE/S 46
  German after Reger, 26 FRE/B 130
  modern and the 19th c, 68 THU 37
  20th c, 26 FRE/B 134, 50 ROM 388, 68 THU 64,
    86, 158, 168, 74 SINZ 97
organ playing
  in Germany, 50 ROM 380
  improvisation in 16th and 17th c Netherlands, 58
    COL 177
  in Moravia, 17th and 18th c, 67 BRN² 123
  performance in 17th c, 57 WÉG 225
  in Poland, 16th and 17th c, 70 BOL 83
  registration, 25 LEIP 232
    French 17th and 18th c, 49 BAS 172
    in Monteverdi, 67 SIE 365, 68 VEN 479
  score-reading as task for 18th c organists, 30 LIÈ
    109
  see also Performing practice
Organology, *see* Instruments
Organum, 58 COL 93
  Notre dame, 56 HAM 135
  outside Notre dame school, 64 SAL i, 25
  peasant, in Iceland, 58 COL 132
  performance of, 58 COL 251

Polish sources, 72 COP 593
Orgelbewegung, *54 STAD*
  in Switzerland, 27 FRE/S 116
Orient, oriental
  Balkan music, element in, *66 GRA*
  Black Africa, music in, 70 YAO 95
  Byzantium, relations with, 66 OXF¹ 267
  chant, 57 PAR 287, 326, 339
    Jewish, 61 JER 366
  directions of music, 68 NEWY 49
  16th to 17th c improvisation, oriental influence
    on, 58 COL 308
  liturgy, *see* Liturgy
  modern oriental music, 38 FLOR 176
  musical civilization, 71 FLOR 27, 53
  musical patronage in, 61 TOK 155
  notation, 27 VIE 317
  scales, 58 MARS 39, 60 PAR¹ 123
  theatre, influence on Craig and Yeats, 59 ROY
    271
    influence on western opera, 64 HAM 116
  variation, 61 TEH 231
  and western music, 56 HAM 24, 56 VIE 238, 61 TEH
    83, 89, 114, 148, 61 TOK 71, 66 MANL 143, 71
    FLOR 67, 95, 141, 157, 197
Ornaments, ornamentation
  general, 61 NEWY i, 425–63
  in Africa, 61 NEWY i, 427
  in English keyboard music 16th to 18th c, 67 BRN²
    128
  in European folk music, 61 NEWY i, 439
  18th c, 75 BLA 9
    development of free in, 70 GRA 147
  in Gregorian chant, 61 NEWY i, 428
  influence of in 17th c church music, 58 COL
    57
  in 16th c motet intabulations, 71 NEWY 475
  interpretation of, 11 LON 259
  or obligatory improvisation, 58 COL 55
  in secular medieval music, 61 NEWY i,
    450
  'Sigel' ornaments, 49 BAS 135
  value of, 00 PAR² 251
  in Vietnam, 61 NEWY i, 445
  vocal, at time of Haydn, 59 BUD 117
  in individual composers
    Chopin, 60 WAR¹ 255, 61 BUD 49
    Corelli, 72 BYD 591
    Liszt, 61 BUD 49
    Monteverdi, 58 COL 284
Orthodox church, 54 VIE 76–93
  chant, *see* Chant
  liturgical music, 62 BERN 32
  psalmody, 54 VIE 82
  reform, 54 VIE 93
  use of western liturgy in church Slavonic, 54 VIE
    89
  see also Russia; Znamenny chant
Ortiz, Diego, *Tratado de glosas sobre clausulas*, 70 BOL
  9
Oskalyd, organ, 26 FRE/B 139
Osterc, Slavko, and style of his day, 70 BON 547
Ostinato, Bach's technique of, 50 LEIP 240
Ottobeurer, organs, 51 OCH 84
Outremonts, musicians in 16th c, 54 ARR 27
Ouvrard, René, and French Baroque theory, 72 COP
  336
Overture, origins of French, 11 LON 149

Pacelli, Asprilio, *Docta schola*, 69 PARM 153

Painting
 and Debussy, 62 PAR 151
 see also Iconography
Paisiello, Giovanni, *L'Elfrida*, 73 SIE 357
Palaeography
 Hungarian contribution to medieval, 56 VIE 176
 see also Notation
Palencia, folksong, 28 PRA 154
Palestine, musical relics, 61 JER 364
Palestrina, Giovanni Pierluiga da, 52 BERN 43, 75
 ROM 147
 as authority and example in 17th c, 68 VEN 253
 biographical, will of Jacobella Palestrina (1527), 03
 ROM 87
 interpretation of, 38 FLOR 166
 in light of style changes, 25 LEIP 245
 and Oratorio of Filippo Neri, 25 LEIP 323
 and Schoenberg, 56 VIE 749
 style, rule of leaps, 24 BAS 211
 teaching methods, 62 KAS 361
 and Verdi, 69 ROM 250
 Vestiva i colli, 72 COP 86–108
 vocal qualities, 50 ROM 327
Pallavicino, Carlo, *Massimo Puppieno*, 72 VEN 273
Palma, and Chopin, 60 WAR¹ 288
Panadés folk dance, 28 PRA 192
Panama, African influence, 58 SJOS 639
Pandora, 57 NEU/S 225
Panizzi, Sir Anthony
 music collections in British Library, 59 CAM 62
Pannonia folk dances, 64 GRA² 109
Panpipe, 72 ROM 31
Pantomime, and ballet *c* 1750, 67 LJU 168
Papius, Andreas de, 32 LIÈ 289
Papua music and songs, 09 VIE 297
Paris
 J. A. André branch (1802–6), 56 VIE 324
 and bourgeois theatre, 75 SIE 33
 chanson 1500–1530, 61 CAM /M 1
 and Enlightenment, 75 *SIE*
 and Italian musicians under Mazarin, 00 PAR² 191
 lute players under Louis XIII, 57 NEU/S 209
 and Mozart, 56 PRA 26, 56 VIE 75, 535
 music *c*1920, 67 LJU 216
 organ in 1600, effect on musicians, 54 PAR¹ 259
 Théâtre italien, 75 SIE 87, 105
 and Verdi, 72 MIL 564
 violin sonatas 1770–85, 72 GRA 20
Parisius, Ludolf, folksong collection, 11 LON 205
Parma, operatic reform, 68 PARM 271
Parody
 cantatas, early 18th c decorated, 56 VIE 203
 in Lassus, 61 NEWY i, 214
 16th c Netherlands parody mass, 49 BAS 179, 50
 ROM 315
 of Psalm 94, 73 HAM 164
 in 17th c, 62 KAS 154
Partita
 documents on, 53 BAM 143
 origin and significance, 52 UTR 404
Part writing
 in Chopin, 60 WAR¹ 145
 in homophonic texture, 25 LEIP 171
Pasquini, Bernardo, 21 PAR 856
Passacaglia, 54 PAL 275
Passamezzo, 50 LÜN¹ 94
Passau organ building school, 54 VIE 246
Passion
 beginnings of German, 49 BAS 39
 history, 30 LIÈ 190

16th c Passion compositions, 58 COL 107
Pasticcio, history, 11 LON 71
Pastorale, influence on opera of 17th c French, 11 LON
 139
Patricij, Andrija, madrigals, 75 BYD 145
Patronage, 61 NEWY ii, 19
 at Brussels court (1540–1559), 54 ARR 169
 in the East, 61 TOK 155
 in India, 61 TOK 159
 in Milan, 68 MIL 17, 23, 35
 in the West, 61 TOK 161, 165
 in 20th c, 68 NEWY 108
Paulo da Firenze, 59 CER 118
Paumann circle in Nuremberg, 50 LÜN¹ 91
Peking music theatre, 59 ROY 89, 99, 66 MANL 114,
 71 ANN 65
Pelpin organ tablature, 60 WAR¹ 628, 70 BOL 75
Pentatonic scale, 60 PAR¹ 161
 in Eskimo music, 26 ROM 15
 in Lapp melodies, 09 VIE 244
Perception
 acoustic studies, 71 BUD² iii, 609–37, 645, 685, 745
 auditory, 14 GÖT 90, 54 WÉG 37, 61 TOK 141
 individual differences, 12 BERL 148
 of intervals, 64 AMS 901, 71 BUD² iii, 617, 685
 melodic, 25 MUN 140
 of pitch, *see* Pitch
 tonality, 56 VIE 55
Performing practice
 general
 acoustic problems, 67 KAS 61, 58 COL 295
 agogic principles, 58 COL 319
 authenticity, 67 KAS 25, 47, 73
 changes in interpretation, 67 BRN² 17
 form in performance, 75 *AUS*
 effects of staging, 75 AUS 52
 musical occasion, 75 AUS 164
 heuristic problems, 67 BRN² 30
 music as style problem, 38 FLOR 67
 natural horns, trumpets and cornetts, 53 BAM
 93
 old instruments, use of, 53 BAM 96, 67 BRN² 34
 phrasing, 70 BON 415
 rhythm, 26 GEN 26, 27 VIE 385
 scordatura, 58 COL 172
 to 1600, 30 LIÈ 55, 52 UTR 33, 67 BRN² 25, 47, 70
 BON 487
 Byzantine 14th to 18th c, 67 BRN² 53
 criteria for voices or instruments, 25 LEIP 225
 ensemble in Dufay's time, 74 NEWY² 61
 French polyphonic music of Renaissance, 67
 BRN² 61
 Gothic music, 67 BRN² 39
 Greek aulos, 62 KAS 300
 Gregorian chant, *see* Gregorian chant
 harp in Pharoah's Egypt, 52 UTR 233
 iconographical sources for 16th c chamber
 music, 71 BRN 37
 Italian sacred music 1475–1525, 71 NEWY 601
 Malines, vocal music, 30 ANT 465
 monodic music, 66 LEIP 208
 prosulae, sequences and organa, 58 COL 251
 Russian vocal, 69 BYD 467
 sacred, 09 VIE 557, 50 ROM 336, 72 BERN 67
 17th c, 09 VIE 147, 61 NEWY i, 220, 231
 Baroque, 57 WÉG 223, 267, 67 KAS 35
 agogics and dynamics, 58 COL 343
 secular and sacred, 38 FLOR 121
 dance music, new source, 72 COP 563
 figured-bass period, 58 COL 76

French, *69 PAR*
  keyboard, 69 PAR 155–239
  mass, 17th to 18th c a cappella, 57 WÉG 177
  tempo, 65 DIJ 162–202
Polish music, 67 BRN² 82
rallentando, 17th to 18th c, 69 PAR 237
tremolo iñ 17th to 18th c instrumental music, 67 BRN² 101
Venetian brass music, 74 GRA² 23
violin, 72 GRA 109–20
18th c, 61 NEWY i, 220, 231
  Bach–Handel period, 75 BLA 64
  Baroque, late in light of automatophones, 67 BRN² 137
  French, *69 PAR*
    keyboard, 69 PAR 155–239
    tempo, 65 DIJ 162–202
  harpsichord, 74 BLA 22
  improvisation, 75 BLA 64–80
    on keyboard instruments, 75 BLA 77
    solo in concertos, 75 BLA 80
  instrumental music, *75 BLA*
  orchestral 1740–70, 70 GRA 98
  notes inégales, 69 PAR 67, 235
  string music, 67 BRN² 92
    at time of young Haydn, *70 GRA*
  trumpet parts, 74 BLA 29
  viola d'amore, 75 BLA 56
  violin, 62 KAS 313, 74 BLA 17
  vocal ornamentation in Haydn's time, 59 BUD 117
19th and 20th c, 62 KAS 293
  intonation, 57 CAM/M 70
  violin, 62 KAS 313, 72 GRA 123–54
see also Bach; Beethoven; Chopin; Corelli; Handel; Handl; Ives; Josquin; Monteverdi; Verdi; Opera: staging; Organ: organ playing; Ornaments, ornamentation
Pergolesi, Giovanni Battista, 52 UTR 127
Peri, Jacopo, *Euridice*, 68 VEN 117
Periodic structure
  in relation to other arts, 38 ZUR 655
  18th c theories, 56 VIE 531
  in Western music, 50 LÜN¹ 200
Periodization, 11 LON 76, 72 BYD 8, 72 COP 185
  Baroque v. Classical, 70 BON 323
  in Czech music, 72 BYD 95
  disintegration caused by mannerism, 70 BRN 121
  relation between the sound and the sterotypes of different epochs, 66 LEIP 499
  in 15th to 16th c instrumental music, 71 WAR 111
  in music 1580–1620, 62 KAS 141
  in 18th c music, 67 LJU 160
Perlus, Hortensjusz, lute compositions, 71 WAR 177
Persia *see* Iran
Personality
  in compositions, 34 TÜB 315
  effect of music on different personalities, 34 TÜB 310
Perti, Giacomo Antonio, 71 WAR 131
  Nerone fatto Cesare, 72 VEN 299
Peru
  evolution of Peruvian music, 39 MEX 25
  scales, 32 LAP 319, 39 MEX 25
Peter von Arberg, Count
  Dat dagelyt von der heilige passien, 70 WÜR 112
Petrarch (Petrarca, Francesco), *Griselda*, 74 VEN 367
Petris, Johann Samuel, 71 GRA 87
Petrucci, Ottaviano dei
  at Fossombrone, 72 COP 295
  Motetti de la Corona, 72 COP 295
Pezzel, Johann, *Faustin*, 71 EIS 147

Philip I of Spain, 54 ARR 51
Philippines
  instruments, 66 MANL 24, 69 KUA 246
  traditional music, 67 BERL 90
  vocal music, 69 KUA 274
  Western music in, 61 TOK 86
Philology, musical, 58 COL 78
Philosophy *see* Aesthetics
Photographone, 08 VIE 563
Phrasing, 70 BON 415
Pianoforte
  automatic pianos, 06 BAS 212
  Beethoven's piano writing and pianos of his time, 70 PIE 129
  building in 17th and 18th c, 50 LÜN¹ 239
  . early pianos in the USA, 59 CAM 179
  electropiano, 71 BUD² iii, 577
  inharmonicity of strings, 53 NET 259
  manufacture in Italy, 21 TUR 217
  Mozart's Hammerflügel, 64 SAL ii, 273
  music
    Czech c1800, 70 BON 531
    Czech before Smetana, 71 BRN 131
    for popularizing music in France, 00 PAR² 289
    principles of teaching, 11 LON 326, 346
    sound and resonance, 00 MUN 347
    tone, machine to judge, 68 TOK¹ vi, 1
    1709 to 1851, 30 LIÈ 146
  see also individual composers
Pibroch, 71 BRN 325
Piccinni, Niccolò, 75 SIE 185
Pictorialism, Baroque in young Haydn 70 GRA 168
Piedmont
  folk sources, 57 CHIE 230
  historical canzoni, 56 VIE 220, 72 BYD 683
Piero (di Firenze), 59 CER 57
Pijper, Willem, 64 AMS 171
Pinpeat music, 69 KUA 196
Pipes
  acoustics, 58 MARS 215, 231
  Irish Uillean, 74 LON 334
  panpipe, 72 ROM 31
  timbre in Japanese, 71 BUD² iii, 597
Pisano, Bernardo, and the early madrigal, 67 LJU 96
Pisendel, Johann Georg, 66 LEIP 247
Pitch
  analysis of in different eras, 71 STU 177
  experiments with highest, 34 TÜB 309
  fundamental and its relation to pitch, 65 LIÈ i, M53
  in lute and vihuela, 57 NEU/S 171
  in harmonics, 71 BUD² iii, 621
  measurements of vibration, 54 WÉG 37
  notation instrument (musical applications), 38 GHE 105
  perception of, 30 BON 15, 50 LÜN¹ 230, 71 BUD² iii, 609, 613, 617
  standardization, 00 PAR¹ 28
  tuner, electronic, 53 NET 220
Pius X, Pope, 54 VIE 98
Pius XII, Pope, 56 VIE 309
Piyyut and its melody from the Geniza, 61 JER 362
Plaine and Easie Code (for notating music), 65 DIJ 156, 65 NEWY 53
Plainsong *see* Gregorian Chant
Plato, on music theory, 56 HAM 196
Platti, Giovanni
  cello style, 49 BAS 203
  concertos, 11 LON 158
Plavec, Gabriel, *Flosculus vernalis*, 72 BYD 323
Pleven, youth music, 72 VIE² 135

Podbielski, Chryszian W., sonatas, 72 BYD 459
Poetry, Poetics *60 WAR²*
  general
    and air de court up to 1620, 53 PAR 211
    and contemporary folksong, 60 WAR² 487
    and folk music, 34 TRT 368, 511
    and music in the 16th c, *53 PAR*
    musical poetry, 64 AMS 745
    and the periodic structure of music, 38 ZUR 655
    and primitive music, 31 PAR 793
  in countries
    and Arab music, 05 ALG 437
    and Bulgarian folksong, 60 WAR² 501
    English poetry, relation of syntax to music, 60 WAR² 203
    and French music, 53 PAR 79
    and French Baroque music, 68 MTA 127
    and French polyphonic music of the Renaissance, 67 BRN² 61
    old High German singable poetry, 56 HAM 225
    and the Italian madrigal, 70 MTA 31
Poglietti, Alessandro, counterpoint theory, 53 BAM 140
Pointillism in Webern, 72 VIE¹ 173
Pokonchi Indian music, 04 STU 403
Poland
  general
    dances outside Poland, 11 LON 201, 60 WAR¹ 572
    evolution of music, 73 WEIM 30
    folk music, 62 WAR 8, 65 BRA 47, 67 RAD 53
      and Chopin, 60 WAR¹ 95, 176, 247
      elements from middle ages to 18th c, 66 BYD 354
      on Polish radio, 54 PAR² 462
      theatre, 28 PRA 200
    and Italy, *69 PARM, 70 BOL, 71 WAR, 74 BOL*
    libraries, *see* Libraries and manuscripts
    lute research, 57 NEU/S 193
    mazurka research, 60 WAR¹ 624
    need for catalogue of Italian manuscripts in Poland, 69 PARM 223
    polka origins, 60 WAR¹ 530
    prelude, beginnings of, 60 WAR¹ 495
    southern influences on Polish music, 09 VIE 156
    violin and folk violin playing, 71 STP 16
  and individual composers
    Chopin, 60 WAR¹ 95, 176, 247
    Debussy, 62 PAR 313
    H. Finck, 62 KAS 119
    Janáček, 58 BRN 226, 60 WAR¹ 618
    Liszt, 75 EIS 53
    B. Milleville, 70 BOL 153
    Mozart, 56 VIE 191
    prewar composers, 62 WAR 86
    G. A. Ristoni, 71 WAR 253
    Szymanowski, 62 WAR 22, 86, 209, 274, 294
    Telemann, 62 MAG 23, 74 BLA 43
  to 1600
    ancient night melodies, 60 PAR² 97
    Carmina patria, origins of, 60 WAR¹ 527
    dances in Italy/Italian dances in Poland, 69 PARM 181
    guilds, musical, beginnings, 75 BYD 235
    history in 2nd half of 15th c, 60 WAR¹ 588
    instruments, early medieval, 60 WAR¹ 551
    Italian Ars nova, influence, 69 CER 465
      music in Poland in Renaissance and Baroque, 69 PARM, 70 BOL
    kolenda songs, medieval, 72 SÁR 165

    kyrial to 16th c, 75 BYD 261
    lute music in 16th c, 60 WAR¹ 630
    monody, medieval, 66 BYD 277
    musical culture, 60 WAR¹ 628, 69 BYD 197, 75 BYD 273
    national style, formation in instrumental Renaissance music, 54 PAR¹ 149
    Netherlands style (1500–1530), 67 LJU 107
    16th c organ style and practice, 70 BOL 33
    Polish–West relations 15th to 17th c, 66 BYD 383
    polyphony, 66 BYD 281
    polystructural musical character in middle ages, 75 BYD 273
    Renaissance, beginnings of, 71 WAR 57
      music in, 60 WAR¹ 640
    role in 14th c music, 64 SAL ii, 188
    sequence repertory, 60 WAR¹ 510, 75 BYD 273
    sources for conductus, organum and medieval motet, 72 COP 593
    study of J. de Muris's *Musica speculativa*, 69 PARM 39
  17th c
    Baroque, 66 BYD 294
      Polish–Italian, *69 PARM, 70 BOL*
      Renaissance break in style, 69 BYD 209
    concertato style in vocal–instrumental music, 69 PARM 89
    choice of means of performance, 67 BRN² 82
    dances in Italy/Italian dances in Poland, 69 PARM 181
    instrumental music, style, 69 PARM 121
    Italian musicians in Poland, 69 PARM 133–81
    Italian song in Poland, 71 WAR 263
    Lombardy instrumental style in Poland, 69 PARM 163
    opera, beginnings of, 69 PARM 173
      first Polish, influence on epoch of Chopin's youth, 11 LON 146
      at Władisław court, *69 WAR*
    Pelpin organ tablature 1620–30, 60 WAR¹ 628, 70 BOL 75
    organ style and practice, 70 BOL 33
    Polish princes' visit to Florence, 70 BOL 191
    polyphony, backward-looking, 71 WAR 277
    Russian–Polish ties, 60 WAR¹ 507
    Venetian polychoral technique, 63 VEN 179
  18th c
    Italian comic intermezzi, 70 VEN 175
    mazurka, 60 WAR¹ 538
    Russian–Polish ties, 60 WAR¹ 507
    symphony, 66 BYD 334
    waltz before Chopin, 60 WAR¹ 613
  19th and 20th c
    contemporary music and Chopin, 74 BOL 129
    gramophone industry in Polish life, 67 ZAG 36
    historical opera in Chopin's youth, 60 WAR¹ 503
    musical culture at beginning of 19th c, and Chopin, 60 WAR¹ 63
    music libraries 1964–73, 73 WEIM 81
    plastic arts in Szymanowski's time, 62 WAR 261
    youth music, 72 VIE² 80
Polka, Polish origin, 60 WAR¹ 530
Polonaise
  J. S. Bach's stylization, 50 LEIP 416
  by W. F. Bach, 60 WAR¹ 578
  Beethoven's development of, 27 VIE 66
  history, 00 PAR² 215
Polonus, Johannes, 60 WAR¹ 514
Polychoral music in 17th c Rome, 58 COL 100
Polynesia, music of, 67 VAN 94

Polyphony
  general
    antique, 58 COL 290
    Byzantine, 72 COP 737
    chromatic step in 16th c, 62 KAS 136
    church, and new fragment at Grottaferrata, 69 CER 305, 315
    in Ciconia, 50 ROM 280
    German polyphonic songs in 15th c, 58 COL 214
    Greek, 54 PAL 243
    Italy, monodic elements 14th to 15th c, 55 WÉG 217
      lauda, 30 LIÈ 155
      and Poland, conservative polyphony, 71 WAR 277
    at Jagiellon court, 27 VIE 164
    St Martial period, 53 BAM 240
    in 14th c mass, 25 LEIP 218
    medieval
      chant as symbol in, 50 ROM 303
      chanson, 21 PAR 784
      German, 50 LÜN¹ 68
      Hungarian, 66 BYD 223
      melismatic, 61 NEWY i, 178
      origins of Western, 61 NEWY i, 161
      Randformen, 70 BON 392
    Netherlands, chanson, 15th to 16th c, 30 LIÈ 168
    lamentations, 15th c, 52 UTR 352
    songs, 15th to 16th c, 30 ANT 453
    Russian polyphonic concerts, 17th to 18th c, 69 BYD 369
    sources and origins, 72 BYD 769, 75 BYD 587
    Sicilian school, 16th to 17th c, 50 LÜN¹ 89, 70 BOL 81, 73 ROM¹ 347
    Slav, sources 13th to 15th c, 75 BYD 381
    West, beginnings among, 60 WAR¹ 567
    Spain, 57 PAR 447
    15th c, 27 VIE 158
    before Flemish musicians, 30 LIÈ 67
    after Flemish musicians, 52 UTR 47
    Baroque, 57 WÉG 91
    11th to 12th c, 09 VIE 101
    12th c, text underlay and rhythmic interpretation, 72 COP 482
    see also individual composers
  sacred
    Christian value of, 50 ROM 330
    classical sacred, 27 BERL 102
    discography, 57 PAR 454
    editions, 57 PAR 431
    modern, 57 PAR 437
    performance of sacred classical, 50 ROM 336
    20th c for proper of mass, 50 ROM 409
    vocal in Roman Catholic liturgy, 54 VIE 154
  folk
    Albania, 56 HAM 229, 58 WÉG 85
    Alpine, 58 COL 316
    Austria, 27 VIE 326
    Balkans, 66 SOF ii, 1067
    Caucasian, 56 HAM 229
    Georgia, 50 LÜN¹ 172, 64 MOS 232
    non-European, 09 VIE 298, 27 VIE 321
    Slav, 64 GRA² 98
    Ukraine, 52 UTR 55
    Venezuela, 58 SJOS 647
    Yugoslavia, 64 MOS 265
Pop music, 72 VIE² 33–140
Popular music
  and Beethoven, 70 BERL² 443, 70 PIE 217
  of Classical period, 70 PIE 143
Populism in music and literature, 61 BUD 11

Porpora, Nicola Antonio (and Haydn), 70 GRA 41
Portugal
  Baroque music, 63 MTA 85
  and Beethoven, 27 VIE 132
  folk music, 63 STT 147, 177, 185
  Gregorian chant, 54 VIE 172
  influenced by Debussy, 62 PAR 263
Potocka, Delphine, Chopin's letters to, 60 WAR¹ 669
Poulenc, Francis (and Apollinaire), 65 STAV 49, 59
Practica musices in Renaissance music theory, 71 WAR 41
Praetorius, Michael
  prefaces, 56 VIE 107
  Rostock MSS, 56 HAM 112
Prague
  cultural centre of Czech and German culture in the interwar years, 70 BRN 381
  Festschrift for Rudolf II's Kapellmeister, 70 BON 520
  and Liszt, 61 BUD 27
  opera staging in 1723, 70 MTA 129
Preclassicism in Würzburg, 27 VIE 208
Precocity, musical, 00 PAR⁴ 97, 10 INN 224
Precolumbian music, 70 LIM 189
  instruments, 52 CAM 54, 62 MEX 369
Prelude, beginnings in Germany and Poland, 60 WAR¹ 495
Pre-romanticism and Mozart, 56 VIE 643
Preservation of traditional music, *61 TEH*
Pressburg *see* Bratislava
Prima prattica, 67 SIE 264
Primitive music
  instrumental style, 53 BAM 212
  and modern Eastern music, 38 FLOR 176
  myth of, 71 FLOR 147
  rhythm in instrumentally-accompanied, 58 COL 72
Printing, music
  1462–1600, 27 VIE 168
  15th and 16th c, 06 BAS 37
Profession, musicological, 62 KAS 321–33
Professionalism, musical, 71 STU 212
Programme music
  imitation of nature in 17th c, 64 AMS 626
  in Liszt, 61 BUD 59, 75 EIS 9
  musical integration of documentary aspects, 66 LEIP 351
  in Schoenberg, 74 BERL 21
Prokofiev, Sergey Sergeyevich
  and Bartók, 71 BUD¹ 137
  and Janáček operas, 68 BRN 219
Proprium de tempore in medieval Poland, 75 BYD 273
Prosa pro defunctis, *Audi tellus*, 60 WAR¹ 565
Prosody
  Italian, 56 HAM 85
  of 16th c, 49 BAS 83
  see also Verse structure; Word setting
Prosula
  performance practice, 58 COL 251
  trope research, 75 ESP 151
Provençal, musical epochs, 55 AVIG 197
Psalm
  and liturgy, 65 MTS 78–82
  notation, 06 BAS 47
  parody of Psalm 94, 73 HAM 164
  of Russian sectarians, 11 LON 187
  tones, evolution, 50 ROM 267
Psalmody, popular, 62 BERN 74
Psalter
  Romanian in 17th and 18th c, 72 BYD 487
  Slavonic 18th c, 57 PAR 346
  see also Huguenot Psalter

Psaltery, Baltic, 73 STOC 7
Psychology (of music) 09 GEN 630, 27 VIE 307, 56 VIE
  99, 727 *see also Index of Titles, Series and
  Sponsors*
  consonance and dissonance, psychological basis, 09
    VIE 330, 58 MARS 61
  and ethnomusicology, 10 INN 256
  experimental, 29 NEWH 384
  functions of music seen by Aristotle, 37 PAR³ ii, 18
  and information theory, 62 KAS 279
  hysterical subjects, musical language of, 05 ROM 476
  metre, 51 STOC 210
  musical ability, research into, 66 LEIP 510
  musical inspiration, 32 COP 7, 37 PAR² 285, 293
  orthosymphonie, 08 FRA 243
  psychophysiology and aesthetics, 11 LON 224
  present state, 61 NEWY i, 121
  recognition, musical, 23 LEIP 182
  of rhythm, 26 GEN 33
  tests, 29 NEWH 284, 406, 48 EDIN 129
  of tone colour, 09 VIE 360
  of tone quality, 39 NEWY 227
  of vibrato, 32 COP 212
  see also Hearing; Memory; Perception; Talent; Taste
Public, 37 FLOR 15, 31, 36, 42, 68, 48 FLOR 75, 68
    NEWY 57
  and composer, 37 FLOR 75, 90, 103, 108, 60 STRT 3,
    5
  and contemporary music, 37 FLOR 25, 47, 57, 83, 90,
    108, 65 BLM 57, 168, 213
  mass audience, 68 SVE 62, 67
  and modern opera, 64 SAL ii, 255
  and musicians, 37 FLOR 31, 98
Publishing, music
  and the composer 1500–1850, 58 COL 340
  early music, 61 NEWY i, 150
  in Italy, 21 TUR 49
  and music libraries, 59 CAM 67
  as profession for the musicologist, 62 KAS 325
  sound recording as form of publication, 68 NEWY
    84
Puccini, Giacomo
  exotic elements, 71 FLOR 141
  use of Gozzi fables, 74 SIE 193
Pueblos, Indian music, 28 PRA 168
Puglia, 'tarantismo' in, 60 PAR² 95
Pulaer, Louis von, Mass 'Christus resurgens', 30 LIÈ 91
Pulse in Mozart's music, 56 VIE 261
Purcell, Henry
  and Bach, 00 PAR² 210
  use of recorder, 59 CAM 227
Pygmy, Babinga music, 56 WÉG 105
Pyrenees, touloulou, 56 WÉG 55
Pythagorus
  system in China, 58 COL 174
  tuning, 25 LEIP 417–25

Quarter tone
  experiments, 27 BON 118
  historical basis, 27 VIE 359
  music, 29 NEWH 203
  and musicology, 25 LEIP 304
Quodlibet, origins and national aspects, 61 NEWY i, 30

Radio, 33 FLOR 43, 52, 61, 37 FLOR 145, *54 PAR²*
  contemporary music on, 37 FLOR 125
  as educating medium, *see* Education: application,
    means
  and church music, 57 PAR 630

  and folk music, 71 HIN 111
  German, 33 FLOR 118
  impact on music, 54 PAR² 367–96
  impact on society, *54 PAR²*
  influence on musical taste, 37 FLOR 129
  libraries, *see* Libraries and librarianship: broadcasting,
    radio music library
  light music, 54 PAR² 559
  music for, 39 NEWY 251
  music critics, use by, 33 FLOR 61
  music history tasks, 50 LÜN¹ 204
  and new music, 37 FLOR 125, 54 PAR² 518, 521, 534
  opera for, 64 HAM 112
  opera on, 37 FLOR 118, 38 FRA 202, 64 HAM 109
  orchestral music on, 37 FLOR 118
  original music for, 54 PAR² 413
  as profession for musicologist, 62 KAS 328
  recital singing on, 38 FRA 199
  and records, 67 ZAG 51, 59
  and singing, 38 FRA 339–65
  sound recording in, 68 NEWY 84
  in therapy, 54 PAR² 468
  voices, character of good, 38 FRA 339
Raga
  classification, 66 MANL 38
  in 20th c, 64 NEWD² 151
Ragazzi, Angelo, Sonate a quattro, 72 COP 356
Ragtime, 65 BLM 91
Raison, André, 69 PAR 183
Rallentando, in 17th and 18th c, 69 PAR 237
Rameau, Jean Philippe (and Beethoven), 30 LIÈ 174
Rapanui, origin of primitive music, 70 LIM 189
Rationalism, in Bach, 50 LEIP 420
Ravel, Maurice, structural problems, 58 COL 289
Rebab, Javanese, 59 CAM 220
Receptivity towards music, *72 VIE²*
Recitative
  compared with melodrama and aria in 18th c, 69
    BRN 59
  in Handel, 59 HAL 135
  in Marschner, 70 BON 461
  in Monteverdi, 68 VEN 157
  in Mozart's instrumental works, 56 PAR 199
  notation, 06 BAS 47
Records, recording
  in relation to different aspects of music
  and composer, 67 ZAG 41
  early uses, 08 VIE 557, 563
  as educating medium, 37 FLOR 166, 67 ZAG 17
  in folk music, 34 TRT 347, 392, 56 CAG 120, 67
    BRN¹ 171, 70 TRČ 151
  as form of publication, 68 NEWY 84
  instruments, 69 STOC 47
  research, use of videotape, 73 ROM² 251
  influence on musical creation, 70 HAMM 12
  and music history, 67 ZAG 44
  and musicology, 61 NEWY i, 404, 418; 67 ZAG 22,
    50
  and other media, 67 ZAG 51, 59
  passing on musical heritage, medium for, 56
    HAM 105
  sonographic research into speech and music, 66
    GRA 40
  as source for speech/song research, 38 FRA 30,
    279
  and youth, 67 ZAG 57
  records, 33 FLOR 76, 109, 37 FLOR 156
  in contemporary life, *67 ZAG*
  criticism, 67 ZAG 33

libraries, *see* Libraries and librarianship
industry, in Hungary, 67 ZAG 37
  in Poland, 67 ZAG 36
  as profession for musicologist, 62 KAS 330
  in Romania, 67 ZAG 56
  repertory, 67 ZAG 21, 22
  sociological aspects, 67 ZAG 14
  wear on, 65 LIÈ i, M63
recording, 68 NEWY 74, 84
  deterioration, 67 PAR 81
  distortion, 67 PAR 81
  international technique, proposals for, 31 UDIN 10
  of melody, 30 BON 31
  modern techniques, 56 HAM 133
  problems, 37 FLOR 261
  stereo, 50 LÜN¹ 243
  subjective judgments, 65 LIÈ i, M62
Recorder, Purcell's use of, 59 CAM 227
Reed
  acoustic studies, 58 MARS 203, 215
  pipe, 59 CAM 218
Regensburg, church music connections with Rome, 50 ROM 90
Reger, Max, *73 NUR*, 56 VIE 563, 73 WEIM 48
  and Catholic church music, 73 NUR 123
  and German organ music, 26 FRE/B 122
  harmony, 73 NUR 55
  influenced by Bach, 73 NUR 3
  interpreted by K. Straube, 73 NUR 21
  and new music, 73 NUR 83
  and Protestant hymns, 73 NUR 113
  style, 68 BRN 303
  variation technique, 62 WAR 142
Registration, harpsichord, 69 PAR 203, 233
Règle de l'octave, 72 COP 556
Reicha, Antonin
  and Beethoven, 70 PIE 13
  fugues, 70 PIE 13
  and Mozart, 56 PRA 79
  wind quintets, 71 BRN 127
Reichardt, Johann Friedrich, 62 KAS 202
  and East European folk music, 60 WAR¹ 601
Reiche, Gottfried, 62 KAS 311
Reichenberg *see* Liberec
Reinken, Johann Adam
  Hortus musicus, arranged by Bach, 49 BAS 160
Religious music *see* Church music
Reményi, Eduard, and Brahms and Liszt, 61 BUD 89
Renaissance, 27 VIE, 39 FLOR 52, 71 WAR 91
  and Baroque, break in style, in Polish instrumental music, 69 BYD 209
  and Baroque and mannerism, 57 WÉG 35
  chromaticism, 53 PAR 225
  composition and aleatoric music, 49 BAS 103
  dance music, 54 PAR¹ 163, 69 BYD 315
  demands of composers on human voice, 67 BRN² 69
  fêtes, *55 ROY, 57 BRUS, 72 TOU*
  form, 54 PAR¹ 165
  French 12th c, 39 NEWY 200
    northern provinces, *54 ARR*
  German 19th c revival, 53 BAM 289
  harmony, 56 VIE 92
  historical conception, 52 UTR 19
  instrumental music, *54 PAR¹*
  styles, 54 PAR¹ 61
  writings, 73 PAR 1
  and mannerism, 57 WÉG 35, 73 ROM¹ 85
  in Netherlands music, concept of, 52 UTR 450
  practica musices in Renaissance musical theory, 71

WAR 41
19th c Rhinelands movement, 25 LEIP 398
Romania, 69 BYD 221–67
  variation technique, 69 PARM 57, 71
Venetian folksongs, 39 NEWY 62
Répertoire internationale des sources musicales
  general, 49 BAS 37, 51 PAR 20–32, 55 BRUS 44, 49, 144, 62 KAS 341
  and Italy, 62 STOC 28
  and theatrical collections, 65 AMS 27
Repertorium musicae universale, 58 COL 221
Repicco, origin and significance, 52 UTR 404
Resia
  Slovenian instrumental ensemble in, 69 STOC 158
  tuning of violins, 69 STOC 163
Resonance, 71 BUD² iv, 1
  in music, 60 PAR¹ 251–79
  in musical scales, *60 PAR¹*
  and rhythm, 65 GEN 141
Restoration
  of Antwerp harpsichords, *70 ANT*
  in instrument collections, 69 NUR 103–117
  reasons for, 70 ANT 28, 72 COP 145
  of string keyboard instruments, *71 GRA*
Reverberation, artificial, 67 PAR 111
Revers introit trope repertory, 75 ESP 97
Revolution
  in Balkan songs, 66 SOF vii, 777
  and music, 74 ZAG v, 113
  music and musicians in 1848, 11 LON 149
  political use of French revolutionary opera, 70 BON 237
Rhapsody, inspiration in 19th and 20th c music, 72 COP 561
Rhetoric and Mattheson, 56 HAM 99
Rhineland
  and Beethoven, 27 VIE 7, 70 VIE 25
  middle Rhine Baroque organ building, 51 OCH 78
  music, 25 LEIP 401
  Renaissance movement in 19th c, 25 LEIP 398
Rhythm
  general, 09 VIE 384, 25 LEIP 445, 460, *26 GEN, 65 GEN*
  analysis, 26 GEN 70, 65 BRA 47–81
  in children, 54 WÉG 64; 62 KAS 286
  primary-school, invention in, 62 KAS 286
  in the cinema and in music, 33 FLOR 209, 37 PAR³ ii, 364
  classical dance, relation with, 65 GEN 154
  concept of, 53 BAM 47, 67 BUC 107
  and improvisation, 65 GEN 148
  indicated by harmonic rhythm, 58 COL 176
  interior, 37 FLOR 265
  in madrigal, 73 ROM¹ 287
  measurement of, 54 WÉG 37
  and metre, 26 GEN 76
  motor co-ordination, 29 NEWH 385
  notation, 21 PAR 810, 26 GEN 82, 52 UTR 377
  in Peking Opera, 66 MANL 114
  in performance, 26 GEN 26, 27 VIE 385
  polyrhythm, 26 GEN 71
  research, 26 GRON 448, 58 COL 113, 69 STOC 53
  and resonance, 65 GEN 141
  structures, 65 GEN 156
  teaching, 26 GEN 82, 179, 65 GEN 22, 136
  word and music, relation to, 58 COL 255
  and individual composers
    Bach, 62 KAS 167
    Beethoven, 27 VIE 45, 70 BON 29–55, 394
    Berlioz, 70 BON 29

Brahms, 62 KAS 217
Chopin, 60 WAR¹ 185, 241
Enesco, 73 BUC 31
Monteverdi, 68 VEN 323
Ockeghem, 58 COL 73
Schubert, 62 KAS 198
Stamic, 70 BON 53
Webern, 72 VIE¹ 52; 73, 100
Oswald von Wolkenstein, 73 NEU/B 51
psychology and aesthetics, 27 HAL 202, 260
biological–cosmic, 26 GEN 39, 350; 27 VIE 45, 66
    LEIP 469, 70 BON 575
correlation with duration, 62 KAS 276
T. Lipp's aesthetics of, 09 VIE 345
psychological aspects, 26 GEN 33, 58 MARS 83
theory of, 58 COL 264
and time elapse, 72 FRE/B 60
Zeitgestalt as basic concept, 62 KAS 268
in folk music and non-western art music, 67 BRN¹
    165, 69 STOC 53
Algeria, 32 CAIR 521
American Indian, 22 RIO 85
Arab, 32 CAIR 131
Bulgarian, 47 PRA 37
Ceylonese, 58 COL 60
classification of folksong, 65 BRA 47–81
Czechoslovakia, 28 PRA 184
Egypt, 32 CAIR 399
Eskimo, 67 VAN 54
Far East, 64 NEWD² 146
Indian, 64 NEWD² 77
Iranian, 58 COL 61
Iraq, 32 CAIR 516
Italian, 73 BEL 40
Morocco, 32 CAIR 521
primitive music with instrumental accompani-
    ment, 58 COL 72
Syria, 32 CAIR 433
Tunisia, 32 CAIR 521
Turkish, 66 SOF ii, 1123
Ukrainian, 09 VIE 276, 11 LON 184
chant
Byzantine, 30 ATH 268
Greek–Roman rhythmic system, 25 LEIP 203
Gregorian, *see* Gregorian chant
and medieval music, 26 GEN 21
cantio, 58 COL 281
conductus, 58 COL 219
lyrics, 49 BAS 45, 56 VIE 7, 61 NEWY i, 3
monody, 52 UTR 377
12th c polyphony, 72 COP 482
Renaissance
14th to 15th c Flemish songs, 24 BAS 376
and metre, in time of humanism, 61 NEWY i, 66
16th c music on rhythm of 17th c, 54 PAR¹ 339
notation in two 16th c prints, 21 PAR 810
20th c, 24 BAS 80, 62 KAS 379
coding rhythmic structure for vocal music, 73 PAR
    66
in serial music, 58 COL 199
Romania
general, 67 BUC 21
Byzantine to 18th c, 66 BYD 419, 67 BRN² 53
chamber music, 67 BUC 162
choral works, 67 BUC 86
epic, connections, with Balkan, 68 GRA 53
folk ballad, 58 WÉG 39
folk music, 11 LON 205, 27 VIE 340, 28 PRA 133,
    67 BERL 186, 67 BUC 60, 69, 137, 75 BYD
    343

folk music instruments, 27 VIE 340, 67 BRN¹ 176,
    75 BRUN 121
harmony, 67 BUC 117
music 1900–29, 73 BUC 49
of psalter in 17th and 18th c, 72 BYD 487
musical culture in 17th and 18th c, 72 BYD 507
national and universal elements, *67 BUC*
record industry, 67 ZAG 56
Renaissance musical culture, 69 BYD 221–67
social basis of art music, 56 VIE 647
violin playing, 67 BUC 80
word setting, 69 BRN 215
14th to 18th c, 66 BYD 403–31
and individual composers
Beethoven, 70 BERL² 135, 70 BON 367
Enesco, 73 BUC 49, 71
Haydn, 59 BUD 177
Janáček, 66 BRN 207
Liszt, 61 BUD 107
Martinů, 66 BRN 207
Mozart, 56 PRA 112
Telemann, 67 MAG i, 101
Ricciotti, Carlo (and Pergolesi), 52 UTR 127
Ricercare, origin and significance of, 52 UTR 404
Riedel, Georg, oratorios, 25 LEIP 373
Riemann, Hugo
Opernhandbuch, revision of, 09 VIE 439
theory of harmonic functions, 00 PAR¹ 56, 56 VIE
    183
Rio de Janeiro and Verdi, 66 VEN 383
*RISM see Répertoire internationale des sources
    musicales*
Ristori, Giovanni Alberto (and Poland), 71 WAR 253
Rock, 71 FLOR 133, 173
Rococo, 60 ROM 387
Roger, Estienne, dating first editions, 53 BAM 273
Rolland, Romain, view of Handel, 59 HAL 219
Romagnoli, Ettore, folk music studies, 54 PAL 95
Romance, history and national importance, 53 PAR
    299
Romanticism, 60 WAR¹ 53, 74 BOL 39
Beethoven as Romantic, 27 VIE 40, 70 VIE 77
and Classicism, 25 LEIP 292
concept, 60 WAR¹ 691
influence on sacred music, 50 ROM 392
Liszt as Romantic, 23 BRUS 368
Mozart and the Romantics, 31 SAL 22
national movements in Germany and Scandi-
    navia, 60 KAS 60, 63 KIE 42
and Szymanowski, 62 WAR 161
violin music, 72 GRA 47
Rome
antiphonary, 50 ROM 248
chant, 50 LÜN¹ 53, 50 ROM 276, 54 PAL 245, 58
    COL 358
church music 1600–1800, 62 KAS 147, 70 BON 406
church music and Regensburg, 50 ROM 90
folksongs, 34 TRT 383
gradual, 50 ROM 207
Greco-Roman art and folk music, 54 PAL 91
Greco-Roman metrical system, 25 LEIP 203
influence on Kapsberger, 67 SIE 288
performances in honour of Polish prince, 70 BOL
    199
17th c polychoral music, 58 COL 100
Schola cantorum, *see* Schola cantorum
theatre and music 1825–50, 03 ROM 157
Ronsard, Pierre de (and music) 53 PAR 105
Rorantists at Wawel, 71 WAR 203
Rossi, Luigi, *Orfeo*, 00 PAR² 191

Rossi, Michel-Angelo, keyboard tablatures, 72 COP 342
Rossini, Giocchino
  conventions of composition, 70 STGE 48
  operas and printed librettos, 67 LJU 194
Rousseau, Jean-Jacques
  as music educator, 62 KAS 282
  view of Italian music, 75 SIE 45
Ruanda music, 56 WÉG 163
Ruckers, Hans
  harpsichords, 70 ANT 23, 44, 53, 77
  workshop, 71 GRA 41
Rudolstadt, cantata librettos, 72 COP 271
Ruffo, Vincenzo, 68 MIL 23
Russia
  general
    Bylina metre, 64 BRA 165
    Byzantine, 48 PAR² 321, 53 THE 120
    folk music, 09 VIE 233
    gusli, history, 67 BRN¹ 134
    musicology, 58 COL 99
    orthodox chant, 00 PAR² 134, 50 ROM 158,52 BERN 38, 53 THE 120, 64 BRA 101, 66 BYD 455
      liturgical music, 62 BERN 32
    religious music, history of, 37 PAR¹ 122
    secular music, 09 VIE 466
    violin school, classical, 72 GRA 149
      modern, 72 GRA 149, 154
  and individual composers
    Bartók, 61 BUD 481
    Beethoven, 70 BERL² 115, 147, 70 BON 135
    Debussy, 62 KAS 241, 62 PAR 199, 315
    Haydn, 59 BUD 61, 85
    Janáček, 65 BRN 72
    Mozart, 56 PRA 106, 56 VIE 365
    Verdi, 66 VEN 458, 69 VER 546
  to 1600
    ecclesiastical chant 12th to 18th c, 66 BYD 455
    performing practice of early vocal music, 69 BYD 467
    services for Slavonic saints in early manuscripts, 75 BYD 211
    Skoromoch, 75 BYD 221
    use of typographical rules in study of ancient forms of singing, 75 BYD 607
  17th c
    anthology with hammer-headed notation, 72 BYD 293
    choral music, development of style, 66 BYD 470
    Polish relations, 60 WAR¹ 507
    polyphonic concerts, 69 BYD 369, 72 BYD 769, 75 BYD 587
    problems in style in 17th and 18th c, 72 BYD 795
  18th c
    classicism, 72 BYD 825
    opera origins, development, 66 BYD 489
    Polish relations, 60 WAR¹ 507
  19th c
    fate of Gozzi's tales, 74 SIE 137
    'Mighty handful' and Chopin, 60 WAR¹ 413
    opera, 70 BON 515
    reception of Liszt's works in 1840s and 1850s, 61 BUD 211
    song, before Glinka, 67 LJU 202
    see also Orthodox church; Znamenny chant; Soviet Union
Rzewuski, Stanisław Mateusz
  music and opera at court, 69 WAR 61

Saar, wind music in industry in 19th c, 74 GRA² 109
Sabah traditional music instruments, 69 KUA 327
Sacchini, Antonio
  centenary, 30 LIÈ 211
  Il renaud, 75 SIE 225
Sacred music *see* Church music
Saess, Heinrich, *Musica plana atque mensurabilis*, 62 KAS 359
St Alessio, 70 BOL 199
St Augustin, 26 GEN 21
St Aycadre, Office, 54 ROU 977
St Césaire, 58 COL 217
St Columban, music and worship, *50 LUX*
St Cyril, 64 BRA 7, 49
St Demetrius, 64 BRA 35
St Gall
  antiphonary, 54 ROU 937
  chant in late middle ages and later, 05 STRS 123
  liturgical MSS, 50 LUX 317
  role in diffusion of Roman chant, 25 BRUG 225
  sequence tradition, 49 BAS 176
St Germain-en-Laye
  performances of *Triomphe de l'amour* (1681), 21 PAR 874
St Julien-des-Ménétiers, 00 PAR⁶ 57
St Martial period, vocal and instrumental style, 53 BAM 240
St Methodius, 64 BRA 7, 49
St Odilon, 49 CLU 51
St Odon of Cluny, 49 CLU 171
St Petersburg, first performance of Beethoven's *Missa Solemnis*, 70 BON 559
St Philibert
  hymns, 54 ROU 343
  rhymed office, 54 ROU 335, 977
Saint-Quentin, Collegiale de
  Josquin Desprez at, 21 PAR 807
  Jumentier, Bernard, at, 53 BAM 279
Saints, cult of in medieval music, 61 TOD 181
Saint-Saëns, Camille, in Scandinavia (1897), 28 OSL 397
Saint-Trond, four-part vocal piece from Abbey, 30 LIÈ 165
Salieri, Antonio, 70 BON 325
Salonika, Hebrew folksong in, 54 PAL 57
Saloum, bow, 45 DAK 248
Saltarello, 57 CHIE 164
Salvatore di Messina, 53 THE 274
Salzburg
  17th c church music, 27 VIE 202
  Mozart memorials, 56 PRA 167
  opera to 1650, 27 VIE 196
  and Toscanini, 67 FLOR 273
Samaritan chant, 65 JER 153
Sammartini, Giovanni Battista, vocal music, 75 SIE 277
Samre, mouth organ among the, 69 KUA 223
San Cassiano, Venice, 72 VEN 97
Sanluri folk music, 57 CHIE 237
Santa Maria del Fiore, Florence
  Marco da Gagliano's sacred music at, 49 BAS 125
São Tomé, Island of, folk music, 56 STOM 101
Sarasin, Lucas, collection of 18th c symphonies, 24 BAS 321
Sardinia, folk music, 40 VEN 357, 382, 48 TUR 120, 54 PAL 89, 73 ROM² 189, 207
Sarri, Domenico, *Didone abbandonata*, 56 HAM 113
Satie, Erik, and Les Six, 68 BRN 321
Savoy fêtes in 1644 and 1645, 70 MTA 49
Saxony (and Thuringia)
  music research, 25 LEIP 385

organs in Protestant churches, 27 FRE/S 102
17th to 18th c sources of music, 58 COL 164
stylistic changes in Saxon era, 60 WAR¹ 633
Scacchi, Marco
  Cribrum musicum, 63 KIE 108, 69 PARM 201, 209
  first book of four-part masses, 71 WAR 217
  opinions on the art of music, 70 BOL 181
Scale *60 PAR¹*
  aesthetics, 68 UPP 811
  Arab, 32 CAIR 593
  assymetry in, 25 LEIP 67
  formation, elements in, 60 PAR¹ 185-223
  influence on development of music, 58 MARS 13
  mathematical analysis of tempered chromatic
    scale, 11 LON 74
  nomenclature, 00 PAR¹ 39
  non-pentatonic, 60 PAR¹ 123
  non-Western, 73 PAR 144
  3-note music, 63 CART 87
  oriental music, development in, 58 MARS 39
  pentatonic, *see* Pentatonic
  of Peru, ancient, 32 LAP 319
  heptaphonic, 39 MEX 25
  resonance in, 60 PAR¹ 21-291
  structure, 28 PRA 102
  · role of 4ths, 5ths and 8ves, 60 PAR¹ 103-49
  theory of, 58 MARS 21-111
  as tone spectrum, 50 LÜN¹ 229
  see also Mode
Scandinavia
  breviaries, 75 ESP 27
  Debussy, influence of, 62 PAR 301
  folksongs, 00 PAR⁵ 62
  Mozart operas in, 56 VIE 387
  music, 47 PRA 13
    1830-1914, 62 KAS 60
    and North German music, *63 KIE*
  register of liturgical fragments, 75 ESP 171-9
  relations with England, 72 COP 263, 75 ESP 11
  Romantic national movement in German and
    Scandinavian music, 62 KAS 60, 63 KIE 42
  Saint-Saëns in, 28 OSL 397
  see also Libraries and Manuscripts
Scapitte, Vincenzo, 70 BOL 173
Scarlatti, Domenico, keyboard works, 00 PAR² 213
Scève, Maurice (and music), 53 PAR 89
Scheidt, Samuel, tablature (1650), 58 COL 196
Schenker, Heinrich
  demonstration of Chopin's part-writing, 60 WAR¹
    145
  theoretical, 56 VIE 183
Schiller, Friedrich von
  influence on Verdi, 62 KAS 222
  and Verdi: *Don Carlos*, 69 VER 156-234
Schleswig-Holstein
  folksongs, 63 KIE 100
  connections with Denmark in 19th c, 63 KIE 48
Schlick, Arnolt (and Cabezón), 54 PAR¹ 217
Schloss Grätz *see* Hradec
Schneider, Willi, 74 GRA² 311
Schnitger, Arp, 27 FRE/S 149
Schoenberg, Arnold
  general, *74 BERL*
    in Berlin, 74 BERL 5
    and *Die blaue Reiter*, 68 STRS 245
    Gesamtausgabe, 70 BON 279
    influence in Vienna c1900, 74 GRA 34
    religious thought, 65 JER 147
    research, 70 BON 279-93
    as theoretician, 70 BON 288

and others
  Bartók and Stravinsky, 68 BRN 331
  Debussy, 62 PAR 319
  Dvořák, 71 BRN 157
  Hába, 70 BRN 407
  Janáček, 58 BRN 236
  Kandinsky, 74 BERL 9
  Palestrina, 56 VIE 749
  Zemlinsky, 74 GRA¹ 55
style
  beginnings of 12-note theory, 70 BON 284
  harmony, 58 COL 305, 72 FRE/B 83
  and programme music, 74 BERL 21
works, general
  chamber, 74 BERL 26
  orchestral, 74 BERL 15
  piano music, 74 BERL 30
  religious, 65 JER 147
  songs, 74 BERL 44
works, specific
  Erwartung, 74 BERL 35
  Harmonielehre, 68 BRN 339, 70 BON 288
  Jane Grey, 72 COP 705
  Moses und Aron, 58 COL 305
  Orchestral pieces op. 16, 70 BON 372, 499, 72
    FRE/B 116
  String Quartet in D Major, 71 BRN 157
  Survivor from Warsaw, 74 BERL 41
Schola Cantorum, Rome, 54 VIE 111
  improvisation, 54 PAL 259
  tradition of Gregorian chant, 54 VIE 120
School
  choirs in Reformation, and wind music, 74 GRA² 31
  see Latin; Education
Schopenhauer, Arthur, theory of music, 29 NEWH 350
Schrecker, Franz
  Fünf Gesänge für eine tiefe Stimme, 74 GRA¹ 111
  and Zemlinsky, 74 GRA¹ 111
Schubert, Franz
  general, *28 VIE*, 56 VIE 289
    character, 28 VIE 141
    and Classical period, 28 VIE 47
    and folksong, 28 VIE 57
    France, cultivation of works in, 28 VIE 87
    genealogy, 28 VIE 77
    size, 28 VIE 81
    and Vienna, 28 VIE 37
  bibliographical
    handwriting, 28 VIE 167
    manuscripts in private hands in Germany, 28 VIE
      155
    manuscripts in Prussian Staatsbibliothek, 28 VIE
      147
    thematic catalogue, 28 VIE 173
  style
    cyclic character of piano dances, 56 VIE 408
    as dance musician, 28 VIE 233
    harmony, 66 LEIP 437
    organic structure, 28 VIE 219
    rhythm, 62 KAS 198
    string instrument handling in chamber music, 28
      VIE 131
    suspensions, 71 BRN 397
    use of same texts, 28 VIE 117
  works, general
    church music, 28 VIE 181
    instrumental, 27 VIE 222
    late works, 58 COL 118
    Lieder, 27 VIE 388, 28 VIE 111, 69 BRN 243
    lyrical piano music, 28 VIE 189

male-voice choruses, 28 VIE 209
sonatas, 28 VIE 199
songs, performance of, 28 VIE 125
works, specific
  Lazarus, 66 LEIP 300
  Piano Sonata in A Major D664, 71 BRN 397
  Schwanengesang, transcription by Liszt, 75 EIS 115
  Winterreise, 66 LEIP 437
Schumann, Robert
  Beethoven, compared with, 27 VIE 91
  Beethoven, view of, 70 BERL[2] 99
  and Chopin, 60 WAR[1] 329, 363
  criticism of Liszt, 75 EIS 131
  documents in Leipzig Stadtarchiv, 66 LEIP 318
  piano pieces opp. 99 and 124, 66 LEIP 313
  piano style, 60 WAR[1] 329
  relationship of word and music, 56 HAM 216
  sketches, 66 LEIP 313
  unpublished letters to Schumann 1834–54, 63 KIE 120
Schütz, Heinrich
  dissonance treatment, 53 BAM 132
  forms of expression, 00 PAR[6] 95
  in light of style changes, 25 LEIP 245
Science
  relation to music, 34 PRA 1073
  relation to musicology, 73 PAR 115
  scientific character of music theory, 70 BERL[1] 49
  scientific and musical theory, 70 BERL[1] 59
Scordatura, 58 COL 172
Score reading
  mistakes in, 38 FLOR 129
  reading and interpreting, 38 FLOR 136
  as task for 18th c organists, 30 LIÈ 109
Scotland
  connections with Renaissance fête, 55 ROY 335
  Highland bagpipe, 53 NET 231
  pibroch, 71 BRN 325
Sebastiani, Johann, and music in Königsberg, 63 KIE 113
Second Viennese School *see* Vienna: 19th and 20th c
Seconda prattica in Ferrara, new music and letters, 72 COP 576
Sedlec Antiphonary, 27 BEL 155
Seger, Josef, figured bass improvisation, 56 VIE 490
Semiotics
  Analysis, 74 KRP 12
  in Czechoslovakia, 73 BEL 27
  evaluation of Beethoven, 70 BERL[2] 405
  of music, *73 BEL*
  and sociology of music, 74 ZAG v, 61, vi, 90
  see also Aesthetics
Seneca, music in Elizabethan tragedies inspired by him, 62 ROY 139
Senfl, Ludwig
  motet and song style, 49 BAS 121
  music in Heidelberg Kapellkatalog, 66 LEIP 186
Sephardic *see* Jewish music
Sequence
  aparallel, 70 BON 467
  Aquitaine, 54 ROU 937
  in archaic Italian style, 54 PAL 289
  Jumièges, 54 ROU 937, 943
  Matergruppe, 56 VIE 276
  origins, 06 BAS 165, 38 ZUR 604
  performance of, 58 COL 251
  in Poland in middle ages, 75 BYD 273
  Polish repertory and place of *Jesu Christe rex sup-*

rerne, 60 WAR[1] 510
St Gall tradition in late middle ages, 49 BAS 176
text underlay, 61 NEWY i, 12
Serbia
  chant, 61 OKH ii, 583, 64 BRA 55, 66 BYD 140, 69 BYD 61, 75 BYD 163
  church music, 72 BERN 84
  flute, 67 BRN[1] 82
  folk music instruments, iconographical sources, 73 BAL 78
  folksong, 31 PAR 710, 66 SOF vii, 883
  instruments in Serbo-Macedonian art, 61 OKH ii, 589
  music 1830–1914, 62 KAS 80
  secular feudal, 66 BYD 117
  Serbo-Croatian folk epic, 56 HAM 241
  shepherd trumpets in north-east, 75 BRUN 76
  wedding songs, compared with Bulgarian, 66 SOF iii, 1088
Serenata and Mozart, 74 ROM 148
Serial music, 55 ARR 175, 60 STRT 49–71
  compositional procedures, 62 KAS 374
  in the orient, 56 VIE 238
  present state, 56 VIE 593
  rhythm in serial technique, 58 COL 199
  in Schoenberg, beginnings, 70 BON 284
  in Webern, 72 VIE[1] 167
Serov, Alexander Nikolayevich (and Mozart), 56 VIE 328
Ševčik, Otakar, 72 GRA 142
Sforza, Antonio (and Josquin Desprez), 68 MIL 17, 71 NEWY 31
Shakespeare
  and Chopin, 64 AMS 187
  last plays and the masque, 71 VAN 156
  musical symbolism, 55 ROY 319
  music as structural element, 71 VAN 174
  The Tempest, 70 MTA 71
  Verdi librettos based on plays, 66 VEN 120
Shalyapin, Feodor Ivanovich (and Verdi), 69 VER 546
Shawm, used by Louis Couperin, 59 CAM 233
Shepherd
  Christmas organ pieces in Westphalia, 75 BRUN 61
  Christmas songs in Slovakia, 75 BRUN 96
  German shepherd idylls, 75 BRUN 106
  instruments in Bulgaria, 75 BRUN 81
  Slovakian research into shepherd music, 75 BRUN 71
  trumpets in North-east Serbia, 75 BRUN 76
Shnorali, Nerses, 75 BYD 421
Shostakovich, Dmitri, string quartets, 71 BRN 455
Sibelius, Jean
  and Bartók, 71 BUD[1] 121
  and Debussy, 68 BRN 307
  and folk music, 53 BAM 207
  as symphonist, 50 LÜN[1] 146
Siciliano
  in Bach and Handel, 54 PAL 301
  evolution, 53 BAM 194
Sicily
  folk music, 54 PAL 37, 89, 95, 73 ROM[2] 229
  Greek-Albanian folksongs in, 54 PAL 329
  history of music, 54 PAL 189
  Italo-Albanian liturgical chant in, 50 ROM 129
  polyphonic school, 50 LÜN[1] 89, 70 BOL 81, 73 ROM[1] 347
Siebeck, Hermann, as music aesthetician, 27 VIE 312
Siefert, Paul
  psalms, 70 BON 522
  quarrel with Scacchi, 63 KIE 108, 69 PARM 209

Siena
Avignon flute players in, 21 PAR 802
dances and instruments in 13th c paintings, 69 CER 83
Sievers, Eduard, theories on interpretation, 24 BAS 110
Sigel ornaments, 49 BAS 135
Sigismund III, musical relations with Austria, 60 WAR¹ 522
Signals, drum, 38 GHE 503, 51 STIS 165
Silbermann, Gottfried
in Alsace, 25 BRUG 224
as organ builder, 26 FRE/B 59
organs, 27 FRE/S 103
organ tuning, 70 BON 487
Silesia, folksong research in, 09 VIE 226
Simon, maître de vièle, 11 MAL 761
Singing
acoustics, 58 MARS 253, 71 BUD² iii, 593, 74 LON 343, 348
art and science, 13 BERL 511
Baroque improvisation, 53 BAM 252
differences between German and Italian, 38 FRA 161
intonation, 38 FRA 253
in Italy in 20th c, 21 TUR 211
phonetic basis of, 38 GHE 207
position of mouth, changes while singing, 38 GHE 77
psychological aspects, 38 FRA 301–36
and radio, 38 FRA 199, 339–65
records and film, use as research sources 38 FRA 30, 279
school movement, 61 NEWY i, 89
'singing formant', 72 COP 679, 74 LON 344
and speech, *38 FRA*
speech training, 38 FRA 279–98
style changes, 33 FLOR 203
of early German opera, 38 FRA 11
teaching, 38 FRA 116–75
phonology in, 09 VIE 309
in schools, 09 VIE 333, 368
text bases for its problems, 30 LIÈ 81
see also Voice
Six, Les (and Satie), 68 BRN 321
Sketches, 56 VIE 616, 58 BRN 220
Beethoven, *see* Beethoven: works (general)
Mozart, 62 KAS 184
Schumann, 66 LEIP 313
Szymanowski, 62 WAR 109
Verdi, 70 BON 412
Skjavetić, Julije, madrigals, 75 BYD 145
Skoromoch, Russian, as medieval minstrel, 75 BYD 221
Skryabin, Alexander Nikolayevich
and Chopin, 60 WAR¹ 335
harmony, 60 WAR¹ 335, 70 BON 438
piano sonatas, 62 WAR 177
piano works, 71 BRN 411
Slav
Baroque in, 67 LJU 310
Byzantine chant influence on early church music, 64 SAL ii, 167, 66 OXF² 119, 141
chant, 57 PAR 346, *64 BRA*
communion cycle, 61 OKH ii, 571
folk dance, 28 PRA 166
idiom in Janáček, 70 BON 603
music, early, 64 BRA 147
song, 64 GRA² 98, 74 KRP 30
instruments, 64 BRA 125–39, 64 GRA² 34

inventory of old Slav sources, 64 BRA 173
Kondakarion notation, 64 BRA 77
liturgical song, origin in 9th c, 52 UTR 456
music, beginnings of, *64 BRA*
musicology in America, 72 BYD 615
notation in 9th c, 50 ROM 114
Oktoechos, 72 COP 766, 75 BYD 175
Petrus liturgy, 64 BRA 23
polyphony, beginning of among West Slavs, 60 WAR¹ 567
sources of in 13th to 15th c, 75 BYD 381
18th c psalter, 57 PAR 346
role in 18th to 19th c music, 64 SAL ii, 237
South Slav, in European music history, 67 LJU 26
influenced by modern Czech, 70 BRN 373
sociological/national changes in 19th c, 74 ZAG v, 125
Slovakia
general
Bartók, influence on, 71 BUD¹ 181
Beethoven, 70 BON 130
Classical modern, 70 BRN 377
compositions in Mozart era, 56 PRA 256
Liszt correspondence with musicians, 61 BUD 125
music, 47 PRA 16
opera and Janáček, 65 BRN 68
to the 18th c, 66 BYD 97
folk
annotated bibliography of folksong collections, 70 TRČ 61
bagpipes, 67 BRN¹ 113
customs, 70 TRČ 119, 127
dances, 70 TRČ 67–93
documentation, 70 TRČ 133–61
music, 28 PRA 150, 65 BRA 57, 67 RAD 85
research, present state, *70 TRČ*
music instruments, 70 TRČ 99–115
in Shepherd Christmas songs, 75 BRUN 96
Shepherd music, research into, 75 BRUN 71
string instrument ensembles, 69 STOC 137
Slovenia
and Chopin in 19th c, 69 WAR¹ 281
folk music instruments, iconographical source for, 73 BAL 77
violin and violin music, 71 STP 48
instrumental ensemble, 69 STOC 158, 165
modern chamber music, 71 BRN 471
style of Protestant music, 69 BYD 47
and Verdi, 66 VEN 413, 69 VER 525
16th to 18th c, 66 BYD 164
1830–1914, 62 KAS 80
Smetana, Bedřich
and Beethoven, 70 BON 450
and Chopin, 60 WAR¹ 304, 324, 347
and Liszt, 61 BUD 131, 139, 241
piano style, 60 WAR¹ 304
as radical democrat, 61 BUD 241
relation of words to music in his works, 69 BRN 107
2nd String Quartet, 71 BRN 143
symphonic poems, 61 BUD 131
Societies, music
organizing amateur, 00 PAR¹ 49
in propagating new music, 37 FLOR 25
for the protection and development of music in France, 00 PAR² 246
Society, sociology, *74 ZAG*
social
aspects of folk music, 73 BAL 39, 73 ROM² 97

aspects of opera librettos at court of Leopold II, 67 NAN 203

aspects of repertory of children's companies in London, 67 NAN 729

background of
classical string quartet, 62 KAS 37
genres, 62 KAS 3–37
isorhythmic motet, 62 KAS 25
restoration anthem, 62 KAS 27
romantic art music, 56 VIE 647
Symphonia concertante, 74 ZAG vi, 9
traditional Malay music, 69 KUA 309
virtuosos, 72 COP 637

position of musicians
Bohemian in Baroque era, 62 KAS 28
in the church in England, 61 NEWY i, 346
in the church in 20th c Germany, 50 ROM 96
French orchestral, economic, 09 VIE 515
Italian, economic, 21 TUR 114, 126
medieval, 58 COL 354
medieval Eurasia and Africa, 56 WÉG 23
in 17th c, 58 COL 210
in 1800, 68 UPP 215
in 19th c, 68 BRN 289
in 20th c, 37 FLOR 9

position of work of art, 68 UPP 215

society
and art, 68 UPP 115–251
creative art in industrial, 61 TOK 18, 178, 181
Eastern traditions in industrial, 61 TOK 170, 173
and music, 73 BEL 173, 74 ZAG v, 43
music in traditional African, 70 YAO 57
and the musician, 61 TEH 125
musical behaviour of youth in industrial, *72 VIE²*
musical expression of classes, 74 ZAG v, 91
and opera, 70 BON 217–47
radio music, impact on, *54 PAR²*

sociology and
aesthetics, 68 UPP 115–251, *74 ZAG*
folk music, 31 SAL 304
musical mythology, 56 WÉG 13
musicology, 56 HAM 193, 70 BON 639
Marxism, 63 PRA 304–11
research into music, 66 LEIP 490, 67 LJU 405
semiology, 74 ZAG v, 61

sociology of
the avant garde, 74 ZAG v, 169
folk music, 63 CART 107, 73 ROM² 97
musical facts, 61 NEWY i, 333
musical life, 50 LÜN¹ 220
music and work, 65 MARB 318
music in a changing world, 71 MOS 242–71
opera staging, 70 BON 242
Polish 16th c music, 69 BYD 197
records, 67 ZAG 14, 41
student songs, 56 VIE 608
style, 69 KUA 345, 71 BUD¹ 83

Solera, Temistocle (and Verdi), 66 VEN 44
Solesmes, rhythm in chant, 27 VIE 240
Solfège, 65 GEN 136
Solfeggio, teaching of, 09 VIE 374
Solmization, 75 BYD 247
Somma, Antonio, *Re Lear*, 66 VEN 110

Sonata
in Bach's time, 50 LEIP 340
terminology, genre problems, 72 COP 478

Sonata da camera, 71 BRN 303
Sonata da chiesa, 71 BRN 303

Sonata form
Beethoven synthesizing qualities, 70 BON 542

character differences through thematic contrasts, 56 VIE 139
early, 09 LIÈ 722
in J. M. Kraus's string quartets, 62 KAS 190
Mozart's development of, 56 PRA 241
themes, 70 BON 323

Song
English 16th c, 53 PAR 121
Flemish 14th and 15th c, 24 BAS 376
history of in 16th c, 24 BAS 72
16th and 17th c Hungarian, 69 BYD 283
intellectual and psychological bases of magic song, 54 WÉG 56
mass songs, 47 PRA 64
medieval, 50 LUN¹ 62, 62 KAS 106, 72 SAR 187
notation, 06 BAS 48
16th to 18th c Romanian, 66 BYD 431
Russian 1800–1820, 67 LJU 202
see also Lied

Song of the Sibyl, 21 PAR 774
Sorbian folksong, 56 HAM 175

Souterliedekens
melodic sources, 52 UTR 193
melodies and German parallels, 52 UTR 438

Soviet Union
chamber music interpretation, 71 BRN 23
Chopin documents, 60 WAR¹ 478
evolution of national traditions in Soviet republics, 71 MOS 166–96
film music, 50 FLOR 129
folk traditions applied to professional music in Eastern republics, 61 TEH 258
library classification system, 73 WEIM 88
and Handel, 59 HAL 261
national and international elements, 71 MOS 102
neoclassicism, 70 BON 257
Union of Soviet Composers, 47 PRA 75
youth leisure and music, 72 VIE² 219
see also Russia

Space in music, 30 HAM² 118, 179, 207

Spain
general
Arab influence, 53 BAM 175, 60 PAR² 107
Arab-Spanish glossary, light on instrumental research, 73 BAL 94
chant, Gregorian, 05 STRS 63
old, 27 VIE 234
Debussy, influence of, 62 PAR 263
Flemish musicians, 52 UTR 47, 54 ARR 51
influence on polyphony, 52 UTR 47
folk music, 28 PRA 151–9, 54 PAL 71
bibliography of, 28 PRA 159
Institute of Musicology, 49 BAS 50
libraries, *see* Libraries and manuscripts
madrigals, 30 LIÈ 225
Monteverdi, influence of, 53 PAR 329
notation, early, 56 VIE 7
opera, origins, 70 MTA 107
popular church music, 50 ROM 291
Sephardic musical legacy from, 69 JER 237
in Verdi's operas, 72 MIL 244
zarzuela, origins of, 70 MTA 107

specific periods
religious polyphony before arrival of Flemish musicians, 30 LIÈ 67
13th c instruments, 11 LON 332
role in 14th c music, 64 SAL ii, 188
polyphony to 15th c, 27 VIE 158
15th c at court of Naples, 53 PAR 35

15th to 17th c organ music, 25 LEIP 227
16th c as source of inspiration for Monteverdi, 53 PAR 329
Baroque music, 63 MTA 85
17th c polyphony, 57 WÉG 91
17th c religious music, 50 ROM 323
opera in 18th c, 30 LIÈ 214
20th c sacred music, 57 PAR 447
Species, and key and mode, 49 BAS 133
Speculum musice, Gregorian modes according to, 49 BAS 72
Speech
acoustic studies, 32 AMS 291, 58 MARS 253, 66 GRA 40, 67 PAR 97, 71 BUD² iii, 657, 74 LON 348
and music, 13 BERL 456, 32 AMS 205, 38 GHE 72, 67 PAR 44, 67 PRA 399, 69 BRN 35
in music theatre, 69 BRN 53
and singing, *38 FRA*
tone colour of singing and speech, 72 COP 679, 715
training, 38 FRA 279-98
Speech melody
in Janáček *see* Janáček, Leoš: style
in Janáček's predecessors, 58 BRN 267
in Janáček's time, 68 BRN 297
in Konjović's operas 69 BRN 259
'meaning' of, 56 HAM 73
measuring, 05 ROM 245
Spilopipa, 75 BRUN 39
Spiz folksong, 28 PRA 150
Spontini, Gaspare
general, *51 IES*
and band music, 51 IES 70
as conductor, 51 IES 86
documents, 51 IES 27, 48, 50
and Forli, 51 IES 50
and German opera, 51 IES 129
as Italian and European, 51 IES 7
and Mendelssohn, 51 IES 95
youth and maturity, 51 IES 23
works
Agnese di Hohenstaufen, 51 IES 105
juvenile works, 51 IES 13
musical style, 51 IES 53
reform of sacred music, 51 IES 59
La vestale, 51 IES 33, 41
Sprechstimme, 67 PRA 1005
Sprezzatura, origin and significance, 52 UTR 404
Squarcialupi, Antonio, 58 COL 65, 59 CER 141
Sri Lanka, music, 58 COL 60, 66 MANL 174
Stage design
in contemporary opera, 64 HAM 96, 98
in Italy, 21 TUR 204
in 17th c Venice, 72 VEN 121, 131, 349, 359
in 18th c Vienna, 73 SIE 513
see also Opera: staging
Stamic, Jan Václav
form in first movements of late symphonies, 70 BRN 235
relation of rhythm and metre, 70 BON 53
Sonats a tre, 09 LIÈ 722
Stanislavsky, Konstantin Sergeyevich, 72 MIL 298
Steinhausen Wallfahrtskirche, 51 OCH 67
Stendhal, *67 PARM*
aesthetic theories of music, 67 PARM 195
and Berlioz, 67 PARM 180
La Chartreuse de Parme, 67 PARM 206
Stieler, Joseph Karl, portrait of Beethoven, 70 BON 557
Stile antico

in 18th c Catholic church music, 27 VIE 244
in Monteverdi's sacred music, 67 SIE 372
Stile nuovo
in Monteverdi's sacred music, 67 SIE 372
Stimmer woodcuts, 59 CAM 261
Štivor, Bosnia, Italian folksongs in, 73 ROM² 243
Stochastic music 61 TOK 134
Stockhausen, Karlheinz, *Ordnung*, 72 FRE/B 205
Stoltzer, Thomas, 58 COL 139
Stradella, Alessandro, 72 VEN 227
Strambotto transcription, 57 NEU/S 37
Strasbourg
music and theatre in 16th c, 75 STRS 557
organs, 32 STRS 172
Straube, Karl, 73 NUR 21
Strauss, Richard
and his librettos, 70 BON 169
style, 68 BRN 303
Stravinsky, Igor
and Bartók and Schoenberg, 68 BRN 331
Debussy traits, 62 KAS 252
and Janáček, 58 BRN 240
music 1915-25, 67 LJU 221
musical language, 48 FLOR 97, 71 VIC 105
music theatre, 64 HAM 78
Wind Quintet, 70 BON 275
String quartet
social history of classical, 62 KAS 37
Strophic song, folk tale as, 54 WÉG 120
Student songs, sociological aspects, 56 VIE 608
Sturm und Drang in music drama, 70 BON 432
Style, 25 LEIP 120
analysis, 65 NEWY 19, 194, 66 MOR 43, 72 COP 43-121
change, 67 LJU 251
in Bach, Beethoven, Palestrina and Schütz, 25 LEIP 245
from Baroque to Vienna classics in Austria, 70 GRA 18
and history of ideas, 65 NEWY 211
method of investigation, 66 LEIP 275
of Monteverdi period, 68 VEN 539
concept of in music, 72 COP 527
instrumental styles in the Renaissance, 54 PAR¹ 61
personal melodic, 25 LEIP 108
vocal and instrumental style, 53 BAM 219-66
see also Language
Styria
Chopin and the Styrian waltz, 60 WAR¹ 374
and Liszt, 61 BUD 301
oldest written German hymn in, 54 VIE 208
wind instruments and music to end of 18th c, 74 GRA² 61
Subbass, range, 66 LEIP 227
Subcontrabassoon, 74 GRA² 233
Subvention, Subsidization of music, 00 PAR¹ 21
provincial theatre, 48 FLOR 133
state and private aid, 65 BLM 251
in the USA, 68 SVE 9
in Yugoslavia, 68 SVE 1
Sudan
terms for instruments, 48 BRUS 103
traditional music, 67 BERL 104, 70 YAO 87
Suite
English 17th c suite composers, 11 LON 93
French influence on development, 21 PAR 853
German printed collections of English 17 c suites, 11 LON 93
Sullivan, Sir Arthur, *70 LAW*
The Grand Duke, 70 LAW 221
hymn tunes, 70 LAW 175

Iolanthe, 70 LAW 107, 63
and Meilhac and Halévy, 70 LAW 91
overtures, 70 LAW 71
Ruddigore, 70 LAW 7
Savoy operas, *70 LAW*
Sulu, Philippines, vocal music, 69 KUA 274
Sulzer, Franz Joseph, 75 BRUN 121
Sumatra, history in music, 50 LÜN¹ 160
Suprasl Hirmologion, 75 BYD 521
Surinam, music, 30 HAM¹ 207, 48 BRUS 266
Swabia
    Baroque music, 51 OCH 40
    Baroque organs, 51 OCH 59, 119
    folk music, 71 HIN 172
    Mozart's Swabian inheritance, 56 PAR 59
    music in 18th c, 25 LEIP 391
Sweden
    general
        church music, Lutheran, 72 BERN 76
        church song history, 30 LIÈ 184
        folksong, 67 RAD 125
        liturgical fragments, 75 ESP 171
        medieval liturgy, 75 ESP 6
        modern music education, 63 KIE 56
        musical life, 56 HAM 33
        nursery tunes, 73 BEL 111
        violinists and dance tunes in 19th c, 11 LON 159
    instruments
        flute, 69 STOC 77
        nyckelharpa, 06 BAS 242
        organs, 09 VIE 91
        sleighbells, 75 BRUN 10
        spilopipa, 75 BRUN 39
        wood trumpet, 67 BRN¹ 87
    and individual composers
        Bach, 50 LEIP 367
        Handel, 59 HAL 251
        Haydn, 09 VIE 429
        Mozart, 56 PRA 189, 56 VIE 416
Swieten, Gottfried van
    chamber music circle, 71 BRN 387
    musical library, 62 KAS 174
Switzerland
    bells, 75 BRUN 20
    history of folk instruments, 75 BRUN 33
    modern chamber organ, 51 OCH 144
    music criticism, 67 GRA 49
    music in reformed church, 62 BERN 43
    music of last 50 years, 24 BAS 147
    Orgelbewegung, 27 FRE/S 116
    Schweizerische Musikgesellschaft, 09 VIE 473
    wind instruments, 74 GRA² 127
    see also Libraries and manuscripts
Symbolism
    instrumental symbolism in art song, 38 FRA 27
    in music, 27 HAL 379, 37 PAR³ ii, 120
    musical symbolism in Shakespeare, 55 ROY 319
    in speech and music, 56 HAM 111
    of *Die Zauberflöte*, 56 VIE 249
Symphonia in the middle ages, 72 COP 541
Symphonic poem and musical form, 11 LON 206
Symphonie concertante, sociological bases, 74 ZAG vi, 9
Symphony
    Basle collections of 18th c, 24 BAS 321
    Classical form, changes in, 09 VIE 141
    French 19th c, 11 ROM 77
    inner unity of classical, 27 VIE 43
    Polish 18th c, 66 BYD 334
    style: origins in toccata, 54 PAR¹ 313

Viennese classical style in 18th c, beginnings of, 25 LEIP 260
Syncopation, 58 COL 277
Syntax
    extending classical, 61 TOK 126
    relation with music in English poetry, 60 WAR² 203
Syria
    liturgical music, 50 ROM 166
    traditional music rhythms, 32 CAIR 433
Szymanowski, Karol
    general, *62 WAR*
        biography, 62 WAR 191
        and Chopin, 60 WAR¹ 300, 415
        and 20th c European music, 62 WAR 37
        influence on Polish music, 62 WAR 22, 86
        and literature, 62 WAR 126
        and plastic arts of his day, 62 WAR 261
        and Polish criticism, 62 WAR 294
        and Polish folk music, 62 WAR 8, 209, 274
        and Romanticism, 62 WAR 161
        sketches, 62 WAR 109
    style
        choral writing, 62 WAR 226
        colour, use of, 62 WAR 75
        harmony, 62 WAR 345
        modality, 68 BRN 201
        technique, 62 WAR 109
        technique, violin, 62 WAR 75
        variation technique, 62 WAR 142
        vocal writing, 62 WAR 305
        word setting, 62 WAR 305
    works, general
        choral, 62 WAR 226
        early, 60 WAR¹ 300
        interpretation of piano works, 62 WAR 67
        mazurkas, 60 WAR¹ 415
        3rd period, 62 WAR 345
        piano sonatas, 62 WAR 177
        programme and absolute music, 62 WAR 136
    works, specific
        Children's Rhymes, 62 WAR 334
        King Roger, 62 WAR 47
        Harnasie, 62 WAR 209
        Slopiewnie, 62 WAR 305
        1st Violin Concerto, 62 WAR 247

Tablature
    articulation marks in 17th c keyboard, 72 COP 342
    Brunswick, 50 LÜN¹ 97
    dances, 16th c, 27 VIE 189
    guitar, 11 LON 354, 58 COL 329
    in Hesse Landesbibliothek, Darmstadt, 24 BAS 276
    and information retrieval, 73 PAR 48
    lute, 09 VIE 220, 54 PAR¹ 177, 57 NEU/S 127,143, 155, 245, 259, 285, 58 COL 329, 70 BON 345, 73 PAR 10
    organ, 24 BAS 243, 57 WÉG 131, 60 WAR¹ 628, 70 BOL 75, 70 BON 609
    score in 17th c, 67 BRN² 106
    transcription, automatic, 73 PAR 25
    in Scheidt, 58 COL 196
Tactus
    in earliest German organ music, 69 CER 176
    and tempo, 62 KAS 145
Talent, 14 GÖT 88, 134, 25 MUN 140, 37 PAR² 397, 38 BAY 133, 66 LEIP 510
Talmud, chants used in study of, 61 JER 366
T'ang dynasty, establishment of schools of secular music, 31 LEID 121
Tantoyuca dances, 47 PAR 335

Tape recorder, 67 PAR 53–71
Tarana, style of singing, 64 NEWD² 22
Tarantella, 28 PRA 175
'Tarantismo', 60 PAR² 95
Tartar, folk music, 64 MOS 343
Tartini, Guiseppe
  and Corelli, 68 FUS 99, 72 BYD 591
  and folk music, 67 LJU 176
Tasso, Torquato
  and Monteverdi, 73 ROM¹ 233
  and music, 54 FER 187
Taste
  and industrial syndrome, 74 ZAG v, 139
  influenceı by radio, 37 FLOR 129
  modern, and early music, 38 FLOR 7, 21, 58
  and personality, 60 ATH 257
  role of critic, 37 FLOR 185
  statistics, 37 FLOR 113
  youth, 72 VIE² 91–142
  see also Public
Tatra brigand song, 56 HAM 172
Tausug vocal music, 69 KUA 274
Tchaikovsky, Peter Ilyich
  on Mozart, 56 VIE 537
  as musician type of 19th c, 70 STGE 59
Teaching, see Education
Technology
  and the composer, 70 STOC 181
    training, 70 STOC 143, 151
  and music, 68 NEWY 25, 35, 69, 74, 84, 95, 68 SVE
    119, 123, 70 STOC
  in Japan, 70 STOC 173
Te Deum
  as Hungarian folksong in middle ages, 72 SÁR 303
  15th and 16th c settings, 62 KAS 117
Tegernsee mensural plainsong notation, 52 UTR 377
Telemann, Georg Philipp
  general, 62 MAG, 67 MAG, 72 BLA, 73 MAG, 62
    KAS 161
  as editor, 72 BLA 47
  and the Enlightenment, 73 MAG 19
  life and works, connections, 67 MAG i, 50
  and music education, 73 MAG
  and Polish music, 62 MAG 23, 74 BLA 43
  as prolific, 67 MAG ii, 18
  social position, 67 MAG ii, 5
  and other people and places
    Corelli, 68 FUS 75
    Darmstadt musicians, 67 MAG ii, 13
    England, 72 BLA 62
    Hamburg opera, 62 MAG 38
    interpreters, 72 BLA 68
    Magdeburg, 66 LEIP 251
    Mizler Societät der musikalischen Wissenschaf-
      ten, 67 MAG ii, 87
    his pupils, 66 LEIP 260
    Romania, 67 MAG i, 101
  style
    chalumeau, 67 MAG ii, 68
    comic opera, 67 MAG i, 73
    early works, 67 MAG i, 61
    figured bass, 67 MAG i, 77, 73 MAG 93
    harmony, 62 MAG 50
    instrumental forces, 75 BLA 33
    oboe d'amore, use of, 72 BLA 41
    orchestration, 67 MAG ii, 40
    tempo, 67 MAG ii, 32
  works
    Admiralitätsmusik(1723), 67 MAG i, 106
    concerto works, 67 MAG ii, 26, 72 BLA 21,74

    BLA 43
    Der getreue Musikmeister, 73 MAG 43
    12 Fantasies for solo flute, 73 MAG 84
    instrumental chamber music, 71 BRN 345
    Kleine Kammermusik 73 MAG 30
    Methodische Sonaten, 73 MAG 60
    opera buffa, 67 MAG i, 92
    Orchestra suite with horn quartet, 62 MAG 64
    Pimpinone 67 MAG i, 88
    Trietti metodichi, 73 MAG 76
Television
  communication of music, 68 NEWY 69
  and folk tradition in music and dance, 70 HAMM 45
  music libraries, 71 STGE 113
Temperament
  advantages and disadvantages, 00 PAR¹ 41
  alternatives to the system, 71 VIC 9
  effect of habituation to equal, 29 NEWH 338
  equal, 52 UTR 191
  mathematical analysis of tempered chromatic
    scale, 11 LON 74
  problems of, and musical language, 48 FLOR 39,
    129
  tempered 19-note system, and notation, 11 LON 279
  unequal, 50 ROM 342, 69 PAR 239
Tempo
  general
    in biological rhythm, 70 BON 575
    and character, 58 COL 185
    indication, independent of rhythm, 58 COL 229
    in oral tradition, 65 DIJ 204
    in performance of 17th and 18th c music, 65 DIJ
      162–204
    and range of divergency, 31 HAM 341
    and reverberation time, 59 STU 979
    subjective measurement, 66 LEIP 459
    and tactus, 62 KAS 145
  and individual composers
    Beethoven, 27 VIE 100
    Brahms, 62 KAS 219
    Chopin, 60 WAR¹ 449
    Handel, 59 HAL 141
    Mozart, 31 SAL 172, 72 COP 720
    Telemann, 67 MAG ii, 32
    Verdi, 72 MIL 238
Tempo rubato
  in Chopin and in Polish folk music, 60 WAR¹ 247
Tenorlied, Germany, catalogue, 71 KAS 38
Terminology
  Byzantine modal, 72 COP 758
  'cantor', meaning of, 49 BAS 134
  'compositio' in 15th and 16th c, 58 COL 104
  development of Latin in middle ages, 72 COP 612
  dictionary of, 52 UTR 155, 211
  and mathematics, 72 FRE/B 33
  'musicus', meaning of, 49 BAS 134
  of music of 20th c, 72 FRE/B
  problems in sonata, 72 COP 478
  'theme', 66 LEIP 380
  'variation', 58 COL 363
Terry, Léonard, 30 LIÈ 73
Tetun, southern, differences in styles, 69 KUA 345
Texts
  arrangement of old foreign, 09 VIE 136
  cataloguing folksong, 70 TRČ 165–9
  choice of, in polyphonic hymns of late middle
    ages, 50 LÜN¹ 75
  distribution in Italian 14th c, 55 WÉG 232
  of Haydn's masses, 09 VIE 542
  see also Word setting; Libretto

Text underlay
in 15th c chanson, 27 VIE 155
Dufay's time, secular music, 74 NEWY² 102
in melismas, 61 NEWY i, 12
12th c polyphony, 72 COP 482
syllabic notation in isolated voices, 72 COP 378
Texture, of 17th c Italian sonata types, 72 COP 478
Thailand
traditional instrumental music, 66 MANL 90
traditional music, 69 KUA 234
Theatre
Asia, *59 ROY*
Baroque, *66 MTA*, 68 VEN 129, 139, *70 MTA*
types of Czech music theatre, 67 LJU 126
Italian 18th and 19th c, 03 ROM 157, 72 COP 531
Japan, 59 ROY 133, 163, 71 ANN 99–189
modern music theatre, *64 HAM*, 66 LEIP 357
Czech, 70 BRN 419
form, 64 HAM 66–82
and Gozzi fables, 74 SIE 143
influence of oriental theatre, 64 HAM 116–30
influence of technical media, 64 HAM 108–14
musical language, 64 HAM 34–43
staging, performance, 64 HAM 86–103
subject matter and libretto, 64 HAM 48–63
Peking, 59 ROY 89, 99, 66 MANL 114, 71 ANN 65
Polish folk theatre, 28 PRA 200
Renaissance, *63 ROY*
Vietnam, 59 ROY 203
Théâtre de la Foire, Paris, influence on comic opera in
France, Germany and England, 09 VIE 193
Theile, Johann, 53 BAM 138
Thematic catalogues, *see* Bibliography
Theory
general, 62 KAS 348–66, *70 BERL¹, 71 STU*
bibliography, 29 ROM iii, 105
connections between science and music theory training, 70 BERL¹ 59
hexachordal, 50 ROM 276
historical and critical, 71 STU 28–108
history of, 65 NEWY 198
new linguistic and old music, 72 COP 652
rationalist basis of musical system, 09 VIE 407
reform of musical system, 00 PAR² 270
teaching, 09 VIE 374, 71 STU 247–318
training, 71 STU 108
specific periods
medieval, 70 BERL¹ 15, 72 COP 388
treatises, authorship of, 62 KAS 353
1200–1500, relation of music theory and composition, 62 KAS 354
Renaissance, 71 WAR 41, 72 COP 432
16th c, 62 KAS 356
16th to 17th c, 70 BERL¹ 23
in Germany, 53 BAM 103–52
17th c Ukrainian, 69 BYD 347
17th to 18th c, 70 BERL¹ 37
individual countries or people
Arab, 72 SÁR 129
Byzantine, 55 IST 287
Greek, 70 BERL¹ 9
M. Hauptmann, 66 LEIP 387
Helmholtz, 70 BERL¹ 49
Moorish, 47 BIS 135
Plato, 56 HAM 196
Schopenhauer, 29 NEWH 350
Therapy, use of radio music, 54 PAR² 468
Thibault, Geneviève, obituary, 57 NEU/S 311
Tibet, religious music, 67 VAN 79
Timbre, 39 NEWY 267, 68 TOK¹ iii, 61

acoustic studies, 58 MARS 135, 145, 185, 193, 203,
239, 245, 71 BUD² iii, 629, 637
aesthetic/psychological studies, 50 LÜN¹ 187
of bells and organs, 53 NET 226
of brass instruments, 72 COP 351, 715
colour, 24 BAS 177
vocal in 17th c Italy, 68 VEN 519, 72 COP 385
comparison with vowel quality, 65 LIÈ i, M66
in computers, 70 STOC 117
hearing, 58 COL 227
of Highland bagpipe, 53 NET 231
'Klangfarbenmelodie', 70 BON 372
notation for, 68 TOK¹ vi, 29
psycho-physiological problems of, 09 VIE 360
in scales, 60 PAR¹ 215
in singing and speech, 72 COP 679
structures in 20th c music, 72 COP 686
see also Bartók; Chopin; Liszt; Webern
Time
feeling of, 30 HAM² 118, 216
music and, 60 ATH 425
timeless musical structures, 66 MANL 152
Timor, differences in styles, 69 KUA 345
Tiompán, in Irish literature, 75 BRUN 84
Tirol
folk violin in, 71 STP 176
musical treatises of folk music of south, 56 VIE
481
Titov, Vasiliy, 72 BYD 847
Toccata, and symphonic style, 54 PAR¹ 313
Todi, laude at, 57 TOD 123
Toledo, folksongs and dances, 28 PRA 158
Tollius, Joannes, 58 COL 203
Tonality
general
in Byzantine Psaltikon, 72 COP 782
concept, 65 BERL¹ 351, 66 LEIP 65–79
in new music, 62 KAS 367, 370
traditional, revision of, 58 COL 332
in ethnomusicology, 74 KRP 26
in folksong, 58 BRN 182, 65 BRA 141
in Gregorian chant, 72 COP 425
late period, 72 COP 705
overcoming of, 48 FLOR 89
perception of, 56 VIE 55
physical basis, 65 LIÈ i, M64
problems in new music, 62 KAS 367
tonal aspects of Cistercian chant, 75 BYD 287
transformation, up to 17th c, 00 PAR² 175
16th c, 61 NEWY i, 44
and individual composers
Bartók, 71 BUD¹ 31
Byrd, 58 COL 322
Chopin, 60 WAR¹ 88
Debussy, 62 PAR 97
Josquin, 71 NEWY 317
Verdi, 69 VER 302, 72 MIL 89
see also Key
Tonary, unknown Carolingian, 58 COL 179
Tone colour, *see* Timbre
Tone painting, in 19th c, 74 GRA² 273
Tone quality, 53 NET 224
acoustics of, 58 MARS 119, 74 LON 341
designing method of reproduced, 65 LIÈ i, M67
of organ flue pipes, 53 NET 237
psychology of, 39 NEWY 227
Tone systems
algebraic model of major – minor, 71 STU 64
Chinese 'Pythagorean', 58 COL 174
in Equiton and Fawcett numbers, 62 KAS 275

Japanese, 66 LEIP 547
Javanese, 39 NEWY 241
19-note tempered, 11 LON 279
origin, 32 AMS 130, 56 HAM 203
sonority in, 58 COL 230
symmetry in European, 47 PRA 31
unsymmetrical, 56 HAM 202
Tonic solfa, 11 LON 364
Tonus peregrinus, origin, 00 PAR² 127
Toruń, music education in 16th to 18th c, 73 MAG 111
Toscanini, Arturo
general, *67 FLOR*
and Beethoven, 67 FLOR 102
biography, 67 FLOR 10
and criticism, 67 FLOR 23
as opera conductor, 67 FLOR 231, 249, 293
opera performances, chronological list, 67 FLOR 337
as organizer, 67 FLOR 64
records, 67 FLOR 128
discography, 67 FLOR 347
repertory, 67 FLOR 137
and young composers, 67 FLOR 152
and places
America, 67 FLOR 83
Austria, 67 FLOR 273
Bologna, 67 FLOR 319
England, 67 FLOR 237
Israel, 67 FLOR 285
Milan, 67 FLOR 55
Turin, 67 FLOR 41
Totentanz, medieval, 70 BON 417
Touloulou, 56 WÉG 55
Tournus
hymns, 54 ROU 343
rhymed office, 54 ROU 335
Traditional music
creating a wider interest in, *67 BERL*
importance for non-European countries, 67 BERL 31
importance for western countries, 67 BERL 44
and innovation, 71 MOS 42–82
traditions in non-European countries, 71 MOS 82
traditions and the present day, *71 MOS*
see also Ethnomusicology; Folk music; individual countries
Traetta, Tommaso
and Mozart, 74 ROM 138
and reform, 73 SIE 343
Tragedy
in Florentine Camerata, 53 PAR 287
Greek renaissance, 53 PAR 275
music in Elizabethan tragedies, 62 ROY 139
Transcription
acoustical measurements as aid, 69 STOC 112
Bach arrangement of Reinken's *Hortus musicus*, 49 BAS 160
of drum music, 58 SJOS 603
Haydn's, for piano of his Symphony no. 96 in D, 58 COL 197
of Italian works by A. Jarzębski, 70 BOL 67
of Josquin's French chansons, instrumental, 71 NEWY 455
Liszt's, 61 BUD 227, 75 EIS 115
lute, 09 VIE 220, 57 NEU/S 37, 143, 259, 277, 285, 73 PAR 25
Moulu motet for organ, 24 BAS 286
of traditional music, 61 TEH 214
see also Notation
Transposition, use of actual sound notation, 00 PAR¹

44
Transylvania
Liszt tours in, 61 BUD 107
and G.B. Mosto, 75 BYD 369
organ music 15th to 18th c, 72 BYD 551
Tregian, Francis, anthology of madrigals etc., 54 PAR¹ 115
Tremolo, performance of instrumental music of 17th and 18th c, 67 BRN² 101
Trent codices, compositional technique at time of, 25 LEIP 219
Trentino, accordion, 34 TRT 352
Treviso, maître de chapelle at, 25 BRUG 222
Trichet, Pierre, letters to Mersenne, 00 PAR³ 311
Trier, *Marienklage*, 49 BAS 118
Trio sonata, style of, and J.S. Bach, 71 BRN 337
Triomphe de l'amour, performances in 1681 at Saint-Germain-en-Laye, 21 PAR 874
Tritone, structural contribution, 70 BON 388
Trope, 62 BERN 55
introit trope repertory at Revers, 75 ESP 97
Jumièges, 54 ROU 959
Kyrie, melodic and rhythmic structure, 50 LÜN¹ 56
Quem quaeritis, 69 BIN 121
research, 75 ESP 123–51
text underlay, 61 NEWY i, 12
Troubadours
in medieval Hungary, 72 SÁR 129
music, 58 AIX 105
origin of, 72 SÁR 129
Trumpet
acoustics, 58 MARS 245
Baroque, music, 70 BON 592
performing practice, 53 BAM 93, 74 BLA 29
repertory of court trumpeter in 17th and 18th c, 74 GRA² 47
Serbian shepherd trumpets, 75 BRUN 76
Swedish wooden, 67 BRN¹ 87
trumpet marine, 72 COP 221, 696
Tuerlinckx family, 13 GHE 311
Tuning, 53 NET 229, 233
brass instruments, 71 BUD² iii, 573
high violin, in Resia, 69 STOC 163
historical temperatures, 71 GRA 57
of instruments, 58 MARS 169
musical implication of standardized frequency, 62 COP i, P52
organ, 20th c, 09 VIE 611, 27 FRE/S 206
pure, 66 LEIP 397
relation of Pythagorean and pure, 25 LEIP 417–25
Silbermann's, 70 BON 487
tempered, 70 BRN 443
Tunisia
folk music instruments, 60 PAR² 113
traditional music, 67 BERL 154
maqamates, 32 CAIR 583
rhythm, 32 CAIR 521
Turin
Don Giovanni in 18th c, 74 ROM 52
17th c opera, 72 VEN 145
Toscanini in, 67 FLOR 41
Turkey
Anatolian dances and music, 73 ANK 315
and Byzantine music, 75 BYD 623
ballet at court of Henri II, 70 MTA 17
contemporary epic song, 66 GRA 83
dance songs, 56 HAM 189
drum, Turkish, 73 ANK 216
folk music, 31 PAR 725, 61 BUD 515, 66 SOF ii, 1123, 67 BERL 160, 73 ANK

instruments, and Western instruments,   73 ANK 178
music,   47 PRA 82
    elements in 18th c,   71 EIS 86
    history of,   62 SIN 145
    and Mozart,   56 PRA 118
Türkü, folksongs,   73 ANK 172
Tuscany
    cappella musicale at court of (1539–1859),   09 VIE
        167
    folksongs,   29 FLOR 66
Twelve-note music, *see* Serial music
Twentieth century
    general,   37 PAR³ ii, 453, 61 BUD 403, 62 KAS 367–
        88, 62 WAR 37, *68 NEWY*, 73 NUR 83
    absolute music,   70 BON 607
    analysis,   71 MOS 210
    avant garde,   66 LEIP 25–41
        dearth of violin music,   72 GRA 56
        social implication of,   74 ZAG v, 169
        and traditional music,   71 MOS 77
    chamber music,   71 BRN 17, 72 GRA 97
        vocal parts,   71 BRN 491
    concerts in Berlin,   72 COP 507
    between East and West,   47 PRA 48
    ethical tasks,   49 BAS 221
    folk music, use of,   71 MOS 90
    function of music today,   71 VIC 83
    influenced by Liszt,   61 BUD 277
    inspired by Balkan and French impressionism,   68
        GRA 80
    the listener,   55 ARR 163
    new classicism,   38 FLOR 172
    notation,   65 BLM 148, 66 LEIP 332, 68 NEWY 62
    the organ,   26 FRE/B 134, 68 THU 37, 64, 86, 158,
        168, *74 SINZ*
    patronage,   68 NEWY 108
    performance of new music,   62 KAS 293, 65 BLM
        18–41
    the public,   37 FLOR 47–108, 65 BLM 57, 168, 213
    and radio,   37 FLOR 125, 54 PAR² 518, 521, 534
    relation to criticism,   47 PRA 41
    renewing musical language,   61 TOK 126–52
    serial,   *see* Serial music
        non-serial,   60 STRT 77–97
    and technology,   68 NEWY 69–84, *70 STOC*
    terminology,   *72 FRE/B*
    traditional forms in new musical idioms,   61
        NEWY i, 100
    traditions of the near East,   71 FLOR 197
    supra-national and sub-national tendencies,   71
        MOS 266
    violin music,   72 GRA 60
    vocal music,   33 LEIP 112
    stylistic aspects
        consonance and dissonance,   58 BRN 261
        form,   60 STRT 133–45, 71 STU 204
        genres,   70 BON 358
        harmony,   24 BAS 118, 125, 37 PAR³ ii, 458
        intonation,   57 CAM/M 70
        language,   *48 FLOR*, 66 LEIP 362
        rhythm,   24 BAS 80, 62 KAS 379
        structure and expression,   64 SAL i, 63
        structure through tone colour layers,   72 COP 686
        tonality,   62 KAS 367, 370
    see also   Opera; individual countries

Uganda, traditional music,   67 BERL 128
Ukraine
    chant,   57 PAR 319
    development in 16th to 18th c,   66 BYD 507

duma,   69 BYD 413
    elements in Chopin,   60 WAR¹ 355, 374
    folksongs,   11 LON 184, 28 PRA 150, 64 MOS 259, 66
        SOF vii, 731
    music theory in 17th c,   69 BYD 347
    oldest music in staff notation,   75 BYD 521
    polyphony in folksongs,   52 UTR 55
    reciting songs,   09 VIE 276
Umbria, folk music,   73 ROM² 217
UNESCO, and libraries,   54 PAL 341
Union des maîtres de chapelle et organistes,   37 PAR¹
    31, 37
Uppsala, Institute of Musicology, sound analysis, rhythm
    research,   69 STOC 53
Uruguay, drum,   65 BLM 23
Uttendals, Alexander, church music,   25 LEIP 335
Uzbek
    evolution of national traditions,   71 MOS 192
    folksong,   64 MOS 243

Valdesi (or Vaudois) valley
    folksongs,   48 TUR 44, 106, 123
    historical canzonas,   56 VIE 220, 72 BYD 683
Val di Mazzara folk melodies,   03 ROM 93
Valdostane folksongs,   34 TRT 397
Valencia folk orchestras,   63 STT 337
Valldemosa, and Chopin,   60 WAR¹ 288
Vallès folk dance,   28 PRA 192
Vallotti, Francesco Antonio,   71 WAR 131
Valois, dramatic performances at the court,   55 ROY 85
Valpolicella folk music,   73 ROM² 223
Vaňhal, Jan Křtitel, Czech folksong in his works,   56
    PRA 70
Varèse, Edgard,   70 BON 299, 307, 313
    and Debussy,   62 PAR 333
Variation
    in Beethoven,   70 BON 487
    in Chopin,   60 WAR¹ 219–24
    in East and West,   61 TEH 231
    in Reger,   62 WAR 142
    in Renaissance,   69 PARM 57, 71
    in Szymanowski,   62 WAR 142
    term,   58 COL 363
    in 19th c,   62 KAS 205
Vatican Council, Second
    church music after,   *64 GRA¹*
    organ building and playing after,   68 THU 120
Vaudeville,   53 PAR 185, 56 VIE 666
Vecchi, Orazio
    Amfiparnasso,   38 FLOR 108
Venezuela
    folk music,   63 CART 73, 65 BLM 7, 176
    folk polyphony,   58 SJOS 647
Venice
    brass music,   74 GRA² 23
    and Chopin,   70 VEN 333
    folksongs of the Renaissance,   39 NEWY 62
    masses, 16th c,   56 VIE 35
    opera, 17th c,   67 VIE 382, 70 BON 336, *72 VEN*
        18th c,   57 VEN¹ 571, 74 VEN 367
    polychoral music,   74 GRA² 23
    polychoral technique in Poland,   63 VEN 179
    17th c school of composers,   67 SIE 264
    theatre,   68 VEN 129, 72 VEN 97, 75 SIE 33, 105
    and Verdi,   66 VEN 328, 367
Verbunkos,   73 BAL 142
    and Bartók,   71 BUD¹ 145
    influence on Gebrauchsmusik of 18th c,   72 BYD 639
Verdi, Giuseppe,   *66 VEN, 69 VER, 72 MIL*
    general

family at S. Agata and Roncole, 66 VEN 216
and Italian patriotism, 66 VEN 417
and musical history, 66 VEN 93
publishers, 66 VEN 431
stylistic criticism of operas, 66 VEN 106, 257
bibliographical
  bibliography and documentation, 66 VEN 446, 72
    MIL 530
  bibliography, regional, 66 VEN 437
  catalogue, 72 MIL 584
  discography, 66 VEN 428, 72 MIL 607
  letters, 66 VEN 67, 69 VER 531, 72 MIL 532
  in Library of Congress, 66 VEN 452
  literature on, 66 VEN 422, 69 ROM 185, 72 MIL
    546
  medals, 72 MIL 587
  periodical on Verdi problems, 66 VEN 443
  Paris Opéra and Verdi, documents, 72 MIL 564
  in Russia, 66 VEN 458
  sketches, 70 BON 412
and others
  Auber, 70 BON 349
  Bartók and Kodály, 66 VEN 97
  Bellini, 66 VEN 184
  Berlioz, 72 MIL 148
  Donizetti, 72 MIL 122
  Fétis, 72 MIL 312
  Manzoni, 72 MIL 274
  Palestrina, 69 ROM 250
  Schiller, 62 KAS 222
  Solera, 66 VEN 44
  Wagner, 69 ROM 1, 304, 328
characteristics
  characters related to Shakespeare, 66 VEN 120
  characters, situation, 66 VEN 268, 69 VER 204,
    412–55
  cruel qualities, 66 VEN 197
  dramaturgy, 69 ROM 272, 69 VER 234, 280, 302,
    72 COP 325, 72 MIL 27, 464
  epic qualities, 66 VEN 197
  honour, 72 MIL 2
  influence of French Grand opera, 69 VER 311
  irrational elements, 69 VER 583
  and 18th c Italian instrumental works, 72 MIL 285
  love, 72 MIL 523
  musical figure of death, 72 MIL 349
  musical knowledge, 72 MIL 250
  naivety, 66 VEN 27
  operatic experience, 66 VEN 116
  poetic qualities, 66 VEN 40
  realism, 72 MIL 408
  religiosity, 66 VEN 208, 69 VER 76, 141
  Risorgimento, 66 VEN 252
  Spain in operas, 72 MIL 244
  storms and battles in works, 72 MIL 322
  verismo, 66 VEN 145, 261
style, 58 COL 247
  ballet music, 69 VER 355
  cavatinas and romances, 66 VEN 59
  6–4 chord, use of, 66 VEN 36
  creative process, 70 STGE 125
  dialogue, 66 VEN 222, 69 VER 193
  duet, 66 LEIP 310
  form, 66 VEN 157, 69 VER 573, 72 MIL 495
  harmony, 66 VEN 36, 72 MIL 166
  late style, 66 VEN 132
  orchestration, 69 ROM 304
  recitative and aria, 72 MIL 56
  relation of text structure to musical structure, 66
    VEN 247

revisions, 72 MIL 189
scena and aria, 69 VER 336, 389
tempo, 72 MIL 238
themes, 72 MIL 178
tonality, 69 VER 302, 72 MIL 89
unity, 64 SAL ii, 249
vocal style, 69 ROM 328, 72 MIL 81
word and music in operas, 69 ROM 255
works
  Aida, 72 MIL 401
  Aroldo, 66 VEN 172
  Ballo in maschera, 70 BON 349
  Battaglia di Legnano, 72 MIL 71
  Corsaro, 66 VEN 276
  Don Carlo/Carlos, 69 VER 2–525, 70 BON 412, 72
    COP 396
  Falstaff, 66 VEN 16, 72 MIL 415
  Macbeth, 66 VEN 176
  Nabucco, 66 VEN 44, 72 MIL 453
  Oberto, 66 VEN 67
  Otello, 72 MIL 20
  Pater Noster, 66 VEN 22
  Quartet, 66 VEN 126
  Rigoletto, 66 VEN 232, 72 COP 325, 72 MIL 166,
    464
  Simon Boccanegra, 62 KAS 222
  Stiffelio, 66 VEN 172
  La traviata, 66 VEN 261, 281, 72 MIL 89
  Il trovatore, 72 MIL 14, 34, 387
librettos
  and Cammarano, 72 MIL 14, 34
  Don Carlos, 69 VER 90, 148–234
  definition, 66 VEN 110
  relation to Shakespeare texts, 66 VEN 120, 72
    MIL 20
  Risorgimento in librettos, 66 VEN 252
  structure, 72 MIL 45
performance
  in Boston, 66 VEN 378
  in Chicago, 66 VEN 336
  Don Carlos, 69 VER 59, 461–516, 546, 550
  and film, 37 FLOR 257
  in Finland, 66 VEN 361
  in France, 69 VER 565, 72 MIL 258, 338
  German-speaking Verdi repertory, building of, 69
    ROM 140
  in Germany, 66 VEN 364
  20th c interpretation, 66 VEN 308, 72 MIL 303
  Italy, fate of minor operas in, 66 VEN 342
  in Japan, 69 VER 560
  in Ljubljana, 66 VEN 346
  in Mexico, 66 VEN 375
  production, 66 VEN 319, 328, 69 VER 573, 588, 72
    MIL 172
  repertory and interpretation in interwar years, 66
    VEN 351
  in Rio de Janeiro, 66 VEN 383
  singing, 66 VEN 314, 323, 72 MIL 443
  in Slovenia, 66 VEN 413
  and Stanislavsky, 72 MIL 298
  in Venice, 66 VEN 328, 367
  Verdi tenor, 66 VEN 298
Verismo
  in Janáček, 68 BRN 67
  in Verdi, 66 VEN 145, 261
Verona folk music, 73 ROM² 223
Vers mésuré, 53 PAR 185
Verse structure
  in Arab poetry and music, 05 ALG 437
  in Beethoven's instrumental music, 70 VIE 97

in English poetry, relation of syntax and music, 60
    WAR[2] 203
of folksong, 65 BRA 73
in Mozart, 74 ROM 107
in Persian poetry and music, 64 MOS 340
see also Word setting
Vibrato, 29 NEWH 224, 32 COP 312
perception of pitch in vibrato singing, 30 BON 15
Viella, 72 COP 453
Vielle à roue, 57 WÉG 260
Vienna
  general
    and Bach, 50 LÜN[1] 129
    fiddle music, 71 STP 129
    and Schubert, 28 VIE 37
    violin school, 72 GRA 133
  17th c
    relations with Venice, 72 VEN 199
    song, 25 LEIP 247
  18th c
    ballet pantomimes, 73 SIE 487, 501
    and Bohemian tradition, 70 BRN 299
    classical composers and Bernolákovo, 70 PIE 113
    Classical style, 72 COP 23
      aesthetics of, 56 VIE 443
      beginnings of in symphony, 25 LEIP 260
      concept of, 27 VIE 29
      obbligato accompaniment in, 25 LEIP 35
    Gluck and Italian culture in Vienna, 73 SIE
  19th and 20th c
    Bartók and Second Viennese School, 71 BUD[1] 77
    church music conference, 56 VIE 309
    Czech music and Second Viennese School, 70
      BRN 407
    and Italian composers, 63 MER 447
    Janáček and Second Viennese School, 65 BRN 55
    Kirchenmusikvereine, 09 VIE 544
    programmes of violin evenings, 1880–1920, 72
      GRA 52
    receptivity at elementary schools, 72 VIE[2] 192
    sound ideal c1840, 71 GRA 105
    and Toscanini, 67 FLOR 273
    and Webern (1929–34), 72 VIE[1] 29
    Zemlinsky and Vienna School, 74 GRA[1]
Vietnam
  musical theatre, 59 ROY 203
  ornamentation in music, 61 NEWY i, 445
  structure in music, 66 MANL 77
  traditional music, 67 BERL 81
Vihuela
  pitch in 17th c music, 57 NEU/S 171
  16th to 17th c music, 54 PAR[1] 205
Villota, 34 TRT 182
Vilna, Jewish musical life, 61 JER 360
Viola d'amore, 37 FLOR 309
  authentic performances, 75 BLA 56
  early history, 72 COP 547
Violin
  general, *72 GRA*
    acoustics, 56 VIE 384, 58 MARS 185, 203, 71
      BUD[2] iii, 561, 581, 601, 72 COP 466, 74 LON
      335, 339, 346, 347
    bows, 72 GRA 295
    fittings, collection of, 59 CAM 251
    in folk music of Europe, *71 STP*
    making, 72 GRA 295–314
    making, research into history, 53 BAM 89
    origins, 37 FLOR 283
    sound since 18th c, 56 HAM 213
    tuning in Resia, 69 STOC 163

vibrato, 29 NEWH 224
music, 37 FLOR 292, 72 GRA 13–97
  dearth of avant-garde, 72 GRA 56
  of Jihlava, 09 VIE 227
  Romantic, 72 GRA 47
  20th c string music, 71 STP 184
playing, performing practice, technique, 72 GRA
  109–154
  Enesco traits in international playing, 67 BUC 202
  performing practice in 18th c, 74 BLA 17
  physiological aspects, 72 GRA 196
  as profession, 72 GRA 259–82
  Romanian school, 67 BUC 80
  Russian school, classical, 72 GRA 149
    modern, 72 GRA 154
  teaching, 11 LON 337, 72 GRA 175–235
  technique, 58 COL 29
    in Austria and Italy in mid 18th c, 70 GRA 114
    in France in 17th and 18th c, 69 PAR 131
    in Szymanowski, 62 WAR 75
    in 18th c and 20th c, 62 KAS 313
    c1800, 72 GRA 123
  Vienna school, 72 GRA 133
Viotti, Giovanni Battista
  chronology of works, 72 COP 644
  new assessment, 72 GRA 41
Virdung, Sebastian
  Musica getutscht und auszgezogen, 24 BAS 7, 71
    GRA 79
Virginal music, new edition of English, 11 LON 369
Virtuoso
  Romantic, 70 STGE 5
  social historical background, 72 COP 637
Visconti emblems in 13th c music, 69 CER 131
Visconti, Pietro Ercole, 57 CHIE 523
Vissungos, 65 BLM 64
Vivace in 18th c England, 65 DIJ 194
Vivaldi, Antonio
  and Bach, 56 HAM 80
  Concerto P217, authenticity, 72 COP 253
  early works, 52 UTR 254
  new catalogue, 72 COP 633
  problems, 49 BAS 195
  reception in Germany, 66 LEIP 247
Võdu music in Dahomey, 60 PAR[2] 121
Vogler, Georg Joseph, documents, 11 LON 134
Voice
  break, 38 FRA 241
  demands of Renaissance composers, 67 BRN[2] 69
  qualities of good radio voice, 38 FRA 339
  registers, 06 BAS 74, 38 FRA 234
  Rufstimme, 38 FRA 311
  training, 11 LON 62
  vocal ornamentation in 18th c, 59 BUD 117
  vocal style in European music, 53 BAM 219–66
Volkmann, Hans, 52 UTR 398
Volkstümlich quality in 18th c, 72 BYD 415
Voluntary for double organ in 17th c England, 56 HAM
  123
Vorarlberg wind music, 74 GRA[2] 145
Vos, Joseph, 68 LIÈ 217
Vowel
  quality compared to musical tone colour, 65 LIÈ i,
    M66
  sounds in singing and speech, 72 COP 679
Vyletel vták, 74 KRP 31

Wagner, Joachim, 27 FRE/S 139
Wagner, Richard
  general

aesthetics in, 50 LÜN¹ 192
Beethoven's 9th Symphony, view of, 72 COP 512
Czech music, relation to, 70 BRN 389
and film, 37 FLOR 257
and Italy, 69 ROM 200
literature in Italy, 69 ROM 14
Mozart, view of, 56 VIE 657
music drama mirrored by Romantic ballad, 62
    KAS 233
nature scenes, 70 BON 199
new interpretation of work, 58 COL 244
relation between music and literature in 19th c, 61
    NEWY i, 314, 323
theatre, problem of, 25 LEIP 312, 314
and Verdi, 69 ROM 1, 304, 328
style
    evolution of compositional procedures after *Lohen-
        grin*, 72 COP 240
    hamony, 70 BON 539
    musico-dramatic concept of form, 69 ROM 290
    orchestration, 69 ROM 304
    vocal style, 69 ROM 328
works
    Die Feen, 74 SIE 69
    Das Liebesverbot, 09 VIE 194
    Lohengrin, 72 MIL 401
    Tristan und Isolde, 70 BON 539
Walloon and French chanson in 16th c, 30 LIÈ 76
Walter, Johann, 62 KAS 129
Waltz, Polish pianoforte waltz before Chopin, 60
    WAR¹ 613
Warsaw
    Grétry at National Theatre, 30 LIÈ 201
    music printed in Warsaw 1800–1830, 60 WAR¹ 593
    music repertory at Saxon theatre, 69 WAR 151
    stage décor at opera of August III, 69 WAR 169
Watermarks
    dating by Beta-radiography and Carbon-14, 72 COP
        447
    dating of 18th c music, 56 VIE 318
    in Handel prints and MSS, 59 HAL 193
Water organs, 59 CAM 189
Wawel, Italian music for Rorantists in 17th c, 71 WAR
    203
Wayang Kulit gamelan orchestra, 69 KUA 290
Waza court, stage sets, 69 WAR 9
Weber, Carl Maria von
    Turandot, 74 SIE 69
    view of Beethoven, 70 BERL² 65
Webern, Anton
    general, *72 VIE¹*
        in America, 72 VIE¹ 153
        creative process, 72 VIE¹ 111
        handwriting, 72 VIE¹ 111
        in Mödling and Maria Enzerdorf, 72 VIE¹ 36
        Moldenhauer archive, 72 VIE¹ 2
        personal recollections, 72 VIE¹ 29
        sources and editing, 72 VIE¹ 198
        succession, 72 VIE¹ 146
        views on Debussy, 62 PAR 319
    style
        continuity and articulation, 72 VIE¹ 100
        in early songs, 72 VIE¹ 127
        harmony, 72 VIE¹ 61
        metrical-rhythmical, 72 VIE¹ 52, 73, 100
        pointillism, 72 VIE¹ 173
        serial aspects, 72 VIE¹ 167
        sound structure, 72 VIE¹ 61
    works, general
        instrumental works, 68 BRN 355, 72 VIE¹ 100

Lieder, 69 BRN 263, 72 VIE¹ 127, 135
    posthumous, 72 VIE¹ 185
    vocal works, 72 VIE¹ 52
works, specific
    Am Ufer, 72 VIE¹ 111
    George-Lieder, 72 VIE¹ 40
    3 Little pieces for cello and piano op. 11, 72 VIE¹
        81
    Orchestral pieces op. 6, 72 VIE¹ 73
    Symphony op. 21, 62 KAS 253
Wedekind, Frank, *Lulu*, 68 STRS 245
Weichlein, Romanus, 56 VIE 689
Weimar
    Liszt and Weimar organist composers, 75 EIS 203
    Liszt's works in Weimar, 61 BUD 193
Weissenfels, and Handel, 59 HAL 53
Werckmeister, Andreas, 53 BAM 149
Werckmeister, Rudolf, 62 KAS 200
Wert, Giaches de
    Ah, dolente partita, 68 VEN 361
    compared with Monteverdi, 68 VEN 361
Western music
    directions of, 68 NEWY 49
    and the East, *61 TOK*, 66 MANL 143
    importance of traditional music in the West, 67
        BERL 44
    improvisation, 64 NEWD² 57
    in India, 61 TOK 82
    Indian music, compared with, 64 NEWD² 43–97
    influence on Asian musical life, 61 TOK 50
    influence on oriental music, 61 TEH 148
    influenced by oriental music, 61 TEH 83, 89, 61 TOK
        71
    in Japan, 61 TOK 77
    patronage, 61 TOK 161, 165
    in the Phillipines, 61 TOK 86
    place in Western life, 61 TOK 40
    rhythm, 64 NEWD² 90
    structure, 64 NEWD² 66
    and the variation, 61 TEH 231
    written by orientals, 61 TEH 114
Westphalia
    music history, 25 LEIP 397
    'shepherd' organ pieces at Christmas, 75 BRUN 61
Westminster Cathedral, music in official liturgy, 50
    ROM 62
Willaert, Adrian
    place in development of chanson, 30 LIÈ 154
    Salmi spezzati, 49 BAS 226
Wind music, *74 GRA²*
    at Dreikönigsgymnasium in Cologne, 74 GRA² 103
    museums, 74 GRA² 175
    in the Saar industries in 19th c and early 20th c, 74
        GRA² 109
    and school choirs at time of Reformation, 74 GRA²
        31
    in Styria to the end of the 18th c, 74 GRA² 61
    in Switzerland, 74 GRA² 127
    Venetian, 74 GRA² 23
    in Vorarlberg, 74 GRA² 145
    in Württemberg, 74 GRA² 187
    see also Instruments: wind
Winde, Paul van, 30 LIÈ 93
Witt, Friedrich, Jena Symphony, 11 LON 158, 58 COL
    279
Wittgenstein, Ludwig, Sprachspiel model, 72 FRE/B 22
Wodzińska, Teresa, Chopin letter to, 60 WAR¹ 675
Wolf, Hugo, compared with Brahms, 50 LÜN¹ 140
Wolkenstein, Oswald von, *73 NEU/B*
    models, 73 NEU/B 285

new edition,   73 NEU/B 219
rhythm,   73 NEU/B 51
training,   73 NEU/B 308
Wolauff, gesell! Wer jagen well   73 NEU/B 37
word setting,   73 NEU/B 68
Women
    composers,   56 HAM 55, 62 KAS 239
    and lutes in France,   23 BRUS 366
Word setting, Relations between words and music
    general,   *69 BRN*, 56 HAM 43, 140, 157, 170, 67 PAR
        44
    aesthetics,   56 VEN 657
    Baroque,   56 HAM 95
    in Bulgarian folksong,   64 MOS 248
    in contemporary opera,   64 HAM 43–63
    in Czech music,   69 BRN 11, 67
    in folk music,   58 BRN 265, 70 TRČ 49, 74 KRP 14,
        46
    in German medieval lyrics,   66 OXF² 96, 118
    in Italian 14th c music,   55 WÉG 149, 239
    in Notre Dame organa,   56 HAM 135
    rhythm,   58 COL 255
    in Romanian music,   69 BRN 215
    in Serbo-Croat folk epics,   56 HAM 241
    in strophic song,   13 BERL 444
    in vernacular texts fitted to Latin compositions,   66
        CHIC 169
    in vocal fugues,   69 BRN 91
    in Western music,   69 BRN 15, 287
    in Znamenny chant and polyphony,   75 BYD 439
    in late 16th and early 17th c music,   69 BRN 27
    in 17th c music,   24 BAS 270
    in 18th c music,   69 BRN 59
    individual composers
        Bach,   56 HAM 95
        Brahms,   56 HAM 97, 62 KAS 217
        Dvořák,   69 BRN 139
        Fibich,   69 BRN 159
        J. A. Herbst,   56 HAM 77
        Janáček,   58 BRN 298, 69 BRN 175
        J. Kapr,   69 BRN 205
        Michna,   69 BRN 81
        Monteverdi,   68 VEN 157, 335, 349, 361
        Mozart,   74 ROM 219
        Schubert,   28 VIE 117, 66 LEIP 300, 69 BRN 243
        Schumann,   56 HAM 216
        Smetana,   69 BRN 107
        Szymanowski,   62 WAR 305
        Verdi,   66 VEN 247, 69 ROM 255
        Webern,   69 BRN 263
        Oswald von Wolkenstein,   73 NEU/B 68
Work songs. Workers' songs   *64 BERL, 65 MARB*
    contemporary,   65 MARB 306
    influence on Hans Eisler,   64 BERL 301
    Georgian,   64 MOS 287
    in German Alps.   65 MARB 325
    Lithuanian,   64 MOS 278
    musical instruments and work,   65 MARB 331
    negro work songs in Brazil,   65 BLM 64
Württemberg
    brass music in the north,   74 GRA² 187
    fêtes (1609–17),   72 TOU 393
    and Hamburg organists,   51 OCH 70
    opera,   09 VIE 186
Würzburg
    and Viennese preclassicism,   27 VIE 208

Xylophone, acoustics,   74 LON 333

Yakut folk music,   64 MOS 319
Yeats, William Butler, influenced by Eastern music
    theatre,   59 ROY 271
Yodelling,   49 BAS 69
    Austrian,   27 VIE 331
    origin,   24 BAS 203
Youth music,   *72 VIE²*, 74 ZAG vi, 47
Yüan drama,   71 ANN 1
Yugoslavia,   *68 SVE*
    acculturation,   74 ZAG v, 217
    composers, training of,   68 SVE 20
    ethnomusicology, place in Yugoslav music study,   68
        SVE 164
    financing music,   68 SVE 1
    folk music,   56 WÉG 149, 56 VIE 760, 64 MOS 265, 67
        BERL 204, 67 RAD 91, 71 HIN 69, 74 ZAG v,
        217
    folk music study,   68 SVE 143
    folk music, influence on art music,   68 SVE 179
    German folksongs from Yugoslavia,   38 FRA 336
    and Janáček,   68 BRN 271–7
    light and pop music,   68 SVE 113
    mass audience and music,   68 SVE 62
    music bibliography,   68 SVE 86
    music criticism,   67 GRA 71
    music education,   68 SVE 35
    musicology,   68 SVE 73, 119
    nationalism in textbooks and other writings,   68 SVE
        194
    partisan songs,   64 BERL 326
    string instruments,   71 STP 38
    trends in contemporary music,   68 SVE 52
    youth music,   72 VIE² 119

Zachs, Jan, quartet symphonies,   71 BRN 109
Zambia, music,   70 YAO 125
Zanger, Johann,   56 VIE 708
Zarzuela, origins,   70 MTA 107
Zelenka, Jan Dismas
    chamber music,   56 VIE 552
    secular works,   74 BLA 35
Zelter, Carl Friedrich,   72 COP 462
Zemlinsky, Alexander,   *74 GRA¹*
    and Berg,   74 GRA¹ 145
    harmony,   74 GRA¹ 137
    influence in Vienna *c* 1900,   74 GRA¹ 34
    Jane Grey,   72 COP 705
    Lyrische Sinfonie,   74 GRA¹ 145
    and Mahler,   74 GRA¹ 101
    operas,   74 GRA¹ 93
    seen by press up to 1911,   74 GRA¹ 80
    and Schoenberg,   74 GRA¹ 55
    and Schrecker,   74 GRA¹ 111
    Sechs Gesänge op 13,   74 GRA¹ 111
    String Quartets,   74 GRA¹ 120
Zen, and musical aesthetics,   64 AMS 843
Zieleński, Mikołaj,   69 PARM 101
Zither,   71 HIN 153
Znamenny chant,   54 VIE 87
    deciphering crook notation,   75 BYD 487
    harmonizing,   64 BRA 117
    origins,   64 BRA 93, 75 BYD 505
    religious poems and monuments of,   75 BYD 535
    role of words,   75 BYD 439